Child Neuropsychology

Second Edition

7

Margaret Semrud-Clikeman · Phyllis Anne Teeter Ellison

Child Neuropsychology

Assessment and Interventions for Neurodevelopmental Disorders

Second Edition

 Springer

Margaret Semrud-Clikeman
Michigan State University
3123 S. Cambridge Road
Lansing MI 48911
USA
semrudcl@msu.edu

Phyllis Anne Teeter Ellison
Department of Educational Psychology
University of Wisconsin
793 Enderis Hall
2400 East Hartford Avenue
Milwaukee WI 53211
USA
teeter@uwm.edu

ISBN 978-0-387-88962-7   e-ISBN 978-0-387-88963-4
DOI 10.1007/978-0-387-88963-4

Library of Congress Control Number: 2008942517

Printed on acid-free paper

springer.com

Foreword

The human brain represents the product of an ongoing, six-billion-year construction project. In its physical form and function, the human brain represents millions upon millions of trial-and-error adaptive adjustments. Comprised of an estimated 100 billion neurons and many more glial cells it is organized into thousands of regions. The human brain, in a seamlessly integrated manner, governs body functions and movement but more importantly, regulates cognition. Not surprisingly, although the brains of different animals may not look exactly alike, they all work according to the same principles and mechanisms. These neurons and glial cells communicate using a nearly infinite number of synaptic connections, yet the entire organ in humans weighs only about three pounds. As authors Sandra Aamodt and Sam Wang eloquently describe in their book, *Welcome to your brain* (2007), billions of years of evolution have resulted in a very complex human brain, yet one that is a jumbled, far from efficient, crowded organ. They describe the neuronal pathways of the human brain as the equivalent of the New York City subway system or the streets of London with layers upon layers of routes each constructed at a different time in a different way. Yet this stunning system, for the most part, develops and works fine for most children.

The adult human brain at between 1300 and 1400 cm is by far not the largest brain among mammals. Consider that a sperm whale's brain is approximately 7800 cm and an elephant's brain is 4700 cm. Thus, bigger brains alone do not necessarily mean smarter or more developed organisms. Although larger brains are associated with higher intelligence to some extent, smaller brains can be advantageous from an evolutionary point of view, particularly if they are equal in intelligence to larger brains. But many additional factors beyond brain size impact intelligence. Brain size in vertebrates such as humans may relate more to social rather than mechanical skills. Lower ratios of brain to body mass may increase the amount of brain mass available for more complex cognitive tasks. For reptiles it is about 1:1500; for birds, 1:220; for most mammals, 1:180 and for humans, 1:50. MRI studies of humans have demonstrated that to some extent brain size has modest correlation with intelligence. Among our ancestors, homo erectus had a brain size of about 980 cm; homo habilis a brain of about 750 cm; homo floresiensis a brain size of about 380 cm; and neanderthals a brain size slightly larger than our current brains. Consider also that an infant is born with a brain of 300–400 cm tripling in size by the adult years. Yet, between birth and the conclusion of the first two decades of life, a nearly infinite acquisition of knowledge and behaviors characterizes human development. Gram for gram the human brain delivers an almost dazzling array of motoric, behavioral, cognitive and emotional capacities nearly impossible to fathom in light of its' size. The brain is a metabolically high cost organ consuming about 20% of the body's metabolic energy providing further evidence of its' complex operations. Further most energy use is devoted to being ready to think and respond rather than thinking per se.

Despite rapid and fascinating advances in our understanding of brain structure, function and complex human behavior, it still remains the case that there is much more that we don't know about how the brain grows, functions and ages. Though neuroimaging techniques have allowed scientists to appreciate the relationship between the anatomy and physiology of the brain and motor functions for example, the basic cognitive operations of the brain remain elusive.

Beyond anatomical structure and physiology, the brain unlike any other organ in the body creates an alter ego, the conscious mind. In his fictional short story *They're made out of meat,* author Terry Bison describes aliens with electronic brains referring to humans as "thinking meat"! The idea that the brain can create consciousness seems like a science fiction phenomena. For thousands of years philosophers and scientists have debated and waxed poetic about the nature of the human mind. The mind appears to be composed of a set of processes driven by language, organized by memory and individualized by each person's unique perception and interpretation of their lives. And yet, the human brain does not appear to possess a localized center of conscious control. Though highly dependent upon the frontal lobes, consciousness is also dependent upon sensory, processing and interpretative abilities distributed throughout the brain. A description of the biological basis of human consciousness continues to elude the best efforts of current researchers. We understand how people lose a sense of consciousness. We also understand how certain conditions are created by alterations in the brain and conscious experience. Yet as we come to appreciate and understand the relationship between certain conscious activities and structures within the brain, it still remains the case that our consciousness extends well beyond the structures and physiology of our brain.

In her extremely cogent and interesting book, *Brain dance* (2004), Dean Falk, a professor of anthropology at Florida State University, describes the conditions and circumstances that allowed a group of ape-like individuals to evolve over a period of at least 5 million years into homo sapiens. During this process, the brain became increasingly more specialized evolving a broad range of abilities as well as right-brain/left-brain and male/female differences. As Falk notes, in less than 2 million years, brain size doubled in the homo species, from around 650 to 1350 cm. Only a small portion of this newly evolved, larger brain was tied to increasing body size. As Falk points out, this process was unprecedented in the evolutionary histories of other mammals. As brain size increased, neurons enlarged and became more widely spaced and the cerebral cortex became more convoluted. As Falk notes, no new structures were found in these larger human brains. However these larger brains set the foundation for an accelerated evolutionary process never before witnessed in any earthbound, mammalian species. In this process, the pre-frontal cortex and the posterior areas of the brain associated with sensory processing in particular became especially convoluted. As Falk points out, the shift in neurochemicals, anatomy of neurons and brain function provided the underlying mechanics of our rapid evolutionary progression, a pattern that was most certainly driven by natural selection.

It is also the case that for hundreds of thousands if not millions of years our ancestors have developed a finely tuned capacity to respond emotionally to events in the environment leading neuronal pathways between emotive centers of the brain stem and cerebral motor control areas to be shorter than those connecting complex, cognitive areas in the frontal lobes. Though as human beings we still process the world first and foremost emotionally, we have developed an impressive capacity to think before acting on emotion alone. Yet it is still the case that stressful experiences may quickly override our capacity for rationale, reflective responding.

Finally, out of this amazing progression forward, we developed language. As Clive Bromhill writes in his book, *The eternal child* (2003), long after we developed the ability to walk on two legs and our brains became larger than those of any other species on the planet, we were still limited in our capacity for complex thinking. For a long period of time, our ancestors' brains grew larger but we appeared to reap few intellectual benefits. However, within the past 50,000 years something happened in the human brain that transformed the already large brains of our ancestors into what they are today. At some point, brain circuitry changed. Our human ancestors through the harnessing of language developed the ability to think. As Bromhall notes, the brain became partitioned, permitting the capacity for subjective experience. In other words, we can simultaneously experience internal thoughts and the external world, a key ingredient in consciousness.

As the center of our consciousness and being, it is fitting that we devote an increasing scientific literature to understanding and facilitating the operation of the developing brain; in particular an appreciation of the developmental disorders and conditions that adversely affect children's transition into adulthood. Children's brains represent an incredible capacity to learn. In the span of 18 months between 1 1/2 and 3 years of age for example, children move from not speaking to telling us how to live our lives! In bilingual homes they master two languages simultaneously.

Clinical child neuropsychologists today and in the future must be scientist practitioners. To do so effectively requires a special type of literature at our fingertips. The first edition of Clinical Child Neuropsychology provided such an essential resource. As research scientists the joint and individual work of Drs. Ann Teeter and Margaret Semrud-Clikeman over the past thirty years has greatly expanded the boundaries of brain neuroscience. I have had the exceptional opportunity to work professionally with both of them. In the second edition of this seminal work, Drs. Ann Teeter and Margaret Semrud-Clikeman have authored a number of new chapters, included case studies in all chapters and completely re-written and updated existing chapters. This volume seamlessly blends current knowledge in pediatric neuroscience with practical, reasoned and reasonable strategies to understand, evaluate and treat the myriad of neurodevelopmental problems children experience as they grow into adulthood. With great pleasure and admiration I will place this volume next to the first edition of this text on my bookshelf.

References

Aamodt, S. A., & Wang, S. (2007) *Welcome to your brain*. New York: Bloomsbury Press.
Bromhill, C. (2003) *The eternal child*. London: Ebury Press.
Falk, D. (2004). *Brain dance* (Revised and Expanded Edition). Gainesville, FL: University Press.

Contents

Part III   Childhood and Adolescent Disorders

Part I
Anatomy and Physiology

Chapter 1
Introduction to Child Clinical Neuropsychology

Child neuropsychology is the study of brain function and behavior in children and adolescents. Brain functioning has a direct impact on the behavioral, cognitive, and psychosocial adjustment of children and adolescents. Thus, disorders must be addressed within an integrated model of child clinical neuropsychology. Further, the development of the central nervous system (CNS) and the neurodevelopmental course of childhood disorders are of importance within an integrated framework. Studies routinely have identified the importance of intact functional cortical and subcortical systems in the overall adjustment of children and adolescents. Further, researchers have recently begun to address specific strategies for treating various brain-related disorders. Initial results suggest reason to be optimistic when interventions consider the child's functional neuro-psychological status.

Clinical child neuropsychologists study and treat a variety of developmental disorders. Children with learning disorders such as dyslexia and pervasive developmental disorders (Semrud-Clikeman, 2007; Wolf, Fein, & Akshoomoff, 2007) are often referred to pediatric neuropsychologists for evaluation and intervention. Children with psychiatric disorders including attention-deficit hyperactivity (Nigg, Blaskey, Huang-Pollock, & Rappley, 2002; M. Semrud-Clikeman, Pliszka, Lancaster, & Liotti, 2006; Teeter, 1998), obsessive-compulsive (Albano, Chorpita, & Barlow, 2003) mood disorders (Hammen & Rudolph, 2003) and conduct disorders (Hinshaw & Lee, 2003) are referred to more fully understand the child's difficulty and to provide suggestions for intervention at home and in school. Children with a variety of medical difficulties are also provided services through pediatric neuropsychology. Children with traumatic brain injury (Donders, 2007; Semrud-Clikeman, 2004); acquired disorders as a result of exposure to teratogenic substances such as alcohol, cocaine, lead, and radiation (Chassin, Ritter, Trim, & King, 2003); recovery from cancer and brain tumors (Nortz, Hemme-Phillips, & Ris, 2007) and other neurological disorders including seizure (Blackburn, Zelko, & Shurtleff, 2007) and movement disorders(Hunter, 2007) can profit from a comprehensive neuropsychological evaluation of their strengths and weaknesses.

The Contribution of Neuroscience

The manner in which disturbances are approached has been revolutionized by neuroscience and medical technologies, such that any serious study of developmental problems must consider neuropsychological theories, methodologies, and empirical findings if the science of childhood and adolescent disorders is to be advanced. For this reason, information has been provided in subsequent chapters about these new technologies. Although a relatively young science, child clinical neuropsychology has been significantly advanced by the use of medical technologies including magnetic resonance imaging (MRI), positron emission tomography (PET), computerized tomography scans (CT), and regional cerebral blood flow (rCBF) (Semrud-Clikeman, 2001). The potential for employing functional magnetic resonance imaging techniques (fMRI) for investigating brain activity by monitoring regional

M. Semrud-Clikeman, P.A. Teeter Ellison, *Child Neuropsychology*, DOI 10.1007/978-0-387-88963-4_1,
© Springer Science+Business Media, LLC 2009

changes in blood flow in children with neurodevelopmental disorders shows promise. New technology called Diffusion Tensor Imaging (DTI) allows us to view the white matter tracts of the brain (the tracts that carry neuronal impulses throughout the brain) and provides an opportunity to evaluate how efficiently the messages are able to travel.

The study of the brain-behavior relationship has been revolutionized by these medical technologies. Many psychiatric disorders of childhood once thought to be mental or functional in nature, and behavioral disorders presumed to be related to noncontingent reinforcement systems and other environmental factors have been found to have a neurodevelopmental or neurochemical basis (Pliszka et al. 2006; Semrud-Clikeman, 2007). For example, children and adolescents with attention-deficit hyperactivity disorders (ADHD) may have dysfunction in alternate cortical pathways depending on the primary behavioral manifestations of the disorder, such as over-arousal, uninhibited, or cognitive deficits (Filipek et al., 1997; Semrud-Clikeman et al., 2006). Further, the presumed central nervous system dysfunction attributed to reading disabilities in some children has been traced to specific cortical regions in the left hemisphere that mediate phonemic awareness and linguistic-semantic processing (Gabrieli, 2003; Shaywitz et al., 2004).

Professional Training Standards

The International Neuropsychological Society (INS), Division 40 (Clinical Neuropsychology) of the American Psychological Association (APA), and the National Academy of Neuropsychology (NAN) are major professional organizations comprised of researchers and clinicians in neuropsychology and child neuropsychology. Professional training standards have been of particular interest to these organizations in an effort to assure the expertise of those individuals practicing clinical child neuropsychology. Table 1.1 summarizes guidelines established and endorsed by INS. Clinicians interested in becoming experts in child neuropsychology should consider the recommended curricula and internship standards. INS recommends Ph.D. training, with core coursework in general psychology,

Table 1.1 Guidelines for doctoral training in neuropsychology (in original text p. 7)

Education May be accomplished through a Ph.D. program in Clinical Neuropsychology offered by a psychology department or medical facility or through completion of a Ph.D. program in a related specialty (e.g., clinical psychology, school psychology) that offers sufficient specialization in clinical neuropsychology.

Required Core
A. Generic psychology core:
  1. Statistics and methodology
  2. Learning, cognition, and perception
  3. Social psychology and personality
  4. Physiological psychology
  5. Life span development
  6. History of Psychology
B. Generic clinical core:
  1. Psychopathology
  2. Psychometric theory
  3. Interview and assessment techniques
    a. Interviewing
    b. Intellectual assessment
    c. Personality assessment
  4. Intervention Techniques
    a. Counseling and psychotherapy
    b. Behavior therapy/modification
    c. Consultation
  5. Professional ethics
C. Neurosciences: Basic human and animal neuropsychology:
  1. Basic neuroscience
  2. Advanced physiological and psychopharmacology
  3. Neuropsychology of perceptual, cognitive, and executive processes
  4. Research design and research practicum in neuropsychology
D. Specific clinical neuropsychology training:
  1. Clinical neuropsychology and neuropathology
  2. Specialized neuropsychological assessment techniques
  3. Specialized neuropsychological intervention techniques
  4. Assessment practicum with children and/or adults
  5. Clinical neuropsychology internship of 1,800 hours, preferably in university setting

Internship The internship must devote at least 50 percent of a one-year full-time training experience to neuropsychology. In addition, at least 20 percent of the training must be devoted to general clinical training to ensure competent background in clinical psychology. Supervisors should be board-certified clinical neuropsychologists.

Source: "INS-APA Division 40 Guidelines for Doctoral Training Program," **Clinical Neuropsychologist**, 1, 1S16.

general clinical psychology, basic neurosciences, and clinical neuropsychology. Internship guidelines specify 1,800 hours, with 50 percent of that time devoted to clinical neuropsychology, including specialization in neuropsychological assessment and intervention techniques, and clinical neurology and neuropathology.

Multicultural Issues in Neuropsychology

Many of the measures utilized for testing in neuropsychological practice have not been standardized on ethnicities beyond middle-class Caucasians. This problem has been present and is currently being studied as to what differences, if any, may exist. One aspect (culture) has only been studied recently in neuropsychology. Previously neuropsychologists have suggested that the study of the brain is nonculturally bound (Wong, Strickland, Fletcher-Janzen, Ardila, & Reynolds, 2000) However, more current studies have suggested that handedness, specialization of the cerebral hemispheres for tasks, and self-reports of behavioral functioning may be related to cultural issues as well as brain development (Best & Avery, 1999; Carlson, Uppal, & Prosser, 2000; DuPaul et al., 2001; Mandal, Ida, Harizuka, & Upadhaya, 1999).

Some have studied the effect of immigration to America and the reasons for such immigration (Llorente, Ponton, Taussig, & Satz, 1999; Llorente, Taussig, Satz, & Perez, 2000). Economic and political factors were found to affect the patterns of immigration to various geographical regions of the United States. These factors were also suggested by the authors to affect normative samples for tests that are commonly used in neuropsychological and psychological practice. One study by Rey, Feldman, Rivas-Vasquez, Levin and Benton (1999) in Florida compared neuropsychological results in three Hispanic groups: Cuban, Mexican and Puerto Rican. Findings indicated differences on neuropsychological test performance that were later related to level of educational attainment. In this study the Cuban population had a higher educational attainment than the other two Hispanic groups. Thus, demographic samples that would include more Cubans than other types of Hispanic groups may bias the results and thus lead to an inappropriate interpretation of the findings. Similar issues have been demonstrated with African-American samples where educational level appeared to be the strongest variable associated with poor neuropsychological performance rather than ethnicity (Peters, Fox, Weber, & Llorente, 2005; Vincent, 1991).

Another aspect that needs to be addressed when considering multicultural issues is differences in language. With the major increase in Spanish-speaking immigrants, neuropsychological testing of these children is affected by language differences. Many neuropsychological (and psychological tests for that matter) are not normed on large Spanish-speaking populations. Most neuropsychologists are not bilingual. One common practice is to translate an English test into Spanish. However, since the norms are unlikely to be appropriate, this can be problematic. There is no easy solution to this problem since test development is expensive and unlikely to be accomplished in the near future. These concerns are present for Asian children as well as Native-American children.

A study by Keith and Fine (2005) focused on possible ethnic differences in learning. Quality and quantity of instruction, previous achievement, and motivation were statistically evaluated across Anglo-American, African-American, Hispanic, Native-American, and Asian-American groups. Higher quality of instruction was found to lead to better achievement across the groups. Quality of instruction appeared to be less important for Native-American groups than quantity of instruction. Quantity of instruction was also found to be important for the Asian-American population. For the Anglo students academic motivation and prior achievement were the best predictors for learning. For African-American and Hispanic students motivation, previous achievement and coursework were strong influences on their resultant learning. For those of Native-American descent academic coursework and motivation were the strongest influences. Thus, these findings indicate that children of different ethnicities may benefit from differing strategies. It is also possible that the patterns of neuropsychological test performance may also differ. This area requires further study to tease apart these issues and determine what influence, if any, cultural differences may play in task performance.

This problem will probably not be resolved quickly. It is important that practitioners become familiar with these issues and that test administration and interpretation be carefully utilized. Sensitivity to multicultural issues is very important and difficulty is likely present when practitioners are not fully in touch with these possible differences. Books that provide additional information about cultural differences that are important include Frisby and Reynolds' (2005) *Comprehensive Handbook of Multicultural School Psychology* and Ethnicity and Family Therapy by McGoldrick, Giordano, and Garcia-Preto (2005). The interested reader is referred to these texts for further information.

Professional Training Issues and Ethics

The guidelines described here are provided for clinicians who may function as child clinical neuropsychologists. Other professionals working with children and adolescents should consider different levels of training. Psychologists in private practice or in schools as well as educational professionals, including diagnosticians and regular, exceptional, and remedial education teachers, may provide some services to assist in the diagnosis and treatment of children. However, these services are not considered practicing neuropsychology. There are ethical issues of providing services without the proper training. At this time most states do not have a specific license for neuropsychology and the practice of providing neuropsychological services is often left up to the discretion of the provider. At the very least to provide neuropsychological services the provider needs to comply with the above guidelines as well as complete an internship and a post-doctoral fellowship that has at least 50 percent of study devoted to neuropsychological training.

Ethical guidelines for the American Psychological Association and the National Association of School Psychologists specify that services should be provided within the competence of the clinician (American Psychological Association, 2002; National Association of School Psychologists, 1997). For school psychologists the NASP ethics specify that the individual has a responsibility to determine his/her competencies to administer tests and to interpret these tests. Without the requisite training in neuropsychology, the use of neuropsychological procedures, measures,

and interpretation should not be conducted. At the very least the school psychologist needs to have doctoral training in neuropsychology, an internship and post-doctoral experience with supervision from a trained neuropsychologist.

For a clinical psychologist, the APA guidelines also state that the practitioner works within his/her competency. With the guidelines from INS, NAN, and Division 40 of the APA as well as the guidelines set by practitioners (Johnstone, Frank, Belar, & Berk, 1995), clinical psychologists must also abide by these training requirements. If a clinical psychologist has completed his/her internship and is currently licensed and now wishes to provide neuropsychological services, the guidelines indicate that the prerequisite coursework and another internship must be completed to deliver these specialized services. While the state licensing boards do not necessarily monitor such changes in practice, nor do most provide a separate license for neuropsychology, ethically practitioners need to monitor themselves and provide only those services for which they have been fully trained.

For clinical and school psychologists who have not received specific and intensive training in neuropsychology but, who work with children with neurological, medical, and/or learning difficulties, basic neurology and neuroanatomy training is important. With children now surviving severe traumatic brain injury as well as cancer and other disorders, it is important to have some basic knowledge of the brain in order to understand when and whether to refer a child for an outside neuropsychological evaluation. Practitioners who have not had the recommended training for neuropsychological practice should not "diagnose" brain difficulties, but should be familiar enough with brain anomalies to know when to refer.

Working in teams with medical professionals, education and clinical professionals can be helpful in designing educational interventions and psychosocial conditions that improve the probability of successful integration of children with severe brain injury, trauma, or disease (e.g., leukemia or brain tumors). Without adequate knowledge, serious problems can arise when the child returns to school after brain surgery or trauma. This concern is illustrated in the story of a child who underwent surgery to remove a large portion of the left hemisphere and received intracranial irradiation as part of his medical treatment for a brain tumor. When the child returned to school after his surgery, the educational staff was unaware of his subsequent neurological status. They were unsure of how his neurological status was related to his present level of academic and intellectual performance, and they did not know what to expect regarding the course of recovery of function for skills that were impaired. Further, the school staff had little confidence in their ability to design effective educational experiences for the child and had little information about what to expect from him in terms of psychosocial functioning.

By working with the child neurologist, the neuropsychologist, and the clinical psychologist, the school staff was able to develop reasonable expectations and to provide a more appropriate education for this child. When the tumor reappeared and later proved fatal, school professionals, again in conjunction with the medical team, were better able to provide the needed psychological support to the child and his family. School staff were also able to help peers and other school personnel deal with the untimely loss of a classmate. By working together as part of a collaborative team, education professionals knowledgeable about brain action and recovery can work effectively to promote the adjustment of children following treatment for brain tumors and other diseases or injuries affecting the CNS.

In another case, school staff were not prepared to integrate a child back into the school system following severe brain injury. Medical records indicated that the child had suffered severe language and memory losses following a prolonged (one week) coma. When the child returned to school, he was immediately referred for a multidisciplinary evaluation. When the school psychologist observed the child, his language processes were significantly better than described in the medical records, although he was struggling with his academic work. Further, in discussions with the mother it became apparent that the family was dealing with a great deal of stress because the child's injury was sustained during a beating from the mother's boyfriend. At the time, the mother was cooperating in a police investigation of the incident and was unable to participate fully in the school's attempt to evaluate her child. In this instance the school staff were unsure about how to proceed in this complex case and needed help in

determining the best course of action for designing an educational intervention plan for the child.

Educational and clinical professionals are often the individuals who first observe behavioral, psychological, and cognitive problems exhibited by children with brain-related disorders. In this position, knowledge about when to refer for further neuropsychological, neurodiagnostic, or medical evaluations is crucial for the proper diagnosis and treatment of some disorders (e.g., seizures, brain tumors, or neurodegenerative diseases). Psychologists who work with very young children often play a pivotal role in identifying subtle neurodevelopmental disorders that respond positively to early intervention or in providing educational interventions for previously diagnosed children. A better understanding of various neurodevelopmental anomalies, normal and abnormal brain development, and effective treatments will no doubt aid in rigorous early and effective intervention programs. Early interventions are particularly important for the optimal development of some children, particularly low birth weight babies, infants with intrauterine exposure to prenatal drugs and alcohol, infants with congenital acquired immune deficiency syndrome (AIDS) infection, and toddlers and preschool children with significant cognitive, speech1 language, and/or motor delays.

Finally, a number of children and adolescents receive medication for various disorders (e.g., Tourette syndrome, seizures, ADHD, depression, and schizophrenia). School and clinical psychologists are in a unique position to provide detailed, systematic feedback to physicians and parents concerning the side effects and efficacy of such medications. Knowledge of common medications and their impact on cognitive, social, and behavioral functioning will greatly facilitate this process. A knowledgeable professional is better informed about the benefits and risks of psychopharmacotherapy and understands the need for combined psychosocial and behavioral treatments for medicated children. Thus, by understanding the neuropsychological basis of other childhood disorders, educational professionals can help design and implement effective interventions. The task of understanding the multiple factors affecting the cognitive, academic, psychosocial, and behavioral development of children is challenging. Increased knowledge will require an expanded curriculum and will no doubt be difficult to manage in rigorous graduate programs in clinical branches of psychology that are already packed with numerous course, practica, and internship requirements. At the very least, all psychologists should be required to take a course in the biological basis of behavior, a requirement that APA enforces for all professional psychology training programs. The potential benefits for children who come in contact with educational professionals who are knowledgeable about neuropsychology, neurodevelopment, and effective interventions for brain-related disorders can hardly be ignored or underestimated.

Important Laws for Delivery of Neuropsychological Services

While ethical guidelines guide the practice of psychology in any arena, it is also important to understand appropriate laws that govern placement in special education programs as well as in practice. These laws include the Individuals with Disabilities Education Act (IDEA), Section 504 of the Americans with Disabilities Act as well as the HIPAA guidelines. The Americans with Disabilities Act of 1990 (ADA) and Section 504 of the Rehabilitation Act of 1973 require that reasonable accommodations be made for individuals at all levels of school and in the workforce. While these laws also apply to the K-12 school environment, they are often overshadowed by the Individuals with Disabilities Education Act (IDEA), which ties federal funding to schools to the mandate that children with disabilities receive a free and appropriate education in the least restrictive environment (Magden & Semrud-Clikeman, 2007). IDEA was reauthorized in 2004 (P.L. 108–446).

IDEA

The Individuals with Disabilities Education Act (IDEA) (IDEA, 1997, 2000) was originally passed by Congress as the Education for All Handicapped Children Act in 1975 (Education for All Handicapped Children Act, 1975) and amended in 1986. Prior to the passage of these laws children with severe disabilities were not in school and there

were few programs devoted to their education in the public schools. Two important civil cases served as the basis for the passage of EACHA and eventually IDEA: *Pennsylvania Association for Retarded Children (PARC) v Commonwealth of Pennsylvania (1971)* and *Mills v Board of Education of District of Columbia* (Mills v Board of Education for District of Columbia, 1980; 1972).

PARC was filed by the parents of children with mental retardation who had been denied access to public education. This court ruling required access to a full education for these children and went beyond basic education to also include training for the children to develop as much self-sufficiency as possible. In addition, the court also required the state of Pennsylvania to locate and identify all school-age persons excluded from public schools and provide them appropriate educational experiences. This practice has evolved into the Child Find provision, which is designed to locate children who may qualify for special education services, but who are either not enrolled or are being served in another manner (such as homeschooling).

In *Mills*, the lawsuit was filed on behalf of seven children with behavioral, emotional, and learning disabilities. The court's decision in this case required the schools to provide schooling, regardless of impairment type. In addition, limits were set on a school's ability to suspend and expel children with severe emotional and behavioral disabilities without due process. Both of these cases set the stage for the eventual passage of EACHA.

EACHA established that children with disabilities were entitled to special education and associated services designed to meet individual student needs (Altshuler & Kopels, 2003). The EACHA became the IDEA when it was reauthorized in 1990. The law was expanded when it was reauthorized in 1997. These requirements and classifications can be found in Table 1.2. The most recent revision of IDEA (P.L. 108–446) contains changes in the way children with learning disabilities are identified, but retains the basic premise of the original EACHA and IDEA 1990. The six aspects defining IDEA include zero reject, non-discriminatory evaluation, a free and appropriate education, least restrictive environment, due process, and parent/child education. Most of these aspects have evolved over the course of IDEA through practice and case law.

Table 1.2 Federal classifications of disabilities in IDEA 2004

1. Deafness/hearing impairment
2. Blindness/visual impairment
3. Speech/language impairment
4. Mental retardation
5. Specific learning disability
6. Orthopedic impairment
7. Emotional disturbance
8. Autistic spectrum disorder
9. Other health impairment
10. Traumatic brain injury
11. Deafness/blindness
12. Multiple handicapped

Zero reject means that all children are served regardless of disability. A free and appropriate education (FAPE) requires that any services the child requires to benefit from his/her education are provided at no additional charge to the parent or guardian. These services can include Occupational Therapy, Physical Therapy, Speech and Language services, counseling, adaptive physical education, and assistive technology (Magden & Semrud-Clikeman, 2007). Within FAPE is the provision of an "appropriate" education. Appropriate is defined through the least restrictive environment and an individual educational plan (IEP) designed for each child depending on his/her needs. The least restrictive environment (LRE) mandates that the child be educated in regular education for as much of the day as appropriate. For some children this may be the majority of classes while for others the most appropriate placement may be residential (Semrud-Clikeman & Cloth, 2005). The IEP is developed by a team of individuals, usually the special education teacher, regular education teacher(s), a school administrator or district representative, the parent(s), and the student (as appropriate). At times a specialist such as a neuropsychologist is most appropriate to help determine appropriate services and time in special education. The IEP consists of specific goals and objectives, the names of specific individuals who are responsible for helping the child meet those goals, and the timeline for their completion.

Due process allows parents or the school to contest the placement, assessment, identification, or provision of FAPE (Jacob & Hartshorne, 2003). A due process hearing is required when disputes cannot be resolved. Finally, parent and student involvement has become an integral part of IDEA and there is funding for support and educational programs for infants, toddlers, and preschool children with special needs and their families (Magden & Semrud-Clikeman, 2007).

Section 504

Section 504 is part of the Rehabilitation Act of 1973. As applied to schools, Section 504 prohibits a child with a disability to be denied access to participation in activities within the educational environment. A disability in Section 504 is not the same as for IDEA and may include disorders that might not affect learning directly (i.e., asthma, allergies, diabetes). It also does not provide for special services for the child that are beyond the scope of regular education. There is no funding for these services. Section 504 is an anti-discrimination statute designed to ensure that the needs of students with disabilities are met at a level that is commensurate with that provided to children without disabilities. While the paperwork for Section 504 is not as onerous as for IDEA it does contain several elements, including a description of the child's concern; the basis for determining whether a disabling condition exists; a description of how major life activities are affected; identification of any necessary medications required by the child; description of the recommended modifications and accommodations needed; a list of participants involved in the education of the child, and a review/reassessment date. Within Section 504 there are also specifications for building and program accessibility. Table 1.3 details the main differences between IDEA and Section 504 in the secondary education setting.

Health Insurance Portability and Accountability Act (HIPAA)

HIPAA was passed in 1996 and was designed to protect privacy and security of patient information. This law went into effect in 2000 and requires strict

Table 1.3 Contrast between IDEA and 504/ADA

	IDEA K-12	Section 504/ADA K-12	College/University
Funding source	Federally funded	Funded by local school district monies	School pays for the provision of accommodations, not personal aids or devices
Legislative authority	U.S. Department of Education	U.S. Office of Civil Rights	U.S. Office of Civil Rights
Notice of placement/ services	Written notice of placement required	Notification of placement required	Students are approved for accommodations following documentation review, but generally must request these every semester
Intent of the law	Insures a child with a disability a FAPE	Federal laws that prohibit discrimination	Federal laws that prohibit discrimination
Disability categories covered	Specific categories receive support	Individuals must meet the definition of a disability set forth in the legislation. Has a broader scope than IDEA and generally includes children with more general, less severe deficits	Individuals must meet the definition of a disability set forth in the legislation
Extent of coverage	Covers children 0–21	Covers all qualified individuals from birth to death	Covers all qualified individuals from birth to death
Parental permission	Formal written permission required	Notification required, but not written permission	Federal privacy laws (e.g., FERPA) limit the information that can be shared with parents or outside agencies without student consent
Assessment procedures/ eligibility	Formal assessment procedures required	Review of existing material may be sufficient	Students must self-identify to appropriate office and provide documentation that meets established guidelines
Evaluation/ documentation	Is the responsibility of the school system. An IEP is developed for each student and reviewed every year. Re-evaluations are scheduled at regular intervals	Is the responsibility of the school system. Students who are designated as "504 only" have a 504 plan, which is reviewed annually	The cost of the evaluation is the responsibility of the student. Once a student is approved for accommodations, additional documentation generally does not need to be submitted unless there is a significant change in the student's functioning, accommodation requests, or the nature of the specific disability changes over time
Notification of teachers, faculty; facilitation of accommodations	Services coordinated by team of individuals. Services may be provided by specialists, including Special Education teachers, depending on the nature of the disability	Accommodations provided by regular classroom teachers who have copies of 504 plan	Once a student is registered for services, he/she must formally request accommodation letters every semester. It is generally the student's responsibility to deliver these to the professors and discuss how these should be implemented in the course
Mandates for physical accessibility	Accessibility not directly mentioned	Detailed regulations for access to facilities to prevent discrimination	Detailed regulations for access to facilities to prevent discrimination

Source: From Magden and Semrud-Clikeman (2007)

adherence to federal and state mandates for record protection, particularly when information is shared electronically. For neuropsychologists this law is important when faxing documents, when billing insurance companies electronically, and when sharing information in any electronic method. HIPAA was designed to protect the consumer and requires the practitioner to notify the patient when any information is to be shared with another and to obtain a signature prior to such sharing. For most psychologists it was already common practice to obtain a signed a release prior to sharing information. HIPAA has now mandated forms that must be provided to each patient prior to such an exchange.

Neuropsychologists need to be conversant on many additional parts to these laws, but such detail is beyond the scope of this book. The interested reader is referred to texts on ethics and law for further information. IDEA was designed to provide instruction to children with disabilities. Section 504 and ADA are non-discrimination laws. Thus, training issues, knowledge of ethical principles that govern practice, and the appropriate laws that apply to our work with children all form the basis for how child clinical neuropsychology has evolved. The following sections seek to discuss our model of child clinical neuropsychology as well as other models that are complementary to the practice of neuropsychology.

Emergence of Child Clinical Neuropsychology

Child clinical neuropsychology has emerged as an important theoretical, empirical, and methodological perspective for understanding and treating developmental, psychiatric, psychosocial, and learning disorders in children and adolescents. Child clinical neuropsychology can be formulated and articulated within an integrative perspective for the study and treatment of child and adolescent disorders. By addressing brain functions and the environmental influences inherent in complex human behaviors, such as thinking, feeling, reasoning, planning, and executive functioning, clinicians can provide much needed service to children with severe learning, psychiatric, developmental, and acquired disorders.

A neurodevelopmental perspective is helpful in understanding childhood disorders for several reasons. First, the influence of developing brain structures on mental development is sequential and predictable. As study of the developing brain has been made possible by new technologies, we are better able to understand how the brain changes with development, what structures vary depending on age, gender, and experience, and what interventions may alter brain activity. Secondly, the effects of brain injury in children have been documented by numerous studies. Children with traumatic brain injury have been more closely studied in the past decade and our understanding of recovery, appropriate interventions, and therapeutic assessment have helped in providing assistance to the child, the school, and medical personnel. Moreover, attention to the scope and sequence of development of cortical structures and related behaviors that emerge during childhood is important to assess the impact of the environment (i.e., enrichment, instructional opportunities, and intervention strategies) on this process.

Thirdly, studies have begun to demonstrate that the nature and persistence of learning problems is dependent on an interaction between dysfunctional and intact neurological systems. Some children respond to one intervention while others profit from another type of strategy. Until recently the ability to evaluate brain activity changes following interventions has not been present. With the advent of such technology, it is now possible to study these changes. Finally, the developing brain is highly vulnerable to numerous genetic and/or environmental conditions that can result in severe childhood disorders (Klein-Tasman, Phillips, & Kelderman, 2007).

A Transactional Approach

Due to the complexity of the brain, particularly the developing brain, a transactional approach to the study and treatment of childhood and adolescent disorders is most appropriate. For this reason theories and research findings from diverse fields, including the neurosciences, neurobiology, behavioral neuropsychology, clinical neuropsychology, cognitive and developmental psychology, social and family systems psychology, and behavioral psychology have been incorporated into this book. A transactional perspective is advanced to illustrate the following: (1) how abnormalities or complications in brain development interact with environmental factors in various childhood disorders; (2) how disorders develop over time depending on the nature and severity of neuropsychological impairment, and (3) how neurodevelopmental, neuropsychiatric, and acquired disorders (i.e., traumatic injury) need to be assessed and treated within an integrated clinical protocol addressing neuropsychological, cognitive, psychosocial, and environmental factors. We propose that all assessment, correctly completed, is therapeutic. In this view the child's performance on appropriate measures, as well as the feedback to the parent and school, provide a basis to assist these involved people in understanding the child's strengths and weaknesses, and to participate in developing appropriate interventions. A transactional approach stresses consultation and collaboration with the caregivers of the child as well as assisting the child in adjusting to his/her areas of challenge. In summary, this book presents child clinical neuropsychology within an integrated framework, incorporating behavioral, psychosocial, cognitive, and environmental factors into a comprehensive model for the assessment and treatment of brain-related disorders in children and adolescents.

Perspectives for the Study of Childhood Disorders

Theoretical orientations have often been pitted against one another: "medical" versus "behavioral," "within-child" versus "environmental," and "neuropsychological" versus "psychoeducational." Further, some have adopted one approach over others in an attempt to describe and treat childhood disorders. Various theoretical orientations in clinical child psychology will be discussed briefly and will be integrated throughout the text whenever possible. An integrated paradigm serves as the foundation of our conceptualization of clinical child neuropsychology. Teeter and Semrud-Clikeman (2007) assert that diverse perspectives should be integrated for a comprehensive approach to neurodevelopmental

disorders and for the advancement of the science of childhood psychopathology. To conduct a comprehensive child study, clinicians need to incorporate various paradigms. Child clinical neuropsychology is then viewed as one essential feature to consider when assessing and treating childhood and adolescent disorders. Differential diagnosis, developmental course, and intervention efficacy should be explored utilizing psychosocial, cognitive, behavioral, and neuropsychological paradigms.

Neuropsychological Paradigm

Neuropsychology is the study of brain-behavior relationships and assumes a causal relationship between the two variables (Lezak et al., 2004). Neuropsychology offers several advantages for child study. It provides a means for studying the long-term sequelae of head injury in children, to support children who are undergoing treatment for cancer and brain tumors, to assist parents and school professionals in understanding the developmental course of learning, social, and behavioral difficulties in children, and to provide assistance in treating various psychiatric disorders. Despite the advent of new methods for studying brain functioning and development, the exact nature of brain functioning and behavior is complex, and our knowledge is incomplete, particularly concerning the developing brain.

Although behavioral psychologists argue that neuropsychology diverts attention from behavioral techniques with documented treatment validity, clinical child neuropsychologists utilize techniques that consider the interaction of psychosocial, environmental, neurocognitive, biogenetic, and neurochemical aspects of behaviors in an effort to more fully understand the relationship between physiological and psychological systems, and frequently incorporate these same behavioral techniques. While neuropsychological approaches provide useful information for understanding and treating childhood disorders, they need to be included with various complementary methods of assessment. Behavioral, psychosocial, and cognitive variables also should be addressed in a comprehensive child clinical study. Critical aspects of each of these paradigms will be reviewed briefly in the following sections.

Behavioral Paradigm

Behavioral approaches have long been recognized for their utility in assessing and treating childhood and adolescent disorders (Kratochwill & Shernoff, 2003) Analysis of the antecedents and consequences of behaviors is an essential feature of behavioral approaches with attention to the impact of the environment on the understanding and remediation of learning and behavioral difficulties in children (Shapiro & Cole, 1999) Assessment and intervention techniques in a behavioral paradigm are closely related and often occur simultaneously. For example, a functional analysis of behavior is an ongoing assessment of the efficacy of a treatment plan (Kratochwill & Shernoff, 2003). Within this perspective, behaviors are targeted for analysis, and subsequent treatment plans are developed to address areas of concern. A functional analysis of behavior is now a required piece of an evaluation for determining appropriateness of a special education placement for behavioral difficulties.

Although some might suggest that behavioral and neuropsychological approaches are mutually exclusive, important information may be lost about a child when these two approaches are not integrated (Teeter & Semrud-Clikeman, 2007). The integration of behavioral assessment and intervention into a clinical neuropsychological paradigm is an important aspect for developing ecologically valid treatment programs of children and adolescents with brain-related disorders. There are several behavioral factors that can interact with neuropsychological functioning. Our understanding of the effects of malnutrition on the developing brain as well as exposure to lead and various environmental toxins has increased in recent years and been found to affect the child's behavior and learning. For example, exposure to lead has been found to decrease attention, increase distractibility and disinhibition (Freeman, 2007). It has also been found to decrease learning abilities and academic performance. At times the effects can be subtle while at other times they are more dramatic. Combining neuropsychological as well as behavioral evaluations assists in developing the most appropriate interventions.

Another example where behavioral and neuropsychological evaluations can equally inform one another is to evaluate the impact of environmental

demands on the child (e.g., school, home, and peer-family interactions) when making predictions about recovery from brain impairment (Semrud-Clikeman, 2004). Children who are at high risk for traumatic brain injury are often those children who come from chaotic homes, have a previous diagnosis of Attention-Deficit Hyperactivity Disorder (ADHD), and who are poorly supervised (Semrud-Clikeman, 2004). These children often show poorer recovery even with mild head injuries than children who come from more intact families (Wade, Carey, & Wolfe, 2006) Thus, working with these families who are at highest risk requires skilled behavioral techniques as well as a strong understanding of the effects of the injury on brain systems. Some studies have found improvement with appropriate behavioral support particularly when a comprehensive evaluation has provided a background for the child's difficulties (Sohlberg & Mateer, 2001). Further, behavioral interventions are frequently incorporated in treatment programs for children with disorders known to have a central nervous system basis, including learning disabilities (Berninger, Abbott, Abbott, Graham & Richards, 2002), attention-deficit hyperactivity disorders (Pelham et al., 2005; Teeter, 1998), and traumatic brain injury (Donders, 2007). Psychosocial and cognitive factors are also considered in an integrated clinical neuropsychological model for studying and treating childhood disorders. The importance of these non-neurologic factors will be discussed briefly in the following section.

Psychosocial and Cognitive Paradigms

The fact that various neurodevelopmental, psychiatric, and behavioral disorders have associated psychosocial and cognitive deficits increases the importance of investigating these features in child clinical neuropsychological assessment and of addressing these deficits in treatment programs. The relationship among cognitive functioning, psychosocial characteristics, and neuropsychological deficits for various childhood disorders is multidirectional or transactional in nature. In some instances neuropsychological functioning may help to explain many of the behavioral, cognitive, and psychosocial deficits found in childhood disorders such as ADHD and dyslexia (Semrud-Clikeman, 2007; P.A. Teeter & Semrud-Clikeman, 1997). In other instances cognitive and/or psychosocial features, such as premorbid intelligence, language and reasoning abilities, and/or social-emotional adjustment, have an impact on function recovery following traumatic brain injury in children and adolescents (Butler, 2007).

The relationship between brain morphology and activity on cognitive and psychosocial functioning has been investigated in children with neuropsychiatric disorders, including ADHD. Brain-related ADHD symptoms (inattention, overactivity, poor impulse control, and behavioral disinhibition) often result in significant social and peer difficulties (Semrud-Clikeman, 2007; Teeter, 1998). Moreover, children with ADHD frequently experience learning disabilities (Martinez & Semrud-Clikeman, 2004), depression (Ostrander & Herman, 2006), and anxiety (Power, Werba, Watkins, Angelucci, & Eiraldi, 2006).

Stimulants are the most frequent intervention for children with ADHD (Wilens, 2004) These medications are known to modify the neurochemical activity of the brain and appear to have a positive impact on cognitive and social functioning in the majority of children with ADHD. Deficits in regulation, planning, and organization skills have been found to have a negative impact on the social and emotional adjustment of children and adolescents with ADHD. For example, children with ADHD are characterized as non-compliant and rebellious and are often described as rigid, domineering, irritating, and annoying in social situations (Barkley, 2003; Nigg et al., 2002) Peer rejection is also common among children with ADHD (Semrud-Clikeman, 2007), particularly when aggression is present (Waschbusch, 2002)

The extent to which these social outcomes are related to impulsivity, distractibility, and disinhibition, which have been found to have a neurobiological basis, needs to be explored within an integrated paradigm. What appears evident is that ADHD can produce persistent social isolation and that it has been found in adults after major symptoms of hyperactivity are no longer present (Wilens, Faraone, & Biederman, 2004) Reports of depression (75%), juvenile delinquency (23–45%), and alcoholism (27%) in older ADHD individuals further suggest the limiting influences of this biogenetic disorder

on psychosocial adjustment even into adolescence and adulthood (Barkley, 2003).

Children and adolescents with ADHD also have associated cognitive disturbances that are severe and chronic in nature. For example, school failure, academic underachievement, and learning disabilities are frequently reported in children and adolescents with ADHD; and few adolescents with ADHD complete college (Martinez & Semrud-Clikeman, 2004). Difficulties in self-regulation and response inhibition may result in academic decline, de- creases in verbal intelligence, and related psychosocial problems. Thus, basic neurochemical and neuropsychological abnormalities interact with social, psychological, and behavioral factors to create significant adjustment problems for children with ADHD.

There are several distinct neurophysiological and neuroanatomical findings that may be related to the associated psychosocial and cognitive problems found in children and adolescents with ADHD, including the following: (1) underactivation or hypoarousal of the reticular activating system (RAS), a subcortical region that activates the cortex (Klove, 1989); (2) subtle anatomical differences in the right caudate nucleus (near the lateral ventricles) (Filipek et al., 1997), and the frontal lobes (Semrud-Clikeman et al., 2000); or (3) smaller genu and/or splenium in the corpus callosum (Castellanos et al., 1996; Giedd et al., 1994; Semrud-Clikeman et al., 1994).

Frontal lobe arousal apparently occurs when methylphenidate is administered. Once activated, the frontal lobes exert a regulatory influence over sub-cortical and cortical regions of the brain that ultimately monitors motor activity and distractibility. Further, the frontal lobes have been found to be underactivated in parents with ADHD who also have ADHD children (Zametkin et al., 1990). Functional studies have found differences in children with ADHD with a history of medication compared to those children with ADHD without such a history (Pliszka et al., 2006). These findings suggest that changes in brain activity can be traced to medication status and may assist in understanding how these brain changes affect behavior.

Barkley (1994) has argued that ADHD is not an attentional disorder, but rather a disorder of dysregulation. Thus, specific symptoms of ADHD (i.e., response disinhibition and poor self-regulation), are likely a result of impairment in executive functions mediated by the frontal cortex (Barkley, 1994). This theory is supported by structural imaging studies that have found changes in the anterior cingulate (a structure in the frontal lobes believed important for directing of attention and error checking) when a medication history is present (Semrud-Clikeman et al., 2006). Such findings suggest that treatment can alter brain structure and also assist in modifying behavior or at least providing an opportunity for the child to "learn" a different method for solving problems.

While various neuropsychological functional systems are involved, children with learning disabilities (LD) also exhibit psychosocial and cognitive deficits that may be related to underlying neural mechanisms. Children with LD who also possess low verbal skills and intact visual-spatial abilities appear to have higher rates of depression than those with average verbal abilities (Palacios & Semrud-Clikeman, 2005). In addition, children with LD who have more social difficulties have also been found to be at higher risk for mood disorders (Martinez & Semrud-Clikeman, 2004). Another example of learning problems affecting poor social adjustment has been found in studies of children with nonverbal learning disabilities (NLD) (Semrud-Clikeman & Hynd, 1990).

Investigating data across divergent paradigms makes it possible to build an integrated model for understanding, assessing, and treating children and adolescents with various disorders. Child clinical neuropsychology can serve as a vehicle for an integrated assessment to determine the nature of disturbances and to develop treatment programs for childhood disorders such as ADHD, dyslexia, and other learning disabilities. Psychiatric disorders such as anxiety and depression may also need to be investigated from a neuropsychological perspective. Once neuropsychological status is assessed, the interaction of environmental-behavioral, psychosocial, and cognitive factors can be explored more fully.

Transactional Paradigm

To date, a transactional neuropsychological paradigm has not been studied systematically across different types of childhood psychopathology. Emerging literature suggests that this is a promising endeavor for studying learning disabilities, ADHD, traumatic head injury, and other neurodevelopmental disorders. This text discusses the neuropsychological correlates of psychiatric, neurodevelopmental, and acquired (e.g., traumatic brain injury) disorders of childhood; the neurodevelopmental course of these disorders, and the impact of moderator variables such as cognitive, social, and behavioral aspects on the overall adjustment of children and adolescents with various disorders. The extent to which neuropsychological weaknesses limit cognitive and psychosocial adjustment or change across different age ranges will be explored within a transactional model. In isolation, neuropsychological approaches have limitations in terms of definitive answers about the relationship between brain dysfunction and the cognitive, psychosocial, and behavioral characteristics of childhood disorders because this is a relatively young science. Within a transactional model, however, it is possible to investigate how intact versus impaired functional neuropsychological systems interact with and limit cognitive-intellectual and psychosocial adjustment in children and adolescents. This text presents a transactional model of child clinical neuropsychology. In a transactional model, basic biogenetic and environmental factors, including prenatal and postnatal toxins or insults, influence the development and maturation of the central nervous system. This relationship is depicted in Fig. 1.1.

The transactional neuropsychological model for understanding childhood and adolescent disorders suggests that regions have a bidirectional influence on various neural functional systems affecting the intellectual and perceptual capacity of the child. These functional systems ultimately interact with and influence the expression of various behavioral, psychological, and cognitive manifestations of childhood disorders. Social, family, and school environments also interact in mutually influential ways to exacerbate childhood disorders or to facilitate compensatory or coping skills in the individual child. Sameroff (1975) and Sameroff & Emde (1988, 1989, 1998) have hypothesized that behavioral and biological functioning need to be incorporated into a model for developmental regulation. In other words, biological vulnerabilities influence and are influenced by coping skills and stresses experienced in the

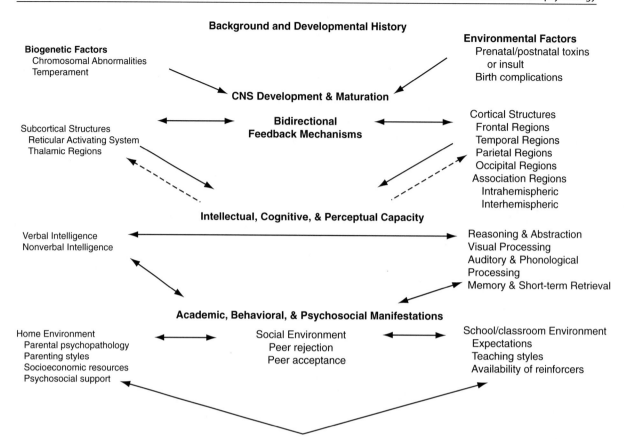

Fig. 1.1 Transactional Neuropsychological Model for Understanding Childhood and Adolescent Disorders

child's life. Sameroff and Emde (1989) further state that psychopathology should be understood not only in terms of the child's ability to cope or not cope with situations, but also in relation to the "continuity of ordered or disordered experience across time interacting with an individual's unique biobehavioral characteristics" (pp. 20–21). Sameroff's developmental approach attempts to identify the variables that impact the child's organization of his or her experience into a method of adaptation. Such adaptation may or may not be efficient or "healthy," but can be viewed as the child's attempt to achieve self-stabilization (Sameroff & Emde, 1989). In such a paradigm, the individual reacts to both internal and external environments as he or she attempts to make his or her way in the world.

In our transactional model, Sameroff's theory of a biobehavioral interaction plays a major role. The transactional model presented in this text assumes a dynamic interaction among the biogenetic, neuropsychological, environmental, cognitive, and

psychosocial systems. Further, biogenetic forces shape the child's experiences and are most predominant during embryogenesis and early infancy (Sameroff & Emde, 1989). As the child becomes more independent, he or she begins to experience influences from the social as well as the cultural environment. In turn, the child's basic temperament also interacts with the social environment and causes changes in that environment. For example, an infant or toddler who is "easy" to manage will fare reasonably well with a caregiver (parent) regardless of the parent's temperamental characteristics (i.e., calm or disruptive). In contrast, a more "difficult," fussy, demanding infant or toddler will not mesh well with a caregiver who is also fussy and demanding (Rothbart & Sheese, 2007). This same "difficult" infant would be more likely to prosper under the care of a parent with an even temperament. The "difficult"/ "difficult" dyad will interact in mutually unsatisfactory ways. This parent-child interaction may be characterized as distant and non-reinforcing, which is more likely to result in attachment or bonding problems. Thus, the child's constitutional temperament forms a template on which psychopathology can develop or is forestalled. In contrast, a "difficult" child/"easy" parent match may be advantageous in that the parent can help reduce the adverse affects of the child's inborn biological tendencies. So, although parental caretaking may not change the biological tendencies of the child, it may buffer biological vulnerabilities (Rothbart & Sheese, 2007).

While our transactional model acknowledges the role of the developing nervous system, it also recognizes that severe childhood disturbances are not necessarily inevitable. Appropriate psychosocial, cognitive, and/or educational interventions, in conjunction with changes in the ecological systems of the child (i.e., home, school, and social environment), can reduce the negative effects of many neuropsychological or biogenetically based disorders. For some childhood disorders, psychopharmacological therapy can also be beneficial. The important point to emphasize is that brain-behavior relationships are dynamic and fluid, and this dynamic transaction should be investigated in the clinical assessment and treatment of childhood disorders. Thus, an integrated model will be used throughout this book as a method to inform neuropsychological assessment and intervention.

Neuropsychological Perspectives on Assessment and Intervention

Child clinical neuropsychological assessment originally focused on identifying the presence or absence of brain damage in individuals, comparing cognitive differences among children and adults following injury, and determining the specific type and nature of cognitive deficits associated with brain damage (Semrud-Clikeman, 2004). Historically, the search for a single item or test to localize and lateralize brain damage was of primary importance (Lezak, 2004). A functional organizational approach to child clinical neuropsychology was subsequently recommended by others, with the emphasis placed on assessment of the sequence and rate of skill development and on the measurement of how disabilities interfere with

and disrupt normal development (Fletcher & Taylor, 1984).

Currently the emphasis is not on determining where damage is given the use of direct measures of brain function, such as MRI and CT scans, in cases involving traumatic brain injury or tumor processes. In contrast to the previous emphasis on localization of brain damage, the focus in neuropsychological assessment with children and adolescents revolves around the following tenets.

1. Neuropsychology distinguishes behaviors that are considered to be within a normal developmental framework from those considered to be alterations of the central nervous system given the child's social-environmental context.
2. Neuropsychology seeks to identify and explain the various learning deficits or disorders that are associated with impaired brain function.
3. Neuropsychology is concerned with evaluating the neurodevelopmental course of specific subtypes of learning disabilities to improve early identification and intervention.
4. Neuropsychologists monitor the recovery of function following brain injury and neurosurgery, and measure the effects of possible deterioration of function associated with degenerative brain diseases.
5. Neuropsychologists focus on understanding the cognitive, behavioral, intellectual, attentional, motoric, memory, and personality deficits associated with traumatic brain injury.
6. Neuropsychology investigates the psychiatric disorders of children with severe neurological disorders.
7. Neuropsychology assists in the design of remediation programs, particularly when used within an integrated clinical framework.

Therefore, this book advances the perspective that clinical neuropsychological assessment should be comprehensive enough to answer referral questions while integrating the behavioral, cognitive-intellectual, psychosocial, and environmental variables within a developmental framework. In a multidisciplinary setting these areas are frequently evaluated by various professionals. In other settings, the child clinical neuropsychologist is responsible for evaluating all of these variables. In both cases, a comprehensive evaluation addresses the main referral question while also screening for additional explanations for the child's areas of concern. Regardless of who actually conducts the evaluation of psychosocial, educational, and family systems problems, the child clinical neuropsychologist will consider these results when formulating diagnostic and intervention plans.

Neurodevelopmental Framework for Child Neuropsychology

There are several misconceptions that are present in the field when comparing adult and child neuropsychology. Adult neuropsychology has a longer history than child neuropsychology. The neuropsychological instruments that have been utilized in the past to evaluate children were often adapted from those used for adults. For this reason there continues to be some confusion over what is child neuropsychology. Some fallacies that have been described in the literature include assuming that children are just "small" adults and that childhood disorders are similar to adult disorders (Fletcher & Taylor, 1984). In addition, tests that are used for both adults and children have been assumed by some to measure the same skills in both populations. This misconceptualization can lead to misinterpretation of test data and to inappropriate interventions. For example, children's motor skills develop over time. One measure that is frequently utilized requires the child/adult to connect numbers, and then numbers and letters, in alternating order as quickly as possible. A child with weak fine motor skills will likely score poorly on this test, not due to problems with working memory, but due to motor difficulty. A neuropsychologist not trained in child development, but who is working with children, may misinterpret these findings.

Similarly, children's development can be very uneven. Some skills may develop at different ages in different children. Development problems with visual-spatial, visual-perceptual, and visual-motor skills appear to be more prominent in younger children with learning problems. Older children are more likely to have difficulty with reasoning and complex language skills. Thus, lags in motor and visual processing abilities in younger children may be

developmentally overcome while deficits in skills that require more complex processing will not become obvious until later ages. Children with reading problems have been found to show delays in motor development that improve with time, but who continue to have problems with phonemic processing. Those with autistic spectrum disorders may show excellent abilities to read single words, but experience significant problems with reading comprehension at older ages. For these children early reading may considered a strength which by fourth grade becomes a weakness. Such difference in skills and types of tasks for different ages needs to be carefully evaluated and a background in these areas is needed for an accurate neuropsychological assessment. Again, a neuropsychologist trained in child development will understand the influence of development on performance and not interpret poor performance inaccurate to brain impairment of deviancy.

In an effort to avoid these fallacies, Fletcher and Taylor (1984) describe a procedure for conceptualizing developmental neuropsychology. The basic postulates of this model (the functional organization approach) emphasize the significance of dividing the behavioral characteristics of developmental disorders into those that form the basis of the disability, and identifying those deficits that are correlated with the disability. One should also consider how moderator variables, including environmental and social factors, influence the basic competencies and disabilities of the child where the central nervous system is viewed as one of several influences. Questions in child clinical neuropsychology begin to focus on the sequence in which skills are developed, the rate at which skills are developed, and the ways these skills change at each developmental stage. Further, there is an emphasis on how disabilities interfere with or disrupt normal develop-ment, rather than on identifying which brain areas are deficient.

Rationale for an Integrated Neuropsychological Model

An integrated neuropsychological paradigm is recommended for making accurate clinical diagnoses, for determining the course and prognosis, and for designing treatment interventions for childhood and adolescent disorders. Adherence to a single theoretical perspective or the adoption of one paradigm to the exclusion of others leads to missed opportunities for more fully understanding the nature of complex human behaviors in children (Teeter & Semrud-Clikeman, 1997). Comprehensive clinical practice, accurate diagnosis, and effective intervention rely on an integrated perspective. Further, educational programming, psychosocial interventions, and psychopharmacological regimes must be multifaceted to be most effective for many childhood disorders. There are several reasons for an integrated approach in assessing and treating child and adolescent disorders. First, research demonstrates that neurodevelopmental deficits identified in young children are associated with later learning disabilities and adjustment problems (Berninger & Hooper, 2006). In some cases a fairly predictable course of development can be anticipated when specific neurocognitive deficits are present, including nonverbal learning disorders (Forrest, 2007), verbal language-related reading disabilities (Berninger et al., 2002), phonemic awareness deficits (Shaywitz, Mody, & Shaywitz, 2006), and impaired temporal processing deficits of auditory information (Tallal, 2003).

Neuropsychological and neurocognitive assessment procedures have been used to identify children with early learning problems. Recent evidence suggests that remediation can be successful for reading-disabled children with phonemic awareness deficits (Gabrieli, 2003). Tallal (2003) also reports that children with linguistic or cognitive impairments show remarkable progress in language comprehension when the rate of acoustic stimuli is modified using computer programs. Understanding the nature of the neuropsychological features underlying specific childhood disorders allows the developmental course of the disorder to be described and treatment planning to be enhanced. Emerging literature suggests that, for some learning disorders, the adverse affects of neurodevelopmental abnormalities can be altered with effective and highly specific early intervention.

Many children with traumatic brain injury and cancer are now surviving their difficulties through improved medical care. The nature and severity of traumatic brain injury is related to cognitive, psychosocial, and adjustment problems in children

(Semrud-Clikeman, 2001). Approximately 1 million children each year sustain brain injuries, with about 20 percent requiring hospitalization (Donders, 2007). Careful evaluation and monitoring of these children is imperative, and federal legislation recognizes traumatic brain injury as a special education need. Nearly 50 percent of children with severe brain injury have been found to develop some psychiatric disturbances post-injury, and related behavioral problems persist long after cognitive deficits improve (Semrud-Clikeman, 2004). Further, social disinhibition is frequently observed in children with closed head injuries. Even mild head injuries can result in various cognitive difficulties, including grade retention, underachievement and, in some cases, increased need for special education or resource support (Semrud-Clikeman, 2007). Knowing the neuropsychological systems involved, the level and degree of injury, the pervasive nature of the injury, and the developmental course of the injury is imperative to successful rehabilitation and reintegration into the school, social, and familial milieu for the child or adolescent with head injuries.

Finally, converging data suggest that many psychiatric disorders have a biochemical basis, and some require psychopharmacological therapy in conjunction with more traditional behavioral and psychosocial interventions. Many childhood disorders are chronic in nature and severely limit the long-term adjustment of children. There is a growing need to utilize an integrated model so that presenting problems and the core features of disorders can be understood in relation to biological indices (Ewing-Cobbs, Prasad, Landry, Kramer, & DeLeon, 2004). Further, the extent to which non-neurological and environmental moderator variables influence this interaction is also of interest. In this manner, behavior, biology, and environment interact with resulting cognitive, social, and emotional functioning.

Overview of Book Chapters

Since the purpose of this book is to provide practical guidance to beginning child clinical neuropsychologists, the remainder of the text addresses practical issues related to the assessment, diagnosis, and treatment of childhood and adolescent disorders. The book is divided into four sections:

1. Background information including neuroanatomy, development issues, and training issues (Chapters 1–4)
2. Clinical assessment issues (Chapters 5–8)
3. Childhood and adolescent disorders (Chapters 9–15)
4. Integrated Intervention Paradigms (Chapters 16–17)

Chapter 1 provides an overview of definitions of neuropsychological practice, appropriate laws that are involved, and training and ethical issues. Chapter 2 presents an overview of the functional neuroanatomy of neurons, subcortical regions, and cortical structures and discusses the functions of these various structures. Chapter 3 describes the stages of brain development and discusses factors affecting this process. Chapter 4 provides an overview of neuroradiological techniques as well as clinical issues and procedures.

In the second section clinical issues and procedures are emphasized. Chapter 5 presents guidelines for making referrals for neurological and neuropsychological examinations and for integrating these results with psychological assessments. Chapter 6 reviews the various neuropsychological domains and measures. Chapter 7 discusses the procedures used in a neuropsychological examination with examples of parent and child feedback as well as a neuropsychological report. Chapter 8 reviews available procedures for neuropsychological assessment, including the Halstead Reitan batteries, the Luria-Nebraska battery, the Boston Hypothesis approach, and other related techniques. A framework for investigating neuropsychological functioning within an integrated assessment paradigm, incorporating measures of psychological, behavioral, and cognitive-intellectual functioning is also presented.

In the third section frequently encountered disorders are discussed from a neuropsychological point of view. Each chapter features a case study of a child to illustrate the issues that may arise. Chapter 9 reviews behavioral disorders of childhood, including Tourette syndrome, ADHD, conduct disorder, and low-incidence disorders. Case

studies are provided at the end of the chapter. Chapter 10 presents the neuropsychological correlates of various mood disorders of childhood, and adolescents are presented within an integrated neuropsychological perspective. Chapter 11 provides information about pervasive developmental disorders and Asperger syndrome. Chapter 12 presents a discussion of neurodevelopmental disorders, including language and articulation impairments, reading disabilities resulting from phonological core deficits, written language disorders, and nonverbal reading disabilities. Select metabolic, biogenetic, seizure, and neuromotor disorders are presented in Chapter 13. Acquired neurological disorders including traumatic brain injury, exposure to teratogenic agents (e.g., alcohol and cocaine), and infectious diseases including meningitis and encephalitis are discussed in Chapter 14. Chapter 15 presents information about childhood cancer including leukemia and brain tumors.

The final section provides information about interventions that include cognitive, behavioral, and pharmacological methods. Chapter 16 presents interventions and treatment approaches for various childhood and adolescent disorders within an integrated neurodevelopmental paradigm. Metacognitive, academic, behavioral, psycho-social, and classroom management techniques will be integrated for a comprehensive, multidimensional intervention plan to address neuropsychologically based disorders. Finally in Chapter 17 pharmacological interventions are provided.

References

Albano, A. M., Chorpita, B. F., & Barlow, D. H. (2003). Childhood anxiety disorders. In E. J. Mash & R. A. Barkley (Eds.), *Child psychopathology* (2nd ed., pp. 279–329). New York: Guilford Press.

Altshuler, S. J., & Kopels, S. (2003). Advocating in schools for children with disabilities: What's new with IDEA? *Social Work, 48*, 320–329.

American Psychological Association. (2002). *Ethical principles of psychologists and code of conduct*. Washington, D.C.: Author.

Barkley, R. A. (1994). Assessment of attention in children. In G. R. Lyon & N. A. Krasnegor (Eds.), *Frames of references for assessment of learning disabilities* (pp. 117–142). New York: Guilford Press.

Barkley, R. A. (2003). Attention-deficit/hyperactivity disorder. In E. J. Mash & R. A. Barkley (Eds.), *Child psychopathology* (2nd ed., pp. 75–143). New York: Guildford Press.

Berninger, V. W., Abbott, R. D., Abbott, S. P., Graham, S., & Richards, T. (2002). Writing and reading: Connections between language by hand and language by eye. *Journal of Learning Disabilities, 35*(1), 39–56.

Berninger, V. W., & Hooper, S. R. (2006). Special issue on writing. *Developmental Neuropsychology, 29*, 61–92.

Best, C. T., & Avery, R. A. (1999). Left-hemisphere advantage for click consonants is determined by linguistic significance and experience. *Psychological Science, 10*, 65–70.

Blackburn, L. B., Zelko, F., & Shurtleff, H. (2007). Seizure disorders. In S. J. Hunter & J. Donders (Eds.), *Pediatric neuropsychological intervention* (pp. 133–150). Cambridge: Cambridge University Press.

Butler, R. W. (2007). Cognitive rehabilitation. In S. J. Hunter & J. Donders (Eds.), *Pediatric neuropsychological intervention* (pp. 444–464). Cambridge: Cambridge University Press.

Carlson, C. I., Uppal, S., & Prosser, M. (2000). Ethnic differences in processes contributing to the self-esteem of early adolescent girls. *Journal of Early Adolescence, 20*, 44–67.

Castellanos, F. X., Giedd, J. N., Marsh, W. L., Hamburger, S. D., Vaiturzis, A. C., & Dickstein, D. P. (1996). Quantitative brain magnetic resonance imaging in attention-deficit hyperactivity disorder. *Archives of General Psychiatry, 53*(7), 607–616.

Chassin, L., Ritter, J., Trim, R. S., & King, K. M. (2003). Adolescent substance use disorders. In E. J. Mash & R. A. Barkley (Eds.), *Child Psychopathology* (2nd ed., pp. 199–232). New York: Guilford Press.

Donders, J. (2007). Traumatic brain injury. In S. J. Hunter & J. Donders (Eds.), *Pediatric neuropsychological intervention* (pp. 91–111). Cambridge: Cambridge University Press.

DuPaul, G. J., Schaughency, E. A., Weyandt, L. L., Tripp, G., Kiesner, J., Ota, K., et al. (2001). Self-report of ADHD symptoms in university students: Cross-gender and cross-national prevalence. *Journal of Learning Disabilities, 34*, 370–379.

Education for All Handicapped children Act 20 U.S.C. Section 401, 20 U.S.C. Section 401 C.F.R. (1975).

Ewing-Cobbs, L., Prasad, M. R., Landry, S. H., Kramer, L., & DeLeon, R. (2004). Executive functions following traumatic brain injury: A preliminary analysis. *Developmental Neuropsychology, 26*, 487–512.

Filipek, P. A., Semrud-Clikeman, M., Steingard, R. J., Renshaw, P. F., Kennedy, D. N., & Biederman, J. (1997). Volumetric MRI analysis comparing subjects having attention-deficit hyperactivity disorder with normal controls. *Neurology, 48*(3), 589–601.

Fletcher, J. M., & Taylor, H. (1984). Neuropsychological approaches to children: Toward a developmental neuropsychology. *Journal of Clinical Neuropsychology, 6*, 39–56.

Forrest, B. (2007). Diagnosing and treating right hemisphere disorders. In S. J. Hunter & J. Donders (Eds.), *Pediatric neuropsychological intervention* (pp. 175–192). Cambridge: Cambridge University Press.

Freeman, N. C. G. (2007). Risk assessment for environmental health. In M. G. Robson & W. A. Toscano (Eds.), *Risk assessment for environmental health* (pp. 315–344). San Francisco: Jossey-Bass.

Frisby, C. L., & Reynolds, C. R. (2005). Comprehensive handbook of multicultural school psychology. Hoboken, NJ: John Wiley & Sons.

Gabrieli, J. D. (2003). *Neuroimaging evidence about the brain basis of dyslexia.* Paper presented at the International Dyslexia Association, San Diego, CA.

Giedd, J. N., Castellanos, F. X., Casey, B. J., Kozuch, P., King, A. C., Hamburger, S. D., et al. (1994). Quantitative morphology of the corpus callosum in attention deficit hyperactivity disorder. *American Journal of Psychiatry, 151*(5), 665–669.

Hammen, C., & Rudolph, K. D. (2003). Childhood mood disorders. In E. J. Mash & R. A. Barkley (Eds.), *Child Psychopathology* (2nd ed., pp. 233–278). New York: Guilford Press.

Hinshaw, S. P., & Lee, S. S. (2003). Conduct and oppositional defiant disorders. In E. J. Mash & R. A. Barkley (Eds.), *Child Psychopathology* (2nd ed., pp. 144–198). New York: Guilford Press.

Hunter, S. J. (2007). Pediatric movement disorders. In S. J. Hunter & J. Donders (Eds.), *Pediatric neuropsychological intervention* (pp. 314–337). New York: Guilford Press.

20 U.S.C. Chapter 33. Amended by Publ.L. No. 105-17 in June 1997, Regulations appear at 34 C.F.R. Part 300 C.F.R. (1997).

IDEA. (2000). *2nd Annual Report to Congress on the Implementation of the Individuals with Disabilities Education Act.* Washington, DC: Department of Education.

Jacob, S., & Hartshorne, T. S. (2003). *Ethics and law for school psychologists.* Hoboken, NJ: John Wiley & Sons, Inc.

Johnstone, B., Frank, R. G., Belar, C., & Berk, S. (1995). Psychology in health care: Future directions. *Professional Psychology: Research and Practice, 26*, 341–365.

Keith, T. Z., & Fine, J. G. (2005). Multicultural influences on school learning: Similarities and differences across groups. In C. L. Frisby & C. R. Reynolds (Eds.), *Comprehensive handbook of multicultural school psychology* (pp. 457–482). Hoboken, NJ: John Wiley & Sons.

Klein-Tasman, B. P., Phillips, K. D., & Kelderman, J. K. (2007). Genetic syndromes associated with intellectual disability. In S. J. Hunter & J. Donders (Eds.), *Pediatric neuropsychological intervention* (pp. 193–223). Cambridge: Cambridge University Press.

Klove, H. (1989). The hypoarousal hypothesis: What is the evidence? In T. Sagvolden & T. Archer (Eds.), *Attention deficit disorder: Clinical and basic research* (pp. 131–136). Hillsdale, NJ: Lawrence Erlbaum Associates.

Kratochwill, T. R., & Shernoff, E. S. (2003). Evidence-based practice: Promoting evidence-based interventions in school psychology. *School Psychology Quarterly, 18*, 389–408.

Lezak, M. D., Howieson, D. B., & Loring, D. W. (2004). Neuropsychological assessment (4th edition). New York: Oxford Press.

Llorente, A. L., Ponton, M. O., Taussig, I. M., & Satz, P. (1999). Patterns of American immigration and their influence on the acquisition of neuropsychological norms for Hispanics. *Archives of Clinical Neuropsychology, 14*, 603–614.

Llorente, A. L., Taussig, I. M., Satz, P., & Perez, L. M. (2000). Trends in American immigration. In E. Fletcher-Janzen, T. L. Strickland, & C. R. Reynolds (Eds.), *Handbook of cross-cultural neuropsychology* (pp. 345–359). New York: Kluwer Academic/Plenum Press.

Magden, J., & Semrud-Clikeman, M. (2007). Bridging neuropsychological practice and educational intervention. In S. J. Hunter & J. Donders (Eds.), *Pediatric neuropsychological practice: A critical review of science and practice.* London: Cambridge Press.

Mandal, M. K., Ida, Y., Harizuka, S., & Upadhaya, N. (1999). Cultural difference in hand preference: Evidence from Indian and Japan. *International Journal of Psychology, 34,* 59–66.

Martinez, R., & Semrud-Clikeman, M. (2004). Emotional adjustment of young adolescents with different learning disability subtypes. *Journal of Learning Disabilities, 37,* 411–420.

McGoldrick, M., Giordano, J., & Garcia-Preto, N. (2005). *Ethnicity and family therapy* (3rd ed.). New York: Guilford Press.

Education of the Handicapped Legislation, contempt proceedings 551 C.F.R. (1980). Mills v Board of Education District of Columbia.

348 F. Suppl. 866 C.F.R. (1972). Mills v Board of Education for District of Columbia.

National Association of School Psychologists. (1997). *Professional conduct manual* (3rd ed.). Bethseda, MD: Author.

Nigg, J. T., Blaskey, L. G., Huang-Pollock, C. L., & Rappley, M. D. (2002). Neuropsychological executive functions and DSM-IV ADHD subtypes. *Journal of the American Academy of Child & Adolescent Psychiatry, 41,* 59–66.

Nortz, M. J., Hemme-Phillips, J. M., & Ris, D. M. (2007). Neuropsychological sequelae in children treated for cancer. In S. J. Hunter & J. Donders (Eds.), *Pediatric neuropsychological Intervention* (pp. 112–132). Cambridge: Cambridge University Press.

Ostrander, R., & Herman, K. C. (2006). Potential cognitive, parenting and developmental mediators of the relationship between ADHD and depression. *Journal of Consulting and Clinical Psychology, 74,* 89–98.

Palacios, E., & Semrud-Clikeman, M. (2005). Delinquency, hyperactivity, and phonological awareness: A comparison of ODD and ADHD. *Applied Neuropsychology, 12,* 94–105.

Pelham, W. E., Burrows-McLean, L., Gnagy, E. M., Fabiano, G. A., Coles, E. K., Tresco, K. E., et al. (2005). Transdermal methylphenidate, behavioral, and combined treatment for children with ADHD. *Experimental and Clinical Psychopharmacology, 13,* 111–126.

Pennsylvania Association for Retarded Children (PARC) v Commonwealth of Pennsylvania 334 F. Supp. 1257 (D.C. E.D. Pa. 1971), 343 F. Supp. 279 (D.C. E.D. Pa. 1972). C. F.R. (1971).

Peters, S. A., Fox, J. L., Weber, D. A., & Llorente, A. L. (2005). Applied and theoretical contributions of neuropsychology to assessment in multicultural school psychology. In C. L. Frisby & C. R. Reynolds (Eds.), *Comprehensive handbook of multicultural school psychology* (pp. 841–860). Hoboken, NJ: John Wiley & Sons.

Pliszka, S. R., Glahn, D. C., Semrud-Clikeman, M., Franklin, C., Perez, R., Xiong, J., et al. (2006). Neuroimaging of inhibitory control areas in children with attention deficit hyperactivity disorder who were treatment naive or in long-term treatment. *American Journal of Psychiatry, 163*(6), 1052–1060.

Power, T. J., Werba, B. E., Watkins, M. W., Angelucci, J. G., & Eiraldi, R. B. (2006). Patterns of parent-reported homework problems among ADHD-referred and non-referred children. *School Psychology Quarterly, 21,* 13–33.

Rey, G. J., Feldman, E., Rivas-Vasquez, R., Levin, B. E., & Benton, A. L. (1999). Neuropsychological test development and normative data on Hispanics. *Archives of Clinical Neuropsychology, 14,* 593–601.

Rothbart, M. K., & Sheese, B. E. (2007). Temperament and emotion regulation. In J. J. Gross (Ed.), *Handbook of emotion regulation* (pp. 331–350). New York: Guilford Press.

Sameroff, A. (1975). Transactional models in early social relations. *Human Development, 18,* 65–79.

Sameroff, A., & Emde, R. N. (1988). *Relationship disturbances in early childhood: A developmental approach.* New York: Basic Books.

Sameroff, A., & Emde, R. N. (1989). *Relationship disturbances in early childhood: A developmental approach.* New York: Basic Books.

Sameroff, A., & Emde, R. N. (1998). *Relationship disturbances in early childhood: A developmental approach.* New York: Basic Books.

Semrud-Clikeman, M. (2001). *Traumatic brain injury in children and adolescents.* New York: Guilford Press.

Semrud-Clikeman, M. (2004). *Traumatic brain jnjury in children and adolescents.* New York: Guilford Press.

Semrud-Clikeman, M. (2007). *Social competence in children.* New York: Springer.

Semrud-Clikeman, M., & Cloth, A. (2005). Least restrictive environment (LRE). In R. Lee (Ed.), *Encyclopedia of school psychology* (pp. 298–301). New York: Sage Publications.

Semrud-Clikeman, M., Filipek, P. A., Biederman, J., Steingard, R. J., Kennedy, D. N., Renshaw, P. F., et al. (1994). Attention-deficit hyperactivity disorder: Magnetic resonance imaging morphometric analysis of the corpus callosum. *Journal of the American Academy of Child & Adolescent Psychiatry, 33*(6), 875–881.

Semrud-Clikeman, M., & Hynd, G. W. (1990). Right hemispheric dysfunction in nonverbal learning disabilities: Social, academic, and adaptive functioning in adults and children. *Psychological Bulletin, 107*(2), 196–209.

Semrud-Clikeman, M., Pliszka, S. R., Lancaster, J., & Liotti, M. (2006). Volumetric MRI differences in treatment-naïve vs chronically treated children with ADHD. *Neurology, 67,* 1023–1027.

Semrud-Clikeman, M., Steingard, R., Filipek, P. A., Bekken, K., Biederman, J., & Renshaw, P. F. (2000). Neuroanatomical-neuropsychological correlates of ADHD. *Journal of the American Academy of Child and Adolescent Psychiatry, 39,* 477–484.

Shapiro, E. S., & Cole, C. L. (1999). Self-monitoring in assessing children's problems. *Psychological Assessment, 11,* 448–457.

Shaywitz, B. A., Shaywitz, S. E., Blachman, B. A., Pugh, K. R., Fulbright, R. K., Skudlarski, P., et al. (2004). Development of left occipitotemporal systems for skilled reading in children after a phonologically-based intervention. *Biological Psychiatry, 55*, 926–933.

Shaywitz, S. E., Mody, M., & Shaywitz, B. A. (2006). Neural mechanisms in dyslexia. *Current Directions in Psychological Science, 15*(6), 278–281.

Sohlberg, M. M., & Mateer, C. A. (2001). *Cognitive rehabilitation: An integrative neuropsychological approach* (2nd ed.). New York: Guilford press.

Tallal, P. (2003). Language learning disabilities: Integrating research approaches. *Current Directions in Psychological Science, 12*(6), 206–211.

Teeter, P. A. (1998). *Interventions for ADHD*. New York: Guilford.

Teeter, P. A., & Semrud-Clikeman, M. (1997). *Child neuropsychology: Assessment and interventions for neurodevelopmental disorders*. Boston: Allyn and Bacon.

Teeter, P. A., & Semrud-Clikeman, M. (2007). *Child neuropsychology*. New York: Springer.

Vincent, K. R. (1991). Black-White IQ differences: Does age make a difference? *Journal of Clinical Psychology, 47*, 266–270.

Wade, S. L., Carey, J., & Wolfe, C. R. (2006). An online family intervention to reduce parental distress following pediatric brain injury. *Journal of Consulting and Clinical Psychology, 74*, 445–454.

Waschbusch, D. A. (2002). A meta-analytic examination of comorbid hyperactive-impulsive-attention problems and conduct problems. *Psychological Bulletin, 128*, 118–150.

Wilens, T. (2004). *Straight talk about psychiatric medications for kids* (2nd ed.). New York: Guilford.

Wilens, T., Faraone, S. V., & Biederman, J. (2004). Attention-deficit/ hyperactivity disorder in adults. *Journal of the American Medical Association, 292*, 619–623.

Wolf, J. M., Fein, D., & Akshoomoff, N. (2007). Autism spectrum disorders and social disabilities. In S. J. Hunter & J. Donders (Eds.), *Pediatric neuropsychological intervention* (pp. 151–174). Cambridge: Cambridge University Press.

Wong, T. M., Strickland, T. L., Fletcher-Janzen, E., Ardila, A., & Reynolds, C. R. (2000). Theoretical and practical issues in the neuropsychological assessment and treatment of culturally dissimilar patients. In E. Fletcher-Janzen, T. L. Strickland & C. R. Reynolds (Eds.), *Handbook for cross-cultural neuropsychology* (pp. 3–18). New York: Kluwer Academic/ Plenum publishers.

Zametkin, A. J., Nordahl, T. E., Gross, M., King, A. C., Semple, W. E., Rumsey, J., et al. (1990). Cerebral glucose metabolism in adults with hyperactivity of childhood onset. *New England Journal of Medicine, 323*(20), 1361–1366.

Chapter 2
Functional Neuroanatomy

The way structures in the developing brain are related to changes in psychological and cognitive development is of interest to child neuropsychologists. There are several ways that this relationship can be explored, including: (1) correlating structural changes in the developing brain with behavioral changes, (2) investigating behavioral changes and making inferences about structural maturation of the brain, and (3) studying brain dysfunction and its relationship to behavioral disorders (Kolb & Fantie, 1989).

Although these approaches can yield useful information about the developing brain, they are not without shortcomings. For example, because of the plasticity of the developing brain following damage, injury in a specific brain region may produce behavioral losses that vary greatly depending on the age of the child. Environmental factors, such as enrichment opportunities and social-cultural experiences, also influence the developing brain and the manner in which behaviors are expressed (Baron, 2004). Thus, the study of the brain-behavior relationship is particularly complex in children, and these factors must enter the equation when drawing conclusions about this relationship. Some have criticized neuropsychological approaches because of the level of inferences made when relating behavior to brain structure and function, and because of the correlational nature of the research (Fletcher & Taylor, 1984). There are now medical technologies and new research protocols that avoid some of these shortcomings. These technologies make it possible to explore the brain during craniotomies under local anesthesia (McDermott, Watson, & Ojemann, 2005), to investigate dendritic morphology with electron microscopic techniques (Scheibel, 1990), to measure sequential brain processing during cognitive tasks using visual evoked potentials (Liotti et al., 2007), and to image the brain while a person is completing a task through functional magnetic resonance imaging (Pliszka et al. 2006).

Our basic understanding of the brain and its relationship to complex human behaviors has been greatly facilitated by technological advances in modern neuroimaging techniques, including computed tomography (CT), magnetic resonance imaging (MRI), regional blood flow (rCBF), and positron-emission tomography (PET). Neuroimaging techniques allow researchers to gather direct evidence linking cognitive, behavioral, and psychosocial disorders to anatomical, physiological, and biochemical processes in the brain (Semrud-Clikeman, 2007). Research findings about the developing brain from these various approaches and methodologies will be used throughout this chapter in an effort to explore the biological basis of childhood disorders. These techniques will be further discussed in Chapter 3. To fully appreciate the brain-behavior relationship in children, an overview of the structure and function of the brain is necessary. This chapter reviews the structures and functions of the neuron and the sub-cortical and cortical regions from a neurodevelopmental perspective. This review serves as a foundation for exploring the complex interaction between anatomical development of the brain and the emergence of childhood behaviors and disorders.

M. Semrud-Clikeman, P.A. Teeter Ellison, *Child Neuropsychology*, DOI 10.1007/978-0-387-88963-4_2,
© Springer Science+Business Media, LLC 2009

Structure and Function of the Neuron

The neuron, the basic cellular structure of the nervous system, transmits nerve impulses throughout a complex network of interconnecting brain cells. The brain contains approximately 180 billion cells, 50 billion of which transmit and receive sensory-motor signals in the central nervous system (CNS) via 15,000 direct physical connections (Carlson, 2007). Investigation of the structure and function of neurons and their synaptic connections provides insight into basic psychopharmacology at the molecular level and may provide a method for describing how various neuropsychiatric disorders emerge and progress (Pliszka, 2003).

The CNS is comprised of two major cell types, neurons and neuroglia (Carlson, 2007). While neurons conduct nerve impulses, the neuroglia ("nerve glue") provide structural support and insulate synapses (the connections between neurons). Glial cells make up about 50 percent of the total volume of the CNS. Glial cells serve various functions, including transmission of signals across neurons, structural support for neurons, repair of injured neurons, and production of CNS fluid (Carlson, 2007). Neuroglia infiltrate or invade surrounding tissue in both the gray and white matter, and in rare instances these cells replicate uncontrollably during tumor activity (Nortz, Hemme-Phillips, & Ris, 2007). Though still relatively infrequent, pediatric brain tumors are the second most common neoplasm in children under 15 years of age, and as many as 1,000–1,500 cases are estimated to occur each year (Sklar, 2002).

Gray matter is located in the core of the CNS, the corpus striata at the base of the right and left hemispheres, the cortex that covers each hemisphere, and the cerebellum (Carlson, 2007). The cell bodies, the neuroglia, and the blood vessels that enervate the CNS are gray-brown in color and constitute the gray matter. White matter covers the gray matter and long axons extending out from the neuron. Axons are generally covered by a myelin sheath, which contains considerable amounts of neuroglia and appears white upon inspection. White matter has fewer capillaries than gray matter (Carlson, 2007).

As the basic functional unit of the CNS, the neuron transmits impulses in aggregated communities or nuclei that have special behavioral functions. Neurons can be modified through experience, and they are said to learn, to remember, and to forget as a result of experiences (Hinton, 1993). Pathological changes in neurons can occur as a result of early abnormal experiences. Although these alterations are thought to have a profound effect on the mature organism, the exact nature of these changes is still under investigation. Genetic aberrations also play a role in the way neurons develop and function (Cody et al. 2005). Damage to or destruction of neurons is also of concern because neurons typically do not regenerate (Swaiman, Ashwal, & Ferriero, 2006). Neurodevelopmental disorders and issues related to recovery of function following brain trauma will be discussed in detail in later chapters (see Chapter 10).

Anatomy of the Neuron

The neuron contains four well-defined cellular parts, including the cell body, dendrites, axons, and axon terminals. The cell body, or soma, is the trophic or life center of the neuron (see Fig. 2.1). Cell bodies vary in size and shape and contain the ribonucleic acid (RNA) and deoxyribonucleic acid (DNA) of the neuron. RNA, the site of protein synthesis, transmits instructions from DNA directing the metabolic functions of the neuron. Biochemical processes of the neuron, which take place in the cytoplasm of the cell body, include the energy-producing functions, the self-reproducing functions, and the oxidating reactions, whereby energy is made available for the metabolic activities of the cell (Carlson, 2007). Destruction or damage to the cell body can result in the death of the neuron.

Dendrites branch off the cell body and receive impulses from other neurons (Carlson, 2007). Dendrites are afferent in nature and conduct nerve impulses toward the cell body. Dendritic spines are the major point of the synapse, the area of transmission from one cell to another. Individuals with cognitive retardation have fewer spines or points of contact across neurons (Klein-Tasman, Phillips, & Kelderman, 2007). Dendrites can transmit neuronal impulses across neurons through either temporal or graded potentials. In

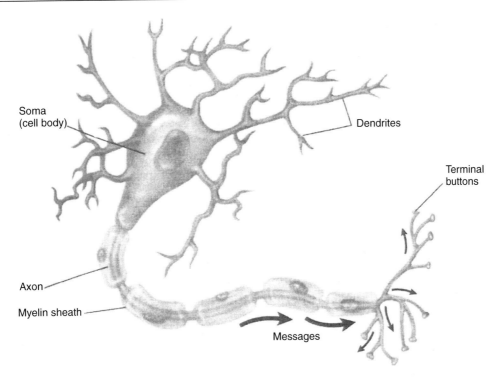

Fig. 2.1 Anatomy of the Neuron
Source: From Neil R. Carlson, *Physiology of Behavior*, 5th edition, p. 21. Copyright © 1994 by Allyn and Bacon. Reprinted by permission

this case, as a neuron receives an impulse it can transmit this impulse if the stimulation is close in time to another impulse or if it is strong enough combined with a previous impulse.

The axon is a long projection or axis from the cell body. Most neurons have only one axon, usually efferent in nature, that conducts nerve impulses away from the cell body. Axons are typically longer than dendrites and can be as much as one yard in length. For example, giant pyramidal cells in the motor cortex send axons to the caudal tip of the spinal cord. The axon hillock is a slender process close to the cell body where action potentials arise. The axon hillock is highly excitable and is activated through electrochemical processes, thereby "turning on" the neuron (Carlson, 2007). The impulse must be of sufficient strength for the neuron to "fire." Axons follow an "all or nothing" rule; if the impulse is not strong enough the neuron will not fire and, thus, will not transmit the message to another neuron. After the neuron fires, there is a period of time when it will not fire again as the neuron "recovers."

Axons are covered by a myelin sheath made up of neurilemma (or Schwann cells), which surround the axon. The myelin sheath gives the axon a white appearance and constitutes most of the white matter in cortical and subcortical areas. Most axons are myelinated at birth particularly in areas necessary for survival (motor-sucking; tactile sensitivity to hot, cold, and pain; auditory, and vision). Some axons continue to myelinate throughout development with myelinization not complete in the frontal lobes until well into the third decade of life. Changes in postnatal brain weight are generally related to increases in dendritic connections and to increases in the number of glial cells that form the myelin sheath along the axon (Shepherd, 2004).

Axons allow the nerve cells to transmit impulses rapidly, particularly along the Nodes of Ranvier. The Nodes of Ranvier are gaps in the myelin and during cell activation, nerve impulses skip from node to node. Myelinated axons permit more rapid transmission of signals, and anesthetics seem to be more effective at the Nodes of Ranvier. The terminal branches of the axon end at the synaptic telodendria.

The presynaptic and postsynaptic sites are both referred to as the synapse. Synapses are specialized for the release of chemicals known as neurotransmitters. Neurotransmitters are released from synaptic knobs at the end foot of the neuron in the presynapse, and they activate neurons at the postsynapse. Neurotransmitters are released from the presynapse (neuron A), travel across the synaptic cleft, and influence the activity of the adjoining neuron (neuron B) (see Fig. 2.2 for a depiction of these activities). There is a collection of vesicles at the synaptic knob at the end of each synapse, where neurotransmitters are stored. Most neurons have thousands of synapses, and each dendritic spine serves as a synapse that is excitatory in nature, which causes neurons to fire. Synapses are quite large for motor neurons and are smaller in the cerebellum and other cortical regions. Synapses usually occur between the axon of one cell and the dendrite of another (axondendritic connections). Although they can connect onto the soma or cell body of another neuron (axosomatic connection), synapses rarely occur from axon to axon (axo-axonal connections).

Types of Neurons

There are two basic types of neurons: efferent and afferent. Efferent neurons originate in the motor cortex of the CNS, descend through vertical pathways into subcortical regions, and culminate in the body's muscles (Gazzaniga, Ivry, & Mangun, 2002). These large descending tracts form columns from the motor cortex connecting higher cortical regions through the brain stem and spinal cord, to the body for the activation of single muscles or muscle groups. Various motor pathways begin to develop prenatally, while postnatal development is marked by changes in primitive reflexes (the Babinski reflex) and automatic reflexes (head and neck righting) (Swaiman et al., 2006).

Afferent neurons, sensory receptors found throughout the body, transmit sensory information into specific cerebral areas. For example, afferent neurons consist of rods and cones (cells that convey information about color or black/white) in the visual system that project into the occipital cortex; hair cells (convey information about tone) in the auditory

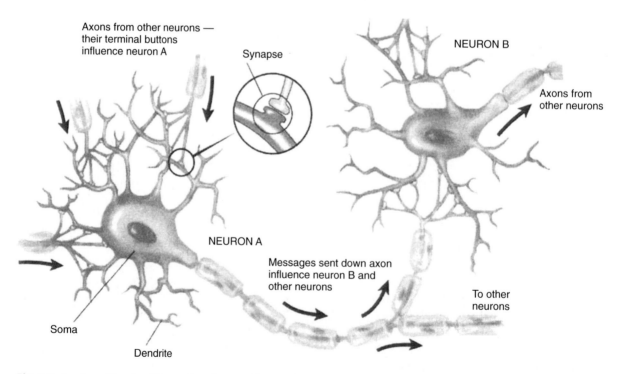

Fig. 2.2 Anatomy Showing Connections between Neuron A and B with Synaptic Cleft
Source: From Neil R. Carlson, *Physiology of Behavior*, 5th edition, p. 23. Copyright © 1994 by Allyn and Bacon. Reprinted with permission

system that project into the temporal cortex, and pain, touch, temperature, and pressure sensors in the skin that project into the parietal cortex. Somesthetic senses are the first to become functional in the fetus, as early as 7–8 weeks gestation, while auditory and visual neural maturation occurs later in embryonic development (Gazzaniga et al., 2002). Other cells in the corpus callosum (a large bundle of fibers connecting the two hemispheres) and the frontal lobes do not become fully functional until the teenage years through the 20s.

Types of Neuroglia

The neuroglia cells serve a number of important functions in the CNS: (1) providing structural support to neurons; (2) aiding in the regeneration of injured nerve fibers; (3) occupying injured sites by producing scar tissue, and (4) transporting gas, water, and metabolites from blood, and removing wastes from nerve cells (Carlson, 2007). The three major types of neuroglia (astrocytes, oligodendroglia, and microglia) have distinct functions and serve multiple purposes in the CNS. Astrocytes have three primary functions: (1) forming the blood-brain barrier; (2) supporting the cellular structure of the brain, and (3) directing the migration of neurons during early development. Astrocytes are the largest in size and the most abundant type of neuroglia (Carlson, 2007). These star-shaped glial cells attach to capillary blood vessels and cover approximately 80 percent of each capillary. Astrocytes, found primarily in the pia matter (fine membrane on the surface of the brain), cover large blood vessels. When injury occurs to the spinal cord or to the brain, through either disease or trauma, astrocytes go into hypertrophy (Morris, Krawiecki, Kullgren, Ingram, & Kurczynski, 2000). These cells multiply quickly, forming a glial scar that fills in gaps in the cellular structure caused by injury. Astrocytes may also serve a phagocytic function by removing destroyed tissue and cleaning up the site of injury. Astrocytoma, a type of primary neoplasm that frequently reoccurs after surgery, is the second most common brain tumor in adults (Hunter et al., 2005); though rare, astrocytomas do occur in children as well.

Astrocytomas in childhood most frequently occur in the cerebellum and the brain stem. These tumors are found equally in males and females. Although astrocytomas can occur at any age, the most frequent incidence is between five and nine years of age (Hunter et al., 2005). Oligodendroglia cells form and maintain the myelin sheath and, when injured, swell in size. Tumors rarely occur in oligodendroglia cells; when they do they grow slowly and are found primarily in the cortex and white matter. While about 40–60 percent of these tumors can be detected by skull X-rays after they calcify (Cohen & Duggner, 1994), radionuclide brain scans, angiography, and computed tomography scans have been helpful in the diagnostic phase of tumor processes. Finally, microglia cells are predominantly found in the gray matter (Carlson, 2007). Following disease or injury, microglia proliferate, move to the site of injury, and perform a phagocytic function by cleaning up damaged tissue. Tumors rarely occur in microglia cells.

These cells develop at different rates depending on location in the brain, experience of the baby, and genetic programming. In order to understand difficulties children have in development it is first important to understand how a typical brain develops. The following section provides a brief overview of the course of neuronal development.

Spinal Cord

The spinal cord serves two major functions: connecting the brain and the body via large sensory and motor neurons. The spinal cord comprises gray matter and white matter. Gray matter is the central, interior region of the spinal cord and is shaped like a butterfly. It appears gray on inspection and is made up of cell bodies. Neurons leave the spinal cord in segments called dermatomes and enter into muscles and organs. Motor commands from higher cortical centers are conducted at these sites. Sensory receptors connect with motor neurons in the gray matter of the spinal cord, via interneurons. Interneurons remain in the spinal cord and mediate motor activity with sensory stimuli. Interneurons also provide for cooperation among different spinal segments, which control distant muscle groups. For example, interneurons connect cervical and lumbar regions of the spinal cord to coordinate forelimbs and legs for walking. White matter surrounds the gray matter and consists of the myelin sheath (Brodal, 2004).

The spinal cord conducts signals to and from higher cortical regions, including the brain stem, the cerebellum, and the cortex. The posterior root of the spinal cord is afferent in nature, where sensory fibers enter into the gray matter, synapse with other neurons, and ascend into higher cortical areas in pathways. Conversely, the anterior root is efferent in nature and is made up of motor fibers that receive motor signals from higher cortical areas and communicate to muscle groups for movement. Nerve fibers enter and leave the spinal cord at regular intervals (dermatomes) and provide sensory and motor innervation to specific body segments. There are a total of 30 segments innervating the spinal cord: eight cervical, 12 thoracic, five lumbar, and five sacral (Brodal, 2004). Damage to the spinal cord at specific sites produces localized sensory and motor dysfunction in the body.

Unlike the brain, the spinal cord has little diversification or specialization, but it does carry out sensory, motor, and integrative functions. Four such functions are carried out in the spinal cord: (1) reflex activity, whereby a stimulus is followed by a coordinated motor response; (2) reciprocal activity, whereby one activity starts or stops another (i.e., excitatory or inhibitory); (3) monitoring activity, whereby incoming messages are controlled, coded, and transmitted, and (4) transmission activity, whereby messages are transmitted to and from the brain through the white matter (Kolb & Whishaw, 2003). In summary, the spinal cord is one of two major divisions of the CNS; the second is the brain.

Structure and Function of the Brain

The nervous system is divided into two basic systems: the peripheral (PNS) and the central nervous system (CNS). The PNS consists of the spinal, cranial, and peripheral nerves that connect the CNS to the rest of the body. Table 2.1 lists the cranial nerves and their functions. The CNS is completely encased in bone, is surrounded by protective coverings (meninges), and consists of two major structures: (1) the spinal cord in the vertebral column, and (2) the brain within the skull.

Table 2.1 Cranial nerves

Number	Name	Function
I	Olfactory	Smell
II	Optic	Vision
III	Oculomotor	Eye movement
IV	Trochlear	Eye movement
V	Trigeminal	Masticatory movement
VI	Abducens	Eye movement
VII	Facial	Face movement
VIII	Auditory	Hearing
IX	Glossopharyngeal	Tongue and pharynx movement
X	Vagus	Heart, blood vessels, viscera, larynx, and pharynx movement
XI	Spinal Accessory	Strength of neck and shoulder muscles
XII	Hypoglossal	Tongue muscles

Role and Function of the Meninges

Both the spinal cord and the brain are surrounded by a protective layer of tissue called the meninges. The meninges comprise three layers: the dura mater, the arachnoid, and the pia mater. The dura mater is the tough outer layer of the spinal cord and the brain, and has the consistency of a thin rubber glove. The dura mater attaches to the bones covering the cranium and receives blood vessels that innervate the brain (Brodal, 2004). Head injury may form an epidural hematoma, causing blood to accumulate in the region between the skull and the dura mater. The dura mater is supplied with blood by tiny vessels on its outermost layer near the skull. The subdural space, a fluid-filled layer, separates the dura mater from the arachnoid space. Accumulation of blood in the subdural area following injury can put enormous pressure on the brain (Swaiman et al., 2006). The arachnoid, a spiderlike web, is a delicate network of tissue under the dura mater. Blood accumulation between the dura mater and the arachnoid following injury is referred to as a subdural hematoma. Finally, the pia mater is the fragile, innermost layer of the meninges and contains small blood vessels. The pia mater surrounds the arteries and veins that supply blood to the brain; it serves as a barrier keeping out harmful substances that might invade the brain.

Bilateral infections that attack the meninges, referred to as meningitis, can have serious consequences for the developing brain (Swaiman et al.,

2006). The first year of life is the time of greatest risk for meningitis. The earlier the infection occurs, the higher the mortality rate. Some of the long-term consequences of meningitis are mental retardation, hydrocephalus, seizures, deafness, and hyperactivity (Swaiman et al., 2006). Cerebrospinal fluid (CSF), a clear, colorless fluid, fills the ventricles and the subarachnoid space (Wilkinson, 1986). CSF contains concentrations of sodium, chloride, and magnesium, as well as levels of neurotransmitters and other agents. An assay of the composition of these chemicals can be important for diagnosing disease processes. CSF reproduces at such a rate that total replacement occurs several times a day. The choroid plexus, located in the floor of the ventricles, produces the CSF, while the lateral ventricles contain the highest amounts of CSF. Infectious and metabolic disorders, such as meningitis, encephalitis, and tumors, as well as traumatic injury, can cause discernible changes in the CSF.

Cerebrospinal fluid has three major functions. Specifically, it (1) protects against injury to the brain and spinal cord; (2) diffuses materials into and away from the brain, and (3) maintains a "special environment" for brain tissues. Interference in the circulation and drainage of CSF can result in hydrocephalus, which causes cranial pressure. Hydrocephalus can have a devastating affect on the developing brain and may cause cognitive delays, particularly for non-verbal information; emotional, psychiatric, or behavioral disturbances, and slow motor development (Fletcher, Dennis, & Northrup, 2000). Surgical shunting drains CSF outside the skull. Recent advances in microsurgery in utero have produced successful results by reducing some of the more severe long-term negative effects of brain dysfunction or damage that can occur when hydrocephalus is untreated. Residual effects of hydrocephaly, ranging from mild to severe, depend on individual variables including the age of the child at the time of shunting and the presence of other neurological or medical complications that often accompany this disorder (Fletcher et al., 2000).

Ventricles

The ventricles, large cavities filled with cerebrospinal fluid (CSF), reside in various regions of the brain. The fourth ventricle, also referred to as the aqueduct of Sylvius, resides in the brain stem at the level of the pons and the medulla. The third ventricle is located in the diencephalon, and the lateral ventricles

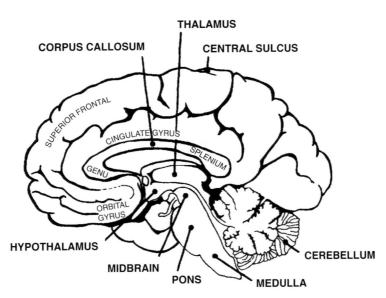

Fig. 2.3 Sagittal Section of the Brain Showing Brain Stem, Midbrain, and Forebrain Structure
Source: Adapted from M. Semrud-Clikeman and P. A. Teeter, "Personality, Intelligence, and Neuropsychology," in D. Saklofske (Ed.), *International Handbook of Personality and Intelligence in Clinical Psychology and Neuropsychology*, copyright © 1995 by Plenum Press, New York

are found in the forebrain region (see Fig. 2.3). Ventricles provide equilibrium as well as the CSF transporting nutrients and wastes throughout the brain. When these ventricles appear enlarged, a diagnosis of a tumor or disease processes, including hydrocephalus, encephalitis, and meningitis, may be made.

Structure and Function of the Brain Stem

The brain stem comprises five areas, including the fourth ventricle, the medulla oblongata, the pons (bridge), the midbrain (mesencephalon), and the diencephalon. Figure 2.4 shows a schematic of these structures and Fig. 2.5 shows a magnetic

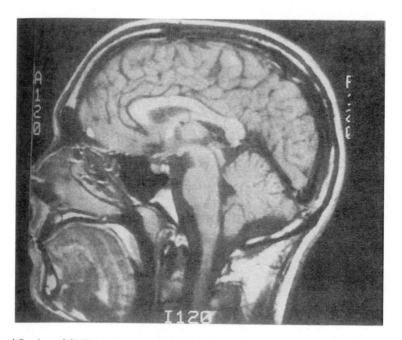

Fig. 2.4 MRI Sagittal Section of CNS Analogous to Brain Areas Depicted in Figure 2.3

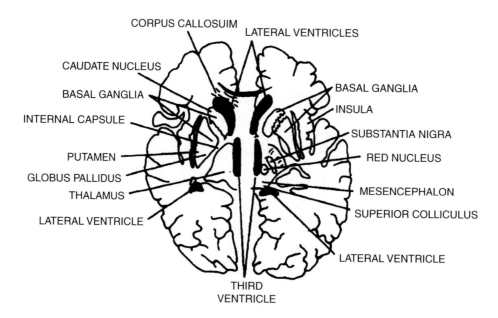

Fig. 2.5 Coronal Section Showing Structures of the Right and Left Hemisphere with Ventricular Systems

resonance image of these same structures. The major regions of the brain stem are discussed in detail in the following sections.

Medulla Oblongata

The medulla is a continuation of the spinal cord and contains nerve tracts similar to those found in the spinal cord. Groups of sensory and motor nuclei are arranged in ascending (i.e., afferent-sensory tracts) or descending (i.e., efferent-motor tracts) cell columns. Projections of the major cranial nerves occur at the level of the medulla, including the hypoglossal (tongue), the glossopharyngeal (pharynx and larynx), and the accessory (neck muscles) nerves. The sensory and motor tracts cross over into the opposite side of the brain at the level of the medulla. The somatosensory (touch, pressure, pain, and temperature) and the motor systems are organized in contralateral fashion, such that sensory information and movement on the right side of the body are primarily controlled by the left hemisphere. Conversely, the left side of the body is controlled by the right hemisphere. The auditory and visual systems also cross in the medulla. These functional systems will be discussed in more detail later in this chapter.

The reticular activating system (RAS) comprises a major portion of the medulla, extends into the midbrain region, and has numerous connections and functions (Brodal, 2004). The RAS, considered the arousal system, plays an important role in maintaining consciousness and attentional states for the entire brain. The RAS has been hypothesized as one of the critical mechanisms involved in ADHD (Sagvolden & Archer, 1989). For example, some RAS functions control blood pressure, blood volume in organs, and heart rate, whereas others regulate sleep and wakefulness.

The RAS receives input from most sensory systems and connects to all levels of the CNS. Because the RAS is directly or indirectly connected to much of the CNS, it can modulate CNS activity. Selective stimuli activate the RAS, which then alerts the cortex to incoming stimuli. Researchers espousing a bottom-up model hypothesize that the RAS may be filtering too much sensory information, thereby not allowing stimulation to reach the higher cortical regions that are necessary for adequate direction and maintenance of attention. When enough information reaches the RAS, it signals the cortex and produces cortical arousal and wakefulness. Thus, in children with ADHD this subcortical filter may not allow sufficient stimuli to reach higher cortical regions. This theory and others will be explored in later chapters.

Secretion of serotonin takes place at the pons, probably in the raphe system. The raphe nuclei are cells located across the medulla, pons, and midbrain regions, with afferent connections to the hypothalamus and limbic system (Brodal, 2004). This region also contains the locus ceruleus (LC), which produces 70 percent of norepinephrine in the brain, and serves as a modulator for other neurotransmitters (Carlson, 2007). The norepinephrine-rich cells in the locus ceruleus connect with the serotonin-rich cells in the raphe nuclei, and each type has a reciprocal affect on the other. Norepinephrine plays a role in vigilance, arousal, filtration of stimuli, and habituation. Finally, the continuation of the RAS at the pontine level appears to mediate sleep.

Serotonin inhibits arousal of the RAS, which then allows the thalamus to bring the cortex to a slow-wave sleep state (Carlson, 2007). Anesthetics appear to depress the RAS, which ultimately depresses the cortex. Fibers in the RAS also project to the limbic system and serve behavioral and emotional mechanisms for the control of pain. Morphine and opiate-like drugs may produce analgesic actions most likely in the raphe system (Shepherd, 2004).

Pons

The pons, between the medulla and midbrain and above the cerebellum, serves as a bridge across the right and the left hemispheres. Major sensory and motor pathways move through the pons, a continuation from the spinal cord and brainstem regions, and enter into higher cortical areas. The pons, in coordination with the cerebellum, receives information concerning movements from the motor cortex and helps modulate movements (Brodal, 2004). Information from the visual cortex is also received at the pontine level, which serves to guide visually determined movements. Finally, information from the hypothalamus and the limbic system converge in the pons and may influence the impact of emotional and motivational factors on motor activity (Brodal, 2004). A number of cranial nerves converge in the pontine region. Cranial nerves innervating the face and head receive sensory information and transmit signals in the pons for swallowing and chewing (trigeminal nerve), moving facial muscles, and affecting the hearing and equilibrium in the inner ear. Cranial nerves innervating the eye muscles (abducens) also pass through the pons.

Midbrain

The most anterior region of the brainstem is the midbrain or mesencephalon. The midbrain serves a major relay function for sensory-motor fibers. The two major divisions in the midbrain are the tegmentum, which falls below the ventricle and is separated by the substantia nigra, and the tectum, which comprises the superior colliculi (upper region involved in vision) and the inferior colliculi (lower region involved in the integration of auditory and kinesthetic impulses). The RAS also continues into the midbrain region. Several cranial nerves are located in the midbrain region. The oculomotor nerve moves the eye (lateral and downward gaze), and regulates the size of the pupil and the shape of the lens. The trigeminal nerve also resides in the midbrain area and serves as the major sensory nerve of the face.

Diencephalon

The diencephalon, the superior region of the brain stem, contains major relay and integrative centers for all the sensory systems except smell. The diencephalon is not clearly demarcated, but includes the thalamus, the hypothalamus, the pituitary gland, the internal capsule, the third ventricle, and the optic nerve (Brodal, 2004). The thalamus receives input from several sensory sources, including: (1) the visual system (projecting into the lateral geniculate body of the

thalamus); (2) the auditory system (projecting into the medial geniculate body), and (3) sensory receptors in the skin for pain, pressure, touch, and temperature.

The hypothalamus, anterior and inferior to the thalamus, plays a role in controlling the autonomic nervous system, including eating, sexual functions and dysfunctions, drinking, sleeping, temperature, rage, and violence. With connections to the limbic system, the hypothalamus influences motivational mechanisms of behavior. The pituitary, following directions from the hypothalamus, secretes hormones that regulate bodily functions. The internal capsule, situated lateral to the thalamus, contains fibers connecting the cortex to lower brain regions including the brainstem and the spinal cord. Major fibers comprise the internal capsule and connect the frontal cortical regions to the thalamus and to the pons. Finally, the optic nerve converges in the diencephalon and forms the optic chiasma (Brodal, 2004). Fibers from the optic nerve cross at the chiasma and project to the lateral geniculate body in the thalamus via the optic tract (Brodal, 2004). Figure 2.6 shows these structures.

Cerebellum

The cerebellum or hindbrain, behind the brain stem, connects to the midbrain, pons, and medulla. The cerebellum receives sensory information about where the limbs are in space and signals where muscles should be positioned. The cerebellum receives information from the semicircular canals (in the inner ear) concerning orientation in space. The cerebellum is involved in the unconscious adjustment of muscles in the body for coordinated, smooth, and complex motor activity. Injury of the cerebellum can result in dystaxia (movement disorders), dysarthria (slurred speech), nystagmus (blurred vision and dizziness), and hypotonia (loss of muscle tone) (Swaiman et al., 2006). Though still relatively uncommon, subtentorial tumors involving the cerebellum and the fourth ventricle are the most frequent type of brain tumor affecting young children (Konczak, Schoch, Dimitrova, Gizewski, & Timmann, 2005).

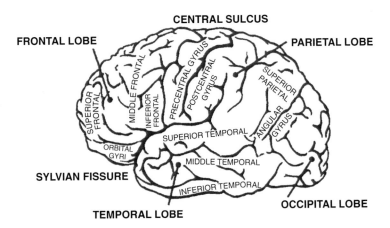

Fig. 2.6 Surface of the Left Hemisphere Showing Sulci, Fissures, and Major Subdivisions of the Cortex
Source: Adapted from M. Semrud-Clikeman and P. A. Teeter, "Personality, Intelligence and Neuropsychology," in D. Saklofske (Ed.), *International handbook of Personality and Intelligence in Clinical Psychology and Neuropsychology*, copyright © 1995 by Plenum Press, New York

Structure and Function of the Forebrain

Neocortex

The neocortex, often referred to simply as the cortex, comprises the highest functional division of the forebrain and makes up about 80 percent of the human brain. The cortex is wrinkled in appearance, with various elevated ridges and convolutions. Ridges are referred to as *gyri*, the deepest indentations are called *fissures*, and the shallower indentations are called *sulci*. The configuration of fissures and large sulci can be identified on visual inspection of the cortex (see Fig. 2.6). The lateral or Sylvian fissure separates the frontal lobe from the temporal lobe, and the central sulcus (fissure of Rolando) separates the frontal from the parietal lobe. The central sulcus is a prominent landmark separating the motor cortex (anterior to the central sulcus) from the sensory cortex (posterior to the central sulcus). The surface areas of posterior temporal and parietal locations are not clearly defined from the occipital regions. Finally, the calcarine sulcus extends from the occipital pole below to the splenium of the corpus callosum. The following sections will describe the structures and functions of the cortex. This brief overview of the structure, function, and development of neurons serves as a foundation for understanding the basic structure of the CNS and will be explored in more detail in a discussion of

brain tumors and head trauma (Chapter 10) and in the discussion of psychopharmacology (Chapter 11). In the following sections, the basic divisions of the nervous system will be explored.

Cerebral Hemispheres

The cerebrum comprises the right and left hemispheres, which appear to have anatomical (asymmetry) as well as functional (lateralization) differences (Brodal, 2004). *Asymmetry* typically refers to the structural or morphological differences between the two hemispheres (Rosen, Galaburda, & Sherman, 1990). Although neuroanatomical differences may underlie behavioral variations documented for each hemisphere, it is not known whether chemical as well as structural differences between the hemispheres also account for functional asymmetries (Witelson & Kigar, 1988). Cerebral lateralization refers to the degree to which each hemisphere is specialized for processing specific tasks. The right and left hemispheres appear to differ in terms of their efficiency in processing certain stimuli, such that both hemispheres are "not equally good at all tasks" (Brodal, 2004). Goldberg and Costa (1981) indicate that significant cytoarchitectural differences exist between the two hemispheres that may be related to neurobehavioral differences. The left hemisphere has a greater ratio of gray matter to white matter, particularly in the frontal, parietal, and temporal regions, compared to the right hemisphere. Conversely, the right hemisphere has greater white-to-gray matter ratios than the left hemisphere.

Major anatomical and functional differences observed in the two hemispheres are described as follows:

1. The left hemisphere has more neuronal representations in modality-specific regions in the three sensory cortices.
2. The right hemisphere has greater association zones, where sensory modalities converge.
3. The left hemisphere is structurally conducive to single modality processing, distinct motor activity, and intraregional integration.
4. The right hemisphere is structurally conducive to multiple modality and intraregional integration.
5. The right hemisphere has a greater capacity for handling informational complexity because of its intraregional connections, whereas the left hemisphere seems best suited for processing unimodal stimuli.

The right hemisphere appears better able to process novel information, whereas the left hemisphere seems able to work more efficiently with information with preexisting codes, such as those found in language activities. These differences will be further explored in a later discussion regarding nonverbal learning disabilities. Although the correlations between structure and function are not perfect, cerebral asymmetry has been of great interest to child neuropsychologists (Baron, 2004). Further, particular anatomical asymmetries between the two hemispheres are present at birth (Kolb & Whishaw, 2003). Measurable differences have been observed in the left planum temporale (near the auditory cortex) by 39 weeks gestation, leading some to suggest that the functional lateralization of language in the left hemisphere is determined prenatally (Witelson & Kigar, 1988). In adults, approximately 70 percent of right-handed individuals show larger planum temporale in the left hemisphere. The planum temporale has been related to phonological coding, a process very important in reading (Semrud-Clikeman, Hynd, Novey, & Eliopulos, 1991). The typical asymmetry of the left hemisphere has not been observed in those with developmental dyslexia and, thus, may

be related to the difficulty in encoding letters and words (Galaburda, Sherman, Rosen, Aboitiz, & Geschwind, 1985; Hynd, Semrud-Clikeman, Lorys, Novey, & Eliopulos, 1990; Larsen, Hoeien, & Oedegaard, 1992).

Early accounts of cerebral lateralization often listed specific functions for each hemisphere in a dichotomous, all-or-nothing fashion, implying that all aspects of a given task were carried out by one hemisphere. This all-or-nothing approach is probably overly simplistic because both hemispheres generally play a role in most complex tasks. One hemisphere, however, is usually considered dominant or most important for a specific task, while the other hemisphere is recessive or nondominant. Table 2.2 summarizes the developmental milestones for anatomical and functional asymmetries.

Witelson (1990) suggests that it is unclear whether functional differences between the two hemispheres are "relative" or "absolute," in such a way that each hemisphere is able to process tasks, but does so less efficiently. Others have proposed that the two hemispheres operate in a domain-specific fashion, whereby each hemisphere acts in an autonomous manner with restricted access to information processed by the other hemisphere.

Table 2.2 Major Division of the Nervous System

Brain Divisions	Brain Structures	Functional Divisions
Telencephalon (endbrain)	Neocortex Basal ganglia Limbic system Olfactory bulb Lateral ventricles	Forebrain
Diencephalon (between-brain)	Thalamus Epithalamus Hypothalamns Pineal gland Third ventricle	
Mesencephalon (midbrain)	Tectum Tegmentum Cerebral aqueduct	Brain stem
Metencephalon (across-brain)	Cerebellum Pons Fourth ventricle	
Myelencephalon (spinal brain)	Medulla oblongata Fourth Ventricle	Spinal cord

Source: Adapted with permission from *Fundamentals of Human Neuropsychology*, 3rd edition, by B. Kolb and I. Q. Whishaw (1990). San Francisco: W. H. Freeman.

Zaidal, Clark, and Suyenobu (1990) suggest the following:

(1) the two hemispheres can operate independently of one another, which reinforces the concept of hemispheric specialization, in some domain-specific functions;
(2) hemispheric specialization is "hard-wired" and is apparently innately directed;
(3) developmental patterns of the two hemispheres may differ, and
(4) while the two hemispheres may share processing resources, they can remain autonomous at any stage of processing.

Functional neuroimaging techniques will help answer these questions and will no doubt add to our understanding of the relative contribution of the two hemispheres, as well as specific structures, during certain activities. Some findings have implicated parts of the right hemisphere (particularly the posterior portion) to be important for visual-spatial and mental rotation tasks (Perez-Fabello, Campos, & Gomez-Juncal, 2007). Others have found more activation in the left hemisphere for processing of language and verbal comprehension (Booth et al., 1999). In addition, studies are beginning to show a right hemispheric preference for processing of emotional information. Facial expression processing has been found to be bilateral and to involve the fusiform gyrus of the temporal lobe (Pierce, Muller, Ambrose, Allen, & Courchesne, 2001). While anatomical differences appear early in development, there is insufficient evidence to conclude that morphological variations between the two hemispheres predict functional capabilities in any perfect sense (Kinsbourne, 2003).

Damage to the left hemisphere can result in a shift of language functions to the right hemisphere, particularly if both the posterior and anterior speech zones are damaged (Kolb & Whishaw, 2003). While language functions can be assumed by the right hemisphere, complex visuospatial functions appear to be in jeopardy (Kolb & Whishaw, 2003); further, complex syntactic processing appears vulnerable. So, although the left hemisphere might be better organized anatomically to deal with the language process, as suggested by the Goldberg and Costa (1981) model, the right hemisphere is able to do so under specific conditions. However, there is a price to be paid when one hemisphere assumes the function of the other, usually involving the loss or compromise of higher level functions. These more complex functions also may be more dependent on the anatomical differences generally found between the two hemispheres that exist early in the developing brain. This difference is most likely a result of the differential ratio of gray-to-white matter between the two hemispheres described by Goldberg and Costa (1981). Recovery and loss of functions will be covered in more detail in subsequent chapters.

Interhemispheric Connections

Large bundles of myelinated fibers connect various intra- and interhemispheric regions. The two hemispheres are connected via several transverse commissures or pathways, including the corpus callosum, the anterior commissure, and the posterior commissure. The corpus callosum, comprising the rostrum, the genu, the body, and the splenium, contains approximately 300 million nerve fibers for rapid interhemispheric communication (Carlson, 2007). The genu connects rostral portions of the right and left frontal lobes, while the body has interconnections between the frontal and parietal regions across the two hemispheres. The splenium connects temporal and occipital regions and is reportedly larger in females (Semrud-Clikeman, Fine, & Bledsoe, 2008). The splenium has been implicated in various childhood disorders, including ADHD (Hynd, Semrud-Clikeman, Lorys, Novey, & Eliopulos, 1991; Semrud-Clikeman et al., 1994) and dyslexia (Fine, Semrud-Clikeman, Keith, Stapleton, & Hynd, 2006). The anterior commissure is smaller than the corpus callosum and connects the temporal lobes of the right and left hemispheres (Kolb & Whishaw, 2003).

Intrahemispheric Connections

Association fibers connect cortical regions within each hemisphere (Kandel, Schwartz, & Jessell, 2000b). Association pathways allow for rapid communication within hemispheric regions for the perception and integration of stimuli and to organize complex output (e.g., emotional responses to stimuli). Short association fibers connect one to another, and longer fibers connect one lobe to another. For example, the arcuate fasciculus connects the frontal and temporal lobes; the longitudinal fasciculus connects the temporal and the occipital lobes with the frontal lobe; the occipitofrontal fasciculus connects the frontal, temporal, and occipital lobes, and the angular gyms connects the parietal and the occipital lobes (Kandel, Schwartz, & Jessell, 2000a). Dysfunction of these pathways can result in a variety of behavioral, cognitive, and personality manifestations including reading, spelling, and computational disorders in children (Zaidel, Iacoboni, Zaidel, & Bogen, 2003).

Structure and Function of the Cortex

The forebrain (telencephalon) comprises the four lobes, the lateral ventricles, the olfactory bulb, the limbic system, the basal ganglia, and the neocortex. Some textbooks also place the thalamus in the forebrain region, while others refer to this as a diencephalic structure (Brodal, 2004). The cortex comprises the right and left hemispheres, each with four major lobes: (1) frontal, motor cortex; (2) parietal, somatosensory cortex; (3) occipital, visual cortex, and (4) temporal, auditory cortex. (See Fig. 2.6 for a view of the cortical regions.) Figure 2.7 illustrates the various functions of the lobes.

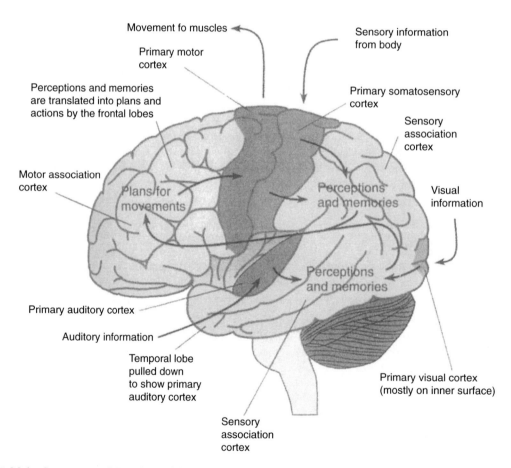

Fig. 2.7 Major Structures and Functions of the Cortex
Source: From Neil R. Carlson, *Physiology of Behavior*, 5th edition, p. 91. Copyright © 1994 by Allyn and Bacon. Reprinted with permission

Frontal Lobes

The frontal lobes are the most anterior cortical structures and comprise the primary motor cortex, the premotor cortex, an area of expressive language (Broca's area), the medial cortex, and the prefrontal cortex (Damasio & Anderson, 2003). Whereas the primary and premotor areas of the frontal lobes have major motor functions, the prefrontal cortex mediates reasoning and planning and monitors other cortical and subcortical functions. The prefrontal cortex matures the most slowly of all of the areas of the lobes.

Lesions or damage to the primary motor cortex can result in paralysis to the contralateral side of the body, whereas lesions to the premotor cortex can produce more complex coordination problems because this region directs the execution of the primary motor area (Kolb & Whishaw, 2003). Lesions or damage to the prefrontal cortex, with its intricate connections to other brain regions, including thalamic, hypothalamic, and limbic areas, often result in affective dissociations, impaired executive functions and judgment, and intellectual deficits (Lezak, Howieson, & Loring, 2004).

Primary Motor Cortex

The motor system comprises the primary motor, the premotor, and to a lesser degree, the prefrontal, with each region assuming differentiated motor functions. The primary motor cortex is involved with the execution and maintenance of simple motor functions; the premotor cortex directs the primary motor cortex; and the prefrontal cortex influences motor planning and adds flexibility to motor behavior as a result of input from internal and external factors (Lezak et al., 2004).

The primary motor cortex resides immediately anterior to the central sulcus and contains giant pyramidal cells (Betz), which control fine motor and highly skilled voluntary movements (Damasio & Anderson, 2003). The primary motor cortex receives afferent (incoming sensory) signals from the parietal lobe, the cerebellum, and the thalamus for the integration of sensory-motor signals, while efferent (outgoing motor) signals are transmitted to the reticular activating system, the red nucleus

(midbrain structure), the pons, and the spinal cord for the production of movement. The primary cortex controls movements to the opposite side of the body and is arranged in a homuncular fashion. A homunculus is a schematic of brain function mapping onto specific body structures. Thus, there is a specific region that is responsible for movement of the thumb, or the ankle, or the nose that maps onto the primary motor cortex.

Specific muscle groups of the body are represented in an inverted pattern stretching across the primary motor area. Stimulation to specific areas of the primary motor cortex produces contractions of highly localized muscle areas. For example, Broca's area resides near the primary motor area in the left hemisphere, controls facial musculature, and mediates speech production (Kolb & Whishaw, 2003).

Premotor Cortex

The premotor cortex, anterior to the primary motor cortex, plays a role in controlling limb and body movements. More complex, coordinated movements appear to be regulated at this level, especially fluid sequential movements. The premotor cortex directs the primary cortex in the execution and maintenance of simple movements. The limbic system also influences the motor cortex, directly and indirectly, primarily in terms of attentional and motivational aspects of motor functions (Damasio & Anderson, 2003).

Prefrontal Cortex

The prefrontal cortex, the most anterior region of the frontal lobe, receives incoming signals from the thalamus, which then project to the hypothalamus. Further, connections to the limbic system allow the prefrontal cortex to mediate, regulate, and control affective, emotional behavior. Prefrontal connections to the temporal, parietal, and occipital association regions allow for a comparison of past and present sensory experiences (Gazzaniga et al., 2002). These intricate connections of the prefrontal cortex with cortical and subcortical regions allow for highly integrative, complex functions. Judgments and insights arise out of prefrontal activity, whereas motor planning, consequential thinking, and ongoing monitoring of behavior also appear to be regulated by prefrontal regions. The limbic system also seems to play a role in complex, intentional, or volitional motor behaviors, though this is not considered part of the motor area. The development of executive control functions is discussed in more detail in later sections of this chapter. Also see Chapter 6 for a discussion of neuropsychiatric disorders (e.g., ADHD and Tourette syndrome) associated with frontal lobe and executive control damage or dysfunction.

Parietal Lobes

The parietal lobe is separated from the frontal regions by the central sulcus and from the temporal lobe by the lateral fissure. The parietal lobes play a central role in the perception of tactile sensory information, including the recognition of pain, pressure, touch, proprioception, and kinesthetic sense. The parietal lobe is comprised of three areas: the primary sensory projection area, the secondary somatosensory area, and the tertiary or association area (Carlson, 2007).

Primary Sensory Cortex

The primary sensory projection area is immediately posterior to the central sulcus, adjacent to the primary motor cortex. Some have argued that there is a great deal of functional overlap between the sensory and motor cortical areas with approximately one-quarter of the points in the motor area also showing sensory capabilities and one-quarter of the points in the sensory area also showing motor capabilities (Brodal, 2004). Thus, regions posterior to the sulcus have been labeled as the sensory-motor area, while regions anterior to the sulcus are labeled the motor-sensory area. What seems most evident from this research is that the sensory-motor regions are highly interrelated, which probably results in increased functional efficiency.

The primary sensory projection area has four major functions: (1) recognition of the source, quality, and severity of pain; (2) discrimination of light pressure and vibration; (3) recognition of fine touch (proprioception) and (4) awareness of the position and movement of body parts (kinesthetic sense) (Lezak et al., 2004). Numerous fibers converge in the primary sensory projection area, including afferents coming from the thalamus, skin, muscles, joints, and tendons from the opposite side of the body. Lesions to the primary parietal regions can produce sensory deficits to the contralateral (opposite) side of the body, and other more complex deficits can occur when the temporoparietal and/ or inferior parietal regions are involved (Tranel, 1992).

Like the primary frontal cortex, the primary sensory projection area is arranged in a homuncular fashion, with the proportion of cortical representation related to the need for sensitivity in a particular body region (Brodal, 2004). For example, the region representing the face, lips, and tongue is quite large because speech production requires multiple sensory input from these various muscles to provide sensory feedback to orchestrate a complex series of movements needed for speaking. The proximity of the primary parietal region to the primary motor regions allows for the rapid cross-communication between sensory-motor systems that is necessary for the execution of motor behavior.

Secondary and Association Cottices

Input from the primary sensory projection regions is synthesized into more complex sensory forms by secondary parietal regions. The tertiary or association region, the most posterior area of the parietal lobe, receives input from the primary sensory projection area and sends efferents into the thalamus. The association region is involved with the integration and utilization of complex sensory information. Gazzaniga et al. (2002) indicate that the association regions synthesize information, whereas the primary areas are involved with finer distinctions and analysis of information. The association region overlaps with other cortical structures, including temporal and occipital areas for the integration of sensory information from different modalities. Although damage to the association region does not produce visual, auditory, or sensory deficits, damage to the association area can result in disorders of the integration of complex sensory information. Cross-modal matching of visual with auditory and sensory stimuli takes place in the association region, which is considered to be the highest level of sensory analysis. Some argue that this region regulates much of what is measured by intelligence tests, including cognitive and mental functions such as thinking, reasoning, and perception (Kolb & Whishaw, 2003).

Occipital Lobes

The most posterior region of the cortex comprises the occipital lobe (primary visual cortex), which is further divided into dorsal (superior) and ventral (inferior) areas. The inferior and superior regions are divided by the lateral-occipital sulcus, while the calcarine fissure extends from the occipital pole into the splenium of the corpus callosum (see Fig. 2.7). The visual cortex receives projections from the retina in each eye via the lateral geniculate nucleus in the thalamus (see Fig. 2.8). The rods and cones in the retina respond to photic stimulation, and photo-chemical processes result in nerve impulses in the optic nerve (Carlson, 2007). Once inside the cerebrum, the optic nerve forms the optic chiasm. The optic chiasm is where nerve fibers partially cross, project to the lateral geniculate in the thalamus, and converge in the visual cortex. Damage anywhere along this pathway can produce a variety of visual defects.

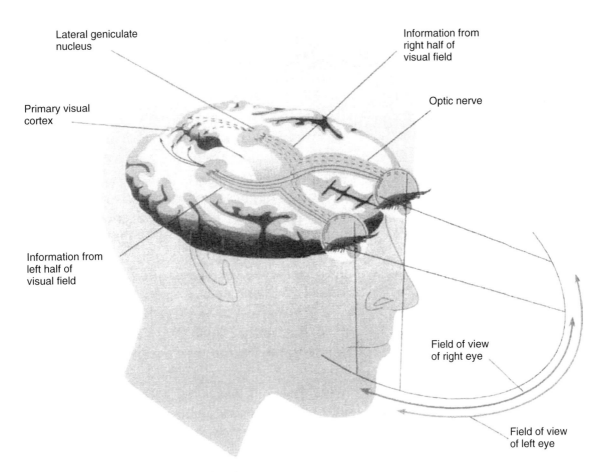

Fig. 2.8 Visual Fields and Cortical Visual Pathways
Source: From Neil R. Carlson, *Physiology of Behavior*, 5th edition, p. 149. Copyright © 1994 by Allyn and Bacon. Reprinted by permission

The occipital lobe comprises primary, secondary, and tertiary or association regions (Kolb & Whishaw, 2003). The primary occipital cortex receives afferent input from the thalamus, which passes through the temporal cortex. Damage to this tract, even if it occurs in the temporal lobe, can produce visual field defects. The association region is involved with complex visual perception, relating past visual stimuli to present stimuli for the recognition and appreciation of what is being seen. Damage to the association region, particularly in the right hemisphere, can produce a variety of visual deficits, including recognition of objects, faces, and drawings.

Temporal Lobes

The temporal lobe has three major divisions: (1) the posterior region of the superior temporal gyrus, which is referred to as Wernicke's area in the left hemisphere; (2) the inferior temporal region, including the occipitotemporal association region, and (3) the mesial temporal aspect, including the hippo-campal and amygdala regions (Tranel, 1992). The temporal lobe has complex interconnections, with afferent fibers coming from the parietal lobe, efferent fibers projecting into the parietal and frontal lobes, and the corpus callosum and the anterior commissure connecting the right and left temporal lobes (Kolb & Whishaw, 2003). Three major pathways connect the temporal lobe with other cortical regions for complex integrated functions. The arcuate fasciculus connects the frontal and temporal lobes, the superior longitudinal fasciculus connects the temporal to the occipital and frontal cortices (i.e., the sensory and motor regions of Wernicke's and Broca's areas), and the occipitofrontal fasciculus connects the frontal-temporal-occipital regions.

The anatomical complexity, including large association regions, suggests that the temporal lobes have diverse functions, including the perception of auditory sensations, the analysis of affective tone in auditory stimuli, and long-term memory storage. Although the temporal lobe has primary auditory perception and association functions related to speech and language processing, it also plays a significant role in memory functions and in facial

(prosopagnosia) and object recognition (Bauer & Demery, 2003).

The primary temporal cortex is involved with the perception of speech sounds, particularly in the left hemisphere, and nonverbal tonal sequences, particularly in the right hemisphere, while the secondary and association regions are more complex and varied in function. The secondary and association regions add the affective quality to stimuli that is essential for learning to take place. When positive, negative, or neutral affective qualities are attached to stimuli, information takes on motivational or emotional importance to the learner. Without this association, all stimuli would be judged as equal and we would respond to all stimuli with the same affect or emotion (Heilman, Blonder, Bowers, & Valenstein, 2003).

The mesial temporal region, including the adjoining hippocampus and amygdala, appears to be linked to memory processes and plays a role in learning or acquiring new information (Tranel, 1992). Lesions in this area result in impaired retention of new memories, as this region appears to be related to the process by which new memories are stored or are retrieved from storage (Lezak et al., 2004). Asymmetry of functions is evident in the temporal lobes. Memory functions appear to be lateralized. The recall of verbal information, including stories and word lists presented either orally or visually, is stored in the left hemisphere, whereas nonverbal recall for geometric drawings, faces, and tunes is stored in the right hemisphere (Kolb & Whishaw, 2003).

Olfactory Bulb

The olfactory system is the only sensory system that converges in the telencephalon. The olfactory bulb receives sensory information concerning smell directly from the olfactory nerve and converges with the olfactory tract; at this juncture, axons cross to the bulb in the opposite hemisphere via the anterior commissure. The olfactory tract projects to the primary olfactory cortex to a small region called the uncus, close to the end of the temporal lobe (Brodal, 2004). Although olfactory assessment is often ignored, the sense of smell is frequently associated with various neuropsychiatric distur-bances found in adults, particularly schizophrenia, Parkinson's disease, multiple sclerosis, subfrontal tumors, and some brain injuries (Heilman & Valenstein, 2003).

Limbic System

The limbic system is a complex deep collection of structures in the forebrain comprising the hippo-campus, amygdale, septum, and cingulate gyms (Kolb & Whishaw, 2003). The limbic system has widespread connections with the neocortex and with the autonomic and endocrinological systems, and is considered a primitive brain structure involved with the olfactory senses. It resides between two brain regions (diencephalon and telencephalon) and serves as an intermediary to cognitive and emotional functions (Wilkinson, 1986). In humans the limbic system has less to do with the olfactory system than with emotional and memory functions that are essential for the survival of the species. It also has preservation functions for the individual.

Wilkinson (1986) describes a number of important functions of the limbic system, including:

(1) analyzing and responding to fearsome, threa-tening situations;
(2) monitoring sexual responses, including repro-ducing and nurturing offspring;
(3) remembering recent and past events, and
(4) sensing and responding to feeling states, including pleasure.

Autonomic responses (e.g., heart rate, breathing, blood pressure, and digestive functions) can be influenced by limbic structures, especially the cingulate gyrus. Aggressive reactions and social indifference have been associated with the cingulate gyrus. The cingulate gyrus has also been associated with error checking and self-monitoring of behavior (Semrud-Clikeman, Pliszka, Lancaster, & Liotti, 2006). Feelings of anxiety, deja vu experiences, rage, and fear have been associated with functions of the amygdala (Gazzaniga et al., 2002). With its connections with other limbic and cortical structures, the hippocampus has broad functions involving learning and memory. Seizure activity in limbic structures, particularly the hippocampus, sometimes includes temporal lobe structures as well (Lockman, 1994). Seizures at this site may result in a temporary loss of consciousness and loss of memory.

Basal Ganglia

The term *basal ganglia* refers to all or some of the masses of gray matter within the cerebral hemi-spheres, including the caudate nucleus, putamen, and globus pallidus. The corpus striatum connects to the neocortex and to the thalamus, and has ascending and descending pathways to midbrain structures (red nucleus and substantia nigra), and to the spinal cord (Brodal, 2004). Serotonin-rich connections from the raphe nuclei also reach the striatum, the prefrontal regions, and the limbic system. These serotonin pathways serve to inhibit motor actions and emotional responses. The basal ganglia are intimately involved with motor func-tions and, when damaged, can produce postural changes, increases or decreases in muscle tone, and movement changes (e.g., twitches, tremors or jerks). Sydenham's chorea, a childhood disease resulting from poststreptoccal rheumatic fever involving the corpus striatum, is characterized by irregular and purposeless movements. This disease usually appears insidiously, gradually worsening with symptoms of hyperkinetic movement disorder, emotional lability, and hypotonia. Rheumatic heart disease is often found in conjunction with Sydenham's chorea and is the cause of mortality in this disorder. The chorea generally dissipates six months after onset, but the emotional lability remains (Cardona et al., in press).

Summary

This chapter's goal was to provide an introduction to the field of neuropsychology. Defining neurop-sychology includes the study of the brain and the transactional effect of neurology and the environment. Neuropsychologists are specialists in assessment and intervention, and specific and intensive training is necessary for practice in this field. Child (pediatric) neuropsychologists require additional training in child development as well as in child assessment. Adult neuropsychologists have separate training in geriatric, adult disorders, and neuroanatomy that is specific to aging, while child neuropsychologists have emphasis in development and in pediatric disorders. To that end, adult neuropsychologists should not complete pediatric assessments without additional training and child neuropsychologists should not complete adult assessments without specific education.

For child neuropsychologists it is important to have knowledge of appropriate laws that apply to education. Since almost all of the children and adolescents that are evaluated are in school, the most effective clinician will be informed about the contents of IDEA, Section 504, and HIPAA to most appropriately serve the population. Providing assessment without such knowledge may result in less than ideal evaluations, inappropriate interventions, and lead parents to expect services that are unlikely to be delivered. Multicultural issues were also discussed and it is very apparent that research and practice in this area is seriously lacking.

This chapter also sought to provide a review of basic anatomy of the brain and neuron in preparation for subsequent chapters on disorders, assessment, and intervention. A review of basic structures as well as their place in gestation and development was provided. Some structures change dramatically during childhood while others are basically formed prior to birth. These changes appear to be linked to stages of cognitive and neurological development, and the informed clinician will utilize these developmental changes when interpreting findings. Many of the aspects of this chapter are important to understand the next chapter on neuroradiological methods.

References

Baron, I. S. (2004). *Neuropsychological evaluation of the child*. New York: Oxford University Press.

Bauer, R. M., & Demery, J. A. (2003). Agnosia. In K. M. Heilman & E. Valenstein (Eds.), *Clinical neuropsychology* (4th ed., pp. 236–295). New York: Oxford.

Booth, J. R., MacWhinney, B., Thulborn, K. R., Sacco, K., Voyvodic, J. T., & Feldman, H. M. (1999). Functional organization of activation patterns in children: Whole brain fMRI imaging during three different cognitive tasks. *Progress in neuro-psychopharmacology & biological psychiatry, 23*, 669–682.

Brodal, P. (2004). *The central nervous system: Structure and function* (Vol. 3). New York: Oxford University Press.

Cardona, F., Ventriglia, F., Cipolla, O., Romano, A., Creti, R., & Orefici, G. (in press). A post-streptococcal pathogenesis in children with tic disorders is suggested by a color Doppler echocardiographic study. *European Journal of Neurology*.

Carlson, N. R. (2007). *Physiology of behavior* (9th ed.). Boston: Allyn & Bacon.

Cody, J., Semrud-Clikeman, M., Hardies, L. J., Lancaster, J., Ghidoni, P., Schaub, R. L., et al. (2005). Growth hormone benefits children with 18q deletions. *American Journal of Human Genetics, 143A*, 1181–1190, 1–7.

Cohen, M. E., & Duggner, P. K. (1994). Tumors of the brain and spinal cord including leukemic involvement. In K. F. Swaiman (Ed.), *Pediatric neurology*. St. Louis, MO: Mosby.

Damasio, A. R., & Anderson, S. W. (2003). The frontal lobes. In K. M. Heilman & E. Valenstein (Eds.), *Clinical neuropsychology* (4th ed., pp. 404–446). New York: Oxford.

Fine, J. G., Semrud-Clikeman, M., Keith, T. Z., Stapleton, L., & Hynd, G. W. (2006). Reading and the corpus callosum: An MRI family study of volume and area. *Neuropsychology, 21*(2), 235–241.

Fletcher, J. M., Dennis, M., & Northrup, H. (2000). Hydrocephalus. In K. O. Yeates, D. M. Ris, & H. G. Taylor (Eds.), *Pediatric neuropsychology* (pp. 25–46). New York: Guilford Press.

Fletcher, J. M., & Taylor, H. (1984). Neuropsychological approaches to children: Toward a developmental neuropsychology. *Journal of Clinical Neuropsychology, 6*, 39–56.

Galaburda, A. M., Sherman, G. P., Rosen, G. D., Aboitiz, F., & Geschwind, N. (1985). Developmental dyslexia: Four consecutive patients with cortical anomalies. *Annals of Neurology, 18*, 222–233.

Gazzaniga, M. S., Ivry, R. B., & Mangun, G. R. (2002). *Cognitive neuroscience: The biology of the mind* (2nd ed.). New York: W.W. Norton & Company.

Goldberg, E., & Costa, L. D. (1981). Hemisphere differences in the acquisition and use of descriptive systems. *Brain and Language, 14*, 144–173.

Heilman, K. M., Blonder, L. X., Bowers, D., & Valenstein, E. (2003). Emotional disorders associated with neurological diseases. In K. M. Heilman & E. Valenstein (Eds.), *Clinical neuropsychology* (4th ed., pp. 447–478). New York: Oxford.

Heilman, K. M., & Valenstein, E. (2003). *Clinical neuropsychology* (4th ed.). New York: Oxford University Press.

Hinton, G. E. (1993). How neural networks learn from experience. In *Mind and brain: Readings from the Scientific American*. New York: W.H. Freeman.

Hunter, S. B., Varma, V., Shehata, B., Nolen, J. D., Cohen, C., Olson, J. J., et al. (2005). Apolipoprotein D expression in primary brain tumors: Analysis by quantitative RT-PCR in formalin-fixed, paraffin-embedded tissue.

The Journal of Histochemistry and Cytochemistry, 53, 963–969.

Hynd, G. W., Semrud-Clikeman, M., Lorys, A. R., Novey, E. S., & Eliopulos, D. (1990). Brain morphology in developmental dyslexia and attention deficit disorder/hyperactivity. *Archives of neurology, 47*, 919–926.

Hynd, G. W., Semrud-Clikeman, M., Lorys, A. R., Novey, E. S., & Eliopulos, D. (1991). Corpus callosum morphology in attention deficit-hyperactivity disorder (ADHD): Morphometric analysis of MRI. *Journal of Learning Disabilities, 24*, 141–146.

Kandel, E. R., Schwartz, J. H., & Jessell, T. M. (2000a). *Principles of neural science* (4th ed.). New York: McGraw Hill.

Kandel, E. R., Schwartz, J. H., & Jessell, T. M. (2000b). *Principles of neural science* (4th ed.). New York: McGraw-Hill.

Kinsbourne, M. (2003). The corpus callosum equilibrates the cerebral hemispheres. In E. Zaidal & M. Iacoboni (Eds.), *The parallel brain: The cognitive neuroscience of the corpus callosum* (pp. 271–281). Cambridge, MA: The MIT Press.

Klein-Tasman, B. P., Phillips, K. D., & Kelderman, J. K. (2007). Genetic syndromes associated with intellectual disability. In S. J. Hunter & J. Donders (Eds.), *Pediatric neuropsychological intervention* (pp. 193–223). Cambridge: Cambridge University Press.

Kolb, B., & Fantie, B. (1989). Development of the child's brain and behavior. In C. R. Reynolds & E. F. Janzen (Eds.), *Handbook of child clinical neuropsychology* (pp. 115–144). New York: Plenum Press.

Kolb, B., & Whishaw, I. Q. (2003). *Fundamentals of human neuropsychology* (5th ed.). New York: Worth Publishers.

Konczak, J., Schoch, B., Dimitrova, A., Gizewski, E., & Timmann, D. (2005). Functional recovery of children and adolescents after cerebellar tumour resection. *Brain: A Journal of Neurology, 128*, 1428–1441.

Larsen, J. P., Hoeien, T., & Oedegaard, H. (1992). Magnetic resonance imaging of the corpus callosum in developmental dyslexia. *Cognitive Neuropsychology, 9*(2), 123–134.

Lezak, M. D., Howieson, D. B., & Loring, D. W. (2004). *Neuropsychological assessment* (4th ed.). New York: Oxford University Press.

Liotti, M. P., Pliszka, S.R., Perez, R., Luus, B., Glahn, D., & Semrud-Clikeman, M. (2007). Electrophysiological correlates of response inhibition in children and adolescents with ADHD: Influence of gender, age, and previous treatment history. *Psychophysiology, 44*, 936–948.

Lockman, L. A. (1994). Nonabsence generalized seizures. In K. F. Swaiman (Ed.), *Pediatric neurology* (2nd ed., pp. 261–270). St Louis: Mosby.

McDermott, K. B., Watson, J. M., & Ojemann, J. G. (2005). Presurgical language mapping. *Current Directions in Psychological Science, 14*, 291–295.

Morris, R. D., Krawiecki, N. S., Kullgren, K. A., Ingram, S. M., & Kurczynski, B. (2000). Brain tumors. In K. O. Yeates, D. M. Ris, & H. G. Taylor (Eds.), *Pediatric neuropsychology: Research, theory and practice* (pp. 74–91). New York: Guilford Press.

Nortz, M. J., Hemme-Phillips, J. M., & Ris, D. M. (2007). Neuropsychological sequelae in children treated for cancer. In S. J. Hunter & J. Donders (Eds.), *Pediatric neuropsychological intervention* (pp. 112–132). Cambridge: Cambridge University Press.

Perez-Fabello, M. J., Campos, A., & Gomez-Juncal, R. (2007). Visual imaging capacity and imagery control in Fine Arts students. *Perceptual and Motor Skills, 104*, 815–822.

Pierce, K., Muller, R. A., Ambrose, J., Allen, G., & Courchesne, E. (2001). Face processing occurs outside the fusiform 'face area' in autism: Evidence from functional MRI. *Brain, 124*, 2059–2073.

Pliszka, S. R. (2003). *Neuroscience for the mental health clinician.* New York: Guilford Press.

Pliszka, S. R., Glahn, D. C., Semrud-Clikeman, M., Franklin, C., Perez, R., Xiong, J., et al. (2006). Neuroimaging of inhibitory control areas in children with attention deficit hyperactivity disorder who were treatment naive or in long-term treatment. *American Journal of Psychiatry, 163*(6), 1052–1060.

Rosen, G. D., Galaburda, A. M., & Sherman, G. F. (1990). The ontogeny of anatomic asymmetry: Constraints derived from basic mechanisms. In A. B. Scheibel & A. F. Wechsler (Eds.), *Neurobiology of higher cognitive function* (pp. 215–238). New York: Guilford Press.

Sagvolden, T., & Archer, T. (1989). *Attention deficit disorder: Clinical and basic research.* Hillsdale, NJ: Lawrence Erlbaum Associates.

Scheibel, A. B. (1990). Dendritic correlates of higher cognitive function. In A. B. Scheibel & A. F. Wechsler (Eds.), *Neurobiology of higher cognitive function* (pp. 239–270). New York: Guilford Press.

Semrud-Clikeman, M. (2007). *Social competence in children.* New York: Springer.

Semrud-Clikeman, M., Filipek, P. A., Biederman, J., Steingard, R. J., Kennedy, D. N., Renshaw, P. F., et al. (1994). Attention-deficit hyperactivity disorder: Magnetic resonance imaging morphometric analysis of the corpus callosum. *Journal of the American Academy of Child & Adolescent Psychiatry, 33*(6), 875–881.

Semrud-Clikeman, M., Fine, J. G., & Bledsoe, J. (2008). *Meta-analysis of empirical literature on NVLD.* Paper presented at the International Neuropsychological Society.

Semrud-Clikeman, M., Hynd, G. W., Novey, E. S., & Eliopulos, D. (1991). Dyslexia and brain morphology: Relationships between neuroanatomical variation and neurolinguistic tasks. *Learning and Individual Differences, 3*(3), 225–242.

Semrud-Clikeman, M., Pliszka, S. R., Lancaster, J., & Liotti, M. (2006). Volumetric MRI differences in treatment-naïve vs chronically treated children with ADHD. *Neurology, 67*(1023–1027).

Shepherd, G. M. (2004). *The synaptic organization of the brain* (5th ed.). New York: Oxford University Press.

Sklar, C. A. (2002). Childhood brain tumors. *Journal of Pediatric Endocrinology and Metabolism, 15*, 669–673.

Swaiman, K. F., Ashwal, S., & Ferriero, D. M. (2006). *Pediatric neurology* (4th ed.). San Diego: Mosby.

Tranel, D. (1992). Functional neuroanatomy: Neuropsychological correlates of cortical and subcortical damage. In S. C. Yudofsky & R. E. Hales (Eds.), *The American Psychiatric Press textbook of neuropsychiatry* (2nd ed., pp. 57–88). Washington, D.C.: American Psychiatric Association.

Wilkinson, J. L. (1986). *Neuroanatomy for medical students.* Bristol BSI: John Wright & Son Ltd.

Witelson, S. F. (1990). Structural correlates of cognitive function in the human brain. In A. B. Scheibel & A. F. Wechsler (Eds.), *Neurobiology of higher cognitive function* (pp. 167–184). New York: Guilford Press.

Witelson, S. F., & Kigar, D. L. (1988). Anatomical development of the corpus callosum in humans: A review with reference to sex and cognition. In D. L. Molfese & S. J. Segalowitz (Eds.), *Brain lateralization in children* (pp. 35–57). New York: Guilford Press.

Zaidal, E., Clark, M., & Suyenobu, B. (1990). Hemispheric independence: A paradigm case for cognitive neuroscience. In A. B. Scheibel & A. F. Wechsler (Eds.), *Neurobiology of higher cognitive function* (pp. 297–356). New York: Guilford Press.

Zaidel, E., Iacoboni, M., Zaidel, D. W., & Bogen, J. E. (2003). The callosal syndromes. In K. M. Heilman & E. Valenstein (Eds.), *Clinical neuropsychology* (4th ed., pp. 347–403). New York: Oxford.

Chapter 3
Development in the CNS

Neuronal development proceeds in an orderly fashion during development of the embryo and fetus. There are certain stages of development that are consistent across individuals during gestation. Following birth, changes in the brain are related to genetics, biology, and environmental stimulation. This chapter will provide an overview of development pre- and postnatally, and discuss challenges that develop due to environmental aspects (stress, substance abuse, toxins, etc.).

Prenatal Course

The fastest rate of brain growth occurs prenatally, when it is estimated that every minute 250,000 brain cells are formed through mitosis (Papalia & Olds, 1992). The increase in the number of cell bodies occurs most rapidly between 25 and 40 weeks gestation (Ivry, & Mangun, 2002). The human brain develops in orderly stages, beginning in the neural tube at 25 days gestation and, though not fully mature, assumes adult features at birth. Finally, this chapter provides information about genetic, environmental, and psychosocial differences that can affect brain development. In pediatric neuropsychology the assessment almost always includes the caretakers and the family unit. Providing services to children requires enlisting the family in treatment and support. The spinal cord, the brain stem, and a large portion of the forebrain are developed at 40 weeks gestation, while the cerebellum has maximum growth by the time of birth and during the first year. Six neuronal layers make up the cytoarchitectonic structure of the cerebral cortex (Kolb & Whishaw, 2003). These layers develop differentially during gestation and through the first year of life. These cortical layers develop in an inside-out fashion, where neurons move into specific regions and are passed by later migrating layers. These layers migrate into various regions, forming the structural organization of the cortex (Kolb & Whishaw, 2003).

While neurons proliferate and migrate to different cytoarchitectonic regions during various prenatal stages, numerous factors can interrupt this process. Environmental toxins (e.g., alcohol and drugs) pose a particular threat to the migration process and, depending on the time and stage of fetal development, different brain regions can be impaired causing significant cognitive and behavioral deficits later in life. These areas of concern are discussed later in this chapter.

Proliferation and Cell Migration

Cell migration is largely defined at birth, and the time and place of migration appear to be regulated by physical as well as chemical processes (Carlson, 2007). The developmental process is marked by an intricate neuron-glial interaction, where neurons are guided along radial glial fibers to their proper location. The migration process occurs rapidly, and several cortical layers appear visible during the fifth month of fetal development (Kolb & Whishaw, 2003). The cortex begins to thicken and shows signs of developing sulci during this period. The

M. Semrud-Clikeman, P.A. Teeter Ellison, *Child Neuropsychology*, DOI 10.1007/978-0-387-88963-4_3,
© Springer Science+Business Media, LLC 2009

sulci develop early, with the longitudinal fissure apparent at 10 weeks, the lateral sulcus at 14 weeks, the parieto-occipital sulcus at 14 weeks, and the central sulcus at 20 weeks gestational age (Carlson, 2007). Within six months of inception, neurons are genetically programmed to proliferate so that the proper number of cells is available.

During the neonatal and postnatal periods neurons also differentiate and migrate into genetically predetermined regions of the brain. Aberrant neuronal development can cause cell to migrate to the wrong locations or cause neurons to make inappropriate synaptic connections. For example, it has been suggested that schizophrenia results from abnormal neuronal connections where mesocortical regions (dopaminergic systems) fail to connect to frontal cortical regions (Buchsbaum et al., 2006). Cell death occurs during these early developmental stages because more neurons are generated than are necessary; thus, strategic or "selective cell death" appears critical in the developing fetal brain (Gazzaniga et al., 2002) with approximately 25–33 percent of neurons in the developing brain being pruned back during the process of neuronal proliferation and migration. Brodal (2004) suggests that as many as 50 percent of motor neurons in the spinal cord are eliminated. It has been hypothesized that neurons compete for a limited amount of the "trophic substance" that keeps the cells alive, so that only a portion of fetal neurons can survive (Brodal, 2004). Neurodevelopmental disorders caused by abnormal cell proliferation, migration, or cell death can have a significant impact on a child's cognitive, behavioral, and psychosocial potential. The impact of these neurodevelopmental anomalies is reviewed in later chapters.

Axon and Synaptic Formations

Once they reach their destination, neurons continue to develop and differentiate. Axons appear to follow or to "grow along" other pioneer axons with high concentrations of chemicals that seem to set the course or direction of growth (Gazzaniga et al., 2002). Brodal (2004) suggests that axons may recognize their developmental path as a result of "chemoaffinity" between the axon terminals and target

neurons. Further, chemical markers may be present only in specific phases of development and then may disappear to ensure selective contact with target neurons. The peripheral nervous system is known to have specific protein nerve growth factor (NGF) that stimulates the outward movement of axons, so that axons grow into these regions and away from areas without NGF. Brodal (2004) suggests that other proteins such as brain-derived neurotrophic factor (BDNF) may play a similar function in the brain. Axons grow at a rapid rate, while cells are still migrating, and cross to form pathways that connect the hemispheres. The anterior commissure which connects the frontal lobes first appears at about three months' gestation, while the corpus callosum (a major bundle of fibers that connects the hemispheres) develops at a slower rate (Brodal, 2004). The hippocampal commissure appears after three months' gestation, followed by the appearance of another set of fibers that eventually develop into the corpus callosum. The corpus callosurn continues to develop postnatally and is fairly well formed by five years of age (Witelson, 1989).

Dendritic and spine growth (visible at about seven months' gestation) occurs at a slower rate than axon development and usually starts after cells have reached their final destination. Dendritic development continues postnatally and is affected by environmental stimulation after birth. Synaptic development is less understood, although synapses have been observed during the fifth month of fetal development (Carlson, 2007). The relationship between synaptic density and cognitive abilities may be an inverse one, because synaptic density appears to decrease with age. Whereas synaptic density was once thought to be indicative of increased functional abilities, the reduction of synapses may be related to efficiency and refinement of function in some qualitative sense (Gazzaniga et al., Ivry, & Mangun, 2002).

Early synaptic redundancy and selective elimination of synapses in later development have been verified in PET studies (Caesar, 1983). The high levels of glucose metabolism recorded during the first year of life begin to decrease during the second year through adolescence. A process similar to selective cell death occurs to eliminate axon collaterals (Brodal, 2004). According to Brodal, this process is best understood in the study of the motor neurons that enervate skeleton muscles. Whereas early stages of development are marked by the emergence of numerous neurons connecting to one muscle, multiple synapses are eliminated in later stages of development. Once motor neurons begin to send signals to the muscle, it appears that the process of synaptic elimination occurs. Brodal (2004) indicates that it is this process of synaptic elimination, once normal activity begins, that allows for precise neural connections. According to Brodal (2004), "meaningful" information rather than simple activity is a key factor in this process. The migration of cells may be disrupted by disorders in genetic programming or as a result of external disruption due to viral infections and disturbances to vascular circulation. Recent advances in brain imaging techniques are shedding new light on differences between genetic and acquired disorders that disrupt cell migration (Cody et al., 2005). Finally, synaptic networks become more elaborate in the postnatal period, where dendritic arborization increases in complexity (Brodal, 2004). In the third trimester the brain enters a major prenatal growth spurt, which continues postnatally until two years of age. Antenatal insults during the third trimester may result in cerebral palsy syndromes (Kolb & Whishaw, 2003)

Postnatal Course

An individual's full quota of neurons is reached by six months' gestational age, but postnatal development is marked by increased cortical complexity (Gilles & Gomez, 2005). In general, myelination increases brain weight from approximately 400 grams at birth to 850 grams at 11 months, to 1,100 grams at 36 months, to 1,350 to 1,410 grams at age 15, and continues to increase through age 60 (Gilles & Gomez, 2005). Four postnatal growth spurts have been found that correspond to Piaget's stages of cognitive development: from two to four years, from six to eight years, from 10 to 12 years, and from 14 to 16 + years (Kolb & Fantie, 1989). Although cognitive development follows time-lines similar to anatomical and physiological growth patterns, the manner in which environmental factors affect brain development through these growth spurts is an area that warrants further study.

Myelination is an important aspect in the brain's maturation. It first occurs in the primary sensory and motor cortices (prior to birth); the secondary areas of the basic senses myelinate within four months postnatally, while the myelination process begins postnatally in the frontal and parietal association regions and continues through the mid-20 s (Fredrik, Macoveanu, Olesen, Tegner, & Klingberg, 2007).

Myelination appears correlated to the development of and changes in visual, motor, social, and cognitive behaviors. Malnutrition, disease, injury, and inadequate stimulation can affect the myelination process, which in turn may affect the learning capacity of the individual. It may be that these environmental events affect the developing brain even more drastically than a more mature brain because they occur before the receptor sites for neurotransmitters are fully established. External medications may interfere with this process, affecting neurological and psychosocial development.

Gestation

The earliest stages of brain development are marked by rapid changes in the embryo. Within seven days of inception, two layers of tissue (the ectoderm and the endoderm) are present and, within nine days, a third layer (the mesoderm) develops and moves between the first two layers in a process referred to as neurulation. The ectoderm forms the neural groove, which in turn forms the neural tube. The process of neurulation is initiated in the first two weeks; embryonic tissue differentiates, forming the neural tube, and is completed by the fourth gestational week. During this process, embryonic tissues thicken, deepen, and close, forming the basic structures of the nervous system. Neurons and glial cells are formed on the outside wall of the neural tube, and the inside wall is covered with glial cells forming a canal that becomes filled with CSF. Throughout this course, neural tissues differentiate and migrate forming columns of spinal and cranial nerves that keep the organism alive. The cranial portion of the neural tube eventually develops into the brain, while the caudal portion becomes the spinal cord. Motor and sensory columns develop from separate structures of the neural tube, and by the end of four weeks the neural tube closes.

Once the process of neurulation ends (4th week), three brain vesicles appear, forming the hindbrain, the midbrain, and the forebrain. These vesicles further differentiate into (1) diencephalon, which eventually forms the thalamus, hypothalamus, and epithalamus, and (2) the telencephalon, which forms the cerebral hemispheres. The lumina or cavities of the brain vesicles develop into the ventricular system, which can be compromised in various developmental or disease processes, such as hydrocephalus. The vesicles continue to develop into the major brain regions.

Although genetic factors map the nature and course of neuronal development, environmental factors have a significant influence on the developing nervous system. Brodal (2004) suggests that "use-dependent stimulation" is crucial during early stages of postnatal development. That is, the developing brain requires proper and adequate stimulation for optimal development. This aspect of neurodevelopment will be explored in later sections of this chapter.

The Development of Higher Cognitive Abilities

The relationship between cognitive-behavioral development and neuroanatomical development is relatively uncharted in young children, with two exceptions: motor and language functions. Changes in myelin formation in specific brain regions are correlated with increased complexity of functions and increased cognitive abilities in children from birth to five years of age. (See Table 3.1 for an overview of this interaction.)

Although there is an obvious interaction among developing brain structures, many of which are developing simultaneously, and behavioral changes, this relationship is highly variable. Brains are distinct in their individual cellular and neural growth patterns, but this process is affected by acculturation (Majovski, 1989) and chemical-environmental factors (Cook & Leventhal, 1992). Despite individual variations in this process, developmental trends in structural and behavioral

interactions can be interpreted with these limitations in mind. The following sections address maturational processes in specific cortical regions. In some instances, sufficient research is not available to determine when structures are fully developed and how structural changes relate to cognitive development; however, there is sufficient evidence to suggest that meaningful patterns are emerging. The following review summarizes the current available research in this area.

Frontal Lobe Maturation

Conel (1939–1959) mapped postnatal frontal lobe development, showing rapid changes in density from birth until 15 months. Synaptic density increases until two years of age, when it is about 50 percent above that of adults, and decreases until about 16 years of age (Gazzaniga et al., Ivry, & Magnun, 2002). A decrease in the number of synapses in the frontal lobes may represent a "qualitative refinement" in the functional capacity of the neurons (Brodal, 2004). That is, cognitive complexity cannot be defined in simple quantitative terms, such as the number of synapses. These structural changes appear to correspond to the development of behaviors mediated by the frontal lobes, namely speech, executive, and emotional functions (see Table 3.1).

Using EEG data to map brain activity, Thatcher (1996) suggests that there are "growth spurts" of cortical connections from the parietal, occipital, and temporal lobes to the frontal lobes. These growth spurts occur at three intervals: (1) from age 1.5 to 5 years; (2) from 5 to 10 years, and (3) from 10 to 14 years. After age 14 the frontal lobes develop at the same rate and continue until age 45. These corticocortical connections differ between hemispheres. The left hemisphere shows a developmental sequence of gradients involving anterior-posterior and lateral-mesial regions, with *lengthening* of connections between posterior sensory regions, and frontal areas, while the right hemisphere involves a *contraction* of long-distance frontal connections to posterior sensory areas. Thatcher (1996) suggests that the expansion of the left hemisphere is due to functional

Table 3.1 Myelination and cognitive development

Age	Visual/motor functions	Social/intellectual functions	Myelination
Birth	Sucking reflex, rooting, swallowing, Moro reflex, grasping, and blinking to light.		Motor root +++; sensory root ++; medial lemniscus ++; superior cerebellar peduncle ++; optic tract ++; optic radiation ±
6 weeks	Neck turning and extension when prone; regards mom's face; follows objects.	Smiles when played with.	Optic tract ++; optic radiation +; middle cerebellar peduncle; pyramidal tract+
3 months	Infantile grasp; volitional sucking; holds head up; turns to objects in visual field; may respond to sound.	Watches own hands.	Sensory root +++; optic trace & radiation +++; pyramidal tract ++; cingulum +; frontopontine tract +; middle cerebellar peduncle +; corpus callosum ±; reticular formation ±
6 months	Grasps with both hands; puts weight on forearms; rolls; supports weight on legs brief periods.	Laughs and shows pleasure. Makes primitive sounds. Smiles at self in mirror.	Medial lemniscus +++; superior cerebellar peduncle ++; middle cerebellar peduncle +; pyramidal tract ++; corpus callosum +; reticular formation +; association areas ±; acoustic radiation +
9 months	Sits and pulls self to sitting position; thumb–forefinger grasp; crawl.	Waves bye-bye; plays pat-a-cake; uses *Dada, Baba*; imitates.	Cingulum +++; formix ++; others as described
12 months	Releases objects. Cruises and walks with one hand held; plantar reflex flexor in 50%.	Uses 2–4 words with meaning; understands nouns; may kiss on request.	Medial lemniscus +++ pyramidal tract +++; fornix +++; corpus callosum +; intracortical neuropil ±; association areas ±; acoustic radiation ++
24 months	Walks up and down stairs; (two feet-step); bends and picks up object; turns knob; partially dresses; plantar reflex flexor 100%.	Uses 2–3 word sentences; uses *I, me,* and *you*; plays simple games; names 4–5 body parts; obeys simple commands.	Acoustic radiation +++ corpus callosum ++; association areas +; nonspecific thalamic radiation ++
36 months	Goes up stairs (one foot) pedals tricycle; dresses self fully except shoelaces, belts, and buttons; visual acuity 20/20/OU.	Asks numerous questions; says nursery rhymes; copies circles; plays with others.	Middle cerebellar peduncle +++
5 years	Skips; ties shoelaces; copies triangles; gives age.	Repeats 4 digits; names 4 colors.	Nonspecific thalamic radiation +++; reticular formation ++; corpus callosum +++; intracortical neuropil & association areas ++
Adult			Intracortical neuropil & association areas ++ to +++

Source: Adapted with permission "Development of the Child's Brain and Behavior" by B. Kolb and B. Fantie (1989), in C. R. Reynolds and E. R. Janzen, eds., *Handbook of Clinical Child Neuropsychology*, pp. 17–40. New York: Plenum Press.
Note: ± minimal amounts; + mild amounts; ++ moderate amounts; +++ heavy.

differentiation of new subsystems, whereas the contraction of the right hemisphere is the functional integration of previously existing subsystems. Thus, experience and stimulation play a direct role in the process of redefining and differentiating neuroanatomy.

Studies of changes in the brain over development using Magnetic Resonance Imaging (MRI) have found differences not only by age but also by gender. Sowell, Trauner, Gamst and Jernigan (2002) found age-related increases in total brain volume as well as in white matter volume in a group of children aged 7–16. Differentiation in white matter was found during this period with increases in volume while gray matter was found to decrease in volume between childhood and adolescence. Cerebrospinal fluid (CSF) was found to show a 2 percent increase with age. Older participants had about 4 percent of the brain volume due to CSF, while younger participants had 2 percent of the total brain volume due to CSF. Additional age effects were found in the areas of the frontal lobe and anterior cingulate with increases in white matter volume in these regions. The caudate and thalamus were found to decrease in volume with age, which was gender-specific. Volumes of the caudate and putamen decreased with age for boys, but not for girls. Similarly, the cerebellum (the region of the brain responsible for fluid movement) was approximately 8 percent larger in boys. The putamen and globus pallidus (other areas deep in the brain and responsible for input of motor information) were also larger in males compared to females.

Male brains have been found to be approximately 7–10 percent larger in volume compared to females during childhood (Giedd, Castellanos, Rajapakse, Vaituzis & Rapoport, 1997; Giedd et al., 1996; Reiss, Abrams, Singer, Ross & Denckla, 1996; Sowell et al., 2002). When brain size was controlled, girls were found to show larger volumes in the gray matter of the temporal cortex, the caudate, thalamus, and regions deep inside the brain (i.e., hypothalamus). In a subsequent study, (Giedd et al., 1997) found that the amygdala (a structure involved in emotional processing) and the hippocampus (a structure involved in setting down memories) volumes increased for both genders with age. The amygdala was found to increase significantly more for males than females, while the hippocampus increased in volume more for females than for males.

Expressive Speech Functions

Scheibel (1990) examined dendritic structures in the frontal lobe to determine the relationship between functional speech abilities and cortical development. In a series of postmortem studies, electron microscopic techniques were applied to brain tissue taken from 17 subjects between the ages of three months and six years. Structural changes in dendritic growth patterns appear related to differences in language functions across the ages and are summarized as follows:

1. Initially, dendritic growth is greater in the right opercular region (motor speech area) than on the left at three months.
2. Dendritic systems on the left increase in higher order speech zones at six months and eventually surpass the right hemisphere.
3. The hemispheres develop in an uneven pattern for the next five years.
4. The dendritic system in the left hemisphere appears more complex by the age of six, and Broca's area resembles the development of adults at this age. Further, these structural changes appear related to differences in functional speech mechanisms present at each stage.

Speech during the first 6–12 months of age is characterized by affective communication patterns, which probably are related to dendritic growth in the right frontal regions (Scheibel, 1990). As the left frontal region develops the child's ability to understand syntax and more complex language forms improves. Development of dendritic processes in the language regions in the left hemisphere catches up to and eventually exceeds development in the right hemisphere corresponding to increases in the use and complexity of language skills. Some suggest that experience and functional differentiation go hand in hand and are necessary for further development.

Scheibel (1990) found that proximal and distal segments of the dendritic branches also differed depending on the hemisphere. Proximal segments (near the cell body) develop early, with distal segments (far) appearing later in development. Proximal segments are longer in the right hemisphere, with distal segments more pronounced in the left hemisphere. The proximal/distal ratio appears complementary, where proximal segments are longer in the absence of distal segments. The importance of distance from the cell body in determining the role of the dendritic processes is unknown. However,

Scheibel (1990) does suggest that distinct dendritic processes in the two hemispheres are probably related to functional differences between the two regions.

Executive Functions

Studies have also focused on the neurobehavioral correlates of frontal lobe development, specifically the emergence of "executive" functions (e.g., planning, flexibility, inhibition, and self-monitoring) that have been attributed to this area. Whereas prefrontal regions have been hypothesized to be involved primarily in executive functions, striatal regions also have been investigated (Castellanos et al., 1996; Semrud-Clikeman, Pliszka, Lancaster, & Liotti, 2006). Because there are rich connections between the frontal lobes and striatal regions (Semrud-Clikeman et al., 2006), it is reasonable to believe that these two areas are intimately involved in executive functions.

It has been strongly suggested that executive functions are subdivided between the dorsal frontal, lateral frontal, and orbital frontal anatomical regions. The dorsal frontal region may be responsible for determining how important a situation is; the lateral frontal is involved in determining if the selected action is worth the effort needed to obtain the result; and the orbital frontal is responsible for determining the social and situational appropriateness of actions. Thatcher (1991) suggests that the interaction of these three functionally relevant areas provides the behavior known as executive function.

In keeping with our transactional model, Denckla (2007) suggests that executive functions have two influences, one neuroanatomical and the other "psychodevelopmental," and that these influences not only interact, but also modify each other. For example, Denckla (2007) cites the example that construct validity of executive action is demonstrated by convergent (a child of X age can do this when he or she can do that) and divergent (a child of X age can do this, but not that) validity. Some suggest that the frontal lobes of children develop rather markedly between the ages of four and seven years, with steady but less dramatic increases from 12 years of age to adulthood (Luria, 1980). Others

suggest that development of executive functioning begins in adolescence and continues up to about 24 years of age (Pennington, 1991). Still others suggest that the frontal lobes develop in cycles rather than with variable development between the hemispheres (Thatcher, 1996).

Experimental studies have shown that children do exhibit behaviors thought to be mediated by the frontal lobes much earlier than adolescence or adulthood. Similar to Denckla's (2007) convergent/divergent validity approach to executive functions, Becker, Isaac, and Hynd (1987) found age variation in skill attainment. Skills thought to be mediated by the frontal lobes were found to be mastered by 10- and 12-year-olds; these included the capability of inhibiting motor responses, remembering the temporal order of visual designs, using strategies for memory tasks, attending to relevant details and ignoring distractors, and employing verbal mediators to enhance performance. Six-year-olds had more difficulty inhibiting motor responses and remembering the temporal order of visual designs. There appeared to be a developmental shift for eight-year-olds, who were able to inhibit motor responses. While subjects at all age levels were able to verbalize directions, younger children, especially those under the age of eight, were not always able to inhibit perseverative responses.

Passler, Isaac, and Hynd (1985) also found that children progress through developmental stages showing mastery of some frontally mediated tasks at six and eight years, while other tasks were not even mastered at the age of 12. Six-year-olds gave flexible, correct responses for a verbal conflict task, but were unable to respond accurately to a nonverbal conflict task. Although eight-year-olds mastered both tasks and were also able to complete a perseveration task, they were unable to complete a series of drawings consistently or to respond correctly to verbal and nonverbal proactive inhibition tasks. Finally, even the 12-year-olds did not obtain full mastery of the verbal and nonverbal retroactive inhibition tasks.

Taken together these findings suggest that the greatest period of development for executive functions occurs between the ages of six and eight, with continued growth beyond the 12-year-old level for more complex tasks. Supporting these findings, children have been found to reach adult levels of performance by 10 years of age on measures of cognitive flexibility (the Wisconsin Card Sorting Test), but did not reach adult levels of performance on a word fluency test even by the age of 17.

Emotional Functions

Models of the neuropsychological basis of emotions indicate that the frontal lobes play a central role in the processing of emotional responses (Semrud-Clikeman, 2007). The two hemispheres appear differentially involved in adults, with damage to the left hemisphere resulting in depression and catastrophic reactions; whereas damage to the right hemisphere results in inappropriate emotional reactions, including indifference or euphoria (Heilman, Blonder, Bowers, & Valenstein, 2003). Developmental patterns have documented that the left hemisphere may be more reactive to emotional stimuli in younger children (9 years of age) than adolescents (14 years of age) and adults (Davidson, 1994). As the right hemisphere matures, it has a modulating effect on the more reactive left hemisphere (Heilman, Watson, & Valenstein, 2003). Moreover, as the corpus callosum matures, the right hemisphere can inhibit or control the left hemisphere more effectively. Thus, depression in children and adults may be a function of underactivation of the frontal regions, or the right hemisphere may be overactivated. It may well be that it is the ratio of activation between the two hemispheres that is important rather than the level of activation of either one. Neurodevelopmental patterns may help to explain why depression seems to increase around puberty, which corresponds to the time when later-developing corpus callosal structures are becoming mature (Zaidel et al., 2003). The temporal lobes may also be important for the perception of emotions (e.g., facial or tonal), and differences between the anterior/posterior regions may be just as important as the right/left hemisphere differences in the control of emotions. For example, posterior regions of the temporal lobe are important for recognition of facial expressions while anterior regions may be implicated in understanding and recalling the labels for such expressions (Semrud-Clikeman, 2007).

Parietal Lobe Maturation

Although it is assumed that the sensory systems are functional prior to birth, very little is known about tactile-sensory development. Whereas evidence suggests that somesthetic senses are the first to develop embryonically, the course of development in infancy and early childhood is less understood. Proton magnetic resonance spectroscopy technology has been used to measure brain metabolism in order to determine regional differences in brain development from childhood into early adulthood (Hashimoto et al., 1995). There was a significant correlation between age and metabolic activity in the right parietal regions, suggesting rapid brain maturation in this region from one month up to the age of two or three years. The frontal regions showed less metabolic activation during the same time frame, suggesting slower development of these regions. The frontal lobes, dense with gray matter, are slower to myelinate and to form synaptic and dendritic connections than the more posterior brain regions.

The course of development for tactile perception has been most thoroughly researched for hemispheric asymmetries. Tactile form perception increases with age (from 8 to 12 years); children usually show a slight superiority in scores using their preferred hand (dominant hand), and scores on the non-preferred hand were much more variable than on the preferred (Baron, 2004). For the 12- to 14-year-old group, children show a more even range of scores and reach adult-like performance on these measures. Tactile finger localization develops more slowly, and most preschool children are unable to name or point to the finger that has been touched (Baron, 2004). This is a difficult task for most seven-year-old children, but by the age of nine few errors are present. When errors do appear, they occur more frequently on adjacent fingers (37.5%), which is four times higher than for adults. Thus, children respond differentially to tactile localization tests on the right and left hands, depending on the type of response mode required (Baron, 2004). Verbal responses seem to increase accuracy when identifying touch to the right hand, whereas nonverbal responses enhance accuracy with the left hand. Witelson and Pallie (1973) found that children do recognize nonsense forms better with the left hand, but recognition of letter shapes does not appear to have a right or left hand advantage.

Occipital Lobe Maturation

The visual system is slow to develop in humans. Myelination of the optic tract is moderately developed at six weeks of age, but is heavily developed by three months (Brodal, 2004). The myelination of the optic radiation is somewhat slower, with minimal development at three months of age and mild development at six weeks. However, heavy myelination occurs in the optic radiation at about the same time as the optic tract. Developmental trends in visual asymmetries have also been investigated in children. Kolb and Fantie (1989) found that the right hemisphere may be specialized for facial recognition in children as young as four years of age, and shows a steady increase in accuracy up to age five, with slower acceleration after this age. Kolb and Fantie hypothesize that the structural hardwire of the brain is sufficiently mature by age five and that further growth in accuracy is dependent on experience. While the six-year-old is adept at facial recognition, matching expressions to situations is not well developed until about 14 years of age. This finding implies that the later task may also require frontal lobe maturation as well as posterior cortical development.

Temporal Lobe Maturation

Developmental patterns have also been investigated for hemispheric asymmetry in the temporal lobes. Asymmetries of the temporal lobe appear to have some relationship between cortical maturation and the development of the corpus callosum (Brodal, 2004). There is sufficient evidence that the left planum temporale is larger than the right and that these differences are present at birth (Witelson & Kigar, 1988). This developmental course is likely related to functional differences between the two hemispheres in their ability to process information. Infants appear to discriminate speech sounds early on, as young as 1–4 months of age (Molfese & Molfese, 2002). Further, researchers have found functional lateralization of the left hemisphere for speech sounds in infants (Molfese & Molfese, 2002) and for music and non-speech sounds in the right hemisphere in infants. See Table 3.2 for a summary of developmental ages when asymmetry between the two hemispheres appears.

Rosen, Galaburda, and Sherman (1990) investigated the ontogeny of lateralization and have generated hypotheses about the mechanisms of asymmetry. In these studies, symmetry in the brain was found to be related to the size of the planum temporale in the right hemisphere. In brains with normal patterns of asymmetrical organization, there was a corresponding decrease in the size of the right hemisphere. This correspondence was not observed in brains that were symmetrical, as there was an abundance of neurons in the temporal regions of the right hemisphere. Further, the corpus callosum in symmetrical brains is larger than in those with normal patterns of asymmetry (Rosen et al., 1990). Rosen et al. (1990) hypothesize that this variation in volume is likely a result of "pruning" of the axons in the corpus callosum that takes place in early developmental stages. Asymmetry may be related to withdrawal of neurons in the corpus callosum, while ipsilateral connections are maintained. Numerous factors impinge upon normal brain development, affecting the manner in which neural systems function and how traits and behaviors are expressed. Genetic as well as environmental factors influence neurodevelopment. These factors will be reviewed briefly in the following sections.

How Genetic Factors Influence Development

Brain development appears to follow relatively fixed sequences of growth and changes in the biological processes that are genetically specified. Defects in the genetic program, intrauterine trauma (e.g., toxins), or other factors can result in serious malformations in brain size and structural organization. See Table 3.3 for a summary of these neurodevelopmental abnormalities.

Cell migration, axonal dendritic formation and growth, synaptic development, and myelination appear compromised. These neurodevelopmental anomalies produce a variety of functional/behavioral deficits, ranging from life-threatening to severely symptomatic to asymptomatic. While a

Table 3.2 Developmental milestones for functional asymmetry and cerebral Lateralization

Functions	Age	Hemisphere	Reference
Motor			
Thumb sucking, right hand preference	15-week fetus	Left	Hepper, Shahidullah, and White (1991)
Head turning[a]	Birth		
Reaching	4 months	Left	Young et al. (1983)
Passive holding		Right	
Moving pegs	3 years	Left	Annett(1985)
Finger tapping	3–5 years	Left	Ingram(1975)
Strength		Left	
Gestures		Left	
Auditory			
Syllables	21 hours	Left	Molfese and Molfese(1979)
Speech	>24 hours	Left	Hammer(1977)
White noise	>24 hours	Right	
Speech sounds	1 weeks–10 months	Left	Molfese, Freeman, and Palermo (1975)
Speech (CV)	22–140 days	Left	Entus(1977)
Music sounds	22–140 days	Right	
Conversational speech	6 months	Left	Gardiner and Walter (1977)
Name of child	5–12 months	Left	Barnet, Vicenti, and Campos (1974)
Visual			
Light flashes	2 weeks	Right	Hahn (1987)
Photography of Mom	4 months	Right	de Schonen, Gil de Diaz, and Mathivet (1986)
Patterns			
Global form	4–10 months	Right	Deruelle and de Schonen (1991)
Tactile			
Dichaptic	4–5 years	Right	Klein and Rosenfield (1980)
Emotions			
Approach expression to sugar H_2O	2 days	Left	Fox and Davidson (1986)
Facial expressivity	Infants	Right	Best and Queens (1989)
Happy facial expressions	10 months	Left	Davidson and Fox (1982)
Crying with separation from Mom	10 months	Right	Davidson and Fox (1989)
Discriminate Emotional faces	5–14 years	Right	Saxby and Bryden (1985)
Emotional tones	5–14 years	Right	Saxby and Bryden (1984)
Emotional reaction	9 years	Left	Davidson (1984)
to negative expression	12 years	Right	

[a]Head turning correlated to same side as thumb sucking at birth.

number of these anomalies are related to defects in embryogenesis (dysplasias, agenesis of the corpus callosum, malformations of the cortex, etc.), both genetic and environmental factors appear to be causative factors. The extent to which other childhood and adolescent disorders, particularly dyslexia and schizophrenia, are genetically transmitted has been investigated. Developmental dyslexia has been the focus of studies demonstrating autosomal dominant (generation to generation) inheritance (Pennington, 2002). Volger, DeFries, and Decker (1984) found that less than half of persons with

dyslexia have parents with a history of reading problems. According to Gilger, Hanebuth, Smith, and Pennington (1996), the genetic linkages will likely increase when cases of dyslexia resulting from injury or environmental damage are excluded from studies. Lubs et al. (1991) conclude that "developmental dyslexia is a heterogeneous group of disorders, some of which are inherited" (p. 74).

Malaspina, Quitkin, and Kaufman (1992) indicate that a number of other neuropsychiatric disorders of childhood and adolescence have a genetic component. Individuals with an affected relative

Table 3.3 Neurodevelopmental abnormalities associated with neurogenesis or abnormal neural migration

Abnormalities	Symptoms	Possible Causes
Size		
Micrencephaly	Brain is smaller than normal. Involves cognitive deficits, epilepsy.	Genetic, malnutrition, inflammatory diseases (e.g., rubella), radiation, maternal exposure to poisons
Megalencephaly	Brain is larger than normal. Intelligence ranges from subnormal to gifted, behavioral deficits.	Genetic
Abnormal tissue growth		
Holoprosencephaly	Hemispheres fail to develop. Single hemisphere or ventricle is present. Medical problems (e.g., apnea, cardiac) exists. Mental and motor retardation are present.	Neurotoxicity, genetic (trisomy 13–15)
Agenesis of corpus callosum	Corpus callosum fails to develop (partial or complete). Linguistic and intellectual deficits are present. Found with other neurological disorders (i.e., hydrocephaly, spina bifida).	Genetic
Cerebellar agnesis Cerebellum fails to develop		Genetic
Cortical malformations		
Lissencephaly	Sulci and gyri fail to develop. Found with agenesis of corpus callosum. Severe mental retardation, epilepsy. Early death.	Etiology unknown
Micropolygyria or polymicrogyria	Numerous small, and poorly formed gyri. Severe retardation to LD.	Intrauterine infections
Abnormalities with hydrocephaly		
Dandy-Walker malformation	Cerebellar malformations, with fourth ventricle enlargement. Other abnormalities (e.g., agenesis of corpus callosum).	Genetic
Abnormalities in neural tube and fusion		
Anencephaly	Hemispheres, diencephalon, and midbrain fail to develop.	Genetic
Hydranencephaly	Hemispheres fail to develop, CDF-filled cystic sac. Looks like hydrocephaly early. Appears normal at birth.	Umbilical cord strangulation. Vascular blockage, ischemia
Porencephaly	Large cystic lesion (bilateral). Mental retardation, epilepsy. Agenesis of temporal lobe. Early death.	Neonatal hemorrhaging following trauma, ischemia
Spina bifida	Neural tube fails to close. Skeletal, gastro-intestinal, cardiovascular, and pulmonary abnormalities, bulging dura mater.	Maternal fever, virus, hormonal imbalance, folic acid deficiency

Source: Adapted from G. W. Hynd and W. G. Willis, *Pediatric Neuropsychology*, Table 4.1, pp.73–77. Copyright © 1988 by Grune & Stratton, Orlando, Florida. Adapted by permission of The Psychological Corporation, Orlando, FL 32887.

seem to be at a higher risk of also developing some disorders, including a 45 percent morbid risk for dyslexia:, a 50 percent morbid risk for Gerstmann-Straussler syndrome (degenerative disease with motor signs and dementia), acute porphyna (motor neuropathy with psychiatric features), and myotonic dystrophy (motoric, intellectual, and psychiatric deterioration); a 25–50 percent risk for leukodystrophy (hyper- or hypotonicity with psychotic symptoms); a 25 percent risk for Lesch-Nyhan syndrome (spastic and movement disorders with retardation); a 24 percent risk for Wilson disease (liver disorder with neuropsychological symptoms); a 12.8 percent risk for schizophrenia; an 8 percent risk for bipolar disorders; a 4 percent risk for epilepsy, and, a 3.6 percent risk for Tourette syndrome (major behavioral disorder with motor and vocal tics). See Malaspina et al. (1992) for an in-depth discussion of the epidemiology and genetic transmission of these and other neuropsychiatric disorders.

The specific abnormal gene(s) involved in these disorders are unknown; further, the role of environmental factors in the expression of these illnesses cannot be overlooked (Malaspina et al., 1992). Even when single autosomal genes are known, the exact nature or presentation of various disorders is unknown. Variable expression of neuropsychiatric disorders depends on a variety of factors, including age at onset of the illness. Further, it has been hypothesized that one genotype may result in multiple phenotypes or vice versa. The latter situation, where one phenotype arises from several genotypes, seems most likely for disorders with heterogeneous etiologies. For example, similar genetic inheritance seems to be present between schizophrenia and bipolar disorders. The critical point at this juncture is that the systematic linking of hereditary factors with environmental factors will likely be useful in advancing our understanding of childhood disorders. Given the importance of environmental and biological interactions for the expression of different types of behavior, it is important to briefly review this transactional aspect.

Biological and Environmental Factors

It has long been recognized that biogenetic (e.g., chromosomal abnormalities), environmental factors, (e.g., pre- and postnatal toxins and insults), and birth complications all affect the developing brain. Traumatic brain injury at an early age and a lack of environmental stimulation are also known to have long-term affects on optimal brain development. Prenatal and postnatal factors known to have an impact on the developing brain will be briefly reviewed.

Prenatal Risk Factors

With the advent of X-ray technology in the 1920s and 1930s, it became apparent that the developing fetus was susceptible to various environmental agents known as *teratogens*. Critical periods during the embryonic (second to eighth week of development) and the fetal stage (9th week to birth) appear particularly susceptible to exposure of teratogens. The central nervous system appears to be particularly vulnerable from the 5th week of embryonic development up to birth. The most detrimental environmental influences affecting neurodevelopment prenatally include alcohol, narcotics, pollutants, maternal disease, and malnutrition (Streissguth et al., 2004)

Maternal Stress, Nutrition, and Health Factors

In addition to numerous prenatal factors that place the developing child at risk for neurological complications, maternal stress, malnutrition, poor health, and age also play a role in the ultimate expression of these risk factors (van den Bergh, Mulder, Mennes & Glover, 2005). Extreme maternal stress is known to increase levels of stress in the fetus and has been associated with low birth weight babies and irritable, restless, colicky infants. Maternal stress may create vasoconstriction reducing circulation that ultimately produces fetal asphyxia, which is known to cause brain damage in the developing fetus. Some findings have indicated that prenatal stress may have long-term consequences with problems in coping and learning, particularly for males, and an increased incidence of mood disorders and schizophrenia (King, Laplante, & Joober, 2005; Mueller & Bale, 2007).

Maternal Nutrition

Nutritional deficiencies during the last three months of fetal life and during the first three months of infancy also can have severe effects on the developing brain, particularly seen as a decrease in the number of brain cells and brain weight (Walker, Thame, Chang, Bennett, & Forester, 2007). Although proper maternal nutrition can reverse infant mortality rates (Morton, 2006), the affects of pre- and postnatal malnutrition on the child's intellectual and behavioral development require additional study.

Maternal Health

Maternal health during pregnancy is generally monitored to ensure normal fetal development. Maternal hypotension may have an adverse affect on the fetal brain as it may result in circulation failures in the developing brain (Martens et al., 2003). Fibromyeline plaques or lesions form in cortical areas called "watershed regions." These ischemic-induced alterations, caused by a temporary loss of blood (perfusion), have been found in the brains of individuals with dyslexia (Duane, 1991).

Ischemia may also be induced by maternal or fetal autoimmune mechanisms. The extent to which these morphological variations are related to or contribute to reading disability will be explored in later chapters. The important point here is that maternal health directly affects the developing fetal brain. Glial cells and specific molecules that direct the migration of cells may be involved in such a way as to alter the cortical architecture of the child's brain (Duane, 1991).

Another maternal health factor that has known effects on the developing brain is rubella (German measles), which often results in deafness in babies if the mother contracts this disease in the first trimester of pregnancy. Eye and heart involvement are other likely outcomes if rubella occurs in the first eight weeks of pregnancy, whereas deafness is more likely to occur if the illness occurs between five and 15 weeks. Maternal herpes simplex 2 is also known to produce mental retardation and learning difficulties because this virus attacks the developing central nervous system of the fetus (Hutchinson & Sandall, 1995).

Concerns have recently been raised about the effects of acquired immune deficiency syndrome (AIDS) on the developing fetus. In the past birth defects including microcephaly as well facial deformities were found with mortality frequently present within five to eight months of symptom onset (Cotter & Potter, 2006). Prior to the new drug regimes, central nervous system involvement was found to be as high as 78–93 percent of children with human immunodeficiency virus (HIV), with signs of motor, visual-perceptual, language, and reasoning delays (Cotter & Potter, 2006; Suy et al., 2006).

Mothers who are likely to contract AIDS often come from high risk populations, including intravenous drug abusers, so other health factors may play a role in the manifestation of symptoms. The extent to which other psychosocial factors play a role in the long-term outcome for children with congenital HIV infection needs further study. When health, poverty, and psychological factors are controlled, infants born to teenagers and mothers over 35 do not appear to be at higher risk for complications (Cotter & Potter, 2006).

Maternal Alcohol Addiction

Heavy maternal alcohol consumption has serious consequences for the developing fetal brain, whereas the effects of drug addiction are less clear (Streissguth et al., 2004). Fetal alcohol syndrome (FAS) occurs frequently in infants born to alcohol-dependent mothers, and estimates suggest that 40,000 children are born with alcohol-related birth defects every year (Streissguth et al., 2004). Characteristic symptoms in children with FAS include pre- and postnatal growth delays; facial abnormalities (e.g., widely spaced eyes, shortened eyelids, small nose); mental retardation; and behavioral problems (e.g., hyperactivity and irritability). Central nervous system symptoms early in life include brain wave abnormalities, impaired sucking responses, and sleep problems, with attentional, behavioral, motor, and learning problems developing and continuing into later childhood (Streissguth et al., 2004). The developing fetal brain is highly susceptible to alcohol damage, and pregnant mothers are advised to eliminate alcohol consumption entirely (U.S. Surgeon General, 2005). Even moderate alcohol consumption (i.e., one to two drinks a day) in mothers who are breast-feeding can produce mild delays in motor development, including crawling and walking delays (Little, Anderson, Ervin, Worthington Roberts, & Clarren, 1989). Although not all children are equally affected, maternal alcohol consumption during pregnancy and lactation is definitely a risk factor, with deleterious affects on the developing brain.

Drugs

Infant and fetal central nervous system signs have been shown to result from heavy maternal consumption of drugs during pregnancy, including marijuana, cocaine, and heroin. Physical signs (i.e., low weight and premature infants), neurological complications, and central nervous system involvement (e.g., tremors and startles) have been found in infants born to mothers with high marijuana usage (Leech, Larkby, Day, & Day, 2006; Noland, Singer, Mehta, & Super, 2003). Cocaine use appears to affect blood flow into the placenta and may affect neurotransmitters in the fetal brain (Snow et al., 2004) Infants born to mothers who use cocaine are at risk for various complications, including spontaneous abortions, prematurity and low birth weight, small head size, and behavioral symptoms (lethargy, unresponsiveness, irritability, and a lack of alertness) (Snow et al., 2004). Leech et al. (2006) described the social interaction and play characteristics of children with intrauterine cocaine exposure. Drug-exposed toddlers were more disorganized, showed signs of abnormal play patterns, showed higher rates of depression and anxiety, and had trouble interacting with peers and adults. Dow-Edwards et al. (2006) also suggest that cognitive and behavioral problems in cocaine-exposed children may not be obvious until later childhood, when damage to frontal lobes and basal ganglia is evident. The long-term effects of cocaine use on the developing brain are difficult to differentiate from the effects of other environmental conditions that might accompany maternal drug use. However, mother-child and child-peer relationships are at risk because infants with symptoms previously described often have trouble with bonding and attachment. Maternal drug addiction may seriously interfere with the mother's ability to care for her infant properly.

Heroin addiction during pregnancy produces risk factors including high mortality rates, prematurity, malformations, and respiratory complications (Burns, Mattick, Lim, & Wallace, 2007) Infants display withdrawal symptoms at birth (tremors, vomiting, fevers, etc), and even though these decrease within months, mothers often have difficulty coping with the behavioral problems (i.e., irritability) that persist in heroin-exposed infants

Postnatal Risk Factors

Many of the prenatal risk factors mentioned previously (infant nutritional deficiencies, maternal

stress, etc.) continue to have an effect on the developing brain in the postnatal period.

Nutritional Deficiencies

Although it is often difficult to isolate the effects of nutritional deficiencies from other socioeconomic complications, severe vitamin deficiencies have a direct influence on the developing brain (Lesage et al., 2006). Hypo- or hypervitaminosis A can lead to developmental and learning disabilities as well as problems with motor, balance, eye problems and mood and emotional disturbance (Marx, Naude, & Pretorius, 2006). Vitamin B depletion can produce neurologic symptoms including ataxia, loss of equilibrium, and impairment of righting reflexes. Neurons and the myelin sheath can be destroyed, moving from peripheral to central brain regions. Thus, numbness and other sensorimotor symptoms appear as early signs (e.g., tingling, muscle tenderness with mental confusion, and learning and memory problems appearing in later stages) (Yoshihiro et al., 2006). Vitamin B_{12} and folic acid deficiencies also have been implicated in structural changes in myelination. Further, low levels of folic acid caused by nutritional deficiencies in breast milk may delay the normal course of EEG development in infants. Other postnatal factors have been known to have long-standing effects on the developing brain, including birth complications, traumatic brain injury, exposure to environmental toxins, and lack of environmental stimulation. The way in which these factors affect the developing brain will be reviewed briefly.

Birth Complications

Birth complications during labor and delivery often produce neurological insults that have been associated with numerous childhood disorders, including psychiatric disorders (Akerman & Fischbein, 1991; Raine, 2002). Of particular concern are complications resulting in significant or prolonged loss of oxygen to the fetus. During the normal delivery process, contractions constrict the placenta and umbilical cord reducing the amount of oxygen to the fetus. In extreme situations, infants produce elevated levels of stress hormones to counterbalance oxygen deprivation and to ensure an adequate blood supply during delivery. Neurological insults are known to follow extreme oxygen deprivation, so electronic fetal monitoring provides vital information about the fetal heartbeat and oxygen level.

A number of birth complications have been found in adults with psychotic symptoms that are consistent with schizophrenia, including long labor, breech presentation, abruptio placenta, neck knot of the umbilical cord, Apgar scores under six, vacuum extraction, meconium aspirated, large placenta infarcts, birth weight under 2,500 or above 4,000 grams, and hemolytic disease (Nasrallah, 1992; O'Reilly, Lane, Cernovsky, & O'Callaghan, 2001).

Environmental Toxins

Exposure to lead, even in low levels, can produce a variety of cognitive and behavioral problems in children (Freeman, 2007). Children with acute lead encephalopathy present severe symptoms, including seizures, lethargy, ataxia, nerve palsy, intracranial pressure, and death in some cases (25%) (Ris, Dietrich, Succop, Berger, & Bornschein, 2004). In about 20–40 percent of cases, children develop epilepsy, severe motor symptoms (hemiplegia and spasticity), and blindness. Inattention and hyperactivity are also known sequelae of lead exposure, although this relationship is not as strong in cases with lower level exposure (Wigg, 2001).

Environmental Stimulation

Postnatal stimulation is a critical factor affecting brain development and the child's capacity for learning. Although the infant appears genetically programmed for many abilities (e.g., sitting, walking, talking), the role of the environment can affect maturation rates in some areas (e.g., vision). Babies who are well-nourished, receive maternal attention and care, and are allowed physical freedom to practice and explore generally will show normal motor development. In extremely deficient environments (e.g., orphanages), motor delays have been documented.

Although infants are born with the ability to learn, learning occurs through experience. Language development, intellectual capacity, and social adaptations are influenced by the environment. The way mothers interact with, talk to, and respond to their infants affects their ability to develop into competent children. However, there appears to be interplay among these genetic-environmental influences. Children evoke differential responses from individuals in their environment depending on their behavior. These responses can reinforce original predispositions and result in more positive interactions with adult caretakers. Infants are highly responsive to attentive, warm, stimulating environments that encourage self-initiated efforts. Inadequate early environments can have a negative impact on a child's early development, but children can recover if they are placed in more responsive environments before the age of two years.

Summary

Neurodevelopmental investigations are beginning to explore how changes in brain structures are related to cognitive development, but this undertaking is far from complete. Further, this area of investigation should be viewed as exploratory and as an emerging field of study that no doubt will evolve with more research and better techniques of inquiry. The extent to which morphological differences are related to various behavioral deficits found in children with learning and reading deficits will be explored in more detail in subsequent chapters. How environmental factors interact with neurodevelopment and cognitive-behavioral development is also critical. Finally, this chapter provided information about genetic, environmental, and psychosocial differences that can affect brain development. In pediatric neuropsychology the assessment almost always includes the caretakers and the family unit. Providing services to children requires the family's participation in treatment and support. All neuropsychologists should understand the impact that family dynamics, family situations, and stresses present during gestation and childhood can have on a child's neurological development. To that end, this chapter sought to provide an overview of some of the most important aspects of which to be cognizant when working with children and their parents.

References

Akerman, B. A., & Fischbein, S. (1991). Twins: Are they at risk? A longitudinal study of twins and nontwins from birth to 18 years of age. *Acta Geneticae Medicae et Gemellologiae: Twin Research, 40,* 29–40.

Annett, M. (1985). Left, right, hand and brain: the right shift theory. Hillsdale, NJ: Lawrence Erlbaum, Associates.

Barnet, A. B., Vincentini, M., & Campos, S. M. (1974). EEG sensory evoked responses (ERs) in early malnutrition. *Paper presented at the Society for Neuroscience,* St. Louis, MO.

Baron, I. S. (2004). *Neuropsychological evaluation of the child.* New York: Oxford University Press.

Becker, M. G., Isaac, W., & Hynd, G. W. (1987). Neuropsychological development of nonverbal behaviors attributed to 'frontal lobe' functioning. *Developmental Neuropsychology, 3,* 275–298.

Best, C. T., & Queens, H. F. (1989). Baby, it's in your smile: Right hemiface bias in infant emotional expressions. *Developmental Psychology, 25,* 264–276.

Brodal, P. (2004). *The central nervous system: Structure and function* (Vol. 3). New York: Oxford University Press.

Buchsbaum, M. S., Friedman, J., Buchsbaum, B. R., Chu, K.-W., Hazlett, E. A., Newmark, R., et al. (2006). Diffusion tensor imaging in schizophrenia. *Biological Psychiatry, 60,* 1181–1187.

Burns, L., Mattick, R. P., Lim, K., & Wallace, C. (2007). Methadone in pregnancy: Treatment retention and neonatal outcomes. *Addiction, 102,* 264–270.

Caesar, P. (1983). Old and new facts about perinatal brain development. *Journal of Child Psychology and Psychiatry, 34,* 101–109.

Carlson, N. R. (2007). *Physiology of behavior* (9th ed.). Boston: Allyn & Bacon.

Castellanos, F. X., Giedd, J. N., Marsh, W. L., Hamburger, S. D., Vaiturzis, A. C., & Dickstein, D. P. (1996). Quantitative brain magnetic resonance imaging in attention-deficit hyperactivity disorder. *Archives of General Psychiatry, 53*(7), 607–616.

Cody, J., Semrud-Clikeman, M., Hardies, L. J., Lancaster, J., Ghidoni, P., Schaub, R. L., et al. (2005). Growth hormone benefits children with 18q deletions. *American Journal of Human Genetics, 143A,* 1181–1190, 1–7.

Conel, J. (1939–1959). *The postnatal development of the human cerebral cortex* (Vol. 1–6). Cambridge, MA: Harvard University Press.

Cook, E. H., & Leventhal, B. L. (1992). Neuropsychiatric disorders of childhood and adolescence. In S. C. Yudofsky & R. E. Hales (Eds.), *The American psychiatric press textbook of neuropsychiatry* (2nd ed., pp. 639–662). Washington, DC: American Psychiatric Association.

Cotter, A., & Potter, J. E. (2006). Mother to child transmission. In J. Beal, J. J. Orrick, & K. Alfonson (Eds.), *HIV/AIDS: Primary care guide* (pp. 503–515). Norwalk, CT: Crown House Publishing Limited.

Davidson, R. J. (1984). Affect, cognition, and hemispheric specialization. In C. E. Izard, J. Kagan, & R. Zajonc (Eds.), *Emotion, cognition, and behavior.* New York: Cambridge University Press.

Davidson, R. J. (1994). Asymmetric brain function, affective style, and psychopathology: The role of early experience and plasticity. *Development and Psychopathology, 6,* 741–758.

Davidson, R. J., & Fox, N. A. (1982). Asymmetrical brain activity discriminates between positive and negative affective stimuli in human infants. *Science, 218,* 1235–1237.

Davidson, R. J., & Fox, N. A. (1989). Frontal brain asymmetry predicts infants' response to maternal separation. *Journal of Abnormal Psychology, 98,* 127–131.

Denckla, M. B. (2007). Executive function: Binding together the definitions of attention-deficit/hyperactivity disorder and learning disabilities. In L. Meltzer (Ed.), *Executive function in education: From theory to practice* (pp. 5–18). New York: Guilford.

Deruelle, C., & de Schonen, S. (1991). Hemispheric asymmetry in visual pattern processing in infants. *Brain and Cognition, 16,* 151–179.

de Schonen, S., Gil de Diaz, M., & Mathivet, E. (1986). Hemispheric asymmetry in face processing in infancy. In H. D. Ellis, M. A. Jeeves, F. Newcome, & A. Young (Eds.), *Aspects of face processing* (pp. 96–120). Dordecht, Nijhoff.

Dow-Edwards, D. L., Benveniste, H., Behnke, M., Bandstra, E. S., Singer, L. T., Hurd, Y. L., et al. (2006). Neuroimaging of prenatal drug exposure. *Neurotoxicology and Teratology, 28,* 386–402.

Duane, D. (1991). Biological foundations of learning disabilities. In J. Obrzut & G. W. Hynd (Eds.), *Neuropsychological foundations of learning disabilities* (pp. 7–27). San Diego: Academic Press.

Entus, A. K. (1977). Hemispheric asymmetry in processing of dichotically presented speech and nonspeech stimuli by infants. In S. J. Segalowitz & F. A. Gruber (Eds.), *Language development and neurological theory* (pp. 63–73). New York: Academic Press.

Fox, N. A., & Davidson, R. J. (1986). Taste-elicited changes in facial signs of emotion and the symmetry of brain electrical activity in human newborns. *Neuropsychologia, 24,* 417–422.

Fredrik, E., Macoveanu, J., Olesen, P., Tegner, J., & Klingberg, T. (2007). Stronger synaptic connectivity as a mechanism behind development of working memory-related brain activity during childhood. *Journal of Cognitive Neuroscience, 19,* 750–760.

Freeman, N. C. G. (2007). Risk assessment for environmental health. In M. G. Robson & W. A. Toscano (Eds.), *Risk assessment for environmental health* (pp. 315–344). San Francisco: Jossey-Bass.

Gardiner, M. F., & Walter, D. O. (1977). Evidence of hemispheric specialization from infant EEG. In S. Harnad, R. Doty, L. Goldstein, J. Jays, & G. Krauthamer (Eds.), *Lateralization in the nervous system* (pp. 481–500). Orlando, FL: Academic Press.

Gazzaniga, M. S., Ivry, R. B., & Mangun, G. R. (2002). *Cognitive neuroscience: the biology of the mind* (2nd ed.). New York: W.W. Norton & Company.

Giedd, J. N., Castellanos, F. X., Rajapakse, J. C., Vaituzis, A. C., & Rapoport, J. L. (1997). Sexual dimorphism of the developing human brain. *Progress in Neuro-Psychopharmacology and Biological Psychiatry, 21*(8), 1185–1201.

Giedd, J. N., Snell, J. W., Lange, N., Rajapakse, J. C., Casey, B. J., Kozuch, P. L., et al. (1996). Quantitative magnetic resonance imaging of human brain development: Ages 4–18. *Cerebral Cortex, 6*, 551–560.

Gilger, J. W., Hanebuth, E., Smith, S. S., & Pennington, B. F. (1996). Differential risk for developmental reading disorders in the offspring of compensated versus noncompensated parents. *Reading and Writing: An Interdiciplinary Journal, 8*, 407–417.

Gilles, F. H., & Gomez, I.-G. (2005). Developmental neuropathology of the second half of gestation. *Early Human Development, 81*, 245–253.

Hahn, W. K. (1987). Cerebral lateralization of function. *From infancy through childhood. Psychological Bulletin, 101*, 376–392.

Hammer, M. (1977). Lateral responses to speech and noise stimuli. Unpublished dissertation, New York University. *Dissertation Abstracts International, 38*, 1439–B.

Hashimoto, T., Tayama, M., Miyazaki, M., Fujii, E., Harada, M., Miyoshi, H., et al. (1995). Developmental brain changes investigated with proton magnetic resonance spectroscopy. *Developmental Medicine & Child Neurology, 37*, 398–405.

Heilman, K. M., Blonder, L. X., Bowers, D., & Valenstein, E. (2003). Emotional disorders associated with neurological diseases. In K. M. Heilman & E. Valenstein (Eds.), *Clinical neuropsychology* (4th ed., pp. 447–478). New York: Oxford.

Heilman, K. M., Watson, R. T., & Valenstein, E. (2003). Neglect and related disorders. In K. M. Heilman & E. Valenstein (Eds.), *Clinical neuropsychology* (4 ed., pp. 296–246). New York: Oxford.

Hepper, P. G., Shadidullah, S., & White, R. (1991). Handedness in the human fetus. *Neuropsychologia, 29*, 1107–1112.

Hutchinson, M. K., & Sandall, S. R. (1995). Congenital TORCH infections in infants and young children: Neurodevelopmental sequelae and implications for intervention. *Topics in Early Childhood Special Education, 15*, 65–82.

Ingram, D. (1975). Motor asymmetries in young children. *Neuropsychologia, 13*, 95–102.

King, S., Laplante, D., & Joober, R. (2005). Understanding putative risk factors for schizophrenia: retrospective and prospective studies. *Journal of Psychiatry and Neuroscience, 30*, 342–348.

Klein, S. P., & Rosenfield, W. D. (1980). The hemispheric specialization for linguistic and non-linguistic tactile stimuli in third grade children. *Cortex, 16*, 205–212.

Kolb, B., & Fantie, B. (1989). Development of the child's brain and behavior. In C. R. Reynolds & E. F. Janzen (Eds.), *Handbook of child clinical neuropsychology* (pp. 115–144). New York: Plenum Press.

Kolb, B., & Whishaw, I. Q. (2003). *Fundamentals of human neuropsychology* (5th ed.). New York: Worth Publishers.

Leech, S. L., Larkby, C. A., Day, R., & Day, N. L. (2006). Predictors and correlates of high levels of depression and anxiety symptoms among children at age 10. *Journal of the American Academy of Child & Adolescent Psychiatry, 45*, 223–230.

Lesage, J., Sebaai, N., Leonhardt, M., Dutriez-Casteloot, I., Breton, C., Deloof, S., et al. (2006). Perinatal maternal undernutrition programs the offspring hypothalamo-pituitary-adrenal (HPA) axis. *Stress: The International Journal on the Biology of Stress, 9*, 183–198.

Little, R. E., Anderson, K. W., Ervin, C. H., Worthington Roberts, B., & Clarren, S. K. (1989). Maternal alcohol use during breast-feeding and infant mental and motor development at one year. *New England Journal of Medicine, 321*, 425–430.

Lubs, H., Rabin, M., Carlan-Saucier, K., Gross-Glenn, K., Duara, R., Levin, B. E., et al. (1991). Genetic bases of developmental dyslexia: Molecular studies. In J. E. Obzrut & G. W. Hynd (Eds.), *Neuropsychological foundations of learning disabilities: A handbook of issues, methods and practice* (pp. 49–78). San Diego: Harcourt Brace Jovanovich.

Luria, A. B. (1980). *Higher cortical functions in man* (2nd ed.). New York: Basic Books.

Majovski, L. V. (1989). Higher cortical functions in children: A developmental perspective. In C. R. Reynolds & E. Fletcher-Janzen (Eds.), *Handbook of clinical child neuropsychology* (pp. 41–67). New York: Plenum Press.

Malaspina, D., Quitkin, H. M., & Kaufman, C. A. (1992). Epidemiology and genetics of neuropsychiatric disorders. In S. C. Yudofsky & R. E. Hales (Eds.), *The American Psychiatric Press textbook of neuropsychiatry* (2nd ed., pp. 187–226). Washington, D.C.: American Psychiatric Association.

Martens, S. E., Rijken, M., Stoelhorst, G. M. S., van Zweiten, P. H. T., Zwinderman, A. H., Wit, J. M., et al. (2003). Is hypotension a major risk factor for neurological morbidity at term age in very preterm infants? *Early Human Development, 75*, 79–89.

Marx, J., Naude, H., & Pretorius, E. (2006). The effects of hypo- and hypervitaminosis A and its involvement in fetal nervous system development and post-natal sensorimotor functioning-A review. *British Journal of Developmental Disabilities, 52*, 47–64.

Molfese, D. L., & Molfese, V. L. (1979). Hemisphere and stimulus differences as reflected in the cortical responses of newborn infants to speech stimuli. *Developmental Psychology, 15*, 505–511.

Molfese, V. J., & Molfese, D. L. (2002). Environmental and social influences on reading skills as indexed by brain and behavioral responses. *Annals of Dyslexia, 52*, 121–137.

Molfese, D. L., Freeman, R. B., & Palermo, D. S. (1975). The ontogeny of brain lateralization for speech and nonspeech stimuli. *Brain and Language, 2*, 356–368.

Morton, S. M. B. (2006). Maternal nutrition and fetal growth and development. In P. Gluckman & M. Hanson (Eds.), *Developmental origins of health and disease.* (pp. 98–129). New York: Cambridge University Press.

Mueller, B. R., & Bale, T. L. (2007). Early prenatal stress impact on coping strategies and learning performance is sex dependent. *Physiology and Behavior, 91*, 55–65.

Nasrallah, H. (1992). The neuropsychiatry of schizophrenia. In S. C. Yudofsky & R. E. Hales (Eds.), *The American psychiatric press textbook of neuropsychiatry* (Vol. 2, pp. 621–638). Washington, D.C.: American Psychiatric Press.

Noland, J. S., Singer, L. T., Mehta, S. K., & Super, D. M. (2003). Prenatal cocaine/polydrug exposure and infant performance on an executive functioning task. *Developmental Neuropsychology, 24*, 499–517.

O'Reilly, R. L., Lane, A., Cernovsky, Z. Z., & O'Callaghan, E. (2001). Neurological soft signs, minor physical anomalies and handedness in schizophrenia. *European Journal of Psychiatry, 15*, 189–192.

Papalia, D., & Olds, S. W. (1992). *Human Development* (5th ed.). New York: McGraw-Hill.

Passler, M., Isaac, W., & Hynd, G. W. (1985). Neuropsychological development of behavior attributed to frontal lobe functioning in children. *Developmental Neuropsychology, 1*, 349–370.

Pennington, B. F. (1991). *Diagnosing learning disorders.* New York: Guilford Press.

Pennington, B. F. (2002). Genes and brain: Individual differences and human universals. In M. H. Johnson, Y. Munakata, & R. O. Gilmore (Eds.), *Brain development and cognition: A reader* (Vol. 2, pp. 494–508). Malden, MA: Blackwell Publishing.

Raine, A. (2002). Annotation: The role of prefrontal deficits, low autonomic arousal and early health factors in the development of antisocial and aggressive children. *Journal of Child Psychology and Psychiatry, 43*, 417–434.

Reiss, A. L., Abrams, M. T., Singer, H. S., Ross, J. L., & Denckla, M. B. (1996). Brain development, gender and IQ in children. A volumetric imaging study. *Brain, 119 (Pt 5)*, 1763–1774.

Ris, M. D., Dietrich, K. N., Succop, P. A., Berger, O. G., & Bornschein, R. L. (2004). Early exposure to lead and neuropsychological outcome in adolescence. *Journal of the International Neuropsychological Society, 10*, 261–270.

Rosen, G. D., Galaburda, A. M., & Sherman, G. F. (1990). The ontongeny of anatomic asymmetry: Constraints derived from basic mechanisms. In A. B. Scheibel & A. F. Wechsler (Eds.), *Neurobiology of higher cognitive function* (pp. 215–238). New York: Guilford Press.

Saxby, L., & Bryden, M. P. (1984). Left-ear superiority in children for processing auditory material. *Developmental Psychology, 20*, 72–80.

Saxby, L., & Bryden, M. P. (1985). Left-visual field advantage in children for processing visual emotional stimuli. *Developmental Psychology, 21*, 253–261.

Scheibel, A. B. (1990). Dendritic correlates of higher cognitive function. In A. B. Scheibel & A. F. Wechsler (Eds.), *Neurobiology of higher cognitive function* (pp. 239–270). New York: Guilford Press.

Semrud-Clikeman, M. (2007). *Social competence in children.* New York: Springer.

Semrud-Clikeman, M., Pliszka, S. R., Lancaster, J., & Liotti, M. (2006). Volumetric MRI differences in treatment-naïve vs chronically treated children with ADHD. *Neurology, 67*(1023–1027).

Snow, D. M., Carman, H. M., Smith, J. D., Booze, R. M., Welch, M. A., & Mactutus, C. F. (2004). Cocaine-induced inhibition of process outgrowth in locus coeruleus neurons: Role of gestational exposure period and offspring sex. *International Journal of Developmental Neuroscience, 22*, 297–308.

Sowell, E. R., Trauner, D. A., Gamst, A., & Jernigan, T. L. (2002). Development of cortical and subcortical brain structures in childhood and adolescence: A structural MRI study. *Developmental Medicine & Child Neurology, 44*, 4–16.

Streissguth, A., Bookstein, F. L., Barr, H. M., Sampson, P. D., O'Malley, K., & Young, J. K. (2004). Risk factors for adverse life outcomes in fetal alcohol syndrome and fetal alcohol effects. *Journal of Developmental and Behavioral Pediatrics, 25*, 228–238.

U.S. Surgeon General. (2005). Advisory on Alcohol Use in Pregnancy. 2005

Suy, A., Martinez, E., Coll, O., Lonca, M., Palacio, M., de Lazzari, E., et al. (2006). Increased risk of pre-eclampsia and fetal death in HIV-infected pregnant women receiving highly active antiretroviral therapy. *AIDS, 20*, 59–66.

Thatcher, R. W. (1991). Maturation of the human frontal lobes: Physiological evidence for staging. Developmental *Neuropsychology, 7*, 397–419.

Thatcher, R. W. (1996). Neuroimaging of cyclic cortical reorganization during human development. In R. W. Thatcher, G. R. Lyon, J. Rumsey & N. A. Krasnegor (Eds.), *Developmental neuroimaging: Mapping the development of brain and behavior* (pp. 91–106). San Diego: Academic Press.

van den Bergh, B. R. H., Mulder, E. J. H., Mennes, M., & Glover, V. (2005). Antenatal maternal anxiety and stress and the neurobehavioural development of the fetus and child: Links and possible mechanisms. A review. *Neuroscience & Biobehavioral Reviews, 29*, 237–258.

Volger, G. P., DeFries, J. C., & Decker, S. N. (1984). Family history as an indicator of risk for reading disability. *Journal of Learning Disabilities, 10*, 616–624.

Walker, S. P., Thame, M. M., Chang, S. M., Bennett, F., & Forester, T. E. (2007). Association of growth in utero with cognitive function at age 6–8 years. *Early Human Development, 83*, 355–360.

Wigg, N. R. (2001). Low level lead exposure and children. *Journal of Paediatrics and Child Health, 37*, 423–425.

Witelson, S. F. (1989). Hand and sex differences in the isthmus and genu of the human corpus callosum. *Brain, 112*, 799–835.

Witelson, S. F., & Kigar, D. L. (1988). Aysmmetry in brain function follows asymmetry in anatomical form: Gross, microscope, postmortem and imaging studies. In F. Boller & J. Grafman (Eds.), *Handbook of neuropsychology* (Vol. 1, pp. 111–142). Amsterdam: Elsevier Science Publishers.

Witelson, S. F., & Pallie, W. (1973). Left hemisphere specialization for language in the newborn: Neuroanatomical evidence of asymmetry. *Brain*(96), 641–646.

Yoshihiro, M., Sasaki, S., Tanaka, K., Yokoyama, T., Ohya, Y., Fukushima, W., et al. (2006). Dietary folate and vitamins B1, 2, 6 and 12 intake and the risk of postpartum depression in Japan: The Osaka maternal and child health study. *Journal of Affective Disorders, 96*, 133–138.

Young, G., Segalowitz, J., Misek, P., Alp, I. E., & Boulet, R. (1983). Is early reaching left-handed? Review of manual specialization research. In G. Young, S. J. Segalowitz, C. Corter, & S. E. Trehaub (Eds.), *Manual specialization and the developing brain* (pp. 13–32). New York: Academic Press.

Chapter 4
Electrophysiological and Neuroimaging Techniques in Neuropsychology

There are technological advances in all areas of medicine, and the techniques to diagnose neuropsychological problems are no exception. These advances have moved neuropsychology from a practice emphasizing assessment to determine focal and diffuse lesions to one of developing interventions to compensate for brain damage or neurodevelopmental differences. Historically, neuropsychology has concentrated on the ability to diagnose cerebral lesions on the basis of behavioral data. This emphasis was necessary because technology was unable to provide the evidence for such diagnoses. With the advent of magnetic resonance imaging (MRI), lesions, brain tumors, and brain conditions that previously could be seen only with surgery or at autopsy can now be observed in the *living* patient. Because the neuropsychologist will consult on cases that utilize neuroradiological and electrophysiological techniques, it is important to understand what these basic techniques involve and what they reveal to the clinician. This chapter will provide information about common neuroradiological and electrophysiological techniques with an emphasis on the information neuropsychologists and psychologists need for their practice.

Electrophysiological Techniques

Procedures utilizing an electrophysiological technique assess electrical activity associated with incoming sensory information. Electrodes are attached to the scalp and electrical brain activity is recorded via computer and an amplifier for the signals. Electrical brain activity provides a weak signal outside of the skull and requires a differential amplifier to record these signals through a translator attached to a personal computer. Each electrode is placed on the scalp according to various conventions, the most common of which is the 20 universal system (Jasper, 1958). Figure 4.1 provides an overview for electrode placement.

Each electrode provides a signal from a particular region, and each signal is referred to a common reference electrode. The function of the reference electrode is to provide a point that is used to subtract the signals from the individual electrodes. Because each electrode provides some natural interference to

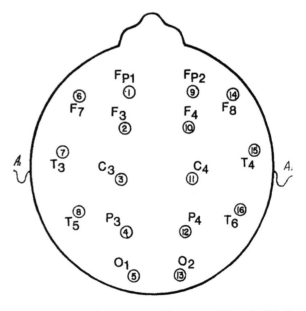

Fig. 4.1 Electrode Placement (Courtesy of Beverly Wical, M.D., pediatric neurologist, University of Minnesota)

M. Semrud-Clikeman, P.A. Teeter Ellison, *Child Neuropsychology*, DOI 10.1007/978-0-387-88963-4_4,
© Springer Science+Business Media, LLC 2009

the signal, the reference electrode serves as a baseline for this interference, and the interference is thus subtracted from each electrode. In this way, each electrode provides information about the unique degree of electrical activity from that selected region of the scalp. Because muscle contractions, muscle movement, and eye movement can interfere with the signal, the patient is observed carefully and brain waves that show such movement are removed. These techniques include electroencephalography and event and evoked potentials. Each of these techniques will be discussed in this chapter, as well as research using such techniques for the study of neurodevelopmental disorders such as learning disabilities and attention-deficit hyperactivity disorders.

Electroencephalography

Electroencephalographs (EEGs) are recorded in patients who are considered at risk for seizure disorders and abnormal brain activity resulting from brain tumors. They are also helpful for use with children who have experienced febrile convulsions, cerebral malformations, brain trauma, vascular events, and coma. Different electrode selections can help in the localization or quantification of EEG results. For example, if seizures are thought to be temporally located, more electrodes will be placed in this region. Different montages can help evaluate seizure activity as well as activation patterns for seizures. EEGs are not foolproof for identifying some types of seizure disorders (Bolter, 1986). At times an EEG may come out normal when in fact there is seizure activity or, conversely, may appear abnormal when no seizure activity exists. For example, a study of normal children found that 68 percent had normal EEGs and 42 percent had abnormal EEGs; 33 percent of normal adolescents registered abnormal EEGs (Harris, 1983**update**).

For some cases, activation procedures can be used to document neurodevelopmental abnormalities more carefully. These activation procedures include induction of sleep, sleep deprivation, hyperventilation, stimulation with flashing lights, and the use of pharmacological agents. These techniques may bring on seizure activity, which can then be recorded through the EEG procedure. Reading an EEG is a complex

and difficult task, particularly with children. Significant variability is found among EEG recordings from different children, with the greatest amount of variability found in neonates (Hynd & Willis, 1988).

Cerebral maturation can also impact EEG recordings. Therefore, it is recommended that a child's mental age, rather than their chronological age, be used for reading the EEG (Black, deRegnier, Long, Georgieff, & Nelson, 2004). Conditions such as illness and metabolic disturbances can also have an impact on the EEG and alter it so that it appears abnormal (Picton & Taylor, 2007).

Evoked Potentials

An *evoked potential* is recorded using electrodes connected to a microcomputer and amplifier. Evoked potentials are recorded in the same manner as EEGs and utilize similar electrode placements. Because an evoked potential is considered a direct response to external sensory stimulation, it is considered to be relatively free from the influence of higher cortical processes. This type of potential is an inexpensive and noninvasive method for assessing the integrity of sensory pathways. With evoked potentials artifacts are more easily screened out compared to EEGs. Evoked potentials, however, have extremely low amplitude (0.1–20 pV), and with such a low voltage, artifacts can have significant impact on the results (Molfese & Molfese, 1994).

The actual brain waves occurring during the artifact can be rejected when compared to typical brain waves associated with the type of evoked potentials. There are distinctive patterns associated with auditory and visual evoked potentials. These will be discussed in more detail.

Auditory Evoked Potentials

Auditory evoked potentials (AEPs) are measures of brain activity from the brain stem to the cortex. The brain stem contains the auditory pathways leading to the cortex. AEPs are one way to assess the integrity of these auditory pathways in infants and young children. The common paradigm is to present auditory stimulation in the form of tones and to evaluate the child's responses to this stimulation. The responses have three phases: early (0–40 ms), middle (41–50 ms), and late (>50 ms).

The early phase is also called the brainstem auditory evoked response (BAER). It consists of 5–7 waves that are thought to coincide with various brain stem nuclei along the auditory pathway (Hynd & Willis, 1988). Figure 4.2 represents a commonly found BAER, in which the first five waves are found in the first 5–6 ms. Waves 6 and 7 are not found in all people. Eighty-four percent of people have wave 6, and 43 percent show wave 7 (Chiappa, 1997).

Wave 5 is considered the most diagnostically important for latency measurement (Chiappa, 1997). This wave appears to be related to the nuclei at the level of the pons or midbrain. It is relevant not only for diagnosing hearing problems, but also for the diagnosis of hydrocephalus, coma, and the effects of toxins, among others (Menkes & Sarnat, 2000). Wave 5 is also important for mapping the neurodevelopment of neonates. As the preterm child develops, the latency for auditory stimulation decreases and approaches that of full-term babies at 38 weeks (Aldridge, Braga, Walton, & Bower, 1999; Novitski,

Huotilainen, Tervaniemi, Naatanen, & Fellman, 2006). Research has found that the BAER is useful in mapping the progression of a disorder of the central nervous system. Disorders such as asphyxia, autism, mental retardation, and hyperglycemia have been found to have differences in the amplitude and latency of various components (Hynd & Willis, 1988).

Visual Evoked Potentials

A visual evoked potential (VER) is a technique to evaluate the integrity of the visual system. Generally, two techniques are used. One involves using a flashing light; the other presents a reversible black and white checkerboard pattern. The pattern-shift paradigm provides a more significant reading for visual deficits. This paradigm results in three peaks which occur at the following latencies: 70, 100, and 135 ms. The VER assists in evaluating the integrity of the visual system in cases of neurofibromatosis (Jabbari, Maitland, Morris, Morales, & Gunderson, 1985). In this study, children with neurofibromatosis (NF) were frequently found to experience tumors on

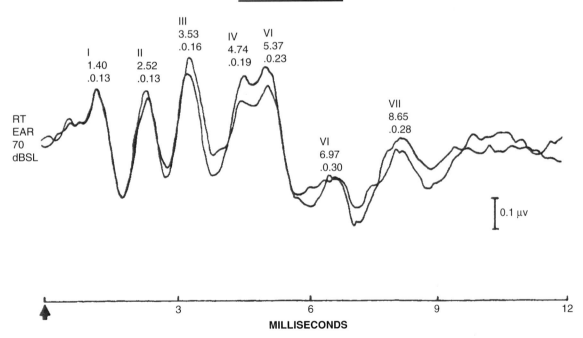

NORMAL BAERS

Fig. 4.2 Common BAER
Source: From G. W. Hynd and G. Willis, 1988, Pediatric Neuropsychology, p. 179. Copyright © 1977 by Allyn and Bacon. Reprinted by permission.

the optic nerves which are difficult to detect in the early stages of growth. Subsequently, early signs were later confirmed through the use of computed tomography (CT) scans.

Similar to the BAER, the VER has been found to be useful in determining the integrity of the visual system in preterm infants. In studies with preterm infants, the latency and amplitude of the waves appears normal with ensuing development (Howard & Reggia, 2007). Thus, the VER is a useful, inexpensive screening device for optic tumors in children as well as for monitoring the development of the visual system in preterm infants.

Event-Related Potentials

In contrast to evoked potentials, *event-related potentials* (ERPs) provide an assessment of later components of the electrical wave forms that are thought to be associated with cognition. ERPs refer to a change in the ongoing waveform that occurs in response to a cognitive event, such as attention or stimulus discrimination. An ERP requires the client to participate in the data gathering process, whereas the client is passive with evoked potentials. ERPs are collected in the same manner as evoked potentials and EEGs, with electrodes, amplifiers, and a computer. The difference lies in stimulus presentation and in the use of later wave components. ERPs consist of complex wave forms comprising several components. These components can be measured for amplitude (size of the wave) and latency (time from stimulus onset). Some components are *exogenous* (automatic responses to stimuli); others are *endogenous* (elicited by psychological characteristics of stimuli). The endogenous ERPs are thought to reflect cognitive processes.

Dyslexia

Electrophysiological techniques are used in the study of learning disabilities to examine the neurobiological mechanisms that underlie these disabilities. ERPs have been used extensively in the study of auditory and visual processes and in study of reading ability (von Koss Torkildsen, Syversen, Simonsen, Moen, &

Lindgren, 2007), making it possible to follow the path of the brain's activity with great precision. Several decades of research have demonstrated different patterns of activation in the brains of children with Learning Disabilities (LD) and those of control groups. One component of interest is the P3, which is a positive component occurring 300 ms after stimulus onset, often used in studies of learning disabilities. P3 is an indicator of the meaningfulness associated to the stimulus; it requires conscious processing and thus is dependent on attention (Taroyan, Nicolson, & Fawcett, 2006).

Abnormal P3 responses have been found in both child and adult LD populations. However, this wave is dependent on attention, and these abnormalities are inconclusive due to the high incidence of comorbid attention problems in subjects with LD. Another component studied in populations with LD is the N4, a negative wave occurring 400 ms after stimulus onset. The N4 is believed to be reflective of semantic and phonological information and, in studies of children with reading problems, has demonstrated a deficit in phonological processing (Guttorm, Leppanen, Tolvanen, & Lyytinen, 2003; von Koss et al., 2007).

The preceding two components involve conscious processing. In contrast, the N200, occurring 100–250 ms after stimulus presentation, is an automatic component that does not require attention. Studies have evaluated the early portion of N2, also called mismatch negativity because it is a negative wave elicited by a deviant stimulus occurring among a series of standard stimuli. These studies have demonstrated that adults and children with reading disabilities process auditory information differently than normal readers. The mismatch negativity response to stimulus change is attenuated in subjects with learning disabilities, indicating low-level auditory processing deficits (Bishop, 2007). This physiological abnormality is also correlated with phonological deficits.

Research utilizing event-related potentials has found differences in the amplitude of the brain wave for both auditory and visual stimuli, with dyslexic children showing smaller amplitude to words, auditory stimuli, and on shape and sound-matching tasks. In addition, those with dyslexia have been found to be less efficient in their processing to auditory material and appear similar to much younger children (Frederici, 2006; Regtvoort, van Leeuwen, Stoel, & van der Leij, 2006; Santos, Joly-Pottuz, Moreno, Habib, & Besson, 2007).

Differences in the response to visual evoked potentials by those with dyslexia have been implicated in dyslexia (Regtvoort et al., 2006). These findings may be related to neuroanatomical differences that subserve these functions found during autopsy studies of dyslexic brains. Autopsy studies have found differences in the lateral geniculate nucleus of the thalamus—a structure important for interpretating visual information (Galaburda, 2005). Research utilizing event-related potentials with people with dyslexia has been problematic in regard to subject selection. Heterogeneous groups of dyslexics have been utilized, and some studies utilized dyslexics who would not qualify for such a diagnosis in current educational practice.

Little to no attention has been given to subtypes in reading deficits and possible differences in their event-related potentials. It is not known whether dyslexic children who experience difficulty with sight word reading, but not with phonics development (surface dyslexia), vary on electrophysiological measures from children with phonological coding disabilities (phonological dyslexia). Moreover, programs for wave form analysis have now been developed that allow not only for comparison across subjects but also for intrasubject comparisons. This development allows reading performance to be compared with different types of reading material. For example, material that requires phonetic processing can be compared with material that primarily requires visual processing. In addition to identification of subtypes, the sample source for studying dyslexia is also problematic. For example, when children identified as learning disabled by objective standardized tests were compared with previously school-identified children for learning disabilities, an overrepresentation of boys in the school-identified sample was found, whereas the objective standardized test method found approximately equal numbers of girls and boys (Shaywitz, Shaywitz, Fletcher, & Escobar, 1990). Similarly, when groups were selected on the basis of objective test results, males have been found to show a more severe type of reading disability than girls (Berninger, Abbott, Abbott, Graham, & Richards, 2002).

Attention-Deficit Hyperactivity Disorders

ERPs have also been helpful with children with attention-deficit hyperactivity disorder (ADHD). Difficulties in sustained attention may cause children with attentional disorders to respond more slowly and variably, and make more mistakes when presented with stimuli. Difficulties with selective attention may cause children not to respond to relevant stimuli. Therefore, it has been important to evaluate both the amplitude and the latency of responses to stimulation.

To evaluate this hypothesis, event-related potentials (ERP) have been used to measure sustained and selective attention. One component of sustained attention that has been most frequently studied in children with attentional disorders has been the P3b component. The P3b is a late positive wave with a latency of 300–800 ms with maximal expression in the parietal region of the cerebral cortex. Amplitude of P3b can be increased by directing attention to novel features presented with low probability. Several studies have found smaller amplitude on P3b for children with ADHD for both frequent and rare stimuli (Burgio-Murphy et al., 2007; Johnstone, Barry, & Clarke, 2007; Rodriguez & Baylis, 2007), while typically developing children show decreases in distractibility from young childhood to adulthood (Wetzel, Widmann, Berti, & Schroger, 2006). However, studies have also found smaller amplitude in diagnostic groups ranging from learning disabilities in mathematics or reading to those with oppositional defiant disorder, which suggests that a reduced P3b may reflect cognitive disturbance rather than a unique characteristic of attention-deficit disorder (Burgio-Murphy et al., 2007).

Administering stimulant drugs has improved accuracy and speed of judgment and to increase P3b amplitude in children diagnosed with ADHD (Klorman, Brumaghim, Fitzpatrick, & Borgstedt, 1994). This finding has been replicated with children with pervasive ADHD and children with ADHD with oppositional/aggressive features, and across age groups (Coons, Klorman,, & Borgstedt, 1987; Klorman et al., 1988).

Holcomb, Ackerman, and Dykman (1985) compared attention-deficit disorder with hyperactivity (ADD/H), attention-deficit disorder without hyperactivity (ADD/noH), and reading-disabled groups and found that only children with ADD/noH had significantly smaller amplitude of their P3b wave to stimuli they were asked to attend to (called target stimuli) than did controls. In a later study (Harter & Anllo-Vento, 1988), children with ADD/H were found to display a larger difference in brain wave amplitudes between targets versus nontargets than did nondisabled children. Children with learning disabilities differed from typically developing children and children with ADHD/H as they had a larger amplitude difference between nontargets than for targets.

Further studies have found that the ERPs are sensitive for specific tasks such as response selection in children with ADHD:predominately inattentive, ADHD:combined, math learning disability and combined reading and math learning disabilities (Klorman et al., 2002). The two subtypes of ADHD performed more poorly than the control group or children with reading and math disability without ADHD.

Medication may also be an important aspect for study. Liotti, Pliszka, Perez, Glahn, and Semrud-Clikeman (in press) studied inhibitory control mechanisms in 36 ADHD-combined type and 30 healthy children using ERPs recorded during an inhibitory task (the Stop Signal Task). The influence of age, gender and previous treatment history was evaluated. The ADHD group showed reduced N200 wave amplitudes. For successful inhibitions, the N200 reduction wave was greatest over right inferior frontal scalp, and only the Control group showed a success-related enhancement of such right frontal N200. Source analysis identified a source of the N200 group effect in right dorsolateral prefrontal cortex. Finally, a Late Positive Wave to Failed Inhibition was selectively reduced in treatment-naïve ADHD children, suggesting that chronic stimulants may normalize late conscious error recognition. Both effects were independent of gender and age.

In contrast to the amplitude component, the latency of the P3b comparing subtypes of children with ADHD to other groups has not been as fully studied. Liotti, Pliszka, Semrud-Clikeman, Higgins, and Perez (in press) found that children with ADHD: combined subtype showed difficulty in response inhibition as measured by the N200 wave and in difficulty processing errors using the P3 wave. In contrast children with reading disorder showed no difficulty with response inhibition as measured by the N200, but did have difficulty on the P3 wave, indicating problems with rapidly orienting to visual and auditory stimuli. These findings are consistent with previous findings of no problems with response inhibition in children with reading disability without ADHD (Facotti et al., 2003; Taroyan et al., 2006), but problems in error detection and late processing of verbal information for children with a sole diagnosis of ADHD (Pliszka, Liotti, & Woldroff, 2000).

Mismatch Negativity

Mismatch negativity (MMN) has been carefully studied in normal children and adults and is believed to reflect the basic mechanism of automatic attention switching to stimulus changes without conscious attention (Naatanen, 1990). MMN is the difference in the N200 (N2) amplitude comparing rare targets and nontargets. Children often need to learn to direct their attention appropriately and to suppress an irrelevant stimuli or response. Research has found that children learn how to direct their attentional orientation and to control distraction over time. There are significant differences in the ability to direct attention and process information that occur over time. Although even young children (aged 6–8) can control distractibility when motivated, such control increases dramatically by the age of 18 to unexpected distractions (Wetzel & Schroger, 2007). It also appears that the locus for mismatch negativity changes over development. Younger children show more activity in the posterior region for mismatch negativity which moves to fronto-central areas during adolescence, with smaller amplitudes also present and becoming similar to adult functioning (Maurer, Bucher, Brem, & Brandeis, 2003). This reduced amplitude of the N2 over development has been related to improved task performance with reaction time and inhibition (Johnstone, Barry, Anderson, & Coyle, 1996).

Some have found that the novelty of a stimulus may capture the attention of a child with ADHD temporarily due solely to the uniqueness of the event (van Mourik, Oosterlaan, Heslenfeld, Konig, & Sergeant, 2007). Because the MMN component is thought to be automatic, it may indicate that it is a 'readiness' to pay attention. Children with ADHD tend to have attenuated N2 amplitudes compared to children without ADHD (Broyd et al., 2005; Smith, Johnstone, & Barry, 2004). These findings have been interpreted to reflect poorer selective attention in children with attention-deficit disorder, particularly when subjects are required to ignore sets of stimuli. When only a single dimension of a target is presented and selective attention is not so overloaded, these differences no longer occur (Barry, Johnstone, & Clark, 2003; Harter & Anllo-Vento, 1988). Therefore, it would be important to gather data on stimuli that require the subject to attend to one task at a time and conditions that require the subject to split her or his attention across tasks. It may be that the deficits in ADHD children often found on behavioral measures of automatized skills are due to hardwired neurological deviations.

Conclusions

In summary, brain wave differences have been found in selective and sustained attention tasks in children with ADHD, particularly when complex tasks are utilized. There is emerging evidence that the subtypes may differ in brain electrical activity, with children with ADHD without hyperactivity symptoms showing the largest amplitude differences from normal controls. If children with ADHD have different patterns of selective attention that can be measured through ERPs, it may well be possible to demonstrate changes in these differences following treatment. For example, children with ADHD without hyperactivity were found to have a larger than normal response to rare stimuli, which may be interpreted to mean that they overreact to novel stimuli. This finding is similar to the behavioral observation that ADHD children tend to be very attentive to rare and/or novel situations, tasks, and experiences. The findings of the processing negativity study indicate that it is almost impossible for these children to inhibit their responses. Therefore, not only do children with ADHD without hyperactivity show better attention to novel stimuli, but they also find it extremely

difficult to ignore or inhibit responses to these rare occurrences. Thus, differences in how the brains of children with ADHD (ADHD with hyperactivity and ADHD without hyperactivity) respond to the environment may provide information for the development of interventions as well as furthering our understanding of the underpinnings of these disorders.

Neuroimaging Techniques

While ERPs allow for a dynamic assessment of brain activity, computed tomography (CT) and magnetic resonance imaging (MRI) techniques allow us to compare possible structural differences in children with developmental disorders to normal controls. Both of these techniques will be briefly discussed in the following sections.

Computed Tomography

Computed tomography (CT) allows for the visualization of the brain anatomy to determine the presence of focal lesions, structural deviations, and tumors. A CT scan uses a narrow X-ray beam that rotates 360 degrees around the area to be scanned. Each CT slice is acquired independently, and that slice can be repeated if a movement artifact occurs. Scanning time is 15–20 minutes per slice. The resulting data are transformed by Fourier analysis into gray scale to create the image. Figure 4.3 illustrates a CT scan image. One advantage of a CT scan is the short acquisition time. Another is the ability to repeat single slices if movement or other artifacts occur. Limitations of CT scans are the relatively poor resolution of gray and white matter structures. Moreover, CT slices are obtained in the axial plane, which limits visualization of the temporal lobes and posterior fossa (Filipek & Blickman, 1992). You may recall from Chapter 2 that the pediatric population is susceptible to tumors of the posterior fossa, which cannot be easily visualized by CT scanning. Although within acceptable ranges, radiation is used in CT scans in order to produce the images.

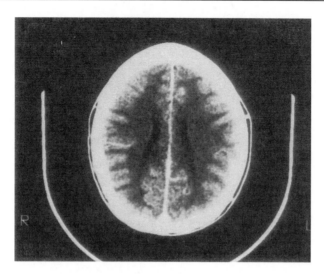

Fig. 4.3 Normal CT scan
Source: Courtesy of William Dobyns, M.D., pediatric neurologist, University of Minnesota.

Magnetic Resonance Imaging

Magnetic resonance imaging (MRI) procedures offer noninvasive investigation of neuroanatomical structures in a *living* brain. MRIs visualize brain tissue at about the level of postmortem studies, with clarity superior to that of CT scans. Figure 4.4 presents a representative MRI scan. The MRI consists of a large magnet with magnetic field strengths up to 3.0 Tesla for use with humans, and up to 7.0 for animals. Tesla is an indication of the magnet strength.

The patient lies on a movable table, which goes inside a doughnut hole-shaped opening. A coil covers the area, to be scanned with an opening over the face in the use of the head coil. To understand how MRI works, it is important to briefly review the physics behind it. In a magnetic field, hydrogen photons align in the same direction as the field. A radiofrequency pulse will deflect these photons into an angle predetermined by the clinician. Once the pulse ceases, the photons return to their original alignment through a series of ever-relaxing and slowing circles (Gazzaniga, Ivry, & Mangun, 2002). Altering the rate, duration, and intensity of the radio frequency pulses allows for the differing visualization of the brain. An MRI is actually several complementary sequences, each an average of 7–10 minutes in length.

In clinical use, routine MRI scans utilize TI- and T2-weighted sequences. T-weighted scans provide visualization generated photons involved in the pulse, whereas T2-weighted scans involve the interaction of the neighboring photons (Cohen, 1986). T1-weighted scans provide excellent anatomical detail with myelin and structural abnormalities. In contrast, T2-weighted scans are sensitive to water content in the tissues and are used to determine the extent of the lesions.

Because MRIs are noninvasive and do not use radiation, they are fairly risk-free. MRIs are expensive and are generally used only when there is suspicion of brain abnormality. They are more sensitive than CTs for locating lesions and, when a contrast agent such as gadolinium is used, the tumor can be differentiated from surrounding swelling.

In the past, neuropsychological assessment was used to *try* to localize brain tumors, lesions, etc. The MRI has supplanted neuropsychological assessment for this process in cases where tumors or lesions are suspected. Neuropsychological assessment is used for intervention planning and for determining *how* the person solves the difficulty. Neuropsychological assessment continues to be sensitive to subtle damage or damage at the microcellular level that the MRI is unable to pinpoint.

Functional MRI

Functional MRI (fMRI) is a relatively new technique which, at present, is used mostly for research. It maps cerebral blood flow or volume as well as changes in cerebral blood volume, flow, and oxygenation. fMRI

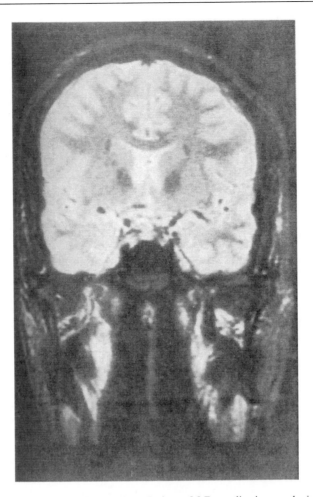

Fig. 4.4 Normal Coronal MRI Scan (Courtesy of William Dobyns, M.D., pediatric neurologist, University of Minnesota)

allows for the study of brain activation through the use of echoplanar imaging (EPI). This technique does not use radioactive agents to visualize the brain. T-weightedthe contrast agent and is currently believed to be risk-free. The obtained images allow for visualization. fMRI technology is one of the most advanced techniques available for measuring brain functions by detecting changes in blood flow during activation. This noninvasive technique allows researchers to explore the relationship between increases in metabolic activity in various local brain regions during cognitive or perceptual tasks; thereby, mapping or identifying cortical regions involved in various functions. Studies have found activation in numerous temporal lobe structures during phoneme awareness tasks and listening tasks (Binder et al., 1994; Roa et al., 1992). Other studies with ADHD children have found less activity when the child is asked to inhibit responding compared to control children particularly in the dorsolateral portion of the frontal lobes (Pliszka et al., 2006).

These fMRI findings suggest that more static or indirect measures of brain function may not be capturing the richness and complexity of brain function, in that both hemispheres were activated during a task thought to be mediated primarily by left temporal regions. These results expand and may challenge fairly well-established patterns (using positron emission tomography (PET) scans) of unilateral left temporal-parietal activation for phonological processing in adult populations of normal readers.

Research with MRI

MRI technology now allows us to obtain pictures of the brain from living children and assess the impact of treatment on the brain's development (Filipek et al., 1989). Because it may be possible to detect neuroanatomical differences before the behavioral problems emerge in response to school requirements, investigating brain measures may allow us to begin studying children at a much younger age and provide earlier interventions.

Dyslexia

Dyslexia Research by Hynd, Semrud-Clikeman, Lorys, Novey, and Eliopulos (1990) and Semrud-Clikeman, Hynd, Novey, and Eliopulos (1991) utilizing MRI scans found differences specific to dyslexia in the neuroanatomical regions involved with language processing. These findings were replicated in several subsequent studies (Duara et al., 1991; Jernigan, Hesselink, Sowell, & Tallal, 1991; Larsen, Hoien, Lundberg, & Odegaard, 1990). Additional findings in these studies indicated no differences in the cerebral hemispheric area or posterior areas in dyslexic subjects. These findings strongly implicate areas thought to be important in language processing. No differences were found in brain size, so reported regional differences more strongly implicate the likelihood of a neurodevelopmental process active during gestation of these regions. Abnormal development is thought to occur somewhere between the 24th and 28th week of gestation.

Fine, Semrud-Clikeman, Keith, Stapleton, and Hynd (2006) studied children with dyslexia within families at risk for learning problems. Findings indicated that better readers show larger midsagittal regions in the middle of the corpus callosum compared to poorer readers. In addition left and right volumes of the corpus callosum were symmetrical and not related to the diagnosis of a reading disability.

Functional Neuroimaging

As technology has improved, we can now view how the brain processes phonemes, words, and strings of words and sounds. Some have now suggested three left-hemispheric neural systems utilized for reading based on neuroimaging research. The anterior system involves the inferior frontal gyrus and is involved in articulation and word analysis. The second system involves the area of the brain in the parietal and temporal juncture and is involved in word analysis. Finally the third system is involved in the occipito-temporal region and is involved in rapid and fluent identification of words (Pugh et al., 2001; Shaywitz, 2003). As a child matures the two posterior regions are involved in learning problems (Shaywitz, Shaywitz, Pugh, Fulbright, & Skudlarski, 2002). The area of the brain that is involved in rapid and automatic processing of written material (occipito-temporal region) has been found to be disrupted in impaired readers (McCrory, Mechelli, Frith, & Price, 2005). This region may also be involved in the word-finding problems that children and adults with dyslexia frequently experience.

Shaywitz et al. (2003) studied participants from the Connecticut Longitudinal Study from five years of age until 22.5 years of age. These participants completed annual assessments of their reading skills throughout this time period. Findings identified three groups of readers: (1) non-impaired; (2) accurate but not fluent readers, and (3) persistently poor readers. fMRI found that when asked to determine if two nonwords rhymed, the accurate but not fluent readers showed disruption of the left-hemispheric posterior reading systems, but not the anterior. The non-impaired readers and the poor readers showed similar activation of the posterior reading system. For the non-impaired readers activation of the posterior systems was correlated with the anterior system. However, for the poor readers activation was present in the frontal regions bilaterally indicating that the memory system was also engaged as the person attempted to read words that were not automatic and thus required additional cognitive resources. The accurate but not fluent readers were more similar to the non-impaired readers and showed similar types of connectivity of frontal and posterior reading systems in the left hemisphere.

Shaywitz et al. (2002) evaluated the histories of these three types of readers. Findings indicated that the persistently poorer readers showed poorer school settings, lower socioeconomic status, and less additional help and tutoring. In contrast the accurate but not fluent readers showed relatively higher IQs compared to the poor readers, better socioeconomic status, and more supportive home environments. These findings are consistent with those from genetic studies that a shared home environment that is enriched is related to higher IQ and better reading ability (Olson, 1999; Shaywitz, Mody, & Shaywitz, 2006).

ADHD

For a regional difference to be predictive, it needs to be unique to a specific disorder. The consistent finding of smaller splenial (the posterior portion of the corpus callosum) measurements in ADHD may be unique to ADHD (Hynd et al., 1990; Semrud-Clikeman et al., 1994). Using a carefully diagnosed sample of ADHD with overactivity symptoms and no codiagnoses, compared to matched non-disabled control subjects, Semrud-Clikeman et al. (1994) were able to demonstrate differences through MRI analysis in the posterior regions of the corpus callosum, with particularly smaller splenial regions for the ADHD group. No differences were found in the anterior regions of the corpus callosum, in callosal length, or callosal total area. When response to medication was evaluated, a trend also was found that may suggest structural differences for the ADD/H sample based on medication response. Subjects who did not respond to methylphenidate, but did respond to desipramine or imipramine, tended to have a smaller corpus callosum splenial measure compared to subjects who were positive methylphenidate responders or control subjects. These results indicate that medication response may be partially mediated by fewer connections between posterior regions of the brain. Given the small number of subjects, the area of medication response and its relationship to brain structure needs further study.

A study by Semrud-Clikeman et al. (1996) explored the utility of using selected brain morphometric indices to predict group membership for children who were developmental dyslexic, ADHD, and a typically developing group. Six brain regions were selected a priori for inclusion in a discriminant function analysis (right and left plana temporale length, right and left insula length, left and right anterior width). This analysis classified participants with an overall accuracy at 60 percent with the best accuracy found for persons with developmental dyslexia and controls. When chronological age and

FSIQ were added to the discriminant analysis, the overall classification accuracy rose to 87 percent with the misclassified participants assigned to one of the clinical groups. This preliminary study supports the hypothesis that selected brain structures can reliably discriminate groups by developmental disorder.

Structural MRI

A structural MRI study by Filipek et al.(1997) found the frontal regions to be smaller volumetrically in children with ADHD compared to normal controls, with greater differences in the right frontal region. Moreover, the region of the brain including the caudate head and other anterior basal ganglia were also found to be volumetrically smaller in the ADHD sample than in the controls. Analyzing the white matter in the frontal area yielded significantly smaller volume in frontal right white matter volume in the ADHD sample. The finding of similar cerebral hemispheric and ventricular volumes in the ADHD cohort without enlarged external cerebrospinal fluid spaces indicates that the underlying pathophysiology is not likely the result of degeneration or atrophy. Rather differences in specific hemispheric regions implicate a neurodevelopmental process which alters neural system configuration, particularly in the right hemisphere, in children with ADHD. Differences have also been found in the corpus callosum, with smaller regions variously reported in the genu and the splenial regions (Giedd et al., 1994; Hynd, Marshall, & Semrud-Clikeman, 1991; Semrud-Clikeman et al., 1994).

The caudate regions have been found to be smaller in several studies in children with ADHD (Castellanos et al., 1994; Hynd et al., 1993; Semrud-Clikeman, 2006; Semrud-Clikeman, Pliszka, Lancaster, & Liotti, 2006).The caudate is intimately involved in the dopaminergic system; a system in which methylphenidate is believed to correct imbalances. Moreover, lesions to the caudate in adults and animals have resulted in behaviors which are very similar to those seen in hyperactive children (Posner & Rothbart, 2007).

These results relate directly to the clinical finding that hyperactivity is a common symptom in caudate infarcts (Caplan, Schmahmann, & Kase, 1990). Hynd et al. (1995) suggested that such a difference may be related to lower levels of neurotransmitter being relayed to the frontal lobes, resulting in compromised levels of complex attentional skills. In contrast, Castellanos et al. (1994) found the right caudate to be smaller and symmetrical with the left caudate in their ADHD sample, while the control sample evidenced R > L caudate volumes. Castellanos et al. (1994) also found that the volume of the caudate decreased significantly with age for the normal controls, with no difference in the ADHD group. Filipek et al. (1997) found smaller volumetric measurements in the left anterior caudate of the ADHD sample compared to normal controls. This finding is consistent with the results of Hynd et al. (1995). Symmetrical caudate volume was found for the ADHD group due to a smaller than expected left caudate. The control group possessed left greater than right caudate volume. Moreover, there was a significant medication effect related to smaller left caudate volume with the ADHD sample who responded favorably to methylphenidate showing the smallest left caudate volume, followed by the sample who did not respond to methylphenidate, and with the normal control group showing the largest left caudate volume.

A more recent study controlling medication history found no asymmetry in the caudate (Semrud-Clikeman et al., 2006). However, findings indicated that the caudate was larger bilaterally in groups of children with ADHD and with and without a medication treatment history, compared to a group of children who were typically developing. There were no laterality differences in the volume of the caudate.

Although there are conflicting findings as to the direction of the caudate asymmetry, the studies to date have found that there are structural differences in the caudate regions of ADHD children compared to normal children. The caudate is intimately involved in the dopaminergic system, a system in which methylphenidate is believed to correct suspected imbalances. Moreover, lesions to the caudate in adults and animals have resulted in behaviors that are similar to those seen in hyperactive children (Posner & Raichle, 1994). Further study is needed to determine the role of the caudate in ADHD as well as the contributions of structural differences in this disorder.

Findings indicate that the anterior cingulate may differ between children with ADHD and controls. Those children without a history of stimulant treatment were found to show smaller volumes in the right ACC compared to children with a history of stimulant treatment and with controls (Semrud-Clikeman et al., 2006). The children with a history of stimulant treatment of at least one year (most of them four years or more) showed anterior cingulate volume equivalent to that of the controls. This is an important finding because the anterior cingulate is a structure that appears to be crucial for directing attention as well as being aware of successful or unsuccessful solutions to a problem. If it is possible for the brain to adapt to input from the environment when appropriate interventions are provided, structural changes indicate that such interventions actually allow neural changes to be implemented that may assist with the processing of information.

These studies are preliminary and must be interpreted with caution because of small numbers and differing methodologies. However, their results suggest that neurodevelopmental anomalies may characterize the brains of children with ADHD and that deviations in structure may be associated and related to prenatal deviations in cellular migration and maturation (Geschwind & Galaburda, 1985; Hynd & Semrud-Clikeman, 1989). The use of three-dimensional MRI as well as subgrouping ADHD may provide further information about the neurodevelopmental underpinnings of this disorder. Investigators have hypothesized that the brain areas implicated in the ADHD:combined subtype are in the anterior regions involved in motor activity modulation, whereas ADHD:predominately inattentive is hypothesized to be related to central-posterior regions affecting attention (McBurnett, Pfiffner, & Frick, 2001; Waldman, Lilienfeld, & Lahey, 1995).

These hypotheses have not been tested empirically, and MRI results may well show anatomical differences among the subtypes. As there appear to be differences in behavior between the subtypes, it is likely that the subtypes differ neurologically. Moreover, the finding that the subtypes of attention-deficit disorder respond differentially to medication further indicates that differing brain mechanisms may be implicated in the subtypes (Millich, Ballentine, & Lynam, 2001). Therefore, since the MRI studies to date have mostly utilized subjects with ADHD:combined subtype, the next step would be to look at subjects with differing expressions of ADHD to determine if neuroanatomical differences exist between the subtypes.

Functional MRI

Functional imaging has found less activation in the dorsolateral regions of the frontal lobes as well as in the ACC (Pliszka et al., 2006). FMRI research in ADHD has primarily focused on inhibitory control. FMRI studies have shown that healthy adults engage the right dorsolateral prefrontal cortex (DLPFC) on inhibition tasks, particularly for successful inhibitions (Garavan, Ross, Murphy, Roche, & Stein, 2002; Rubia, Smith, Brammer, & Taylor, 2003).

While the anterior cingulate cortex (ACC) is also involved when inhibition is successful, it is involved more strongly for unsuccessful inhibitions. After unsuccessful inhibitions, activation of the ACC may increase prefrontal cortex activity on future trials, thus increasing cognitive control after errors (Kerns et al., 2004). After unsuccessful inhibitions, healthy children show more activation in the ACC (Pliszka et al., 2006) or the posterior cingulate cortex (Rubia, Smith, Brammer, Toone, & Taylor, 2005), compared to children with ADHD.

Findings for children with ADHD in the frontal cortex have been more inconsistent, with studies showing both increased (Durston, 2003; Schulz et al., 2004; Vaidya et al., 1998) and decreased activity (Rubia et al., 1999; Rubia et al., 2005) relative to controls during inhibitory tasks. Recently, Pliszka et al. (2006) obtained fMRI on children with ADHD (both medication naïve and those with a history of chronic stimulant treatment) to healthy controls while they performed a stop signal task. ADHD children had increased right PFC activity relative to controls during both successful and unsuccessful inhibitions. During unsuccessful inhibitions, healthy controls showed greater ACC and left ventrolateral PFC (VLPFC) activation than ADHD children. Studies of children with ADHD on social understanding types of tasks using fMRI, volumetric MRI, or DTI are not present in the literature.

To date, most of the research has either used samples of children with ADHD: combined subtype or without specifying the subtype. It is rare that

children with ADHD: predominately inattentive type have been studied, and no studies were identified with children with ADHD: PI using functional neuroimaging. We were unable to locate any published studies utilizing DTI in children with ADHD: PI. The one study we located utilized children with ADHD: C with some on medications and others not (Ashtari et al., 2005). Findings were of decreased fractional anisotropy (FA) in the areas of the left cerebellum, right striatal region, and in the right premotor areas. It will be of interest to study children with ADHD: PI using fMRI and DTI to determine whether these findings also apply to the PI subtype.

Autism

Structural imaging in autistic spectrum disorder (ASD) has found a variety of cerebral anomalies. Some findings have indicated differences in the corpus callosum, particularly in thinning and in the midsagittal area and in white matter density in persons with ASD (Chung, Dalton, Alexander, & Davidson, 2004; Hardan, Minshew, & Keshavan, 2000; Vidal et al., 2006). These differences have been linked to difficulties with language processing and in working memory (Just, Cherkassky, Keller, & Minshew, 2004; Koshino et al., 2005). Structural imaging findings show increased brain size in children with ASD, specifically enlargement in the regions of the parietal, temporal, and occipital lobes found for children (Courchesne, Carper, & Akshoomoff, 2003; Piven, Arndt, Bailey, & Andreasen, 1996). The enlargement is due to greater volumes of white matter, but not gray (Filipek et al., 1997). For adolescents and adults with autism, increased brain size was not found, but increased head circumference was identified (Aylward, Minshew, Field, Sparks, & Singh, 2002). Findings have also implicated the caudate in children with ASD. Sears et al.(1999) found increased volume bilaterally in the caudate of adolescents and young adults with HFA. Caudate enlargement was found to be proportional to the increased total brain volumes also identified. To determine whether these findings were specific to the sample studied, the results were replicated with a different sample of participants with ASD. Thus, it will be of interest to evaluate the caudate volume in children and adolescents to determine whether the finding of larger caudates bilaterally are present in younger participants but not in older participants. Previous studies have found that the caudate volume in typically developing children decreases at puberty (Giedd, 2004). For the Sears et al. (1999) study this decrease did not occur. Increased caudate volumes were also not present for the ADHD population (Semrud-Clikeman et al., 2006).

In typically developing adults, right-sided activation has been found for the FG, the STG, and the amygdala when viewing social faces (Schultz et al., 2003). These findings seem to corroborate the hypothesis that the right hemisphere is more heavily involved in social processing than the left (Winner, Brownell, Happe, Blum, & Pincus, 1998). Studies of adults with high functioning autism (HFA) or Asperger Syndrome (AS) have found differences in these regions using structural and functional imaging with finding less activation or smaller volumes (Abell et al., 1999; Baron-Cohen et al., 1999). Some studies have found underactivation in the prefrontal areas in participants with ASD (Schultz et al., 2000) with higher activation in controls particularly in the left prefrontal regions. Significant metabolic reduction has been found in the anterior cingulate gyrus, an area important for error monitoring, and in the frontostriatal networks involved in visuospatial processing (Ohnishi et al., 2000; Silk et al., 2006). The amygdala and striatal regions have been implicated in processing of emotional facial expressions (Canli, Sivers, Whitfield, Gotlib, & Gabrieli, 2002; Killgore & Yurgelun-Todd, 2005; Yang et al., 2002). Studies involving the amygdala have found that patients with bilateral lesions show difficulty in judging emotional facial expressions (Bechara, Damasio, & Damasio, 2003). Faces that were negative in nature were found to produce slower activation than those which were neutral in controls (Monk et al., 2003; Simpson, Öngür, Akbudak, Conturo, & Ollinger, 2000). Positive stimuli was found to increase activity in the amygdala with happy expressions resulting in faster response times (Canli et al., 2002; Pessoa, Kastner, & Ungerleider, 2002; Somerville, Kim, Johnstone, Alexander, & Whalen, 2004).

Hare, Tottenham, Davidson, Glover, and Casey (2005) found longer latencies for negative facial expressions when the amygdale was activiated in normal adult controls, while activation of the

caudate was present when the participant was avoiding positive information. These findings point to the neural networks that underlie the processing of positive and negative emotions. It would appear crucial to determine how emotional cues may influence behavior that interferes with this processing, as is frequently seen in children and adults with ASD. Similarly, Ashwin, Wheelwright, and Baron-Cohen (2006) studied the amygdala in adults with HFA and AS using fMRI when viewing fearful (high and low fear) and neutral faces. Findings indicated that the control sample showed more activation in the left amygdala and left orbitofrontal regions, compared to the HFA/AS group when viewing the fearful faces. In contrast, the HFA/AS group showed more activation in the anterior cingulate and the superior temporal cortex when viewing all of the faces.

Specific areas implicated in ASD using fMRI include the superior temporal gyrus (STG) (Allison, Puce, & McCarthy, 2000; Baron-Cohen et al., 1999) and the amygdala (Amaral, Price, Pitkanan, & Carmichael, 1992; Carmichael & Price, 1995). When a child with ASD is asked to view faces, functional imaging has found less activation in the right fusiform face gyrus (FG) (Critchley et al., 2000; Dierks, Bolte, Hubl, Lanfermann, & Poustka, 2004; Pierce, Muller, Ambrose, Allen, & Courchesne, 2001; Schultz et al., 2001; Schultz, Romanski, & Tsatsanis, 2000). The fusiform face gyrus appears to be selectively engaged when the person views faces. Children with ASD appear to pay less attention to the face and may not activate this region in the same manner as typically developing children (Schultz et al., 2003).

Differences in activation have not been solely found for viewing of faces. Just et al. (2004) found more cortical activation in children with HFA when processing verbal material compared to a control group. This finding may indicate that more brain resources are needed to process verbal information in children with ASD. This inefficiency may slow down their processing and take resources away from understanding the intent or speaker's prosody or interpreting of facial expressions. Kana, Keller, Cherkassky, Minshew, and Just (2006) found that children with HFA show poorly synchronized neural connectivity when asked to process material using their imagination. Moreover, the children with ASD were also found to use parietal and occipital regions associated with imagery for tasks that had low imagery as well as high imagery requirements. Controls only utilized these regions for the high imagery tasks.

A finding of difference in activation when participants with ASD view faces is important for our understanding of ASD. Animal studies have found that the temporal cortex responds to the perceptual aspects of social stimuli (Hasselmo, Rolls, & Baylis, 1989; Perrett & Mistlin, 1990). Human studies have also found a relationship between the perception of eyes and mouths in the superior temporal cortex (Adolphs, 2001; Haxby, Hoffman, & Gobbini, 2000). The superior temporal lobe may be involved in perceiving social stimuli with the connections to the amygdala and frontal lobes for interpretating these stimuli. Findings from participants with ASD have repeatedly shown that these areas are important to process facial expressions.

There have been few studies using DTI in children with ASD. Alexander et al. (2007) used DTI with ASD children and found reduced volumes in the corpus callosum and reduced fractional anisotropy (FA) of the genu, splenium, and total corpus callosum in children with ASD. Medication status and the presence of comorbid diagnoses were not found to have an effect on the DTI measures. Similarly, Boger-Megiddo et al. (2006) scanned young children with ASD and found that the corpus callosum area was disproportionately small compared to total brain volume for these children, compared to typically developing children. Children with a more severe form of ASD showed the smallest corpus callosal area. Future research needs to utilize quantitative imaging to more fully capture the relation between the corpus callosum connectivity and ASD. Taken together these findings suggest that children with ASD may be inefficient in their use of neural networks and that their networks show poor connectivity compared to same-aged peers.

Neuroradiological Techniques

Although techniques involving neuroradiology are not used by neuropsychologists and are of necessity research-based, it is important for neuropsychologists to be familiar with the burgeoning evidence these techniques provide. These techniques generally use radioactive isotopes and require very expensive equipment, and are seldom used with children given that radioactivity is administered. However, results from studies using these measures can provide information on the brain processes at the metabolic level.

PET and SPECT Scans

Positron emission tomography (PET) imaging can provide a direct measure of cerebral glucose metabolism. Zametkin et al. (1990) studied adults with ADD and hyperactivity (ADD/H) through the use of PET with 5–6 mm resolution. A radioactive tracer injected into the subjects was partially metabolized by the neurons and emitted radiation images through the PET scanner. These 25 ADD/H adults had onset of ADD/H in childhood and were also parents of ADD/H children. Subjects with conduct disorder or those using stimulant medication in childhood were eliminated from the sample. Cerebral glucose metabolism (CGM) was measured in 60 regions and the ADD/H group was found to have a CGM approximately 8 percent lower than the controls, with 50 percent of the regions showing significantly lower metabolism than the controls ($p < 0.05$). The regions with significant hypometabolism were in the cingulate, right caudate, right hippocampal, and right thalamic regions. In addition, reduced metabolism was found in the left parietal, temporal, and rolandic structures for the ADHD subjects. Statistical difficulties are present in this study in that 60 t-tests were used for analysis, introducing the possibility of inflated significant results due to experiment-wise error. Zametkin has written additional information about his study and, when his results were studied using the Bonferonni method of correction, the areas that continued to be significant were in the superior prefrontal and premotor regions (Zametkin & Cohen, 1991).

In contrast to PET scans, single photon emission tomography (SPECT) is a direct measure of regional cerebral blood flow (rCBF) with neuronal glucose metabolism inferred from the rCBF. Thus SPECT is a vascular measure, whereas PET is a neuronal measure. Results from PET and SPECT studies may not be directly comparable because of this difference in acquisition. Lou, Hendriksen, and Bruhn (1984) utilized SPECT in 13 children with dysphasia and ADHD. Only two of these children had pure ADHD. The remaining 11 had variations of dysphasia, mental retardation, and visual-spatial delays, although two did not have a diagnosis of ADHD. All children were attending a school for children with learning disorders. The contrast group was selected from the siblings of these children. Given that Lou et al. (1984) did not provide information about the functioning of these children and of the finding of substantial learning and attentional problems in siblings of ADHD children, it may be that the contrast group was not a true control group. Despite these methodological problems, the findings from this study are intriguing. All children with ADHD ($n = 11$) were found to have less blood perfusion in the white matter of the middle frontal regions, including the region of the genu of the corpus callosum.

Hypoperfusion was also found in the caudate region. The caudate region was inferred from the scan, as the caudate nucleus is smaller than the 17 mm resolution of the scanner. Therefore, the hypoperfusion may also have involved the lateral wall of the anterior horn of the lateral ventricle as well as the caudate, in addition to other areas of the basal ganglia. When methylphenidate was administered to the ADHD group, increased flow was found in the central region of the brain most likely encompassing the basal ganglia region. Theoretically these findings make sense. Frontal regions have feedback loops into the caudate. However, the primary output for the caudate is the thalamus, and it is not clear why the thalamus was not found to be hypoperfused also. The thalamic region was found to have lower perfusion in only three of the children; two with mental retardation and one without ADHD.

Lou, Henriksen, Bruhn, Borner, and Nielson (1989) expanded their study to include 19 additional subjects, six of whom were identified as "pure ADHD." The remaining 13 had ADHD as their primary diagnosis, along with other neurological deficits. Of these 13, three had mild mental retardation, nine had dysphasia, and six had visuospatial problems. The control group was the same as in the initial study. In this follow-up study, the mesial frontal region did not show significant hypoperfusion as was found in the 1984 study. Instead, hypoperfusion in the right striatal area encompassing the anterior

corpus callosum, internal capsule, and part of the thalamus in addition to the caudate was found in the children with ADHD. Hyperperfusion was found in the occipital region for the group with ADHD and in the left anterior parietal and temporal regions. Methylphenidate normalized perfusion in the left striatal area but not the right, as well as in the association regions in the posterior region of the brain.

In a 1991 letter to the *New England Journal of Medicine*, Lou stated that statistical analysis was not performed on the SPECT scans in the initial 1984 study. Scans were analyzed through "visual analysis," and when the prefrontal region measures were statistically analyzed with corrections for multiple analyses performed, the regional difference was not statistically different. Therefore, Lou et al.'s (1989) statistically significant finding of hypoperfusion in the striatal region and hyperperfusion in the posterior regions may implicate these regions in ADHD. With statistical correction Zametkin et al. (1990) reported that the superior prefrontal and premotor areas continued to show significant differences. Further study with controlled statistical procedures, as well as subjects without comorbid diagnoses, would clarify knowledge in this area, and it is hoped that these researchers will pursue this end.

Conclusions

In summary, MRI imaging of the brains of ADHD children and adults has shown differences in the frontal regions of the brain as well as in the corpus callosum. Finding these differences in the caudate nucleus is particularly interesting and important, as a structural anomaly in the caudate region in other disorders has been found to be important for the ability to inhibit behavior (Pennington, 1991). Studies have not addressed issues of comorbidity of disorders nor of adult-child similarities in these structures when both present with ADHD. Most important, the relationship between structural differences and behavioral measures needs to be investigated. The question of behavioral measures predicting structural differences in ADHD remains largely unexplored.

The areas found to differ on MRI may also show differences in metabolism and blood flow as measured by the SPECT and PET studies of Lou and Zametkin. Methodological problems in these metabolism and blood flow studies make their results equivocal and further investigation appears to be warranted. The development of these techniques is promising not only for clinical reasons, but also for furthering our knowledge of brain function and links to behavior. fMRI, spectroscopy, and PET scans evaluate the structure and function. It is likely that the next decade will add exponentially to our understanding of various disorders and, we hope, lead to the development of appropriate interventions.

References

Abell, F., Krams, M., Ashburner, J., Passingham, R., Friston, K., Frackowiak, R., et al. (1999). The neuroanatomy of autism: A voxel-based whole brain analysis of structural scans. *Cognitive Neuroscience, 10*, 1647–1651.

Adolphs, R. (2001). The neurobiology of social cognition. *Current Opinion in Neurobiology Cognitive Neuroscience., 11*, 231–239.

Aldridge, M. A., Braga, E. S., Walton, G. E., & Bower, T. G. R. (1999). The intermodal representation of speech in newborns. *Developmental Science, 2*, 42–46.

Alexander, A. L., Lee, J. E., Lazar, M., Boudos, R., Dubray, M. B., Oakes, T. R., et al. (2007). Diffusion tensor imaging of the corpus callosum in autism. *NeuroImage, 34*, 61–73.

Allison, T., Puce, A., & McCarthy, G. (2000). Social perception from visual cues: Role of the STS region. *Trends in Cognitive Sciences, 4*, 1364–1366.

Amaral, D. G., Price, J. L., Pitkanan, A., & Carmichael, S. T. (1992). Anatomical organization of the primate amygdaloid complex. In J. Aggleton (Ed.), *The amygdala: Neurobiological aspects of emotion, memory and mental dysfunction*. New York: Wiley.

Ashtari, M., Kumra, S., Bhaskar, S. L., Clarke, T., Thaden, E., Cervellione, K. L., et al. (2005). Attention-deficit/hyperactivity disorder: A preliminary diffusion tensor imaging study. *Biological Psychiatry, 57*, 448–455.

Ashwin, C., Wheelwright, S., & Baron-Cohen, S. (2006). Attention bias to faces in Asperger Syndrome: A pictorial emotion Stroop study. *Psychological medicine, 36(6)*, 835–843.

Aylward, E. H., Minshew, N. J., Field, K., Sparks, B. F., & Singh, N. (2002). Effects of age on brain volume and head circumference in autism. *Neurology, 59*, 175–183.

Baron-Cohen, S., Ring, H. A., Wheelwright, S., Bullmore, E. T., Brammer, M. J., Simmons, A., et al. (1999). Social intelligence in the normal and autistic brain: An fMRI study. *European Journal Neuroscience, 11*, 1891–1898.

Barry, R. J., Johnstone, B., & Clark, C. A. (2003). A review of electrophysiology in attention-deficit/hyeractivity disorder: II. Event-related potentials. *Clinical Neurophysiology, 114*, 184–198.

Bechara, A., Damasio, H., & Damasio, A. R. (2003). The role of the amygdala in decision making. *Annals of the New York Academy of Sciences, 985*, 356–369.

Berninger, V. W., Abbott, R. D., Abbott, S. P., Graham, S., & Richards, T. (2002). Writing and reading: connections between language by hand and language by eye. *Journal of Learning Disabilities, 35*, 39–56.

Bishop, D. V. M. (2007). Using mismatch negativity to study central auditory processing in developmental language and literacy impairments: Where are we, and where should we be going? *Psychological Bulletin, 133*, 651–672.

Black, L. S., deRegnier, R. A., Long, J., Georgieff, M. K., & Nelson, C. A. (2004). Electrographic imaging of recognition memory in 34–38 week gestation intrauterine growth restricted newborns. *Experimental Neurology, 190*, S72–S83.

Boger-Megiddo, I. B., Shaw, D. W., Friedman, S. D., Sparks, B. F., Artru, A. A., Giedd, J. N., et al. (2006). Corpus callosum morphometrics in young children with autism spectrum disorder. *Journal of Autism and Developmental Disorders, 36*, 733–739.

Bolter, J. R. (1986). Epilepsy in children: Neuropsychological effects. In J.E. Obzrut & G.W. Hynd (Eds.), *Child neuropsychology: Clinical practice* (pp. 59–81). New York: Academic Press.

Broyd, S. J., Johnstone, S. J., Barry, R. J., Clarke, A. R., McCarthy, R., Selikowitz, M., et al. (2005). The effect of methylphenidate on response inhibition and the event-related potential of children with Attention Deficit/Hyperactivity Disorder. *International Journal of Psychophysiology, 58*, 47–58.

Burgio-Murphy, A., Klorman, R., Shaywitz, S. E., Fletcher, J. M., Marchione, K. E., Holahan, J. M., et al. (2007). Error-related event-related potentials in children with attention-deficit hyperactivity disorder, oppositional defiant disorder, reading disorder, and math disorder. *Biological Psychology, 75*, 75–86.

Canli, T., Sivers, H., Whitfield, S. L., Gotlib, I. H., & Gabrieli, J. D. (2002). Amygdala response to happy faces as a function of extraversion. *Science, 296(5576)*, 2191.

Caplan, L. J., Schmahmann, J. D., & Kase, C. S. (1990). Caudate infarcts. *Archives of Neurology, 47*, 133–143.

Carmichael, S. T., & Price, J. L. (1995). Limbic connections of the orbital and medial prefrontal cortex in macaque monkeys. *The Journal of Comparative Neurology, 363*, 615–641.

Castellanos, F. X., Giedd, J. N., Eckburg, W. L., Marsh, A. C., Kaysen, D., Hamburger, S. D., et al. (1994). Quantitative morphology of the caudate nucleus in attention deficit hyperactivity disorder. *American Journal of Psychiatry, 151*, 1791–1796.

Chiappa, K. H. (1997). *Evoked potentials in clinical medicine*. Philadelphia, PA: Lippincott-Raven.

Chung, M. K., Dalton, K. M., Alexander, A. L., & Davidson, R. J. (2004). Less white matter concentration in autism: 2D voxel-based morphometry. *NeuroImage, 23*, 242–251.

Cohen, D. J. (1986). *Pediatric magnetic resonance imaging.* Philadelphia, PA: W.B. Saunders.

Courchesne, E., Carper, R., & Akshoomoff, N. (2003). Evidence of brain overgrowth in the first year of life in autism. *The Journal of the American Medical Association, 290,* 337–344.

Critchley, H. D., Daly, E. M., Bullmore, E. T., Williams, S. C. R., Van Amelsvoort, T., Robertson, D. M., et al. (2000). The functional neuroanatomy of social behavior: Changes in cerebral blood flow when people with autistic disorder process facial expressions. *Brain, 123,* 2203–2212.

Dierks, T., Bolte, S., Hubl, D., Lanfermann, H., & Poustka, F. (2004). Alterations of face processing strategies in autism: A fMRI study. *NeuroImage, 13,* 1016–1053.

Duara, B., Kushch, A., Gross-Glenn, K., Barker, W. W., Jallad, B., Pascal, S., et al. (1991). Neuroanatomic differences between dyslexic and normal readers on magnetic resonance imaging scans. *Archives of Neurology, 48,* 410–416.

Durston, S. (2003). Differential patterns of striatal activation in young children with and without ADHD. *Biological Psychiatry, 53,* 871.

Facotti, A., Lorusso, M. L., Paganoni, P., Cattaneo, C., Galli, R., & Mascetti, G. G. (2003). The time course of attentional focusing in dyslexic and normally reading children. *Brain and Cognition, 53,* 181–184.

Filipek, P. A., & Blickman, J. G. (1992). Neurodiagnostic laboratory procedures: Neuroimaging techniques. In R. B. David (Ed.), *Pediatric neurology for the clinician.* Norwalk, CT: Appleton-Lang.

Filipek, P. A., Semrud-Clikeman, M., Steingard, R. J., Renshaw, P. F., Kennedy, D. N., & Biederman, J. (1997). Volumetric MRI analysis comparing subjects having attention-deficit hyperactivity disorder with normal controls. *Neurology, 48,* 589–601.

Fine, J. G., Semrud-Clikeman, M., Keith, T. Z., Stapleton, L., & Hynd, G. (2006). Reading and the corpus callosum: An MRI family study of volume and area. *Neuropsychology, 21,* 235–241.

Frederici, A. D. (2006). The neural basis of language development and its impairment. *Neuron, 52,* 941–952.

Galaburda, A. M. (2005). Neurology of learning disabilities: What will the future bring? The answer comes from the successes of the recent past. *Learning Disabilities Quarterly, 28,* 107–109.

Garavan, H., Ross, T. J., Murphy, K., Roche, R. A., & Stein, E. A. (2002). Dissociable executive functions in the dynamic control of behavior: Inhibition, error detection, and correction. *NeuroImage, 17,* 1820–1829.

Gazzaniga, M. S., Ivry, R. B., & Mangun, G. R. (2002). *Cognitive neuroscience: The biology of the mind* (2nd ed.). New York: W.W. Norton & Company.

Geschwind, N., & Galaburda, A. M. (1985). Cerebral lateralization: Biological mechanisms, associations, and pathology: I. A hypothesis and a program for research. *Archives of Neurology, 42,* 521–552.

Giedd, J. N. (2004). Structural magnetic resonance imaging of the adolescent brain. *Annals of the New York Academy of Sciences, 1021,* 1308–1309.

Giedd, J. N., Castellanos, F. X., Casey, B. J., Kozuch, P., King, A. C., Hamburger, S. D., et al. (1994). Quantitative morphology of the corpus callosum in attention deficit hyperactivity disorder. *American Journal of Psychiatry, 151,* 665–669.

Guttorm, T. K., Leppanen, P. H., Tolvanen, A., & Lyytinen, H. (2003). Event-related potentials in newborns with and without familial risk for dyslexia: Principal component analysis reveals differences between the groups. *Journal of Neural Transmission, 110,* 1059–1074.

Hardan, A. Y., Minshew, N. J., & Keshavan, M. S. (2000). Corpus callosum size in autism. *Neurology, 55,* 1033–1036.

Hare, T. A., Tottenham, N., Davidson, M. C., Glover, G. H., & Casey, B. J. (2005). Contributions of amygdala and striatal activity in emotion regulation. *Biological Psychiatry, 57,* 624–632.

Harris, R. (1983). Clinical neurophysiology in paediatric neurology. In E.M. Brett (Ed.), Paediatric neurology (pp. 582–600). Edinburgh, Scotland: Churchill Livingston.

Harter, M. R., & Anllo-Vento, L. (1988). Separate brain potential characteristics in children with reading disability and attention deficit disorder: Color and letter relevance effects. *Brain and Cognition, 7,* 115–140.

Hasselmo, M. E., Rolls, E. T., & Baylis, G. C. (1989). The role of expression and identity in the face-selective responses of neurons in the temporal visual cortex of the monkey. *Behavioural Brain Research, 32,* 203–218.

Haxby, J. V., Hoffman, E. A., & Gobbini, M. I. (2000). The distributed human neural system for face perception. *Trends in Cognitive Sciences, 4,* 223–233.

Holcomb, P. J., Ackerman, P. T., & Dykman, R. A. (1985). Cognitive event-related brain potentials in children with attention and reading deficits. *Psychophysiology, 22,* 656–667.

Howard, M. F., & Reggia, J. A. (2007). A theory of the visual system biology underlying development of spatial frequency lateralization. *Brain and Cognition, 64,* 111–123.

Hynd, G. W., Hall, J., Novey, E. S. (1995). Dyslexia and corpus callosum morphology. *Archives of Neurology, 52,* 32–38.

Hynd, G. W., Hern, K. L., Novey, E. S., Eliopulos, D., Marshall, R., Gonzalez, J. J., et al. (1993). Attention deficit-hyperactivity disorder and asymmetry of the caudate nucleus. *Journal of Child Neurology, 8,* 339–340.

Hynd, G. W., Marshall, R. M., & Semrud-Clikeman, M. (1991). Developmental dyslexia, neurolinguistic theory and deviations in brain morphology. *Reading and Writing, 3,* 345–362.

Hynd, G. W., & Semrud-Clikeman, M. (1989). Dyslexia and brain morphology. *Psychological Bulletin, 106,* 447–482.

Hynd, G. W., Semrud-Clikeman, M., Lorys, A. R., Novey, E. S., & Eliopulos, D. (1990). Brain morphology in developmental dyslexia and attention deficit disorder/hyperactivity. *Archives of Neurology, 47,* 919–926.

Hynd, G. W., & Willis, W. G. (1988). *Pediatric neuropsychology.* Orlando, FL: Grune & Stratton.

Jabbari, B., Maitland, C. G., Morris, L. M., Morales, J., & Gunderson, C. H. (1985). The value of visual evoked potential as a screening test in neurofibromatosis. *Archives of Neurology, 42*, 1072–1074.

Jasper, H. H. (1958). The ten twenty system of the international federation. *Electroencephalography and Clinical Neurophysiology, 10*, 371–375.

Jernigan, T. L., Hesselink, J. R., Sowell, E., & Tallal, P. (1991). Cerebral structure on magnetic resonance imaging in language- and learning-impaired children. *Archives of Neurology, 48*, 539–545.

Johnstone, S. J., Barry, R. J., Anderson, J. W., & Coyle, S. F. (1996). Age-related changes in child and adolescent event-related potential component morphology, amplitude, and latency to standard and target stimuli in an auditory oddball task. *International Journal of Psychophysiology, 24*, 223–238.

Johnstone, S. J., Barry, R. J., & Clarke, A. R. (2007). Behavioural and ERP indices of response inhibition during a stop-signal task in children with two subtypes of attention-deficit hyperactivity. *International Journal of Psychophysiology, 66*, 37–47.

Just, M. A., Cherkassky, V. L., Keller, T. A., & Minshew, N. J. (2004). Cortical activation and synchronization during sentence comprehension in high-functioning autism: evidence of underconnectivity. *Brain, 127*, 1811–1821.

Kana, R. K., Keller, T. A., Cherkassky, V. L., Minshew, N. J., & Just, M. A. (2006). Sentence comprehension in autism: Thinking in pictures with decreased functional connectivity. *Brain, 129*, 2484–2493.

Kerns, J. G., Cohen, J. D., MacDonald, A. W., Cho, R. Y., Stenger, V. A., & Carter, C. S. (2004). Anterior cingulate conflict monitoring and adjustments in control. *Science, 303*, 1023–1026.

Killgore, W. D., & Yurgelun-Todd, D. A. (2005). Social anxiety predicts amygdala activation in adolescents viewing fearful faces. *Neuroreport, 16*, 1671–1675.

Klorman, R., Thatcher, J. E., Shaywitz, S. E., Fletcher, J. M., Marchione, K. E., Holahan, J. M., et al. (2002). Effects of event probability and sequence on children with Attention-Deficit/Hyperactivity, reading, and math disorder. *Biological Psychiatry, 52*, 795–804.

Klorman, R., Brumaghim, J. T., Fitzpatrick, P. A., Borgstedt, A. D. (1994). Clinical and cognitive effects of methylphenidate on children with attention deficit disorder as a function of aggression/oppositionality and age. *Journal of Abnormal Psychology, 103*, 206–221.

Koshino, H., Carpenter, P. A., Minshew, N. J., Cherkassky, V. L., Keller, T. A., & Just, M. A. (2005). Functional connectivity in an fMRI working memory task in high-functioning autism. *NeuroImage, 24*, 810–821.

Larsen, J. P., Hoien, T., Lundberg, I., & Odegaard, H. (1990). MRI evaluation of the size and symmetry of the planum temporale in adolescents with developmental dyslexia. *Brain and Language, 39*, 289–301.

Liotti, M., Pliszka, S. R., Perez, R., Glahn, D. C., & Semrud-Clikeman, M. (2001). Electrophysiological correlates of response inhibition in children and adolescents with ADHD: Influence of gender, age, and previous treatment history. *Psychophysiology, 44*, 936–948.

Liotti, M., Pliszka, S. R., Semrud-Clikeman, M., Higgins, K., & Perez, I., R. (in press). Evidence for specificity of ERP abnormalities during response inhibition in ADHD *Brain and Cognition.*

Lou, H. C., Hendriksen, L., & Bruhn, P. (1984). Focal cerebral hypoperfusion in children with dysphasia and/or attention deficit disorder. *Archives of Neurology, 41*, 825–829.

Lou, H. C., Henriksen, L., Bruhn, P., Borner, H., & Nielson, J. B. (1989). Striatal dysfunction in attention deficit and hyperkinetic disorder. *Archives of Neurology, 46*, 48–52.

Maurer, U., Bucher, K., Brem, S., & Brandeis, D. (2003). Development of the automatic mismatch response: From frontal positivity in kindergarten children to the mismatch negativity. *Clinical Neurophysiology, 114*, 808–817.

McBurnett, K., Pfiffner, L. J., & Frick, P. J. (2001). Symptom properties as a function of ADHD type. An argument for continued study of sluggish cognitive tempo. *Journal of Abnormal Child Psychology, 29*, 207–213.

McCrory, E., Mechelli, A., Frith, U., & Price, C. J. (2005). More than words: A common neural basis for reading and naming deficits in developmental dyslexia? *Brain, 128*, 261–267.

Menkes, J. H., & Sarnat, H. B. (2000). *Child neurology.* Philadelphia, PA: Lippincott, Williams, & Wilkins.

Millich, R., Ballentine, A. C., & Lynam, D. R. (2001). ADHD-combined type and ADHD-predominately inattentive type are distinct and unrelated disorders. *Clinical Psychology, Science, & Practice, 8*, 463–488.

Molfese, D. L., & Molfese, V. J. (1994). Short-term and long-term developmental outcomes. In G. Dawson & K.W. Fischer (Eds.), *Human behavior and the developing brain* (pp. 493–517). New York: Guilford Press.

Monk, C. S., McClure, E. B., Nelson, E. E., Zarahn, E., Bilder, R. M., & Leivenluft, E. (2003). Adolescent immaturity in attention-related brain engagement to emotional facial expressions. *NeuroImage, 20*, 420–428.

Naatanen, R. (1990). The role of attention in auditory information processing as revealed by event-related potentials and other brain measures of cognitive function. *Behavior and Brain Sciences, 13*, 112–130.

Novitski, N., Huotilainen, M., Tervaniemi, M., Naatanen, R., & Fellman, V. (2006). Neonatal frequency discrimination in 250–4000 Hz range: Electrophysiological evidence. *Clinical Neurophysiology, 118*, 412–419.

Ohnishi, T., Matsuda, H., Hashimoto, T., Kunihiro, T., Nishikawa, M., Uema, T., et al. (2000). Abnormal regional cerebral blood flow in childhood autism. *Brain, 123*, 1838–1844.

Olson, R. K. (1999). Genes, environment, and reading disabilities. In R. Sternberg & L. Spear-Swerling (Eds.), *Perspectives on learning disabilities* (pp. 3–22). Oxford: Westview Press.

Pennington, B. F. (1991). *Diagnosing learning disorders.* New York: Guilford Press.

Perrett, D. I., & Mistlin, A. J. (1990). Perception of facial characteristics by monkeys. In W. C. Stebbins & M. A. Berkley (Eds.), *Comparative perception* (pp. 187–215). Oxford: John Wiley & Sons.

Pessoa, L., Kastner, S., & Ungerleider, L. G. (2002). Attentional control of the processing of neutral and emotional stimuli. *Cognitive Brain Research, 15,* 31–45.

Picton, T. W., & Taylor, M. J. (2007). Electrophysiological evaluation of human brain development. *Developmental Neuropsychology, 3,* 249–278.

Pierce, K., Muller, R. A., Ambrose, J., Allen, G., & Courchesne, E. (2001). Face processing occurs outside the fusiform 'face area' in autism: Evidence from functional MRI. *Brain, 124,* 2059–2073.

Piven, J., Arndt, S., Bailey, J., & Andreasen, N. (1996). Regional brain enlargement in autism: A magnetic resonance imaging study. *Journal of the American Academy of Child & Adolescent Psychiatry, 35,* 530–536.

Pliszka, S. R., Liotti, M., & Woldroff, M. G. (2000). Inhibitory control in children with attention-deficit/hyperactivity disorder: Event-related potentials identify the processing component and timing of an impaired right-frontal response-inhibition mechanism. *Biological Psychiatry, 48,* 238–246.

Posner, M. I., & Raichle, M. E. (1994). *Images of mind.* New York: Scientific American Library.

Posner, M. I., & Rothbart, M. K. (2007). Research on attention networks as a model for the integration of psychological science. *Annual Review of Psychology, 58,* 1–23.

Pugh, K. R., Mencl, W. E., Jenner, A. R., Katz, L., Frost, S. J., Lee, J. R., et al. (2001). Neurobiological studies of reading and reading disability. *Journal of Communication Disorders, 34,* 479–492.

Regtvoort, A. G. F. M., van Leeuwen, T. H., Stoel, R. D., & van der Leij, A. (2006). Efficiency of visual information processing in children at-risk for dyslexia: Habituation of single-trial ERPs. *Brain and Language, 98,* 319–331.

Rodriguez, P. D., & Baylis, G. C. (2007). Activation of brain attention systems in individuals with symptoms of ADHD. *Behavioural Neurology, 18,* 115–130.

Rubia, K., Overmeyer, S., Taylor, E., Brammer, M. J., Williams, S. C. R., Simmons, A., et al. (1999). Hypofrontality in attention deficit hyperactivity disorder during higher-order motor control: A study with functional MRI. *American Journal of Psychiatry, 156,* 891–896.

Rubia, K., Smith, A. B., Brammer, M. J., & Taylor, E. (2003). Right inferior prefrontal cortex mediates response inhibition while mesial prefrontal cortex is responsible for error detection. *NeuroImage, 20,* 351–358.

Rubia, K., Smith, A. B., Brammer, M. J., Toone, B., & Taylor, E. (2005). Abnormal brain activation during inhibition and error detection in medication-naïve adolescents with ADHD. *American Journal of Psychiatry, 162,* 1067–1075.

Santos, A., Joly-Pottuz, B., Moreno, S., Habib, M., & Besson, M. (2007). Behavioural and event-related potentials evidence for pitch discrimination deficits in dyslexic children: Improvement after intensive phonic intervention. *Neuropsychologia, 45,* 1080–1090.

Schultz, R. T., Gauthier, I., Klin, A., Fulbright, R. K., Anderson, A. W., Volkmar, F., et al. (2000). Abnormal ventral temporal cortical activity during face discrimination among individuals with autism and Asperger Syndrome. *Archives of General Psychiatry, 57,* 331–340.

Schultz, R. T., Grelotti, D. J., Klin, A., Kleinman, J., Van der Gaag, C., Marois, R., et al. (2003). The role of the fusiform face area in social cognition: Implications for the pathobiology of autism. *Philosophical Transactions of The Royal Society of London, 358,* 415–427.

Schultz, R. T., Grelotti, D. J., Klin, A., Levitan, E., Cantey, T., Skudlarski, P., et al. (2001). *An fMRI study of face recognition, facial expression detection, and social judgment in autism spectrum conditions.* Paper presented at the International Meeting for Autism Research.

Schultz, R. T., Romanski, L. M., & Tsatsanis, K. D. (2000). Neurofunctional models of autistic disorder and Asperger syndrome: Clues from neuroimaging. In A. Klin, F. R. Volkmar, & S. S. Sparrow (Eds.), *Asperger syndrome.* New York: The Guilford Press.

Schulz, K. P., Fan, J., Tang, C. Y., Newcorn, J. H., Buchsbaum, M. S., Cheung, A. M., et al. (2004). Response inhibition in adolescents diagnosed with attention deficit hyperactivity disorder during childhood: An event-related fMRI study. *American Journal of Psychiatry, 161,* 1650–1657.

Sears, L. L., Vest, C., Mohamed, S., Bailey, J., Ranson, B. J., & Piven, J. (1999). An MRI study of the basal ganglia in autism. *Progress in neuro-psychopharmacology & biological psychiatry, 23,* 613–624.

Semrud-Clikeman, M. (2006). Neuropsychological aspects for evaluating LD. *Journal of Learning Disabilities, 38,* 563–568.

Semrud-Clikeman, M., Filipek, P. A., Biederman, J., Steingard, R. J., Kennedy, D. N., Renshaw, P. F., et al. (1994). Attention-deficit hyperactivity disorder: Magnetic resonance imaging morphometric analysis of the corpus callosum. *Journal of the American Academy of Child & Adolescent Psychiatry, 33,* 875–881.

Semrud-Clikeman, M., Hooper, S. R., Hynd, G. W., Hern, K., Presley, R., & Watson T. (1996). Prediction of group membership in developmental dyslexia, attention deficit hyperactivity disorder, and normal controls using brain morphometric analysis of magnetic resonance imaging. *Archives of Clinical Neuropsychology, 11,* 521–528.

Semrud-Clikeman, M., Hynd, G., Novey, E. S., & Eliopulos, D. (1991). Dyslexia and brain morphology: Relationships between neuroanatomical variation and neurolinguistic tasks. *Learning and Individual Differences, 3,* 225–242.

Semrud-Clikeman, M., Pliszka, S. R., Lancaster, J., & Liotti, M. (2006). Volumetric MRI differences in treatment-naïve vs chronically treated children with ADHD. *Neurology, 67.*

Shaywitz, B. A., Shaywitz, S. E., Pugh, K., Fulbright, R. K., & Skudlarski, P. (2002). Disruption of posterior brain systems for reading in children with developmental dyslexia. *Biological Psychiatry, 52,* 101–110.

Shaywitz, S. E. (2003). *Overcoming dyslexia: A new and complete science-based program for reading problems at any level.* New York: Alfred A. Knopf.

Shaywitz, S. E., Mody, M., & Shaywitz, B. A. (2006). Neural mechanisms in dyslexia. *Current Directions in Psychological Science, 15,* 278–281.

Shaywitz, S. E., Shaywitz, B. A., Fletcher, J. M., & Escobar, M. D. (1990). Prevalence of reading disability in boys and girls: Results of the Conneticut Longitudinal Study. *The Journal of the American Medical Association, 264,* 998–1003.

Shaywitz, S. E., Shaywitz, B. A., Fulbright, R. K., Skudlarski, P., Mencl, W. E., Constable, R. T., et al. (2003). Neural systems for compensation and persistence:

Young adult outcome of childhood reading disability. *Biological Psychiatry, 54*, 25–33.

Shaywitz, Silk, T. J., Rinehart, N., Bradshaw, J. L., Tonge, B., Egan, G., O'Boyle, M. W., et al. (2006). Visuospatial processing and the function of prefrontal-parietal networks in autism spectrum disorders: a functional MRI study. *American Journal of Psychiatry, 163*, 1440–1443.

Simpson, J. R., Öngür, D., Akbudak, E., Conturo, T. E., & Ollinger, J. M. (2000). The emotional modulation of cognitive processing: An fMRI study. *Journal of Cognitive Neuroscience, 12*, 157–170.

Smith, J. L., Johnstone, S. J., & Barry, R. J. (2004). Inhibitory processing during the Go/NoGo task: an ERP analysis of children with attention-deficit/hyperactivity disorder. *Clinical Neurophysiology, 115*, 1320–1331.

Somerville, L. H., Kim, H., Johnstone, T., Alexander, A. L., & Whalen, P. J. (2004). Human amygdala responses during presentation of happy and neutral faces: Correlations with state anxiety. *Biological Psychiatry, 55*, 897–903.

Taroyan, N. A., Nicolson, R. I., & Fawcett, A. J. (2006). Behavioural and neurophysiological correlates of dyslexia in the continuous performance task. *Clinical Neurophysiology, 118*, 845–855.

Vaidya, C. J., Austin, G., Kirkorian, G., Ridlehuber, H. W., Desmond, J. E., Glover, G. H., et al. (1998). Selective effects of methylphenidate in attention deficit hyperactivity disorder: A functional magnetic resonance study. *Neurobiology, 95*, 14494–14499.

van Mourik, R., Oosterlaan, J., Heslenfeld, D. J., Konig, C. E., & Sergeant, J. A. (2007). When distraction is not distracting: A behavioral and ERP study on distraction in ADHD. *Clinical Neurophysiology, 118*, 1855–1865.

Vidal, C. N., Nicolson, R., DeVito, T. J., Hayashi, K. M., Geaga, J. A., Drost, D. J., et al. (2006). Mapping corpus callosum deficits in autism: An index of aberrant cortical connectivity. *Biological Psychiatry, 60*, 218–225.

von Koss Torkildsen, J., Syversen, G., Simonsen, H. G., Moen, I., & Lindgren, M. (2007). Brain responses to lexical-semantic priming in children at-risk for dyslexia. *Brain and Language, 102*, 243–261.

Waldman, I. D., Lilienfeld, S. O., & Lahey, B. B. (1995). Toward construct validity in the childhood disruptive behavior disorders: Classification and diagnosis in DSM-IV and beyond. *Advances in Clinical Child Psychology, 17*, 323–363.

Wetzel, N., & Schroger, E. (2007). Cognitive control of involuntary attention and distraction in children and adolescents. *Brain Research, 1155*, 134–146.

Wetzel, N., Widmann, A., Berti, S., & Schroger, E. (2006). The development of involuntary and voluntary attention from childhood to adulthood: A combined behavioral and event-related potential study. *Clinical Neurophysiology, 117*, 2191–2203.

Winner, E., Brownell, H., Happe, F., Blum, A., & Pincus, D. (1998). Distinguishing lies from jokes: Theory of mind deficits and discourse interpretation in right hemisphere brain-damaged patients. *Brain Language, 62*, 89–106.

Yang, T. T., Menon, V., Eliez, S., Blasey, C., White, C. D., Reid, A. J., et al. (2002). Amygdalar activation associated with positive and negative facial expressions. *Neuroreport: For Rapid Communication of Neuroscience Research, 13*, 1737–1741.

Zametkin, A. J., & Cohen, R. M. (1991). Cerebral glucose metabolism in hyperactivity (letter to the editor). *New England Journal of Medicine, 324*, 1216–1217.

Zametkin, A. J., Nordahl, T. E., Gross, M., King, A. C., Semple, W. E., Rumsey, J., et al. (1990). Cerebral glucose metabolism in adults with hyperactivity of childhood onset. *New England Journal of Medicine, 323*, 1361–1366.

Part II
Clinical Assessment

Chapter 5
Integrating Neurological, Neuroradiological, and Psychological Examinations in Neuropsychological Assessment

This chapter provides guidelines to help psychologists determine when to refer a child or adolescent for neuropsychological assessment, neurological examination, or other neurodiagnostic testing (e.g., CT scan or MRI). Children and adolescents often need neurological, neuroradiological, and/ or neuropsychological assessments. Although not every child seen for cognitive, academic, psychiatric, or behavioral problems requires further assessment apart from traditional psychoeducational evaluations, some disorders do need further attention by specialists to investigate the child's neurological or neuropsychological status. Clinical and school psychologists should be apprised of conditions that typically require further attention. The nature of neurologic, neuroradiologic, and neuropsychological assessment will be discussed, along with guidelines for making referrals. Further, aspects of psychological, psychosocial, and academic functioning are discussed, as these areas may be seriously compromised by brain-related disorders of childhood. Integration of these various evaluation findings are discussed.

The Neurological Examination

Neurological examinations are conducted by neurologists generally specializing in childhood and adolescent neurology. Because it is sometimes difficult to differentiate normal developmental variations from abnormal neurodevelopment in the first few years of life, it is important to access child neurologists when there is a question about chronic and serious

neurodevelopmental delays. The neurologist will identify disease, injury, developmental, or genetic processes that interfere with CNS functioning. The neurological examination usually consists of the following: (1) an in-depth review of medical and developmental history; (2) an assessment of mental status; (3) an assessment of the functional capacity of the CNS, including the cranial nerves; (4) an evaluation of motor systems; (5) an assessment of sensory functions, and (6) an assessment of autonomic functions (Swaiman, Ashwal, & Ferriero, 2006). Each area is systematically evaluated through a series of activities designed to measure muscle tone, cranial nerves, and primitive and autonomic reflexes. Interpreting information from the neurological examination is complicated by the child's age and intellectual and functional capacity. A look inside the examination room with a neurologist and patient would show the physician initially conducting an in-depth developmental interview. Since the child is present during this procedure and the physician notes the child's participation, attention, and language. Moreover, the child's facial movements are noted with attention to head nodding, eye blinking, staring, tics, and movement disorders. In addition, the physician observes the child's behavior with regard to his or her impulsivity, dependence on the parent, and activity level. Additional observations of parent-child interaction are obtained. Swaiman et al. (2006) suggests that the physician consider the following questions: "Does the child respond positively to the parent's interaction? Does the child attempt to manipulate the parent? Is the response transient or persistent? Is the parent's attitude one of caring or hostility?"

M. Semrud-Clikeman, P.A. Teeter Ellison, *Child Neuropsychology*, DOI 10.1007/978-0-387-88963-4_5,
© Springer Science+Business Media, LLC 2009

After age four, a motor screening examination is conducted. The neurologist has the child stand in front of him or her and demonstrate the required motor acts. The child is asked to hop on one foot and then the other, to walk forward and backward, to walk on tiptoes, and to walk on heels with toes pointed up. Additionally, the child is asked to rise from a squatting position, and to stand with feet together, eyes closed and arms and hands outstretched from the body and parallel with the floor. These maneuvers are designed to check for balance, extraneous unnecessary movement, and the Romberg sign. The Romberg sign is indicative by the child's inability to stand still when his or her eyes are closed (Swaiman et al., 2006). The child then is asked to touch his or her nose with the finger, both with eyes closed and with eyes open. Based on this initial screening, the neurologist will follow up on any abnormalities in motor coordination. The next portion of the examination involves testing reflexes. Both deep tendon reflexes (also known as muscle stretch reflexes) and reflexes appropriate at various ages are assessed. For the deep tendon reflexes, the neurologist elicits the reflex with a rubber reflex hammer while the child is seated quietly. Hyper reflexes (contraction of muscles that generally are not involved in the reflex) are a sign of corticospinal dysfunction. Hypo reflexes are most often associated with motor unit abnormalities of the spinal cord (Swaiman, 1994) or of the cerebellum. Cerebellar functions are assessed by asking the child to first touch his or her nose and then the examiner's finger at various positions. The child is also asked to run his or her heel down the shin of the opposite leg. Inability to complete these tasks smoothly may indicate cerebellum dysfunction.

Cranial nerves are evaluated next. Congenital anomalies as well as traumatic injury can produce observable neurological signs. See Table 5.1 for a review of some common anomalies that might be identified when conducting an examination of the cranial nerves.

The sensory system is assessed next. The ability to sense vibrations, position of limb, and joint sense is evaluated. To evaluate the child's ability to localize tactile information, the neurologist touches various places both unilaterally and bilaterally with the child's eyes closed. The inability to localize touch is associated with parietal lobe dysfunction

(Swaiman et al., 2006). The child is also asked to recognize various objects which are placed in his or her hand (stereognosis) with eyes closed. Although these tasks are believed to provide information as to the integrity of the parietal lobes, attention to task can interfere with performance.

Muscle strength is also assessed. The child is asked to push against the examiner's hand with his or her hand or foot as hard as possible. He or she may also be requested to push his/her head against the neurologist's hand as hard as possible, or walk on his or her hands while the examiner holds the child's feet. Once the child's feet are placed on the floor, the child is asked to stand up. Inability to stand without aid is another measure of muscle strength. To evaluate gait, the child is asked to walk back and forth and to run. Running exacerbates problems with gait and can show additional signs of spasticity or jerking movements (Swaiman, 1994). This section was a brief overview of a typical neurological examination. The interested student may wish to observe a neurological examination in order to obtain a first-hand experience. You may wish to ask a parent if you can accompany him or her to such an examination.

When to Refer for a Neurological Evaluation

A neurological examination should be considered under the following conditions:

1. Sudden, unexplained, and prolonged nausea accompanied by high fever, headache, and lethargy that might suggest meningitis or encephalitis
2. Rapid blinking eye movements, visual aura (auditory and sensory auras are not uncommon), blank stares, or head or muscle jerks/spasms that might suggest seizure activity
3. Visual or olfactory hallucinations
4. Sudden motor clumsiness or cerebellar ataxia
5. Prolonged viral infections producing symptoms listed under item 1
6. Head trauma producing nausea, blurred vision, loss of consciousness, or dilated pupils
7. Cranial nerve involvement producing unilateral or bilateral motor weaknesses (e.g., droopy mouth, eyes, or facial muscles, or tongue protrusion)

Table 5.1 Common anomalies revealed during examination of the cranial nerves

Number	Name and function	Anomalies	Contributing factors
I	Olfactory (smell)	Asnomia-loss of smell	Severe head trauma
			Frontal lobe gliomas
			Olfactory groove meningiomas
			Temporal lobe epilepsy
II	Optic (vision)	Uncoordinated movement	Congenital blindness
		Asymmetric nystagmus	Gliomas or craniopharyngiomas
		Exophthalmos	Congenital disorders
		Papilloedema	Increased cranial pressure
		Macula discoloration	Tay-Sachs, metachromatic dystrophy, Batten's disease
		Retinal bleeding	Intracranial pressure, bleeding, or leukemia
III	Oculomotor (eye movement)	Pupil dilation	
		Eyes downward	
IV	Trochlear	Depression of eye movement	
VI	Abducens	Eye turns medially	
		Restricted lateral eye movement	
V	Trigeminal (masticatory movement)	Hyperactive jaw	Cerebral trauma
			Pseudobulbar palsy
		Hypoactive jaw	Bulbar palsy
VII	Facial (facial movement)	Symmetry, upper and lower face	Lesions
		Odd auditory perceptions	Lesions
		Impaired taste and salivation	Bell's palsy
VIII	Auditory (hearing)	Vestibular dysfunction	
		Vertigo, nystagmus, ataxic gait	
		Audition	Medication
			Neuromas or skull factures
		Tinnitus (ear ringing)	Otosclerosis or toxins (streptomycin or aspirin)
IX	Glossopharyngeal (tongue and pharynx)	Taste buds	
X	Vagus (heart, blood vessels, viscera, larynx, and pharynx)	Swallowing	
		Language expression	
XI	Spinal accessory (movement, strength of neck and shoulder muscles)	Paralysis of head/ neck muscles	Lesions
		Atrophy	
XII	Hypoglossal (tongue muscles)	Atrophy of tongue	Lesions
		Protrusion of tongue	
		Eating problems	
		Dysarthria	

Note: See Hynd and Willis (1988) for more details on cranial nerve damage.

8. Sudden, unexplained diminution of cognitive, language, speech, memory, or motor functions following normal development

A number of tumor processes, CNS leukemia, CNS infections (meningitis, encephalitis, and intracranial abscesses), neuromuscular diseases, and genetic disorders (e.g., neurofibromatosis, Sturge-Weber syndrome, and tuberous sclerosis) produce some of these symptoms (Hynd & Willis, 1988). These conditions typically require ongoing neurological examination and follow-up. Neurologic examination is usually part of the diagnostic and treatment protocol that follows when children display the symptoms described here. In some instances, neurologists will recommend further neuroradiological follow-up to ascertain the nature and range of CNS involvement. In other instances (head injury or suspected brain tumor or lesion), CAT scans and MRI studies may be warranted immediately. CT scans, MRI scans, and regional cerebral blood flow (rCBF) procedures were described in detail in Chapter 4.

Neuroradiological Evaluation

Despite their research potential, CT scans and MRI procedures are not necessarily part of the typical diagnostic process for identifying developmental disorders unless there are other accompanying neurologic signs (e.g., seizures, dysphasia). CT and MRI techniques are relatively expensive and for the most part are reserved for diagnosing and treating medical or neurological conditions affecting the CNS.

When to Refer for Neuroradiolgical Evaluation

A physician generally refers a child or adolescent for neuroradiological techniques under the following conditions:

1. Head trauma
2. CNS tumor processes
3. CNS disease processes involving white matter degeneration

4. Neurodevelopmental anomalies affecting the size or formation of brain structures, such as hydrocephaly or agenesis of the corpus callosum
5. Cerebrovascular diseases (e.g., sickle cell anemia)
6. Dyslexia or other neurodevelopmental disorders when there is a history of seizures, neurological signs, and/or significant language or speech delays

Positive signs on the neurological examination (see previous section) also may warrant further neuroradiologic evaluation. Children with neurodevelopmental disorders that affect brain size, tissue growth, cortical formations, and neural tube and fusion abnormalities usually require initial diagnostic and ongoing neuroradiological follow-up.

Finally, repeated neuroradiologic evaluations are routinely conducted on children with brain trauma to measure changes in neurologic status (Donders, 2007). Neuropsychological evaluations utilize measures and methods for determining the neurobehavioral status of children with various disorders. Guidelines for referral for neuropsychological evaluation will be explored next.

Neuropsychological Assessment

Neuropsychological assessment procedures are described in detail in Chapter 6. Neuropsychological tests are generally administered to investigate the brain-behavior relationship in children and adolescents and to determine whether cognitive, academic, and psychiatric disorders are related to abnormal brain function.

When to Refer for Neuropsychological Evaluation

Neuropsychological evaluations are generally recommended under the following conditions:

1. Conditions affecting the CNS that were previously described under neurological and neuroradiological referrals (e.g., head trauma, CNS diseases)

2. Chronic and severe learning disabilities that do not respond to traditional special education or remedial programming, particularly when there is evidence of a pattern of right or left hemisyndrome (lateralizing sensory-motor neurological signs)

3. Severe emotional or behavioral disturbances accompanied by significant learning, intellectual or developmental delays (e.g., motor, speech/language, perceptual) that are particularly resistant to traditional psychopharmacological, psychological, or behavioral interventions

4. Acute onset of memory, cognitive, academic, motor, speech/language, behavioral, and personality deficits that cannot be explained by other psychoeducational evaluations

Neuropsychological evaluations can be used to diagnose various neurodevelopmental disorders (e.g., LD), brain injuries, and CNS diseases, and for measuring treatment efficacy and recovery of function (Donders, 2007). See later chapters for methods of developing interventions for specific childhood disorders.

The Integration of Neurological, Neuroradiological, and Neuropsychological Data

Medical and university labs and clinics are exploring integrated research protocols including neuroradiological and neuropsychological data in an effort to more fully understand the nature of childhood disorders. Clinicians and researchers that are prominent in this effort include Castellanos et al. (2002), Giedd et al. (2004), Papanicolaou (2003), Gabrieli (2003), Semrud-Clikeman et al. (2006), and Shaywitz et al. (2004), to name a few. In these efforts, researchers are revealing evidence linking neurocognitive and neuropsychological deficits to functional brain regions or systems. In essence, these investigators are providing information to establish the bidirectional nature of the neuroanatomical/morphological neuropsychological-functional link. (This relationship is depicted in Fig. 1.1). While the link between anatomy and function has generally been downward, these efforts start at the functional and neuropsychological level and build upward, establishing a function-to-structure linkage that may lead to a better understanding of childhood disorders.

Researchers postulate neurobiological models of childhood disorders, such as dyslexia, and, in an effort to test these models empirically, information from divergent sources is analyzed. Typically theories about how the brain functions are tested by administering neuropsychological tests to carefully defined groups of children (e.g., dyslexic children with language-related deficiencies), and then by studying morphological variations in brain structures using neuroimaging techniques and, more recently, fMRI procedures. The degree to which specific neurolinguistic deficiencies are related to morphological abnormalities or functional differences in brain activation can thus be investigated. In doing so, researchers are beginning to answer questions such as these: Do children with language-related reading disorders have structures that are similar to those typically found in children in regions presumably mediating language processes? And, are the measured linguistic difficulties a function of these unique patterns of brain asymmetry? Shaywitz, Shaywitz, Pugh, Fulbright, and Skudlarski (2002) have discussed these morphological-functional relations for children with dyslexia in detail. The reader is also referred to Pliszka et al. (2006) for a better understanding of these brain/behavior interactions in children with ADHD.

The next logical and critical step in developing a neurobiological model of childhood disorders is to investigate the extent to which children with cognitive-processing and/or linguistic deficits respond to differential intervention programs. Efforts to identify cognitive correlates of reading deficits have been reviewed by Eden and Moats (2002). A meta-analysis of phonologically based approaches to remediation found that stressing phonological processing skills for poor readers improves reading performance (National Reading Panel, 2000). These interventions will be explored in more detail in Chapter 10.

In summary, efforts linking neuroradiological and neuropsychological findings are underway establishing the bidirectional nature of the relationship between brain structure and brain function. Integrated research paradigms are important in this effort, and will advance our basic understanding of childhood disorders. In the clinical setting, children referred for neuropsychological evaluation do not necessarily receive neurological or neuroradiological testing unless there is accompanying brain damage or suspected CNS disease. Cognitive, academic, behavioral and psychosocial functioning are also of interest to the neuropsychologist because these factors may affect test performance on neuropsychological measures. Thus it is important to explore alternative hypotheses (e.g., attentional deficits, motivational variations, depression, anxiety, and/or oppositional defiance) before making inferences about brain pathology on the basis of neuropsychological test results. Tests of psychological functioning that are commonly incorporated into neuropsychological evaluations are reviewed next. Psychological factors that have a negative impact on the neuropsychological evaluation are also explored.

Psychological Assessment of Children with Neurodevelopmental, Neuropsychiatric, and Other CNS Disorders

Achenbach (1990, 2005) suggests that at least six microparadigms be incorporated in the study of childhood disorders: biomedical, behavioral, psychodynamic, sociological, family systems, and cognitive. By drawing from each of these diverse approaches, questions about childhood disorders can be framed into an integrated "macroparadigm." Achenbach describes a model of multiaxial assessment with specific suggestions for measuring child behavior:

Axis I: Parent reports, Child Behavior Checklist (Achenbach, 1991)
Axis II: Teacher reports, Child Behavior Checklist Teacher's Report Form
Axis III: Cognitive assessment, WISC-IV or WAIS-III
Axis IV: Physical assessment, height, weight, and neurologica/medical exam
Axis V: Direct assessment, Semistructured Clinical Interview and Youth Self Report (Achenbach & Rescorla, 2001).

Neuropsychological evaluations could be appropriately incorporated into Axis IV of this model. Various components and techniques recommended for use in a comprehensive psychological evaluation are discussed briefly. Information gathered from this evaluation informs the neuropsychologist and others about the child's overall cognitive-intellectual, psychosocial, and academic functioning. This information is helpful in describing the extent to which brain-related dysfunction affects these important functional areas of the child.

Impact of Psychological Functioning on Neuropsychological Results

A number of psychological conditions or factors can have an impact on neuropsychological evaluations that should be considered when evaluating children and adolescents. These factors may interact differentially depending on whether the child's condition is a result of acquired anomalies (e.g., traumatic brain injury) or developmental anomalies (e.g., learning or neuropsychiatric disorders). First, children sustaining traumatic brain injury may display symptoms of "psychic edema" that interfere with performance on neuropsychological tests. Inattention, distractibility, and motivational problems may be present soon after injury. Although these features frequently subside within weeks of injury, once the child has stabilized, initial or baseline neuropsychological evaluation may be contaminated by these short-term problems (Semrud-Clikeman, 2004). Furthermore, these psychological aspects may mask other deficits that could ultimately be long-lasting (e.g., impaired reasoning and planning). For example, tests of executive functioning (e.g., Wisconsin Card Sort or Category Test) may be sensitive to these psychological problems.

If a child is inattentive and distractible, then careful and thoughtful analysis is lacking. Impulsive responses may be inaccurate. Some children with TBI do continue to display ADD-like symptoms long after recovery, but the clinician is advised to consider the initial impact on test results if inattention and distractibility are observed, particularly when the child's history does not suggest that the problems were present preinjury. Second, language and/or reading delays may make some neuropsychological items difficult. If a child does not understand the verbal directions of a test and responds inaccurately, this may indicate a language comprehension problem rather than a deficit in the underlying neuropsychological function of interest. For example, instructions on some psychological and neuropsychological measures tests (i.e., Trails B from the Halstead Reitan) may prove too complicated for a child with a receptive language delay. In this instance, it is imperative to determine whether low scores result from true reasoning or planning deficits, or from problems in comprehension. Testing the limits or simplifying instructions may be helpful in this determination. Further, cognitive delays also may produce poor performance on measures of global (e.g., reasoning, abstract formation, memory) versus specific brain functioning (e.g., motor speed).

Third, children with conduct-related or oppositional defiant disorders may show signs of passive aggressiveness and poor motivation. Refusal or poor effort should not be confused with neuropsychological deficits. It is also not uncommon for children with these psychiatric problems to have poor frustration tolerance. They may give up quickly and become easily frustrated when they begin to struggle on items that are difficult (e.g., reasoning tasks). Efforts to improve frustration tolerance may include using reinforcers (e.g., a soda, a candy bar) or shorter testing intervals. Fourth, children with ADHD also may make careless, impulsive errors. Testing on and off medication often gives the clinician a better picture of the child's underlying neuropsychological problems beyond the impulsivity and distractibility that may be paramount in ADHD. Breaking testing periods into shorter periods may also improve performance.

Finally, depression and/or anxiety may interfere with a child's ability to put forth sustained effort. Children may appear apathetic, withdrawn, or overly nervous. It is important to build rapport with the child and to create a supportive, reinforcing testing climate. Again, testing the child both on and off medication may be indicated, especially for children who take antidepressants. The neuropsychological report should reflect any special testing administration changes or modifications,

and should describe the conditions under which the behaviors were elicited. It may be helpful to conduct a follow-up evaluation (three to six months later) if the clinician believes that psychological factors have rendered the interpretation of neuropsychological findings suspect or contaminated. An important part of the neuropsychological evaluation process is a comprehensive presentation of the information gathered on the child's behavior and method of interacting with the examiner.

Conclusion

With the advent of new examination methods for the neurological functioning of children, neurologists and neuropsychologists are better equipped to concentrate on areas of strength and weakness as well as remediation, instead of the previous emphasis on location of damage or diagnosis. Understanding when to refer a child for a neuropsychological examination is just as important as understanding the basic measures that are utilized. Neuropsychological reports should not only report testing results, but also provide interventions and understanding of the results. Many cases that are referred for a neuropsychological evaluation will often also have psychiatric overtones. A comprehensive examination provides information about the child's social and emotional functioning. For adolescents and adults the MMPI-A and MMPI-2 are instruments that are frequently utilized. For children self-report rating scales are generally useful. For some clients who are either unwilling or unable to describe their difficulties or who have poor insight, a projective measure will be helpful.

Thus, a comprehensive neuropsychological evaluation encompasses a good psychological assessment and adds knowledge about brain function as well as possible aspects of development that may negatively impact brain development and functioning. These issues are illustrated in the neuropsychological report provided in this chapter.

The following chapter briefly reviews basic domains of neuropsychological functioning. It also provides a brief discussion of the commonly utilized tests for these areas. Further discussion of set neuropsychological batteries is provided in Chapter 8.

Hospital: Developmental/Behavioral Program

Patient Name:	**Sam**
Medical Record Number:	
Date of Birth:	
Date of Evaluation:	**8/5, 8/12, 8/26/**
Chronological Age:	**13–10**
Neuropsychologist:	

Reason for Referral

Sam was referred for evaluation by Dr. K to evaluate his current level of intellectual and academic functioning. Dr. K evaluated Sam and diagnosed him with ADHD: combined type, Conduct disorder: adolescent onset, Anxiety disorder NOS with rule outs for Bipolar disorder, and learning disorders. Dr. R, child psychiatrist, is evaluating Sam concurrently with this evaluation. Sam is not currently prescribed any medications.

Background Information

The following information was obtained through review of medical records, discussion with Dr. K, and parent and child interviews. Additional information is available through Dr. K's report to the interested professional. The following is a summary of Sam's history. Sam has a long history of acting out behaviors and sadness/anxiety disorder. Significant deficits have been found in attention, social skills, and activity level. His family history is positive for incarceration and substance abuse and has been notably unstable. He has been at a juvenile detention center twice with the most recent stay in the past school year. He was at the juvenile detention center most recently due to significant behavioral difficulties at home, school refusal, and suicidal ideation. Sam's older brother has been reportedly arrested several times and is currently in prison for burglary. His mother also has a history of incarceration and substance abuse, but is currently working on turning her life around, and she reported she has been clean for 18 months.

The pregnancy was complicated by the use of heroin, caffeine, and nicotine during the first trimester, substances which were discontinued at that time. Pregnancy and delivery were reported as normal and delivery was by Cesarean Section. Sam was reported to be an active and fussy baby, but met all developmental milestones within normal limits. Sam's mother reports that he has significant difficulty sleeping and frequently doesn't sleep until early morning. Sam attends school at the ALC and has a history of suspensions and expulsions prior to his attendance at ALC. His achievement was reported to be in the average range. Sam has not had a psychological or neuropsychological evaluation. Dr. K's report indicates the presence of depression, anxiety, conduct problems, and peer problems. These findings were present on both home and school behavioral checklists and consistent with self-report measures completed by Sam.

Speech and Language assessment conducted at the hospital found Sam's language skills to be within normal limits for his age. An audiological evaluation through CHOA found an auditory processing deficit with recommendations for a repeat evaluation in one year.

Behavioral Observations

Sam was accompanied to the assessment by his mother. He was tested during two consecutive Thursday appointments for approximately three hours each. Sam was friendly throughout the evaluations and seemed to enjoy the tasks at hand. His language was age-appropriate and his speech was clear and unpressured. He reported that he had not slept well the nights before the assessments and was tired. Sam did appear to be lethargic during the testing which affected his attention at times. He responded well to redirection and worked on the tasks at hand. On tasks that were challenging for him Sam would give up easily and appeared to lack confidence in his abilities. He worked hard throughout the tests, but did not push himself if he didn't know the answer. He did not become unduly frustrated on tasks that were challenging for him. Given his high level of cooperation, the following results are felt to be a reliable and valid representation of his level of current functioning.

Tests Administered

Differential Abilities Scales (DAS), Wechsler Individual Achievement Test-II (WIAT-II), California Verbal Learning Test-Children's Version (CVLT-C), Stroop Color Word Test, Test of Variables of Attention, Wisconsin Card Sorting Test (WCST), Judgment of Line Orientation (JLO), Rey-Osterreith Complex Figure Test, Rorschach Inkblot Test, Behavior Assessment System for Children—parent form (BASC), Review of Medical Records, Clinical Interview

Test Interpretations

Cognitive Functioning

The Differential Abilities Scales (DAS) consists of core and diagnostic tests of general cognitive ability. The cognitive subtests assess the child's ability to understand and use language, complete puzzles and block designs, and interpret visual information. The diagnostic subtests evaluate the child's short- and long-term memory as well as his speed of information processing. Sam shows average overall functioning achieving a general cognitive index of 91 that places him at the 27th national percentile. There is a 90 percent assurance that his true ability lies between 86 and 95. There is a significant difference between his verbal and nonverbal skills; his verbal ability is in the strong average range and his nonverbal reasoning skills is below the average for his age. Sam's spatial abilities are in the average range. On the verbal subtests Sam shows age-appropriate ability to define words and use abstract language concepts. He also shows average perceptual skills. Weakness is present in Sam's nonverbal reasoning skills particularly in his ability to recognize patterns and complete sequencing tasks. The diagnostic tests indicate very good visual memory, both short- and long-term. His ability to process information quickly and his recall of auditory information are in the low average range for his age.

Academic Functioning

The Wechsler Individual Achievement Test is a measure of general academic functioning in the areas of reading, arithmetic and writing. On the reading subtests the child is asked to read single words and also to read a passage and answer questions about content. On the arithmetic subtests the child is asked to solve word problems as well as general calculation problems. The writing subtests require the child to spell words and then to write a story on a topic.

Sam's reading skills are within expectations for his age and grade placement. He shows better abilities understanding what he has read and appears to use context clues in order to understand passages. His ability to sound out words is not as well developed and he would not attempt to sound out words that he did not know. Sam's mathematics abilities are his weakest area particularly in his ability to complete calculation tasks. He has not mastered fractions and shows poor understanding of decimals. Sam's spelling skills are in the below average range and his ability to write a paragraph is significantly below his age and ability measures. His story was marked by poor word usage, lack of punctuation and capitalization, run-on sentences, and limited word usage. Sam shows adequate development of his ideas. Compared to his ability, particularly compared to his verbal ability, Sam meets criteria for a learning disability in mathematics and written expression.

Learning and Memory

The California Verbal Learning Test-Children's Version (CVLT-C) was administered to assess Sam's ability to learn verbal material after several exposures. The task also provides measures of recall and recognition of previously learned material. Sam's scores on this measure are listed below. Sam shows average ability to encode and store auditory information. When asked to recall information after a short period of time, Sam's scores are significantly below average. Strategies for recalling information do not improve his score either in the short- or long-term.

The findings from the memory measures have important implications for Sam's school performance. He does not spontaneously generate efficient strategies for encoding, and may need to be taught more effective means of remembering new material. It also appears that new learning may be taking place, but Sam is having difficulty with retrieval. Thus, he should be provided with a system of cueing himself to help him to remember information that he has just learned. Additionally, new learning should be rehearsed often to help render retrieval somewhat easier. These findings are consistent with the possibility of a central auditory processing disorder.

Executive Functioning

The Wisconsin Card Sorting Test is a measure of executive or frontal lobe functioning, including the ability to form concepts, generate an organizational strategy, and use examiner feedback to shift strategy to the changing demands of the task. Sam's performance is summarized below:

Sam shows excellent executive functioning skills. He is able to utilize examiner feedback to change his answers and to respond flexibly to a cognitive task. Sam did show difficulty in staying on the task and became distracted by additional stimuli. This finding indicates that he can be distracted from the task at hand and this hampers his ability to respond.

The Stroop Color Word Test was also administered to measure Sam's ability to inhibit responding. The Stroop has three parts: the first part requires him to read color words as quickly as possible, then colors, then words that are printed in opposing colors (the word red is printed in green ink and the child reads the color of the ink). Sam scored in the low average range in his ability to read color words quickly and for the colors. He scored in the below average range in his ability to inhibit his response when asked to complete the task where he reads the color, but not the word. He became increasingly frustrated at this task and this frustration also contributed to his very low score.

Attention

Sam was administered the Test of Variables of Attention (TOVA) to evaluate his abilities. He was administered the TOVA off of any medication, then on 10 mgs of methylphenidate. His scores without medication showed difficulties in all areas. With the medication his scores fell within average ranges.

These findings are consistent with observations during the evaluation as well as an interview with Sam and his mother. He endorsed eight symptoms of inattention, three of poor impulse control and four of high activity level. These findings are similar to those reported by Dr. K.

Perceptual-Motor Functioning

The Rey-Osterreith Complex Figure test requires the adolescent to copy a very detailed figure. Sam scored in the average range on this task showing good visual-motor skills, as well as good planning and organizational abilities.

Sam's basic visual-perceptual skills were assessed using the Judgment of Line Orientation test which requires the adolescent to determine the correct directional orientation of a line pattern. On this measure, Sam showed significant deficits in his ability to match patterns. This finding is consistent with his difficulty on the DAS nonverbal reasoning tasks. Sam achieved a score of 14 which places him 3.5 standard deviations below expectations for his age.

Sam also completed the Purdue Pegboard. The Purdue Pegboard requires him to place pegs in a pegboard as quickly as possible with each hand individually and then with both simultaneously. He scored in the average range with his ability to place pegs with his right (dominant) and left hands as well as with both hands together. He also completed the Finger Tapping Test, which requires him to tap on a tapper as quickly as possible with each hand for 10 seconds. Sam scored well within the average range on the measure. These findings indicate that Sam does not have significant motor task problems, but he does have difficulty with perception and with the integration of perception and motor, a task that is important for writing.

Emotional Functioning

Sam completed the Behavioral Assessment System for Children-Self-report (BASC), an integrated system designed to facilitate the differential diagnosis and classification of a variety of emotional and behavioral disorders of children and to aid in the design of treatment plans. His mother had previously completed the BASC as well as his teacher during the evaluation with Dr. K. Findings indicated highly clinically significant difficulties present in learning, social functioning, activity level, and attention in school. At home significant problems were reported in attention, activity level, aggression, conduct, and self-esteem.

Sam's ratings indicate that he is feeling most stress in school and that his attitude toward school and teachers is problematic. He does not consider teachers as people who can help him, that they are unfair, and that they only look at the bad things you do. He also does not feel that school is a helpful place and that he really doesn't care about school and wants to get out as soon as possible. In addition, Sam indicates that he prefers excitement and will seek out such situations if they are not present. The risk for antisocial behavior is very high based on the BASC and he shows little anxiety about getting in trouble with authority figures. There are indications of concerns about his sense of worth and that he does not have the motivation to attempt tasks when they are more difficult. He reports adequate self-esteem and self-reliance, but problematic relationships with his parents.

The Rorschach Inkblot Test was also administered to attempt to uncover areas of emotional functioning that Sam did not appear free to discuss. Sam's protocol indicates that he directs his behavior through internal means and attempts to keep his feelings aside when in coping situations so that their influence on his decisions is, at best, modest. This coping style is very marked and not very flexible—in other words, he will persist in his behavior even in a situation in which an intuitive or trial-and-error style may be more appropriate. Sam is also showing significant signs of situational stress that appears to be interfering with his ability to direct his behavior in a more appropriate manner. He shows a conflict between possibly unmet dependency needs and his need to isolate himself—given his history he may feel that he needs to protect himself from opening up to anyone. He shows a tendency toward cognitive distortion that may make it more difficult for him to interpret interpersonal behavior appropriately. His protocol indicates the risk for antisocial behavior and he does not perceive that people work together toward a goal. Positively, Sam shows an interest in people,

but may not process human relationships very well. He shows signs of dysthymia as well as some indications that he sees himself as damaged or inadequate.

Summary and Recommendations

Sam is a 13-year, 10-month-old male with a history of aggressive behavior, attendance at a juvenile detention center, and a problematic childhood. Cognitive assessment indicates average ability in verbal and spatial skills with below average nonverbal reasoning skills. Achievement testing indicates age-appropriate reading skills with deficits present in mathematics and written expression. He shows significant problems with attention which is improved with medication. Sam also has a history of social skills deficits as well as our finding of visual-spatial skill deficits. These findings are consistent with a diagnosis of a nonverbal learning disability. His difficulty in understanding appropriate social actions as well as containing his impulses make it difficult for him to participate in many social interactions. Instead Sam has developed behaviors that remove him from this difficulty through acting out. One cannot rule out that some of these behaviors may be related to his early development and his mother's probable substance abuse during pregnancy and after birth.

Sam shows good skills in utilizing feedback to change his behavior. However, he shows difficulty recalling information when presented orally—a finding consistent with his performance on the auditory processing test recently completed at the hospital. Emotionally Sam shows indications of being at high risk to develop antisocial behavior. He seeks out situations that are exciting for him and has a very low tolerance for boredom. There are indications of dysthymia in the projective testing as well as unmet needs for nurturance. Sam's difficulty in trusting adults in authority make it problematic for him to change his behavior and his defiance is his way of asserting control over a situation. These feelings are likely grounded in his early experience where his mother was unavailable to him and his needs were not met in a timely manner. The picture presented by Sam is of an adolescent who is torn between a need to be cared for and nurtured, and a need to reject human contact. These concerns are complicated by his difficulty in perception that may frequently lead him to misinterpret people and their motives.

These findings are not consistent with a diagnosis of bipolar disorder, but are consistent with that of conduct disorder, ADHD, and a learning disability. It is believed that Sam is at a crossroads at this time and is at high risk to continue down his path of antisocial behavior. He requires intensive intervention assist him in preventing this possibility.

Given the above findings, the following recommendations are offered:

1. It is strongly recommended that his school convene a multidisciplinary team meeting to determine Sam's eligibility for special education services in the areas of OHI and LD.
2. A sleep study is recommended to determine the cause of Sam's history of sleep difficulty.
3. Individual cognitive-behavioral therapy is recommended and can be arranged through the hospital.
4. Continuation of parent training with Dr. K. is strongly recommended. Moreover, continuation of therapy with Dr. R is also strongly recommended as well as consideration for medication.
5. It is very important that auditory information which requires encoding be paired with visual cues to improve Sam's ability to remember what he has learned.
6. Additional memory strategies are provided as follows:

Strategies for Improved Memory Skills

Teaching Behaviors which are helpful:

1. Break tasks into small steps
2. Use extensive repetition
3. Teach strategies for memory, such as verbal rehearsal, clustering or chunking, imagery, associations, note taking, etc.
4. Use massed and distributed practice

Focus on the following:

A. Working Memory: Teach the child how to remember directions and keep it in mind long enough to complete the task. Younger children especially forget what they are supposed to do and start to "drift away." Use cues like "make yourself remember. . ." "This is important. . ." Do the first few items with the child, pointing out what is important.
B. Present information in short segments: Two sentences may be overwhelming. Monitor comprehension.
C. Get the child involved actively whenever possible. Use many visual aids, demonstrate, repeat, give many pages of the same idea. Your goal is comprehension, retention, and mastery.
D. The child needs memory strategies such as:

   • visualization (make a picture in your mind as you listen)
   • note taking (or buddy note taker)
   • repeating words in chunks
   • learning to associate related ideas
   • using "silly" cues such as, *Joe's Present* . *Joe* was born on *Sunday* , *July* 4th, in *Seattle* , *WA* , *USA* on *Book Street* . He got a *Ninja Turtle* from *Toys R' Us* . These sentences have all the rules for *capitalization* .

E. Only present the important information; leave out the frills and elaborations. Simplify, make it interesting, make it fun. Avoid long paragraphs or small print.

7. Techniques to help students with attentional problems in the classroom

Physical Arrangement of Room

1. Have student seated near teacher
2. Move student's desk away from hallway, outside windows, etc.
3. Use desk dividers or study carrels if possible
4. Seat appropriate models next to students with attentional problems
5. Stand near student when giving directions or presenting lesson. Use the student's worksheet as an example
6. Use rows for seating arrangement. Avoid tables with groups of students, if possible

Lesson Presentation

1. Provide an outline, key concepts, or vocabulary prior to lesson presentation

2. Include a variety of activities during each lesson
3. Make lessons brief
4. Actively involve the student during the lesson presentation:

   - Use cooperative learning activities
   - Develop learning stations
   - Provide self-correcting materials
   - Enable the student to make frequent responses
   - Interact frequently (verbally and physically) with the student

5. Use the student's name during your presentation
6. Pair students to check work
7. Arrange for peer tutoring to help students review concepts
8. Use colored chalk during presentations when using chalk board

Worksheets and Tests

1. Use larger type
2. Keep page format simple:

   - Don't include extraneous pictures
   - Provide only one or two activities per page
   - Have white spaces on each page

3. Write clear, simple directions
4. Underline key direction words, vocabulary words, etc.
5. Draw borders around parts of page you want emphasized
6. Add reminders on worksheets to check work, etc.
7. Give frequent short quizzes and avoid longer tests
8. If necessary, allow student to take tests orally
9. Provide practice tests
10. Shorten assignments

Behavior

1. Implement a classroom behavior management system
2. Implement an individual behavior program and consistently chart progress (earn points for on-task time)
3. Use kitchen timer to help students stay on task
4. Use visual and auditory cues as behavioral reminders
5. Develop contracts/ behavior management systems in conjunction with parents to reinforce specific behaviors at home and at school

6. Implement a social skills curriculum
7. Give students choices ("You may work on your report or finish your math sheet")
8. Praise *specific* behaviors ("I like how you remembered to check your work before turning it in to me")
9. Define and review class rules each day
      Post rules where students can see them
10. Be as consistent as possible in following through on classroom and individual behavior programs
11. Set hourly, daily, weekly, or monthly goals with the student and provide frequent feedback on student's progress

Thank you for the opportunity to work with this young man and his family. If you have any questions about this report, please do not hesitate to contact me at the XXX-XXXX.

Dr. X. Ph.D.
Licensed Psychologist
cc: Dr. K
      Dr. R

Psychometric Summary

Differential Abilities Scale-2

Average standard scores for the general cognitive index are between 85 and 115 with average T-scores for the individual subtests being between 40 and 60.

	Standard Score	Percentile
Verbal Cluster	105	63
Nonverbal Reasoning	81	10
Spatial	91	27
General Conceptual Ability	91	27

Core Subtests	T-Score	Percentile
Verbal Subtests		
Word Definitions	54	66
Similarities	53	62
Spatial Subtests		
Recall of Designs	45	31
Pattern Construction	45	31

Nonverbal Reasoning
Subtests

Matrices	38	14
Sequential and Quantitative Reasoning	40	16

Diagnostic Subtests

Recall of Digits	45	31
Recall of Objects— Immediate	57	76
Recall of Objects— Delayed	54	66
Speed of Information Processing	47	38

Wechsler Individual Achievement Test-II

Average standard scores are between 85 and 115. Sam's scores are as follows:

	Standard Score	Percentile
Basic Reading	86	18
Word Attack	73	3
Reading Comprehension	101	53
Reading Composite	**90**	**25**
Mathematics Reasoning	83	13
Numerical Operations	73	4
Mathematics Composite	**74**	**4**
Spelling	82	12
Written Expression	75	5
Writing Composite	**77**	**6**

California Verbal Learning Test-Children's Version
Scores have a mean of 0, with standard scores of -1.0 to +1.0 indicating performance within the broad average range.

	Raw Score	Standard Score
List A, Trial 1	7	0.0
List A, Trial 5	12	0.0
Trials 1–5	45	42
List B Free Recall	6	−0.5
List A Short Delay Free Recall	6	−2.0
List A Short Delay Cued Recall	7	−2.0
List A Long Delay Free Recall	8	−1.0
List A Long Delay Cued Recall	7	−2.0
Correct Recognition Hits	7	−3.5
Discriminability	66.67%	−5.0
Learning Slope	1.2	−0.5

Wisconsin Card Sorting Test

Categories Achieved:	6	Normal range = 5–6
Failure to Maintain Set	4	Normal range = 0–1

	Raw Score	Standard Score (100 + 15)
Total Errors	15	116
Perseverative Responses:	11	108
Perseverative Errors:	0	109
Non-perseverative Errors:	5	118
Percent Conceptual Level Responses	82%	118

Test of Variables of Attention-Visual
Average scores run between 85 and 115

	Off Ritalin	On 10 mg
Omissions	65	103
Commissions	66	105
Response Time	77	110
Variability	55	95

Stroop Color Word Test
Average scores range between 40 and 60

Words	47
Colors	45
Color/Words	32

Behavior Assessment Scale for Children— Self-Report

Domain	T-Score	Percentile
Attitude to School	74*	99
Attitude to Teachers	74*	99
Sensation Seeking	70	97
School Maladjustment	*78**	*98*
Atypicality	69+	94
Depression	49	64
Somatization	65+	91
Anxiety	49	64
Sense of Inadequacy	62+	86

Social Stress	54	69
Clinical Maladjustment	57	75
Personal Adjustment	*39+*	*14*
Emotional Symptoms		
Index	*55*	*73*

For the following scales, higher scores are desirable

Relations with Parents	30*	7
Interpersonal		
Relations	41	15
Self-Esteem	50	37
Self-Reliance	46	26

+ at risk

*high scores indicate problem behaviors

References

Achenbach, T. M. (1990). Conceptualization of developmental psychopathology. In M. Lewis & S. R. Miller (Eds.), *Handbook of developmental psychopathology* (pp. 3–13). New York: Plenum Press.

Achenbach, T. M. (1991). *Manual for the child behavior checklist and revised child behavior profile.* Burlington, VT: T.M. Achenbach.

Achenbach, T. M. (2005). Advancing assessment of children and adolescents: Commentary on evidence-based assessment of child and adolescent disorders. *Journal of Child and Adolescent Psychology, 34*, 541–547.

Achenbach, T. M., & Rescorla, L. A. (2001). *Manual for the ASEBA school-age forms & profiles.* Burlington, VT: University of Vermont, Research Center for Children, Youth, and Families.

Castellanos, F. X., Lee, P. P., Sharp, W., Jeffries, N. O., Greenstein, D. K., Clasen, L. S., et al. (2002). Developmental trajectories of brain volume abnormalities in children with adolescents with attention-deficit/hyperactivity disorder. *The Journal of the American Medical Association, 28* (4), 1740–1749.

Donders, J. (2007). Traumatic brain injury. In S. J. Hunter & J. Donders (Eds.), *Pediatric neuropsychological intervention* (pp. 91–111). Cambridge: Cambridge University Press.

Eden, G., & Moats, L. C. (2002). The role of neuroscience in the remediation of students with dyslexia. *Nature Neuroscience, 5*, 1080–1084.

Gabrieli, J. D. (2003). *Neuroimaging evidence about the brain basis of dyslexia.* Paper presented at the International Dyslexia Association, San Diego, CA.

Giedd, J. N. (2004). Structural magnetic resonance imaging of the adolescent brain. *Annals of the New York Academy of Sciences, 1021*, 1308–1309.

Hynd, G. W., & Willis, W. G. (1988). Pediatric neuropsychology. Orlando, FL: Grune & Stratton.

National Reading Panel. (2000). *Teaching children to read: An evidence-based assessment of the scientific research literature on reading and its implications for reading instruction.* Washington, DC: National Institute of Child Health and Human Development.

Papanicolaou, A. C. (2003). *Brain imaging in normal and impaired reading: A developmental-educational perspective.* Paper presented at the International Dyslexia Association.

Pliszka, S. R., Glahn, D. C., Semrud-Clikeman, M., Franklin, C., Perez, R., Xiong, J., et al. (2006). Neuroimaging of inhibitory control areas in children with attention deficit hyperactivity disorder who were treatment naive or in long-term treatment. *American Journal of Psychiatry, 163* (6), 1052–1060.

Semrud-Clikeman, M. (2004). *Traumatic brain injury in children and adolescents.* New York: Guilford Press.

Semrud-Clikeman, M., Pliszka, S. R., Lancaster, J., & Liotti, M. (2006). Volumetric MRI differences in treatment-naïve vs chronically treated children with ADHD. *Neurology, 67*, 1023–1027.

Shaywitz, B. A., Shaywitz, S. E., Blachman, B. A., Pugh, K. R., Fulbright, R. K., Skudlarski, P., et al. (2004). Development of left occipitotemporal systems for skilled reading in children after a phonologically-based intervention. *Biological Psychiatry, 55*, 926–933.

Shaywitz, B. A., Shaywitz, S. E., Pugh, K., Fulbright, R. K., & Skudlarski, P. (2002). Disruption of posterior brain systems for reading in children with developmental dyslexia. *Biological Psychiatry, 52*, 101–110.

Swaiman, K. F. (1994). Cerebellar dysfunction and ataxia in childhood. In K. F. Swaiman (Ed.), *Pediatric neurology* (Vol. 2, pp. 261–270). St. Louis: Mosby.

Swaiman, K. F., Ashwal, S., & Ferriero, D. M. (2006). *Pediatric neurology* (4th ed.). San Diego: Mosby.

Chapter 6
Neuropsychological Domains of Functioning

Chapter 8 discusses various approaches to neuropsychological testing including the Reitan batteries and Boston Process techniques. The goal of this chapter is to provide a brief overview of the various domains generally associated with a neuropsychological evaluation. These domains include traditional components of a psychological evaluation such as cognitive ability, achievement, and social-emotional functioning. In addition, domains such as attention, executive functioning, fine motor skills, and visual-perceptual abilities are also presented as typically contained in a neuropsychological evaluation. This chapter is not an exhaustive review of the available measures; such a discussion is available in many sources, primary of which is Strauss, Sherman, and Spreen (2006).

Cognitive Ability

Selected instruments for measuring cognitive-intellectual functioning are reviewed including the following: (1) the Woodcock-Johnson Cognitive Battery-III (WJ-III); (2) the Weschler Intelligence Scale for Children-IV (WISC-IV); (3) the Differential Ability Scale-2 (DAS-2); (4) the Kaufman Assessment Battery for Children-2 (K-ABC-2), and (5) the NEPSY 2.

Woodcock-Johnson Tests of Cognitive Ability-III

The Woodcock-Johnson Tests of Cognitive Ability (WJ) was developed by Woodcock and Johnson

(1977), revised (WJR) in 1989 by Woodcock and Johnson (1989) and again revised in 2001 (Woodcock, McGrew, & Mather, 2001a). The WJ-III is based on the intellectual model of crystallized and fluid intelligence (Cattell & Horn, 1978) and has been found useful for measuring cognitive ability, scholastic aptitude, and achievement (Woodcock, 1990). There are scales that measure intelligence (a brief and general scale) as well as measures of attention, executive functioning, working memory, verbal ability, thinking ability and cognitive flexibility. Although it is sometimes difficult to abandon the verbal-perceptual organization model of intelligence underlying the Weschler scales, the WJR offers a conceptual alternative to this framework that might be extremely useful for some childhood disorders, particularly learning disabilities. The WJIII has strong psychometric properties and offers a method of gathering benchmark measures of visual and auditory processing, memory and retrieval, and reasoning abilities in children and adolescents.

Wechsler Intelligence Scale for Children-IV

The Wechsler scales have enjoyed a long history of use for measuring intelligence in children and adolescents (Sattler, 2001), and the Wechsler Intelligence Scale for Children-IV (WISC-IV) is the latest revision for children (Wechsler, 2003). The WISC-IV departs from the previous revisions and provides four indices of performance: Verbal Comprehension, Perceptual Reasoning, Working

M. Semrud-Clikeman, P.A. Teeter Ellison, *Child Neuropsychology*, DOI 10.1007/978-0-387-88963-4_6,
© Springer Science+Business Media, LLC 2009

Memory, and Processing Speed as well as a Full Scale IQ (FSIQ). Though not originally developed as a measure of brain functioning, the Wechsler scales are almost always used as part of a neuropsychological evaluation (Baron, 2004). T*he* WISC-IV *or the* WJIII: *Which is best?*

In general, neuropsychologists do not incorporate both the WISC-IV and the WJIII in an evaluation of children, primarily due to time constraints. However, deciding which cognitive-intelligence instrument to use may be a difficult choice. In making this determination, consider using the WISC-IV

1. when the impact of injury or CNS disease on the child's intelligence is of concern
2. when long-term intellectual competencies are in question, and
3. when identifying functional sequelae of focal injury is of interest (i.e., verbal comprehension deficits related to injury of temporo-parietal regions or perceptual-organization weaknesses following injury to parieto-occipital regions).

The WJIII may be more useful

1. when perceptual processing and memory functions are of primary interest (i.e., phonological core deficits)
2. when deficits of concept formation and abstract reasoning are of concern (i.e., injury to frontal regions)
3. when there are signs of visual agnosia, aphasia, or significant academic deficits in language-related or math skills (i.e., dyslexia), or
4. when the WISC-IV or other cognitive measures do not seem to adequately reflect the child's ability, as evidenced by adaptive behavior levels.

There also seems to be historical precedence for selecting the WISC-IV, although important data can be gleaned from the WJIII that are quite distinct from those obtained with other intelligence measures. The WJIII was developed with multiple intelligences as the theoretical framework, which may prove to be very useful for more clearly articulating the complexities of specific cognitive abilities as they relate to specific brain function. Further research exploring the relative contributions of the WISC-I11 and the WJR to neuropsychological evaluation is needed to clarify these issues.

Differential Ability Scal-2 (DAS-2)

The Differential Ability Scale (AS) comprises a cognitive and an achievement scale and was developed for children and adolescents between the ages of 2 ½ and 17 years (Elliott, 2007). The Cognitive Battery has a total of 20 subtests for the Preschool and the School-Age Level. The Preschool Level measures the following cognitive abilities General Conceptual Ability (GCA), which comprises Pattern Construction, Vocabulary Comprehension, Picture Similarities, and Naming Vocabulary for children aged two to six, to three to five. The GCA is divided into Verbal Ability and Nonverbal Ability for children three to six, to five to 11. For children between the ages of six to 0, and 17 to 11, the GCA consists of Verbal Ability, Nonverbal Reasoning Ability, and Spatial. In addition it provides a scale for children who have English as a second language or who are hearing impaired.

The normative sample for the DAS-2 includes children who are learning disabled; speech- and language-impaired, cognitively retarded, gifted and talented, severely emotionally disturbed, and mildly impaired on visual, auditory, or motoric functions. The DAS-2 was designed to measure profiles of cognitive abilities as well as differences between cognitive and achievement abilities. The DAS-2 is new and there are few validity and reliability studies that have been conducted beyond what is reported in the manual. Studies with the DAS, however, indicate its utility for describing subgroups of LD (McIntosh & Gridley, 1993) and ADHD students (Gibney, McIntosh, Dean, & Dunham, 2002). The extent to which the DAS-2 becomes a useful tool for clinical neuropsychologists is undetermined at this time, but the DAS-2 appears to have minimized some of the weaknesses inherent in less psychometrically sound batteries.

Kaufman Assessment Battery for Children (KABC II)

The Kaufman Assessment Battery for Children (K-ABC) (Kaufman & Kaufman, 1983) was developed on the basis of neuropsychological theory (i.e., Sperry and Luria) as a measure of simultaneous and sequential processing. The KABC-2 was revised in 2004 (Kaufman & Kaufman, 2004). The KABC-2 was designed to measure how a child processes information, where simultaneous processing is thought to be holistic in nature and consistent with right-hemisphere processing, whereas sequential processing is linear and analytic, reflecting left-hemisphere processing. The battery has five global scales: Sequential, Simultaneous, Planning, Learning, and Knowledge. It provides a Mental Processing Index as well as a Nonverbal Index for global scores.

The KABC-2 is currently being studied. Initial factor analysis findings indicate that the factor structure is consistent with the five broad abilities hypothesized in the manual (Reynolds, Keith, Fine, Fisher, & Low, 2007). This measure is somewhat different than the original KABC and further study is needed to determine whether the previous weaknesses of the measure (low ceiling for some tests, problems with test interpretation, and factor structure) remain. The manual for the KABC-2 indicates attention to theory and research in the revised version.

The NEPSY II (Korkman, Kirk, & Kirk, 2007) is a neurocognitive measure for children aged three to 16. It requires approximately 45 minutes to administer the general assessment and 90 minutes for preschoolers for the entire battery, and 2–3 hours for older children. Depending on the age of the child there are six domains provided with 32 total subtests possible. The six domains include:

- Attention and Executive Functioning
- Language
- Memory and Learning
- Sensorimotor
- Social Perception
- Visuospatial Processing

Compared to the previous version of the NEPSY there are measures added for theory of mind, affect recognition, animal sorting, inhibition geometric puzzles and picture puzzles. In addition, tests can be used alone or in combination to evaluate certain areas of difficulty for a particular child. Psychometric properties are reported to be good. Clinical studies of children with various types of disorders have also been reported to strengthen the NEPSY II's ability to discriminate difficulties in these populations.

Academic Functioning

Most psychological evaluations include a measure of academic achievement in a comprehensive evaluation of children. Generally the Wide Range Achievement Test III (WRAT-III) (Wilkinson & Robertson, 2005) is used as a screening measure. To obtain more comprehensive measures of achievement, the Woodcock Johnson Tests of Achievement-Revised (WJA-III) (Woodcock, McGrew & Mather, 2001b) or the Wechsler Individual Achievement Tests (Psychological Corporation, 2002) (WIAT-II) are recommended.

Woodcock-Johnson Tests of Achievement-III

The WJIII Tests of Achievement Standard Battery include Reading, Mathematics, Written Language, Oral Language, and Knowledge. Each of the main academic areas now contain a measure of fluency. Three discrepancy scores can be generated comparing intra-cognitive discrepancies (e.g., Auditory versus Visual Processing), intra-achievement discrepancies (e.g., Reading versus Mathematics), and cognitive-achievement discrepancies when the WJ-III cognitive and achievement batteries are both employed. There are several advantages to incorporating these tests into a neuropsychological battery. First, the WJIII Tests of Achievement have strong technical properties. Second, these measures are conormed with the same population as the WJIII Tests of Cognitive Ability. This reduces the weaknesses inherent in comparing a child's intellectual and achievement abilities on tests with different standardization groups and norms. Finally, the discrepancy scores provide a method for making normative comparisons and for determining individual strengths and weaknesses across various measures.

This measure also possesses some strengths that are particularly important for a neuropsychological examination. There are measures for understanding directions, verbal memory as well as naming that are also present in separate tests, but having them in one measure is helpful for the clinician. Strauss et al. (2006) found the validity of the cluster scores to not be established at this time, particularly for groups of individuals often seen in a neuropsychological practice.

Wechsler Individual Achievement Test-II (WIAT-II)

The Wechsler Individual Achievement Test-II (WIAT-II) was developed and linked with the WISC-IV. Linking intelligence and achievement tests on the same population decreases statistical and measurement error that may be present for tests that are not linked. The WIAT-II provides measures of reading, math, oral language, and written language. It was designed to identify children and adults with problems with achievement and has sufficient floor to do so. For gifted individuals there is not sufficient ceiling on some of the subtests, thus limiting how effective this measure is for high achieving individuals. Psychometric principles are reported to be sound with strong norms, easily administered measures and good materials (Strauss et al., 2006).

Although the Wide Range Achievement Test III (WRAT-III) is often used for screening purposes, these measures are not sufficient for diagnosing learning disabilities in children. The WJ-III or the WIAT-II should be included to fully assess the academic performance of children.

Executive Functioning

Executive functioning is a construct describing behaviors that are associated with skills in planning, cognitive flexibility, response inhibition, organization, and working memory (Semrud-Clikeman, 2007). They have been defined as "those capacities that enable a person to engage successfully in independent, purposive, self-serving behavior" (Lezak, Howieson, & Loring, 2004, p. 42). Barkley (2000) further defines executive functions as the "when or whether aspects of behavior, whereas nonexecutive functions involve the what or how" (p. 1065).

As such these skills are believed to be an integral part of a "supervisory" system that works to control behaviors and allows the individual to engage in goal-directed behaviors (Gioia, Isquith, Guy, & Kenworthy, 2000). In addition, these skills are particularly important when faced with a novel situation or problem which requires the development of appropriate strategies and solutions (Strauss et al., 2006). Difficulties in executive functioning generally are seen to be present in organizational problems, difficulties following through with tasks, prioritizing tasks, remembering what one was about to do or following directions (working memory) and in cognitive flexibility. These problematic areas often create difficulty in the school setting with completing assignments, having materials that are needed to finish a project, and with organizational skills in writing. In social settings they can translate into problems with sharing, taking turns in conversation and in play, and in having difficulty with inhibiting a response (i.e., saying the first thing that pops into one's head).

Executive functions have generally been associated with frontal lobe functioning. Patients who have frontal lobe damage often have difficulties with behavior regulation and response inhibition (Gazzaniga, Ivry, & Mangun, 2002). As described in Chapter 2, the frontal lobes are responsible for movement, planning, organization, and behavioral regulation. In addition, the frontal lobes play a major role in working memory skills. Working memory is the ability to retain information while solving a problem. A simple example of working memory is the ability to recall a phone number after looking it up in the phone book within the time it takes to reach the phone. Working memory is a skill that allows one to keep information for a short period of time in order to facilitate a task.

The ability to inhibit responding to a stimulus is an important skill that has also been associated with the frontal lobes. In order to inhibit a behavior one needs to establish control over the behavior. Such inhibition allows one to "filter" out extraneous stimuli in order to solve the problem at hand. For example, if you attend to all stimuli at the same time you can be easily overwhelmed. Inhibition includes a filter that allows one to attend to the most important aspect of a task and then complete it. When inhibition fails, working memory is affected; you get distracted, lose your place, and then forget what you were doing. Different neuronal networks activate to assist in inhibition and studies have found that these networks differentially activate, depending on the task at hand (Shimamura, 2000).

Goal-oriented behavior ability has also been linked to the frontal lobes (Gazzaniga et al., 2002). In order for a person to succeed at a goal the task generally needs to be broken down into smaller steps or behaviors that need to be completed before the overall goal can be obtained. For a child to succeed on an exam it is likely required that he complete the reading, have sufficient sleep and food, and be relaxed enough to think clearly. All of these aspects can be further broken down. People who are successful at completing tasks are able to prioritize these tasks, break down the steps that are needed to complete the tasks, and then see the task through to completion.

In addition to the frontal lobes, the anterior cingulate cortex (ACC) may be an executive attentional system; that is, it directs attention to the task at hand by marshalling various areas of the brain needed for the successful completion of the task. Thus, there are many connections between the ACC and other brain regions often accomplished by signals transported across long white matter tracks that connect the anterior and posterior systems of the brain (the superior longitudinal fasciculus, the inferior longitudinal fasciculus, and others). This system, when working properly, is highly efficient and provides coordination between knowledge and skills that have been previously learned and a problem that requires solving. Neuroimaging studies have found that the ACC is highly activated when the person is facing a difficult or novel situation or when behavior requires correcting or inhibiting (Posner & Rothbart, 2007).

One issue that is found in many neuropsychological reports is the erroneous use of the word "frontal lobe" tests. The tests that may measure executive functioning require many different regions of the brain to solve the issue, not just the frontal lobes. These tests have not been found to be diagnostic of a frontal lobe lesion, and to use the frontal lobe task synonymously with executive functioning is incorrect (Strauss et al., 2006).

Table 6.1 provides a listing of the major measures of executive functioning. These tests can be used with various aged children and most require additional training in order to correctly administer, score, and interpret.

Table 6.1 Common neuropsychological measures

Measure	Age range	Administration time	Tasks	Ability measured
Executive function tests				
Delis-Kaplan executive function system (Delis, Kaplan, & Kramer, 2001)	8–89	90 minutes for entire battery Subtests may be used separately	Child must connect letters and numbers as quickly as possible	Trails: visual scanning working memory, motor speed
			Child provides words in different categories quickly	Verbal Fluency: working memory, word retrieval
			Child copies figures as quickly as possible	Design Fluency: working memory, visual-motor
			Child reads words, colors, and then words printed in contrasting colors	Color-Word Interference: Response inhibition, cognitive flexibility
			Child is asked to sort objects using differing rules	Sorting: Problem-solving, concept formation, cognitive flexibility
			Child is asked to answer questions to figure out the answer	Twenty Questions: concepts, use of feedback
			Child must supply the word to fit the situation	Word context: Reasoning, abstraction
			Child must place rings on sticks with as few of moves as possible to match a model	Tower Test: Planning, response inhibition
			Child must tell what a proverb means	Proverb Test: higher order reasoning

Table 6.1 (continued)

Measure	Age range	Administration time	Tasks	Ability measured
Stroop test (Golden, 2003)	4–16	15 minutes		3 conditions Word reading: speed of reading Color reading: speed of color identification Color-Word reading: response inhibition
Verbal fluency (FAS)	7–90 +	5 minutes	Child provides words that begin with specific letters as quickly as possible. Other forms require categories such as fruit, furniture, etc.	Several forms available as well as contained in the DK-EFS, NEPSY, WJIII, and CELF-4 Measures word retrieval ability
Wisconsin card sorting test (Heaton, 2003)	5–89	25 minutes on average	Child must sort deck of cards to match one of 4 cards presented in some manner and is given immediate feedback	Measure of cognitive flexibility as well as working memory
Tower of Hanoi (Simon, 1975); Tower of London (Culbertson & Zillmer, 2000); Tower from NEPSY (Korkman, Kirk, & Kemp, 1997)	Various forms ages 7/8-adults	15 minutes on average	Child must place rings on pegs to match a model as quickly as possible following several rules	Measure of planning, cognitive flexibility
Behavior rating inventory of executive function (Gioia et al., 2000)	5–18	10–15 minutes	Parent and teacher provide ratings as to the child's behavior	Parent and Teacher Rating Forms: Factors are for behavioral regulation, emotional regulation, and metacognition (working memory, initiation, planning) Self-report (ages 11–22)

Attention

Measure	Age range	Administration time	Tasks	Ability measured
Brief test of attention (Schretelen, 1997)	6–14 Adult form also	10 minutes	Child must repeat numbers and letters and then must reorder the numbers and letters in order	Auditory divided attention
Children's color trails test (Llorente, Williams, Satz, & D'Elia, 2003)	8–16	10 minutes	Child must connect colors in alternating order (yellow and pink) for part A Part B requires the child to connect numbers 1–15 alternating between pink and yellow circles	Measures Attention, visual scanning, and working memory
Comprehensive trail making test (Reynolds, 2002)	8–75	5–10 minutes	5 conditions: connecting numbers 1–25; connecting numbers 1–25 with 29 empty circles as distractors;	Attention, visual scanning, visual processing speed, working memory

Table 6.1 (continued)

Measure	Age range	Administration time	Tasks	Ability measured
			same task with 2 types of distractors, connect Arabic numbers alternating with the written number word, connect numbers and letters in alternating form with 50 empty circles serving as distractors	
D2 Test of attention (Brickenkamp & Zillmer, 1998)	9–59	20 minutes	Child must quickly cross out all d's with 2 marks of any kind—each line is given 20 seconds and then the child is asked to move to the next one	Selective and sustained attention, visual scanning speed
Test of everyday attention for children (Manly, Robertson, Anderson, & Nimmo-Smith, 1999)	6–16	30–45 minutes	Several subtests that measure different aspects of attention	Selective, sustained, divided and alternating attention, cognitive flexibility
CHIPASAT (Johnson, Roethig-Johnson, & Middleton, 1988)	8–14	15–20 minutes	Instructions are on tape. The child is asked to add the numbers together that he/she hears. For example, 2 3 Answer is 5, next number is 1, answer is 4 (3 + 1) and so on	Divided attention, sustained attention, working memory, processing speed
PASAT (Diehr, Heaton, Miller, & Grant, 1998)	16–74	15–20 minutes	Same as CHIPASAT only more complex	Divided attention, sustained attention, working memory, processing speed
CPTs				
Conners' Continuous Performance Test (Conners, 2000)	6–55 +	14 minutes	Child must press the space bar to all stimuli except when X is shown	Measures sustained attention, inhibition, impulsivity and response speed
IVA + Plus (Sanford & Turner, 2004)	6–99	15 minutes per condition	Two stimuli are presented alternating between visual and auditory stimuli. The child must respond to the targets when they appear either visually or orally	Measures response control, attention, impulsivity, response speed. Has two conditions, auditory and visual
TOVA (Greenberg, Kindschi, & Corman, 2000)	4–80	22 minutes per condition	Child must push the button when the small square is at the top of the large square but not when it is at the bottom. For the auditory TOVA the child must respond to high tones but not low tones	Measures sustained attention, inhibition/ impulsivity, response speed and variability of responding. Has 2 conditions: auditory and visual

Table 6.1 (continued)

Measure	Age range	Administration time	Tasks	Ability measured
Language				
Auditory analysis test (Rosner & Simon, 1971)	5–12	8–10 minutes	Child repeats a word after deleting specific sounds (say the word belt without the 't').	Measures phonological processing and awareness—the ability to segment words and understand the sound structure of words
Comprehensive test of phonological processing (Wagner, Torgesen, & Rashotte, 1999)	5–24		Includes 13 measures including sound blending, sound matching, digit naming, repetition of words and nonwords, rapid color naming and segmenting words and nonwords	Used to identify children who have problems with phonological processing
				Provides scores in phonological awareness, phonological memory, and rapid naming.
Boston naming test-2 (Kaplan, Goodglass, & Weintraub, 2001)	5-adult	15 minutes	Child names a picture that is presented. The pictures increase in difficulty. If the name is not provided, a semantic cue is provided (it is something you eat). If still not successful a phonemic cue of the first letter is provided.	Measure of word knowledge, word retrieval and confrontational naming
Rapid automatized naming (Denckla & Rudel, 1974)			4 cards are presented with 50 stimuli on each card. Cards have colors, numbers, letters or objects. The child must quickly name the stimuli	The child's ability to name colors, letters, numbers and objects quickly has been tied to problems with reading as well as with attention. The test requires visual and verbal connections as well as processing speed
Peabody picture vocabulary test III (Dunn & Dunn, 1997)	2 ½–90 +	15 minutes	Child must chose a picture from 4 presented that most closely describes the examiner provided word	Measure of Receptive vocabulary—conormed with the Expressive Vocabulary test
Expressive vocabulary test (Williams, 1997)	2–90	10–12 minutes	The test has 38 labeling items and 152 questions requiring a synonym for a supplied word	Measure of expressive vocabulary as well as naming for the first 38 items
Expressive one-word picture vocabulary test-3 (Brownell, 2000a)	2–18	10–15 minutes	The child must verbalize a one-word response to a picture	Conormed with Receptive One-Word Picture Vocabulary Test-Third Edition
				Tests expressive ability as well as naming skill

Table 6.1 (continued)

Measure	Age range	Administration time	Tasks	Ability measured
Receptive one-word picture vocabulary test-3 (Brownell, 2000b)	2–18	10–15 minutes	The examiner orally presents a stimulus word, and the examinee must identify the illustration that depicts the meaning of the word	Conormed with the EOWPT-3 it provides a measure of receptive language as well as listening comprehension
Token test (De Renzi & Vignolo, 1978)	2-adult	10–15 minutes	The child is asked to point to different colored disks of various shapes. The examiner asks the child to follow increasingly more difficult directions. (show me a circle; show me the yellow square, etc.	This is a measure of listening comprehension, working memory, concepts, and attention
Clinical evaluation of language fundamentals-4 (Semel, Wiig, & Secord, 2003)	5–21	30–60 minutes	There are several subtests to measure various aspects of language. The receptive tests require the child to repeat sentences, answer a question about a read paragraph, chose pictures that represent the same category, and select a picture that tells about a sentence. The expressive tests require the child to formulate sentences from presented words, define words, assemble a grammatically appropriate sentence, and relate two similar words	This test provides information as to how well the child is able to understand and recall information, express him or herself, and to hold information in mind while solving a problem
Preschool language scle-3	Birth-6	20–45 minutes	Child is asked to point to pictures, name pictures, and follow directions	Provides a measure of expressive, receptive, and total language ability in preschool children
Memory				
California verbal learning test-children's version (Delis et al., 1994)	4–16	15–20 minutes	Child is asked to repeat a list of words from memory. The list is read 5 times and the child repeats the list after each reading. Then a distractor list of words is read. 20 minutes later the child is asked to recall the list read 5 times first	Provides a measure of learning initially and over trials. Also provides a measure of the child's response to cues as well as recognition ability. Measures are for initial recall, delayed recall, learning slope and for recognition. In

Table 6.1 (continued)

Measure	Age range	Administration time	Tasks	Ability measured
			without a cue and then with a cue. After that he/she is asked to recognize the words from the first list from a longer list of words	addition, measures are provided as to the strategy the child used to recall the words—serial versus semantic
Rey auditory verbal learning test (Bishop, Knights, & Stoddart, 1990)	6–89	10–15 minutes	15 words are provided to the child and the child is asked to recall as many as possible with 4 additional trials provided. A distractor list is then read. Free recall of the first list is then required and 30 minutes later another recall of this list	This test provides information as to how the child learns with information repeated. In addition, it provides a measure of learning and of delayed recall. It has been reported to be simpler than the CVLT-CR (Bishop et al., 1990)
Children's memory scale (Cohen, 1997)	5–16	30–45 minutes	There are several subtests on the CMS. The child is asked to recall stories, word pairs and word lists (auditory/verbal). Also to recall spatial location, recognize human faces, and recall pictured scenes (visual/nonverbal). Finally there are measures of digit span, recall of information (reciting the days of the week backwards) and recalling where pictures are on a page once it is removed (attention/concentration)	The rest provides measures of general memory. In addition there are measures of immediate and delayed verbal memory, immediate and delayed visual memory, learning, and attention/concentration
Test of memory and learning-2 (Reynolds & Voress, 2007)	5–60	30 minutes for core; 60 minutes for core and supplementary	Test has several subtests including memory for stories, facial memory, word selective reminding, visual selective reminding, object recall, abstract visual memory, digits forward, visual sequential memory, paired recall, memory for location, manual imitation, letters forward, digits backward, and letters backward	This test provides measures of verbal memory, nonverbal memory, and a composite memory. The supplementary battery provides measures that tap the child's ability to recall information after a delay, a learning index, an attention/concentration index, and a free recall index. There is also an index for recalling information when provided a cue

Table 6.1 (continued)

Measure	Age range	Administration time	Tasks	Ability measured
Wide range assessment of memory and learning-2nd edition (Sheslow & Adams, 2005)	5–90	Core Battery requires less than one hour; screening battery requires		
Wechsler memory scale III (Wechsler, 1997)	16–89	30–35 minutes	Provides measures of the adolescent's ability to listen and retell stories, recall pairs of words, complete letter-number sequencing, learn word lists, mental control (count backwards from 100 by 7, say the alphabet from Z to A, etc.) provide general information and orientation, reproduce designs from memory, reproduce a sequence of moves based on an examiner provided model, and repeat digits	This test provides measures of auditory and visual immediate memory, an index of working memory, and delayed recall memory that contributes to a general memory score
Visual perception				
Judgment of line orientation (Benton, Varney, & Hamsher, 1978)	7–96	15–20	Child views an array of lines and then must match 2 lines to the correct lines in the array	This test measures visual perception without a motor component
Facial recognition test (Benton, Sivan, Hamsher, Varney, & Spreen, 2004)	6- adult	Long form 10 to15 minutes; short form 7 to 10 minutes	Child is shown a face(s) and then must recall the face when shown an array of faces	This test measures the child's ability to recall unfamiliar faces
Hooper visual orientation test (Hooper, 1958)	5–91	Long Form 10 to 15 minutes	Child is shown drawings which are cut into 2 or more pieces. He/she is asked to name the object. Norms were updated in 1994(Seidel, 1994)	This is a measure of spatial relations—the ability of the child to put together pieces of a picture to form a whole. It also requires working memory
		Short form: less than 10 minutes		
Motor free visual perception test-3 (Colarusso & Hammill, 2002)	4–95	25 minutes	Child is asked to match figures, find figures that are hidden, identify figures that are incompletely drawn, recall visual information, and discriminate forms	This is a measure of visual perception that utilizes different modalities to evaluate the child's perceptual skills. It does not include a motor component so it is good for children

Table 6.1 (continued)

Measure	Age range	Administration time	Tasks	Ability measured
				with significant motor difficulties to determine whether perceptual problems exist
Test of visual-perceptual skills-3 (Martin, 2002)	4–19	30–40 minutes	Child must discriminate forms, recall what has been seen, look at pictures that have been cut apart and determine how they would look if reassembled, recall what has been seen in the same order, and complete incomplete figures	This is a measure of visual perception without motor involvement. It works with preschoolers as well as older children with motor difficulties as a measure of visual perception
Visual-motor				
Beery developmental test of visual-motor integration (Beery, Buktenica, & Beery, 2006)	3–18	30 minutes for whole battery	The child is asked to trace a stimulus form with a pencil without going outside of the lines, to choose which of 3 forms are identical to the stimulus, and to copy 24 increasingly more complex geometric forms	This is a measure of motor coordination, visual perception, and visual-motor skills
Wide range assessment of visual-vmotor abilities (Adams & Sheslow, 2005)	3–17	4–10 minutes per subtest	The child is asked to copy figures of increasing complexity. The child is also asked to match pictures and to complete a pegboard	This is an omnibus measure of visual perception as well as visual-motor ability.
Developmental test of visual perception-2	4–10	45 minutes	The child is asked to put pegs in a board as quickly as possible, to copy figures, to show eye-hand coordination, to understand position in space, to find hidden figures, and to identify pictures that are incompletely drawn	This is an omnibus measure of visual perception, eye-hand coordination, visual-motor ability, and understanding of spatial relations
Rey-Osterreith complex figure (Meyers & Meyers, 1995)	6–93	10–15 minutes	Child is asked to copy a complex figure, then draw it within 3 minutes from memory, and then draw it again 30 minutes later	This is a measure of visual-spatial skills as well as organization and planning. As the child draws the figure it is important for the examiner to evaluate the order drawn (i.e., does the child draw the overarching parts of the figure or start with details)

Table 6.1 (continued)

Measure	Age range	Administration time	Tasks	Ability measured
Motor				
Finger tapping (Reitan, 1969)	5–85	10 minutes	Child is asked to tap on a tapper as quickly as possible with each hand	This is a measure of finger speed. It is generally expected that the dominant hand will be faster but unless there is a highly significant difference across measures, this is not diagnostic
Grip strength (Reitan & Wolfson, 1985)	6–85	5 minutes	The child is asked to squeeze a dynamometer as hard as he/she can	This is a measure of strength. Again it is expected that the dominant hand will be stronger but unless there is a highly significant difference across measures, this is not diagnostic
Grooved pegboard (Matthews & Klove, 1964)	6–85	5 minutes	The child is asked to place pegs in a pegboard with each hand as quickly as possible. The pegs only fit in the holes one way	This is a measure of manual dexterity and motor speed
Purdue pegboard (Tiffin, 1968)	5–89	5 minutes	The child must place the pegs in holes as quickly as possible first with his/her dominant hand, then nondominant hand, then both hands together	This is a measure of fine motor dexterity and motor speed. It is also a measure of how well the child can coordinate hands

Attention

Attention is a construct that can be very difficult to define. It includes the ability to sustain attention, to selectively attend to a specific stimulus, to divide one's attention among two or more items, and to alternate attention. Memory and attention are related in that if you don't pay attention to an item, you generally will not recall that item. We have a limited capacity for attention and thus can become overwhelmed when too much is asked at one time. When the capacity is overloaded, some people will shut down while others will become agitated and overstimulated. The brain has the ability to prevent this from happening through filtering of stimuli (generally thought to be a thalamic-cortical process). When such filtering is not operational, you may see attentional deficits for some individuals (ADHD) while others will show agitation or experience actual pain from being overwhelmed (autistic spectrum disorder).

Children and adolescents with ADHD may show difficulties in one or more areas of attention. Some believe that children with ADHD: combined subtype show problems in selective and sustained attention while those with ADHD: predominately inattentive type show problems with overfocusing or with sustained attention (Barkley, 1997). Complicating the picture, most tests that measure attention will often evaluate more than one aspect of attention, as well as executive functions such as working memory and response inhibition. Strauss et al. (2006) argued that many tests are a combination of attention and executive functioning and that the differentiation between tests of executive functioning and attention is artificial.

Attention is believed to require several areas for processing depending on the task at hand. For visual attention, the occipital lobe has been implicated while the parietal lobe works with the occipital for visual-spatial analysis. Attention to auditory stimuli requires the temporal lobe, particularly in the language centers of the brain. Coordination of these systems appears to be an important function of the ACC, the frontal cortex, and subcortical structures such as the basal ganglia and the thalamus.

Imaging work with children with ADHD has found that the caudate, a structure important for dopamine production, differs in volume depending on diagnosis (ADHD vs. non-ADHD) (Liotti, Pliszka, Perez, Glahn, & Semrud-Clikeman, in press; Pliszka et al., 2006) and medication status (treated vs. non-treated) (Semrud-Clikeman, Pliszka, Lancaster, & Liotti, 2006). Such variations in structure may also be related to differences in neuropsychological functioning on measures of attention and executive functions (Semrud-Clikeman, Pliszka, & Liotti, in press). It is believed the commonly prescribed stimulant medications work on the subcortical as well as frontal lobe regions to normalize neurotransmitters and activity level in these regions (Pliszka, 2003).

Attention is also an area that is highly susceptible to damage. Many children and adolescents with traumatic brain injury experience significant problems with attention in the early stages of recovery (Semrud-Clikeman, 2004). For some children, particularly those with severe head injuries, the attentional problems continue following recovery. Children with seizure disorders, those with long-term effects from cancer treatment, and those with several genetic disorders (neurofibromatosis, tuberous sclerosis, etc.) also show attentional problems (Semrud-Clikeman, 2007).

Table 6.1 lists the major attentional tasks most frequently utilized with children. There are four basic types of attention evaluation. The first type is a structured interview with the parent to determine the presence of sufficient symptoms to warrant a diagnosis of ADHD. The second are parent and teacher behavior rating scales. These scales are generally utilized to determine the presence of symptoms, and how the child compares to others his/her age in severity and frequency of the symptoms. Some of the measures are designed to solely measure attentional skills (i.e., Connor's or Brown's

ADHD scales) while others are omnibus measures such as the BASC or CBCL.

The third type uses computerized measures. These tests require the child to select a target from other targets and provide measures of attention, inhibition, reaction time, and variability of response. The child's performance is compared to others his/her age as well as to a sample of children with ADHD. Finally, there are paper and pencil measures that directly evaluate the child's skills on selective, sustained, and divided attention. Other measures of attention are present in most of the ability measures, as well as in some of the memory skills. As cautioned by Strauss et al. (2006), measures that are not solely designed to evaluate a child's attentional skills may be one-dimensional and, thus, will not fully evaluate the child's ability. It is strongly suggested that a neuropsychological evaluation include measures of attention as well as a good interview and the use of behavior rating scales to provide a full picture of the child's functioning.

Memory

Memory and learning go hand in hand. Learning is acquiring new information while memory is retrieving this information for later use (Gazzaniga et al., 2002). In order to remember an item it must first be encoded, then stored, and then available for retrieval to be used. At any point, difficulty may occur and cause problems with learning and, hence, memory. As mentioned in the attention section, attention is an important aspect in memory—if something isn't paid attention to, it will not be stored.

There are various forms of memory. The fastest type of memory is sensory memory—this is when you are looking, hearing, or feeling something and you are processing it in milliseconds to seconds. Sensory memory is not stored—it is registered by the brain without processing. Short-term memory is information that is stored for just a few minutes and is also not placed into permanent memory stores. Working memory and short-term memory are related constructs. For items that may be later stored, the initial input is through short-term memory. Not all information is converted into long-term memory—it depends on the nature of the information as well as the goals of the individual. A phone number that is used only once is unlikely to be stored while one that is needed several times will eventually be stored in long-term memory.

Baddeley (2003) has a model of working memory where there are three parts that interact depending on the task at hand. The phonological (articulatory) loop processes speech-based material while the visual-spatial sketchpad stores visual information. These are controlled by the central executive that controls these inputs. Finally there is an episodic buffer that integrates the information. This is basically a limited-capacity memory and attentional system that helps with strategy selection as well as coordination of higher order cognitive processing. Digit Span from the Wechsler measures is an example of the phonological loop working memory, while spatial memory from the TOMAL (Reynolds & Bigler, 1994) is an example of the visual sketchpad form of working memory.

Long-term memory is generally divided into implicit (unconscious/procedural) and explicit (language/situational) memory (Schacter, Wagner, & Buckner, 2000). A typical task for implicit memory is the ability to read words from incomplete fragments (s _ oe = shoe). This task requires the person to make the connection between a word that has been previously seen and fill in the blank. These are skills that have been previously learned but are now applied to a new situation. Some subtests of the WJ Cognitive III battery test this skill. Explicit memory is generally learning new information and then later queried as to these words. An example would be the California Verbal Learning Test-Children's Version (CVLT-C) (Delis, Kramer, Kaplan, & Ober, 1994) where the person is asked to learn a list of words over five trials and then later queried as to how many he/she can remember. Most neuropsychological measures tap explicit memory but not implicit memory. It is recommended to include both types in a comprehensive neuropsychological evaluation. Table 6.1 provides a sampling of memory tasks.

Areas of the brain that have been implicated in memory are widespread and dependent on the type of memory that is being tapped. The initial sensory memory includes the hardwired areas of the brain that receive visual (occipital), auditory (temporal), tactile, or kinesthetic (parietal) information. Working memory has been linked to systems in the dorsolateral regions of the frontal lobes for monitoring of the information, and the ventrolateral regions for maintaining the information (Schacter et al., 2000). In addition, the limbic system may be active in the transfer of experiences into memory with the emotional coloring that is attached to such memories and to language (Markowitsch, 2000). The left hemisphere has been implicated in retrieval of language and facts while the right is important for episodic and social interaction memory (Markowitsch, 2000).

Long-term memory requires a consolidation of information. Such consolidation is a chemical process that can take place over hours, days, or months and lays down neural traces of the memory for later retrieval (Moscovitch et al., 2005). The localization for this process for storage of explicit memory items begins in the hippocampus and then storage occurs throughout the brain; somewhat like files in a storage cabinet that can be accessed as needed (Nadel, Samsonovich, Ryan, & Moscovitch, 2000). Moscovitch (2004) suggests that this process is automatic and requires hippocampal involvement even for retrieval of previously learned material. He further hypothesizes that the frontal lobes work in concert with the hippocampus in the selection of what memories are retrieved and subsequently organized into information. In this view the frontal lobes basically organize and control the information and mediate memories brought to mind by the hippocampus and thalamic nuclei involved in the initial laying down of these memories.

Implicit memory is believed to be related to what the task involves. For perceptual tasks the brain regions responsible for processing of these skills are generally in the parietal and occipital lobes. When language is also present, then the temporal lobes are brought into the loop. The recall of the word horse can be done through perceptual priming (a picture of the horse) as well as through the language connection of the picture to the word.

Many of these higher level cognitive processes overlap and are linked and are a challenge for the neuropsychologist to separate (if possible) areas of strength and weakness. Memory tests are sometimes difficult to interpret due to interference with attention, and at times with language. The following section briefly discusses language from a neuropsychological viewpoint.

Language

Language involves precepts that include spoken (expressive) and listening (receptive) aspects as well as the ability to name objects. Expressive language involves that which one uses to communicate to another person or to oneself. Receptive language is the ability to listen, comprehend, and appropriately form a response. The basic part of language is the word. These words are stored in the brain in what has been termed a mental lexicon. This lexicon includes the word's meaning as well as the sound, spelling, and usage of the word. It has been estimated that the average adult has 5,000 words in his/her lexicon and can understand two to three times more than that. This lexicon, to be usable, needs to be organized and efficient. Thus, words that are frequently used are stored in an area that is more accessible while those that are more unusual may not be as readily available.

Each word is also made up of phonemes—small units of sound such as the sounds for the letters m and n. These sounds are characteristic of a particular language and will change depending on the language and culture of the user. Theorists have suggested that the lexicon is arranged not by letter or sounds like the dictionary, but by information-specific networks (Levelt, Roelofs, & Meyer, 1999). These networks are organized through the relationship of the words to each other as well as sound families. Words such as freight and eight rhyme, have similar sounds and would be arranged near to each other on a conceptual node, but not directly to each other as they mean very different things. When learning words, those that sound similar also assist in learning as well as words that are in the same category. The pair of raccoon and acorn is a bit easier to recall than clown and truck for this reason. Many measures of memory also have these pairs together and are confounded by language difficulties when these problems arise.

Expressive language uses many of these phonemes and acoustic signals to communicate to others. The area of the brain most implicated with expressive language is also called Broca's area. This region lies in the ventral lateral left frontal cortex in an area known as pars triangularis and pars opercularis. When a patient has a lesion in this area and the underlying white matter, problems are seen in pronunciation of words (also referred to as Broca's aphasia). Their language is very difficult to understand and often sounds like gibberish.

Listening comprehension and receptive language requires decoding of the aural signal. This signal is then translated into a phonological code that has previously been stored in the mental lexicon. This information is then decoded into the word and subsequently the meaning of the word. Reading also involves these steps as the reader must analyze the word's sound to understand what the word is saying. Perceptually the reader first utilizes the visual system (discussed in Chapter 2), the auditory system, and then the lexical system. The listener has another challenge because there is no visual feedback, so words that may be pronounced similarly require the listener to decipher the meaning based on context. Words such as lettuce and let us are very different but when slurred together can sound remarkably the same. Speech rhythm and pitch as well as intonation generally help the listener to discern what is being said. Prosody, another terms for speech intonation, is an important communication device to assist in understanding the speaker's intent.

Structures that are important for receptive language lie in the region of the temporal lobe also frequently referred to as Wernicke's area. This area is generally in the superior temporal gyrus and near the auditory processing regions surrounding the lateral sulcus. Studies have found that for true difficulties in this area (also called Wernicke's aphasia) damage must be present in these regions as well as in the posterior temporal lobe or in the white matter that connects Wernicke's area to the other language areas. Patients with these kinds of difficulties generally have problems with language comprehension either from the spoken or written language (also referred to as Wernicke's aphasia). They can speak fluently, but often their speech is meaningless.

In situations where damage is present to the connections between Wernicke's and Broca's areas, problems are seen in speech production as well as in word repetition and word usage (Gazzaniga et al., 2002). This difficulty is referred to as conduction aphasia. In this case, the patient is able to understand and produce language, but has difficulty with repeating words and word usage.

Naming ability is another important aspect of language. Children with learning problems as well as language difficulties may experience problems in naming objects. Some tests provide phonetic prompts to assist the child in word retrieval while others provide pictures or semantic prompts. Naming is a skill that can be affected by traumatic brain injury, brain tumors/cancer, or learning problems to name a few areas. At times word retrieval problems can be identified through awareness of how the child completes the Picture Completion subtest of the WISC III. In this case, the child may be able to point at what is missing but not supply the name. Additional testing of these skills is certainly warranted when the examiner finds the child unable to complete these types of tasks.

Measures of language functioning often include receptive and expressive language as well as naming ability. For children and adolescents, unless there is a direct brain insult or a stroke, aphasia is not frequently seen. However, difficulties in receptive and expressive language can pose significant problems for many children and have been related to difficulties with learning. Chapter 12 discusses these issues in more detail. Table 6.1 lists the major measures of receptive and expressive language and many of these are utilized by speech pathologists as well as by psychologists.

Motor Abilities

Tests of motor ability are important to determine how well the child can complete tasks evaluating his/her motor speed, motor coordination, and strength. Comprehensive neuropsychological examinations need to include a screening of motor abilities ranging from simple motor speed to more complex measures involving pegboards. These skills are also related to visual-motor abilities which are described in the next section.

Motor tasks generally evaluate the child's ability to use his/her preferred (or dominant) hand as well as working with both hands together. Tapping tests measure the child's ability to quickly tap on a board while pegboards measure the child's ability to quickly put pegs in first with the dominant hand, then the nondominant, and

for some tests, with both hands together. These tests are generally quick to administer and many children enjoy them. They can be used as an icebreaker particularly with a reluctant or shy child. Motor skills are important for daily living skills such as buttoning and tying as well as for feeding and taking care of one's needs. Table 6.1 lists the main motor tasks.

Visual-Spatial and Visual-Motor

Tests of visual-motor ability are important parts of a neuropsychological assessment. These tests allow the examiner to determine whether difficulties in perception or an integration of motor and perception are creating difficulties in the child's ability to put items together or to copy figures or complete a handwriting task. Visual-motor tasks require integration between what is seen and how it is represented.

There are two systems are involved in visual perception. The inferior longitudinal fasciculus (ILF) carries information as to "what" the object is named. This pathway runs from the visual region of the brain to the naming areas of the brain in the temporal lobe. The "where" pathway connects the visual regions of the brain to the parietal lobe via the superior longitudinal fasciculus (SLF). Some children experience difficulties with naming (discussed earlier in the language section), while others have difficulty understanding objects in space as well as being able to copy these objects appropriately. Problems with spatial analysis can be seen in the child's ability to complete the block design task or other tasks that require spatial analysis. Table 6.1 lists the main tests used to evaluate perceptual abilities.

In addition to visual perceptual tasks, children are often asked to copy figures in order to understand how they are able to translate visual information into written form. For these types of tests there is integration between visual perception and motor skills. The previous section discussed some of the main motor tasks. For an assessment, it is often good to attempt to sort out the differing types of skills contained within a task that are visual-motor in nature. If a child experiences problems on visual-motor tasks, one must rule out the contributions of motor difficulty as well as perceptual problems. Children may experience integration of these skills and these problems may be related to integrated difficulties as well as executive functions of planning and organization (Baron, 2004). If perceptual and/or motor problems are ruled out and the child continues to experience problems with copying and handwriting, then analysis of the child's executive functioning as well as integration abilities needs to be evaluated.

Psychosocial Functioning

Assessing a child's psychosocial adjustment is best accomplished using behavioral rating scales, clinical interviews, and observational techniques. These techniques are useful to determine comorbid psychiatric problems and to rule out other disorders that may result in reasoning, problem solving, and social interaction difficulties that affect overall adjustment and impact on treatment plans. Clinicians may opt to start with instruments that measure broad-band personality disorders, and then utilize tests designed for specific problems such as ADHD, depression, and/or anxiety. Several instruments will be described briefly.

Child Behavior Checklist (CBL)

The Child Behavior Checklist (CBCL) is a well-developed, psychometrically sound instrument measuring two broad-band personality syndromes: externalizing and internalizing disorders (Achenbach, 1991). The CBCL can be used for children and adolescents across a wide age range (6–18 years) and includes rating scales for parents and teachers and a self-report form for older children (Achenbach, 1991). Structured Interview and Observation forms have also been developed for the CBCL. Externalizing disorders measured by the CBCL include aggressive, hyperactive, schizoid, delinquent, and sex problems. Internalizing disorders comprise depressive, anxious, and social withdrawal problems. Teacher ratings are highly correlated with observations of the child, and parent ratings are associated with other well-established measures of behavior problems (Achenbach & McConaughy, 2003). The CBCL offers a comprehensive method for obtaining data from a variety of sources to identify comorbid personality disorders in children and adolescents.

Behavior Assessment System for Children

The Behavior Assessment System for Children-2 (BASC-2) (Reynolds & Kamphaus, 2004) was developed as a "multimethod, multidimensional approach to evaluating the behavior and self-perceptions of children aged 4–18 years" (Reynolds & Kamphaus, 2004, p. 1). The BASC-2 includes five methods for assessing the child's behavior:

1. A self-report for children aged 8–18 years, which allows the child to answer "true" or "false" to questions about feelings and perceptions of the self and of others
2. A teacher behavioral rating scale
3. A parent behavioral rating scale
4. A structured developmental history that can be used as an interview or questionnaire format
5. A system for systematically observing and recording the child's behavior

The BASC-2 measures both adaptive and clinical dimensions of the child's behavior. The wording on the BASC-2 rates observable behavior, thus decreasing subjectivity on the part of the rater. The system measures the child's behavioral and emotional functioning from a variety of sources to provide a more comprehensive picture of the total child. The BASC-2 is not intended to provide a diagnosis, placement decision, or treatment plan. It is, rather, designed to compile information about the child's behavior from many sources and to help design and determine the most appropriate intervention. The BASC can provide useful data to be used as a follow-up for further interviews and evaluation.

Social Skills Questionnaire

Social Responsiveness Scale (Constantino, 2002) Rutter, Bailey, and Lord (2003) developed the Social

Responsiveness Scale to systematically measure social skills problems in children and adolescents. The SRS contains rating scales for parents, and teachers, and provides a method for determining the child's social interaction skills, social awareness, reciprocal social communication ability degree of avoidance of social situations, and preoccupations that are present. It is appropriate for ages 4 to 18. This is a relatively new instrument and may prove to be a valuable addition to a comprehensive evaluation of child and adolescent disorders. Particularly in the areas of autism and Asperger's disorder. This scale provides a measure of the degree of impairment across numerous items. It also provides the ability to measure severity of the disorder. There are 5 scales in addition to the Total score that are included in this scale; receptive, cognitive, expression and motivational aspects of social behavior are included as well as the level of preoccupation the child shows to objects or topics that may interfere with social functioning. Ratings are not only provided for the two settings (school and home) but are also divided by gender.

Social Communication Questionnaire

The Social Communication Questionnaire (SCQ) (Rutter, Bailey, & Lord, 2003) is a parent report measure that evaluates the possible presence of autistic spectrum behaviors. This measure can be used to screen out the possibility of autistic spectrum disorders. Positive scores indicate that a further evaluation is necessary. The SCQ was designed as a screening tool that is followed up by the Autism Diagnostic Interview-Revised (ADI-R) (Rutter, Le Couteur, & Lord, 2003). The age range for the SCQ is from four years of age to adulthood and has two forms: lifetime and current. The lifetime form should be used if the measure is for screening while the current form should be used to measure therapeutic progress.

The items are designed to reflect the items on the ADI-R that were most predictive of an ASD diagnosis. This measure utilizes a cut-off score of 15. The SCQ is sensitive to social communication problems and, emerging research suggests, children with ADHD, LD, and other types of neurodevelopmental disorders. For this reason the measure may be very helpful in designing treatment plans for children that have social difficulties.

Conclusion

While this chapter cannot possibly provide a guide for every test that may be used in a neuropsychological examination, the major ones that are used in several clinics with which we have worked are discussed or presented in the table. It is important to provide a screening of the major areas in a neuropsychological exam at the very least and to follow-up the screening with a more intensive evaluation when difficulties are identified. The main domains include cognitive, academic, executive functioning/attention, memory, perceptual/sensory/motor, and social and emotional functioning. A good neuropsychologist has a very good psychological background and provides a link between the two areas. Given that many neurological problems have psychiatric consequences, as well as some masquerading as psychiatric diagnosis, it is important for the neuropsychologist to be aware of this duality particularly when working with significantly complex cases.

The next chapter discusses three main approaches to neuropsychological assessment. One of these approaches uses a set battery such as in the Reitan Neuropsychological Battery. The Austin Neuropsychological System and the Boston Process system use a combination of measures to evaluate children and adolescents.

References

Achenbach, T. M. (1991). *Manual for the child behavior checklist and revised child behavior profile.* Burlington, VT: T.M. Achenbach.

Achenbach, T. M., & McConaughy, S. H. (2003). The Achenbach system of empirically based assessment. In C. R. Reynolds & R. W. Kamphaus (Eds.), *Handbook of psychological and educational assessment of children: Personality, behavior, and context* (Vol. 2, pp. 406–432). New York: Guilford Press.

Adams, W., & Sheslow, D. (2005). *Wide range assessment of visual-motor abilities.* Odessa, FL: PAR.

Baddeley, A. D. (2003). Working memory: Looking back and looking forward. *Nature Reviews: Neuroscience, 4,* 829–839.

Barkley, R. A. (1997). Behavioral inhibition, sustained attention, and executive functions: Constructing a unifying theory of ADHD. *Psychological Bulletin, 121,* 65–94.

Barkley, R. A. (2000). Genetics of childhood disorders: XVII. ADHD, Part 1: The executive functions and ADHD. *Journal of the American Academy of Child & Adolescent Psychiatry, 39*(8), 1064–1068.

Baron, I. S. (2004). *Neuropsychological evaluation of the child.* New York: Oxford University Press.

Beery, K. E., Buktenica, N. A., & Beery, N. A. (2006). *Developmental test of visual-motor integration-5.* San Antonio: Pearson.

Benton, A. L., Sivan, A. B., Hamsher, K., Varney, N. R., & Spreen, O. (2004). *Contributions to neuropsychological assessment: A clinical manual* (2nd ed.). New York: Oxford University Press.

Benton, A. L., Varney, N. R., & Hamsher, K. (1978). Visuospatial judgment: A clinical test. *Archives of Neurology, 35,* 364–367.

Bishop, E. G., Knights, R. M., & Stoddart, C. (1990). Rey Auditory-Verbal Learning Test: Performance of English and French children aged 5 to 16. *The Clinical Neuropsychologist, 5,* 125–142.

Brickenkamp, R., & Zillmer, E. A. (1998). *d2 test of attention.* Seattle, WA: Hogrefe and Huber Publishers.

Brownell, R. (2000a). *Expressive one-word picture vocabulary test-III.* Novato, CA: Academic Therapy Publications.

Brownell, R. (2000b). *Receptive one-word picture vocabulary.* Novato, CA: Academic Therapy Publications.

Cattell, R. B., & Horn, J. L. (1978). A check on the theory of fluid and crystallized intelligence with description of new subtest designs. *Journal of Educational Measurement, 15,* 139–164.

Cohen, M. S. (1997). *Children's memory scale.* San Antonio, TX: Harcourt Publishing Company.

Colarusso, R. R., & Hammill, D. D. (2002). *Motor free visual perception test-3.* Austin, TX: Pro-Ed.

Conners, C. K. (2000). *Conners' continuous performance test (CPT III) computer programs for Windows technical guide and software manual.* North Tonawanda, NY: Multi-Health Systems, Inc.

Constantino, J. N. (2002). *The Social Responsiveness Scale.* Los Angeles, CA: Western Psychological Services.

Culbertson, W. C., & Zillmer, E. A. (2000). *Tower of London-Drexel University.* Chicago, IL: Multi-Health Systems Inc.

De Renzi, E., & Vignolo, L. (1978). Development of a shortened version of the Token Test. *Cortex, 14,* 41–49.

Delis, D. C., Kaplan, E., & Kramer, J. H. (2001). *Delis-Kaplan executive functioning system: Examiner's manual.* San Antonio, TX: the Psychological Corporation.

Delis, D. C., Kramer, J. H., Kaplan, E., & Ober, B. A. (1994). *California verbal learning test-children's version.* Bloomington, MN: Pearson Assessments.

Denckla, M. B., & Rudel, R. (1974). Rapid "automatized" naming of pictured objects, colors, letters, and numbers by normal children. *Cortex, 10,* 186–202.

Diehr, M. C., Heaton, R. K., Miller, W., & Grant, W. (1998). Paced Auditory Serial Addition Task (PASAT): Norms for age, education and ethnicity. *Assessment, 5,* 375–387.

Dunn, L. M., & Dunn, L. M. (1997). *Examiner's manual for the Peabody picture vocabulary test* (3rd ed.). Circle Pines, MN: American Guidance Service.

Elliott, C. D. (2007). *Differential abilities scale II.* San Antonio, TX: Pearson Education, Inc.

Gazzaniga, M. S., Ivry, R. B., & Mangun, G. R. (2002). *Cognitive neuroscience: the biology of the mind* (2nd ed.). New York: W.W. Norton & Company.

Gibney, L. A., McIntosh, D. E., Dean, R. S., & Dunham, M. (2002). Diagnosing attention disorder with measures of neurocognitive functioning. *International Journal of Neuroscience, 112,* 539–564.

Gioia, G. A., Isquith, P. K., Guy, S. C., & Kenworthy, L. (2000). *BRIEF: Behavior rating inventory of executive function professional manual.* Lutz, FL: PAR.

Golden, C. J. (2003). *Stroop color and word test children's version for ages 5–14.* Wood Date, IL: Stoelting Company.

Greenberg, L. M., Kindschi, C. L., & Corman, C. M. (2000). *Test of variables of attention: Clinical guide.* Los Alamitos, CA: Universal Attention Disorders.

Heaton, R. K. (2003). *Wisconsin card sorting test: Computer version* (4th ed.). Austin, TX: The Psychological Corporation, Inc.

Hooper, H. E. (1958). *The Hooper visual organization test.* Beverly Hills, CA: Western Psychological Services.

Johnson, S. K., Roethig-Johnson, K., & Middleton, J. (1988). Development and evaluation of an attentional test for head-injured children: 1. Information processing capacity in a normal sample. *Journal of Child Psychology and Psychiatry, 2,* 199–208.

Kaplan, E., Goodglass, H., & Weintraub, S. (2001). *Boston naming test* (2nd ed.). Philadelphia, PA: Lea & Febiger.

Kaufman, A. S., & Kaufman, N. L. (1983). *Kaufman assessment battery for children.* Circle Pines, MN: American Guidance System.

Kaufman, A. S., & Kaufman, N. L. (2004). *Kaufman assessment battery for children-2.* Circle Pines, Mn: American Guidance Service.

Korkman, M., Kirk, S., & Kirk, U. (2007). *NEPSY II.* San Antonio: Pearson.

Korkman, M., Kirk, U., & Kemp, S. (1997). *NEPSY: A developmental neuropsychological assessment.* San Antonio: The Psychological Corporation.

Levelt, W. J. M., Roelofs, A., & Meyer, A. S. (1999). A theory of lexical access in speech production. *Behavioral Brain Science, 22,* 1–75.

Lezak, M. D., Howieson, D. B., & Loring, D. W. (2004). *Neuropsychological assessment* (4th ed.). New York: Oxford University Press.

Liotti, M., Pliszka, S. R., Perez, R., Glahn, D. C., & Semrud-Clikeman, M. (in press). Electrophysiological correlates of response inhibition in children and adolescents with ADHD: Influence of gender, age, and previous treatment history. *Psychophysiology, 143B,* 936–948.

Llorente, A. M., Williams, J., Satz, P., & D'Elia, L. F. (2003). Children's color trains test (CCTT). In. Odessa, FL: Psychological Assessment Resources.

Manly, T., Robertson, I. H., Anderson, V., & Nimmo-Smith, I. (1999). *TEA-Ch: the test of everyday attention for children.* Bury St. Edmunds, England: Thames Valley Test Company.

Markowitsch, H. J. (2000). Neuroanatomy of memory. In E. Tulving & F. I. M. Craik (Eds.), *The Oxford book of memory* (pp. 465–484). New York: Oxford University Press.

Martin, N. A. (2002). *Test of visual-perceptual skills-3*. Austin, TX: Pro-Ed.

Matthews, C. G., & Klove, K. (1964). *Instruction manual for the adult neuropsychology test battery*. Madison, WI: University of Wisconsin Medical School.

McIntosh, D. E., & Gridley, B. E. (1993). Differential ability scales: Profiles of learning-disabled subtypes. *Psychology in the Schools, 30*, 11–24.

Meyers, J. E., & Meyers, K. R. (1995). *Rey complex figure test and recognition trial (RCFT)*. Odessa, FL: Psychological Assessment Resources, Inc.

Moscovitch, M. (2004). Amnesia. In N. B. Smesler & O. B. Baltes (Eds.), *The international encyclopedia of social and behavioral sciences* (pp. 1–26). Oxford: Pergamon/Elsevier Science.

Moscovitch, M., Wesmacott, R., Gilboa, A., Addis, D. P., Rosenbaum, S., Viskontas, I., et al. (2005). Hippocampal complex contribution to retention and retrieval of recent and remote episodic and semantic memories: Evidence from behavioral and neuroimaging studies of healthy and brain-damaged people. In N. Ohta, C. M. MacLeod, & B. Uttl (Eds.), *Dynamic cognitive processes* (pp. 333–380). Tokyo: Springer-Verlag.

Nadel, L., Samsonovich, A., Ryan, L., & Moscovitch, M. (2000). Multiple trace theory of human memory: Computational, neuroimaging, and neuropsychological results. *Hippocampus, 10*, 352–368.

Pliszka, S. R. (2003). *Neuroscience for the mental health clinician*. New York: Guilford Press.

Pliszka, S. R., Glahn, D. C., Semrud-Clikeman, M., Franklin, C., Perez, R., Xiong, J., et al. (2006). Neuroimaging of inhibitory control areas in children with attention deficit hyperactivity disorder who were treatment naive or in long-term treatment. *American Journal of Psychiatry, 163*(6), 1052–1060.

Posner, M. I., & Rothbart, M. K. (2007). Research on attention networks as a model for the integration of psychological science. *Annual Review of Psychology, 58*, 1–23.

Psychological Corporation. (2002). *Wechsler individual achievement test II*. San Antonio: Psychological Corporation.

Reitan, R. M. (1969). *Manual for administration of neuropsychological test batteries for adults and children*. Tucson, AZ: Neuropsychology Press.

Reitan, R. M., & Wolfson, D. (1985). *The Halstead-Reitan neuropsychological test battery: theory and interpretation*. Tucson, AZ: Neuropsychology Press.

Reynolds, C. R. (2002). *Comprehensive trail-making test*. In. Austin, TX: Pro-Ed.

Reynolds, C. R., & Bigler, E. D. (1994). *Test of memory and learning examiner's manual*. Austin, TX: Pro-Ed.

Reynolds, C. R., & Kamphaus, R. W. (2004). *Behavior assessment system for children-2*. Circle Pines, MN: Pearson Assessments.

Reynolds, C. R., & Voress, J. K. (2007). *Test of memory and learning-second edition*. Austin, TX: Pro-Ed.

Reynolds, M. R., Keith, T. Z., Fine, J. G., Fisher, M., & Low, J. A. (2007). Confirmatory factor structure of the Kaufman assessment battery for children-second edition: Consistency with Cattell-Horn-Carroll theory. *School Psychology Quarterly, 22*, 511–539.

Rosner, J., & Simon, D. P. (1971). The auditory analysis test: An initial report. *Journal of Learning Disabilities, 4*, 384–392.

Rutter, M., Bailey, A., & Lord, C. (2003). *The social communication questionnaire*. Los Angeles: Western Psychological Services.

Rutter, M., Le Couteur, A., & Lord, C. (2003). *Autism diagnostic interview-revised*. Los Angeles: Western Psychological Services.

Sanford, J. A., & Turner, A. (2004). *IVA + Plus: Integrated visual and auditory continuous performance test interpretation manual*. Richmond, VA: Brain Train, Inc.

Sattler, J. M. (2001). *Assessment of children: Cognitive approaches*. San Diego: Author.

Schacter, D. L., Wagner, A. D., & Buckner, R. L. (2000). Memory systems of 1999. In E. Tulving & F. I. M. Craik (Eds.), *The Oxford handbook of memory* (Vol. 627–643). New York: Oxford University Press.

Schretelen, D. (1997). *Brief test of attention professional manual*. Odessa, FL: Psychological Assessment Resources.

Seidel, W. T. (1994). Applicability of the Hooper visual organization test to pediatric populations: Preliminary findings. *Clinical Neuropsychologist, 8*, 59–68.

Semel, E., Wiig, E. H., & Secord, W. A. (2003). *Clinical evaluation of language fundamentals manual* (4th ed.). San Antonio: Pearson.

Semrud-Clikeman, M. (2004). *Traumatic brain injury in children and adolescents*. New York: Guilford Press.

Semrud-Clikeman, M. (2007). *Social competence in children*. New York: Springer.

Semrud-Clikeman, M., Pliszka, S., & Liotti, M. (in press). Executive functioning in children with ADHD: Combined type with and without a stimulant medication history. *Neuropsychology, 22*, 329–340.

Semrud-Clikeman, M., Pliszka, S. R., Lancaster, J., & Liotti, M. (2006). Volumetric MRI differences in treatment-naïve vs chronically treated children with ADHD. *Neurology, 67*(1023–1027).

Sheslow, D., & Adams, W. (2005). *Wide range assessment for memory and learning-2*. Lutz, FL: Psychological Assessment Resources.

Shimamura, A. P. (2000). The role of the prefrontal cortex in dynamic filtering. *Psychobiology, 28*, 207–218.

Simon, H. A. (1975). The functional equivalence of problem solving skills. *Cognitive Psychology, 7*, 268–288.

Strauss, E., Sherman, E. M. S., & Spreen, O. (2006). *A compendium of neuropsychological tests* (3rd ed.). New York: Oxford University Press.

Tiffin, J. (1968). *Purdue pegboard: Examiner manual*. Chicago: Science Research Associates.

Wagner, R. K., Torgesen, J. K., & Rashotte, C. A. (1999). *Comprehensive test of phonological processing*. Austin, TX: Pro-Ed.

Wechsler, D. (1997). *Wechsler memory scales, examiner's manual* (3rd ed.). San Antonio, TX: The Psychological Corporation.

Wechsler, D. (2003). *Wechsler intelligence scale for children (WISC-IV)* (4th ed.). San Antonio, TX: The Psychological Corporation.

Wilkinson, G. S., & Robertson, G. J. (2005). *Wide range achievement test* (4th ed.). Lutz, FL: Psychological Assessment Resources.

Williams, K. T. (1997). *Expressive vocabulary test.* Circle Pines: American Guidance Service.

Woodcock, R. W. (1990). Theoretical foundations of the WJ-R measures of cognitive ability. *Journal of Psychoeducational Assessment, 8,* 231–258.

Woodcock, R. W., & Johnson, M. B. (1977). *Woodcock-Johnson Psycho-Educational Battery.* Allen, TX: DLM.

Woodcock, R. W., & Johnson, M. B. (1989). *Woodcock-Johnson Tests of Cognitive Ability: Examiner's Manual.* Allen, TX: DLM.

Woodcock, R. W., McGrew, K. S., & Mather, N. (2001a). *Woodcock-Johnson III test of cognitive abilities.* Rolling Meadows, IL: Riverside Publishing.

Woodcock, R. W., McGrew, K. S., & Mather, N. (2001b). *Woodcock-Johnson III tests of achievement.* Itasca, IL: Riverside.

Chapter 7
The Neuropsychological Assessment Process

When a practitioner begins an assessment there are three major parts to the evaluation. These sections include the intake interview, the assessment, and the feedback. Each of these areas will be described in greater detail as well as the mechanics of neuropsychological report writing.

The Intake Interview

The first contact the patient has with the examiner is often following a phone call to schedule an appointment. Most neuropsychologists have established a routine form that asks specific questions to determine whether the referral is appropriate for the practice. These questions are important to determine whether the referral question is within the bounds of the clinician's competencies, whether it is warranted, and to explain what the evaluation entails. Parts of this process can be handled by a trained receptionist, but it is up to the individual clinician to determine whether or not the case is appropriate.

The conversation with the parent or guardian needs to discuss the costs involved, the amount insurance (if you take insurance) is likely to cover, how long the assessment will take, whether the entire assessment is done on the same day or on additional days, and what the parent can expect from the results. Dealing with these issues up front can assist in a smooth relationship with the parent.

Following the intake phone call it is advisable to have an in-person interview with the main caregivers. It is preferable to have both parents present if at all possible. The intake interview helps you get to know the parent and enables the parent to feel comfortable with you. It also provides a time to explain the testing process as well as time frames for when the testing will be done, when the results will be provided, and when to expect the report. In addition, this is a good idea to complete a written release of information form to obtain previous testing, to talk to the child's teacher, and to obtain any other additional medical information. At this time, you may consider having the parent complete the behavior rating scales as well as a developmental history form so that you can have these available before the assessment begins.

One example of a parent interview format is provided below. It is helpful to obtain information about the presenting concern of the parent—when the parent first became concerned about his/her child and what has been attempted to solve the problem. In addition, basic demographic information is important. Who does the child live with? Who else lives in the home? What is the educational level and occupation of the parent(s)?

During this time one needs to also ask about the child's developmental history (achievement of developmental milestones, birth and delivery history, etc.). The medical history is also important to obtain to document possible head injuries, severe illnesses and/or fevers, and chronic diseases and disorders. The child's school and academic history is an important area to investigate. How does the child get along with others, does he/she have a favorite teacher, a teacher that didn't work for him, a school setting that was particularly helpful or problematic? Has the child received tutoring or behavioral assistance—if so what kind and what was the result?

At this time it is also helpful to inquire about any learning, emotional, or behavioral problems that are present in the parent or siblings. Having the parent

M. Semrud-Clikeman, P.A. Teeter Ellison, *Child Neuropsychology*, DOI 10.1007/978-0-387-88963-4_7,
© Springer Science+Business Media, LLC 2009

describe the child's behavior, temperament, coping strengths and weaknesses is an important aspect of the intake interview. A description of the child's interactions with others in the family as well as with his/her peers can provide information as to the child's social development.

Insert Developmental History Form About Here

Preparing the Child for the Assessment

It is helpful to assist the parent in preparing the child for the assessment. Many times children assume they will "fail" the assessment, or believe the outcome of the assessment will determine if they "pass" their current grade. It is far better for the parent to discuss the upcoming visit the night before the appointment to give the child an opportunity to ask questions as well as to adjust to the idea. It is not a good idea to label the tasks that are going to be done during the testing as "games." In this case, the child believes he/she will be coming to have fun and be very disappointed as most of the tasks are not games, but are work. I generally recommend that the parent describe the various tasks that will be done with the child and provide specific examples like building with blocks, looking at pictures, drawing, and answering questions.

For children with high anxiety, autistic spectrum disorders, or any disorder that requires additional transition time, it is helpful to prepare the child in sufficient time prior to the meeting. For some children that are particularly emotionally fragile or brittle, it is a good idea to have the child visit the office so that he/she can become more comfortable with the surroundings. It is not a good idea for these children to attempt to do the testing all in one day—rather it is better to parcel the testing into smaller amounts. The better the child is prepared for the evaluation, the easier the testing will be and the more applicable the results will be to estimate the child's current level of functioning.

The Evaluation

For the most part, a neuropsychological evaluation is similar to a psychological evaluation. It is the examiner's job to provide a comfortable and safe environment for the evaluation whether the examiner is the neuropsychologist or a technician. It is very helpful to give the child time to become acclimated to the room. Furniture should be the appropriate size and be comfortable. Setting the rules for the room often is very appropriate particularly for children that have behavioral difficulties or those who are anxious. The basic rules often regard not hitting, leaving the room, talking quietly, and not breaking materials. It is often very helpful to have tangible rewards particularly for children that may be recalcitrant or resistant to the testing.

It is not generally recommended to have the parent present in the evaluation room unless the child is unable to separate after a try or if the child is very young and requires the parent's presence. Often a parent will believe that she/he needs to be present, but if the examiner is firm and appears confident the child will often not require such presence. For more difficult cases it is possible for the parent to initially be present (with the caution to not answer for the child) and then leave after the child is comfortable. Many children can manage this type of separation, particularly if they know that the parent is in the waiting room.

If the examiner has decided to utilize a non-battery approach, then the appropriate tests should be readily available. For beginning practitioners it may be helpful to have a list ready, while for more advanced examiners may not need a list. If the testing is to be done by a technician, then it is important to prepare the technician for the tests that may be needed and to be available if testing results require flexibility. As will be discussed in Chapter 8, neuropsychological testing from a hypothesis testing approach provides flexibility to determine what measures may be utilized to best answer the question.

The initial portion of the evaluation can be simply talking with the child and getting to know him/her. It is very appropriate to talk to them about their likes and dislikes as well as querying why they believe they have come to see you. Depending on the developmental age of the child, I find it helpful to begin with tasks and then gradually talk about feelings and issues as the child becomes more comfortable with me. For other children who need to talk about why they are present, a discussion of why the testing is occurring and how the child feels about it is appropriate. Interviewing is an art and relies on the examiner being adept at sensing and interpreting the child's mood and affect, and adjusting the questioning appropriately (Semrud-Clikeman, 1995). Some children really need to talk about their concerns immediately while others need time to get comfortable with the examiner.

Testing should begin with measures that are relatively easy and fun so the child can ease into the situation. As the child's comfort increases, it is possible to bring out some of the more challenging measures. It is also strongly suggested that the tests be alternated so that the challenging measures are not all grouped together, but instead interspersed with measures that may be easier. It is also important to end the session with a task for which the child feels success. In this manner the child is more likely to leave with a good feeling about how she/he has performed and happy about returning for another visit. For children who are anxious or rigid, it is often helpful to tell how many tests will be used for that period of time and to cross out the tests as they are completed. This strategy offers a feeling of completion and lets the child see there is an end to what is being asked of him/her. Moreover, as appropriate, the examiner can let the child choose which test is used. For example, we have often said, "Today we have to do a mathematics test and drawing test—which test would you like to do first?" In this manner the child has some control over the situation and feels a part of the decision.

At the end of the session, it is appropriate to tell the child that he/she has worked well and that there were a lot of things that he/she could do well—listing the tasks that he/she felt most comfortable with is helpful. If there is another appointment, it is very appropriate to state, "I will see you again in five days" or a specific date for older children. If the testing is completed, it is very appropriate to tell the child/adolescent that the testing is done and that you will meet with him/her in the near future to discuss the results.

Feedback Session

It is important to be cognizant of the parent's level of anxiety as they approach the feedback session. For many parents there are great fears that the neuropsychologist will actually find something seriously wrong with their child or that it is their fault. The feedback session can be very therapeutic if managed in a careful way. Work to keep jargon out of the feedback and, for beginning neuropsychologists, it may be difficult to realize what jargon is for the lay person. For example, one student began a feedback with a parent in this way:

> Thank you for coming today. Joey completed the WISC III, the WIAT II, and the Rey-Osterreith in our first session. We found that he had difficulties with working memory, processing speed, phonological coding and visual-spatial integration. These problems are consistent with LD as well as possibly sensory-integration difficulty.

One can see that a lay person would likely have no idea what was being said. Most parents will not stop you and ask, "what does this mean?" These mistakes are most common with beginning practitioners, but we have had parents who have received a feedback from an experienced practitioner ask for a reinterpretation of the results because, "I didn't understand anything that he/she said." To utilize the assessment in the most therapeutic manner requires that the findings be presented in *plain English*.

Keep in mind the main goal for the feedback is not just to provide scores and information to the parent (Handler, 2007), but to provide a forum to discuss possible interventions and remediation of difficulties. For example, it is a good idea to begin the feedback by summarizing the main reason the parent has sought the evaluation. This can be done simply, for example:

> I want to thank you for coming today to discuss the results of Cindy's testing. As we talked in our first meeting, I understand you are concerned about Cindy's difficulty with completing her work and following directions. You were concerned whether Cindy has any attentional problems or whether the work is too hard for. Cindy and I completed many tests to look at these issues and I'd like to talk to you about the results at this time. Please do not hesitate to stop me and ask a question if what I am saying is not clear.

In beginning the feedback it is advantageous to provide examples of how the child related to the examiner as well as the behaviors that were noted. For example if the child had difficulty remaining seated or paying attention it is appropriate to remark on these behaviors and then ask if the parent sees this type of behavior at home or in school. As one begins the feedback try to remember that the parent is going to be very anxious, wondering what the bottom line (diagnosis) is. It is important to convey to the parent that you really know their child and that you care. Relating an anecdote of how the child worked on a task is one way to convey your knowledge of the child. If the clinic or hospital in which you work uses technicians for the testing, it is important that you met and interacted with the child. This helps you build a rapport with the parent and lends credibility to the later recommendations.

It can be very helpful to provide concrete examples of areas of strength and/or weakness. If the child has difficulty with Block Design on the WISC IV then phrasing this problem as, "Cindy had difficulty using blocks to copy a model in a short period of time. When I gave her extra time to do this task, she was able to copy the model. It appears that the difficulty in her skills is not that she cannot interpret what she sees, but that it takes her longer." The neuropsychologist can also discuss tasks where the child succeeded. "Cindy is very good at explaining what words mean. She approaches many tasks by using her excellent verbal skills to solve the problem."

As the feedback continues, check with the parent to determine if the neuropsychologist's observations are consistent with what is happening at home. Anticipating questions and prompting parents to give examples of what you have seen are very helpful in engaging the parent in the process, and to ensure that the information may be more readily

used when the parent communicates with the school or interested parties (Baron, 2004). Generally, relating the findings should not focus on the scores but rather on the broad picture. Stating something like:

"Cindy shows good overall ability with her scores in the high average range for her age. She shows particular strengths in her verbal ability to answer questions, define words, and recall facts. She has more difficulty when she is asked to solve a problem in her head (like 2×12) quickly or copy a block design quickly. Cindy has difficulty on tasks that require her to complete them quickly and which are monotonous. Her attention on these tasks started out well but then as the boring task continued she began to fidget and have difficulty staying with me. She would return to the task when I asked her to, but then would again need to be drawn back to the task at hand—are these behaviors you see at home?

In this manner the parent is drawn into the feedback and begins to relate the findings to the real world. Of course if they ask for the numbers you need to provide them. I often will utilize a normal curve and then mark the areas of strength in one color and the areas that are problematic in another.

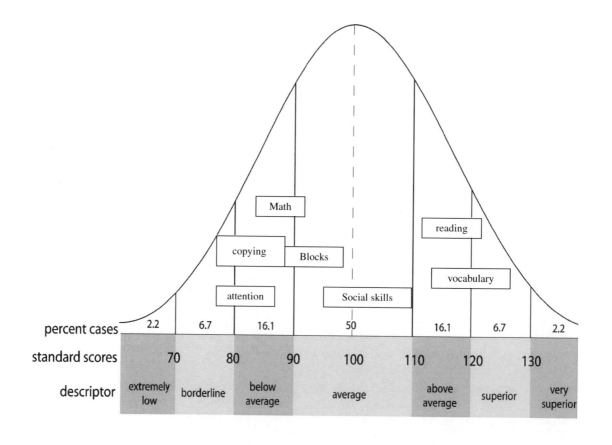

This graph can then be taken home to help the parent explain the results to the teacher. I use a similar one with the child during feedback, emphasizing the child's strengths as well as areas that could be strengthened.

It is important to provide the diagnosis for the child, if there is one, and to discuss what the diagnosis means. During this discussion, explore how the parent understands the diagnosis and whether he/she agrees with it. At times there may be disagreement between the parents and the practitioner can assist with resolving some of these issues. One parent may be comfortable with the diagnosis while another may dispute the findings. It is important to stay calm and collected during these discussions and to not become combative or defensive. Helping the parent to think about what the disagreement is about, as well as trying to come to a resolution, is an important part of the feedback. Sometimes the disagreement is due to having fewer interactions with the child over the problems or not attending school meetings and thus being less informed. At other times, the disagreement may be due to the diagnosis hitting too close to home—in other words the parent has a similar problem and has not resolved the issue for him or herself.

If the child has a learning disability, it is important that you be very aware of the laws that are present in your state and nationally to obtain services (Magden & Semrud-Clikeman, 2007). It is disconcerting to the parent to be told a child qualifies for an educational service (such as a learning disability program) only to find out that the state law does not support such a conclusion. Thus, the practitioner needs to be cognizant of the rules and to write his/her report and conduct the feedback accordingly. It is imperative that the practitioner be aware whether the child is most appropriately referred for a special education evaluation or for a Section 504 evaluation (Magden & Semrud-Clikeman, 2007). It is also important for the practitioner to be able to discuss the difference and provide support in contacting appropriate school personnel.

Finally, and the most important part of the feedback, is discussing interventions. Provide concrete and direct suggestions to help the child in school and at home. The interventions also need to be realistic. At times the practitioner will use a "shot-gun" approach and recommend everything to be done at once. It is easy to lose sight of the fact that financial resources at home and school may be stretched and purchasing individual physical therapy in addition to school physical therapy may not be feasible. It is also important to realize that emotional resources may also be strained. Helping the parent to prioritize interventions can be very helpful and prevent burnout as the parent attempts to do everything at once. I find it helpful to say the first priority is . . . and then name it. If the child has a learning disability, then that is the first priority area to obtain services. If the child is ADHD, then determining whether a medication trial is appropriate should take precedence.

For a few patients it may take more than one session to fully manage the findings and secure appropriate interventions. For others, the feedback session may be followed up by a phone call to support the parent's efforts. Providing the written report at the end of the feedback session is very appropriate and allows the parent to read and reflect upon it. I always offer that they can come back and talk more if needed. Finally ending the session with a short summary of what was discussed is very helpful so that everyone understands what was said.

Child Feedback

It is also appropriate to offer to provide feedback to the child. This feedback can either be done after the main feedback to the parent or on another day. It should be done at the child's developmental level and may take a few minutes or longer, depending on the age and the nature of the child's questions. Similar to the parent feedback, the use of a visual chart can be very helpful to assist the child's understanding. Using examples of the tests to illustrate weaknesses and strengths helps the child to understand what the results mean. Providing numbers is not helpful and should be used. When the child feedback is discussed with the parent, it is helpful to have advance agreement whether the parent is comfortable not attending or whether they insist on being present. I generally suggest to the parent that it works better to ask the child if she/he wants the parent present. Usually the child assents to having the parent attend the feedback.

For adolescents, the feedback is a bit different and while most are comfortable having their parent present during the feedback, some are not and this is a good avenue for discussion. Coaching the findings in terms of strengths and weaknesses is helpful, as is relating the findings to the adolescent's experience in school and at home. Discussing the main interventions is also important since many of the interventions with adolescents are only successful if the individual agrees to them. Explaining what a learning disability is provides information that the adolescent may not have; he/she may be assuming that they can't read because they are "stupid." Explaining some of the brain differences that have been found for these disorders can often lessen fears that the problem is unchangeable and insurmountable.

It is very appropriate and ethical to provide the parent with the report at the end of the final session (Semrud-Clikeman, Fine, & Harder, 2005). To make the parent wait an unreasonable amount of time for the report is not only poor clinical practice, it is unethical. At the very least, the report should follow the feedback within two weeks.

The following section discusses the neuropsychological report in detail and provides a model. While there are many different styles for writing a neuropsychological report most include sections for background and developmental history, behavioral observation, tests used, test results and interpretation, summary (or case formulation) and recommendations. Each of these areas is briefly discussed below.

Neuropsychological Reports

Reason for Referral

This section should briefly describe the reasons the client is currently being referred for testing, indicate who referred the child and what the main question is. In addition, this section should briefly describe where the client is currently, what grade he/she is in, and if he/she is in any special programs.

Background and Developmental History

A developmental and background history is important for a number of reasons. First, a developmental

history can be important to identify risk factors during pregnancy and delivery that have been associated with neurodevelopmental disorders of childhood of a specific (e.g., learning disabilities) or global (e.g., cognitive disabilities) nature. Second, previous head trauma and/or other health factors (e.g., recurring ear infections, high fevers, or febrile seizures) can be uncovered in a review of developmental history. Third, a careful history is important to determine the presence of similar or related disorders in other family members or hereditary linkages that might be helpful to understand the etiology of a particular disorder. Fourth, a history of when the child attained motor and language milestones (walking, talking, etc.) is essential to determine the nature and extent of the developmental correlates of the child's problem. Fifth, background history is essential to determine the presence of coexisting disorders (e.g., conduct disorders, depression, anxiety) that affect long-term outcomes for children with various neurodevelopmental disorders. These conditions often must be addressed separately in treatment plans. It is important to include any pertinent medical and medication history. Finally, background information will shed light on the child's educational, psychosocial, and academic opportunities, which may assist in the proper diagnosis of a disorder (i.e., reading deficits). It is important to briefly discuss interventions that have been attempted and the success of these interventions in this section.

The extent to which environmental, genetic, and experiential factors affect the manner in which some CNS disorders progress or influence treatment approaches can be explored with a complete review of the child's history. This information is crucial for accurate differential diagnoses, particularly when the clinician is trying to determine whether the problem is neurodevelopmental in nature or the result of a lack of opportunity to learn, or the absence of appropriate modeling, stimulation, or reinforcement.

There are several methods for obtaining reliable background information, including the structured parent and child interviews from the Child Behavior Checklist (Achenbach, 1991) and the Behavior Assessment for Children-2 (Reynolds & Kamphaus, 2004). Most neuropsychological clinics use semi-structured interviews [i.e., K-SADS; (Kaufman, Birmaher, Brent, Rao, & Ryan, 1997)] for gathering information, and many utilize questionnaires designed specifically to investigate a particular disorder, such as ADHD. Medical and school records also provide crucial information for identifying the child's biogenetic, health, and environmental history. A careful review of these materials often reveals risk factors and predisposing conditions that may interact with the child's specific problem, and this information may be useful in designing effective interventions.

Behavior Observations

Behavioral observations allow the person reading the report to truly understand what it was like to be in the room testing the client. At the very least the behavioral observations need to describe the client's language abilities, attention to task, ability to manage frustration, and his/her mood and affect. This section should describe how the child/adolescent communicated— was it with full sentences or just one word responses? Was he/she distractible? If so, was the examiner able to bring the client back to the task at hand? Most reports also provide information about how the child reacted to encouragement and praise, and how the client responded to frustration. Was the child's affect flat, animated, expansive, appropriate to the situation? How did the child approach certain tasks? Did she/he talk their way through the task? All of these behaviors can assist in understanding the findings. In this section, also, if changes needed to be made to standardized tests, then those changes need to be enumerated and qualified.

Tests Administered and Results

This section lists the tests that were administered. It then discusses the findings generally in the various neuropsychological domains (i.e., cognitive, academic, executive functioning, attention, memory, psychosocial). A good neuropsychological report provides not just the scores, but an interpretation that is understandable to the lay reader. Each domain should be presented clearly but concisely so that the findings are usable. We find it helpful

to provide a short summary at the end of each domain that includes the strengths and weaknesses in that domain. This section provides the backbone of the report and the interpretation of what these findings mean.

In this section of the report it is often helpful to put the measures into a context with which the reader is familiar. For example, we generally state that standard scores are in the average range when they fall between 85 and 115, with similar statements made for scaled scores and for T scores. Many neuropsychologists prefer to have the body of the report to reflect the findings and attach a separate psychometric summary at the end of the report. See the attached report for a model.

Summary and Recommendations

This section is the most difficult to write and yet the most important section of the report. It ties together all of the issues involved and meshes the findings with the tests and recommendations. Some neuropsychologists will not include a diagnostic formulation here while others do. We suggest that when the diagnosis using DSM axis format is helpful, then it should be used and included.

The summary is also described as a case formulation. In this section the developmental history, medical history, school history, family history as well as the test results are integrated. In addition this section discusses findings that are unusual or difficult to understand and attempts to place them in a framework for the reader. Scores and statistics should not be present in this section. The summary is also the aspect of the report in which specialists (neurologist, psychiatrist, etc.) are generally most interested. Some practitioners now put this section at the beginning of the report.

The interventions need to be appropriate to the case at hand and reasonable. Many school professionals bristle at reports that tell them the child needs one-on-one intervention; a practice that is likely unfeasible. The interventions should also be tied to the diagnosis. For example, if ADHD is diagnosed there should be interventions that address problems with organization, attention, possible medical interventions, and impulse control problems. Likewise, if a learning disability is present it is helpful to explain what types of reading and/or mathematics assistance and methods are appropriate (Semrud-Clikeman, 2006).

Neuropsychological Report Example

The following is an example of a neuropsychological report. Different clinics and hospitals have varying forms and the astute clinician will adapt the report accordingly. This is but one example of a report.

Hospital

Developmental/Behavioral Program

Patient Name: Sam

Medical Record Number:

Date of Birth:

Date of Evaluation: 8/5, 8/12, 8/26/

Chronological Age: 13–10

Neuropsychologist:

Reason for Referral: Sam was referred for evaluation by Dr. K to evaluate his current level of intellectual and academic functioning. Dr. K evaluated Sam and diagnosed him with ADHD: combined type, Conduct disorder: adolescent onset, Anxiety disorder NOS with rule outs for Bipolar disorder, and learning disorders. Dr. R, child psychiatrist, is evaluating Sam concurrent with this evaluation. Sam is not currently prescribed any medications.

Background Information: The following information was obtained through review of medical records, discussion with Dr. K, and parent and child interviews. Additional information is available through Dr. K's report to the interested professional. The following is a summary of Sam's history. Sam has a long history of acting out behaviors and sadness/anxiety disorder. Significant deficits have been found in attention, social skills, and activity level. His family history is positive for incarceration and substance abuse and has been notably unstable. He has been at a juvenile detention center twice with the most recent stay in the past school year. He was at the juvenile detention center most recently due to significant behavioral difficulties at home, school refusal, and suicidal ideation. Sam's older brother has been reportedly arrested several times and is currently in prison for burglary. His mother also

has a history of incarceration and substance abuse, but is currently working on turning her life around and she reported she has been clean for 18 months.

The pregnancy was complicated by the use of heroin, caffeine, and nicotine during the first trimester, substances which were discontinued at that time. Pregnancy and delivery were reported as normal and delivery was by Cesarean Section. Sam was reported to be an active and fussy baby, but met all developmental milestones within normal limits. Sam's mother reports that he has significant difficulty sleeping and frequently doesn't sleep until early morning. Sam attends school at the ALC and has a history of suspensions and expulsions prior to his attendance at ALC. His achievement was reported to be in the average range. Sam has not had a psychological or neuropsychological evaluation. Dr. K's report indicates the presence of depression, anxiety, conduct problems, and peer problems. These findings were present on both home and school behavioral checklists and consistent with self-report measures completed by Sam.

Speech and Language assessment conducted at the hospital found Sam's language skills to be within normal limits for his age. An audiological evaluation through CHOA found an auditory processing deficit with recommendations for a repeat evaluation in one year.

Behavioral Observations: Sam was accompanied to the assessment by his mother. He was tested during two consecutive Thursday appointments for approximately three hours each. Sam was friendly throughout the evaluations and seemed to enjoy the tasks at hand. His language was age-appropriate and his speech was clear and unpressured. He reported that he had not slept well the nights before the assessment and was tired. Sam did appear to be lethargic during the testing which affected his attention at times. He responded well to redirection and worked on the tasks at hand. On tasks that were challenging for him Sam would give up easily and appeared to lack confidence in his abilities. He worked hard throughout the tests but did not push himself if he didn't know the answer. He did not become unduly frustrated on tasks that were challenging for him. Given his high level of cooperation, the following results are felt to be a reliable and valid representation of his level of current functioning.

Tests Administered: Differential Abilities Scales (DAS), Wechsler Individual Achievement Test-II (WIAT-II), California Verbal Learning Test-Children's Version (CVLT-C), Wisconsin Card Sorting Test (WCST), Judgment of Line Orientation (JLO), Rey-Osterreith Complex Figure Test, Rorschach Inkblot Test, Behavior Assessment System for Children–parent form (BASC), Review of Medical Records, Clinical Interview.

Test Interpretations

Cognitive Functioning: The Differential Abilities Scales (DAS) consists of core and diagnostic tests of general cognitive ability. The cognitive subtests assess the child's ability to understand and use language, complete puzzles and block designs, and interpret visual information. The diagnostic subtests evaluate the child's short- and long-term memory as well as his speed of information processing. Sam shows average overall functioning achieving a general cognitive index of 91 that places him at the 27th national percentile. There is a 90 percent assurance that his true ability lies between 86 and 95. There is a significant difference between his verbal and nonverbal skills; his verbal ability is in the strong average range and his nonverbal reasoning skills are below average for his age. Sam's spatial abilities are in the average range. On the verbal subtests Sam shows age-appropriate ability to define words and use abstract language concepts. He also shows average perceptual skills. Weakness is present in Sam's nonverbal reasoning skills, particularly in his ability to recognize patterns and complete sequencing tasks. The diagnostic tests indicate very good visual memory, both short- and long-term. His ability to process information quickly and his recall of auditory information are in the low average range for his age.

Academic Functioning: The Wechsler Individual Achievement Test is a measure of general academic functioning in the areas of reading, arithmetic and writing. On the reading subtests the child is asked to read single words and also to read a passage and answer questions about content. On the arithmetic subtests the child is asked to solve word problems as well as general calculation problems. The writing subtests require the child to spell words and then to write a story on a topic.

Sam's reading skills are within expectations for his age and grade placement. He shows better abilities understanding what he has read and appears to use context clues in order to understand passages. His ability to sound out words is not as well developed and he would not attempt to sound out words that he did not know. Sam's mathematics abilities are his weakest area, particularly his ability to complete calculation tasks. He has not mastered fractions and shows poor understanding of decimals. Sam's spelling skills are in the below average range and his ability to write a paragraph is significantly below his age and ability measures. His story was marked by poor word usage, lack of punctuation and capitalization, run-on sentences, and limited word usage. Sam shows adequate development of his ideas. Compared to his ability and, most particularly, compared to his verbal ability, Sam meets criteria for a learning disability in mathematics and written expression.

Learning and Memory: The California Verbal Learning Test-Children's Version (CVLT-C) was administered to assess Sam's ability to learn verbal material after several exposures. The task also provides measures of recall and recognition of previously learned material. Sam's scores on this measure are listed below. Sam shows average ability to encode and store auditory information. When asked to recall information for a short period of time, Sam's scores are significantly below average. Strategies for recalling information do not improve his score in either the short- or long-term.

The findings from the memory measures have important implications for Sam's school performance. He does not spontaneously generate efficient strategies for encoding, and may need to be taught more effective means of remembering new material. It also appears that new learning may be taking place, but that Sam is having difficulty with retrieval. Thus, he should be provided with a system of cueing himself to help him remember information that he has just learned. Additionally, new learning should be rehearsed often to help render retrieval somewhat easier. These findings are consistent with the possibility of a central auditory processing disorder.

Executive Functioning: The Wisconsin Card Sorting Test is a measure of executive or frontal lobe functioning, including the ability to form concepts, generate an organizational strategy, and use examiner feedback to shift strategy to the changing demands of the task. Sam's performance is summarized below:

Sam shows excellent executive functioning skills. He is able to utilize examiner feedback to change his answers and to respond flexibly to a cognitive task. Sam did show difficulty staying on task and became distracted by additional stimuli. This finding indicates that he can be distracted from the task at hand and, when that happens, his ability becomes hampered in changing his method of response.

The Stroop Color Word Test was also administered to measure Sam's ability to inhibit responding. The Stroop has three parts—the first part requires him to read color words as quickly as possible, then colors, then words that are printed in opposing colors (the word red is printed in green ink and the child reads the color of the ink). Sam scored in the low average range in his ability to read color words quickly and for the colors. He scored in the below average range in his ability to inhibit his response when asked to complete the task where he reads the color, but not the word. He became increasingly frustrated at this task and this frustration also contributed to his very low score.

Attention: Sam was administered the Test of Variables of Attention (TOVA) to evaluate his abilities. He was administered the TOVA off of any medication, then on 10 mgs of methylphenidate. His scores without medication showed difficulties in all areas. With the medication his scores fell within average ranges.

These findings are consistent with observations during the evaluation as well as an interview with Sam and his mother. He endorsed eight symptoms of inattention, three of poor impulse control and four of high activity level. These findings are similar to those reported by Dr. K.

Perceptual-Motor Functioning: The Rey-Osterreith Complex Figure test requires the adolescent to copy a very detailed figure. Sam scored in the average range on this task, showing good visual-motor skills, but also good planning and organizational abilities.

Sam's basic visual perceptual skills were assessed using the Judgment of Line Orientation test which requires the adolescent to determine the correct directional orientation of a line pattern. On this measure, Sam showed significant deficits in his ability to match patterns. This finding is consistent with his difficulty on the DAS nonverbal reasoning tasks. Sam achieved a score of 14 which places him 3.5 standard deviations below expectations for his age.

Emotional Functioning: Sam completed the Behavioral Assessment System for Children-Self-report (BASC), an integrated system designed to facilitate the differential diagnosis and classification of a variety of emotional and behavioral disorders of children, and to aid in the design of treatment plans. His mother and teacher had previously completed the BASC during the evaluation with Dr. K. Findings indicated highly clinically significant difficulties present in learning, social functioning, activity level, and attention in school. At home significant problems were reported in attention, activity level, aggression, conduct, and self-esteem.

Sam's ratings indicate that he is feeling most stress in school and that his attitude toward school and teachers is problematic. He does not consider teachers as people who can help him, that they are unfair, and that they only look at the bad things you do. He also does not feel that school is a helpful place, and he really doesn't care about school and wants to get out as soon as possible. In addition, Sam indicates that he prefers excitement and will seek out such situations if they are not present. The risk for antisocial behavior is very high based on the BASC and he shows little anxiety about getting in trouble with authority figures. There are indications of concerns about his sense of worth and that he does not have the motivation to attempt tasks when they are more difficult. He reports adequate self-esteem and self-reliance, but problematic relationships with his parents.

The Rorschach Inkblot Test was also administered to attempt to uncover areas of emotional functioning that Sam did not appear to feel free to discuss. Sam's protocol indicates that he directs his behavior through internal means and attempts to keep his feelings aside when in coping situations so that their influence on his decisions is, at best, modest. This is a very marked and not very flexible coping style—in other words, he will persist in his behavior even in a situation in which an intuitive or trial-and-error style may be more appropriate. Sam is also showing significant signs of situational stress that appear to be interfering with his ability to direct his behavior in a more appropriate manner. He shows a conflict between possibly unmet dependency needs and his need to isolate himself—given his history he may feel that he needs to protect himself from opening up to anyone. He shows a tendency toward cognitive distortion that may make it more difficult for him to interpret interpersonal behavior appropriately. His protocol indicates the risk for antisocial behavior and he does not perceive that people work together toward a goal. Positively, Sam shows an interest in people, but may not process human relationships very well. He shows signs of dysthymia as well as some indications that he seems himself as damaged or inadequate.

Summary and Recommendations: Sam is a 13-year, 10-month-old male with a history of aggressive behavior, attendance at a juvenile detention center, and a problematic childhood. Cognitive assessment indicates average ability in verbal and spatial skills with below average nonverbal reasoning skills. Achievement testing indicates age-appropriate reading skills with deficits present in mathematics and written expressions. He shows significant problems with attention which is improved with medication. Sam also has a history of social skills deficits as well as our finding of visual-spatial skill deficits. These findings are consistent with a diagnosis of a nonverbal learning disability. His difficulty in understanding appropriate social actions as well as containing his impulses make it difficult for him to participate in many social interactions. Instead Sam has developed behaviors that remove him from this difficulty through acting out. One cannot rule out that some of these behaviors may be related to his early development and his mother's probable substance abuse during pregnancy and after birth.

Sam shows good skills in utilizing feedback to change his behavior. However, he shows difficulty recalling information when presented orally—a finding consistent with his performance on the auditory processing test recently completed at the hospital. Emotionally Sam shows indications of being at high risk to develop antisocial behavior. He seeks out situations that are exciting for him and has a very low tolerance for boredom. There are indications of dysthymia in the projective testing as well as unmet needs for nurturance. Sam's difficulty in trusting adults in authority make it problematic for him to change his behavior, and his defiance is his way of asserting control over a situation. These feelings are likely grounded in his early experience where his mother was unavailable to him and his needs were not met in a timely manner. The picture presented by Sam is of an adolescent who is torn between a need to be cared for and nurtured, and a need to reject human contact. These concerns are complicated by his difficulty in perception that may

frequently lead him to misinterpret people and their motives. It is believed that Sam is at a crossroads at this time and is at high risk to continue down his path of antisocial behavior. He requires intensive intervention at this time to provide as much assistance as possible to prevent such a possibility.

Given the above findings, the following recommendations are offered:

1. It is strongly recommended that his school convene a multidisciplinary team meeting to determine Sam's eligibility for special education services in the area of OHI and LD.
2. A sleep study is recommended to determine the cause of Sam's history of sleep difficulty.
3. Individual cognitive-behavioral therapy is recommended and can be arranged through the hospital.
4. Continuation of parent training with Dr. K. is strongly recommended. Moreover, continuation of therapy with Dr. R is also strongly recommended as well as consideration for medication.
5. It is very important that auditory information which requires encoding be paired with visual cues to improve Sam's ability to remember what he has learned.
6. Additional memory strategies are provided as follows.

Strategies for Improved Memory Skills

Teaching Behaviors which are helpful:

1. Break tasks into small steps
2. Use extensive repetition
3. Teach strategies for memory, such as verbal rehearsal, clustering or chunking, imagery, associations, note taking, etc.
4. Use massed and distributed practice

Focus on the following:

A. Working Memory: Teach the child how to remember directions and retain them long enough to complete the task. Younger children especially forget what they are supposed to do and start to "drift away." Use cues like "make yourself remember..." "This is important..." Do the first few items with the child, pointing out what is important.
B. Present information in short segments: Two sentences may be overwhelming. Monitor comprehension.

C. Get the child actively involved whenever possible. Use many visual aids, demonstrate, repeat, give many pages of the same idea. Your goal is comprehension, retention, and mastery.

D. The child needs memory strategies such as:

- visualization (make a picture in your mind as you listen)
- note taking (or buddy note taker)
- repeating words in chunks
- learning to associate related ideas
- using "silly" cues such as, *Joe's Present. Joe was born on Sunday, July 4th, in Seattle, WA, USA on Book Street. He got a Ninja Turtle from Toys R' Us.* These sentences have all the rules for *capitalization.*

E. Only present the important information, leave out the frills and elaborations. Simplify, make it interesting, make it fun. Avoid long paragraphs or small print.

Techniques to Help Students with Attentional Problems in the Classroom

Physical Arrangement of Room

1. Have student seated near teacher
2. Move student's desk away from hallway, outside windows, etc.
3. Use desk dividers or study carrels if possible
4. Seat appropriate models next to students with attentional problems
5. Stand near student when giving directions or presenting lesson. Use student's worksheet as an example
6. Use rows for seating arrangement. Avoid tables with groups of students, if possible

Lesson Presentation

1. Provide an outline, key concepts, or vocabulary prior to lesson presentation
2. Include a variety of activities during each lesson
3. Make lessons brief
4. Actively involve the student during the lesson presentation:

- Use cooperative learning activities
- Develop learning stations
- Provide self-correcting materials
- Enable the student to make frequent responses
- Interact frequently (verbally and physically) with the student

5. Use the student's name during your presentation
6. Pair students to check work
7. Arrange for peer tutoring to help students review concepts
8. Use colored chalk during presentations when using chalk board

Worksheets and Tests

1. Use larger type
2. Keep page format simple:

- Don't include extraneous pictures
- Provide only one or two activities to a page
- Have white spaces on each page

3. Write clear, simple directions
4. Underline key direction words, vocabulary words, etc.
5. Draw borders around parts of page you want emphasized
6. Add reminders on worksheets to check work, etc.
7. Give frequent short quizzes and avoid longer tests
8. If necessary, allow student to take tests orally
9. Provide practice tests
10. Shorten assignments

Behavior

1. Implement a classroom behavior management system
2. Implement an individual behavior program and consistently chart progress (earn points for on-task time)
3. Use kitchen timer to help students stay on task
4. Use visual and auditory cues as behavioral reminders
5. Develop contracts/ behavior management systems in conjunction with parents to reinforce specific behaviors at home and at school
6. Implement a social skills curriculum
7. Give students choices ("You may work on your report or finish your math sheet")

8. Praise *specific* behaviors ("I like how you remembered to check your work before turning it in to me")

9. Define and review class rules each day. Post rules where students can see them

10. Be as consistent as possible in following through on classroom and individual behavior programs

11. Set hourly, daily, weekly, or monthly goals with the student and provide frequent feedback on student's progress

Thank you for the opportunity to work with this young man and his family. If you have any questions about this report, please do not hesitate to contact me at the Hospital.

Dr. X. Ph.D.

Licensed Psychologist

Psychometric Summary

Differential Abilities Scale-2
Average standard scores for the general cognitive index are between 85 and 115; average T-scores for the individual subtests are between 40 and 60.

	Standard Score	Percentile
Verbal Cluster	105	63
Nonverbal Reasoning	81	10
Spatial	91	27
General Conceptual Ability	91	27
Core Subtests	**T-Score**	**Percentile**
Verbal Subtests		
Word Definitions	54	66
Similarities	53	62
Spatial Subtests		
Recall of Designs	45	31
Pattern Construction	45	31
Nonverbal Reasoning Subtests		
Matrices	38	14
Sequential and Quantitative Reasoning	40	16
Diagnostic Subtests		
Recall of Digits	45	31
Recall of Objects—Immediate	57	76
Recall of Objects—Delayed	54	66
Speed of Information Processing	47	38

Wechsler Individual Achievement Test-II

Average standard scores are between 85 and 115. Sam's scores are as follows:

	Standard Score	Percentile
Basic Reading	86	18
Word Attack	83	14
Reading Comprehension	101	53
Reading Composite	**90**	**25**
Mathematics Reasoning	83	13
Numerical Operations	73	4
Mathematics Composite	**74**	**4**
Spelling	82	12
Written Expression	75	5
Writing Composite	**77**	**6**

California Verbal Learning Test-Children's Version Scores have a mean of 0, with standard scores of -1.0 to $+1.0$ indicating performance within the broad average range.

	Raw Score	Standard Score
List A, Trial 1	7	0.0
List A, Trial 5	12	0.0
Trials 1–5	45	42
List B Free Recall	6	−0.5
List A Short Delay Free Recall	6	−2.0
List A Short Delay Cued Recall	7	−2.0
List A Long Delay Free Recall	8	−1.0
List A Long Delay Cued Recall	7	−2.0
Correct Recognition Hits	7	−3.5
Discriminability	66.67%	−5.0
Learning Slope	1.2	−0.5

Wisconsin Card Sorting Test

Categories Achieved:	6	Normal range = 5–6
Failure to Maintain Set	4	Normal range = 0–1
	Raw Score	**Standard Score (100 + 15)**
Total Errors	15	116
Perseverative Responses:	11	108
Perseverative Errors:	10	109
Non-perseverative Errors:	5	118

(continued)

Percent Conceptual
 Level
Responses   82%   118

Test of Variables of Attention-Visual
    Average scores run between 85 and 115

	Off Ritalin	On 10 mg
Omissions	65	103
Commissions	66	105
Response Time	77	110
Variability	55	95

Stroop Color Word Test
Average scores range between 40 and 60

Words	47
Colors	45
Color/Words	32

Behavior Assessment Scale for Children—Self-Report

Domain	T-Score	Percentile
Attitude to School	74*	99
Attitude to Teachers	74*	99
Sensation Seeking	70	97
School Maladjustment	*78**	*98*
Atypicality	69+	94
Depression	49	64
Somatization	65+	91
Anxiety	49	64
Sense of Inadequacy	62+	86
Social Stress	54	69
Clinical Maladjustment	*57*	*75*
Personal Adjustment	*39+*	*14*
Emotional Symptoms Index	*55*	*73*

For the following scales, higher scores are desirable.

Relations with Parents	30*	7
Interpersonal Relations	41	15
Self-Esteem	50	37
Self-Reliance	46	26

+at risk
*high scores indicate problem behaviors

Developmental and Family History

Child's Name _____   Birth date _____   Age _____

Home Address _____
            Street   City   Sate   Zip

Phone

Child's school _____   Teacher's Name _____

Is Child in Special Education?   Yes   No   If so, what category? _____
                                   _____

Father _____   Age _____   Education (yrs) _____

Employment _____

Mother _____   Age _____   Education (yrs) _____

_____

Employment _____

Is child adopted?   Yes   No   If yes, what age at adoption? _____
           _____

Parent status   Married   Separated   Divorced
_____

Race/Ethnicity (birth father) _____

Race/Ethnicity (birth mother) _____

Race/Ethnicity (child) _____

Family and Extended Relationships

Please list all other children in the family:

Name	Age	School grade	Please list any problems the child is experiencing

Please list all other people living in the home:

	Relationship (i.e., Uncle, Friend, etc.)	Age	Please list any difficulties the individual is experiencing

Pregnancy and Delivery

A. Length of pregnancy (e.g., full term, 40 weeks, 32 weeks, etc.)	
B. Length of delivery (number of hours from initial labor pains to birth)	
C. Child's birth weight	

E. Did the mother experience any of the following conditions during pregnancy/delivery?

1. Bleeding	No Yes
2. Excessive weight gain (more than 30 lbs.)	No Yes
3. Toxemia/preeclampsia	No Yes
4. Rh factor incompatibility	No Yes
5. Frequent nausea or vomiting	No Yes
6. Serious illness or injury	No Yes

7. Took prescription medications
   a. If yes, name of medication:
   _____
	No
	Yes

8. Took medications or recreational drugs on your own	No Yes

9. Used alcoholic beverage
   a. If yes, approximate number of drinks per week:
   _____
	No
	Yes

10. Smoked cigarettes
   a. If yes, approximate number of
   cigarettes per day (e.g., 1/2 pack):_____
	No
	Yes

13. Had a breech delivery	No Yes
14. Had a cesarean section delivery	No Yes
15. Other problems—please describe	No Yes

Pregnancy and Delivery (continued)

F. Did any of the following conditions affect your child during delivery or within the first few days after birth?

1. Injured during delivery	No Yes
2. Delivered with cord around neck	No Yes
3. Had trouble with heartbeats ("distress") during delivery	No Yes
4. Had trouble breathing following delivery	No Yes
5. Needed oxygen	No Yes
6. Was cyanotic, turned blue	No Yes
7. Was jaundiced, turned yellow	No Yes
8. Had an infection	No Yes
9. Had seizures	No Yes
10. Was given medications	No Yes
11. Born with a congenital defect	No Yes
12. Was in hospital more than 7 days	No Yes

Infant Health and Temperament

A. During the first 12 months, was your child:

1. Difficult to feed	No / Yes
2. Difficult to get to sleep	No / Yes
3. Colicky	No / Yes
4. Difficult to put on a schedule	No / Yes
5. Alert	No / Yes
6. Cheerful	No / Yes
7. Affectionate	No / Yes
8. Sociable	No / Yes
9. Easy to comfort	No / Yes
10. Difficult to keep busy	No / Yes
11. Overactive, in constant motion	No / Yes
12. Very stubborn, challenging	No / Yes

Early Developmental Milestones

A. At what age did your child first accomplish the following:

1. Sitting without help	
2. Crawling	
3. Walking alone, without assistance	
4. Using single words (e.g., "mama," "dada," "ball," etc.)	
5. Putting two or more words together (e.g., "mama up")	
6. Bowel training, day and night	
7. Bladder training, day and night	

Health History

A. Date of child's last physical exam: _____

B. At any time has your child had the following:

1. Asthma	Never Past Present
2. Allergies	Never Past Present
3. Diabetes, arthritis, or other chronic illnesses	Never Past Present
4. Epilepsy or seizure disorder	Never Past Present
5. Seizures with a fever	Never Past Present
6. Chicken pox or other common childhood illnesses	Never Past Present
7. Heart or blood pressure problems	Never Past Present
8. High fevers (over 103°)	Never Past Present
9. Broken bones	Never Past Present
10. Severe cuts requiring stitches	Never Past Present
11. Head injury with loss of consciousness	Never Past Present
12. Lead poisoning	Never Past Present
13. Surgery	Never Past Present
14. Hospitalization for more than one night	Never Past Present
15. Speech or language problems	Never Past Present

16. Chronic ear infections	Never Past Present
17. Hearing difficulties	Never Past Present
18. Eye or vision problems	Never Past Present
19. Fine motor/handwriting problems	Never Past Present
20. Gross motor difficulties, clumsiness	Never Past Present
21. Appetite problems (overeating or undereating)	Never Past Present
22. Sleep problems (falling asleep, staying asleep)	Never Past Present
23. Soiling problems	Never Past Present
24. Wetting problems	Never Past Present
25. Sensory-integration difficulties (sensitivity to light, touch, noise)	Never Past Present
26. Other health difficulties—please describe	

Evaluation and Treatment History

| Has your child ever been evaluated previously for developmental, behavioral, or learning problems? | Yes No |

If so, when, who provided the evaluation, what type of evaluation did the child have, and what were you told about your child regarding the results of any evaluations?   *[Circle one]*

_____

_____

_____

_____

_____

_____

| Has your child ever been seen or treated by a neurologist? | Yes No |

[Circle one]

If so, when, who was the doctor, what tests (EEGs, brain scans) were done, and what medications were prescribed?

_____

_____

| Has your child ever received any psychiatric or psychological treatment? | Yes No |

[Circle one]

If so, what type of treatment did he/she receive and how long did the treatment last?

_____

_____

Who provided this treatment to your child?

_____

| Has your child ever received any *medication* for his/her behavior or emotional problems? | Yes No |

If so, who was the doctor, what type of medication did your child take, at what dose and for how long?   *[Circle one]*

_____

_____

_____

References

Achenback, T. M. (1991). *Manual for the Child Behavior Checklist and Revised Child Behavior Profile.* Burlington, VT: T. M. Achenbach.

Baron, I. S. (2004). *Neuropsychological evaluation of the child.* New York: Oxford University Press.

Handler, L. (2007). The use of therapeutic assessment with children and adolescents. In S. R. Smith & L. Handler (Eds.), *The clinical assessment of children and adolescents* (pp. 53–72). Mahwah, NJ: Lawrence Erlbaum Associates, Publishers.

Kaufman, J., Birmaher, B., Brent, D., Rao, U., & Ryan, N. (1997). Schedule for affective disorders and schizophrenia for school-age children-present and lifetime version (K-SADS-PL): Initial reliability and validity data.

Magden, J., & Semrud-Clikeman, M. (2007). Bridging neuropsychological practice and educational intervention. In S. J. Hunter & J. Donders (Eds.), *Pediatric neuropsychological practice: A critical review of science and practice.* London: Cambridge Press.

Reynolds, C. R., & Kamphaus, R. W. (2004). *Behavior assessment system for children-2.* Circle Pines, MN: Pearson Assessments.

Semrud-Clikeman, M. (1995). *Child and adolescent therapy.* Needham Heights, MA: Allyn and Bacon.

Semrud-Clikeman, M. (2006). Neuropsychological aspects for evaluating LD. *Journal of Learning Disabilities, 38,* 563–568.

Semrud-Clikeman, M., Fine, J. G., & Harder, L. (2005). Providing neuropsychological services to learners with learning disabilities. In R. C. D'Amato, E. Fletcher-Janzen, & C. R. Reynolds (Eds.), *Handbook of school neuropsycholgoy* (pp. 403–424). Hoboken, NJ: John Wiley & Sons.

Chapter 8
Neuropsychological Assessment Approaches and Diagnostic Procedures

The purpose of this chapter is twofold. First, we will briefly review three generally accepted approaches to neuropsychological assessment. Second, we will present our transactional assessment approach. This discussion will include evaluation methods for selected functional areas of the central nervous system. The conceptual framework underlying each battery and research with each approach will also be presented.

Approaches to Child Clinical Neuropsychological Assessment

Halstead-Reitan-Indiana Assessment Procedures

The Halstead-Reitan neuropsychological procedures are the most commonly used batteries available in this country (Nussbaum & Bigler, 1997), and the most well researched neuropsychological battery available. Halstead originally developed a series of tests to measure frontal lobe dysfunction in adults, and Reitan later added new tests and recommended the battery for various types of brain damage in children (Reitan & Wolfson, 2004). The Halstead-Reitan batteries contain measures necessary for understanding the brain-behavior relationship in children and adolescents.

Conceptual Model for the Halstead-Reitan Methods

Reitan and Wolfson (1985) indicate that attempts to develop a set of assessment measures resulted in a conceptual model of brain function that is incorporated in the Halstead-Reitan Battery. The battery consists of six categories representing the behavioral correlates of brain function: (1) input measures; (2) tests of concentration, attention, and memory functions; (3) tests of verbal language abilities; (4) tests of visual-spatial, sequential, and manipulatory functions; (5) tests of abstraction, reasoning, concept formation, and logical analysis, and (6) output measures (Reitan & Wolfson, 1985, p. 4).

Reitan and Wolfson (1985) further argue that a neuropsychological battery must have three components: (1) items that measure the full range of psychological functions of the brain; (2) strategies that allow for interpretation of individual brain functions, and (3) valid procedures demonstrated through empirical and clinical evaluation and applications. The neuropsychological batteries for children and adolescents were developed with these components in mind.

Halstead-Reitan Neuropsychological Batteries for Children

Reitan designed two batteries for children, the Halstead-Reitan Neuropsychological Battery for Older Children (HRNB-OC; 9–14 years) and the Reitan-Indiana Test Battery (RINTB; 5–8 years); see Table 8.1. Adolescents 15 years and older are evaluated using the Halstead-Reitan Battery for Adults. Reitan and Wolfson (2004a, 2004b) developed a screening battery for both the HRNB-OC and the RINTB. See Reitan and Wolfson (1992a, 1992b, 2004a, 2004b) for an in-depth description

M. Semrud-Clikeman, P.A. Teeter Ellison, *Child Neuropsychology*, DOI 10.1007/978-0-387-88963-4_8,
© Springer Science+Business Media, LLC 2009

Table 8.1 Subtests of the Halstead-Reitan neuropsychological test batteries

Functional Skills	Halstead-Reitan battery (9–14 Years)	Reitan-Indiana battery (5–9 Years)
Motor functions	Finger tapping	Finger tapping
	Grip strength	Grip strength
	Tactual performance test (total time)	Tactual performance (total time)
		Marching test
Visual-spatial[a]	Trails Part A	Matching figures
		Matching V's
		Matching pictures
		Star drawing
		Concentric squares
		Target
Sensory-perceptual	Tactile perception	Tactile perception
	Tactile form recognition	Tactile form Recognition
	Tactile localization	Tactile localization
	Fingertip writing	Fingertip writing
Alertness and concentration[b]	Speech sound perception	Progressive figures
Immediate memory	TPT-memory	TPT-memory
	TPT-localization	TPT-localization
Reasoning	Category test	Category test
	Trails Part B	Color form

[a]Reitan includes Picture Arrangement, Block Design, and Object Assembly from Wechsler scales.
[b]Reitan includes Coding from Wechsler scales.

of the HRNB-OC, the RINTB, and the two screening batteries. Table 8.2 lists the various subtests and the abilities associated with each of these measures.

One of the major shortcomings of the CHRNB has been inadequate norms, and insufficient reliability and validity information (Davis, Johnson, & D'Amato, 2005; Strauss, Sherman, & Spreen, 2006). Over the years Reitan developed and expanded his approach for analyzing the CHRNB (9–14 years) and the RINB (5–8 years). Interpretation typically focuses on a Multiple Inferential Approach, including an investigation of Level of Performance, Pathognomonic Signs, Patterns of Performance, and Right-Left Comparisons. Reitan (1986a, 1987) also developed the Neuropsychological Deficit Scale (NDS), a scoring and interpretation model for these batteries, which incorporates multiple factors. The Functional Organization Approach, proposed by Fletcher and Taylor (1984), is less inferential and places neuropsychological measures within a developmental and contextual framework. Each of these approaches will be briefly described and critiqued.

Multiple Levels of Inference

Reitan (1969) and Selz and Reitan (1979b) developed an interpretive system using four levels of inference: Level of Performance, Pathognomonic-Sign, Differential/Pattern of Scores, and Right-Left Differences.

Level of Performance

Interpretive guidelines for the batteries have discussed the importance of determining the Level of Performance by comparing the child's scores to those of a normative group. In an attempt to expand available norms, Findeis and Wright (1995) developed metanorms from 20 published articles from 1965 to 1990. Tombaugh (2003) also expanded norms for the Trail Making Tests A and B for the 18–89-year-old group, but not for the younger ages.

Standard score comparisons are typically employed in this method, where two standard deviations below the mean are often used as the

Table 8.2 Abilities assessed by the HRNB and HINB in children and adolescents

Function	Subtest	Requirements	R/L Differentiation	Abilities	Localization
Motor	Finger tapping	HINB and NRNB: Children tap mounted key 5–10 second trials with dominant and nondominant hand	Dominant hand expected 10% faster	Motor speed and coordination	Frontal lobe
Motor	Grip strength	HINB and HRNB: Squeeze on dynamometer, alternate hands, 3 trials dominant/non-dominant	Dominant hand expected to be stronger	Sensitive to R/L weaknesses in motor cortex	Frontal lobe
Motor	Tactual performance test (TPT)	HINB & HRNB: (a) Place 6 blocks onto board while blind-folded with dominant/nondominant	Expect 1/3 improvement over trials	Motor and sensory functions, kinesthetic functions	Frontal lobe
Memory		(b) Draw location of blocks from memory	No	Spatial memory	Global
Visual	Trails A[a]	HRNB: Child connects circles sequentially as quickly as possible	No	Motor speed Visual-perception and symbol recognition	
Sensory	Tactile perception test	HRNB and HINB: Back of hand and face are touched either separately or together with eyes closed	Errors on RH-implicates left hemisphere and LH errors implicate right hemisphere	Sensory stimulation	Contralateral parietal lobe
	Auditory perception test	Examiner stands behind child and lightly rubs fingers together. Child indicates where sound is (unilateral or bilateral presentations)	Yes	Auditory stimulation	Temporal lobe
	Visual perception	Examiner produces a finger movement at eye level, above and below eye level	Yes	Visual fields peripheral, unilateral, and bilateral	Visual pathway Visual fields
	Tactile form recognition TRF	Child extends hand through opening in board, and a cross, square, or triangle is placed in hand	Yes	Tactile form recognition (stereognosis)	Parietal lobe
	TRF	Child points to same shape on front of board			
Sensory	Fingertip writing (FTW)	HRNB: Numbers are traced on palm while child watches. Then, 3–are traced on fingertips with eyes closed.	Yes	Tactile perception, attention can be a factor in performance	Peripheral nervous system parietal lobe

Table 8.2 (continued)

Function	Subtest	Requirements	R/L Differentiation	Abilities	Localization
	Finger localization test	HINH: X's and O's are traced. Examiner lightly touches each of child's fingers with eyes closed. Child indicates which finger was touched.	Yes. Errors on RH implicates left hemisphere and RH errors implicates right hemisphere.	Tactile perception discrimination and attention to tactile stimulation	Unilateral errors implicatecontralateral parietal lobe-can also occur with bilateral errors
Alertness and Concentration	Speech[a] sounds perception test	60 nonsense words presented on tape recorder. Child underlines correct sound from 4 alternatives	No	Attention Auditory discrimination cross-modal matching	Global anterior left-hemisphere deficits (Teeter, 1986)
	Rhythm[a]	Thirty pairs of rhythms are presented on tape recorder. Child writes S or D if pair is same or different.	No	Attention, auditory perception, and concentration	Global
Abstract reasoning logical analysis	Category test	80 items HINB, 168 items HRNB: Visual stimulus is projected on screen, and child selects one of four stimuli that corresponds to the original. If correct, bell rings. Incorrect: A buzzer sounds	No	Abstract concept formation, mental efficiency and flexibility, learning skills	Global Sensitive to right frontal lobe dysfunction in older children (Rourke et al., 1983)
	Trails B[a]	Series of circles alternating between letters (A–G) and numbers (1–8). Child connects circles alternating numbers-letters-numbers, etc.	No	Simultaneous processing, flexibility in planning	Global
Language	Aphasia screening test	HRNB items: Naming, drawing, reading, math, and spelling	Yes	Receptive language and expressive language, dyspraxia, word naming	Language items relate to left hemisphere. Constructional items related to right hemisphere reading, calculation, articulation, right/left discrimination

The following items are in HINB for younger children only:

Function	Subtest	Requirements	R/L Differentiation	Abilities	Localization
Visual-spatial	Matching pictures that are identical, then in same category	No	Perception generalization reasoning	Global	

Table 8.2 (continued)

Function	Subtest	Requirements	R/L Differentiation	Abilities	Localization
	Matching V's and figures, concentric square, and star	Matching group of figures, or group of V's of differing widths; copying complex concentric square and star	No	Visual-perception and motor abilities	Association areas
	Target test	Consists of large cardboard poster with nine printed dots. Examiner taps out a series of dots and after 3-second delay child reproduces series on protocol	No	Visual and spatial memory abilities	Association areas
Motor	Marching test	Child follows a sequence of circles connected by lines up a page touching each circle as quickly as possible, using right, left, and both hands	Yes	Gross motor function and coordination	Global
Alertness and concentration	Progressive figures	8 large shapes with small shapes inside. Child moves from the small shape inside to a large figure with same shape	No	Visual perception, motor speed, concentration, and cognitive flexibility	Global
Reason	Color form test	Geometric shapes of different colors on board. Child touches one figure then another, moving from shape-color-shape-color, etc.	No	Simultaneous processing and flexibility in planning	Global

Note: Reitan Indiana Neuropsychological Battery (HINB); Halstead-Reitan Neuropsychological Battery (HRNB).
[a]In HRNB for older children only.

benchmark for consideration as significantly below normal, and 1.5 standard deviations below the mean suggests mild impairment. While a normative approach may be essential for children in the five- to 15-year range, there are reasons to use caution with a Level of Performance analysis in isolation (Nussbaum & Bunner, in press). First, normal or abnormal levels of performance do not unequivocally confirm or disconfirm abnormal brain function (B. P. Rourke, 1981). Recovery of function may affect a child's level of performance such that a brain-injured child may reach normal performance. Other children may be falsely identified as neuropsychologically impaired as a result of other factors, including motivation, psychopathology or significant language deprivation (Teeter, 1986). Barron (2003) also suggests that there other factors that affect performance on these tests including a lack of motivation, inattention and low frustration tolerance. To be most reliable and valid, the Level of Performance approach should be used in conjunction with other interpretive factors.

Pathognomonic Sign Approach

One of the most common methods of analyzing neuropsychological data has been the deficit or pathognomonic sign approach. This approach was developed from research findings showing that certain items on neuropsychological batteries, particularly those items from the Aphasia Screening Test, occurred almost exclusively in brain-damaged individuals and not in normal individuals (Wheeler & Reitan, 1962).

The pathognomonic approach has been moderated by other findings demonstrating that false negatives can be common when this approach is used in isolation (Boll, 1974). Analyzing these signs is also particularly complicated in children because of wide developmental variations in acquiring some skills in typically developing children (Teeter, 1986). To be considered pathognomonic, it must be proved that the child at one time had acquired the skill prior to injury or insult. Although this is usually easier to establish in older children and adults, the pathognomonic sign approach is rarely advocated in isolation.

Pattern of Performance Approach

The differential score or Pattern of Performance approach involves developing an overall gestalt of the various performance patterns of the individual. In this method, the examiner builds a profile of individual strengths and weaknesses on test scores and begins to make inferences about the neuropsychological status of specific and global brain function based on these patterns. For example, a pattern of clear right-handed weaknesses on sensory and motor measures (e.g., elevated time for the right hand Tactual Performance Test (TPT) score and low tapping speed with the right hand), in conjunction with poor performance on the Speech Sounds Perception test and borderline Verbal Intelligence (IQ) scores (compared to normal Performance IQ), might suggest a pattern of left-hemisphere weaknesses. Reitan (1971) also reports that children and adults show similar patterns of performance on some tests: low scores on Part B of Trails compared to good scores on Part A has been found in individuals with left-hemisphere weaknesses, and poor performance on the Speech Sounds Perception Test is often found in individuals with left-hemisphere impairment.

Rourke, Bakker, Fisk, and Strang (1983) indicate that this method of interpretation is problematic for young, severely involved children. However, the Pattern of Performance approach has been broadly adopted by some neuropsychologists in their quest to identify meaningful subtypes of learning disabilities (Nussbaum & Bigler, 1986; B. Rourke, 1989).

Right-Left Differences

Reitan (1986a, 1987) suggests that Right-Left Differences can be a useful adjunct to understanding a child's neuropsychological performance. Table 8.3 reports right-left sensory and motor signs based on the Halstead-Reitan batteries for children. Reitan (1987) states that right-left indices can be a useful method for comparing the status of the two cerebral hemispheres, because even young children (5–8 years) have developed consistent hand preferences for simple motor tasks. Reitan (1987) further argues that right-left differences rely on "basic

Table 8.3 Right–left sensory and motor signs on the Halstead-Reitan neuropsychological test battery

Motor and sensory items	Left-Hemisphere signs[a]	Right-Hemisphere signs
Finger-tapping	Lower right hand tapping	Lower left hand tapping
Tactual performance test	Lower right hand scores	Lower left hand scores
Grip strength	Lower right hand scores	Lower left hand scores
Finger localization	Higher errors–right hand	Higher errors–left hand
Fingertip writing	Higher errors–right hand	Higher errors–left hand
Tactile perception	Higher errors–right hand	Higher errors–left hand

Note: Right-dominant individuals.
[a]Divide nondominant hand by dominant hand and subtract from 1. Use Neuropsychological Deficit Scale to determine significant differences between right and left hands.

neuroanatomical structure and organization rather than higher-level neuropsychological functions that have been developed through educational and environmental influences and experiences" (p. 6).

The extent to which right-left differences differentiate between brain-damaged and normal children is also of interest. Reitan (1987) found that this method of analysis had less overlap between a normal control group and children with brain damage when compared to the Level of Performance or the Aphasia Screening Test. Reitan also argues that it is important to identify children who lag behind in the basic biological organization of the brain (e.g., sensory and motor functions), which can be related to learning problems that may require remediation. Sensory and motor pathways are "essentially equivalent among younger children, older children and adults" (Reitan, 1987, p. 40). While the right-left approach can differentiate brain-damaged from normal children, it is not recommended in isolation or as a substitute for a comprehensive neuropsychological evaluation.

Neuropsychological Deficit Scale Approach

The Neurological Deficit Scale (NDS) incorporates a method for determining the child's Level of Performance, Right-Left Differences, Dysphasia and Related Deficits, and cutoff scores for differentiating brain-damaged from normal youngsters for each battery. The NDS also provides a total score for measuring the overall adequacy of neuropsychological functioning in children. Raw scores are weighted as Perfectly Normal (score = 0), Normal (score = 1), Mildly Impaired (score = 2), or Significantly Impaired (score = 3) on the basis of normative comparisons. When using the NDS approach, the examiner takes the following steps: (1) converts raw scores on each test to corresponding weights (0, 1, 2, or 3) based on normative tables provided by Reitan (1986a, 1987); (2) calculates right-left difference scores by dividing the score of the nondominant hand by that of the dominant hand, subtracting from 1.00, and converting to weighted scores; (3) makes clinical judgments following Reitan's (1984) guidelines for scoring the Aphasia Screening Test and assigns NDS scores; (4) totals weighted scores across each factor, Level of Performance, Right-Left Differences, and Aphasia Test, and (5) totals the weighted scores on 45 variables for older children and 52 variables for younger children to obtain a Total NDS Score. Reitan provides cut-off scores for brain-damaged versus normal children on the Total NDS score and for each of the factor scores.

Separate tables are available to analyze the neuropsychological test results of older children (Reitan, 1986a) and younger children (Reitan, 1987). Although the NDS approach seems to be an extension of an earlier standardized scoring procedure ("Rules for Neurological Diagnosis;" Selz and Reitan (1979a)), the normative group used to develop the weighted scores reported in the tables is not clearly described in recent test manuals available for the child batteries.

Several other methodologies use and interpret the Halstead-Reitan battery including the normative analysis, the biobehavioral, and the pragmatic approach. These approaches are briefly described.

Normative Analysis of the Halstead-Reitan Neuropsychological Tests

The normative analysis differs from the "level of performance" approach (+ 2 Standard Deviations above the mean) by analyzing scores on a continuum rather than cut-offs scores; brain damage is either present or absent. Clinicians use the meta-norms to determine a child's performance within a normative framework (Findeis & Wright, 1995) rather than as dichotomous criteria for determining brain damage versus no brain damage (Nussbaum & Bigler, 1997; Nussbaum & Bunner, 2008).

Biobehavioral Approach

The Biobehavioral Approach employs a broader, more comprehensive method for interpreting test data and was first proposed by Taylor and Fletcher (1990). This model assumes that neuropsychological functioning occurs with a context, with behavioral as well as neurocognitive, biological and genetic variables interacting and affecting how a disability is manifested (Nussbaum & Bunner, 2008). First, neuropsychological assessment includes information from four major sources: (1) presenting problems; (2) cognitive and psychosocial characteristics; (3) environmental, sociocultural and historical variables (e.g., family and school history), and (4) biological and genetic vulnerabilities (i.e., family history).

Second, the biobehavioral approach assesses other child and environmental factors that impact the child's basic neurocognitive functions in order to determine the intensity of the disability. These factors may also diminish the disability. Third, it is likely that an uneven profile of performance is associated with disabilities and it is critical to understand the variability to fully appreciate the nature of the disability. Fourth, the clinician must determine the impact of the environment on the neurocognitive functioning of the child. Fifth, neurocognitive deficits influence and ultimately limit the behavioral competencies of the child. These deficits are moderated by family and environmental factors. Finally, neurocognitive deficits must be interpreted within a developmental framework, and are considered correlational and not causal.

Pragmatic Approach

The Pragmatic Approach offers a more flexible model (Barron, 2003). Barron suggests a more fluid, non-battery approach for neuropsychological assessment. He advocates a tailored assessment of the child's strengths and weaknesses that can yield information for targeted interventions. Barron suggests other tests to assess a full spectrum of the child's assets and deficits.

Research Findings with CHRNB and HINB

While there have been relatively few studies on the CHRNB and HINB over the past decade, two studies are noteworthy. First, Vanderslcie-Barr, Lynch, and McGaffrey (2008) found that the screening batteries for the older and younger child produced a high percentage of correct classifications for determining normal or impaired function using archival data from a neuropsychological clinic. The authors found that the screening battery, neuropsychological deficit scale score (SBNDS) for older children had an 85 percent accuracy rate (cut-off scores 16/17), while a cut-off of 22/23 was 100 percent accurate for younger children.

Bello, Allen, and Mayfield (2008) investigated the sensitivity of the Children's Category Test level 2 (CCT-2) to determine brain dysfunction in children with attention–deficit hyperactivity disorder (ADHD) and children with structural brain damage. Although the Category test was found to be psychometrically sound, it did not differentiate children with brain damage from those with ADHD. The CCT-2 was not particularly sensitive to brain damage; further, both groups performed within the normal range. The authors conclude "we would recommend against the use of the CCT-2, including its factor and subtest scores, for clinical and research applications that aim to draw conclusions regarding the impact of brain injury on abstraction and problem solving abilities" (Bello et al., 2008, p. 338). They recommend using the longer version of the Category test within a comprehensive, larger battery.

Historically, studies utilizing the HRNB-OC and HINB have focused on the ability of these batteries either to distinguish between children with brain damage and those with learning disabilities, or to elucidate the profiles achieved by differing disorders (e.g., conduct disorder, psychiatric disorders). The longer Category test is the best discriminator for children with learning disabilities. Results of studies attempting to distinguish children with learning disabilities from those with brain damage and typically developing children suggest that children with LD have normal motor development with consistent weaknesses on the Category test (Shurtleff et al., 1988). Moreover, a relationship between reading and/or math difficulty and the Category test has been found (Shurtleff et al., 1988; Strom, Gray, Dean, & Fischer, 1987).

Intelligence scores show moderate correlations with the HRNB-OC (Shurtleff et al., 1988). In a review of studies that attempted to differentiate learning-disabled from brain-damaged children using the HRNB-OC, Hynd (1992) suggested that differential performance on intelligence tests may account for much of the ability of the HRNB-OC to discriminate between the two groups. On the other hand, Strom et al. (1987) found that the HRNB-OC provided unique data that were not redundant with data from the WISC-R. Because the issue of the overlap between the WISC-R and the HRNB-OC has not been resolved, it is important that the clinician recognize the overlap between the two measures and take intelligence into consideration when interpreting results.

In addition to the caution as to the influence of intelligence on performance on this battery, children with psychiatric disorders have also performed poorly on the HRNB-OC (Tramontana, Hooper, & Nardillo, 1988). The HRNB-OC's ability to distinguish children with psychiatric disorders from children with brain damage is not clear from existing research. This finding is consistent with the adult Reitan Battery, which also is not diagnostically specific for brain damage versus psychiatric disorder (Hynd & Semrud-Clikeman, 1992). The length and expense of the battery for general use with clients is another concern. The average amount of time to administer the battery ranges from six to 12 hours. Reitan (1986b) suggested that although reducing the length of the battery or developing a screening protocol would have value, the information necessary to answer referral questions makes the

development of a screening protocol problematic. Alth-ough Reitan demonstrated a remarkable hit rate for his ability to determine brain damage (Selz & Reitan, 1979a, 1979b), there has not been sufficient documentation of the battery's ability to localize dysfunction or predict recovery from brain injury (Hynd, 1992). Furthermore, the HRNB-OC does not have adequate norms, and lacks detailed information on the validity and reliability of the battery.

Finally, the HRNB-OC requires intensive training for administration and interpretation of results, which also can be problematic for its use in general clinical or school environments. It may be more appropriate for general clinicians to use other measures to screen for possible neuropsychological involvement and to refer clients to a trained neuropsychologist for a full evaluation if areas of concern are identified. "In terms of future directions for the HRNB-OC and the RINB, if the HRNB-OC is to remain relevant and employed as a battery, then it should be updated with broader and more indepth measures, particularly in areas such as memory and attention" (Nussbaum & Bunner, 2008, p. 264).

Luria Theory of Neuropsychological Assessment for Children

Few would question the importance of the contributions made by the Russian neuropsychologist A. R. Luria, although some have been skeptical about the manner in which his clinical procedures have been standardized into a battery for assessing brain functions (Lezak, 1983). Luria originally described assessment procedures that varied from patient to patient depending on the specific brain area of concern. Attempts to standardize these procedures have been met with enthusiasm by some neuropsychologists and criticism by others. While the Luria-Nebraska Neuropsychological Battery for Children-Revised (LNNB-CR) was an attempt to standardize Luria's approaches, the battery is rarely used in clinical practice. Newer cognitive and neurocognitive assessment procedures represent innovative applications of Luria's conceptual model.

Luria's Conceptual Model

Luria (1980) described brain activity in terms of functional that incorporated elements of localization and equipotential theories. Localization theorists argued that specific brain regions were responsible for discrete brain functions with visual functions in the occipital lobe, auditory functions in the temporal lobe, and so on (Kolb & Whishaw, 2003). Equipotential theorists pointed out that complex human behaviors are controlled by functional CNS regions in such a way that when one portion is damaged, another adjacent or analogous region can assume its function (Kolb & Whishaw, 2003).

Luria's theory was different from other hypotheses at the time because he made four major assumptions:

1. Only specific parts of the brain (not all) are involved in forming a behavior.
2. No equipotentiality of brain tissue is hypothesized. Rather, brain tissue is conceptualized as being specialized for function, both psychologically and physiologically.
3. Behavior is conceived as a function of systems of brain areas working in concert rather than unitary and specific areas producing set behaviors. Therefore, a given behavior will be impaired when any part of the functional system responsible for the behavior is impaired.
4. Luria proposed that alternative functional systems exist—that is, a given behavior can be produced by more than one functional system. Therefore, the clinician will at times see no deficits when such deficits are expected given the locus of damage and at other times see deficits when no known damage is present. If the nature of the task is changed, then the locus of information processing will be changed and another input or output modality utilized. Thus, damage to areas controlling lower skills can be compensated for by areas controlling higher skills.

Research supports aspects of each of these theories in various degrees because functions appear localized to some extent; however, a particular behavior may be impaired because of damage to a number of different brain areas. Kolb and Whishaw (2003) suggest that the important questions center on how damage to a particular site can affect specific behaviors or performance. Luria's functional systems approach conceptualizes brain function as follows. Luria (1980) discussed three functional units as: (1) the arousal unit; (2) the sensory receptive and integrative unit, and (3) the planning, organizational unit (see Table 8.4). The nature of each functional unit is briefly described.

Functional Unit I

In Luria's theory (1980) the arousal system is the first unit and comprises the reticular activating system (RAS), the midbrain, the medulla, the thalamus, and the hypothalamus. Visual, auditory, and tactile stimulation comes through this unit to higher cortical regions. The structures work together in concert in Unit I to regulate energy level and to maintain cortical tone. This unit raises or lowers cortical arousal depending on internal needs. When cortical tone is too low, the brain loses its ability to discriminate between stimuli. Another function of this unit is to filter out irrelevant stimuli. The RAS prevents the cortex from being flooded by unimportant stimuli that could interfere with cortical functioning. If the RAS filters out too much stimulation, sensory deprivation and hallucinations may be present as the cortex attempts to generate its own activity to keep itself aroused. Severe injury to Unit I can result in marked deterioration of wakefulness, with loss of consciousness and possible death. Less severe injury can result in disorganization of memory, distractibility, attentional problems and insomnia. If Units II and III are functional, then in later development or in adulthood these units can assume the functions of Unit I and monitor hyperactive and/or impulsive behavior. Methylphenidate has also been found to activate Unit I and thereby decrease behaviors of impulsivity and poor attention.

Functional Unit II

Unit II is considered the sensory system and consists of the parietal, temporal, and occipital lobes; its major function is sensory reception and integration. Therefore, the areas of Unit II correspond to their sensory modality (temporal for auditory, parietal for sensory

Table 8.4 Selected research with the Halstead-Reitan neuropsychological batteries

Reference	Population	Age	Major findings
Batchelor and Dean (1993)	Learning	9–14 years	1. Two distinct clusters across ages. Group 1 = diffuse deficits. Group 2 = spatial memory deficits. 2. Diffuse deficits may not change with age. 3. Specific deficits deem to change with age.
Berman and Siegal (1976)		CD, normal	1. CD > normals on every HRNB task. 2. CD lowest on verbal mediation, concept formation, and perceptual.
Boyd, Tramontana, and Hopper (1986)	Psychiatric	9–16 years	1. DE = WISC-R + Aphasia test. 79% rate for prediction. LNNB-C status. 2. DE valid as screening device.
Coutts et al. (1987)	LD, non-LD	11–12 years	1. LD > non-LD on Category test. 2. Minimal practice effect after 3 weeks for LD. 3. Category test may be useful for measuring treatment efficacy.
Gamble, Mishra, and Obrzut (1988)	Referred-learning	6–8 years	1. Category test loaded on psychomotor Speed Factor. 2. TPT loaded on Memory Factor. 3. Use Reitan-Indiana with caution with young LD children.
Newby and Matthews (1986)	Clinic-referred	6–14 years	1. Specific neuropsychological function not predicted by PIC.
Nussbaum et al. (1988)	Referred-learning	7–12 years	1. Anterior deficits related to Social Withdrawal Aggression, Hyperactivity, and Externalized scales on CBCL. 2. Posterior deficits high on ANX.
Reitan and Boll (1973)	Normal, MBD, BD	5–8 years	1. BD > MBD > normals. 2. 84% overall accuracy rate classification. 3. 96% BD, 89% MBD, 64% normals.
Selz and Reitan (1979a)	Normal, LD, BD	9–14 years	1. LD normal on motor tasks. 2. LD similar to BD on cognitive and attentional tasks. 3. 80% accuracy, error-impaired groups as less impaired.
Selz and Reitan (1979b)	Normal, LD, BD	9–14 years	1. Classification rules. 2. BD < LD > normals performance. 3. 73% accuracy rate for classification.
Shurtleff, et al. (1988)	Learning	10–12 years	1. Low to moderate correlations of HRNB and WISC-R. 2. Speech Sounds related to Reading decoding and spelling. 3. Category related to math.
Strang & Rourke (1983)	LD	9–14 years	1. Low math/normal reading/spelling group scores low on Category, bilateral tactile-motor, and visual-perceptual-organization.

Table 8.4 (continued)

Reference	Population	Age	Major findings
Strom et al. (1987)	LD	11 years	2. Low math related to low reasoning and sensory-motor. 1. 28% variance in reading accounted for by HRNB. 2. 15% variance in math accounted for by HRNB. 3. Unique contributions of HRNB not measured by WISC-R.
Teeter (1985)	Normal	5—8 years	1. RINB accurate for discriminating high, average, and low readers. 2. RINB more predictive than McCarthy Scales for spelling, reading, and math. 3. Predictive variable stable over two years.
Tramontana et al. (1980)	Psychiatric	9—15 years	1. 60% mild impairment on HRNB using Selz and Reitan rules. 2. 25% moderate impairment. 3. Impairment > chronic psychiatric.
Tramontana and Hooper (1987)	CD, depression		1. No distinct neuropsychological features for INT and EXT disorders.
Tramontana and sherrets (1985)	Psychiatric		1. 50% abnormal HRNB or LNNB-C 2. Impairment > young boys with chronic psychiatric history.
Tramontana, Hooper, and Nardillo (1988)	Psychiatric	8—16 years	1. Impairment > with more severe behavior problems. 2. Mostly in young children with INT disorders. 3. EXT disorders no distinct neuropsychological features.

Notes: **BD** = brain damaged; **MBD** = minimal brain dysfunction; **LD** = learning-disabled; **CD** = conduct-disordered; **RINB** = Reitan Indiana Neuropsychological Battery; **HRNB** = Halstead-Reitan Neuropsychological Battery; **LNNB-CR** = Luria Nebraska Neuropsychological Battery for Children-Revised; **INT** = Internalized Scale on the Child Behavior Checklist; **EXT** = Externalized Scale on the Child Behavior Checklist.

tactile, and occipital for vision). Unit II has been hypothesized to be guided by three functional laws: (1) hierarchical structures of cortical zones do not remain the same during ontogenesis; (2) hierarchical zones decrease in their specificity of function with development, and (3) progressive lateralization of function within hierarchical zones in-creases with development (Luria, 1980). This hierarchy is further divided into three zones: primary, secondary, and tertiary. The primary zones are responsible for sorting and recording sensory information. The secondary zones organize the sensory information and code it for later retrieval. The tertiary zones combine data from various sources in order to lay the basis for organized behavior.

Primary Zones

The primary zones generally consist of sense receptors with point-to-point relationships to the peripheral sense organs. These zones are predetermined by genetics and are the most hardwired of the areas. The primary auditory zone is in the temporal lobe and involves auditory perception. The primary tactile zone is in the sensory strip of the parietal lobe and involves tactile perception. Finally, the primary visual zone is in the occipital lobe and involves visual perception.

Secondary Zones

The secondary zones are generally involved in input of data and integration of information. These zones process information sequentially and have a link, with more than one stimulus being received by the brain at a time. For the auditory secondary zone, the locus is in the secondary regions of the temporal lobe and involves the analysis and synthesis of sounds and the sequential analysis of phonemes, pitch, tone, and rhythm. The secondary tactile zone is in the parietal lobes next to the sensory strip and is involved in two-point discrimination, movement detection, and recognition of complex tactile stimuli (i.e., identifying shapes by touch). The secondary visual zone surrounds the primary visual center of the occipital lobe and is involved in visual discrimination of letters, shapes, and figures.

There is specialization in the secondary zones, with the left hemisphere predominantly responsible for analyzing verbal material and language while the right hemisphere is important for the analysis of non-verbal material such as music, environmental sounds, and prosody of language. Both hemispheres play a role in reading, with the right hemisphere important for recognizing unfamiliar shapes. Once words and letters have been learned, recognition of these shapes becomes a process of the left hemisphere. Both hemispheres are involved in comprehension, with the left hemisphere more involved with semantic and syntactic analysis and the right hemisphere with processing the emotional quality and tone of the passage. Lateralization of function is also found for writing, with the right hemisphere activated primarily when the task is a novel visual-motor task and the left hemisphere activated primarily once a task is learned.

Intelligence tests are hypothesized to measure Unit II functions. Given that Unit II is the center for the analysis, coding, and storage of information, damage to this region results in difficulty in learning basic reading, writing, and mathematics skills.

Tertiary Zones

Tertiary zones allow for cross-modal integration of information from all sensory areas. Information is processed simultaneously and involves integration of various modalities. For example, the reading process is an integration of auditory and visual material; language is an integration of grammatical skills, analysis of auditory information, and comprehension of auditory material, and mathematics involves the integration of visual material with knowledge of number and quantity. These zones are the primary region that intelligence tests are thought to directly measure. Damage to this association area can result in a lowered IQ score, poor reading, writing, and mathematics ability, and language comprehension.

Functional Unit III

Unit III is responsible for output and planning. It is located in the frontal lobes which are further demarcated into three hierarchical zones. The primary zone, in the motor strip of the frontal lobe, is concerned with simple motor output. The secondary zone, in the primary premotor regions, is involved in sequencing motor activity and speech production. The tertiary zone located in the orbitofrontal region of the frontal lobe (the prefrontal region) is the last region to myelinate and develop. Development continues until the third decade of life. The tertiary zone of Unit III is primarily involved with planning, organization, and evaluation of behavior, functions similar to the executive functions. Damage to this area has been linked to problems in delaying gratification, controlling impulses, learning from past mistakes in behavior, and focusing attention. In many cases damage to this zone can be difficult to distinguish from psychiatric and behavior problems. When dysfunction occurs in Unit I, later development of Unit III can compensate or modulate levels of arousal. Moreover, Unit III can activate other parts of the brain and has rich connections to all regions of the brain.

Developmental Considerations

Luria's conceptual framework is based on the theory that certain skills are acquired at different rates depending on the neurodevelopmental stage of the child (Golden, 1981). Further, specific problem solving strategies, behaviors, and skills are dependent on biochemical as well as physiological maturation, including myelination and the growth of cells, dendritic networks, and interconnecting neuronal pathways. Although physiological development is related to psychological maturation, this relationship can be altered by adverse environmental events. Table 8.5 outlines the five major developmental stages described by Golden (1981).

Injury during any one of these stages is thought to produce various deficits depending upon the site and severity of injury. Golden (1981) suggests that damage to the developing brain during Stage 1 is likely to produce deficits in arousal and that, when severe damage ensues, death or mental retardation may result. Damage after 12 months of age is less likely to produce attentional deficits, although physiological hyperactivity is associated with damage prior to 12 months. Paralysis, deafness, blindness, or tactile deficits may result from unilateral injury

to the primary sensory areas during Stage 2 development. In some instances, sensory or motor functions may be transferred to the opposite hemisphere if damage occurs during this stage. Although damage after this developmental stage is likely to produce more serious deficits, there are still compensatory factors that play a role in recovery of function. Golden cautions, however, that bilateral damage is more serious, producing deafness, blindness, and/or paralysis, where compensation is less likely. During Stage 3 development, the two hemispheres begin to show differentiation of function in terms of verbal and nonverbal abilities (Golden, 1981). Unilateral damage is likely to result in loss of language functions if injury is sustained in the left hemisphere once verbal skills are present, at about the age of two years. Damage prior to age two may result in transfer of language to the right hemisphere, whereas damage after age two begins to mimic recovery of functions similar to what is seen in adults (Golden, 1981). However, Golden (1981) suggests that plasticity (i.e., transfer of function) is less likely when injuries are diffuse in nature, or in cases of mild injury. Thus, small injuries early in development can have more deleterious effects than larger injuries later in life. Recovery of function will be explored in more detail in later chapters.

Golden (1981) suggests that learning during the first five years of life is primarily unimodal in nature, with little cross-modal, integrative processing. Early reading during this stage is characterized by rote strategies involving memorization of individual letters, words, or letter sounds. The visual symbol is meaningful only in its relationship to spoken language. Cross-modal learning is possible during Stage 4 when tertiary association regions of the sensory cortices are developing. Injury to these association regions can result in significant learning impairments, such as mental or cognitive deficits or learning disabilities. The type of deficit depends on the location and severity of the injury, and even small insults can affect the integration of one or more sensory modalities (Golden, 1981). Golden (1981) suggests that injuries to tertiary regions are not always evident until Stage 4 development. Injury in one stage may not produce observable deficits until a later stage because the brain regions subserving specific psychological and behavioral functions are not mature. For example, a child sustaining injury to

Table 8.5 Major systems and behavioral correlates of Luria's functional Units

Functional system	Brain units	Behavioral correlates
Unit 1: Arousal System	Reticular activating system pons and medulla through thalamus to cortex	Modulate cortical arousal
		Filters incoming stimuli
		Attention and concentration
Unit 2: Sensory System	Primary temporal lobes	Auditory perception
	Secondary temporal lobes	Analysis and synthesis acoustic sounds and sequential analysis
		Phoneme, pitch, tone, and rhythm
	Primary parietal lobes	Tactile perception
	Secondary parietal lobes	Two-point discrimination
		Movement detection
		Recognition of complex tactile stimuli (e.g., shapes)
	Primary occipital lobes	Visual perception
	Secondary occipital lobes	Visual discrimination (letters, shapes, etc.)
		Cross-modal integration
	Tertiary parital occipital/temporal region	Simultaneous processing
		"Intelligence" (e.g., reading, writing, math, language, syntax, grammar, stereognosis, spatial rotation, angle discrimination)
Unit 3: Output/ Planning	Primary frontal lobes	Simple motor output
	Secondary frontal lobes	Sequencing motor activity
		Speech production
	Tertiary frontal lobes	Decision making and evaluation
		Impulse control
		Delay of gratification
		Focused attention

tertiary regions at the age of two may appear normal at age three, but may show serious learning deficits at age 10 (Golden, 1981). Golden further indicates that predicting future deficits is complicated by these neurodevelopmental factors, and that neuropsychologists must consider these issues when injury is sustained early in life. Finally, according to Golden (1981), Stage 5 involves the development of the prefrontal regions of the brain, which begins during adolescence. According to this neurodevelopmental theory, deficits resulting from injury to frontal regions may not begin to emerge until 12–15 years of age or later. Others have argued that frontal lobe development may occur at earlier stages than suggested by Golden (1981). For example, Becker, Isaac, and Hynd (1987) and Passler, Isaac, and Hynd (1985) describe a progression of frontal lobe development beginning at age six. In these studies it was found that some tasks thought to be mediated by the

frontal lobes begin at six years of age (e.g., flexibility during verbal conflict tasks), continue to emerge at age eight (e.g., inhibition of motor responses), and still are incomplete at age 12 (e.g., verbal proactive inhibition). Neurodevelopmental stages are of primary importance in child neuropsychology, and further research is needed to more clearly map these stages of brain development. Although the question of frontal lobe development will be of continued interest to researchers and clinicians in the next decade, the relationship between brain development and psychological and behavioral function has a strong empirical base.

Although the Luria-Nebraska Children's Battery Revised (LNCB-R) was designed to assess brain functioning based on Luria's model, the test has not been adequately researched. Attempts to standardize and validate the LNCB-R have been slow and "the lack of current research findings present a major concern" (Leark, 2003, p. 155). "Several contemporary neuropsychological assessment tools are available to assess skills similar to those tapped by the Luria-Nebraska domains and were designed solely for children" (Hale & Fiorello, 2004, p. 137). There are several newer batteries that were developed using Luria's conceptualizations of brain functions. The NEPSY and the Cognitive Assessment System (CAS) will be briefly reviewed next.

NEPSY: A Developmental Neuropsychological Assessment

The NEPSY, first developed in 1998 (Korkman, Kirk, & Kemp, 1998), has been revised (Korkman, Kirk, & Kemp, 2007). The NEPSY-II assesses complex cognitive functions as well as subcomponents across functional domains. The instrument is designed to assess neuropsychological development in preschool and school-aged children (ages 3–16 years) including children with Attention-deficit Hyperactivity Disorder, Autism and Asperger's disorder, emotional disturbance, deaf and hearing impaired, language disorders, intellectual disabilities, math and reading disabilities, and traumatic brain injury. Clinicians may use the NEPSY-II for the following: to assess the neurocognitive development of children; to create a tailored assessment to answer specific referral questions, and to diagnose various disorders and to develop intervention plans (Korkman et al., 2007).

Six major domains are measured including: Attention and Executive Functioning, Language, Memory and Learning, Sensorimotor, Social Perception, and Visuospatial. See Korkman et al. (2007) for an in-depth description of the subtests for each domain.

Attention and Executive Functioning

The Attention and Executive Function Scale measures inhibition of learned and automatic responses, monitoring and self-regulation, vigilance, selective and sustained attention, nonverbal problem solving, planning and organizing complex responses, and figural fluency.

Language

The Language Scale measures major phonological processing, repetition of nonsense words, identification of body parts, verbal semantic fluency, rhythmic oral sequences, and the comprehension of oral instructions.

Memory and Learning

The Memory and Learning Scale measures immediate memory for sentences; narrative memory and free recall, cued recall and recognition recall; recall with interference, and immediate and delayed memory for designs, faces and lists.

Sensorimotor

The Sensorimotor domain measures hand movements, repetitive finger movements, and use of a pencil with speed and precision.

Social Perception

The Social Perception domain measures facial affect recognition, comprehension of others' perspectives, and intentions and beliefs.

Visuospatial

The Visuospatial domain measures line orientation, copying geometric figures, three-dimensional designs, mental rotation of objects, whole-part relations, and schematic map reading.

Research Findings with NEPSY

Korkman (1999) provides a nice review of validity studies with the NESPY. Specifically the NEPY appears to have validity for differentiating subtypes of learning difficulties, discriminating ADHD from other learning disabilities, and identifying deficits in infants with prenatal alcohol exposure. Further, Korkman reports that children with brain damage had deficits on the NEPSY, but did not have lateralizing effects. This is consistent with findings that children show functional reorganization of the brain with early brain damage, and that children tend to have more diffuse rather than focal brain dysfunction.

The NEPSY can also be used to identify neurodevelopmental deficits in a number of clinical populations. Mikkola et al. (2005) found that extremely low birth weight (ELBW) infants had decreased performance on measures of the NEPSY (i.e., Attention, Language, Sensorimotor, Visuospatial, and Verbal Memory) compared to controls. Shum, Neulinger, O'Callaghan, and Mohay, (2008) also reported poor performance on verbal memory and attention on the NESPY and low scores on the Trail Making B test. These problems were associated with parent and teacher ratings of attentional difficulties. Young children at risk for ADHD were also found to have deficits on NEPSY measures of executive tasks [e.g., Attention, Fluency (Perner, Kain, & Barchfeld, 2002)

CAS: Cognitive Assessment System

The Cognitive Assessment System (CAS) was designed to assess the cognitive functioning of children 5–18 years of age (Naglieri & Das, 1997). The CAS was developed to identify specific cognitive problems underlying learning and attentional difficulties. The authors indicate that the CAS has utility for assessing cognitive and neuropsychological functions from multiple dimensions or domains, differential diagnosis for learning and attentional difficulties, and intervention planning. The CAS is theory-driven, based on neuropsychological and cognitive theories— Luria's model and the PASS model. The PASS theory suggests that four basic functions underlie cognitive functions including planning, attention, successive and simultaneous processes.The CAS has strong psychometric properties (Naglieri & Das, 1997; Strauss et al. 2006).

Planning

The Planning scale measures mental processes for determining, selecting, applying, and evaluating problems. Performance on this scale is dependent on retrieval of knowledge and impulse control, and is reflective of prefrontal lobe functions.

Attention

The Attention scale measures selective focus on stimuli, while inhibiting other responses. Selective attention, focused cognitive activity, resistance to distractions, orienting to tasks, and vigilance reflect reticular activating system functions.

Simultaneous

The Simultaneous scale measures the ability to perceive and integrate parts into a whole or group. The parietooccipital regions are primarily involved with this mental process.

Successive

The Successive scale measures the ability to integrate stimuli in a sequential, serial order.

Research Findings with CAS

The CAS appears to have been well conceived and researched. While initial factor analyses support the four-factor solution of the PASS model (Naglieri & Das, 1999), others have not found the same results (see Strauss et al., 2006 for a review).Research has shown that the CAS has utility for measuring cognitive processing deficits in clinical groups including children with reading difficulties (Joseph, McCachran, & Naglieri, 2003), children with written expressive disorders (Johnson, Bardos, & Tayebi, 2003), children with ADHD (Naglieri &

Das, 2005), and children with moderate to severe TBI (Gutentag, Naglieri, & Yeates, 1998).The following results have been reported: (1) Children with ADHD had lower scores on the Planning scale of the CAS compared to children without ADHD; (2) the Planning scale best discriminates children with and without written expressive disorders, and (3) children with TBI show low scores on the Planning and Attentions scales.

The CAS is correlated with achievement measures, other intelligence and neuropsychological tests, including the NEPSY (Naglieri, DeLauder, Goldstein, & Schwebach, 2005; Naglieri & Bornstein, 2003). Specifically, low scores on the Successive Processing scale is related to poor reading scores, while low Planning scores are related to decreased performance on calculation, dictation and writing scores on the WJ-R (Naglieri & Bornstein, 2003)

Neuropsychological Protocol: Austin Neurological Clinic

Nussbaum et al. (1988) describe a neuropsychological protocol that reflects neurobehavioral functioning along an anterior/posterior (AP) axis or gradient. This framework is formulated on the anatomical divisions of the cortex along the frontotemporal and parietooccipital axis. Frontal (A) regions have been associated with motor, attentional, sequential processing, reasoning, and abstract thinking abilities, while parietotemporal (P) regions have been associated with tactile, visual perceptual, word recognition, and spelling functions (Nussbaum et al., 1988). On the basis of theoretical and research findings with children and adults, Nussbaum et al. (1988) have included test items from the Halstead-Reitan battery (i.e., finger tapping, tactual performance test, sensory perceptual exams); the Benton Visual Retention Test (BVRT); the Kaufman Assessment Battery for Children (K-ABC) (i.e., Number Recall, Word Order, Gestalt Closure, and Spatial Memory); the Wechsler Scales for Children-Revised (WISC-R) (i.e., Similarities, Digit Span), and the Wide Range Achievement test (WRAT). See Table 8.6 for a

detailed description of Anterior and Posterior measures. While Nussbaum et al. (1988) recognize that this conceptualization is somewhat artificial, they provide this model for heuristic purposes and discuss the importance of developing models to investigate functional asymmetries in children with various learning and personality disorders. Initial findings with the A/P model suggest that children with weaknesses on anterior measures are likely to exhibit psychological and behavioral problems. These findings may be important for clinicians when developing behavioral management interventions.

Boston Process Approach

The Boston Hypothesis Testing Approach utilizes an initial cadre of tests to sample specific behaviors, including memory, language, visual-motor skills, and attention. From these measures, additional tests may be added to further evaluate areas of possible deficit.

The Boston Process Approach is not a published approach and can vary depending on the clinician. It is also called the Boston Hypothesis Testing Approach. The approach suggests that basic areas of functioning are screened and from this screening hypotheses are developed and additional measures are added (Lezak, 1983; 1995). The Boston Process Approach has its foundation in the belief that both the qualitative nature of behaviors and the quantitative scores are important in order to understand the client's deficits and to develop the treatment programs (Kaplan, 1988).

The Boston Process Approach emphasizes the utilization of information about the client's age, handedness, and previously developed skills, which is gathered through the interview process. Such information not only informs the conduct of the evaluative process, but also puts into focus how these skills are affected or spared from brain damage. In addition, these skills are assessed to determine which strategies the client may employ to compensate for his or her impairments. Emphasis is also placed on "testing the limits"-that is, asking the client to answer questions above the ceiling level. Because

Table 8.6 Austin neurological clinic: a paradigm of anterior/posterior measures

Neuropsychological measures	Anterior function assessed
Finger oscillation, dominant and non-dominant hands	Fine motor coordination
Similarities-WISC-R	Verbal abstract reasoning, cognitive flexibility
Digit span-WISC-R	Sequential processing, attention, cognitive flexibility
Number recall-K-ABC	Sequential processing, attention
Word order-K-ABC	Sequential processing, attention
Tactual performance test (TPT)-both hands[a]	Motor coordination
	Posterior function assessed
Sensory perceptual exam	
Tactile	Tactile perception
Visual	Visual perception
Finger recognition	Tactile gnosis
	Sensory integration
Fingertip Number writing	Tactile graphesthesia, Sensory integration
TPT-both hands[a]	Tactile perception, Spatial abilities, Sensory integration
TPT memory	Memory for tactile information
TPT localization	Spatial memory
Testalt closure-K-ABC	Simultaneous visual processing, Figure-ground discrimination
Spatial memory-K-ABC	Visuospatial memory
Wide range achievement test	
Reading	Reading recognition skills
Spelling	Spelling skills

[a]The TPT for Both Hands is included in the Anterior composite score when the TPT-Both Hands is impaired, and when the Sensory Perceptual Exam (SPE) and the Benton Visual Retention Test (BVRT) are in the normal range. The TPT for Both hands is included in the Posterior composite score when the TPT-Both Hands is impaired, and when the SPE and the BVRT are impaired.

Source: Adapted from *Archives of Clinical Neuropsychology*, Vol. 3, N. L. Nussbaum, E. D. Bigler, W. R. Koch, J. W. Ingram, L. Rosa, and P. Massman, "Personality/Behavioral Characteristics in Children: Differential Effects of Putative Anterior versus Posterior Cerebral Asymmetry," pp. 127–135, copyright © 1988, with kind permission from Elsevier Science Ltd., The Boulevard, Langford Lane, Kidlington 0X5 1 GB, UK.

patients with brain damage are often able to do difficult tasks past their ceiling level (Milberg & Blumstein, 1981), it is important to determine these limits through testing to verify if the failure lies in the client's inability, retrieval problems, or less efficient strategies due to brain damage. This modification is important not just for verbal tasks, but also for timed performance tasks. On these timed tasks it is important to determine whether the problem is one of power (mastery) or speed.

A process approach allows flexibility in assessment with an eye to how this assessment informs the treatment plan. Kaplan (1988) suggests that the process approach is helpful to provide insights into brain-behavior relationships. Both standardized and experimental measures are utilized. Therefore, the goal of the process approach is to evaluate the current behavioral functioning in light of intuited brain-behavior relationships.

Instruments utilized in the Boston Process Approach are described in the following section; they include tests of reasoning, verbal language and memory, and perception. See Table 8.7.

Table 8.7 Neuropsychological test procedures: modified boston battery

History
Neuropsychological screening examination
Wechsler intelligence scale for children—3rd edition
Symbol digit modalities test (optional if digit symbol not used)
Wisconsin card sorting test
WRAML
Rey auditory verbal learning test
Neuropsychological screening test
Boston naming test
Rey-Osterreith complex figure
Finger tapping test
Hooper visual organization test
Wide range achievement Test-revised (optional)

Note: September 1986.

Tests of Reasoning

Stroop Color Word Test

The Stroop consists of 100 words (random color names) printed in three different colors. In separate trials, the child will be asked to read the color word (maybe printed in a different color) and then call out the color (maybe a different color word). The time taken to read the color words is usually recorded. Young ADHD children had trouble inhibiting habitual responding on this task (Boucugnani & Jones, 1989).

Wisconsin Card Sorting Test

The Wisconsin Card Sorting Test (WCST) was developed as a measure of frontal lobe dysfunction. The child must match 128 cards to four key cards on the dimensions of color, form, or number. The criteria for correct responses change unexpectedly, and the child must alter the response pattern. Several scores can be derived from the test, including the total number of errors and the number of perserverative errors. Heaton, Chelune, Talley, Kay, and Curtiss (1993) provide a revised and expanded manual for the WCST, with extensive norms for children and adolescents. The WCST measures reasoning, concept formation, and flexibility, and has been shown to be sensitive to frontal lobe activity in children (Chelune, Fergusson, Koon, & Dickey, 1986).

WRAML

The Wide Range Assessment of Memory and Learning (WRAML) contains a Screening Index for memory and new learning ability. This screening index includes the ability to scan pictures and then recall items that have been changed. In addition, the child is shown four pictures of increasing complexity and, after a 10-second delay, is asked to reproduce the figure. The screening index also includes a measure of verbal learning. This subtest requires the child to learn a list of simple words within four trials. This test yields a learning curve over trials. The child then goes on to an additional test with delayed recall of this list following the intervening task. Finally, the child is read two stories and is asked to recite the stories back to the examiner. The child is asked to recall these stories after an intervening task. An optional story recognition format presents the details from a story in a multiple-choice manner. Children who are unable to recall story details spontaneously may be able to elicit this information from memory when prompts are provided.

Rey-Osterreith Complex Figure Test

The Rey-Osterreith Complex Figure Test was standardized by Osterreith in 1944. This task requires the child to copy a complex figure using six different colors: red, orange, yellow, blue, green, and purple. Every 45 seconds, the child is asked to switch colors. If the child completes the figure before using all colors, the examiner notes the final color utilized and the time needed. After 20 minutes, the child is asked to draw the figure from memory.

Tests of Verbal Language and Memory

Boston Naming Test

The Boston Naming Test (BNT), developed by Kaplan, Goodglass, and Weintraub (1978), requires the child to name increasingly difficult black and white pictures. If the child misperceives or fails to recognize a picture, he or she is given a cue as to a category (i.e., if a banana is called a "cane," the examiner might say, "No, it's something to eat"). Phonemic cues are also provided by giving the child the beginning sound of the target word. This cue is given after an incorrect response or no response. Norms for children are being developed for this test, but remain incomplete at this time. The BNT has successfully differentiated children with reading problems from those without (Wolf & Goodglass, 1986) Results from children with language disorders found their performance to be similar to that of children with learning disabilities (Rubin & Liberman, 1983). McBurnette et al. (1991) also found that males with conduct disorders show significantly discrepant scores on this measure, suggesting that these children have verbal expressive disabilities. A total error score can be derived for this instrument.

Controlled Oral Word Association Test

The Controlled Oral Association Test (COWA) requires the child to say as many words beginning with the letter "F" as he/she can think of within one minute; then words beginning with "A," the "S." These letters were selected by how frequently they appear in the English language. This test is sensitive to brain dysfunction in adults, particularly in the left frontal region, followed by the right frontal area (Lezak, 1994).

California Verbal Learning Test

The California Verbal Learning Test-Children's Version (CVLT-C) was developed to assess memory-related strategies and processes for verbal material for children five to 16 years of age (D. C. Delis, Kramer, Kaplan, & Ober, 1994). The test was developed as an adjunct to intellectual and neuropsychological evaluations for children with learning, attentional, intellectual, psychiatric, and other neurological disorders. The test measures memory and verbal learning skills using a hypothetical shopping list in an effort to use everyday, meaningful stimuli. Learning strategies, learning rate, interference (proactive and retroactive conditions), memory enhancement using cuing, and short and longer delay retention are variables of interest in the CVLT-C.

The CVLT-C comprises the following subtests: List A, Immediate Free-Recall; List B, Immediate Free-Recall; List A, Short-Delay Free-Recall; List A, Short-Delay Cued-Recall; List A, Long-Delay Free-Recall; List A, Long-Delay Cued-Recall, and List A, Long-Delay Recognition. The Test Manual presents normative data; a description of the standardization group; administration, scoring, and interpretation guidelines, and reliability and validity studies with the CVLT-C. Nine-hundred-twenty children were selected from a representative sample across gender, racial, and age categories using U.S. Bureau of Census data.

Initial research suggests that the CVLT-C has adequate reliability and validity (D. C. Delis et al., 1994). The CVLT-C could be used to investigate memory and verbal learning abilities of children with various disorders, including Down syndrome and fetal alcohol syndrome (FAS) (Mattson, Riley, Delis, Stern, & Jones, 1996), ADHD (Loge, Staton, & Beatty, 1990), developmental verbal learning disability without ADHD (Shear, Tallal, & Delis, 1992), and dyslexia (Knee, Mittenburg, Bums, DeSantes, & Keenan, 1990). Developmental differences appear on the use of semantic clustering (Levin et al., 1991) and on beginning (primacy) and ending (recency) portions of the lists. Learning curves (average number of words learned across five trials) also were found to differ across ages, with older children displaying steeper curves than younger children (D. C. Delis et al., 1994). Finally factor analysis yielded six major factors that appear consistent with the theoretical principles of the CVLT-C. The factor structure is also similar to the solution found on the Adult CVLT.

At present, the CVLT-C appears psychometrically sound and measure skills not readily measurable with other neuropsychological tests.

Neurosensory Center Comprehensive Examination for Aphasia

The Spreen-Benton Aphasia Tests or the Neurosensory Center Comprehensive Examination for Aphasia (NCCEA) comprises 20 subtests measuring language functions, and four subtests measuring visual and tactile skills (Spreen & Benton, 1969). Spreen and Benton (1977) describe the revised NCCEA tests in detail and list the following tests for the language domain: Visual Naming, Description of Use, Tactile Naming (right hand), Tactile Naming (left hand), Sentence Repetition, Repetition of Digits, Reversal of Digits, Word Fluency, Sentence Construction, Identification by Name, Identification by Sentence (Token Test), Oral Reading (Names), Oral Reading (Sentences), Reading Names for Meaning, Reading Sentences for Meaning, Visual-Graphic Naming, Writing Names, Writing to Dictation, Writing from Copy, and Articulation. The NCCEA items cover a range of language functions and were selected to be sensitive to aphasic symptoms, but not to mild intellectual impairment.

Tests of Perception

Hooper Visual Organization Test

The Hooper Visual Organization Test is comprised of 20 cut-up pictures that the subject is asked to write or name. The test has been shown to be related to frontal lobe functioning in children (Kirk & Kelly, 1986). A total accuracy score can be derived.

Benton Visual Perceptual Tests

The Benton Visual Retention Test, the Benton Facial Recognition Test, the Benton Judgment of Line Orientation Test, and the Benton Visual Form Recognition Test can be used as part of a larger, more comprehensive battery for children between the ages of six and 14 years. Hynd (1992) suggests that the Facial Recognition and the Line Orientation tests may be most useful clinically.

Judgment of Line Orientation

The Judgment of Line Test requires the child to estimate the relationship between line segments by matching a sample to an array of 11 lines in a semicircular array of 180″. The test includes 30 items, with five practice items to teach the test. There are two forms, H and V, which present identical items in different order.

Test of Facial Recognition

This test requires the child to match faces with three different conditions: identical view orientation, matching front view with three-quarter views, and front view with lighting differences. The first six items require a match of only one pose with six selections. The final 16 items require the child to match three selections to the sample. This test is sensitive to language comprehension difficulties as well as to visual-spatial processing problems.

Cancellation Tasks

The Cancellation Task requires the child to select a target visually and repetitively, as quickly as possible. One task that may be used (D2 task) requires the child to cross out all the Ds with two marks above them. There are 15 lines of Ds, and the child is asked to cross out the Ds in each line for 20 seconds and then to switch to the next line. Lower scores may indicate problems in visual scanning, inhibition problems, and inattention.

Clients with difficulties in sequencing and inattention do poorly on this task compared to those individuals without these problems (Spreen & Strauss, 1991; Sohlberg & Mateer, 1989). The Symbol Search task from the WISC-III and the Visual Matching and Cross-Out Tasks from the Woodcock-Johnson are additional tasks that require quick visual scanning and attention to task, and which may be utilized if this area is of concern. There are several more measures which may be utilized to more fully evaluate various aspects of functioning. The astute clinician will seek out these measures in order to determine their appropriateness for various children or adolescents.

Summary and Conclusions

In summary, the Boston Process Approach begins with a sampling of behaviors and then fine tunes the evaluation depending on the initial findings. The strength of the Boston Process Approach is also its weakness; namely, the ability to determine the client's areas of strength and deficit through qualitative data. Qualitative information has improved the prediction of brain damage found on radiological evidence to more than 90 percent (Milberg et al., 1986). Heaton, Grant, Anthony, and Lehman (1981) also found that qualitative data gathered by clinicians using the Reitan battery also showed significant improvement over quantitative scales.

The weakness of the Boston Process Approach lies within the examiner. To avail him- or herself of this approach, the clinician not only must have a wide array of measures in his or her knowledge base, but also sufficient experience in which to apply behavioral observations to brain-behavior relationships. It is also imperative that the clinician have a good database of a "normal" child's performance at various ages.

Although there is a beginning database for the use of the Boston Process Approach with adults (Lezak, 1994; Milberg et al., 1986), data on its efficacy with children are limited. The astute clinician will recognize that best practice will always dictate careful observation of how the child solves the tasks presented to him or her. Although the Boston Approach may be intuitively appealing, further research is needed to determine the benefit of this approach with children.

Delis-Kaplan Executive Function System (D-KEFS)

D. Delis, Kaplan, and Kramer (2001) designed the Delis-Kaplan Executive Function System (D-KEFS) for individuals between the ages of eight to 89 years. The D-KEFS is comprised of nine individually administered tests, and the "battery offers one of the first psychometrically sound, nationally normed set of tests designed exclusively for the assessment of verbal and nonverbal executive functions in children, adolescents and adults" (Shunk, Davis, & Dean, 2006, p. 275). While the D-FEFS contains new tests, other tests have been modified. The battery has an empirical basis and reflects the principles and procedures from the extensive body of literature on executive functions (EF).

The test is organized into four domains: Concept Formation, Flexibility, Fluency and Productivity, and Planning. The D-KEFS contains improved versions of older tests previously described, including the following (Shunk et al., 2006): (1) D-KEFS Trail Making Test measures visual scanning and motor speed; (2) D-KEFS Word Context measures abstract thinking and deductive reasoning; (3) D-KEFS

Sorting Tests measures verbal and nonverbal concept formation; (4) D-KEFS Twenty Questions measures object naming and recognition, visual attention and perception; (5) D-KEFS Tower Test measures planning and problem solving, learning, inhibition of impulsivity, and maintenance of instructional sets; (6) D-KEFS Color-Word Interference test is a version of the Stroop test, and measures inhibition and attention; (7) D-KEFS Verbal Fluency Test measures verbal fluency; (8) D-KEFS Design Fluency Test measures verbal fluency in the spatial domain, and (9) D-KEFS Proverb Test measures verbal abstraction.

The technical adequacy of the D-FEFS is an improvement over earlier EF measures particularly with newer, expanded norms and modified measures (Shunk et al., 2006). Initial research with the D-FEFS shows promise with special populations including ADHD (Wodka et al., 2008), and individuals with autism and Asperger's disorders. However, additional reliability and validity research for children is needed (Barron, 2003).

A Transactional Approach to Neuropsychological Assessment

Neuropsychological assessment from a transactional model encompasses evaluation of a child's functioning in many areas of his or her life. Given the basic premise of our model that the child's bio-behavioral status acts and is acted on by the environment, it is important that this assessment evaluate home, school, and community functioning as well as neuropsychological performance. The assessment is generally based on the referral question, but must also address additional issues that may be raised during the evaluation process.

This approach avoids many of the shortcomings inherent in other methods of interpretation. The functional approach emphasizes the major behavioral characteristics of each disorder, analyzes how behavioral and cognitive variables correlate with one another, analyzes how these behaviors affect development and change over time, and investigates the neurological substrates of behavioral and cognitive characteristics of a disorder. Further emphasis is placed on determining how non-neurological factors (e.g., family and education) interact with and moderate biological factors (i.e., neurochemical imbalances or structural damage).

In concordance with the functional organizational approach, the transactional neuropsychological approach includes the following: (1) a description of the neuropsychological correlates of the disorder; (2) identification of behavioral characteristics of various childhood disorders; (3) considers moderator variables such as family, school, and community interactions, and (4) determines how the existing neuropsychological constraints interact with the child's coping ability and developmental changes that occur at various ages.

The transactional model further provides a systematic study of the interaction of the child's behavior with his or her neurobiology, not only as a means of assessment but for measuring treatment efficacy (Bergquist & Malec, 2002). This approach is ecologically valid and recognizes the interplay of the child's acts and predispositions to his or her environment and the resulting neuropsychological findings. Thus medical interventions such as psychopharmacology will be measured in juxtaposition with psychosocial interventions and vice versa.

In keeping with these assumptions, a neuropsychological assessment based on the transactional approach includes several domains for examination. The initial approach would be a comprehensive developmental interview with the parents. Such an interview would detail information about the child's birth, temperament, developmental milestones, and social, medical, family, and school history. Medical history needs to include information about the existence of seizure disorder, head injury, illnesses, and any medications the child is currently taking. Not only is it important to gather this information, it is also crucial to gather as much information from parents about their perceptions of the child's strengths and weaknesses, as well as questions they may have about their child's neuropsychological functioning.

The evaluation also needs to contain reports from the child's teacher, which should include behavior rating scales by at least two teachers who know the child well. We find it instructional to use the main teacher plus a teacher of a subject that is less structured than formal academics, such as art or gym. These less structured classes can provide a window into the child's ability to handle situations that may be less predictable. Art, music, and gym classes also frequently provide additional information about the child's social skills. If a special education teacher is providing any services to the child, it is very important that this teacher also complete a behavior rating scale.

The next part of the evaluation involves direct observation of the child. If the child is to be observed in his or her classroom, this should be done before the assessment begins. Although it is always good practice to observe the child in the classroom setting, clinicians in private practice or in clinics generally are unable to do so. If this is the case, then a phone interview (with the parents' permission, of course) with the teacher is strongly suggested to ascertain areas of concern in that setting, consistency of behavior across settings (particularly important with regard to assessing behavioral problems such as ADHD, conduct disorders, and social skills deficits), and interventions that have been attempted and that have failed or succeeded. Observation of the child also takes place during the assessment process. How the child separates from his or her parents, how he or she relates to the examiner and copes with a novel situation, and his or her language skills, affect, and problem-solving strategies during the session are all important areas of observation.

Finally, the transactional assessment process includes information about the presenting problem and selection of measures for that concern as well as any additional areas that emerge during the assessment. Incorporating these data and evolution of an evaluation strategy are integral to the transactional approach to neuropsychological assessment. The domains to be assessed will vary depending on the referral question and on the child's age and developmental level. Screening of areas not believed to be involved is desirable, but not always possible. For example, a child who is suspected of having ADHD but who is performing adequately in school does not need a full achievement battery; if there are recent standardized test scores or group achievement tests, then further evaluation is not required. The examiner can then concentrate on measures of distractibility, attention, impulse control, and activity level. In contrast, a child referred to assess for a possible learning disability may not need a full assessment of attention or emotional functioning, particularly when there is no evidence that these are problem areas. The assessment should be tailored to the child and not the child to an assessment protocol. Therefore, we recommend this approach over a battery approach.

Table 8.8 contains the various domains that are often evaluated in a neuropsychological assessment, along with some suggested measures. It is hoped that these suggestions will assist the clinician in using these measures either to determine the existence of a problem that requires a full neuropsychological evaluation or to gain needed information for the development of an intervention program.

Several of these measures were described earlier in Chapter 4. The interested reader is also referred to the test manuals of standardized tests for more details (e.g., Woodcock-Johnson Psychoeducational Battery-Revised: Cognitive; Clinical Evaluation of Language Fundamentals; Token Test; Differential Ability Test). Many of these measures take little time to administer and can be used as screening devices to confirm a diagnosis or area of concern. Many of the measures listed in Table 8.8 are routinely used by the generally trained clinical or school psychologist. The interpretation of these measures

Table 8.8 Domains for neuropsychological assessment and suggested measures

Gross motor	Fine motor	Visual perceptual
Marching (HINB)	Grooved pegboard	Matching figures, V's, concentric squares, and stars (HINB)
Motor scale (MSCA)	Purdue pegboard	K-ABC subtests
Motor scale (LNNB-CR)	Finger tapping	Rey-Osterreith complex figure
Grip strength test	Tactual performance test	Judgment of line Test
	Bender-gestalt test	Facial recognition
	Trails A	Bender-Gestalt test
	Rhythm (LNNB-CR)	Beery visual-motor integration test
		Hooper visual organization test
Sensory-motor	Verbal fluency	Expressive language
Tactile, visual, auditory (HRNB, HINB)	Controlled oral word association-FAS	Clinical evaluation of language fundamentals (CELF-R)
Tactile form recognition	Verbal fluency (MSCA)	Vocabulary subtest (SB: FE & WISC-III)
Fingertip writing (HRNB, HINB)		Boston naming test
		Aphasia screening test (HRNB)
Receptive language	Memory	Abstraction reasoning
CELF-R	Benton visual-retention	Category test (HRNB, HINB)
Token test	Tactual performance test	Wisconsin card sort (WCST)
Peabody picture Vocabulary-Revised	Wide range assessment of Memory and learning (WRAML)	Concept formation test (WJ-R)
Picture vocabulary (WJ-R)	Children's auditory verbal Learning Test (CAVLT)	Trails B (HRNB)
	Rey auditory verbal learning test sentence memory (SB:FE)	Color form test (HINB)
		Ravens progressive matrices
Learning	Executive functions	Attention
CAVLT	Wisconsin card sort	Continuous performance test
WRAML	Category test	Cancellation tests (WJ-R; D2)
Rey-auditory verbal learning test	Matching familiar figures (HINB)	Stroop test
Auditory-verbal learning (WJ-R)	Verbal fluency tasks	Seashore rhythm test (HRNB)
		Speech-sounds perception test (HRNB)
		Progressive figures test (HINB)
		Serial 7's

Note: Halstead-Indiana Neuropsychological Battery (HINB); Halstead-Reitan Neuropsychological Battery for Children (HRNB); Kaufman Assessment Battery for Children (K-ABC); Luria Nebraska Neuropsychological Battery-Children Revised (LNNBB-CR); McCarthy Scales of Children's Ability (MSCA); Stanford-Binet Intelligence Scale, Fourth Edition (SB:FE); Woodcock-Johnson Cognitive Battery-Revised (WJ-R); Wechsler Intelligence Scales for Children-Third (WISC-III).

from a functional neuropsychological perspective is what differs between the evaluations. In the transactional approach it is important to assess the varying domains and determine how the results affect the child's ability to relate to his or her environment and to adapt to the resulting environmental reaction. The transactional model interprets the results of these measures and develops an appropriate intervention program.

References

Barron, I. S. (2003). *Neuropsychological evaluation of the child*. New York: Oxford Press.

Batchelor, E. S., & Dean, R. S. (1993). Empirical derivation and classification of subgroups of children with learning disorders at separate age levels. *Archives of Clinical Neuropsychology, 8*, 1–15.

Becker, M. G., Isaac, W., & Hynd, G. W. (1987). Neuropsychological development of non-verbal behaviors attributed to "frontal lobe" functioning. *Developmental Neuropsychology, 3*, 275–298.

Bello, D. T., Allen, D. N., & Mayfield, J. (2008). Sensitivity of the children's category test level 2 to brain dysfunction. *Archives of Clinical Neuropsychology, 23*, 329–339.

Bergquist, T. E., & Malec, J. F. (2002). Neuropsychological assessment for treatment planning and research. In P. J. Eslinger (Ed.), *Neuropsychological interventions: Clinical research and practice* (pp. 38–58). New York: Guilford Press.

Berman, A., & Siegal, A. (1976). Adaptive and learning skills in juvenile delinquents: A neuropsychological analysis. *Journal of Learning Disabilities, 9*, 51–58.

Boll, T. J. (1974). Behavioral correlates of cerebral damage in children aged 9-14. In R. M. Reitan & L. Davison (Eds.), *Clinical neuropsychology: Current status and application* (pp. 91–120). Washington, DC: V. H. Winston & Sons.

Boucugnani, L., & Jones, R. W. (1989). Behaviors analogous to frontal lobe dysfunction in children with attention deficit hyperactive disorder. *Archives of Clinical Neuropsychology, 4*, 161–174.

Boyd, T. A., Tramontana, M. G., & Hopper, S. R. (1986). Cross-validation of a psychometric system for screening neuropsychological abnormality in older children. *Archives of Clinical Neuropsychology, 1*, 387–391.

Chelune, G. J., Fergusson, W., Koon, R., & Dickey, T. (1986). Frontal lobe disinhibition in attention deficit disorder. *Child Psychiatry and Human Development, 16*, 221–234.

Coutts, R. L., Lichstein, L., Bermudez, J. M., Daigle, M., Mann, R., Charbonnel, T. S., Michaud, R., & Williams, C. R. (1987). Treatment assessment of learning disabled children: Is there a role for frequently repeated neuropsychological testing? *Archives of Clinical Neuropsychology, 2*, 237–244.

Davis, A. S., Johnson, J. A., & D'Amato, R. C. (2005). Evaluating and using longstanding school neuropsychological batteries: The Halstead and the Luria-Nebraska neuropsychological batteries. In R. C. D'Amato, E. Fletcher-Janzen, & C. R. Reynolds (Eds.). *Handbook of school neuropsychology* (pp. 236–263). Hoboken, NJ: John Wiley & Sons, Inc.

Delis, D., Kaplan, E., & Kramer, (2001). Delis-Kaplan executive function system (D-FEFS). San Antonio, TX: The Psychological Corporation.

Delis, D. C., Kramer, J. H., Kaplan, E., & Ober, B. A. (1994). *CVLT-C Children S California verbal learning test: Manual*. San Antonio, TX: The Psychological Corporation.

Findeis, M. K., & Wright, D. G. (1995). *Meta-norms for Indiana-Reitan and Halstead-Reitan neuropsychological test batteries for children, age 5–14*. Unpublished manuscript. Brigham Young University.

Fletcher, J., & Taylor, H. (1984). Neuropsychological approaches to children: Toward a developmental neuropsychology. *Journal of Clinical Neuropsychology, 6*, 35–56.

Gamble, C. M., Mishra, S. P., & Obrzut, J. E. (1988). Construct validity of neuropsychological instrumentation with a learning disabled population. *Archives of Clinical Neuropsychology, 3*, 35P–368.

Golden, C. J. (1981). The Luria-Nebraska children's battery: Theory and formulation. In G. W. Hynd & J. E. Obrzut (Eds.), *Neuropsychological assessment and the school-age child: Issues and procedures* (pp. 277–302). Orlando, FL: Grune & Stratton.

Gutentag, S., Naglieri, J. A., & Yeates, K. O. (1998). Performance of children with traumatic brain injury on the Cognitive Assessment System. *Assessment, 5*, 263–272.

Hale, J. B., & Fiorello, C. A. (2004). *School neuropsychology: A practitioner's handbook*. New York: Guilford Press.

Heaton, R. K., Chelune, G. J., Talley, J. L., Kay, G. G., & Curtiss, G. (1993). *Wisconsin card sorting test manual*. Odessa, FL: Psychological Assessment Resources.

Heaton, R. K., Grant, I., Anthony, W. Z., & Lehman, R. A. W. (1981). A comparison of clinical and automated interpretation of the Halstead-Reitan Battery. *Journal of Clinical Neuropsychology, 3*, 121–141.

Hynd, G. W. (1992). *Neuropsychological assessment in clinical child psychology*. Newbury Park, CA: Sage Publications.

Hynd, G. W., & Semrud-Clikeman, M. (1992). Neuropsychological batteries in assessment of intelligence. In A. S. Kaufman (Ed.), *Adolescent and adult intelligence testing* (pp. 638–695). New York: Guilford Press.

Johnson, J. A., Bardos, A. N., & Tayebi, K. A. (2003). Discriminant validity of the Cognitive Assessment System for students with written expressive disabilities. *Journal of Psychoeducational Assessment, 21*, 180–195.

Joseph, L. M., McCachran, M. E., & Naglieri, J. (2003). PASS cognitive processing, phonological processed, and basic reading performance for a sample of referred primary-grade children. *Journal of Research in Reading, 26*(3), 304–314.

Kaplan, E. (1988). A process approach to neuropsychological assessment. In T. Boll & B. K. Bryant (Eds.), *Clinical neuropsychology and brain function* (pp. 125–167). Washington, DC: American Psychological Association.

Kaplan, E., Goodglass, H., & Weintraub, S. (1978). *Boston naming test*. Boston: E. Kaplan & H. Goodglass.

Kirk, U., & Kelly, M. (1986). Children's differential performance on selected dorsolateral prefrontal and posterior cortical function: A developmental perspective. *Journal of Clinical Experimental Neuropsychology, 7,* 604.

Knee, K., Mittenburg, W., Bums, W. J., DeSantes, M., & Keenan, M. (1990). Memory indices of LD readers using the CVLT-C. *The Clinical Neuropsychologist, 4,* 278.

Kolb, B., & Whishaw, I. Q. (2003). *Fundamentals of human neuropsychology* (5th ed.). San Francisco: W. H. Freeman & Co.

Korkman, M. (1999). Applying Luria's diagnostic principles in neuropsychological assessment of children. *Neuropsychology Review, 9,* 89–105.

Korkman, M., Kirk, U., & Kemp, S. (1998). *NEPSY.* San Antonio, TX: Psychological Coorporation.

Korkman, M., Kirk, U., & Kemp, S. (2007). *NEPSY – second edition (NEPSY-II).* San Antonio, TX: Psychological Coorporation.

Leark, R. A. (2003). Luria-Nebraska neuropsychological battery-children's revision. In M. Hersen (Eds.), *Comprehensive handbook of psychological assessment* (Vol. 4, pp. 147–156). New York: Wiley & Son.

Levin, H. S., Culhane, K. A., Hartman, J., Evankovich, K., Mattson, A. J., Haward, H., et al. (1991). Developmental changes in performance on tests of frontal lobe functioning. *Developmental Neuropsychology, 7,* 377–395.

Lezak, M. D. (1983). *Neuropsychological assessment.* New York: Oxford University Press.

Lezak, M. D. (1994). *Neuropsychological assessment* (4th ed.). New York: Oxford University Press.

Lezak, M. D. (1995). *Neuropsychological assessment* (3rd ed.). New York: Oxford University Press.

Loge, D. V., Staton, R. D., & Beatty, W. W. (1990). Performance of children with ADHD on tests sensitive to frontal lobe dysfunction. *Journal of the American Academy of Child and Adolescent Psychiatry, 29,* 540–545.

Luria, A. R. (1980). Higher cortical functions in man (2nd ed.). New York: Basic Books.

Mattson, S., Riley, E. P., Delis, D. C., Stern, C., & Jones, K. L. (1996). Verbal learning and memory in children with fetal alcohol syndrome. *Alcoholism: Clinical and Experimental Research, 20*(5), 810–816.

McBurnette, K., Lahey, B. B., Frick, P. J., Risch, C., Loeber, R., Hart, E., Christ, M. A., & Hanson, K. (1991). Anxiety, inhibition, and conduct disorder in children. *Journal of American Academy of Child and Adolescent Psychiatry,* 30, 192–196.

Mikkola, K., Ritari, N., Tommiska, V., Salokorpi, T., Lehtonen, L., Tammela, O., et al. (2005). Neurodevelopmental outcome at 5 years of age of a national cohort of extremely low birth weight infants who were born in 1996–1997.*Pediatrics, 116*(6), 1391–1400.

Milberg, W. B., & Blumstein, S. E. (1981). Lexical decisions and aphasia: Evidence for semantic processing. *Brain and Language, 28,* 154–168.

Milberg, W. B., Hebben, N., & Kaplan, E. (1986). The Boston Process Approach to neuropsychological assessment. In I. Grant & K. M. Adams (Eds.), *Neuropsychological assessment and neuropsychiatric disorders* (pp. 65–86). New York: Oxford University Press.

Naglieri, J. A., & Bornstein, B. T. (2003). Intelligence and achievement: Just how correlated are they? *Journal of Psychoeducational Assessment, 21*(3), 244–260.

Naglieri, J. A., & Das, J. P. (1997). Construct and criterion-related validity of planning, simultaneous, and successive processing task. *Journal of Psychoeducational Assessment, 5,* 353–363.

Naglieri, J. A., & Das, J. P. (1999). *Cognitive assessment system.* Rolling Meadows, IL: Riverside Publishing.

Naglieri, J. A., & Das, J. P. (2005). Planning, attention, simultaneous, successive (PASS) theory (pp. 120–135). In D. P. Flanagan & P. L. Harrison (Eds.), *Contemporary intellectual assessment* (2nd). NY: Guilford Press.

Naglieri, J. A. Goldstein, S., Delauder, B. I., & Schwebach, A. (2005). Relationships between WISC-III and the Cognitive Assessment System with the Conners' rating scales and continuous performance tests. *Archives of Clinical Neuropsychology, 20,* 385–401.

Newby, R. F., & Matthews, C. G. (1986). Relationship between the "cognitive triad" from the personality inventory for children and an extended Halstead-Reitan neuropsychological battery. *Archives of Clinical Neuropsychology, I,* 157–164.

Nussbaum, N. L., & Bigler, E. D. (1986). Halstead-Reitan test batteries for children. In C. R. Reynolds & E. Fletcher-Janzen (Eds.), *Handbook of clinical child neuropsychology* (pp. 181–192). New York: Plenum Press.

Nussbaum, N. L., & Bigler, E. D. (1997). Halstead-Reitan test batteries for children. In C. R. Reynolds & E. Fletcher-Janzen (Eds.), *Handbook of clinical child neuropsychology* (2nd ed., pp. 219–236). New York: Plenum Press.

Nussbaum, N. L., Bigler, E. D., & Koch, W. R., Ingram, J. W., Rosa, L., & Massman, P. (1988). Personality/behavioral characteristics in children: Differential effects of putative anterior versus posterior cerebral asymmetry. *Archives of Clinical Neuropsychology, 3,*127–135.

Nussbaum, N. L., & Bunner, M. R. (2008). Halstead-Reitan neuropsychological test battery for children. In C. R. Reynolds & Fletcher-Janzen, E. (Eds.), *Handbook of clinical child neuropsychology* (3rd ed., pp. 247–266). New York: Plenum Press.

Passler, M., Isaac, W., & Hynd, G. W. (1985). Neuropsychological development of behavior attributed to frontal lobe functioning in children. *Developmental Neuropsychology, 1,* 349–370.

Perner, J., Kain, W., & Barschfield, P. (2002). Executive control and higher order theory of mind in children at risk for ADHD. *Infant and Child Development, 11*(2), 141–158.

Reitan, R. M. (1969). *Manual for administration of neuropsychological test batteries for adults and children.* Indianapolis, IN: Author.

Reitan, R. M. (1971). Sensorimotor functions in brain-damaged and normal children of early school age. *Perceptual and Motor Skills, 33,* 671–675.

Reitan, R. M. (1984). Aphasia and sensory-perceptual deficits in children. Tucson, AZ: Neuropsychological Press.

Reitan, R. M. (1986a). Theoretical and methodological bases of the Halstead-Reitan neuropsychological test battery. Tucson, AZ: Neuropsychological Press.

Reitan, R. M. (1986b). Theoretical and methodological bases of the Halstead-Reitan neurological test battery. In I. Grant & K. M. Adams (Eds.), *Neuropsychological assessment of neuropsychiatric disorders* (pp. 3–30). New York: Oxford University Press.

Reitan, R. M. (1987). *Neuropsychological evaluation of children*. Tucson, AZ: Neuropsychological Press.

Reitan, R. M., & Wolfson, D. (1985). *The Halstead-Reitan neuropsychological battery: Theory and clinical interpretation*. Tucson, AZ: Neuropsychological Press.

Reitan, R. M., & Wolfson, D. (1992a). *Neuropsychological evaluation of older children*. Tucson, AZ: Neuropsychology Press.

Reitan, R. M., & Wolfson, D. (1992b). *Neuropsychological evaluation of younger children*. Tucson, AZ: Neuropsychology Press.

Reitan, R. & Wolfson, D. (2004a). The trail making test as an initial screening procedure for neuropsychological impairment in older children. *Archives of Clinical Neuropsychology, 19*, 281–288.

Reitan, R. & Wolfson, D. (2004b). Use of the progressive figures test in evaluating brain damaged children, children with academic problems, and normal controls. *Archives of Clinical Neuropsychology, 19*, 305–312.

Rourke, B. P. (1981). Neuropsychological assessment of children with learning disabilities. In S. B. Filskov & T. J. Boll (Eds.), *Handbook of clinical child neuropsychology*. New York: Wiley Interscience.

Rourke, B. (1989). Nonverbal learning disabilities: The syndrome and the model. New York: Guilford Press.

Rourke, B., Bakker, D., Fisk, J., & Strang, J. (1983). *Child neuropsychology: An introduction to theory, research, and clinical practice*. New York: Guilford Press.

Rubin, H., & Liberman, I. (1983). Exploring the oral and written language errors made by language disabled children. *Annals of Dyslexia, 33*, 111–120.

Selz, M., & Reitan, R. (1979a). Neuropsychological test performance of normal, learning-disabled, and brain-damaged older children. *Journal of Nervous and Mental Disorders, 167*, 298–302.

Selz, M., & Reitan, R. (1979b). Rules for neuropsychological diagnosis: Classification of brain function in older children. *Journal of Consulting and Clinical Psychology, 47*, 258–264.

Shear, P. K., Tallal, P., & Delis, D. C. (1992). Verbal learning and memory in language-impaired children. *Neuropsychologia, 30*, 451–458.

Shum, D., Neulinger, K., O'Callaghan, M., & Mohay, H. (2008). Attentional problems in children born very premature or with extremely low birth weight at 7-9 years. *Archives of Clinical Neuropsychology, 23*(1), 103–112.

Shunk, A. W., Davis, A. S., & Dean, R. S. (2006). Test review: Delis Kaplan Executive Function System (D-FEFS). *Applied Neuropsychology, 13*(4), 275–279.

Shurtleff, H. A., Fay, G. E., Abbott, R. D., & Berninger, V. W. (1988). Cognitive and neuropsychological correlates of academic achievement: A levels of analysis assessment model. *Journal of Psychoeducational Assessment, 6*, 298–308.

Sohlberg, M. M., & Mateer, C. A. (1989). *Introduction to cognitive rehabilitation*. New York: Guilford Press.

Spreen, O., & Benton, A. L. (1969). *Neurosensory center comprehensive examination for aphasia (NCCEA)*. Victoria, BC: University of Victoria.

Spreen, O., & Benton, A. L. (1977). *Neurosensory center comprehensive examination for aphasia (NCCEA)-revised*. Victoria, BC: University of Victoria.

Spreen, O., & Strauss, E. (1991). *A compendium of neuropsychological tests*. New York: Oxford University Press.

Strang, J. D., & Rourke, B. (1983). Concept-formation1 nonverbal reasoning abilities of children who exhibit specific academic problems in arithmetic. *Journal of Clinical Child Psychology, 12*, 33–39.

Strauss, E., Sherman, E. M., & Spreen, O. (2006). *A compendium of neuropsychological tests* (3rd ed.). New York: Oxford University Press.

Strom, D. A., Gray, J. W., Dean, R. S., & Fischer, W. E. (1987). The incremental validity of the Halstead-Reitan neuropsychological battery in predicting achievement for learning-disabled children. *Journal of Psychoeducational Assessment, 2*, 157–165.

Taylor, H. G., & Fletcher, J. M. (1990). Neuropsychological assessment of children. In G. Goldstein & M. Hersen (Eds.), *Handbook of psychological assessment*. New York: Pergamon.

Teeter, P. A. (1985). A neurodevelopmental investigation of academic achievement: A report of years 1 and 2 of a longitudinal study. *Journal of Consulting and Clinical Psychology, 53*, 709–717.

Teeter, P. A. (1986). Standard neuropsychological batteries for children. In J. E. Obrzut & G. W. (Eds.), *Child neuropsychology, Volume 2: Clinical practice* (pp. 187–228). Orlando, FL: Academic Press.

Tombaugh, T. N. (2003). Trail Making Test A and B: Normative data stratified by age and education. *Archives of Clinical Neuropsychology, 19*(2), 203–214.

Tramontana, M., & Hooper, S. (1987). Discriminating the presence and pattern of neuropsychological impairment in child psychiatric disorders. *International Journal of Clinical Neuropsychology, 9*, 111–119.

Tramontana, M., & Sherrets, S. D. (1985). Brain impairment in child psychiatric disorders: Correspondences between neuropsychological and CT scans. *Journal of American Academy of Child Psychiatry, 24*, 333–596.

Tramontana, M., Sherrets, S. D., & Golden, C. J. (1980). Brain dysfunction in children with psychiatric disorders: Application of Selz-Reitan rules for neuropsychological diagnosis. *Clinical Neuropsychology, 2*, 118–123.

Tramontana, M., Hooper, S., & Nardillo, E. M. (1988). Behavioral manifestations of neuropsychological impairment in children with psychiatric disorders. *Archives of Clinical Neuropsychology, 3*, 369–374.

Vanderslcie-Barr, J. L., Lynch, J. K., & McCaffrey, R. J. (2008). Screening for neuropsychological impairment in children using Reitan and Wolfson's preliminary neuropsychological test battery. *Archives of Clinical Neuropsychology, 23*, 243–249.

Wheeler, L., & Reitan, R. M. (1962). The presence of laterality of brain damage predicted from responses to short aphasia screening test. *Perceptual and Motor Skills, 15*, 783–799.

Wodka, E. L., Mostofsky, S. H., Prahme, C., Gidley Larson, J. C., Loftis, C., Denckla, M. B., et al. (2008). Process examination of executive function in ADHD: Sex and subtype effects. *The Clinical Neuropsychologist, 22*(5), 826–841.

Wolf, M. M., & Goodglass, H. (1986). Dyslexia, dysnomia, and lexical retrieval: A longitudinal investigation. *Brain and Language, 28*, 154–168.

Part III

Childhood and Adolescent Disorders

Chapter 9
Neuropsychological Correlates of Childhood and Adolescent Psychiatric Disorders: Disruptive Behavior Disorders

Externalizing disorders have been defined as those disorders in which overt behavior is present (American Psychiatric Association [APA], 2000). Externalized disorders are characterized by numerous dysfunctional behaviors, which pose difficulties in management in the social and psychological aspects of the child's life. The externalized disorders to be reviewed include Attention-Deficit Hyperactivity Disorder and conduct disorder. Severe neuropsychiatric disorders, including Tourette syndrome, are discussed here because of the similarities in the brain areas that are implicated and in the neurotransmitter systems that are thought to be involved. Many of the symptoms of ADHD and frontal lobe dysfunction are also found with autism and Tourette syndrome. Biochemical and neuropsychological models of these disorders will be discussed in more detail in the following sections, including the effects on these neuropsychiatric disorders on the psychosocial and academic functioning of children.

Biochemical and Neuropsychological Models of Psychiatric Disorders of Childhood

Investigating the causes of neuropsychiatric disorders of childhood has led researchers to appreciate the role of neurochemicals, specifically neurotransmitters, and their effect on behavior. Three major neurotransmitters have received attention: (1) serotonin (SE), (2) dopamine (DA), and (3) norepinephrine (NE). Neurotransmitters are not evenly distributed throughout the brain but appear concentrated in specific brain regions (Pliszka, 2003; See Table 9.1)

High levels of DA apear in the caudate, putamen (striaturn) and frontal lobes. In general, NE is more widespread in the brain. The hypothalamus has high concentrations of SE and NE, while the limbic and frontal lobes also have high levels of SE. These various brain regions play different roles in the control and regulation of motor activity, emotional responsivity, and emotions.

Neurotransmitters are part of the electrochemical mechanisms by which neurons communicate to initiate, regulate, and inhibit simple and complex activities. An over- or under-abundance of neurotransmitters appear related to some psychiatric problems in children and adults. See Table 9.2 for a summary of the behavioral effects of neurochemical levels and psychiatric disorders. Although evidence suggests that neurotransmitter models are viable explanations for psychiatric disorders, there are billions of neurons in the brain and the complexity of the interactions are almost unfathomable. The chemical balance of neurotransmitters is interactive; that is, increases or decreases in one neurotransmitter affect the levels of other chemicals in various brain regions. Furthermore, medications that move one transmitter to normal levels may have a negative influence on other transmitters.

Medication Effects on Neurotransmitters

Neurotransmitters are released at the synaptic cleft (see Chapter 2 for an explanation of the anatomy of the neuron), and if they remain at the synapse neurons fire. To keep neurons from constant firing, neurotransmitters are either broken down or reabsorbed into the presynapse (neuron originating the signal).

M. Semrud-Clikeman, P.A. Teeter Ellison, *Child Neuropsychology*, DOI 10.1007/978-0-387-88963-4_9,
© Springer Science+Business Media, LLC 2009

Table 9.1 Neurotransmitter circuits, brain regions, and functional activity

Neurotransmitters	Brain circuits	Functional activity
Dopamine (DA)	• Nigrostriatal pathway Substantia nigra → caudate → striatum	Stimulates movement ↓ DA ↑ muscle rigidity & tremors (e.g., Parkinson's) ↓ DA ↑ jerky movements, tics (e.g., Tourette)

	• Mesocortical-limbic pathway
	  Brain stem → prefrontal
	  Brain stem → limbic system
		Modulates emotions
		↑ DA ↑ hallucinations and paranoia (e.g., schizophrenia)
		↓ DA disinhibition of subcortex
		↓ DA ↑ hyperactivity
		    ↑ inattention
		    ↑ temper
		    ↑ aggression

	• Tuberoinfundibular pathway Hypothalamus ® pituitary	
Norepinephrine (NE)	• Locus ceruleus (LC) → spinal cord • LC → cerebellum • LC → thalamus • LC → frontal → limbic	Regulaes DA and NE in prefrontal Alternative hypothesis for Tourette syndrome and ADD
Serotonin	• Caudal raphe nuclei → cerebellum • Rostral raphe nuclei → thalamus • Rostral raphe nuclei → prefrontal → limbic	Inhibits large brain regions • Frontal (ADHD) • Striatum (tics) • Hippocampus (memory and learning) • Septum and limbic (emotional lability)

	• Feedback loop
	  Raphe nuclei inhibits
	  Habenual → feedback → inhibits raphe nuclei
		May increase/decrease symptoms
		
		Decreased serotonin
		• Alcoholism
		• ADHD
		• Aggression
		• Borderline personality
		• Bulimia
		• Depression
		• Impulsivity & inattention
		• Self-multilation (Lesch-Nyhan)
		• PMS
		• Tourette syndrome
		• Violent behavior
		• Violent suicide

Monoamine oxidase (MAO) is one of the enzymes that breaks down neurotransmitters. Thus, medications that inhibit this breakdown process (MAO inhibitors) allow the neuron to continue firing. MAO inhibitors are used to treat depression and serve to increase the amount of neurotransmitters at the synapse. Other antidepressants, such as the ticyclics, inhibit the reuptake process, thereby enhancing the activity of dopamine, norepinephrine, and serotonin.

Transmitters can stimulate or inhibit neural activity and are classified as either agonists, because they stimulate receptor activity, or antagonists, because they inhibit receptors (e.g., Haloperidol inhibits dopamine). Neurotransmitters can stimulate or inhibit cell activity (e.g., serotonin inhibits cellular activity). See Table 9.3 for a summary of medication effects on neurotransmitter systems.

Table 9.2 Neurotransmitter levels, psychiatric disorders, and behavioral effects

Psychiatric Disorders	Neurotransmitters	Behavioral effects
Tourette syndrome	↓ DA frontal regions	Frontal lobe syndrome
	↑ DA nucleus accumbens and striatum	Motor and vocal tics
	↓ DA substantia nigra	ADHD symptoms
		Learning and conduct problems
		Mimics frontal lobe syndrome
	↓ SE	Aggression and self-injury
		Hypersuxuality
ADHD	↓ DA frontal regions	Disinhibition of subcortex
		Hyperactivity and irritability
	↓ SE	Aggression
Schizophrenia	↑ NE	Hyperarousal
	↑ SE	Particularly in brain atrophy
	↓ SE	Two types of schizophrenia
Depression	↓ NE	Depression
	↑ NE	Mania
	↓ SE	Severe depression
Anxiety	↑ NE	Anxiety and fear
Obsessive-compulsive disorder (OCD)	Hypersensitive SE receptors	OCD symptoms
		Linkage of depression, anxiety, and aggression in OCD

Note: DA = dopamine; SE = serotonin; NE = norepinephrine.

Table 9.3 Medication effects on neurotransmitters

Medications	Neurotransmitter effects	Behavioral effects
Stimulants	↑ DA in frontal regions	Frontal lobe inhibits subcortex
		Decreases ADHD symptoms
		Increases Tourette symptoms
Haldol	Stimulates synthesis and turnover of DA	
	↑ SE	Decreases aggression
		Decreases Tourette symptoms
		Decreases self-injury
Cylert	↑ SE	Decreases ADHD symptoms
Clonidine	↓ NE	Decreases anxiety and panic attacks
	↑ SE ↑ DA frontal regions	Decreases ADHD
	Inhibits production of NE	Decreases Tourette symptoms
Tricyclics	↓ Locus ceruleus activity	Decreases depression
	↑ NE	
Imipramine	Inhibits reuptake of NE	Decreases depression
Clomipramine	↑ SE	Decreases obsessive-compulsive symptoms
		Decreases panic attacks
Prozac	↑ SE	Decreases depression
	Increases synthesis or decreases reuptake of SE	

Note: DA = dopamine; SE = serotonin; NE = norepinephrine.

Although neurochemical models of psychiatric disorders are far from complete, many researchers suggest that the biochemistry of neurotransmitter systems holds the key to better understanding and treating many severe disorders of childhood. Further, research that investigates the effects of combined psychopharmacology and psychosocial interventions may shed further light on how biochemical and environmental factors interact. It may also indicate how psychosocial or behavioral therapies augment medication and vice versa. Future clinical and research trials should investigate this interaction. The MTA Cooperative Group (2008a, 2008b) has completed research for combined treatments for ADHD. Efforts of this nature may prove useful for other disorders, such as conduct disorders and depression. The following sections provide a review of severe neuropsychiatric disturbances, including Tourette syndrome and externalized, disruptive disorders.

Tourette Syndrome

The essential features of Tourette syndrome (TS) are multiple motor and vocal tics (APA, 2000), and is etiologically similar to obsessive-compulsive disorders (Pennington, 2002). TS is associated with significant social impairment and often interferes with normal school adjustment. For diagnostic purposes, symptoms of TS must be present before 18 years of age and must include both motor and vocal tics which are not the result of medication (e.g., stimulants) or other medical conditions (e.g., encephalitis).

Motor tics may include the following: facial regions (e.g., eye blinking, eye rolling, squinting, licking lips, sticking tongue out, smacking lips, etc.); head and neck movements (touching shoulder to chin, throwing head back); shoulders (e.g., shrugging); arms (failing, extension, or flexion); hands (e.g., biting nails, finger signs or copropraxia, picking at skin); diaphragm (e.g., inhaling or exhaling); legs and feet (e.g., kicking, stooping, stamping, tapping, toe curling), or others (e.g., banging, chewing on clothes, flapping arms, smelling fingers, body jerking, picking lint).

Vocal tics present unique problems for individuals with TS and are involuntary in nature. Compulsive swearing or coprolalia is one of the more disturbing features of TS. The compulsive, repetitive nature of the swearing has a negative impact on the individual's ability to interact with others. Although swearing appears high in severe TS, in milder cases swearing appears to occur less frequently. An interesting aspect of the disorder is the child's ability to control the tics for periods of time during the day (Pennington, 2002). This often leads

to misunderstanding and misdiagnosis, as the child may display the symptoms while at home but not in school. Stress appears to increase the rate of tics, and the presence of early TS symptoms appears related to more severe cases of the disorder.

Genetic Correlates and Brain Mechanisms of TS

Although TS appears to be an inherited disorder in a majority of cases, some children do not have a familial history of the disorder (APA, 2000). About 80 percent of the genome has been eliminated as the location of TS, thus multiple genetic risk factors are more likely (Pennington, 2002). Pauls and Leckman (1986) found that approximately one in 83 people are carriers of the gene that transmits TS.

Frontal-subcortical circuits (FSC) and superior medial frontal regions appear to be implicated in TS (Miller & Cummings, 2007). Individuals with TS appear to have decreased activation of orbitofrontal, cingulated and insular brain regions (Peterson, Leckman, & Cohen, 1995). Further, neuroimaging studies have found that brain regions implicated in OCD, TS and anxiety disorders overlap (Pennington, 2002).

Prevalance of TS

TS may occur more often than previously suspected. Prevalence rates are estimated to be 5–30 per 10,000 in young children with lower rates in adults [1–2 per 10,000 (APA, 2000)]. The fact that TS may occur with other disorders also may mask an accurate diagnosis when symptoms are mild.

Associated Features of TS

TS can coexist with numerous other childhood disorders, including autism, Asperger's syndrome, ADHD, borderline personality disorder, schizophrenia, and manic-depressive and depressive disorders (APA, 2000). The linkages among these various disorders may depend on activity levels and the intricate balance among the neurotransmitters (DA, SE, and NE), as well as on the site of primary neurological involvement (frontal, striatal, or limbic regions). Other associated features of TS include learning problems, reading and speech deficits, motivational problems, sleep disorders, attentional deficits, and motor coordination problems (Comings, 1990).

Implications for Assessment

The diagnosis of TS depends on a comprehensive evaluation, including careful history taking and behavioral descriptions. An assessment of psychosocial interactions and cognitive-academic functioning should be included. Neuropsychological evaluation may be helpful to identify frontal lobe deficits, speech, language, memory, and learning problems associated with TS. Deficits on measures of executive control skills may be present, but studies have not been conclusive on this finding (Pennington, 2002).

Medical consultation may be helpful to identify genetic linkages and for ruling out other neurological disorders (e.g., Lesch-Nyhan and myoclonus) that may present like TS symptoms. Pennington (2002) also reports that one-third of individuals with TS have autoimmune disorders from streptococcal infections that attack the basal ganglia.

Implications for Interventions

Interventions may include medication in conjunction with other psychosocial and behavioral therapies depending upon the diagnostic picture. Medical treatments of TS are varied including DA agonists, neuroleptics and atypical neuroleptics, and SSRIs (Pennington, 2002). The selection of psychosocial intervention strategies depends on the number and severity of other comorbid disorders (e.g., ADHD, depression, OCD). Individual case analysis with careful monitoring is then the key to successful programming for children with TS.

Pharmacological Interventions

Pennington (2002) indicates that medications are the main treatment for TS, and are helpful when the child's behaviors significantly interfere with adjustment, and when the behavioral pattern cannot be controlled through other behavioral and psychosocial interventions. Increased structure at home or in school may be warranted, and educational interventions such as tutoring may alleviate learning and academic difficulties.

Common medications that control TS symptoms are haloperidol and clonidine. The child's overall quality of life should be considered when assessing the need for medication. Dosage levels should be "the smallest dose that provides just enough change in the chemical balance so the child, or adult, can function as near to normal as possible" (Comings, 1990, p. 538). Tics may be the easiest to control, while other associated behaviors may require additional medications. For example, stimulants may be useful for ADHD symptoms. In some instances, haloperidol and clonidine are administered together, and clonopin may be added for children who do not respond to single medications (Comings, 1990). It is always best to start with low doses and to increase dosage levels when needed. This basic approach may reduce the negative side effects associated with medications.

Psychosocial and Behavioral Interventions

Nonpharmacological interventions will do nothing to reduce tics, but may help reduce associated behavioral problems (Comings, 1990). Many children do not get better with medication alone, so combined interventions are recommended. However, medication may increase the likelihood of success of nonpharmacological treatments (Comings, 1990).

Comings (1990) suggests that parents can and should discipline for antisocial behavioral problems (e.g., lying, stealing, refusal to complete chores, disrespect, talking back, oppositional confrontational, temper tantrums), but not for tics, attentional problems, obsessive-compulsive behaviors, or learning problems. There are a number of effective techniques including short-term natural consequences, rewards, behavioral contracts, skill building for appropriate behaviors, and family sibling therapy (Comings, 1990). Parents are advised to avoid prolonged restrictions, spankings, arguing back and being drawn into the angry outburst, abdicating the parenting role, and inconsistent parenting. A careful plan for handling rage attacks is needed. Some parents find that holding the child until the rage subsides works well, while others find that removing themselves from the angry outburst works, too. For example, if the child loses control and begins to yell obscenities, the parent disengages by repeating that the decision stands and that the conversation is over. Other techniques for controlling physical or verbal outbursts can be gleaned from Patterson's work with oppositional and conduct-disordered youth. The clinician should work closely with the parent to have a plan of action and to seek out alternatives if the plan fails. These types of interventions are time-consuming and can be taxing for the family, so family therapy may be necessary to address the stress involved in raising a child with TS.

Family dynamics and stress factors should be addressed. A patient who was treated by one of the authors was placed in an out-of-state residential treatment facility because his parents could no longer tolerate his behavioral problems and he was an embarrassment to the family. When discussing his feelings about this rejection, the teenager became more agitated, and his tics and involuntary swearing increased. It was important to improve the family cohesion and to initiate efforts to reinstate the youngster back into the family.

School-based interventions should focus on the child's strengths and attempt to bypass weaknesses if possible (Comings, 1990). Strength approaches may include untimed tests, small work units, simple instructions, child-paced work, reduced workload, oral exams, the use of tape recorders and computers, and individual tutoring. Children with TS may require special education services, and an individualized educational plan (IEP) may be needed.

Attention-Deficit Hyperactivity Disorder

Attention-Deficit Hyperactivity Disorder (ADHD) involves disturbances in attention, self-regulation, activity level, and impulse control. According to recent reports from the National Survey of Children's Health, ADHD is among the most commonly diagnosed disorders in childhood (Blanchard, Gurka, &

Blackman, 2006). While general population estimates of children ages 6–17 years old suggest that it has a prevalence rate of 8.8 percent (Blanchard et al., 2006), incidence rates have ranged from 3 to 11 percent (Daley, 2005). The prevalence rate for learning disabilities, which may be found in as many as 11.5 percent of the school-age population, is the most common childhood disorder (Blanchard et al., 2006). Epidemiological studies of preschool children suggest that as many as 1.0–5.7 percent have ADHD (Blanchard et al., 2006; Egger & Angold, 2006). The Center for Disease Control (CDC) data indicates that of those diagnosed with ADHD, a little more half receive medication (Visser, Lesesne, & Perou, 2007).

Recent studies have begun to apply empirical methodologies to further refine and clarify the diagnostic subtypes of ADHD. Specifically, latent class analysis (LCA), a statistical technique that partitions individuals into phenotypically homogenous groups based on profiles of symptoms, have revealed interesting sub-typologies (Volk, Henderson, Neuman, & Todd, 2006). Studies using LCA have reported that there may be as many as seven population-based profiles of ADHD symptoms (Few Symptoms, Mild Inattentive, Severe Inattentive, Talkative-Impulsive, Mild-Combined, Severe-Combined, and Hyperactive; Volk et al., 2006; Volk, Neuman, & Todd, 2005). The most prevalent profiles were the Few Symptoms (53.4%), Mild Inattentive (12.3%), and Severe Inattentive (12.1%) groups (Volk et al., 2005). The extent to which these population-based studies inform clinical practice is still not determined. The results certainly show the heterogeneity of ADHD and may explain the differences in clinical presentation particularly in population versus clinical samples.

Three empirically based subtypes of ADHD may be most clinically relevant based on endorsed levels of impairment and competency—the Severe Inattentive, Mild-Combined, and Severe-Combined subtypes (Volk et al., 2006). Children classified into one of these three groups were found to have significantly greater social impairment than the other four latent classes identified (Few Symptoms, Talkative-Impulsive, Mild Inattention, and Hyperactive). School functioning was also significantly lower for the Severe-Combined, Mild-Combined, and Severe-Inattentive groups compared to the other latent classes. Finally, while the Severe-Combined class had the most impairment in total competency scores, we should not ignore the finding that mild competency impairment was also found for the Severe Inattentive, Mild Inattentive, and Mild-Combined classes (Volk et al., 2006). These findings have clear implications for treatment as the Mild-Combined subtype is often left undiagnosed despite impairment in important competency areas. Furthermore, twin heritability studies have recently suggested that Mild and Severe-Combined ADHD have different genetic influences (Volk et al., 2006).

In addition to considering subtype classification, Frick and Lahey (1991) suggest that it is important to differentiate primary symptoms from associated problems in children with ADHD. The primary deficits associated with ADHD include inattention/ disorganization and motor hyperactivity/impulsivity. Associated problems include poor academic achievement, impaired peer relationships, and low self-esteem. Other problems that are commonly reported include language impairments, impaired motor coordination and perception, lower cognitive functioning, greater accidental injuries, and greater sleep disturbances (Bruce, 2006; Cortese, Konofal, Yateman, Mouren, & Lencdreaux, 2006; Daley, 2005; Faraone, Biederman, & Monuteaux, 2002; Miller, Miller, Bloom, Hynd, & Craggs, 2006).

Compared to typically developing (TD) children, children and adolescents with ADHD have significantly lower full scale IQ and math achievement, and significantly higher rates of a learning disability, with reading achievement differences approaching significance (Faraone et al., 2002). Incidence rates for repeating grades also vary for TD youths versus those with ADHD. Approximately 5–13 percent of children and adolescents without ADHD repeat a grade, while as many as 18–31 percent of children and adolescents with ADHD repeat a grade (Faraone et al., 2002). Common sleep disturbances of ADHD children include more movements during sleep, greater daytime drowsiness, and higher indexes of apnea-hypopnea (Cortese et al., 2006).

Comorbidity: ADHD with Other Childhood Disorders

The rate of comorbidity is pertinent since as many as 87 percent of children with ADHD have at least one other comorbid disorder, and as many as 67 percent had at least two additional diagnoses (Kadesjö & Gillberg, 2001). Prevalence rates of other *DSM-IV* disorders suggest that some of the most common comorbid diagnoses associated with ADHD include: oppositional defiant disorder (ODD; 60%), developmental coordination disorder (47%), reading/writing disorder (40%), and tic disorders (33%), although internalizing problems such as anxiety and depression were not examined (Kadesjö & Gillberg, 2001). Biederman and colleagues (Biederman et al., 1992; Biederman, Newcorn, & Sprich, 1991) found that approximately 30 percent of children with ADHD tend to develop affective disorders. Children with ADHD also tend to have parents and/or siblings with ADHD or other affective disorders.

Continuity rates for ADHD from childhood into adulthood varies across studies, with 50–66 percent of subjects retaining the symptoms (Barkley, 2006). Longitudinal study data appear to vary due to differences in the severity of ADHD in the baseline sample, the diagnostic criteria used to determine ADHD, and the method/source of obtaining diagnostic information (adult self- report versus parent report). Barkley suggests that current DSM criteria are increasingly less sensitive to the disorder in later adolescence and adulthood. For the adolescent or adult with ADHD, continuing difficulty with the law, substance abuse problems, difficulty holding a job, and problems with interpersonal relationships are also prominent (Barkley, 2006; Biederman & Steingard, 1989). When prevalence rates of conduct disorder and depression are examined concurrently in a clinical sample, as many as 25 percent of children and 30 percent of adolescents have comorbid major depression, whereas approximately 15 percent of children and 23 percent of adolescents have been found to have a comorbid conduct disorder (CD; Faraone et al., 2002).

If comorbidity is examined by ADHD subtype, ODD remains the most prevalent, with 48.3 percent of children with ADHD-C, 33.3 percent of children with ADHD-HI, and 23.3 percent of children with ADHD-PI meeting criteria for comorbid ODD (Volk et al., 2005). Comorbid depression is slightly less prevalent, with approximately 10.3 percent of children with ADHD-C, 8.7 percent of children with ADHD-HI, and 8.6 percent of children with

ADHD-PI found to have a co-occurring depressive disorder (Volk et al., 2005).

Comorbid or associated behaviors complicate the diagnostic process and have led some to conclude that they are part of the disorder. In an attempt to clarify the diagnostic issue, researchers have separated correlated symptoms from the major features of ADHD. The National Institute of Mental Health (NIMH) collaborative Multisite Multimodal Treatment Study of Children with Attention-Deficit/Hyperactivity Disorder (MTA) reported that there may be three distinct clinical profiles of ADHD comorbidity (Jensen et al., 2001). Separate profiles of ADHD with co-occurring internalizing disorders (primarily anxiety; ADHD + ANX), ADHD with co-occurring oppositional defiant disorder/conduct disorder (ADHD + ODD/CD), and ADHD with both comorbid problems (ADHD + ANX + ODD/CD) evolved based on consistent differences in clinical baseline characteristics, outcomes, and response to treatment. These findings suggest the need to discriminate among comorbid subtypes of ADHD (Jensen et al., 2001). Specifically, those children with both anxiety and ADHD responded differently to ADHD treatments when compared to other groups. The ADHD + ANX group, regardless of ODD/CD status, tended to be more responsive to treatment than the children with ADHD + ODD/CD or ADHD-only groups. In addition, children with ADHD + ANX responded positively to any of three treatments (behavioral, medication management, or combined treatment), whereas the ADHD + ANX + ODD/CD had the greatest benefits from the combined treatment. Finally, the ADHD + OCC/CD or ADHD-only groups generally only responded to the treatments with medication (Jensen et al., 2001).

The long-term outcome for children with ADHD and conduct disorder is the poorest compared with any other childhood disorder (Barkley, Fischer, Smallish, & Fletcher, 2006; Mannuzza & Klein, 2000). Poor long-term functioning occurs across multiple domains, including educational, occupational, financial, criminal, emotional, and social realms, and persists into adolescence and adulthood (Barkley et al., 2006; Mannuzza & Klein, 2000).

Further complications of differentiating core ADHD behaviors from comorbid disorders is the potential genetic overlap of childhood disorders (Pliszka et al., 1999). A large genetic comorbidity twin study found that shared genetic heritability estimates were strong for comorbid reading disabilities and ADHD-PI (31%), conduct disorder and ADHD-HI (37%), and oppositional defiant disorder with ADHD-HI (42%; Martin, Levy, Pieka, & Hay, 2006). Future research is needed to determine whether the genetic connections are due to similar shared biological pathways or to the environmental impact one set of behaviors has in the development of other destructive behaviors.

Neurological Study of ADHD

Reaction time to alertness tasks has also been found to be highly variable in children with AD/HD compared to controls, which may result from core symptoms of inattention (Dreschler et al., 2005). Children with ADHD have been found to make more false alarms and produce fewer correct responses on spatial interference/inhibitory control tasks which are often indicative of hyperactivity/impulsivity (Dreschler et al., 2005). Finally, processing speed has also been found to be an area of weakness (Calhoun & Mayes, 2005).

The neurophysiology and neuropsychology of AD/HD continues to be extensively studied using multiple techniques, including magnetic resonance imaging (MRI; Eliez & Reiss, 2000; Miller et al., 2006), functional magnetic resonance imaging (fMRI; Booth et al., 2005; Konrad, Neufang, Hanisch, Fink, & Herpertz-Dahlmann, 2006; Vaidya et al., 2005; Zang et al., 2005), magnetoencephalography (MEG; Mulas et al., 2006), cerebral blood flow (Kim, Lee, Shin, Cho, & Lee, 2002), and tests of executive functioning (Dreschler, Brandeis, Földényi, Imhof, Steinhausen, 2005; Fischer, Barkley, Smallish, & Fletcher, 2005).

Brain imaging techniques have found lowered metabolism in the prefrontal brain regions on sustained attention tasks in both children and adults with ADHD (Lou, Henriksen, & Bruhn, 1984; Zametkin et al., 1990). Structural and functional neuroimaging of children and adults with ADHD often report abnormalities in right frontal cortex areas, the basal ganglia particularly in the caudate nucleus, the corpus callosum, and the cerebellum

(Eliez & Reiss, 2000; Miller et al., 2006; Roth & Saykin, 2004; Vaidya et al., 2005). Magnetic Resonance Imaging (MRI) studies have found smaller total brain volume, smaller global and posterior parietal-occipital white matter volumes, and smaller cerebral volume in children with ADHD. While the degree of asymmetry of the caudate nucleus, a subcortical basal ganglia structure, has been found to significantly predict ADHD inattentive behaviors as opposed to hyperactive/impulsive symptomatology (Schrimsher et al., 2002), research is inconsistent as to whether abnormalities are primarily in the right or left hemisphere (Eliez & Reiss, 2000; Roth & Saykin, 2004; Schrimsher et al., 2002). Studies investigating abnormalities of the corpus callosum have found that the anterior and posterior sections of the corpus callosum are smaller in individuals with ADHD, particularly in the rostral areas, genu, and splenium areas (Eliez & Reiss, 2000). Finally, several studies have found decreased volume in the cerebellar region, particularly posterior vermis and inferior posterior vermis areas (Eliez & Reiss, 2000; Roth & Saykin, 2004).

Using single photon emission computerized tomography (SPECT), atypical cerebral blood flow patterns have been found in ADHD children, compared to controls during a resting state specifically in prefrontal cortex areas (Kim et al., 2002). Areas of decreased cerebral blood flow have been found in the right lateral prefrontal cortex, both orbital prefrontal cortexes, and the cerebellum (Kim et al., 2002). Areas of increased blood flow may include mainly posterior cortex regions such as the upper parietal cortex (left and right postcentral gyrus, left and right angular gyrus) and the left parieooccipital cortex [inferior and superior occipital gyrus (Kim et al., 2002)].

These structural and functional abnormalities of the frontal cortex, basal ganglia, and cerebellum have been corroborated using functional MRI (fMRI) techniques (Vaidya et al., 2005; Zang et al., 2005). One study investigated children with ADHD on and off methylphenidate (MPH) to controls on a task developed to elicit a Stroop effect [where an interference condition requires greater response time and greater activation volumes of brain regions than a neutral condition (Zang et al., 2005)]. Children with ADHD off MPH had smaller activation volumes of the prefrontal cortex in both the neutral and interference condition compared to the controls. Activation volumes of the basal ganglia, insula, and cerebellum were also smaller in the interference condition for children with ADHD off MPH than controls. Finally, when MPH was administered, there was increased activation volume and increased behavioral reaction time (Stroop effect), suggesting that ADHD is a disorder of hypofrontality and may also involve subcortical structures, specifically the basal ganglia and cerebellum (Zang et al., 2005).

Primary Symptoms

Primary symptoms of ADHD include inattention, hyperactivity, and impulsivity form the bases for DSM-IV subtypes (Barkley, 2006). Cognitive models of ADHD emphasize deficits in executive functions and problems with disinhibition (Nigg, 2006). "Executive functioning is not unitary; it reflects distinct operations that may differentially recruit distinct aspects of the prefrontal-subcortical neural loops involved in behavior regulation, working memory, and attention" (Nigg, 2006, p. 140).

Inattention

The inability to control and direct attention to the demands of a task is central to ADHD (Barkley, 2006). In fact, attention problems may be secondary to a disorder of behavioral regulation and inhibition (Barkley, 2006). The term *distractibility* is often used to describe a deficit in *focused attention* or an inability to focus attention (Mirsky, 1987; Posner & Boies, 1971). Brain structures in Luria's first functional unit, the reticular formation, control basic alertness and attention, with higher functions of disinhibition controlled by the network of connections to the upper brain or cortex. Focused attention is thought to be one of the first aspects of attention to develop.

Problems with distractibility appear to be a function of declining persistence or effort when responding to tasks that have little intrinsic appeal or have minimal immediate consequences for completion. When alternative activities that promise immediate reinforcement or gratification are available, children with ADHD may appear distracted because their attention shifts off task in order to engage in the more rewarding, competing activity. Thus, the problem may be one of disinhibition rather than distraction.

The child with ADHD is capable of orienting to specific stimuli, but unable to resist or disinhibit responses to competing stimuli that appear more interesting and reinforcing.

Disinhibition of response to extraneous stimulation is also implicated in the second component of attention to develop: *sustained attention*, or the ability to maintain a behavioral response for a continuous or repetitive activity. *Vigilance* is the term often used to describe this type of attention. This component of attention is most easily measured using a continuous performance test and K-ABC hand movements. Difficulties with maintaining attention while resisting other impulses indicate that there may be a basic problem at the arousal level within Luria's first functional level and may explain why the use of stimulants helps attention, because stimulants may raise the level of basic arousal to within a normal range.

Sustained attention for more complex tasks is probably controlled in later development by the frontal lobes, which regulate behavior. Because the frontal lobes are the last areas of the brain to develop fully, it may be that hyperactive symptoms are due in part to a significant maturational lag in the development of the inhibitory mechanisms of motor responses controlled by the frontal lobes (Becker, Isaac, & Hynd, 1987; Passler, Isaac, & Hynd, 1985).

Suggestion that these regions are at least partially compromised has been supported by cerebral blood flow studies with single-photon emission computed tomography (SPECT; Lou et al., 1984; Lou, Henriksen, Bruhn, Borner, &Nielson, 1989; Gustafsson, Thernlund, Ryding, Rosen, & Cederblad, 2000), in PET studies (Zametkin et al., 1990), and in fMRI studies (Zang et al., 2005). These neurological studies have generally found decreased blood flow and diminished metabolism in prefrontal frontal regions (particularly right prefrontal regions) and pathways connecting to the limbic system (caudate nucleus in the striatum) and the cerebellum (Barkley, 2006). Differences in metabolic and activation patterns appear related to symptom presentation and executive deficits.

Selective attention is a complex behavior that requires the maintenance of a response involving activation or inhibition of another response. These filtering mechanisms, which are necessary to block out or attend to input, probably involve maintaining arousal of the first functional unit as well as the information-processing capacity of the primary and secondary zones of the second functional unit. This component of attention is most easily measured using cancellation tasks, the Stroop, and the Trails tests.

Dysfunction in selective attention would compromise academic achievement, especially when the information presented is complex and of some length, requiring both sustained attention and information processing simultaneously. This area is also thought to be implicated in sensory localization. When the symptoms of cognitive sluggishness, confusion, hypoactivity, and anxiety are displayed, finger agnosia on the left side was found with ADD and may relate to difficulties in selective attention (Goodyear & Hynd, 1992; Lorys, Hynd, & Lahey, 1990).

There is support for the hypothesis that children with ADD/H may have difficulties in sustained attention while selective attention is related to ADD. Trommer, Hoeppner, Lorber, and Armstrong (1988) found significant differences between the ADD subtypes in impulse control. ADD children were as impulsive as ADD/H children on a choice task in the initial portion of the task. However, ADD children displayed significant improvement as training continued, while ADD/H showed no lessening of impulsivity. Similarly, children with ADD have exhibited slower rates of processing speed and more difficulties in selective attention than children with ADD/H (Barkley, Fischer, Edelbrock, & Smallish, 1990).

The most complex forms of attention are *alternating attention* and *divided attention*. Both of these involve the ability to time-share mental operations when there is competition for attention. Alternating attention includes measures such as the WSCT and the Category test. There is no current measure for divided attention. These functions are highly dependent on the executive functioning of Luria's third unit to organize and orchestrate the associated complex responses.

Differences in subtypes of ADHD have been suggested by Barkley (2006). Children with ADD:

Combined Type show poor sustained attention that improves with stimuli that are novel. Individuals with ADHD: Inattentive Type show problems in focused attention, which appears to be more of a cognitively driven (as opposed to behavioral) disorder. Barkley suggests that measures of attention need to assess the interrelationship between the environment the child is in and his or her behavior. Further, there is a functional relationship between the behavior and the environment; that is, each influences the other. Thus, in his view, attentional problems are deficits in facilitating, sustaining, or disengaging these behaviors in relation to the environment. Moreover, attention involves rules and instructions that are associated with the task either explicitly or implicitly.

Hyperactivity (Motor Disinhibition)

Hyperactivity generally refers to "excessive or developmentally inappropriate levels of activity" and is expressed as "restlessness, fidgeting, and generally unnecessary gross bodily movements" (Barkley, 2006, p. 82). Studies have consistently found that hyperactivity is a problem for at least a subset of children with ADHD. Overactivity may be situational (occurs in one environment) or pervasive (occurs in most environments, e.g., home and school). Hyperactivity is often observed in situations that are not stimulating, novel or interesting, and can be particularly problematic in social, school or work situations where self-control is needed and valued. Studies of ADHD in adulthood show that hyperactivity is experienced more as a feeling of restlessness, excessive verbalization, and fidgetiness (Murphy & Barkley, 1996).

In addition to motor disinhibition, Nigg (2006) indicates that children with ADHD have difficulty with motor control and timing. Motor coordination problems have been found in children with ADHD including clumsiness, fine motor difficulties, time perception and temporal information processing. Barkley (2006) also suggests that sense of time and the capacity to "manage behavior relative to time" involves the ability hold information in working memory, and focused attention to internal and external cues (p. 309). See Nigg (2006) for a discussion of how immature frontal regions, particularly

premotor and motor areas, subcortical regions, particularly the cerebellum and cerebellar-frontal connections play a role in time perception and temporal information processing. Nigg indicates that it is important "to understand that motor control delays are distinct from motivational, cognitive or other self-control problems" (p. 171).

Impulsivity (Executive Functioning or Cognitive Control)

In his discussion of impulsivity, Barkley (2006) describes two major aspects of impulsivity—poor behavioral inhibition including hyperactivity, and aspects of executive control (e.g., inability to delay gratification, low effort, poor self-regulation, poor planning). Dysfunction at the executive level would be seen in diminished complex problem solving strategies, organizational skills, and less efficient memory strategies characteristic of ADHD children (Barkley, 2006).

Nigg (2006) uses executive functioning and cognitive control interchangeably, and suggests that it is multifaceted including behavior regulation or response suppression, working memory, and attention or interference control. Working memory deficits may be interfering with executive functions, particularly spatial working memory, when planning and executing complex behaviors.

The neural mechanisms of executive functions involve widespread brain regions. Nigg (2006) indicates that the prefrontal regions are involved with many, but not all executive functions. The basal ganglia, the thalamus, and the cerebellum also play a role in behavioral inhibition. The impact of executive control dysfunction has profound effects on the child's overall adjustment and may be more devastating than effects of hyperactivity or inattention. This line of research may provide a better understanding of ADHD and warrants further inquiry.

Self-Regulation Theory of ADHD

Barkley (2006) presents an integrated theory of self-regulation to explain the underlying cognitive mechanisms in ADHD. The theory is built on the construct of executive functions which is based on behavioral disinhibition (e.g., control prepotent responses, interrupt ongoing responses, and interference control). Barkley describes four executive functions including nonverbal working memory, verbal working memory, self-regulation of emotions/motivation/arousal, and reconstitution or analysis and synthesis of behavior. See Barkley (1997, 2006) for an extensive overview of his theory of ADHD, and research that supports aspects of the model of self-control and executive functions.

Transactional Model of ADHD

Our conceptual model of ADHD is transactional in nature, where neuropsychological dysfunction arises from genetic factors and/or temperamental variations. While prenatal or postnatal insult may result in ADHD characteristics, environmental factors are not considered causal. See Table 9.4 for an overview of the interactional nature of ADHD.

Neuropsychological tests that measure complex problem solving, response inhibition, and sustained effort believed to be primarily executive functions may be important in the diagnosis of ADHD (Nigg, 2006). In addition to interhemispheric disinhibition, frontal lobe inhibitory circuits are also believed to play a role in ADHD (Zang et al., 2005). The prefrontal lobes have a rich network of reciprocal pathways with the reticular formation and diencephalic structures that regulate arousal and the ability to suppress responses to stimuli that are not task-relevant. The failure of children with ADHD to inhibit inappropriate responses and sustain goal-directed behavior may be due to their inability to suppress and control higher level inhibitory cortical reflexes. This theory would support age-related changes in some of the symptoms of ADHD children as they get older. During adolescence, many of the hyperactive symptoms diminish in intensity, and improvements are seen in impulse control attention span (Fischer, Barkley, Smallish, & Fletcher, 2005). Although the primary symptom of hyperactivity may improve, up to 80 percent of youths identified with ADHD continue to show systems in adolescence. Associated difficulties and comorbidities persist, creating unusual challenges for teens.

Genetic Factors

There is compelling evidence that there is an interaction between genetics and environment which affects how ADHD is manifested. Analysis of data reported from 20 recent twin heritability studies of ADHD suggest that heritability rates average around 76 percent, with studies reporting anywhere from 60 percent to over 95 percent heritability (Faraone et al., 2005). These variations in heritability rates are likely due to differences in how studies define and classify ADHD, differences in environment, and differences in rates of comorbidity (Levy, Hay, & Bennet, 2006). For example, heritability estimates derived from twin studies using DSM-IV criteria for diagnosing ADHD have frequently been extremely high (between 90 and 95%), while twin studies employing empirical methods (i.e., Child Behavior Checklist scales or the Conner's Rating scales) to identify the presence of ADHD have reported somewhat lower rates of genetic influence [60–70% (Hudziak, Derks, Althoff, Rettew, & Boomsma, 2005)].

Further analyses suggest that genetic dominance factors may comprise 48 percent of a model of ADHD, additive genetic factors 30 percent, and unique environmental factors contributing another 22 percent of an ADHD model (Hudziak et al., 2005). This finding has led researchers to argue for the use of dimensional models to identify attention problems. These allow for phenotypic variation and rely on normative data for comparison which may reduce the large estimates of rater bias of ADHD symptom criteria in twin heritability studies and enable us to better determine genetic dominance (Hudziak et al., 2005). Other nongenetic, environmental risk factors (maternal alcohol consumption and cigarette smoking during pregnancy, elevated lead exposure, exposure to streptococcal infection, etc.) may also play a role in the etiology of the disorder (Barkley, 2006).

There is growing evidence that variants in dopamine-related genes have been implicated in children, adolescents and adults with ADHD. Swanson et al. (1997, 2001) investigated the dopamine D4 receptor gene (DRD4), while others have investigated the dopamine transporter gene [DAT1 (Cook, Stein, Leventhal, 1997)]. Casey et al. (2001) found that variations in the dopamine-related genes were associated

Table 9.4 Summary of specific deficits associated with attention deficit hyperactivity disorder (ADHD)

Biogenetic Factors	*Environmental Factors/Prenatal/Postnatal*
– 59 – 84% MZ	– Multifactorial, polygenetic, cultural, and environmental
– 33 – 29% DZ	transmission seem unlikely
– Independent genetic code differs from reading	– Poverty, overcrowding, chaotic family style, pollution,
– Familial ADD transmitted single gene	food additives account for very little variance
– Single gene has not been isolated; probably domapamine	– Common environmental factors: 0 – 30% variance
receptor gene	
Temperament	*Birth Complications*
– Genetic linkage	– No known correlates

- Activity level
- Distractibility
- Psychomotor activity
- Attentional problems, school competence, and behavioral problems

CNS Factors
– Underactivated frontal lobe
– Bilaterally smaller anterior cortex
– Reversed asymmetry of anterior cortex (right < left)
– Reversed asymmetry of caudate nucleus (left < right)
– Reduced metabolic activity in right caudate region
– Smaller left caudate nucleus
– Right-hemisphere deficits (disinhibition of left hemisphere)
– Left-hemisphere underactivation
– Genu (corpus callosum) smaller
– Rostrum and rostral bodies smaller

Intellectual	*Perceptual*	*Memory*	*Attentional*
– Range of IQ		– Low verbal	– Sustained
– Low coding		– Less efficient	– Selective
			– Alternatiting/divided

Reasoning
– Response inhibition
– Sustained effort
– Complex problem solving
– Executive functions
– Organizational skills

Academic/Behavioral	*Psychosocial*	*Family*
– Motivational problems	– Rejected	– Disorder exacerbates
– Underachievers	– Ignored	– Parental psychopathology
– Comorbid LD	– Comorbid INT/EXT	– Related to CD/ADHD
– Work completion	– Comorbid aggression	

Note: DZ = dyzgotic; MZ = monzygotic; INT = internalized disorders; EXT = externalized disorders; LD = learning disabilities; CD = conduct disorders; ADHD = attention deficit hyperactivity disorder.

with variations in cognitive control measures for children with ADHD. Specifically, the 7-repeat allele version of the DRD4 receptor (transmits inhibitory signals) has been found in a sizeable portion of ADHD children, adolescents and adults (DiMaio, Grizenko, & Jooper, 2003), while the 10-repeat form of the dopamine transporter gene (DAT1) has been found in children with ADHD and may be related to poor response to methylphenidate (Winsberg & Comings, 1999).

Family Factors

Although exploring the genetic basis of ADHD is promising, biological predispositions or vulnerabilities likely interact with environmental variables (e.g., parental psychopathology, parenting styles) to develop a more severe type of ADHD. In a study of ADHD sibling pairs, parents report significantly more problems in family cohesiveness, expressiveness, achievement orientation, organization, and conflict in comparison to control families, as well as significantly higher conflict, organization, and achievement-orientation problems than control "distressed families" without ADHD (Pressman et al., 2006). Family environment variables account for approximately 40 percent of ADHD impairment in models of sibling ADHD impairment, whereby the sibling correlation of impairment dropped from 67 to 38 percent when family conflict was controlled. Furthermore, parental psychopathology (i.e., parental mood disorders or substance abuse) accounted for between 3 and 9 percent of the variability in ADHD impairment, and tended to be linked to sibling impairment through family conflict as a mediator. In most instances, the eldest sibling was the most vulnerable to a negative family environment (Pressman et al., 2006). Thus, children with ADHD who have parents with ADHD, parents with additional comorbid psychopathology, or who live in a chaotic environment may be at the highest risk for the disorder to appear and for comorbid disorders to also be present (Pfiffner, McBurnett, Rathouz, & Judice, 2005). Given that a higher incidence of parental psychopathology is present in families of children with **ADHD**, a chaotic and/or conflictual family environment may exacerbate or increase the signs of this disorder.

Just as ADHD children have negative interactions with their peers, they also experience similar difficulties at home. Dysfunctional interaction patterns have been found in families with ADHD children, with these parents frequently engaging in highly directive, controlling, and negative interactions with their child. Fewer incidences of reward and responsivity to the child's needs have also been found (Befera & Barkley, 1985). Moreover, these interactions tend to improve when the child begins medication and parent-child relationships improve (Barkley, Karlsson, Pollard, & Murphy, 1985).

Psychosocial Factors

Another area of impairment that is often related to ADHD involves the social domain, including poor social skills and/or social competence (Semrud-Clikeman & Schafer, 2000). Significant differences in social competence are revealed between children who are overactive with inattention and those with inattention without overactivity. Furthermore, ADHD children with aggressive behavioral problems are less popular, more disliked, and more likely to be rejected by their peers (Atkins & Pelham, 1991). Although children with ADHD and aggression do not necessarily demonstrate social skill deficits, they have extreme difficulty carrying out their intentions in a social situation. In contrast, children with ADD and more withdrawn behaviors are often isolated and seem to lack important skills needed for social interactions (Hynd et al., 1991). A higher risk for mood disorders, including anxiety and depression, has been found in the latter group (Hynd et al., 1991).

The presence of depression complicates interactions and increases social impairments. For example, a recent community sample study comparing ADHD children with and without comorbid depression found that children who present with comorbid ADHD + depression have even greater impairments in social functioning than those children with ADHD-only (Blackman, Ostrander, & Herman, 2005). Because inattention symptoms explained nearly all of the depression variance, this suggests that the link between ADHD and depression goes beyond simple association. Contrary to previous research, which tended to use clinical samples and single method formats allowing for potential rater bias, no differences were found in academic achievement, ADHD severity, or conduct problems between children with ADHD + depression and those with ADHD-only, although these results need to be further studied (Blackman et al., 2005).

Finally, in the social domain, individuals with hyperactivity have been found to have significantly fewer close friends, a greater number of social problems, shorter duration of dating relationships, become sexually active at a younger age (15.5 compared to 16.3), and had more sexual partners within the last year compared to controls (Barkley et al., 2006). The social relations of children with ADHD appear to produce a number of outcomes including a sense of isolation and rejection which may increase depression over time.

Intellectual, Perceptual, Attention, and Memory Functioning

Current research shows that children with ADHD have lower levels of intellectual performance than non-ADHD peers (Frazier, Demaree, & Youngstrom, 2004). Estimates suggest that the average difference is nine points with a range between 7–15 points on intelligence tests (Fischer, Barkley, Edelbrock, & Smallish, 1990). These deficits may be partially related to difficulties across a spectrum of cognitive and executive functions including poor working memory, internalized speech and the development of verbal thinking (Barkley, 2006). While the coexistence of learning disabilities may be related to lower intelligence scores, Barkley, DuPaul and McMurray (1990) found that the learning disabilities groups had lower IQs, but the ADHD groups still had lower abilities than non-disabled control groups. Barkley suggests that children with ADHD will have intellectual development crossing the spectrum from gifted to mild intellectual deficits.

Academic and School Adjustment

Academic difficulties have been documented in numerous studies of children with ADHD [see (Barkley, 2006) for a review]. Studies show that children have significantly lower achievement standard scores (10–30 points) compared to classmates on reading, spelling, math and reading comprehension (Fischer et al., 1990; Semrud-Clikeman et al., 1992). Academic performance is related to difficulties with work completion and productivity, inattention, impulsive, and restless behaviors in the classroom setting (Barkley, 2006). Others suggest that academic difficulties are related to cognitive-intellectual weaknesses (Rapport, Scanlan, & Denney, 1999).

Barkley and colleagues followed a sample of children with hyperactivity over a minimum of 13 years and found significantly higher rates of grade retention, greater number of suspensions, higher rates of

special education, lower grade point averages, lower college enrollment status, fewer years of education completed, and lower graduation rates, with as many as 32 percent failing to complete high school (Barkley et al., 2006). Ongoing problems persisted into adulthood with higher rates of being fired from a job (more than twice as often), owing money to others (twice as much as controls), more trouble paying bills, and lower prevalence of credit card ownership and having a savings account (Barkley et al., 2006). Other longitudinal studies report higher rates of arrests, multiple arrests, and incarcerations among individuals with ADHD in comparison to controls (Mannuzza & Klein, 2000).

Predictors of overall functional outcomes were also examined by these authors, including high school graduation, employment stability, work performance, age of sexual initiation, parenthood involvement, number of close friends, and social problems (Barkley et al., 2006). The best predictors of high school graduation status included severity of childhood hyperactivity, number of lifetime CD symptoms, and grade retainment. Employment stability was best predicted by total ADHD symptoms and severity of ODD symptoms, whereas current job performance was predicted by employer-rated ADHD symptoms and the intensity of childhood hyperactivity. Age of sexual activity initiation predictors included the number of lifetime CD symptoms, severity of childhood CD, and IQ. Involvement during a pregnancy was predicted by lifetime CD symptoms and child hyperactivity severity. Finally, the number of close friendships and social problems were best predicted by the severity of childhood hyperactivity and severity of current ADHD and hyperactivity, respectively (Barkley et al., 2006). Early aggressive tendencies plus neuropsychological delays in early childhood have been found to be highly predictive of delinquent behavior in adolescence and criminal behavior in adulthood (Mannuzza, Klein, Abikoff, & Moulton, 2004; Toupin, Déry, Pauzé, Mercier, & Fortin, 2000).

Implications for Assessment

The assessment of AD/HD generally consists of a number of behavioral measures and approaches including clinical interviews with parents and teachers, global and AD/HD specific behavioral rating scales (e.g., parent, teacher, and self-ratings), and observational methods. See Barkley & Edwards (2006), Achenbach & McConaughy (2003), Achenbach & Rescorla (2001), Kamphaus & Frick (2005), and Reynolds & Kamphaus (2002) for a more in-depth review of various multi-dimensional rating scales for assessing psychosocial and behavior problems and measuring symptoms of AD/HD in children and youth. While clinical assessment includes multiple behavioral measures and techniques, they do not adequately measure the attentional and executive control deficits associated with AD/HD.

Objective assessment of attention and behavioral disinhibition may have inherent difficulties with ecological validity; that is, many tasks may not be demanding enough to tax the attentional system or frontal lobe, executive functions (Stuss, 2007). Often the tasks utilized are initially interesting, last only a few minutes, and are administered under direct adult supervision. To measure the component of sustained attention and executive functions accurately, for example, the tasks must be of sufficient length and repetition to ensure potential boredom. In addition, adult supervision must not be seen as a discriminating stimulus to remain on task. These findings suggest that neuropsychological tasks should not be used alone to diagnose ADHD; however, such tasks may be useful in describing the cognitive and neuropsychological functioning of a subgroup of ADHD (Barkley, 2006). Denckla (1994) suggests that assessment of attention and executive functions need tasks that provide a delay between stimulus and response, require an internally represented view of the task, require response inhibition and efficiency of response, and require active and flexible strategies for solutions. All of these aspects need not be present, but the majority should be for a complete assessment of attentional—executive functions.

The role of frontal dysfunction in ADHD continues to be widely discussed (Barkley, 2006). Beyond the neuroanatomical findings of possible frontal involvement in ADHD, recent research has suggested that children diagnosed with ADHD display neurological deficits with greater consistency on tests evaluating neuropsychological functions mediated by the frontal and prefrontal cortex

(Hynd, Voeller, Hem, & Marshall, 1991). The frontal lobes are important to regulate motor output and to organize and manage behavior, such as developing plans, allocating resources, and inhibiting behaviors that interfere with goal achievement. An individual suffering frontal disturbance may have totally normal basal-posterior functions, including normal or even high intelligence, but be unable to use these abilities effectively. Chelune et al. (1986) found that subjects with attention deficits were impaired in the Wisconsin Card Sorting Task (WCST). The WCST, which requires sustained attention, cognitive flexibility, and regulation of goal-directed activity through the use of environmental feedback, is believed to reflect frontal lobe functioning. Chelune et al. (1986) suggest that the WCST may be assessing disinhibition and not hyperactivity or attentional deficits. Other studies (Barkley, 2006) failed to replicate data supporting the use of WCST due to inconsistent findings and low overall accuracy of classification.

Studies using other measures, such as the Stroop Test, have found inconsistent differences between subjects with ADHD and normal controls. These inconsistent results may be a function of the use of varying ADHD subtypes, failure to control for co-occurrence of comorbid disorder, or severity of ADHD. Each of these factors may influence the subject's performance on the WCST. Studies investigating the Conner Continuous Performance Tests II (Conners & MHS Staff, 2003) suggest promise, but high false-negative rates diminish their diagnostic utility (Barkley, 2006).

More complicated tasks pose greater demands for planning, organization, and executive regulation of behavior. Children with ADHD display fewer attentional or behavior problems in novel or unfamiliar settings or when tasks are unusually different, colorful, or highly stimulating (Barkley, 2006). Symptoms of ADHD are noticeable when the demands of the environment or the task exceed the child's capacity to sustain attention, regulate activity, and/or restrain impulses. Examples of this poor regulation and inhibition of behavior include responding quickly to situations without understanding what is required, failing to consider consequences, having difficulty waiting one's turn, and seeking immediate gratification or rewards that require less work to achieve rather than working toward a long-term goal and a larger reward. Thus, poor inhibition and regulation of behavior may appear as an attention deficit, but is explained more clearly as a dysfunction of behavioral inhibition.

This complex interplay of attention, behavioral inhibition, motivation, overactivity, and brain maturation mustbe addressed in treatment of ADHD children. In addition to attentional difficulties in ADHD, recent studies have supported a hypothesis of a generalized self-regulatory deficit that affects information processing, inhibition of responses, arousal/alertness, planning, executive functions, metacognition, and self-monitoring abilities that span the various sensory modalities (Barkley, 2006). An inability to inhibit excess behavior and stimulation has a negative impact on the child's ability to learn in the classroom not only in terms of negative classroom behavior, but also in terms of impact on attentional resources. Because attention is not directed, the child takes in irrelevant as well as relevant detail. Thus, an interaction between inattention and disinhibition has a negative impact on information processing and, thus, on school achievement. These deficits may also be dependent on the situation the child faces. For children with ADHD, attentional problems become more evident in situations where attention is required to be sustained on a repeated task (Nigg, 2006) or in structured situations (Barkley, 2006). Moreover, on tasks that are novel or when behavioral consequences are immediate, children with ADHD show great ability to contain attentional problems (Douglas, 1983). Some suggest that the primary difference in ADHD children may not be in attention, but in the way the child's behavior is regulated by consequences (Barkley, 2006).

There may also be differences in how children with ADD/H and ADHD-PI respond to consequences and to their environment. All of these areas deserve further empirical investigation. Children with ADHD frequently experience concomitant learning difficulties (Semrud-Clikeman et al., 1992). A review of the literature by Semrud-Clikeman et al. (1992) found that 30 percent of children with ADHD also have learning disabilities while another 25–35 percent have learning delays. The extent of learning difficulties found in over 50 percent of the ADHD population may relate not only to attentional problems, but also to the self-regulatory deficit proposed by Douglas (1988). If children with ADHD cannot learn to plan, organize, and evaluate their learning (i.e., metacognitive skills), they will likely experience significantly more problems performing academically as they develop, since most of their educational experiences after third grade will require independent work skills. Moreover, if, as Sohlberg and Mateer (1989) propose, attentional resources are hierarchical, then difficulties with selective or sustained attention may predispose a child to self-regulatory deficits. Thus, regulation of self and others and attention are not dichotomous characteristics of ADHD.

It is reasonable to speculate that regulation and attention may be inextricably interrelated and mutually reciprocal. Thus, a child who is motorically active may not necessarily show significant attentional problems or learning deficits once the overactivity is controlled. These children respond readily to medication and may be the children who are later found to "outgrow" their hyperactivity. Conversely, a child who has attentional and self-regulatory deficits may respond partially to medication but often will continue to have learning difficulties and require additional support (Barkley, 2006). It is these children who may need continuing support throughout life (Weiss & Hechtman, 1986, 1993).

Tasks that are sensitive to frontal lobe functioning (i.e., executive function deficits) include a perseveration score on the WCST, Tower of Hanoi and London, Go/No-Go tasks, motor sequencing, and continuous-performance tests. These tasks require either flexible problem solving (WCST, Tower of Hanoi or London) or response inhibition (continuous performance test, Go/No-go). However, their utility for diagnostic purposes has not been established and more research is needed before these measures are recommended for clinical diagnoses.

Gender

Gender differences have been reported as the ratio of males to females with ADHD ranges from 2:1 to 10:1, depending on the study (Barkley, 2006). These differences may result from referral biases due to the finding that males often present with higher rates of aggression and antisocial behaviors. In recent studies of gender differences, Biederman et al. (2002) found that girls with ADHD had higher risks for depression, anxiety and bipolar disorder compared to males in earlier studies. Girls also tended to have lower rates of externalizing disorders compared to males, with lower incidence of conduct and oppositional defiant disorders. Girls with ADHD showed lower intelligence, reading and math scores compared to female peers, and did not differ from males with ADHD on these measures. The extent to which girls receive needed treatment for ADHD is still unresolved. Some studies suggest they are less likely to receive medication for ADHD (Safer & Malever, 2000), while others show equitable services for boys and girls with ADHD, including special education, tutoring, counseling and medication (Biederman et al., 2002).

Implications for Treatment

The AACAP Practice Parameters (AACAP Author, 2007) focus on the comprehensive assessment, diagnosis and treatment of AD/HD with a developmental framework. The extensive guidelines describe evidence-based medical treatments options, and suggest the need for a multimodal approach including parent education and support, appropriate educational services, and well-controlled and properly managed medication.

The Multimodal Treatment Study of ADHD (MTA) is the first large scale clinical treatment study of ADHD funded by the National Institute of Mental Health (NIMH). The MTA study reported superior outcomes for children receiving a combination of behavioral treatments (i.e., parent training, intensive summer school program, and ongoing ADHD consultation in the school setting), and carefully managed medications [i.e., double-blind, placebo controlled titration (MTA Cooperative Group, 2004a, 2004b)]. All treatment groups in the study outperformed a control group receiving routine community care (CC), even though the majority of children in the CC group received medication. The MTA medication alone and combined treatment groups received more carefully monitored and managed medication, and higher doses of medication than found in the community. The combined groups received slightly lower medication doses than the medication alone groups, most likely due to the added benefits of behavioral interventions. Improvements were documented on measures of ADHD and oppositional/aggressive problems. Children with anxiety also showed improvement in all MTA treatment groups compared to CC groups even though anxiety was a target of the treatment protocol. Families receiving public assistance reported lower rates of closeness when their children were medicated, although there were no differences in positive parenting practices across groups.

At two-year follow-up some of the initial (14-month follow-up) superiority of combined treatment and medication treatment over behavioral treatment alone were no longer present. While the combined treatment group appeared to outperform other groups, differences between the medication alone and combined groups were no longer statistically significant. At 24-month follow-up all study treatments were discontinued and parents were free to seek routine community care.

Other intensive treatment programs have also shown positive findings for various treatment approaches, including an intensive summer treatment program (Pelham et al., 1988), the California-Irvine/Orange County Department of Education (UCI-OCDE), and the University of Massachusetts Medical School (UMASS) for kindergarten children [see (Barkley, 2006) for a review]. The first two programs were included in the MTA study protocol for the behavioral alone and the combined treatment groups.

In any treatment paradigm, it is important to consider the child's age and developmental level. In infancy and toddlerhood it is recommended to emphasize building positive parent-child relationships (Teeter, 1998). Teeter (1998) suggests that a warm and responsive style coupled with flexibility would be the best parenting response to an infant and toddler with ADHD. Kern et al. (2007) also found that parent training and multicomponent interventions were equally effective in reducing aggression and improving social skills at home in young children with ADHD. As the child matures the parents need to develop effective parenting skills that utilize consistent limit setting and tying consequences to both appropriate and inappropriate behaviors. In addition work with children in developing appropriate social skills, self-control, and organizational problem solving techniques needs to start in elementary school and continue throughout the school experience (Abramowitz & O'Leary, 1991). In adolescence, additional instruction in social judgment, problem solving, and managing typical teenage concerns, including substance abuse, sex, and peer pressure (Robin & Foster, 1989), is warranted. Bussing et al. (2007) also found that adolescent ADHD stigma perceptions do affect treatment receptivity. Some stigma perceptions are more strongly perceived by African-American youth and poor youth who appear to already experience heightened levels of discrimination. Thus, stigma and treatment receptivity need to be addressed in therapy with ADHD adolescents. For a comprehensive review of treatment approaches, see DuPaul and Stoner (2003) and Teeter (1998) for school-based treatments and interventions through the lifespan.

Conduct Disorder

Aggressive behaviors that do not consider the feelings of others and that can be dangerous and hurtful are becoming more visible in today's society. Individuals who display such behaviors often have a history of antisocial behavior stretching back into early childhood. Conduct disorder (CD) is "a repetitive and persistent pattern of behavior in which the basic rights of others or major age-appropriate societal norms or rules are violated" (APA, 2000, p. 93). These behaviors fall into four major categories including aggressive behaviors that cause or threaten physical harm to people or animals, non-aggressive conduct that damages property, theft or deceitfulness, and serious rule violations. These behaviors have a negative impact on the child's academic and social functioning. The diagnosis of conduct disorder appears to be stable across environments and informants (Patterson, 1986).

There are three major subtypes of conduct disorder: Childhood-Onset, Adolescent-Onset, and Unspecified Onset (APA, 2000). Children with early onset aggression are more likely to have persistent antisocial problems later in life, while adolescent onset antisocial behaviors are more time-limited (Hinshaw & Lee, 2003). Adolescents who develop conduct problems as

teens are less likely to have significant psychopathology that is seen in children with early-onset CD.

Estimates from twin studies suggest that CD is influenced by both genetics and environment, where children who have either biological or adoptive parents with antisocial personality disorder (ASP) are at greater risk for CD (APA, 2000; Hinshaw & Lee, 2003). Other biological parental psychopathology increases the risk for CD in children, including substance abuse disorders and mood disorders, and/or a parental history of ADHD and CD.

Incidence

Prevalence rates vary from 1 to more than 10 percent (APA, 2000). Conduct disorder is the most common reason for referral to mental health services (Wells & Forehand, 1985). Moreover, children with conduct disorder are heavily represented in school classrooms for children with behavioral disturbances (Pullis, 1991).

Gender

Conduct disorders vary as a function of gender (APA, 2000). While studies generally report lower rates of CD in girls, these gender differences are reduced in adolescence [see (Hinshaw & Lee, 2003) for a review]. Males are more likely to have early-onset CD and are more likely to exhibit "fighting, stealing, vandalism, and school discipline problems," while females are more likely to exhibit "lying, truancy, running away, substance use, and prostitution" (APA, 2000, p. 97). In general, males are more likely to be involved with illegal behaviors (Pennington, 2002).

Developmental Course

There is a high concordance between conduct problems in early childhood and antisocial personality disorders in adulthood (APA, 2000). Early-onset CD is associated with a more serious form of the disorder, and increases risk for later substance abuse, mood, anxiety, and somatoform disorders. Current research suggests that there is a developmental trajectory of disruptive behavior disorders based on dimensions of overt-covert and destructive-nondestructive behaviors (Frick et al., 1992). Studies suggest that children may show behaviors consistent with Oppositional Defiant Disorder (ODD) at an early age (2–3 years or earlier), which predicts the development of CD (Hinshaw & Lee, 2003). The development of adult ASP also follows a similar progression, with CD proceeding ASP in adulthood. This pattern is extremely common in boys, but girls are less likely to have lifetime ASP.

There may be at least two differing expressions of conduct disorder (Patterson, DeBaryshe, & Ramsey, 1990). The first is that of the child who begins with oppositional behaviors in preschool and the elementary years and develops into aggressive behavior and lying and stealing in middle childhood, with significant behavioral difficulties in adolescence. The second pathway is that of the child who first exhibits conduct problems in adolescence after a fairly normal childhood. The prognosis is poorer for the early starter than the later starter; further, oppositional defiant disorder in early childhood is considered a significant risk factor (White, Moffitt, Earls, & Robins, 1990).

Comorbid Disorders

The development of antisocial personality disorder (APD) occurs in as many as 8.7 percent of children with CD (Fergusson, Horwood, & Ridder, 2005). Young children between the ages of seven to nine years have an increased risk for criminal activities such as property offending, violent offending, arrests and convictions, repeated traffic offenses, and imprisonment (Fergusson et al., 2005). Research also shows that children have an increased risk for substance use/abuse (nicotine, illicit drug dependence) and mental health problems (MDD, anxiety disorder, antisocial personality disorder, suicide attempts). Fergusson et al. (2005) report that 42.1 percent of children with severe conduct

problems have comorbid MDD or anxiety by age 25, and as many as 14.6 percent of adults with a diagnosis of CD in childhood become addicted to an illegal drug (Fergusson et al., 2005).

Interpersonal relationships also appear problematic particularly sexual/partners and education/employment difficulties, including higher risks of having multiple partners, becoming pregnant or getting one pregnant, parenthood, being involved in interpartner violence, no educational or employment qualifications, failing to obtain a university degree, unemployment for 12 months or more, or welfare dependency (Fergusson et al., 2005). These risk factors were found even after controlling for gender, ethnicity, SES, parental adjustment problems, child abuse, child attention problems, and child IQ.

While comorbidity is high in children with CD, the developmental trajectory of physical aggression in children through adolescence is highly variable. Most children with antisocial behavior problems do not develop serious adult problems (Brame, Nagin, & Tremblay, 2001); however severe aggression in childhood is predictive of aggression in adolescence and adulthood (Brame et al., 2001).

While reasoning problems may play a role in the development and progression of conduct-related disorders, it is not clear which variables are correlated and which are causative (Teeter Ellison et al., in press). Studies exploring poorly developed language skills in aggressive children and adolescents with conduct disorders suggest that there may be involvement of the left hemisphere (Coy, Speltz, DeKlyen, & Jones, 2001). In addition to the behavioral problems, interventions should also target the cognitive, reasoning, and language deficits that have been linked to delinquent behavior and conduct disorder.

Genetic Influences

Conduct disorder is likely the result of the interaction of several genetic correlates and environmental variables (Pennington, 2002). Heritability of CD symptoms also varies with age ($h^2 = 0.66$ for older males and $h^2 = 0.57$ younger males) and gender [$h^2 = 0.48$ for older females and $h^2 = 0.24$ for younger females; see (Pennington, 2002)]. Pennington indicates that studies of CD with other comorbid disorders have stronger heritability indices; for example, CD with ODD have moderate heritability ($h^2 = 0.65$) for males and girls ($h^2 = 0.53$). Finally, a study of adopted children found that conduct problems were highly correlated with antisocial personality disorder in the biological parent and were not correlated with their adoptive family (Jarey & Stewart, 1985). Studies of aggression and ASB are not as clearcut as those investigating the genetic basis of ADHD. While environmental influences are stronger, hereditability appears to increase with age, suggesting a dynamic interplay between genes and environment (Hinshaw & Lee, 2003).

The degree to which genetic and environmental factors interact to predict ASB in children has been the focus of twin studies (Kim-Cohen, Moffitt, Taylor, Pawlby, & Caspi, 2005). Kim-Cohen et al. (2005) found that maternal depression after the birth of twins was associated with the development of ASB and CD in childhood, while maternal depression before the birth was not predictive. Depressed and antisocial mothers were more likely to have multiple problems with child care practices, were more likely to engage in physical maltreatment, had high rates of maternal hostility, and also had high rates of exposure to domestic violence (Kim-Cohen et al., 2005)

Family Influences

"At the outset, we alert the reader to the obvious but often overlooked point that in biological families, familial influences on child development may be psychological in nature, may be genetically mediated, or may result from correlated (or interacting) joint influences of genes and environment" (Hinshaw & Lee, 2003, p. 174). There are a number of family factors associated with ASB, including poor early attachment relationships, family conflict and aggression, and maternal depression (Teeter Ellison et al., in press). Disorganized attachment styles are associated with family adversity, hostile parenting, and parental depression, and do predict school-age aggressive behavior (Lyons-Ruth, 1996).

In families of children with conduct disorder there is evidence of considerable stress (McGee, Silva, & Williams, 1984; Patterson, 1982), frequent parental substance abuse and criminality (West, 1982), and a higher incidence of familial psychopathology (Frick et al., 1992). Families with a history of conduct disorder have patterns of coercive, inconsistent and highly punitive child management practices (Patterson, 1982). Similarly, these families do not consistently reinforce positive behaviors nor do they evidence prosocial relationships. Therefore, negative parent-child interactions, fraught with negative interactions and very few positive exchanges, are highly predictive of childhood conduct disorder (Patterson, 1982). See Hinshaw and Lee (2003) for an in-depth overview for family issues.

In addition to negative parent-child interactions, families of children with conduct disorder are more likely to engage in substance abuse than are those of other children (Frick et al., 1992). In studies designed to untangle the relationship between substance abuse, parental antisocial personality disorder, and childhood conduct disorder, parental substance abuse was not associated with criminality in children, while parental antisocial personality disorder was highly associated (Frick et al., 1992).

Physiological Signs

Researchers have investigated psychophysiological responses of children with antisocial behavioral (ASB) problems. In a meta-analysis, Ortiz and Raine (2004) found that youth with ASB had significantly lower resting heart rate and lower heart rate during a stressor. These were robust findings across gender, culture, or country of origin. Effect size was moderate ($d = 0.44$) for resting heart rate, with larger effect size for heart rate during a stressor ($d = -0.76$). Ortiz and Raine (2004) also reported similar findings were present in parents of youth with ASB; that is, parents with a criminal past had low resting heart rates. Ortiz and Raine suggest that this supports a genetic transmission or predisposition for ASB.

Research suggests that physiological responses to stress and resting heart rate may be a specific marker of ASB (Teeter Ellison et al., in press).

Significantly lower physiological reactions to aversive stimuli have been found in youths with CD alone or with comorbid ADHD; these are lower than those found in other childhood disorders including ADHD and psychiatric controls, or healthy comparisons (Herpertz et al., 2005; Ortiz & Raine, 2004). Differences are reported across various measures (self-reports, skin conductance, and heart rate). There are numerous theories to explain these physiological variations and why they are markers for ABS, including stimulation-seeking theories, fearlessness theories, and biosocial theories. Neurophysiologic research suggests that other processes may be involved (Ortiz & Raine, 2004), specifically that low heart rate may be an artifact of right hemisphere dysfunction. The right hemisphere controls heart rate and other autonomic functions, and has been shown to be implicated in antisocial populations and those with reduced noradrenergic functioning.

In summary, identifying clear-cut lateralizing signs may not be as important as determining the types of associated neuropsychological deficits (i.e., language and reasoning problems), and assessing their effect on later psychophysiological, psychosocial, and emotional development (Teeter Ellison et al., in press).

Neuropsychological Correlates

Research investigating the nature and extent of neuropsychological difficulties in children with CD has not produced clear patterns of deficits although weaknesses in language, executive functions and nonverbal reasoning have been found (Teeter Ellison et al., in press). In general children with CD tend to have lower IQs (1/2 standard deviation below the mean) than controls, particularly lower verbal IQ (Pennington, 2002). Language deficits may underlie difficulties in understanding the consequences of behaviors and an inability to adequately monitor and control behaviors. Thus, children with a predisposition to develop a conduct disorder with poorly developed language skills and/or overall lower cognitive ability are at a higher risk for significant antisocial behaviors as an adolescent and as an adult. Tramontana and Hooper (1989)

suggest that difficulties in language may translate into impulsive acting out when the child faces a provoking situation because verbal reasoning and judgment skills are deficient. Support for this hypothesis comes from studies that have found 15-point verbal < performance scores on the WISC-R to be highly predictive of recidivism in adjudicated delinquents (Haynes & Bensch, 1981).

In addition to language difficulties, executive functioning deficits may emerge at an early age. In a study of children with CD between seven to 12 years of age, Toupin et al. (2000) found no differences in verbal abilities compared to non-CD controls, but did find significantly worse performance on almost all EF measures of inhibition\impulsivity, cognitive flexibility, and planning/organization. These differences were observed even when ADHD was controlled. The Rey-Osterrieth Complex Figure Test (ROCF) was particularly sensitive to discriminating groups, as children with CD had difficulties on this measure of visual-motor-spatial organization and construction, planning strategy, and sustained attention. Several factors were predictive of the development of CD, and are ranked in order of importance: greater ADHD symptoms, impaired performance on the ROCF, a history of parental punishment, and lower socioeconomic status (Toupin et al., 2000). See Teeter Ellison et al. (in press) for a more complete discussion.

Pennington and Ozonoff (1996) found that executive deficits are most pronounced in children with CD and comorbid ADHD. White, Moffitt, & Silva (1989) found that children with conduct disorder showed higher measures of impulsivity than other groups even with IQ and social class controlled. Pennington and Bennetto (1993) suggest that children with CD and concomitant verbal and executive function deficits are at higher risk for significant aggressive and antisocial behaviors.

Intellectual/Academic

Children with conduct disorder (CD) have been shown to have significantly lower intelligence than children without CD (Semrud-Clikeman, Hynd,

Lorys, & Lahey, 1993). In general, higher intelligence may protect against the development of delinquent behavior in high-risk children and adults (White, Moffitt, & Silva, 1989). Although academic failure is associated with delinquency, a 15-year longitudinal study examining causal pathways found that both academic achievement and later delinquent behaviors were influenced by the common effects of early behavior problems and low IQ (Fergusson & Horwood, 1995).

Studies have examined the response of CD children to reward and punishment. Children with CD have a greater tendency to respond to the reward cues (Newman, Patterson, & Kosson, 1987) and have trouble managing their behaviors when rewards are present. A study investigating sensitivity to reward found that children with CD are exquisitely sensitive to reward and unable to inhibit responding in mixed-incentive situations (Shapiro, Quay, Hogan, & Schwartz, 1988). Daugherty and Quay (1991) also found a preseverative response set; that is, children with CD continued maladaptive response patterns even though such responses resulted in loss of rewards.

Cognitive factors are related to conduct problems (Dodge, 1993). Children with conduct disorder have a negative response bias and interpret even ambiguous stimuli as negative and hostile toward them (Dodge, Price, Bachorowski, & Newman, 1990). Difficulties with problem solving skills, a rigid response style, and stereotyped responses to conflictual situations have frequently been found in children with conduct disorder (Short & Shapiro, 1993; Spivack, Platt, & Shure, 1976).

Unfortunately, poor achievement in middle school and adolescence is predicted by disruptive behaviors in first grade (Tremblay, Masse, Perron, & Leblanc, 1992). Although students showed academic difficulties in 1st and 4th grades, disruptive behavior in 1st grade was significant for predicting delinquency at age 14 years.

In addition to difficulties in learning, children with conduct disorder experience peer rejection (Patterson et al., 1990). Perhaps in reaction to such rejection, children with similarly disruptive and aggressive behavior tend to group together and form gangs that become involved in delinquent behaviors in adolescence (Dishion & Loeber, 1985).

Implications for Assessment

Because conduct disorder is rarely diagnosed before age six, most young preschoolers with behavioral difficulties are frequently diagnosed as having oppositional defiant disorder (Webster-Stratton, 1993). A diagnosis of conduct disorder requires that the behavioral difficulties must have lasted for at least six months and that at least three of the following symptoms are present (APA, 2000): cruelty to people and/or animals, stealing or breaking and entering, lying and cheating in school activities, aggression, setting fires, school truancy, and/or, running away from home at least twice.

Diagnosis of conduct disorder is behavioral in nature, and a clinical structured interview is the preferred method of analysis (Webster-Stratton, 1993). The key elements for diagnosing a severe conduct disorder are as follows: (1) early onset of conduct problems; (2) presence of the problem behaviors in many settings; (3) greater frequency, intensity, and severity of conduct difficulties; (4) presence of several types of misbehavior; (5) covert behavioral difficulties such as stealing and lying, and (6) family characteristics.

Implications for Intervention

The earlier the child develops oppositional and conduct problems, the more severe the problem, so it is surprising that there are so few early screening and intervention programs. Webster-Stratton (1993) suggests that early intervention programs would be appropriate to allow parents and teachers to modify target behaviors before peer rejection has taken place and negative school reputations are in place.

Intervention programs have focused mainly on parent training programs. An exemplary training program was developed by the Oregon Social Learning Center (Patterson, Reid, Jones, & Conger, 1975). The parents are taught parenting skills by utilizing a task analysis approach that breaks down the task and builds each succeeding skill upon skills that are already mastered. As part of this approach, the parent is directly taught how to reward appropriate behavior and modify inappropriate behavior, as well as discipline procedures, how to supervise children, and problem solving and child negotiation skills. Patterson and Chamberlain (1988) reported that almost one-third of the time in training is devoted to dealing with parental adjustment issues. Another program developed by McMahon and Forehand (1984), based on a model introduced by Hanf and Kling (1973), was specifically developed for working with younger children with conduct disorders. This program stresses teaching the parent to play with his or her child and, in so doing, teach prosocial behaviors. The goal is to teach the parent to reward appropriate behavior and forestall the punitive parenting process frequently seen in these families.

Finally, a program developed by Webster-Stratton (1984) combines the McMahon and Forehand approach with the Patterson strategies. In addition, a program to deal with the personal issues of the parent has been developed that encompasses skills such as anger management, developing coping skills for negative feelings, promoting effective communication skills, and improving problem solving skills (Webster-Stratton, 1993). This program utilizes videotaped vignettes of models appropriately demonstrating the necessary skills as well as less appropriate methods of discipline. All of these programs have evidenced good reviews from parents and short-term evaluation. Improvement has been documented in parental change through home observation and generalization of appropriate behaviors to other settings and to untreated behaviors. Unfortunately, these improvements do not generalize to the school setting.

Direct child training combined with the parent programs has been an effective and ecologically valid method of intervention. These programs include social skills training, academic and social skills training, and training in behavioral self-control skills. Additional programs target helping children to develop cognitive awareness of their feelings and their ability to see situations from more than one perspective.

Conclusion

Further research is necessary to shed light on the neurological and neuropsychological underpinnings of severe psychiatric and externalized disorders of children. Although there appear to be strong neurochemical models that help to explain the high rates of comorbidity of these disorders, it is still unclear why neurotransmitter imbalances result in different behavioral patterns (e.g., TS vs. ADHD or TS vs. conduct disorders). The picture is further complicated by the repeated finding that frontal lobe dysfunction is prominent in a number of neuropsychiatric disorders (e.g., TS, ADHD, autism). It may be that further research using rCBF imaging techniques will be helpful in this investigation, particularly if this technology can more clearly demonstrate differences in activation in the various frontal-limbic regions that correspond to specific neurochemical pathways (e.g., NE, DA, and SE brain circuits).

In externalizing disorders, the environment, genetics, and behavior interact with the child, and he or she in turn acts on the environment. The genetic and neurochemical evidence discussed in relation to the disorders in this chapter sets the stage and needs to be considered as a constraint the child works against, works with, or works around. Family interactions are another level that overlay the child's genetic background and development. Assessment of all of these areas is crucial to fully understand not only the child, but also brain-behavior functioning. Research on the neuropsychological and neurochemical underpinnings of these disorders is in its infancy, and the contribution of neuropsychological measures to treatment planning is just beginning. The extent to which executive control deficits can be reliably measured and ultimately altered through psychosocial or behavioral interventions may presage future models of neuropsychiatric disorders of childhood.

The child neuropsychologist and the clinical or school psychologist have a wealth of information among them, none of which is solely within the purview of one specialty. Neuropsychological assessment should be in addition to an educational assessment or a child clinical assessment and can provide knowledge about the child's functional level. Differential diagnosis of ADHD versus depression or anxiety, of conduct disorder versus information-processing deficits, and obsessive-compulsive disorder versus ADHD are just some of the possibilities. This chapter was designed to give the reader an overview of the genetic and neuropsychological correlates of the more commonly seen neuropsychiatric disorders. A further goal of this chapter was to discuss these disorders so that astute school and clinical psychologists, in addition to the neuropsychologist, recognize the interplay of brain function and behavior and glean suggestions for assessment that are within his or her expertise. The two roles are complementary and not distinct. One of the purposes of this book is to provide the child clinician with basic understanding of these disorders, as well as methods for screening these possibilities when confronted with the dilemma of differential diagnosis.

The following presentation is a case illustration of a child with ADHD. It is provided by Dr. Sam Goldstein at our request. The case is typical of others seen in many tertiary settings.

Case: Combined Type of Attention-Deficit Hyperactivity Disorder
With Comorbid Oppositional Defiant Disorder, and Reading and Mathematics Disabilities

Reason for Evaluation

Alex has been diagnosed and treated for Attention-Deficit Hyperactivity Disorder and Oppositional Defiant Disorder. He has a history of disruptive, non-compliant, argumentative and inattentive behavior. Evaluation was requested by his physician to provide a broad overview of Alex's adjustment and development to assist with treatment planning and support.

Background Information

Alex's mother and her second husband were interviewed to review Alex's social and developmental history. Alex's father passed away in a work accident three months before Alex was born. He completed high school. He evidently had a history of learning disabilities and ADHD. There is a history of depression on his side of the family. Alex's mother is employed as a jail clerk. She completed two years of college. She noted a history of depression in herself and her family. Alex's stepfather has known him for two years. He reported that they get along well

although it has been a learning process for him to understand that Alex's behavior is not always the result of non-compliance. Alex's mother has an 11-year-old child from a previous marriage who is doing well. The family also has a seven-week-old child. Alex and his half-sibling often fight. He is aggressive towards her. He has threatened her with objects when upset. He appears to have sibling rivalries. She can antagonize him at times. He frequently complains about fairness at home.

Alex was the product of an uncomplicated pregnancy, labor and delivery. As an infant he had "a lot of gas." He did not sleep well. As a toddler he was constantly into things and disruptive. He could be distracted very easily. He struggled with transition and would cry frequently. People were very aware of his emotions. He tended to have a low emotional threshold and a high intensity of reaction. He demonstrated no sensory threshold problems.

Alex suffers from eczema. He has had pressure equalization tubes placed three times. He was hospitalized once in November 2001 for influenza. Most of the time he settles down to sleep. He has had some nightmares. He is a restless sleeper, being described as "like a little race car." He also snores in his sleep. He does not eat very much, a problem that pre-dated his initiation to medication. He was initially tried on Adderall with a good response, but side effects. He has been taking Vyvanse at 50 mgs qd over the past year. The medication appears to work well.

Alex met developmental milestones within normal limits. Pre-academic milestones appeared to be reached appropriately. Alex is athletic. He has been a risk taker. His handwriting is poor because he rushes, but he may also have limited abilities.

Alex appears to understand directions and situations as well as others. Intellectually he appears average.

Alex's mother was concerned about him before he entered school because he was struggling to master knowledge of numbers and letters. The initiation of medication in preschool appeared to significantly help his achievement. He is still receiving reading assistance at school. Despite behavioral improvements at school, he continues to struggle with reading and spelling.

Alex seeks out and is sought out by peers for friendship. He has a best friend. Children call him and he attends birthday parties. Nonetheless, at times he can be aggressive, bossy and controlling.

Alex has a history of biting his fingernails, cuticles and picking at his nose. He has a hard time settling down when things are exciting. He has problems following through with instructions. He shifts from one uncompleted activity to another. Alex "talks non-stop." At times he does not appear to listen. He has a history of boundless energy and poor judgment as well as poor self-control. He frustrates easily and is quick to lose his temper. A number of times per week he has an outburst. Tantrums can last over an hour.

Alex has had problems with orthographic skills and visual association. He did not appear to have problems early on with language, label and association but possibly sequencing.

Alex enjoys legos and will stick to these activities for long periods of time. He has a negative mindset about his reading skills. He often acts like he is driven by a motor. When upset he has destroyed things at home. He works well for short-term rewards, but not quite as well for long-term rewards. He does not always benefit from experience and creates more problems at home than his sister. Time-out at times can be effective, but not in the long run. Alex's parents have attended a parenting class for children with ADHD.

Alex was initially enrolled in a Children's Center kindergarten program, but appeared to become more aggressive in a short time there. He was withdrawn and put into the public school. He has been seen once for outpatient counseling. Alex attends a parochial school.

Alex enjoys riding his dirt bike, playing with legos and cars. He dislikes chores, cleaning, schoolwork and following instructions. He has a big heart, a sweet nature and a creative mind.

Assessment Procedures

Conners Parent Rating Scale—Revised (Form L)
Conners Teacher Rating Scale—Revised (Form L)
Child Behavior Checklist
Home Situations Questionnaire
Social Attributes Checklist (parent and teacher form)
Teacher Observation Checklist
Elementary School Situations Questionnaire
Review of Academic File

Peabody Picture Vocabulary Test—IIIA
Expressive Vocabulary Test
Wechsler Intelligence Scale for Children—IV
Test of Memory and Learning
Gordon Diagnostic System
Purdue Pegboard
Developmental Test of Visual Motor Integration
Human Figure Drawing
Letter and Number Writing Sample
Woodcock-Johnson III Tests of Achievement
Revised Children's Manifest Anxiety Scale
Clinical Interview

Adaptive Functioning

For comparative purposes, Parent and Teacher Conners' Rating Scales appear below providing age-adjusted T-scores (mean = 50; s.d. = 10). It should be noted these observations are based on Alex's functioning while receiving the currently prescribed Vyanase.

	Parent	Teacher
Oppositional Behavior	74	61
Cognitive Problems/Inattention	70	57
Hyperactivity	66	75
Anxious/Shy	53	48
Perfectionism	57	84
Social Problems	45	51
Psychosomatic	43	n/a
Conners' ADHD Index	73	62
Conners' Global Index		
Restless-Impulsive	73	69
Emotional Lability	84	53
Total	78	64
DSM-IV		
Inattentive	68	53
Hyperactive-Impulsive	68	68
Total	71	61

Parents report seven inattentive and five hyperactive-impulsive symptoms to a clinical degree. Alex's first grade teacher reported three inattentive and six hyperactive-impulsive symptoms to a clinical degree.

Parent responses to the Child Behavior Checklist placed Alex at the following age-adjusted percentiles (50th percentile is average; high score indicates problem):

	Percentile (mean = 50th)
Withdrawn	84th
Somatic Complaints	50th
Anxious/Depressed	70th
Social Problems	60th
Thought Problems	50th
Attention Problems	93rd
Delinquent Behavior	95th
Aggressive Behavior	98th

Alex is argumentative and quick to demand attention. He loses his temper easily. He has trouble sitting still and often acts impulsively. Alex is prone to cry quickly. A number of times in public he has pulled his pants down thinking that this behavior is humorous.

On the Home Situations Questionnaire, Alex's parents noted moderate to significant problems when playing with others, at meals, when dressing, when washing or bathing, with behavior in public places, when asked to do chores and doing homework. No problems are noted when playing alone, with other routines or with behavior when visitors are in the home or visiting others.

On the Social Attributes Checklist, Alex's parents noted that he has a positive mood, but at times can be dependent upon adults. He demonstrates empathy and humor. He can approach others positively and express wishes and preferences clearly. He is less consistent in asserting rights and needs appropriately and expressing anger and frustration effectively. He gains access to peers and is accepted by other children. He takes turns, but is less consistent in entering conversation, showing interest, negotiating and compromising. At times he can draw inappropriate attention to himself.

School Functioning

A number of additional questionnaires were completed by Alex's first grade teacher. His teacher notes that during the first grade year Alex appeared self-confident, but demonstrated limited and narrow motivation in the classroom. He could adapt to new situations and did not seek extra attention. His approach to problems was moderately careful. He could follow simple instructions, but often required individual help. Alex learned and worked slowly in most

situations. He demonstrated some ability to tolerate frustration, but would often demand attention and speak out of turn. Vocabulary and language skills were rated as average. Alex was reported to be average in large motor skills, but below average in fine motor and perceptual skills. Alex was reported to be very poor in reading achievement and below average in mathematics.

On the School Situations Questionnaire, his teacher noted Alex's moderate to significant problems when arriving at school, during individual task work, during small group activities, during free time, during class lectures, in the hallways, bathroom, on field trips and assemblies. During instruction Alex would often be "playing with pencils and paper."

On the Social Attributes Checklist, his teacher noted that Alex had a positive mood. At times he could be dependent upon adults. He demonstrated empathy and humor. He was inconsistent in approaching others positively, expressing wishes and preferences clearly, asserting rights and needs appropriately and expressing anger and frustration effectively. Alex at times could gain access to peers and at times was accepted. He was inconsistent in entering a conversation, taking turns, negotiating and compromising. He often drew inappropriate attention to himself.

A review of Alex's school records noted concerns about fighting with other students. Academic screening placed Alex below average on the Dynamic Indicators of Basic Early Literacy Skills with minimal progress reported during the school year for phonemic awareness.

Behavioral Observation

Alex is a child of average size and appearance, was well-groomed and neatly dressed. He was seen for two assessment sessions with a lunch time break. He completed additional instruments in the afternoon session with the examiner. Alex had taken the prescribed Vyvanse on the day of the evaluation.

Eye contact was appropriate. Alex demonstrated mild receptive language problems. Expressive articulation was adequate. Alex maintained and initiated conversation. No overt signs of anxiety, sadness or emotional lability were noted. Alex was calm and emotionally stable. Alex was alert, attentive and concentrated reasonably well. He was cooperative and attempted all tasks presented. Alex was motivated to perform, but required some prompting to persist. No muscular tension or significant individual mannerisms were noted. Alex would periodically bite his nails.

Alex presented with a normal activity level. He squirmed and wriggled occasionally. Overall he was not distracted. Alex appeared moderately competent in his skills and related well to the examiners. His approach at times to some test tasks was mildly impulsive. His thoughts overall were logical, focused and relevant. It was not difficult to establish a working relationship with this pleasant child.

Assessment Results and Interpretation

Language

The Peabody was administered as a simple measure of one word receptive vocabulary. Alex completed this test with a standard score of 90, equivalent to the 19th percentile.

The Expressive Vocabulary Test was administered as a simple synonym measure of expressive language. Alex completed this test with a standard score of 87, equivalent to the 19th percentile.

Intellectual

The Fourth Edition of the Wechsler Intelligence Scale was administered as an overall screening of intellectual ability and achievement. Age-adjusted scaled scores appear below:

	Scaled Scores (mean = 10; s.d. = 3)
Verbal Comprehension	
Similarities	5
Vocabulary	8
Comprehension	11
Information	6
Word Reasoning	10
Perceptual Reasoning	
Block Design	12
Picture Concepts	13
Matrix Reasoning	11

	Scaled Scores (mean = 10; s.d. = 3)
(continued)	
Working Memory	
Digit Span	8
Letter-Number Sequencing	6
Processing Speed	
Coding	16
Symbol Search	8

	Standard Scores	90% Confidence Interval (mean = 100; s.d. = 15)
Verbal Comprehension	89	84–95
Perceptual Reasoning	112	105–117
Working Memory	83	78–91
Processing Speed	110	103–118
Full Scale	99	95–103

Alex demonstrates markedly better perceptual reasoning than verbal comprehension skills. Simple working memory appears below average, but processing speed appears above average.

Learning and Working Memory

The Test of Memory and Learning was administered as an overall screening. Age-adjusted scaled scores appear below:

	Scaled Scores (mean = 10; s.d. = 3)
Verbal Subtests	
Memory for Stories	10
Word Selective Reminding	13
Object Recall	12
Digits Forward	6
Paired Recall	11
Nonverbal Subtests	
Facial Memory	9
Visual Selective Reminding	13
Abstract Visual Memory	12
Visual Sequential Memory	11
Memory for Location	11
Delayed Recall Scores	
Memory for Stories	10
Facial Memory	7
Word Selective Reminding	12
Visual Selective Reminding	11

	(mean = 100; s.d. = 15)	Percentile
Verbal Memory Index	103	58th
Nonverbal Memory Index	108	70th
Composite Memory Index	106	65th
Delayed Recall Index	100	50th

Executive/Neuropsychological Skills

The Cognitive Assessment System was administered as a neuropsychological screening. Age-adjusted scaled scores appear below:

	Scaled Scores (mean = 10; s.d. = 3)
Matching Numbers	8
Planned Codes	12
Nonverbal Matrices	15
Verbal-Spatial Relations	11
Expressive Attention	8
Number Detection	12
Word Series	4
Sentence Repetition	8

	IQ	Percentiles	90% Confidence Interval
Planning	100	50th	92–108
Simultaneous	117	87th	108–123
Attention	100	50th	92–109
Successive	78	7th	73–87
Full Scale	98	45th	91–106

Though Alex demonstrates an atypical pattern of neuropsychological processes, despite an overall average Full Scale score he appears to possess very poor successive processes, average planning and attention processes, but well above average simultaneous processes. The latter reflects his ability to problem solve nonverbally.

Attention

The Gordon was administered as a computerized measure of Alex's ability to sustain attention and inhibit impulsive responding. On the Delay tasks he performed within the normal range despite an extremely impulsive approach. He could not understand the seven-year-old instructions on the Vigilance task. He was administered the five-year-old version. His performance was still within the abnormal range, demonstrating significant patterns of impulsivity.

Motor/Perceptual

Alex held a pencil in his right hand with a four-finger pincer grip. Casual observation did not indicate any large motor abnormalities. Fine motor skills for motor speed and coordination, based on the Purdue Pegboard performance, appeared in the high average range.

Alex's reproductions of the figures on the Developmental Test of Visual Motor Integration yielded a standard score of 111, equivalent to the 77th percentile. Alex's Human Figure Drawing reflects this level of development. The figure was drawn very quickly. The figure appears below in reduced size. Of interest are the pointed teeth which Alex did not comment upon when asked.

Academic

The Woodcock was administered as a screening of Alex's academic abilities and fluency. Age-adjusted standard scores appear below:

	Standard Scores (mean = 100; s.d. = 15)
Letter/Word Identification	75
Story Recall	105
Understanding Directions	104
Calculation	73
Math Fluency	81
Spelling	75
Passage Comprehension	74
Applied Problems	87
Writing Samples	72
Word Attack	87
Oral Language	105
Brief Achievement	73

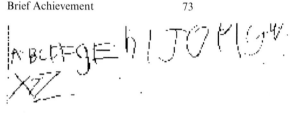

Total Achievement	77
Brief Reading	75
Basic Reading Skills	79
Brief Math	78
Math Calculation Skills	74
Brief Writing	70
Academic Skills	69
Academic Application	73

Alex's academic achievement appears well below expectation based upon his entering grade and age. In light of his significant successive processing problems, however, this overall profile academically is not unexpected.

Alex was unable to write the alphabet in sequence without error. He was able to write numbers 1–20 with multiple reversals. Alex's alphabet sample appears below

Emotional/Personality

Alex's responses to the Manifest Anxiety Scale suggests that he fosters strong anxious thinking. His overall score was at the 97th percentile. Alex reported getting nervous when he makes mistakes, getting mad easily, worrying what his parents will say to him, feeling that people don't like the way he does things, worrying what other people think about him, often feeling alone, having his feelings hurt easily, feeling that other people are happier, finding it hard to keep his mind on his schoolwork and believing that a lot of people dislike him.

During a brief clinical interview, Alex was open and responsive with the examiner. He tended to perseverate on discussions about dirt bikes. He spoke about a normal range of emotions, but reported he became angry more intensely and more often and others, explaining "I don't know how to control my anger." Alex spoke about a best friend and a number of social activities. He described himself as a "cry baby" and "mean" to others. He reported he wished he could be "better."

Alex described his favorite part of school as math and his least favorite as "schoolwork." He felt he was smart in school, but that school was "boring." He reported that second grade was going to be hard and that he was not going to "do very good." Alex reported the medication he takes "sometimes helps me be good." He denied any significant side effects. Alex reported that even if allowed to he would not stop attending school, indicating he was proud of math at school. He agreed that he had difficulty completing work, listening and staying in his seat. He reported that others at school find schoolwork easier.

Alex described his father as "he bought a dirt bike for me" and his mother as "she takes good care of me." He complained about his father's spanking, reporting that he got spanked for misbehaving and it "really hurts bad." He reported that he had been spanked three times that morning for going outside in his underwear. Alex reported that he wasn't treated fairly at home because "they won't let me stay up as late as my sister." This led to a long discussion about fairness and Alex's insistence that he should have the same privileges as his sister. He agreed that he created problems at home, sometimes on purpose. He reported spankings as the worst thing that happens to him and "being really good the whole day" as the best thing. He reported not getting along well with his sibling.

Alex reported it was difficult to fall asleep, but then he slept well. He reported intermittent headaches as hurting in his forehead. He noted that sometimes he lies down, usually he takes aspirin. Overall, Alex reported he was not satisfied with his life.

Alex presents as a child with adequate reality testing and age-appropriate thought processes. Though bonded to his parents, it is clear that because of his impulsive temperament he has developed a very negative view of himself and the manner in which he is treated by others. Youth with this emerging personality style as they enter their adolescent years are prone to feel misunderstood and unappreciated. They tend to project the source of their problems onto others, frequently complaining that life is unfair. In the face of stress they are prone to develop anxious and depressive symptoms.

Diagnostic Impression

Alex has been diagnosed and treated for ADHD and Oppositional Defiant Disorder. Concerns continue to be raised about his general behavior and achievement. Family history is noted by learning disabilities and ADHD. Alex has a history of impulsive and hyperactive behavior. Early academic milestones appeared to be reached appropriately. Later milestones have been slow in developing. Parent and teacher reports reflect high levels of oppositional, restless, impulsive and emotional behavior with a generally equal pattern of complaints at school and at home despite current medication use. Alex was also reported to be very poor in reading achievement and below average in mathematics achievement.

Alex took the prescribed stimulant medication on the day of the assessment. His intellectual abilities appear average with weak verbal comprehension and above average perceptual reasoning. Receptive and expressive language skills appear low average. Memory skills appear average. Neuropsychological processes are noted by strong nonverbal reasoning, but very weak successive processing. The latter skill is a key component in basic achievement. Thus, it is not surprising given the combination of Alex's impulsivity and successive processing weakness that he is struggling academically. His academic skills appear at a late kindergarten level. He demonstrates problems with academic application and fluency.

Alex presents as a child with adequate reality testing and generally age-appropriate thought processes. However, the quality of some of his responses during the assessment clearly reflects his weak overall verbal comprehension skills. Youth with his emerging personality style are prone to feel misunderstood and unappreciated. Alex is somewhat obsessed about fairness. He demonstrates problems with anger management and behavioral impairment that is driven by his impulsive temperament.

Alex's presentation meets the diagnostic criteria for the Combined Type of Attention-Deficit Hyperactivity Disorder and Oppositional Defiant Disorder. This examiner is concerned that despite treatment with stimulant medication and the improvements noted, reports from home and school continue to reflect clinically elevated symptoms related to impulsivity, inattention and hyperactivity. Relative to his basic intellect, Alex's academic achievement lags behind, consistent with diagnoses of Reading and Mathematics Disorders.

Recommendations

It is strongly recommended that Alex's physician review the current evaluation and consider a careful retitration of Alex's medications at home and at school. Should adjustments be made this examiner is prepared to assist in the collection of behavioral data within the home and school settings.

Alex's parents would benefit from additional ideas and resources to assist Alex at home. The text by this examiner and Robert Brooks, *Raising a Self-Disciplined Child*, is suggested as a helpful resource.

It is strongly recommended that Alex's educational team review the current evaluation and consider special education services for Alex. Current assessment suggests he should qualify under the IDEIA as a student with a Specific Learning Disability. This examiner is prepared to consult further with Alex's educational team.

Alex's parents may wish to consider private academic tutoring to augment school experiences. The text by Sam Goldstein and Nancy Mather, *Overcoming Underachieving*, and Jack Naglieri and Eric Pickering, *Helping Children Learn*, are suggested as helpful resources.

It is recommended that Alex be considered for short–term, problem-focused therapy to help him better understand his way of thinking about the world and develop more effective coping and self-management skills. A cognitive behavioral approach is recommended.

It is recommended that Alex be reevaluated during his fifth grade year.

Case: Combined Type of Attention-Deficit Hyperactivity Disorder With comorbid Oppositional Defiant Disorder, and Reading and Mathematics Disabilities

NAME:	XXXX XXXX
CA:	7 years 5 months
ENTERING GRADE:	Second

Reason for Evaluation

XXXX has been diagnosed and treated for Attention-Deficit Hyperactivity Disorder and Oppositional Defiant Disorder. He has a history of disruptive, non-compliant, argumentative and inattentive behavior. Evaluation was requested by his physician, XXXX M.D., to provide a broad overview of XXXX's adjustment and development so as to assist with treatment planning and support.

Background Information

Ms. XXXX and her second husband, XXXX, were seen to review XXXX's social and developmental history. XXXX's father passed away in a work accident three months before XXXX was born. He completed high school. He evidently had a history of learning disabilities and ADHD. There is a history of depression on his side of the family. Ms. XXXX-XXXX is employed as a jail clerk. She completed two years of college. She noted a history of depression in herself and her family. XXXX's stepfather has known XXXX for two years. He reported that they get along well although it has been a learning process for him to understand that XXXX's behavior is not always the result of non-

compliance. Ms. XXXX-XXXX has an eleven-year-old child from a previous marriage who is doing well. The XXXXs have a seven-week-old child. XXXX and his half-sibling XXXX often fight. He is aggressive towards her. He has threatened her with objects when upset. He appears to have sibling rivalries. She can antagonize him at times. He frequently complains about fairness at home.

XXXX was the product of an uncomplicated pregnancy, labor and delivery. As an infant he had "a lot of gas." He did not sleep well. As a toddler he was constantly into things and disruptive. He could be distracted very easily. He struggled with transition and would cry frequently. People were very aware of his emotions. He tended to have a low emotional threshold and a high intensity of reaction. He demonstrated no sensory threshold problems.

XXXX suffers from eczema. He has had pressure equalization tubes placed three times. He was hospitalized once in November 2001 for influenza. Most of the time he settles down to sleep. He has had some nightmares. He is a restless sleeper, being described as "like a little race car." He also snores in his sleep. He does not eat very much, a problem that pre-dated his initiation to medication. He was initially tried on Adderall with a good response, but side effects. He has been taking Vyvanse at 50 mgs qd over the past year. The medication appears to work well.

XXXX met developmental milestones within normal limits. Pre-academic milestones appeared to be reached appropriately. XXXX is athletic. He has been a risk taker. His handwriting is poor because he rushes, but he may also have limited abilities.

XXXX appears to understand directions and situations as well as others. Intellectually he appears average.

XXXX's mother was concerned about him before he entered school because he was struggling to master knowledge of numbers and letters. The initiation of medication in preschool appeared to significantly help his achievement. He is still receiving reading assistance at school. Despite behavioral improvements at school, he continues to struggle with reading and spelling.

XXXX seeks out and is sought out by peers for friendship. He has a best friend. Children call him and he attends birthday parties. Nonetheless, at times he can be aggressive, bossy and controlling.

XXXX has a history of biting his fingernails, cuticles and picking at his nose. He has a hard time settling down when things are exciting. He has problems following through with instructions. He shifts from one uncompleted activity to another. XXXX "talks non-stop." At times he does not appear to listen. He has a history of boundless energy and poor judgment as well as poor self-control. He frustrates easily and is quick to lose his temper. A number of times per week he has an outburst. Tantrums can last over an hour.

XXXX has had problems with orthographic skills and visual association. He did not appear to have problems early on with language, label and association, but possibly sequencing.

XXXX enjoys legos and will stick to these activities for long periods of time. He has a negative mindset about his reading skills. He often acts like he is driven by a motor. When upset he has destroyed things at home. He works well for short-term rewards, but not quite as well for long-term rewards. He does not always benefit from experience and creates more problems at home than his sister. Time-out can be effective, but not in the long run. XXXX's parents have attended a parenting class for children with ADHD.

XXXX was initially enrolled in a Children's Center kindergarten program, but appeared to become more aggressive in a short time there. He was withdrawn and put into the public school. He has been seen once for outpatient counseling. XXXX attends a parochial school, XXXXX.

XXXX enjoys riding his dirt bike, playing with legos and cars. He dislikes chores, cleaning, schoolwork and following instructions. He has a big heart, a sweet nature and a creative mind.

Assessment Procedures

Conners Parent Rating Scale—Revised (Form L)
Conners Teacher Rating Scale—Revised (Form L)
Child Behavior Checklist
Home Situations Questionnaire
Social Attributes Checklist (parent and teacher
  form)

Teacher Observation Checklist
Elementary School Situations Questionnaire
Review of Academic File
Peabody Picture Vocabulary Test—IIIA
Expressive Vocabulary Test
Wechsler Intelligence Scale for Children—IV
Test of Memory and Learning
Gordon Diagnostic System
Purdue Pegboard
Developmental Test of Visual Motor
  Integration
Human Figure Drawing
Letter and Number Writing Sample
Woodcock-Johnson III Tests of Achievement
Revised Children's Manifest Anxiety Scale
Clinical Interview

Adaptive Functioning

For comparative purposes, Parent and Teacher Conners' Rating Scales appear below providing age-adjusted T-scores (mean = 50; s.d. = 10). It should be noted these observations are based on XXXX's functioning while receiving the currently prescribed Vyvanse:

	T-scores	
	Parent	Teacher
Oppositional Behavior	74	61
Cognitive Problems/Inattention	70	57
Hyperactivity	66	75
Anxious/Shy	53	48
Perfectionism	57	84
Social Problems	45	51
Psychosomatic	43	n/a
Conners' ADHD Index	73	62
Conners' Global Index		
Restless-Impulsive	73	69
Emotional Lability	84	53
Total	78	64
DSM-IV		
Inattentive	68	53
Hyperactive-Impulsive	68	68
Total	71	61

Parents report seven inattentive and five hyperactive-impulsive symptoms to a clinical degree. XXXX's first grade teacher reported three inattentive and six hyperactive-impulsive symptoms to a clinical degree.

Parent responses to the Child Behavior Checklist placed XXXX at the following age-adjusted percentiles (50th percentile is average; high score indicates problem):

	Percentile (mean = 50th)
Withdrawn	84th
Somatic Complaints	50th
Anxious/Depressed	70th
Social Problems	60th
Thought Problems	50th
Attention Problems	93rd
Delinquent Behavior	95th
Aggressive Behavior	98th

XXXX is argumentative and quick to demand attention. He loses his temper easily. He has trouble sitting still and often acts impulsively. XXXX is prone to cry quickly. A number of times in public he has pulled his pants down thinking that this behavior is humorous.

On the Home Situations Questionnaire, XXXX's parents noted moderate to significant problems when playing with others, at meals, when dressing, when washing or bathing, with behavior in public places, when asked to do chores and doing homework. No problems are noted when playing alone, with other routines or with behavior when visitors are in the home or visiting others.

On the Social Attributes Checklist, XXXX's parents noted that he has a positive mood, but at times can be dependent upon adults. He demonstrates empathy and humor. He can approach others positively and express wishes and preferences clearly. He is less consistent in asserting rights and needs appropriately and expressing anger and frustration effectively. He gains access to peers and is accepted by other children. He takes turns, but is less consistent in entering conversation, showing interest, negotiating and compromising. At times he can draw inappropriate attention to himself.

School Functioning

A number of additional questionnaires were completed by XXXX's first grade teacher, Ms. XXXX. Ms. XXXX notes that during the first grade year

XXXX appeared self-confident, but demonstrated limited and narrow motivation in the classroom. He could adapt to new situations and did not seek extra attention. His approach to problems was moderately careful. He could follow simple instructions, but often required individual help. XXXX learned and worked slowly in most situations. He demonstrated some ability to tolerate frustration, but would often demand attention and speak out of turn. Vocabulary and language skills were rated as average. XXXX was reported to be average in large motor skills, but below average in fine motor and perceptual skills. XXXX was reported to be very poor in reading achievement and below average in mathematics.

On the School Situations Questionnaire, Ms. XXXX noted XXXX's moderate to significant problems when arriving at school, during individual task work, during small group activities, during free time, during class lectures, in the hallways, bathroom, on field trips and assemblies. During instruction XXXX would often be "playing with pencils and paper."

On the Social Attributes Checklist, Ms. XXXX noted that XXXX had a positive mood. At times he could be dependent upon adults. He demonstrated empathy and humor. He was inconsistent in approaching others positively, expressing wishes and preferences clearly, asserting rights and needs appropriately and expressing anger and frustration effectively. XXXX at times could gain access to peers and at times was accepted. He was inconsistent in entering a conversation, taking turns, negotiating and compromising. He often drew inappropriate attention to himself.

A review of XXXX's school records noted concerns about fighting with other students. Academic screening placed XXXX below average on the Dynamic Indicators of Basic Early Literacy Skills with minimal progress reported during the school year for phonemic awareness.

Behavioral Observation

XXXX, a child of average size and appearance, was well-groomed and neatly dressed. He was seen for two assessment sessions with a lunch time break. He completed additional instruments in the afternoon session with Ms. XXXX. XXXX had taken the prescribed Vyvanse on the day of the evaluation.

Eye contact was appropriate. XXXX demonstrated mild receptive language problems. Expressive articulation was adequate. XXXX maintained and initiated conversation.

No overt signs of anxiety, sadness or emotional lability were noted. XXXX was calm and emotionally stable.

XXXX was alert, attentive and concentrated reasonably well. He was cooperative and attempted all tasks presented. XXXX was motivated to perform, but required some prompting to persist.

No muscular tension or significant individual mannerisms were noted. XXXX would periodically bite his nails.

XXXX presented with a normal activity level. He squirmed and wriggled occasionally. Overall he was not distracted. XXXX appeared moderately competent in his skills and related well to the examiners. His approach at times to some test tasks was mildly impulsive. His thoughts overall were logical, focused and relevant. It was not difficult to establish a working relationship with this pleasant child.

Assessment Results and Interpretation

Language

The Peabody was administered as a simple measure of one word receptive vocabulary. XXXX completed this test with a standard score of 90, equivalent to the 19th percentile.

The Expressive Vocabulary Test was administered as a simple synonym measure of expressive language. XXXX completed this test with a standard score of 87, equivalent to the 19th percentile.

Intellectual

The Fourth Edition of the Wechsler Intelligence Scale was administered as an overall screening of intellectual ability and achievement. Age-adjusted scaled scores appear below:

	Scaled Scores (mean = 10; s.d. = 3)
Verbal Comprehension	
Similarities	5
Vocabulary	8
Comprehension	11
Information	6
Word Reasoning	10
Perceptual Reasoning	
Block Design	12
Picture Concepts	13
Matrix Reasoning	11
Working Memory	
Digit Span	8
Letter-Number Sequencing	6
Processing Speed	
Coding	16
Symbol Search	8

	Standard Scores (mean = 100; s.d. = 15)	Percentiles	90% Confidence Interval
Verbal Comprehension	89	23rd	84–95
Perceptual Reasoning	112	79th	105–117
Working Memory	83	13th	78–91
Processing Speed	112	79th	103–118
Full Scale	99	47th	95–103

XXXX demonstrates markedly better perceptual reasoning than verbal comprehension skills. Simple working memory appears below average, but processing speed appears above average.

Learning and Working Memory

The Test of Memory and Learning was administered as an overall screening. Age-adjusted scaled scores appear below:

	Scaled Scores (mean = 10; s.d. = 3)
Verbal Subtests	
Memory for Stories	10
Word Selective Reminding	13

(continued)

	Scaled Scores (mean = 10; s.d. = 3)
Object Recall	12
Digits Forward	6
Paired Recall	11
Nonverbal Subtests	
Facial Memory	9
Visual Selective Reminding	13
Abstract Visual Memory	12
Visual Sequential Memory	11
Memory for Location	11
Delayed Recall Scores	
Memory for Stories	10
Facial Memory	7
Word Selective Reminding	12
Visual Selective Reminding	11

	(mean = 100; s.d. = 15)	Percentile
Verbal Memory Index	103	58th
Nonverbal Memory Index	108	70th
Composite Memory Index	106	65th
Delayed Recall Index	100	50th

Executive/Neuropsychological Skills

The Cognitive Assessment System was administered as a neuropsychological screening. Age-adjusted scaled scores appear below:

	Scaled Scores (mean = 10; s.d. = 3)
Matching Numbers	8
Planned Codes	12
Nonverbal Matrices	15
Verbal-Spatial Relations	11
Expressive Attention	8
Number Detection	12
Word Series	4
Sentence Repetition	8

	I.Q. (mean = 100; s.d. = 15)	Percentiles (mean = 50)	90% Confidence Interval
Planning	100	50th	92–108
Simultaneous	117	87th	108–123
Attention	100	50th	92–109

(continued)

	I.Q. (mean = 100; s.d. = 15)	Percentiles (mean = 50)	90% Confidence Interval
Successive	78	7th	73–87
Full Scale	98	45th	91–106

Though XXXX demonstrates an atypical pattern of neuropsychological processes, despite an overall average Full Scale score he appears to possess very poor successive processes, average planning and attention processes, but well above-average simultaneous processes. The latter reflects his ability to problem solve nonverbally.

Attention

The Gordon was administered as a computerized measure of XXXX's ability to sustain attention and inhibit impulsive responding. On the Delay tasks he performed within the normal range despite an extremely impulsive approach. He could not understand the seven-year-old instructions on the Vigilance task. He was administered the five-year-old version. His performance was still within the abnormal range, demonstrating significant patterns of impulsivity.

Motor/Perceptual

XXXX held a pencil in his right hand with a four-finger pincer grip. Casual observation did not indicate any large motor abnormalities. Fine motor skills for motor speed and coordination, based on the Purdue Pegboard performance, appeared in the high average range.

XXXX's reproductions of the figures on the Developmental Test of Visual Motor Integration yielded a standard score of 111, equivalent to the 77th percentile.

XXXX's Human Figure Drawing reflects this level of development. The figure was drawn very quickly. The figure appears below in reduced size. Of interest are the pointed teeth which XXXX did not comment on when asked.

Academic

The Woodcock was administered as a screening of XXXX's academic abilities and fluency. Age-adjusted standard scores appear below:

	Standard Scores (mean = 100; s.d. = 15)
Letter/Word Identification	75
Story Recall	105
Understanding Directions	104
Calculation	73
Math Fluency	81
Spelling	75
Passage Comprehension	74
Applied Problems	87
Writing Samples	72
Word Attack	87
Oral Language	105
Brief Achievement	73
Total Achievement	77
Brief Reading	75
Basic Reading Skills	79
Brief Math	78
Math Calculation Skills	74
Brief Writing	70
Academic Skills	69
Academic Application	73

XXXX's academic achievement appears well below expectation based upon his entering grade and age. In light of his significant successive processing problems, however, this overall profile academically is not unexpected.

XXXX was unable to write the alphabet in sequence without error. He was able to write numbers one through 20 with multiple reversals. XXXX's alphabet sample appears below in reduced size:

Emotional/Personality

XXXX's responses to the Manifest Anxiety Scale suggests that he fosters strong anxious thinking. His overall score was at the 97th percentile. XXXX reported getting nervous when he makes mistakes, getting mad easily, worrying what his parents will say to him, feeling that people don't like the way he does things, worrying what other people think about him, often feeling alone, having his feelings hurt easily, feeling that other people are happier, finding it hard to keep his mind on his schoolwork and believing that a lot of people dislike him.

During a brief clinical interview, XXXX was open and responsive with the examiner. He tended to perseverate on discussions about dirt bikes. He spoke about a normal range of emotions, but reported he became angry more intensely and more often than others, explaining "I don't know how to control my anger." XXXX spoke about a best friend and a number of social activities. He described himself as a "cry baby" and "mean" to others. He reported he wished he could be "better."

XXXX described his favorite part of school as math and his least favorite as "schoolwork." He felt he was smart in school, but that school was "boring." He reported that second grade was going to be hard and that he was not going to "do very good." XXXX reported the medication he takes "sometimes helps me be good." He denied any significant side effects. XXXX reported that even if allowed to he would not stop attending school, indicating he was proud of math at school. He agreed that he had difficulty completing work, listening and staying in his seat. He reported that others at school find schoolwork easier.

XXXX described his father as "he bought a dirt bike for me" and his mother as "she takes good care of me." He complained about his father's spanking, reporting that he got spanked for misbehaving and it "really hurts bad." He reported that he had been spanked three times that morning for going outside in his underwear. XXXX reported that he wasn't treated fair at home because "they won't let me stay up as late as my sister." This led to a long discussion about fairness and XXXX's insistence that he should have the same privileges as his sister. He agreed that he created problems at home, sometimes on purpose. He reported spankings as the worst thing that happens to him and "being really good the whole day" as the best thing. He reported not getting along well with his sibling.

XXXX reported it was difficult to fall asleep, but then he slept well. He reported intermittent headaches as hurting in his forehead. He noted that sometimes he lies down and usually he takes aspirin. Overall, XXXX reported he was not satisfied with his life.

XXXX presents as a child with adequate reality testing and age-appropriate thought processes. Though bonded to his parents, it is clear that because of his impulsive temperament he has developed a very negative view of himself and the manner in which he is treated by others. Youth with this emerging personality style as they enter their adolescent years are prone to feel misunderstood and unappreciated. They tend to project the source of their problems onto others, frequently complaining that life is unfair. In the face of stress they are prone to develop anxious and depressive symptoms.

Diagnostic Impression

XXXX has been diagnosed and treated for ADHD and Oppositional Defiant Disorder. Concerns continue to be raised about his general behavior and achievement. Family history is noted by learning disabilities and ADHD. XXXX has a history of impulsive and hyperactive behavior. Early academic milestones appeared to be reached appropriately. Later milestones have been slow in developing. Parent and teacher reports reflect high levels of oppositional, restless, impulsive and emotional behavior with a generally equal pattern of complaints at school and at home despite current medication use. XXXX was also reported to be very poor in reading achievement and below average in mathematics achievement.

XXXX took the prescribed stimulant medication on the day of the assessment. His intellectual abilities appear average with weak verbal comprehension and above-average perceptual reasoning. Receptive and expressive language skills appear low average. Memory skills appear average. Neuropsychological processes are noted by strong nonverbal reasoning, but very weak successive processing. The latter skill is a key component in basic achievement. Thus it is not surprising given the combination of XXXX's impulsivity and successive processing weakness that he is struggling academically. His academic skills appear at a late kindergarten level. He demonstrates problems with academic application and fluency.

XXXX presents as a child with adequate reality testing and generally age-appropriate thought processes. However, the quality of some of his responses during the assessment clearly reflects his weak overall verbal comprehension skills. Youth with his emerging personality style are prone to feel misunderstood and unappreciated. XXXX is somewhat obsessed about fairness. He demonstrates problems with anger management and behavioral impairment that is driven by his impulsive temperament.

XXXX's presentation meets the diagnostic criteria for the Combined Type of Attention-Deficit Hyperactivity Disorder and Oppositional Defiant Disorder. This examiner is concerned that despite treatment with stimulant medication and the improvements noted, reports from home and school continue to reflect clinically elevated symptoms related to impulsivity, inattention and hyperactivity. Relative to his basic intellect, XXXX's academic achievement lags behind, consistent with diagnoses of Reading and Mathematics Disorders.

Recommendations

It is strongly recommended that XXXX's physician review the current evaluation and consider a careful retitration of XXXX's medications at home and at school. Should adjustments be made this examiner is prepared to assist in the collection of behavioral data within the home and school settings.

XXXX's parents would benefit from additional ideas and resources to assist XXXX at home. The text by this examiner and Robert Brooks, *Raising a Self-Disciplined Child*, is suggested as a helpful resource.

It is strongly recommended that XXXX's educational team review the current evaluation and consider special education services for XXXX. Current assessment suggests he should qualify under the IDEIA as a student with a Specific Learning Disability. This examiner is prepared to consult further with XXXX's educational team.

XXXX's parents may wish to consider private academic tutoring to augment school experiences. The text by Sam Goldstein and Nancy Mather, *Overcoming Underachieving*, and Jack Naglieri and Eric Pickering, *Helping Children Learn*, are suggested as helpful resources.

It is recommended that XXXX be considered for short-term, problem-focused therapy in an effort to help him better understand his way of thinking about the world and develop more effective coping and self-management skills. A cognitive behavioral approach is recommended.

It is recommended that XXXX be reevaluated during his fifth grade year.

References

AACAP Author. (2007). Practice parameter for the assessment and treatment of children and adolescents with attention deficit/hyperactivity disorder. *Journal of Child and Adolescent Psychopharmacology, 46*(7), 894–921.

Abramowitz, A. J., & O'Leary, S. G. (1991). Behavioral interventions for the classroom: Implications for students with ADHD. *School Psychology Review, 20*, 220–234.

Achenbach, T. M., & McCoaughy, S. H. (2003). The Achenbach system of empirically based assessment. In C. R. Reynolds & R. W. Kamphaus (Eds.), *Handbook of psychological & educational assessment of children: Personality, behavior, and context* (2nd ed.) (pp. 406–432). New York: Guilford Press.

Achenbach, T. M., & Rescorla, L. (2001). *Manual for the ASEBA school-age forms and profiles*. Burlington: University of Vermont, Research Center for Children, Youth and Families.

American Psychiatric Association. (2000). *Diagnostic and statistical manual of mental disorders* (4th ed., Text revision). Washington, DC: Author.

Angold, A., Costllo, E. J., & Erkanli, A. (1999). Comorbidity. *Journal of Child Psychology and Psychiatry, 40*, 57–87.

Atkins, M. S., & Pelham, W. E. (1991). School-based assessment of attention deficit–hyperactivity disorder. *Journal of Learning Disabilities, 24*, 197–204.

Barkley, R. A. (1997). *ADHD and the nature of self-control*. New York: Guilford Press.

Barkley, R. A. (2006). *Attention-deficit hyperactivity disorder: A handbook for diagnosis and treatment* (3rd ed.). New York: Guilford Press.

Barkley, R. A., DuPaul, G. J, & McMurray, M. B. (1990). A comprehensive evaluation of attention deficit disorder with and without hyperactivity. *Journal of Consulting and Clinical Psychology, 58*, 775–789.

Barkley, R. A., Fischer, M., Edelbrock, C. S., & Smallish, L. (1990). The adolescent outcome hyperactive children diagnosed by research criteria: I. An 8-year prospective follow-up. *Journal of the American Academy of Child and Adolescent Psychiatry, 29*, 546–557.

Barkley, R. A., Fischer, M., Smallish, L., & Fletcher, K. (2006). Young adult outcome of hyperactive children: Adaptive functioning in major life activities. *Journal of the American Academy of Child and Adolescent Psychiatry, 45*, 192–202.

Barkley, R. A., Karlsson, J., Pollard, S., & Murphy, J. V. (1985). Developmental changes in the mother-child interactions of hyperactive boys: Effects of two dose levels of Ritalin. *Journal of Child Psychology and Psychiatry, 26*, 705–715.

Becker, M., Isaac, W., & Hynd, G. W. (1987). Neuropsychological development of nonverbal behaviors attributed to "frontal lobe" functioning. *Developmental Neuropsychology, 3*, 275–298.

Befera, M. & Barkley, R. A. (1985). Hyperactive and normal girls and boys: Mother-child interactions, parent psychiatric status and child psychopathology. *Journal of the American Academy of Child and Adolescent Psychiatry, 34*, 629–638.

Biederman, J., Mick, E., Faraone, S. V., Braaten, E., Doyle, A., Spencer, T., et al. (2002). Influence of gender on attention deficit hyperactivity disorder in children referred to a psychiatric clinic. *American Journal of Psychiatry, 159*, 36–42.

Biederman, J., Faraone, S. V., Keenan, K., Benjamin, J., Krifcher, B., Moore, C., et al. (1992). Further evidence for family-genetic risk factors in attention deficit hyperactivity disorder. *Archives of General Psychiatry, 49*, 728–738.

Biederman, J., Newcorn, J., & Sprich, S. (1991). Comorbidity of attention deficit hyperactivity disorder with conduct, depressive, anxiety, and other disorders. *American Journal of Psychiatry, 148*, 564–577.

Biederman, J., & Steingard, R. (1989). Attention deficit hyperactivity disorder in adolescents. *Psychiatric Annals, 19*, 587–596.

Blackman, G. L., Ostrander, R., & Herman, K. C. (2005). Children with ADHD and depression: A multisource, multimethod assessment of clinical, social, and academic functioning. *Journal of Attention Disorders, 8*, 195–207.

Blanchard, L. T., Gurka, M. J., & Blackman, J. A. (2006). Emotional, developmental, and behavioral health of American children and their families: A report from the 2003 National Survey of Children's Health. *Pediatrics, 117*, e1205–e1212.

Booth, J. R., Burman, D. D., Meyers, J. R., Lei, Z., Trommer, B. L. Davenport, N. D., et al. (2005). Larger deficits in brain networks for response inhibition than for visual selective attention in attention deficit hyperactivity disorder (ADHD). *Journal of Child Psychology and Psychiatry, 46*, 94–111.

Brame, B., Nagin, D. S., & Tremblay, R. E. (2001). Developmental trajectories of physical aggression from school entry to late adolescence. *Journal of Clinical Psychology and Psychiatry, 42*, 503–512.

Bruce, B. (2006). ADHD and language impairment. *European Child and Adolescent Psychiatry, 15*, 52–60.

Bussing, R., Teeter Ellison, A., Mason, D., Garvan, C. W., Cheng, Y., & Smith, P. L. (2007,. October). Adolescents with ADHD stigma perceptions: Relationship to self disclosure and treatment receptivity. 54th Annual Meeting of the American Academy of Child and Adolescent Psychiatry (AACAP). Boston, MA.

Calhoun, S. L., & Mayes, S. D. (2005). Processing speed in children with clinical disorders. *Psychology in the Schools, 42*,333–343.

Casey, B. J. (2000). Disruption of inhibitory control in developmental disorders: A Mechanistic model of implicated frontostriatal circuitary. R. S. Siegler & J. L. McClelland (Eds.), *Mechanisms of cognitive development: The Carnegie Symposium on Cognition* (Vol. 28). Hillsdale, NJ: Erlbaum.

Casey, B. J., Durston, S., & Fossella, J. A. (2001). Evidence of a mechanistic model of cognitive control. *Clinical Neuroscience Research, 1*, 267–282.

Chelune, G. J., Fergusson, W., Koon, R., & Dickey, T. (1986). Frontal lobe disinhibition in attention deficit disorder. *Child Psychiatry and Human Development, 16*, 221–234.

Comings, D. E. (1990). *Tourette syndrome and human behavior.* Durante, CA; Hope Press.

Conners, C. K., & MHS Staff. (2000). *Conners continuous performance test II.* Tonawanda, NY: Multi-Health Systems.

Cook, E. H., Stein, M. A., & Leventhal, D. L. (1997). Family-based association of attention-deficit hyperactivity disorder and the dopamine transporter. In K. Blum (Ed.), *Handbook of psychiatric genetics* (pp. 297–310). New York: CRC Press.

Cortese, S., Konofal., E., Yateman, N., Mouren, M.C., & Lencdreaux, M. (2006). Sleep and alertness in children with attention-deficit/hyperactivity disorder: A systematic review of the literature. *Sleep, 29*, 504–511.

Coy, K., Speltz, M. L., DeKlyen, M., & Jones, K. (2001). Social-cognitive processes in preschool boys with and without oppositional defiant disorder. *Journal of Abnormal Child Psychology, 29*, 107–119.

Daley, D. (2005). Attention deficit hyperactivity disorder: A review of the essential facts. *Child: Care, Health, & Development, 32*, 193–204.

Daugherty, T. K., & Quay, H. C. (1991). Response perseveration and delayed responding in childhood behavior disorders. *Journal of Child Psychology and Psychiatry, 32*, 455–461.

Denckla, M. B. (1994). Measurement of executive function. In R. Lyon (Ed.), *Frames of reference for assessment of learning disabilities* (pp. 117–142). New York: Guilford Press.

DiMaio, S., Grizenko, N., & Jooper, R. (2003). Dopamine genes in attention-deficit hyperactivity disorder: A review. *Journal of Pediatric Neuroscience, 28*, 27–38.

Dishion, T. J. & Loeber, R. (1985). Adolescent marijuana and alcohol use: The role of parents and peers revisited. *American Journal of Drug and Alcohol Abuse, 11*, 1–15.

Dodge, K. A. (1993). Social-cognitive mechanisms in the development of conduct disorder and depression. In L. W. Porter & M. R. Rosenzweig (Eds.), *Annual review of psychology* (pp. 559–584). Palo Alto, CA: Annual Reviews, Inc.

Dodge, K. A., Price, J. M., Bachorowski, J., & Newman, J. P. (1990). Hostile attributional biases in severely aggressive adolescents. *Journal of Abnomzal Psychology, 99*, 385–392.

Douglas, V. I. (1983). Attention and cognitive problems. In M. Ruttter (Ed.), *Developmental neuropsychiatry* (pp. 280–329). New York: Guilford Press.

Douglas, V. I. (1988). Cognitive deficits in children with attention deficit with hyperactivity disorder. In L. M. Bloomingdale & J. M. Swanson (Eds.), *Attention deficit disorder: Criteria, cognition, intervention* (pp. 65–82). New York: Pergamon Press.

Drechsler, R., Brandeis, D., Földényi, M., Imhof, K., & Steinhausen, H.C. (2005). The course of neuropsychological functions in children with attention deficit hyperactivity disorder from late childhood to early adolescence. *Journal of Child Psychology and Psychiatry, 46*, 824–836.

DuPaul, G. J., & Stoner, G. (2003). *ADHD in the schools: Assessment and intervention strategies* (2nd ed.). New York: Guilford Press

Egger, H. L., & Angold, A. (2006). Common emotional and behavioral disorders in preschool children: Presentation, nosology, and epidemiology. *Journal of Child Psychology and Psychiatry, 47*, 313–337.

Eliez, S., & Reiss, A. L. (2000). Annotation: MRI neuroimaging of childhood psychiatric disorders: A selective review. *Journal of Child Psychology and Psychiatry, 41*, 679–694.

Faraone, S., Biederman, J., & Monuteaux, M. C. (2002). Further evidence for diagnostic continuity between child and adolescent ADHD. *Journal of Attention Disorders, 6*, 5–13.

Faraone, S. V., Perlis, R. H., Doyle, A. E., Smoller, J. W., Goralnick, J. J., Holmgren, M. A., et al. (2005). Molecular genetics of attention-deficit/hyperactivity disorder. *Biological Psychiatry, 57*, 1313–1323.

Fergusson, D. M., & Horwood, L. J. (1995). Early disruptive behavior, IQ, and later school achievement and delinquent behavior. *Journal of Abnormal Child Psychology, 23*, 183–199.

Fergusson, D. M., Horwood, J., & Ridder, E. M. (2005). Show me the child at seven: The consequences of conduct problems in childhood for psychosocial functioning in adulthood. *Journal of Child Psychology and Psychiatry, 46*, 837–849.

Fischer, M., Barkley, R. A., Smallish, L., & Fletcher, K. (2005). Executive functioning in hyperactive children as young adults: Attention, inhibition, response perseveration, and the impact of comorbidity. *Developmental Neuropsychology, 27*, 107–133.

Fischer, M., Barkley, R. A., Edelbrock, C. S., & Smallish, L. (1990). The adolescent outcome of hyperactive children diagnosed by research criteria: 11. Academic, attentional, and neuropsychological status. *Journal of Consulting and Clinical Psychology, 58*, 580–588.

Frazier, T. W., Demaree, H. A., & Youngstrom, E. A. (2004). Meta-analysis of intellectual and neuropsychological test performance in attention-deficit/hyperactivity disorder. *Neuropsychology, 18*, 543–555.

Frick, P., & Lahey, B. B. (1991). Nature and characteristics of attention deficit hyperactivity disorder. *School Psychology Review, 20*, 163–173.

Frick, P. J., Lahey, B. B., Loeber, R., Stouthamer-Loeber, M., Christ, M. A. G., & Hanson, K. (1992). Familial risk factors to oppositional defiant disorder and conduct disorder: Parental psychopathology and maternal parenting. *Journal of Consulting and Clinical Psychology,60*, 49–55.

Goodyear, P., & Hynd, G. W. (1992). Attention deficit disorder with (ADD/H) and without (ADD/WO) hyperactivity: Behavioral and neuropsychological differentiation. *Journal of Clinical Child Psychology, 21*, 273–304.

Gustafsson, P., Thernlund, G., Ryding, E., Rosen, I., & Cederblad, M. (2000). Associations between cerebral blood-flow measured by single photon emission computer tomography (SPECT), electroencephalogram (EEG), behavior symptoms, cognition, and neuropsychological soft sings in children with attention-deficit hyperactivity disorder (ADHD). *Acta Paediatrica, 89*, 830–835.

Hanf, E., & Kling, J. (1973). *Facilitating parent-child interactions: A two-stage training model*. Portland: University of Oregon Medical School.

Haynes, J. P., & Bensch, M. (1981). The P > V sign of the WISC-R and recidivism in delinquents. *Journal of Consulting and Clinical Psychology, 49*, 480–481.

Herpertz, S. C., Mueller, B., Qunaibi, M., Lichterfeld, C., Konrad, K., & Herpertz-Dahlman, B. (2005). Response to emotional stimuli in boys with conduct disorder. *American Journal of Psychiatry, 162*, 1100–1107.

Hinshaw, S. & Lee, S. S. (2003). Conduct and oppositional defiant disorder. In E. J. Mash & R. A. Barkley (Eds.), *Child psychopathology* (2nd ed., pp. 144–198). New York: Guilford Press.

Hudziak, J. J., Derks, E. M., Althoff, R. R., Rettew, D. C., & Boomsma, D. I. (2005). The genetic and environmental contributions to attention deficit hyperactivity disorder as measured by the Conner's rating scales-revised. *American Journal of Psychiatry, 162*, 1614–1620.

Hynd, G. W., Lorys, A. R., Semrud-Clikeman, M., Nieves, N., Huettner, M. I. S., & Lahey, B. B. (1991). Attention deficit disorder without hyperactivity (ADD/WO): A distinct behavioral and neurocognitive syndrome. *Journal of Child Neurology, Supplement, 69*, S35–S41.

Hynd, G. W., Voeller, K. K. S., Hem, K. & Marshall, R. (1991). Neurological basis of attention deficit hyperactivity disorder (ADHD). *School Psychology Review, 20*, 174–186.

Jarey, M. L., & Stewart, M. A. (1985). Psychiatric disorder in the parents of adopted children with aggressive conduct disorder. *Neuropsychobiology, 13*, 7–11.

Jensen, P.S., Hinshaw, S., Swanson, J., Greenhill, L., Conners, K., Arnold, E., et al. (2001). Findings from the NIMH multimodal treatment study of ADHD (MTA): Implications and applications for primary care providers. *Developmental and Behavioral Pediatrics, 22*, 60–73.

Kadesjö, B., & Gillberg, C. (2001). The comorbidity of ADHD in the general population of Swedish school-age children. *Journal of Child Psychology and Psychiatry, 42*, 487–492.

Kamphaus, R. W., & Frick, P. J. (2005). *Clinical assessment of child and adolescent personality and behavior - second edition*. New York, NY: Springer Science.

Kern, L., DuPaul, G. J., Volpe, R., Sokol, N., Lutz, J. G., Arbolino, L., et al. (2007). Multi-setting assessment-based interventions for young children at-risk for ADHD: Initial effects on academic and behavioral function. *School Psychology Review, 36*(2), 237–255.

Kim, B. N., Lee, J. S., Shin, M. S., Cho, S. C., & Lee, D. S. (2002). Regional cerebral perfusion abnormalities in attention deficit/hyperactivity disorder: Statistical parametric mapping analysis. *European Archives of Psychiatry and Clinical Neuroscience, 252*, 219–225.

Kim-Cohen, J., Moffitt, T.E., Taylor, A., Pawlby, S., & Caspi, A. (2005). Maternal depression and children's antisocial behavior: Nature and nurture effects. *Archives of General Psychiatry, 62*, 173–181.

Levy, F., Hay, D. A., & Bennet, K. S. (2006). Genetics of attention deficit hyperactivity disorder: A current review and future prospects. *International Journal of Disability, Development, and Education, 53*, 5–20.

Lorys, A. R., Hynd, G. W., & Lahey, B. B. (1990). Do neurocognitive measures differentiate attention deficit disorder (ADD) with and without hyperactivity? *Archives of Clinical Neuropsychology, 5*, 115–135.

Lou, H. C., Henriksen, L., & Bruhn, P. (1984). Focal cerebral hypoperfusion in children with dysphasia and/or attentional deficit disorder. *Archives of Neurology, 41*, 825–829.

Lou, H. C., Henriksen, L., Bruhn, P., Borner, H., &Nielson, J. B. (1989). Striatal dysfunction in attention deficit and hyperkinetic disorder. *Archives of Neurology, 46*, 48–52.

Lyons-Ruth, K. (1996). Attachment relationships among children with aggressive behavior problems: The role of disorganized early attachment patterns. *Journal of Consulting and Clinical Psychology, 64*, 32–40.

Mannuzza, S., & Klein, R. G. (2000). Long-term prognosis in attention-deficit/hyperactivity disorder. *Child and Adolescent Psychiatric Clinics of North America, 9*, 711–726.

Mannuzza, S., Klein, R. G., Abikoff, H., & Moulton, J. L. (2004). Significance of childhood conduct problems to later development of conduct disorder among children with ADHD: A prospective follow-up study. *Journal of Abnormal Child Psychology, 32*, 565–573.

Martin, N. C., Levy, R., Pieka, J., & Hay, D. A. (2006). A genetic study of attention deficit hyperactivity disorder, conduct disorder, oppositional defiant disorder, and reading disability: Aetiological overlaps and implications. *International Journal of Disability, Development and Education, 53*, 21–34.

McGee, R., Silva, P. A., & Williams, S. M. (1984). Perinatal, neurological, environmental and developmental characteristics of seven-year-old children with stable behavior problems. *Journal of Child Psychology and Psychiatry and Allied Disciplines, 25*, 573–586.

McMahon, R. J., & Forehand, R. (1984). Parent training for the noncompliant child: Treatment outcome, generalization and adjunctive therapy procedures. In R. F. Dangel & R. A. Polster (Eds.), *Parent training: Foundations of research and practice* (pp. 298–328). New York: Guilford Press.

Miller, B. L., & Cummings, J. L. (2007). *The human frontal lobes* (2nd ed.). New York: Guilford Press.

Miller, S. R., Miller, C. J., Bloom, J. S., Hynd, G. W., & Craggs, J. G. (2006). Right hemisphere brain morphology, attention-deficit hyperactivity disorder (ADHD) subtype, and social comprehension. *Journal of Child Neurology, 21*, 139–144.

Mirsky, A. F. (1987). Behavioral and psychophysiological markers of disordered attention. *Environmental Health Perspectives, 74*, 191–199.

MTA Cooperative Group. (2004a). National Institute of Mental Health Multimodal Treatment Study of attention-deficit/hyperactivity disorder. *Pediatrics, 113*, 754–761.

MTA Cooperative Group. (2004b). National Institute of Mental Health Multimodal Treatment Study of ADHD follow-up: Changes in effectiveness and growth after the end of treatment. *Pediatrics, 113*, 762–769.

MTA Cooperative Group. (2008a). Evidence, interpretation, and qualification from multiple reports of long-term outcomes in the Multimodal Treatment Study of Children with ADHD (MTA): Part I: Executive summary. *Journal of Attention Disorders, 12*(1), 3–13.

MTA Cooperative Group. (2008b). Evidence, interpretation, and qualification from multiple reports of long-term outcomes in the Multimodal Treatment Study of Children with ADHD (MTA): Part II: Supporting details. *Journal of Attention Disorders, 12*(1), 14–41.

Mulas, F., Capilla, A., Fernández, S., Etchepareborda, M. C., Campo, P., Maestu, F., et al. (2006). Shifting-related brain magnetic activity in attention-deficit/hyperactivity disorder. *Biological Psychiatry, 59*, 373–379.

Murphy, K., & Barkley, R. A. (1996). Attention deficit hyperactivity disorder in adults. *Comprehensive Psychiatry, 37*, 393–401.

Newman, J. P., Patterson, C. M., & Kosson, D. S. (1987). Response perseveration in psychopaths. *Journal of Abnormal Psychology, 96*, 145–148.

Nigg, J. T. (2006). *What causes ADHD? Understanding what goes wrong and why*. New York: Guilford Press.

Ortiz, J., & Raine, A. (2004). Heart rate level and antisocial behavior in children and adolescents: A meta-analysis. *Journal of the American Academy of Child and Adolescent Psychiatry, 43*, 154–162.

Patterson, G. R. (1982). *Coercive family process*. Eugene, OR: Castalia Publications.

Patterson, G. R. (1986). Performance models for antisocial boys. *American Psychologist,41*,32–444 .

Patterson, G. R., & Chamberlain, P. (1988). Treatment process: A problem at three levels. In L. C. Wynne (Ed.), *The state of the art in family therapy research: Controversies and recommendations* (pp. 189–223). New York: Family Process Press.

Patterson, G. R., DeBaryshe, B. D., & Ramsey, E. (1990). A developmental perspective on antisocial behavior. *American Psychologist, 44*, 329–335.

Patterson, G. R., Reid, J. B., Jones, R. R., & Conger, R. W. (1975). *A social learning approach to family intervention* (Vol. 1). Eugene, OR: Castalia Publications.

Passler, M., Isaac, W., & Hynd, G. W. (1985). Neuropsychological behavior attributed to frontal lobe functioning in children. *Developmental Neuropsychology, 1*, 349–370.

Pauls, D., & Leckman, J. F. (1986). The inheritance of Gilles de la Tourette's syndrome and associated behaviors. *New England Journal of Medicine, 315*, 993–997.

Pelham, W. E., Schnedler, R. W., Bender, M. E., Miller, J., Nilsson, D., Budow, M., et al. (1988). The combination of behavior therapy and methylphenidate in a treatment of hyperactivity: A therapy outcome study. In L. Bloomingdale (Ed.), *Attention deficit disorders* (pp. 2948). London: Pergamon Press.

Pennington, B. F. (2002). The development of psychopathology: Nature and nurture. New York: Guilford Press.

Pennington, B. F., & Bennetto, L. (1993). Main effects or transactions in the neuropsychology of conduct disorder? Commentary on "The neuropsychology of conduct disorder." *Development and Psychopathology, 5*, 153–164.

Pennington, B. F., & Ozonoff, S. (1996). Executive functions and developmental psychopathology. *Journal of Child Psychology and Psychiatry, 37*, 51–87.

Peterson, B. S., Leckman, J. F., & Cohen, D. J. (1995). Tourette's syndrome: A genetically predisposed and an environmentally specified developmental psychopathology. In D. Ciccetti & D. J. Cohen (Eds.), *Developmental psychopathology* (pp. 213–242). New York: Wiley.

Pfiffner, L. J., McBurnett, K., Rathouz, P. J., & Judice, S. (2005). Family correlates of oppositional and conduct disorders in children with attention deficit/hyperactivity disorder. *Journal of Abnormal Child Psychology, 33*, 551–563.

Pliszka, S. R. (2003). *Neuroscience of mental health clinicians*. New York: Guilford Press.

Pliszka, S. R., Carlson, C. L., & Swanson, J. M. (1999). *ADHD with comorbid disorders*. New York, NY: Guilford Press.

Posner, M. I., & Boies, S. J. (1971). Components of attention. *Psychological Review, 78*, 391–409.

Pressman, L., J., Loo, S. K., Carpenter, E. M., Asarnow, J. R., Lynn, D., McCracken, J. T., et al. (2006). Relationship of family environment and parental psychiatric diagnosis to impairment in ADHD. *Journal of the American Academy of Child and Adolescent Psychiatry, 40*, 1169–1183.

Pullis, M. (1991). Practical considerations of excluding conduct disordered students: An empirical analysis. *Behavior Disorders, 17*, 9–22

Rapport, M. D., Scanlan, S. W., & Denney, C. B. (1999). Attention-deficit/hyperactivity disorder and scholastic achievement: A model of dual developmental pathways. *Journal of Child and Adolescent Psychiatry, 45*, 346–354.

Robin, A. L., & Foster, S. (1989). *Negotiating parent-adolescent conflict.* New York: Guilford Press.

Roth, R. M., & Saykin, A. J. (2004). Executive dysfunction in attention-deficit/hyperactivity disorder: cognitive and neuroimaging findings. *Psychiatric Clinics of North America, 27*, 83–96.

Reynolds, C. R., & Kamphaus, R. W. (2004). *Behavior Assessment System for Children- Second Edition.* Circle Pines, MN: American Guidance Service.

Safer, D. J., & Malever, M. (2000). Stimulant treatment in Maryland public schools. Pediatrics, *106*(3), 533–539.

Schrimsher, G. W., Billinsgly, R. L., Jackson, E. F., & Moore, B. D. (2002). Caudate nucleus volume asymmetry predicts attention-deficit hyperactivity disorder symptomatology in children. *Journal of Child Neurology, 17*, 877–884.

Semrud-Clikeman, M., Biederman, J., Sprich-Buckminister, S. Lehamn, B., Faraone, S., & Norman, D. (1992). Comorbidity between ADHD and learning disability: A review of and report in a clinically referred sample. *Journal of the American Academy of Child and Adolescent Psychiatry, 31*, 439–448.

Semrud-Clikeman, M., Hynd, G. W., Lorys, A. R., & Lahey, B. B. (1993). Differential diagnosis of children with ADD/H and ADD/with co-occurring conduct disorder: Discriminant validity of neurocognitive measures. *School Psychology International, 14*, 361–370.

Semrud-Clikeman, M., & Schafer, V. (2000). Social and emotional competence in children with ADHD and/or learning disabilities. *Journal of Psychotherapy in Independent Practice, 1*, 3–19.

Shapiro, S. K., Quay, H. C., Hogan, A. E., & Schwartz, K. P. (1988). Response perseveration and delayed responding in undersocialized conduct disorder. *Journal of Abnormal Psychology, 97*, 371–373.

Short, R. J., & Shapiro, S. K. (1993). Conduct disorders: A framework for understanding and intervention in schools and communities. *School Psychology Review, 22*, 362–375.

Spivack, G., Platt, J. J., & Shure, M. B. (1976). *The problem solving approach to adjustment.* San Francisco: Jossey-Bass.

Sohlberg, M., & Mateer, C. (1989). *Introduction to cognitive rehabilitation.* New York, NY: Guilford Press.

Stuss, D. T. (2007). New approaches to prefrontal lobe testing. In B. L. Miller & J. L. Cummings (Eds.). *The human frontal lobes* (2nd ed., pp. 292–305). New York: Guilford Press.

Swanson, J., Posner, M., Fusella, J., Wasdell, M., So, T., & Fan, J. (2001). Genes and attention deficit hyperactivity disorder. *Current Psychiatric Report, 3*, 100.

Swanson, J., Sunohara, G., Kennedy, J., Regino, R., Fineberg, E., Wigal, E., et al. (1997). Association of the dopamine receptor D4 (DRD4) gene with a refined phenotype of attention deficit hyperactivity disorder (ADHD): A family-based approach. *Molecular Psychiatry, 3*, 38–42.

Tamm, L., McCandliss, B., Liang, A., Wigal, T., Posner, M. & Swanson, M. (2008). Can attention be trained? Attention training for children at-risk for ADHD. In K. McBurnett, L. Pfiffner, R. Schacher, G. Elliott, J. Nigg (Eds.), Attention *Deficit/Hyperactivity Disorder: A 21st Century Perspective.* New York: Marcel Dekker.

Teeter, P. A., (1998). *Interventions for ADHD: Treatment in developmental context.* New York: Guilford Press.

Teeter Ellison, P. A., Eckert, L., Nelson, A., Platten, P., Semrud-Clikeman, M., & Kamphaus, R. W. (2008). Assessment of behavior and personality in the neuropsychological diagnosis of children. In C. R. Reynolds & Fletcher-Jensen, E. (Eds.), *Handbook of clinical child neuropsychology* (2nd ed.). New York: Plenum Press.

Toupin, J., Déry, M., Pauzé, R., Mercier, H., & Fortin, L. (2000). Cognitive and familial contributions to conduct disorder in children. *Journal of Child Psychology and Psychiatry, 41*, 333–344.

Tramontana, M. G., & Hooper, S. R. (1989). Neuropsychology of child psychopathology. In C. R. Reynolds & E. Fletcher-Janzen (Eds.), *Handbook of clinical child neuropsychology* (pp. 87–106). New York: Plenum Press.

Tremblay, R. E., Masse, B., Perron, D., & Leblanc, M. (1992). Early disruptive behavior, poor school achievement, delinquent behavior, and delinquent personality: Longitudinal analyses. *Journal of Consulting & Clinical Psychology, 60*, 64–72.

Trommer, B. L., Hoeppner, J. B., Lorber, R., & Armstrong, K. (1988). Pitfalls in the use of a continuous performance test as a diagnostic tool in attention deficit disorder. *Developmental and Behavioral Pediatrics, 9*, 339–345.

Vaidya, C. J., Bunge, S. A., Dudukovic, N. M., Zalecki, C. A. , Elliott, G. R., & Gabrielli, J. D. E. (2005). Altered neural substrates of cognitive control in childhood ADHD: Evidence from magnetic resonance imaging. *American Journal of Psychiatry, 162*, 1605–1613.

Visser, S. N., Lesesne, C., A. & Perou, R. (2007). National estimates and factors associated with medication treatment for childhood attention-deficit/hyperactivity disorder. *Pediatrics, 119*(S1), S99–S106.

Volk, H. E., Henderson, C., Neuman, R. J., & Todd, R. D. (2006). Validation of population-based ADHD subtypes and identification of three clinically impaired subtypes. *American Journal of Medical Genetics Part B (Neuropsychiatric Genetics), 141B*, 312–318.

Volk, H. E., Neuman, R. J., & Todd, R. D. (2005). A systematic evaluation of ADHD and comorbid psychopathology in a population-based twin sample. *Journal of the American Academy of Child and Adolescent Psychiatry, 44*, 768–775.

Webster-Stratton, C. (1984). Randomized trial of two parent training programs for families with conduct disordered children. *Journal of Consulting and Clinical Psychology, 52*, 666–678.

Webster-Stratton, C. (1993). Strategies for helping early school-aged children with oppositional defiant and conduct disorders: The importance of home-school partnerships. *School Psychology Review, 22*, 437–457.

Weiss, G., & Hechtman, L. (1986). *Hyperactive children grown up.* New York: Guilford Press.

Weiss, G., & Hechtman, L. (1993). *Hyperactive children grown up* (2nd ed.). New York: Guilford Press..

Wells, K. C., & Forehand, R. (1985). Conduct and oppositional disorder. In P. H. Bornstein & A. E. Kazdin (Eds.), *Handbook of clinical behavior therapy with children* (pp. 3–5). Homewood, IL: Dorsey.

West, D. J. (1982). *Delinquency: Its roots, careers and prospects*. London: Heinemann.

White, J., Moffitt, T., Earls, F., & Robins, L. (1990). Preschool predictors of persistent conduct disorder and delinquency. *Criminology, 28*, 443–454.

White, J. L., Moffitt, T. E., & Silva, P. A. (1989). A prospective replication of the protective efforts of IQ in subjects at high risk for juvenile delinquency. *Journal of Consulting and Clinical Psychology, 57*, 719–724.

Winsberg, B. G., & Comings, D. E. (1999). Association with the dopamine transporter gene (DAT1) with poor methylphenidate response. *Journal of the American Academy of Child and Adolescent Psychiatry, 38*, 1474–1477.

Zametkin, M. D., Nordahl, T. E., Gross, M., King, A. C., Semple, W. E., Rumsey, et al. (1990). Cerebral glucose metabolism in adults with hyperactivity of childhood onset. *New England Journal of Medicine, 323*, 1361–1366.

Zang, Y. F., Jin, Z., Weng, X. C., Zhang, L., Zeng, Y. W., Yang, L., et al. (2005). Functional MRI in attention-deficit hyperactivity disorder: Evidence for hypofrontality. *Brain & Development, 27*, 544–550.

Chapter 10
Neuropsychological Correlates of Childhood and Adolescent Internalized Disorders: Mood and Anxiety Disorders

This chapter explores childhood mood and anxiety disorders within a transactional model. Genetic, prenatal, and postnatal history will be discussed in light of how these factors interact with neuropsychological, executive, cognitive, perceptual, and memory functioning. Moreover, the impact these factors have on the child's functioning (i.e., family, school, and social interactions) will be discussed within a transactional framework; that is, social and familial factors play a role in environmentally induced mood and anxiety disorders which, in turn, interfere with social interactions and interpersonal well-being.

Mood Disorders

Although some believe that internalizing disorders in children are more closely related to brain dysfunction than externalizing disorders (Tramontana & Hooper, 1989), there is a paucity of published research to support this hypothesis. As with all taxonomies, the distinction between externalizing and internalizing disorders becomes blurred in real practice with children and adolescents who meet criteria for both diagnoses. For example, this picture is complicated by the finding that mood and anxiety disorders co-occur with disruptive behavior disorders (Jensen, Martin, & Cantwell, 1997; Jensen et al., 2001; Semrud-Clikeman & Hynd, 1991). Approximately 25 to 40 percent of children with ADHD also experience depression and/or anxiety disorders (Barkley, 2006). Spencer, Wilens, Biederman, Wozniak, and Harding-Crawford (2000) found that 38 percent of children seen in clinics for ADHD had comorbid

major mood disorders (MMD), and these children had a worse outcome than children with either disorder alone. Moreover, children with ADHD have a significantly higher tendency to have parents with diagnoses of anxiety disorder and/or depression than typically developing children or children with other psychiatric diagnoses. Thus, it is often difficult to obtain a sample of children with only mood disorders or internalizing symptomatology, and research that has done so is rare (Kusche, Cook, & Greenberg, 1993).

Research investigating the neuropsychological correlates of these disorders has exploded in the past decade. The following sections are not meant to be exhaustive of all mood disorders. The disorders that are included in this review are major depression and bipolar disorders. See Mash and Barkley (2006) for a more thorough review of childhood psychopathologies and treatment options.

Childhood Depression

Childhood depression as defined by Diagnostic and Statistical Manual of Mental Disorders (4th ed. - text revision; DSM-TR) requires that the child must have experienced the following symptoms for six months or longer nearly every day: sad or dysphoric mood (in children, mood can be irritable), loss of interest in previously enjoyable events, significant weight gain or loss, sleeping problems (e.g., too little or too much sleep), lack of energy; excessive guilt or feelings of worthlessness, difficulty with concentration, and thoughts of death or suicide

M. Semrud-Clikeman, P.A. Teeter Ellison, *Child Neuropsychology*, DOI 10.1007/978-0-387-88963-4_10,
© Springer Science+Business Media, LLC 2009

(APA, 2000, p. 356). In the school setting, children with depression may appear withdrawn, resist social contact, at times refuse to attend school and show academic difficulties.

Depression in childhood may last for years and extend into adulthood (Reinherz, Gianconia, Hauf, Wasserman, & Paradis, 2000; Weissman et al., 1999); may lead to suicidality, and may be more widespread than previously recognized (Hammen & Rudolph, 2003). Silver (1988) reported that a diagnosis of depression was present in 17.9 percent of all children under age 18 admitted to psychiatric hospitals. Overall prevalence for depression has been estimated to be 14% in adolescents, with an additional 10 percent with minor depression (Avenenoli, Knight, Kessler, & Merikangas, 2007; Kessler & Waters, 1998; Lewinson, Hops, Roberts, Seeley, & Andrews, 1993); while, the full-fledged diagnosis of major depression among all children ages 9 to 17 has been estimated at 5 percent (Shaffer et al., 1996). Incidence rates of depression are lower in younger children (Anderson, Williams, McGee, & Silva, 1987; Hankin et al., 1998); however, children who present with depression at early age appear to be at greater risk for a host of serious problems later in life including more impaired social and occupational adjustment, a more negative view of life, increased rates of life-long depression, more medical and psychiatric comorbidities, increased suicide attempts, and greater and more severe symptoms with recurring episodes of depression (Zisook et al., 2007). There are no gender differences in rates of depression until the middle to late teen years (Hammen & Rudolph, 2003). In fact gender ratios are basically equal before adolescence and after age 30 years (Satcher, 1999).

Comorbidity

Depression in childhood has been found to co-occur with anxiety, other mood disorders and disruptive behavior disorders. Depression has been found to occur concurrently with anxiety disorders (Angold, Costello, & Erkanli, 1999; Munir, Biederman, & Knee, 1987; Strauss, Last, Hersen, & Kazdin, 1988), conduct disorders (Alessi & Magen, 1988), and attention-deficit hyperactivity disorder (Biederman, Baldessarini, Wright, Knee, & Harmatz, 1989; Jensen et al., 1997; Steingard, Biederman, Doyle, & Sprich Buckminster, 1992). It has been hypothesized that

children with a dual diagnosis will evidence a more severe disorder and have a poorer prognosis (Kovacs, 1989).

Although Biederman, Munir, Keenan, and Tsuang (1991) found that depression co-occurs with attention-deficit hyperactivity disorder (ADHD) at approximately an incidence level of 30 percent to 40 percent, Jensen et al. (2001) reported lower rates of comorbid affective disorders (between 1% to 7.4%) for children in a large scale study of ADHD treatments. In a review of comorbidity in childhood disorders, Pliszka, Carlson, and Swanson (1999) report that incidence rates of ADHD and depression vary from 0 percent to 38 percent depending on the study type (epidemiological versus clinical), with rates of comorbidity highest for the clinic samples (32% to 38%). Pliszka et al. suggest that children with depression and ADHD may share some common genetic mechanisms, but more research is needed to resolve this issue.

It is crucial that the child be evaluated for other disorders as well as for the presenting symptoms of depression. There may be a tendency to develop an affective disorder, and unique environmental and familial factors mediate how the disorder is expressed in individual children. Although work in the area of comorbidity is progressing, there are few studies that have evaluated dual-diagnosed disorders outside of a clinical sample.

Genetic and Family Factors

Family studies of depression show strong heritability rates, and clear evidence that adult depression runs in families (Sullivan, Neale, & Kendler, 2000). The percentage of persons with major depression who have been found to have family members with depression is six times greater than those without depression (Downey & Coyne, 1990). Twin studies have found a 65 percent concordance rate for affective disorders for monozygotic twins versus 14 percent for dizygotic twins. Genome-wide linkage studies investigating affective disorder susceptibility have found association in numerous chromosomal regions (Venken et al., 2005). While these findings suggest a genetic risk factor for depression, environment and biology may interact in this disorder (Teeter Ellison et al., 2009). Mothers who are depressed may interact differently with their children and an insecure attachment may occur (Quay et al., 1985). Such insecure attachment is a significant risk factor in the development of childhood depression (Hammen & Rudolph, 2003).

Dawson, Grofer Klinger, Panagiotides, Hill, and Spieker (1992) found that infants of mothers with depression had more activation in the right versus left frontal lobe, even when placed in neutral conditions. This is considered to be an atypical pattern of activation, and is also found in subjects who are in remission for depressive symptoms (Henriques & Davidson, 1990). What is not clear is whether the patterns of brain activity are the consequence of the environmental impact of a depressed episode or episodes, or if a biologically mediated depressive tendency is present (Teeter Ellison et al., 2009). Thus, depression, as with many other disorders, appears to have multiple facets that likely interact to produce the syndrome.

The STAR*D-Child Sequenced Treatment Alternatives to Relieve Depression, the nation's largest NIMH-funded study investigating the treatment of childhood depression, investigated 151 child-mother pairs to determine the effects of maternal depression on children (Weissman et al., 2006). In the STAR*D-Child study, 11 percent of children whose mothers were successfully treated for depression no longer met criteria for depression and one-third of children went into remission (Weissman et al., 2006). Further, only 12 percent of children went into remission if their mothers remained depressed. This study provides insight into the gene by environment interaction in the transmission of depression, and that successful treatment of maternal depression serves to protect vulnerable children.

Brain Anatomy and Neurochemistry

Current theories of depression, based on findings from neuroanatomical as well as functional studies, implicate prefrontal and striatal systems that regulate limbic and deep brain structures that ultimately modulate emotions (Drevets, 2001a, 2001b). Drevets (2001a, 2001b) further suggests that these complex neural networks underlie the cognitive, motivation, and behavioral features of depression. In a review of PET and fMRI studies, Phan, Wager, Taylor, and Liberzon (2002) found that there are separate brain regions involved in different aspects of emotions (i.e.,

emotional responses, processing stimuli that illicit emotional responses). The basic brain regions implicated in emotions are: (1) prefrontal cortex processes emotions; (2) the amygdala processes fear; (3) subcallosal cingulated regions are involved with feelings of sadness; (4) occipital lobes and amygdala are involved with emotional response to visual stimuli; (5) anterior cingulate and insula involved with emotional recall and imagery, and (6) anterior cingulated and insula involved with emotional tasks that also have a cognitive component (Phan et al., 2002).

Much of the research investigating the neuroanatomical, functional and neurochemical basis of depression has been conducted on adults, with few studies completed on children (Hammen & Rudolph, 2003). Structural differences have been found in the volume of left frontal regions and regions of the basal ganglia, particularly in the caudate and putamen, and enlarged lateral ventricles in late onset depression (Pennington, 2002). In a summary of neuroimaging research, Pennington reports two major findings: (1) decreased blood flow to frontal lobes and to the cingulate gyrus, primarily in the left hemisphere, and (2) increased flow in the amygdala. Frontal lobe blood flow is normalized with antidepressive medications, so that top-down control (frontal regions) is exerted over bottom-up (amygdala) components of the emotional regulation system. See Pennington for more details.

In an effort to better understand the influence of the frontal circuits, Hasler et al. (2008) investigated PET scans of unmedicated patients with a history of depression that were in remission. When given drugs that depleted dopamine and norepinephrine, depression symptoms reappeared while control subjects with no prior history of depression had only minor changes in mood. Dopamine inhibits emotional circuits and, when depleted, this braking system does not properly exert control over mood. Increased brain activation patterns showed that the emotional circuit was not actively inhibited by higher brain regions. The authors suggest that even when in remission, patients with depression are vulnerable to symptoms when dopamine and norepinephrine are reduced.

In general, symptoms of psychiatric disorders affecting mood stability, depression, apathy, obsessive-compulsive thoughts, and mania are related to various frontal-subcortical circuits (FSC) including the dorsolateral prefrontal-subcortical circuit (DLPFC), the superior medial frontal (SMF), the lateral orbitofrontal-subcortical circuits (OFC), and the medial OFC (Chow & Cummings, 2007). These large brain circuits, with complex connections from the frontal lobes and other brain regions, are rich in neurotransmitters including dopamine, serotonin, and norepinephrine. Emotional, affective and social behaviors are affected by dysregulation of these various frontal-subcortical circuits. Bipolar disorders appear to have abnormal functions in major FSC systems (DSM-IV TR). fMRI studies show reduced DLPFC activity during depression, with reduced superior frontal and OFC during manic states (Haldane & Frangou, 2004). Mood stabilizers normalize these activation patters. See Chow and Cummings (2007) for an in-depth discussion of the frontal-subcortical circuits.

PET studies also have investigated brain metabolic changes in frontal-limbic regions in control subjects. Decreased metabolic activity was found in the "dorsolateral prefrontal cortex, the dorsal and posterior cingulated gyrus, and the inferior parietal lobe" and "increases in orbitofrontal prefrontal cortex, the dorsal and hippocampus" (see Pliszka, 2003, p. 215). These differences are similar to the metabolic imbalances found in untreated patients with depression.

Although research on children is limited in scope, MRI research suggests that the frontal lobes are implicated in the pathogenesis of early-onset depression (Steingard et al., 1996). Data from neuroimaging studies of childhood depression report abnormalities in the hippocampus and amygdala. Children with depression have significantly smaller left and right amygdala volumes, compared to non-affected children (Rosso et al., 2005). White matter hyperintensities, which are areas of possible increased water density, have been found in the frontal regions of children with unipolar depression or bipolar disorders (Lyoo, Lee, Jung, Noam, & Renshaw, 2002).

Current neurological theories suggesting neurotransmitter imbalances have led researchers to focus on the hypothalamic-pituitary-adrenal (HPA) axis, as this system appears to be dysregulated in adults with depression (Hammen & Rudolph, 2003). The HPA system regulates response mechanisms in stress situations. Adults with depression show three major abnormalities: "higher basal cortisol, abnormal cortisol regulation as indicated by the dexa-methasone suppression test (DST) and abnormalities of corticotrophin-releasing factor" (Hammen & Rudolph, 2006, p 246). Resea-

rch findings with children and adolescents have been less consistent, particularly when basal cortisol levels and CRR infusion are measured; however, nonsuppression on the DST is similar for both children and adults (Birmaher et al, 1996; Kaufman, Martin, King, & Charney, 2001). See Hammen and Rudolph (2006) for a detailed discussion of the regulatory role of the HPA system.

Neuropsychological Correlates: Cognitive, Perceptual, Attention and Memory Functioning

Cognitive impairments, particularly difficulties in attention, concentration and alertness, have been found in individuals with depression and are likely related to dysfunction of the prefrontal cortical and striatal systems that regulate limbic and brainstem regions (Drevets, 2001a, b; Pliszka, 2003). In addition, Mayberg (1997) found that positive medication response increased activity in the anterior cingulate gyrus (limbic structure) which is important in "executive attention, recruiting effort for a task" (Pliszka, 2003, p. 215).

In a study comparing internalizing-only, externalizing-only, and mixed symptoms groups, Kusche et al. (1993) evaluated found neuropsychological weaknesses in the clinical groups. Although all groups performed more poorly than a control group, the mixed symptom group showed the most severe deficits. The internalizing-only group was the closest to the control group and showed the least amount of neuropsychological impairment, while the externalizing-only group showed moderate amounts of impairment (Teeter Ellison et al., 2009).

Family and Home Factors

Individuals with major depression are six times more likely to have family members with depression than those without depression (Downey & Coyne, 1990; Hammen, 1990). While these findings suggest a genetic risk for depression, environment and biology interact to express this disorder. Mothers who are depressed may interact differently with their children resulting in insecure attachment (Quay et al., 1985). Such insecure attachment has been found to be a significant risk factor in the development of childhood depression (Cummings & Cicchetti, 1990).

A number of family factors influence the development of depression in children and adolescents, including dysfunctional parent-child relations, parental psychopathology, and hostile-rejecting family dynamics (Hammen & Rudolph, 2006). The mechanisms by which family and contextual factors impact childhood and adolescent depression are complex and bidirectional; that is, parental difficulties influence the child's well-being while the child's difficulties have negative influences on parents and family functioning. The pathways for transmission are multidimensional, but often persistent, interpersonal difficulties are at the center of the problem (Hammen & Brennan, 2001). Parenting difficulties and impaired attachment also seem likely contributors to the development of childhood depression. Dawson and colleagues further suggest that impaired mother-child interactions alter the development of brain circuits in ways that place children at risk for emotional difficulties and depression (Dawson, Frey, Panagiotides, Osterling, & Hessl, 1997).

While having a parent with depression is one of the most predictive factors for childhood and adolescent depression, adverse psychosocial factors also influence the development of depression (see Hammen & Rudolph, 2003 for a review). Adverse events include stressful life events, impaired parent-child relationships, and marital discord. Furthermore, it is interesting to note that Silberg et al. (1999) found there is an increased heritability of depression in adolescent girls, where genetic vulnerabilities interacted with environmental factors including stressful life events. The fact that familial and environmental factors interact has led to a number of cognitive and psychosocial theories to explain depression (e.g., negative cognitive schemas, depressive attributional styles, diathesis-stress models, etc.). See Hammen and Rudolph (2003) and Hankin and Abela (2005) for an in-depth review of depression.

Implications for Assessment

Depression has been found to affect cognition, memory and concentration which indirectly impact neuropsychological and psychological performance (Teeter Ellison et al., 2009). Slower response and completion times, particularly on speeded tasks, may be problematic. For example, a child or adolescent with major depression may have decreased attention to detail or lowered reaction speed which, in turn, reduces scores on performance subtests of cognitive-intellectual tests as well on timed tasks such as Trails A and B, the Tactual Performance Test, Stroop, and others.

In addition to attention problems, depressed clients experience problems with new learning (Caine, 1986). When the same information is presented in a very structured format, learning improves dramatically (Weingartner et al., 1981). For something to be learned it must first be attended to; thus, if attention is deficient poor performance follows (Cohen, Weingarten, Smallberg, & Murphy, 1982). Retrieval deficits are also frequently seen in depressed clients (Firth et al., 1983). Problems in both remote and newly acquired information are found. These difficulties ameliorate after recovery from depression (Caine, 1986).

Children with depression may present in much the same manner as those with medical problems. The astute clinician will recognize such overlap and seek to differentiate, if at all possible, between the two types of disorders. Clues for differentiation may be found in specific areas of the child's social functioning/ relationships (e.g., isolation, rejection, withdrawal, etc.) and emotional adjustment/well-being (e.g., overwhelming feelings of sadness; prolonged, chronic feelings of sadness/depression, etc.). In cases where such a distinction is not possible, retesting should be pursued after a trial of medication and/or therapy is attempted.

Diagnosing depression involves gathering information about the client and matching this information to the DSM-IV criteria for a diagnosis of depression. It is recommended that the diagnosis be made on the basis of a multi-informant, multi-method procedure. Although multi-method procedures provide the best information, it is important to recognize that poor concordance has been found between raters (Semrud-Clikeman & Hynd, 1991). Particularly important is the finding that the child/adolescent is a reliable source of information about his or her subjective feelings of depression (Kazdin, 1987). Therefore, an assessment for suspected depression should include information gathered directly from the child or adolescent as well as information from teachers and parents.

Clinical interviews. Clinical interviews are one of the most sensitive methods of assessment (Semrud-Clikeman, Bennett, & Guli, 2003; Teeter Ellison et al., 2009). Interviews allow information to be gathered from multiple sources, answer queries about the severity, duration, and frequency of depressive symptoms more fully, and provides a comparison of the child or adolescent's feelings with his or her developmental and mental age.

Self-Report Scales. The Children's Depression Inventory (CDI; Kovacs, 1992) is the most frequently utilized rating scale and has had the greatest amount of research. The CDI consists of 27 items with three alternatives to each question measuring severity of symptoms (the higher the number, the more severe). The CDI may be best used as a screening measure, after which further diagnosis may rest on clinical interviews and other rating scale measures (Semrud et al., 2003).

Other self-report scales include the Reynolds Child Depression Scale (Reynolds, 1989), the Children's Depression Rating Scale-Revised (Pomanski et al., 1984), the Hopelessness Scale (Kazdin, French, Unis, Esveldt-Dawson, & Sherick, 1983), the Depression Self-Rating Scale (Birleson, 1981), and the Hamilton Depression Rating Scale (Hamilton, 1967). Although these scales may also be used, the results may be redundant with the CDI, and all of these measures take a longer time to administer. See Semrud et al. (2003) for an in-depth discussion of the assessment of childhood depression.

If depression is suspected, use of both the structured interview and the CDI can most efficiently and reliably answer the diagnostic questions posed to the examiner. In cases where difficulty remains in diagnosis due to an unwillingness by the child or adolescent to discuss his or her feelings, projective techniques such as the Rorschach, Roberts Apperception Test, or Thematic Apperception Test should be considered. These measures are beyond the confines of this book, and the interested reader is referred to Allen and Hollifield (2003) and DuPree and Prevatt (2003). If an omnibus rating scale is indicated, clinicians are advised to use either the Behavioral Assessment Scale for Children II (BASC-II; Reynolds & Kamphaus, 2004) or the Achenbach System of Empirically Based Assessment (ASEBA; Achenbach & Rescorla, 2001).

Implications for Intervention

Treatment of depression must be conducted by professionals with training and sensitivity to the subjectively felt distress of the child or adolescent. Disturbances in concentration, feelings of guilt and worry, self-destructive thoughts, and social withdrawal are extremely painful and have repercussions for present and future adjustment. Relapses following treatment or poor progress in the initial stages of treatment may exacerbate the disorder and prolong the subjective feelings of hopelessness, helplessness, and sadness (Stark et al., 2006). Treatment of depression often combines pharmacotherapy and Cognitive Behavioral Therapy (CBT).

Pharmacotherapy. Knowledge of the etiology of depressive disorders has been expanded by examining neurotransmitter systems affected by antidepressant medications. Antidepressant medications affect the brain systems in which the primary neurotransmitters are norepinephrine and for serotonin. Antidepressants alter these functional systems by increasing or decreasing the release of neurotransmitters at the presynapse or by enhancing neurotransmitter reuptake mechanisms at the postsynapse.

Since the first edition of this book, NIMH funded a large scale study of treatment for adolescent depression (Treatment for Adolescents with Depression Study Team [TADS], 2004). In this hallmark study 439 adolescents with depression, between 12–17 years of age, were randomly assigned to three treatment groups: medication alone, Cognitive-Behavioral Treatment (CBT) alone, and medication with CBT. Combined treatments were superior to both medication and/or CBT alone treatment. Suicidal ideation was reduced in all treatment groups. It was necessary to monitor adverse effects (i.e., gastrointestinal track events, sedation, and insomnia) for medicated youths. NIMH also funded two other large scale studies of treatment resistant depression. See Chapter 17 for a more in-depth discussion of results from the *Treatment for Adolescents with Depression Study (TADS)*, *STAR*D Sequenced Treatment Alternatives to Relieve Depression*, and the *Treatment Of Resistant Depression In Adolescents, TORDIA*.

Clinicians suggest that given the long-term course of depression, the possible morbidity, and the psychic pain experienced, medication is warranted if the child shows a severe form of depression, psychosocial treatment has not been successful, and hospitalization is considered. Frequent communication between home, school, and physician is recommended, particularly with regard to assignment completion and rate of social interaction. Therefore, it is important that the child's progress be closely monitored, consultation between school, home, and physician be maintained, and psychosocial interventions be continued.

Cognitive Behavioral Therapy for Depression

Cognitive Behavioral Therapy (CBT) and interpersonal therapy (IPT) are among the most common forms of therapy for adolescents with depression (Stark et al., 2006). These approaches have much in common and include strategies to improve social interactions, emotional regulation, and social skills. Cognitive-behavioral treatments include problem solving therapy, training in self-monitoring, and self-control training.

While CBT is considered to be a "promising practice," more research is needed to determine its efficacy. Initial research suggests that a number of therapies including CBT may be helpful for adolescents with depression (Michael & Crowley, 2002). See Stark et al. (2006) for an in-depth review of research on CBT and IPT.

NIMH is currently funding a multi-year study to determine the efficacy of CBT in girls with depression (ACTION; Stark et al., 2006). Components of the study target goal setting, affective education, coping skills training, problem solving training, cognitive restructuring, and building a positive sense of self. There is some evidence that CBT can be an effective treatment for adolescents with depression, particularly when combined with medication. The TADS study showed that a combination of Prozac with CBT produced the most favorable results when weighing both risks and benefits for adolescents with major depression (March, Silva, & Vitiello, 2006).

In summary, the efficacy of pharmacological intervention for childhood depression is not clear at this time. The emergence of studies that utilize psychosocial intervention indicates improvement when cognitive-behavioral treatment is used. As controlled studies of pharmacological and therapeutic techniques appear, the field may well discover the most efficacious methods of treatment. Major depression

may be related to environmental factors as much as to biological factors. Treatment of familial difficulties along with multimodal child treatment may be the best avenue for success.

Pediatric Bipolar Disorder

Mood disorders also include two forms of bipolar disorder: Bipolar I and Bipolar II (APA, 2000). The essential features of the bipolar disorders are recurring bouts of mania in addition to bouts of depression. Approximately 10 percent to 15 percent of adolescents with recurring major depression are later diagnosed with Bipolar I disorder (APA, 2000). Bipolar disorders (BPD) are rare in children, with greater frequency of occurrence found in adolescents. Early onset bipolar disorders appear to have more severe problems including higher rates of anxiety and substance abuse disorders, suicide attempts and recurrences (Perlis et al., 2004).

There is a great deal of controversy concerning the diagnosis of childhood bipolar disorders (McClellan, Kowatch, & Findling, 2007). There has been a 40-fold increase in the diagnosis of BPD in children and adolescents, and it is unclear whether children display all the same adult symptoms that are outlined in DSM-IV. Children and adolescents may have high rates of irritability and impulsivity, but it is not certain that these are separate from other broader mood disorders rather than BPD per se. Although 65 percent of adults with BPD report having symptoms in adolescence, it is unclear whether children currently diagnosed with BPD will continue to have the disorder in adulthood. Another of the major diagnostic issues is the overlap of symptoms of BPD with ADHD, where as many as 60 percent of children have a dual diagnosis (Dickstein et al., 2004). Others are concerned that diagnosis is difficult because children present with a number of symptoms that are difficult to differentiate from other schizo-affective, schizoid personality and other mood and anxiety disorders (Gorwood, 2004). Geller and Tillman (2005) have established conservative diagnostic criteria for childhood BPD in order to improve the validity of the disorder.

Bipolar and major depressive disorders differ not only in terms of symptomatology, but also in terms of genetic contributions (APA, 2000; Hammen & Rudolph, 2006). Bipolar depression is likely a genetically based disorder, whereas major depression is related to both genetic and environmental contributions. Torgesen (1986) studied 151 same-sex twins for incidence of bipolar and major depression, and found that 10 had bipolar depression, 92 had major depression, 35 had dysthymia, and 14 had adjustment disorder with depressed mood. Torgesen reported a 75 percent concordance rate for bipolar depression in monozygotic twins and close to 0 percent concordance in dizygotic twins. Furthermore, data indicated a 27 percent concordance rate for major depression in monozygotic twins and a 12 percent rate for dizygotic twins, with a 40 percent concordance rate for psychotic depression in monozygotic twins, compared to 15 percent in dizygotic twins. Torgesen (1986) concluded that major depression and bipolar disorders are two different disorders, with bipolar and severe (i.e., psychotic) depression more likely to be genetically transmitted.

Dickstein et al. (2004) found that children with bipolar disorder show deficits in attentional set shifting and visuospatial memory tasks from the Cambridge Neuropsychological Test Automated Battery. Children with bipolar depression also experience more difficulty on performance-based tasks rather than on verbal measures (Dencina et al., 1983).

Typical first line treatments for BPD include mood stabilizers and atypical antipsychotic medication (McClellan et al., 2007). Behavioral therapies may also be used to address violent outbursts and violence in some adolescents with juvenile mania. The National Institute of Mental Health is funding the Systematic Treatment Enhancement Program for Bipolar Disorder (STEP-BD) study to follow a cohort of children diagnosed with BPD. Additional studies are also underway to determine treatment efficacy of early onset mania, and to examine the effectiveness of family-based treatments and medications (see NIMH Bipolar Facts, 2008).

Anxiety Disorders

For purposes of this chapter, Generalized Anxiety Disorder, which includes Overanxious Disorder of Childhood as defined by DSM-IV-TR (APA, 2000),

will be discussed. The essential features of GAD are excessive anxiety and worry or apprehension that is difficult to control. Anxiety causes considerable distress that impairs social, academic and other important daily functions. One of six symptoms must be present to meet criteria for GAD: restlessness or feeling keyed up, easily fatigued, difficulty concentrating, irritability, muscle tension, and sleep disturbance (APA, 2000, p. 476).

Additional types of anxiety disorders found in childhood include separation anxiety disorder, social phobia, panic disorder, obsessive-compulsive disorder and posttraumatic stress disorder. Obsessive-compulsive disorder (OCD) is diagnosed when recurrent and distressing thoughts or drive lead to a repetitive or irrational behavior, which in turn causes anxiety when resisted (APA, 2000). OCD typically begins in adolescence or early adulthood, but it can begin in early childhood (APA, 2000; Spence, Rapee, McDonald, & Ingram, 2001). Early onset of anxiety increases the risk for comorbidity and, if left untreated, anxiety may persist into adulthood (Albano, Chorpita, & Barlow, 2006).

Posttraumatic stress disorder (PTSD) is characterized by anxiety symptoms following an emotionally distressing event that is unusual in normal human experience. The child may have been exposed to a variety of traumatic events including war, natural disaster, actual or threatened death, serious injury or physical threat to self or others (APA, 2000). Responses to the trauma may include intense fear or horror, helplessness, frightening nightmares, acting or feeling that the event will reoccur (i.e., hallucinations, flashbacks), intense psychological distress, and physiological reactions to events that resemble the trauma. Individuals with PTSD seek to avoid stimuli that are similar to the trauma which may result in a lack of interest in activities, inability to recall the event, restricted range of emotions (blunting, inability to feel love), feelings of detachment, and a sense of hopelessness as it relates to the future.

Incidence

Prevalence rates for childhood anxiety disorders estimated from data gathered through the 2003 National Survey of Children's Health (NSCH) suggest that 2–4 percent of children have anxiety or depression (Blanchard, Gurka, & Blackman, 2006). In the National Comorbidity Replication study (NCS-R), Shear, Jin, Ruscio, Walters, and Kessler (2006), reported prevalence rates of 4.1 percent of lifetime separation anxiety in children and 6.6 percent in adults, with 1/3 of the children showing persistent anxiety into adulthood.

Blanchard et al. (2006) found that anxiety and depression maybe under-diagnosed in children where 36 percent of parents surveyed indicated concerns over anxiety or depression. The study also revealed that emotional problems were more frequent in school-aged versus preschool children. In a longitudinal study of a community sample of children aged 9–13 years of age participants were followed until the age of 16 years. Costello, Mustillo, Erkanli, Keeler, and Angold (2003) found that anxiety disorders (social anxiety and panic disorders) increased over the study period.

Comorbidity

Children with generalized anxiety disorders are at high risk to develop concurrent mood disorders, and other anxiety disorders (APA, 2000). In a longitudinal study of individuals living in New Zealand, Moffitt et al. (2007) reported that 72 percent of individuals with lifetime anxiety had a history of depression. In adulthood, 12 percent had comorbid generalized anxiety disorders with major depression, which placed them at risk for significant mental health needs including psychiatric medication (47%), attempted suicide (11%), sought mental health services (64%), and high recurrence rates of generalized anxiety (47%) with major depression (67%).

Externalizing behavioral difficulties have also co-occurred with anxiety disorders, including ADHD (Jensen et al., 2001). In addition individuals with generalized anxiety disorders are at risk for substance abuse disorders (APA, 2000). Costello et al. (2003) also reported that there was considerable continuity of having one diagnosis than another over time, particularly from depression to anxiety, depression to anxiety, and conduct disorder with anxiety to substance abuse.

The neuropsychological differences between children with comorbid internalizing and externalizing disorders (i.e., conduct disorders and anxiety or depression) and those with co-occurring internalizing disorders (i.e., anxiety and depression) have not been investigated (Teeter Ellison et al., 2009). Children with various comorbid psychiatric disorders may well have underlying weaknesses in neuropsychological functions that ultimately affect treatment strategies and outcomes. Further research is needed in this area to more fully determine if there are unique characteristics for various combinations of comorbid disorders, and to determine how comorbidity affects treatment outcome. See the discussion of Implications for Treatment for a more detailed discussion.

Genetic Factors

Research on the genetic basis of anxiety disorders has significantly increased over the past 15 years (Albano et al., 2006). Although anxiety and other mood disorders typically run in families, researchers have not isolated any specific gene area or region for anxiety (Pliszka, 2003). Gratacos et al. (2001) have found that chromosome 15 may be involved with several anxiety disorders (i.e., panic, agoraphobia, social and simple phobia). Apparently OCD differs from the other anxiety disorders due to its high co-occurrence with tic disorders. Pliszka (2003) suggests that tic disorders and OCD have been found in individuals recovering from encephalitis, and other autoimmune diseases such as strep throat. "Pediatric autoimmune neuropsychiatric disorders associated with strep" or (PANDAS) have been reported. Pliszka suggests that genetic vulnerability may be to autoimmune weaknesses rather than to OCD.

Twin studies report that heritability estimates for anxiety disorders range from 30 percent to 40 percent (see Kendler, Neale, Heath, & Eaves, 1992, 1993). Studies utilizing twins have found a high concordance rate for anxiety disorder in identical twins (Torgesen, 1986). There is a tendency for children who are behaviorally inhibited at an early age to have parents who are under treatment for panic disorder and agoraphobia (Rosenbaum, 1988). On follow-up these children were at increased risk for anxiety disorders in late adolescence and early adulthood (Rosenbaum, 1988).

It appears that biological dispositions may interact with environmental stressors and result an increase in anxiety disorders in children born to parents who have been diagnosed as affectively disordered. A review of twin studies by Rapoport (1986) found a concordance of 80 percent for obsessive-compulsive disorder in monozygotic and dizygotic twins. This high rate of concordance is suggestive of genetic transmission and needs to be studied further. This area of study is just beginning, and further information is needed to determine the relationship that genetics and environment has on the risk factor of later developing an anxiety disorder.

Brain and Neurochemistry

Pennington (2002) discusses the brain mechanisms underlying anxiety and explains the shift from single neurotransmitter theories (i.e., norepinephrine) to more complex theories involving the amygdale and the hypothalamic-pituitary-adrenal axis (HPA), and other neurotransmitters (serotonin, GABA, corticotrophin-releasing factor, and cholecystokinin). While there are few neuroimaging studies, Davidson, Abercrombie, Nitschke, and Putman (1999) report that greater amygdala and right prefrontal activation patterns were found in children with anxiety compared to nonanxious controls.

According to Teeter Ellison and Nelson (2008), negative emotions and emotional deprivation affect stress-responsive systems, particularly the sympathetic adrenal medullary (SAM which is the fight/flight system) and the HPA [counteracts or suppresses acute stress reactions (Adam, Klimes-Dougan, & Gunnar, 2007)]. While hormones in the HPA system (cortisol) sustain brain development, cortisol can also be detrimental to the developing neurons. "More recently, the link between early experience, brain development, and both normal and disordered functioning has become increasingly evident and better understood, due largely to evidence that early experience (especially deprivation experiences) reduces neural plasticity to stress experienced later in life (e.g., Mirescu, Peters, & Gould, 2004) and even permanently silences genes critical to the regulation of the stress response (e.g., Weaver et al., 2004)" (Adam et al., 2007, p. 266). Cortisol levels change at different stages, first when anticipating the stressor, second

when reacting to the stressor, and finally recovering to pre-stress levels. Cortisol responses can be buffered with secure early attachment to the primary caregiver, whereby the HPA system becomes under social regulation (Teeter Ellison & Nelson, 2008).

Positive mother-child interactions, with responsive care buffer cortisol levels, ultimately reduce the distress infants feel, while unresponsive, insensitive interactions have negative affects on the infant's stress responses (Teeter Ellison & Nelson, 2008). "Although parents can clearly serve as buffers on the effects of social environments on young children's HPA-axis, they can also serve as a profound source of social strain if their behavior is threatening or fails to provide appropriate comfort" (Adam et al., 2007, p. 274).

Long-term alterations of the HPA system often occur in children exposed to severe deprivation (institutions) and those who experience physical and sexual abuse (Teeter Ellison & Nelson, 2008). Fearful, anxious children and undercontrolled children also have altered cortisol levels as a result of negative peer interactions in childhood and adolescence. Peer rejection, stressful social interactions, social isolation, and chronic social strain appear to influence the HPA system.

Differences in HPA-axis activity have been found in a number of childhood disorders including both internalizing and externalizing disorders, memory and cognitive deficits, and poor educational performance (Teeter Ellison & Nelson, 2008). However, positive early childhood care and school environments may buffer the adverse affects of high cortisol levels (see Adam et al., 2007).

Elevated blood pressure and heart rate responses are related to anxiety arousal (Matthews, Manuck, & Saab, 1986). Use of electrophysiology has found increased arousal in the limbic system of inhibited children (Kagan, Arcus, Snidman, & Feng-Wang-Yu, 1994). It has been hypothesized that such arousal contributes to the development of anxiety disorders. It is also possible that biological dispositions interact with environmental stressors, subsequently resulting in the higher-than-expected incidence of anxiety disorder in children of parents with anxiety and/or depressive disorder. Evidence gained through PET and CT scans in individuals with OCD has found increased metabolic rates for glucose, particularly in regions of the orbital gyrus and caudate nucleus (Baxter et al., 1987; Luxenberg et al., 1988).

Academic and School Adjustment

Anxiety disorders have not been found to be related to low intelligence. In contrast, children with anxiety disorders tend to have at least average ability (Rachman & Hodgson, 1991). Anxious children experience significant psychosocial difficulty, including impaired peer relations, depression, low self-concept, poor attention span, and deficits in academic per-formance (Strauss, Frame, & Forehand, 1987). Children with anxiety disorder have been found to be as disliked by their peers as those children with conduct disorder (Strauss et al., 1988). Children with anxiety also have been found to be socially neglected, isolated, withdrawn, and lonely (Strauss, 1990). Anxious children are more likely to experience test anxiety and difficulty in presenting before their classmates. Children with obsessive-compulsive disorder are absent from school frequently because of peer ridicule (Clarizio, 1991) and social isolation (Allsop & Verduyn, 1990), and are at higher risk for suicide (Flament et al., 1988, 1990) and substance abuse (Friedman, Utada, Glickman, & Morrissey, 1987).

It is important to note that anxious children rarely pose significant overt behavioral difficulties in school, and often are not referred for assessment by their teacher. Teachers have frequently described these children as well-behaved and eager to please (Strauss, 1990). However, such anxiety can impair the child's social and academic functioning, and teachers need to be familiar with these difficulties through in-service and direct training.

Family and Home Factors

There appears to be a relationship between socioeconomic status and anxiety in children (Strauss, 1990). Separation anxiety disorder has been found to be more prevalent in families of lower socioeconomic status (SES; Last, Hersen, Kazdin, Finkelstein, & Strauss, 1987), while overanxious children are found in greater concentration in middle to higher SES families. Moreover, avoidant disorder also has been found to be more prevalent in middle to higher SES families than in lower SES families (Francis, Last, & Strauss, 1992). In addition, there is an increased incidence of psychopathology in close relatives of children and adolescents with obsessive-compulsive disorders (Templer, 1972). Families of children with OCD tend to be highly verbal, socially isolated and withdrawn, emphasize cleanliness and etiquette, and have a tendency to be extremely frugal with money (Adam et al., 1995). Clark and Bolton (1985) found that adolescents with OCD believed their parents held very high expectations for them, and these expectations were higher than those perceived by adolescents with anxiety disorders. These authors reported that the parents of OCD and anxious adolescents did not differ in their expectations for their children.

Implications for Assessment

It is important to utilize a multi-method approach to the diagnosis of anxiety disorders. Semi-structured interviews, rating scales, self-report scales, and observations are important pieces of an assessment. As discussed in the section on childhood depression, semi-structured and structured interviews are helpful in diagnosing anxiety disorders (Loney & Frick, 2003). Last et al. (1987) found good concordance across informants using a semi-structured clinical interview to diagnose anxiety disorders. Children reported more anxiety symptoms than parents, possibly indicating that because of the internal nature of these signs, children are more aware of these types of difficulties than their caregivers (Edelbrock, Costello, Dulcan, Kalas, & Conover, 1986). However, interviews with children under the age of nine years have low reliability [see (Loney & Frick, 2003) for a review]. The Dominic-R was developed to address these weaknesses for assessing young children with anxiety (Valla, Bergerson, & Smolla, 2000). The Dominic-R assesses DSM-III-R criteria and is presented in a picture format. The pictorial format, combined with verbal questions, increased the reliability and validity of the diagnostic interview in young children (Loney & Frick, 2003).

The neuropsychological underpinnings of anxiety disorders in childhood have not been as extensively investigated compared to other disorders of childhood (Teeter Ellison et al., 2009). Shaffer et al., (1996) also reported that children with anxiety and withdrawal had a higher risk of developing long-term problems due to dependent behavior coupled with signs of motor clumsiness, associated movements, and/or fine motor delays in childhood (Teeter Ellison et al., 2009).

Rating Scales

Self-report rating scales are frequently used to assess general anxiety levels. These scales are not developed to determine various types of anxiety disorders. One of the most popular rating scales used is the Revised Children's Manifest Anxiety Scale (Reynolds & Richmond, 1978), which provides a global score. It is confounded by symptoms of depression in the scale and may be best utilized as a general measure of psychic distress. Behavioral rating scales such as the Achenbach and BASC are useful to screen for anxiety disorders with children showing elevated scores on more intensive measures, including a structured clinical interview and observations. Such a multistage method of evaluation can decrease false positives and increase the specificity of diagnosis in order to facilitate selecting the most appropriate treatment.

Implications for Treatment

Treatment of anxiety disorders is typically multifaceted and may involve behavioral techniques, cognitive-behavioral therapy, and/or pharmacology (Chorpita & Southam-Gerow, 2006). Specific behavioral interventions generally include systematic desensitization, flooding, modeling, and reinforcement. Systematic desensitization involves the gradual exposure of fear-evoking situations paired with a nonanxiety arousing situation. This technique has been most successful with phobias. Flooding involves placing the child in the feared situation for an extended period of time to evoke an intense reaction which gradually diminishes. Although this technique has been effective with school phobia, it is not recommended for other types of disorder because of the aversive nature of the treatment and the availability of less stressful methods. The use of positive reinforcement, shaping, and extinction

have been most helpful with phobias. One of the most important components of this technique is to reduce parental attention when the child becomes fearful, thus removing a very powerful reinforcement for the anxious behavior.

Modeling is another behavioral technique in which the child imagines or watches a model successfully interact with the fear producing stimulus. This technique is helpful in reducing common childhood fears. Modeling can take a variety of forms: (1) symbolic where pictures or videos show successful interactions, (2) covert modeling where the child imagines the model interacting successfully, and (3) peer or adult models where others confront the fearful stimulus and model coping strategies (Chorpita & Southam-Gerow, 2006).

Cognitive behavioral interventions are used to modify cognitions that underlie the anxiety and emotional distress. Included in this type of intervention are methods of cognitive restructuring, self-instruction, and self-monitoring. These techniques have been successful in treating treatment anxiety disorders in childhood. Psychopharmacology will be discussed in Chapter 17.

Effects of Comorbidity on Treatment Outcomes

Children with both anxiety and ADHD respond differently to ADHD treatments when compared to other groups. The ADHD + ANX group, regardless of ODD/CD status, tended to be more responsive to treatment than either children with ADHD + ODD/CD or ADHD-only groups. In addition, children with ADHD + ANX responded positively to any of three treatments (behavioral, medication management, or combined treatment), whereas the ADHD + ANX + ODD/CD had the greatest benefits from the combined treatment. Finally, the ADHD + OCC/CD or ADHD-only groups generally only responded to treatments with medication (Jensen et al., 2001).

Conclusions

Children with internalizing and externalizing psychiatric disorders appear to present with both functional (behavioral) and neuropsychological (biogenetic) markers. These domains are intertwined and difficult to separate out. It seems safe to conclude that children who have more than one disorder are more likely to be referred for assessment and are more likely to demonstrate severe types of psychopathology and neuropsychological dysfunction.

The next section provides a clinical case study of a child with Major Depressive Disorder, Generalized Anxiety Disorder, and Panic Disorder.

Depression Case Study

Learning Characteristics Assessment

Identifying Information:

Name: Mr. L.M.
Age (Date of Birth): 17
Education: 12 years

Procedures Administered:

Clinical Interview
Test of Malingering (TOMM)
Wechsler Adult Intelligence Scale – 3rd Edition (WAIS-III)
Woodcock Johnson Achievement Battery – 3rd Edition (WJ-III)
Wechsler Individual Achievement Test – 2nd Edition (WIAT-II; selected tests)
Nelson-Denny Reading Test
Delis-Kaplan Executive Function System (D-KEFS; Selected tests)
Test of Variables of Attention (TOVA)
Wechsler Memory Scale – 3rd Edition (WMS-III)
California Verbal Learning Test – 2nd Edition (CVLT-II)
Rey Complex Figure Test (RCFT)
Beck Depression Inventory (BDI)
State-Trait Anxiety Inventory (STAI)
Minnesota Multiphasic Personality Inventory – 2nd Edition (MMPI-2)

Referral Question

Mr. M. is a 17-year-old, right-handed male who is planning to attend the local community college in the fall. He was referred for evaluation by his parents who are concerned about possible difficulties that may arise in college in writing and reading. Mr. M.'s stated goals for the assessment were to determine if he had a writing disability and to receive recommendations for improving his writing. During the clinical interview, he reported that he has problems with academic writing in the social sciences, especially due to his difficulties sustaining attention while writing and developing a cohesive argument.

Developmental History

The following information was obtained through the learning assessment questionnaire completed by Mr. M. and a clinical interview.

Birth and Developmental Milestones

Mr. M. reported that he was born after a full-term pregnancy and his mother did not have complications with his pregnancy or delivery. His mother was 26-years-old when he was born. Mr. M. reported reaching all developmental milestones (walking, talking, and crawling) at appropriate times without difficulty.

Family

Mr. M. described his parents as typical and conservative. Mr. M. also reported that during his middle school years, his parents were not very strict and he often argued and yelled at them. While he does not remember what they argued about, he indicated that he remembers just wanting to get his way. He reported that his parents eventually concluded that they "could not control him and let him go." His mother has a high school diploma and his father went on to earn some college credits. They are employed as managers in a large company. Mr. M.has one younger brother who is in elementary school and doing well.

Family Medical and Psychiatric History

There is no history of any medical difficulties or psychiatric problems for Mr. M.'s family. Mr. M. did not report experiencing any medical problems during his lifetime. He reported that he has been very healthy.

Academic History

Early Academic Performance

Mr. M. attended a small private elementary school where he reports performing well academically. In the 7th grade, however, he began attending a public school and his grades dropped to mostly Cs and Ds, and deficiency notices were sent home to his parents. Mr. M. reported that while his parents expected him to do well in school, they did not help him with schoolwork. In high school, he continued to do poorly and failed some of his classes, reportedly because he did not apply himself. He did, however, earn his high school diploma.

During this time, Mr. M. did not receive any remedial services or academic tutoring. His favorite subject was science and his least favorite was history, because he reported having no connection or interest in the subject. Throughout middle and high school, Mr. M. reported that he had a good group of friends and stayed out of trouble.

Behavioral Observations

Mr. M. appeared for each testing session on time or early, well-groomed, and casually dressed. He indicated that he is right-handed, does not have any hearing problems, but does wear glasses to correct his vision problems. English is his native language.

During the first assessment session, Mr. M. was very lively and talkative. During the clinical interview, Mr. M. was candid and open to answering each question to the best of his ability. He was cooperative and motivated during testing and even made jokes. For example, during WAIS-III Digit-Symbol Coding, Mr. M. asked if I had ever tested

someone who finished the subtest incredibly fast "like Rain Man." He did, however, appear somewhat nervous. He was frequently observed biting his nails, picking with his skin, and scratching his head. He took great care in responding to the items on the BDI-II. He read each item carefully and asked questions about any items he did not understand.

During the subsequent assessment sessions, Mr. M. appeared less energetic and somewhat sad and stressed. When given a self-report anxiety measure on the second day of testing, Mr. M. said that he had a paper due that day and his responses were largely influenced by his school concerns. During this testing session, we completed some of the writing assessment measures. He did not appear to have trouble during the WJ-III Achievement Writing Fluency subtest, where he wrote very quickly. During the WJ-III Achievement Writing Samples subtest, however, he frequently crossed out what he had written and started again. During the WIAT-II Written Expression subtest, Mr. M. said that his "mind went blank," but it was "not because he was tired." He began the essay by creating a short outline of his main points. While writing the essay for this subtest, Mr. M. frequently erased what he had written. He also placed a great deal of pressure on the pencil as he wrote. The table even moved with the force of his writing. After 10 minutes had passed, Mr. M. had only written 4–5 lines of text. He also held his face very taut, with his lips firmly pressed together during this and other writing exercises.

Mr. M. was administered a measure of malingering, which fell within normal limits (TOMM). In sum, the assessment results are thought to be a valid and reliable representation of Mr. M.'s psychological, cognitive, and academic functioning.

Test Results

Intellectual Functioning

Mr. M.'s general cognitive abilities were assessed using the WAIS-III. On the WAIS-III, Mr. M.'s overall intellectual abilities fell within the high average to significantly above average range. He obtained a Full Scale IQ of 120, which falls at the

91st percentile when compared to others at the same education level. The chances that the range of scores from 116 to 124 includes his true IQ are about 95 out of 100. Mr. M. obtained a Verbal IQ of 115 and a Performance (nonverbal) IQ of 124. The difference between his Verbal IQ and Performance IQ was not statistically significant. Therefore, Mr. M.'s Full Scale IQ score is the most appropriate index of his overall intellectual abilities.

Mr. M.'s performance on tests of verbal comprehension was in the average range. The verbal comprehension subtests required him to answer oral questions that measure factual knowledge, provide meanings of words, exhibit reasoning ability, and adeptly express his ideas in words. Among these verbal subtests, Mr. M.'s performance on a test that required him to describe how two things are similar was a relative weakness.

His performance on tests of perceptual organization was in the superior range. The perceptual organization subtests required him to integrate visual stimuli, use nonverbal reasoning skills, and apply visual-spatial and visual-motor skills to solve the kinds of problems that are not taught in school. Among these perceptual subtests, Mr. M.'s very superior performance on a task that required him to use blocks to create a model in three-dimensional space based on a two- or three-dimensional example model was a strength. His superior performance in this domain suggests that his nonverbal thinking and visual motor coordination are well developed.

On tests of working memory, he performed in the superior range. These subtests required him to respond to oral stimuli that involve handling numbers and letters in a sequential fashion and displaying a non-distractible attention span. These results suggest that his sequential processing ability is very well developed.

Mr. M.'s processing speed was in the high average range. The processing speed subtests required him to demonstrate extreme speed in solving an assortment of nonverbal problems. These tests measured speed of thinking as well as motor speed. His performance in this domain suggests that his response speed, the ability to quickly scan, discriminate between, and sequentially order visual information, is in the high average range.

There was a significant difference between Mr. M.'s superior performance on perceptual organization and working memory subtests, and his average verbal comprehension performance. This indicates that his verbal conceptualization, knowledge, and expression abilities are a relative weakness.

Overall, Mr. M. exhibited superior intellectual abilities. His perceptual organization and working memory skills were strengths, while his verbal comprehension ability was a relative weakness.

Scholastic Achievement

Mr. M.'s overall performance on the WJ-III Achievement Battery was in the high average range. Mr. M.'s overall reading achievement was in the average range.

His reading comprehension and his ability to recognize words were in the high average range. Mr. M.'s reading fluency was in the low average range. Mr. M.'s vocabulary, comprehension, and reading rate were also in the average range when tested using the Nelson-Denny Reading Test.

Mr. M.'s scores on written achievement were in the high average range. His ability to produce meaningful written sentences in response to a variety of tasks was in the average range (Writing Samples subtest). His spelling was also in the average range. His writing speed was in the high average range as measured by the Writing Fluency which required him to write complete sentences using a given set of words and matching picture. When writing single sentences in the structured format of the Writing Fluency subtest, Mr. M.'s performance is in the high average range. Mr. M.'s written achievement was also tested using the WIAT-II. On this test, his spelling and written expression were in the average range.

Mr. M.'s overall math achievement fell in the high average range. His mathematic calculation skills (Calculation subtest) and his ability to solve mathematic word problems (Applied Problems subtest) were both in the average range. His performance on Math Fluency, a timed task that requires examinees to calculate addition, subtraction, and multiplication problems quickly, was in the high average range.

Overall, Mr. M.'s scholastic achievement skills were in the high average range. Specifically, his overall mathematics and written language skills were in the high average range and his reading skills were in the average range. Because his academic achievement is within cognitive expectations, Mr. M. does not meet criteria for a learning disorder.

Working Memory and Attention

Mr. M.'s performance on working memory tasks was in the superior range on both the WAIS-III and the WMS-III. On the D-KEFS Trail Making Test, a task measuring working memory, visual scanning, attention, number-letter sequencing, and visual-motor abilities, Mr. M.'s performance was in the average to high average range.

The Auditory and Visual T.O.V.A. was used to assess Mr. M.'s attention and impulse control. The test resembles a computer game where the examinee is directed to press a switch whenever a specific stimulus appears. When compared to those of his same age and gender, Mr. M.'s performance suggested he has a significant problem with sustained attention.

Executive Functioning

The D-KEFS Color-Word Interference Test was used to assess Mr. M.'s verbal inhibition and cognitive flexibility. This test consists of four timed conditions. In the first condition of this test, Mr. M. was shown a sheet with color patches aligned in rows and asked to name each of the colors as quickly as possible. In the second condition, he was shown a list of color words and asked to read them as quickly as possible. Mr. M.'s performance in both of these conditions was in the average range. The third condition required him to inhibit the written color word and, instead, name the color of ink, and his performance was in the high average range. He also performed in the high average range during the fourth condition, which required him to switch back and forth between naming the dissonant ink color and reading the conflicting word. His high average performance during these conditions indicates that he took less time than others of similar education level to complete the task.

The D-KEFS Verbal Fluency Test was used to assess Mr. M.'s cognitive flexibility and strategic thinking. This test required him to generate as many words as possible beginning with a given letter or belonging to a specific category within a short period of time. Mr. M.'s performance on this test was in the average to high average range, indicating that his cognitive fluency is within normal limits.

The D-KEFS Sorting Test was used to assess Mr. M.'s executive functioning, concept formation, and problem solving abilities. This test required him to sort various cards into groups, describe the concepts he used to generate each sort, and identify the correct categorization rule or concept used to generate sorts created by the examiner. Mr. M.'s performance on these tasks was in the average to high average range suggesting that his ability to implement and perceive conceptual relationships in both verbal and nonverbal modalities is within age and education level expectations.

The D-KEFS Tower Test was used to assess Mr. M.'s spatial planning and rule learning skills. His performance on this task was in the average range.

Overall, Mr. M. demonstrated average to high average executive functioning.

Memory Functioning

Mr. M.'s general memory abilities, as measured by the WMS-III, were in the high average range. His ability to recall visual information immediately and after a 25-minute delay were in the high average and average ranges, respectively. His ability to recall oral information immediately and after a 25-minute delay were both in the high average range.

Mr. M.'s auditory learning and memory were also tested using the CVLT-II. On this test, Mr. M. was given several oral presentations of a 16-word list and asked to recall the list after each presentation. Mr. M.'s recall after the initial presentation of the first word list was in the high average range. After the fifth trial of oral presentation of the words, Mr. M.'s performance was significantly above average. His overall ability to recall words with repeated exposure to the list of words was in the average range as indicated by his learning slope score. When orally presented with a second list of words, Mr. M. scored in the superior range, recalling 14 out of the 16 words. His performance was significantly above average when he was asked to recall the first list of words after a short and long delay. An analysis of his memory performance revealed that across all five trials, Mr. M. used a less efficient method for learning the words, recalling them in the order given. While Mr. M.'s performance on this test was in the high average to superior range, he did not use the most effective learning strategy, reorganizing the target words into categorical groups, to pull the words from memory.

In sum, results from both the WMS-III and the CVLT-II indicate that Mr. M.'s general memory abilities are in the high average range. His somewhat less developed visual memory skills and his slower processing speed may be influencing his overall memory abilities and his current reading difficulties.

Overall, Mr. M.'s memory abilities were in the high average range to superior range.

Visual-Motor-Spatial Skills

The Rey-Osterreith Complex Figure test (ROCF) was used to measure Mr. M.'s visual-motor-spatial memory and construction skills. This test first required him to make a copy drawing of a complex figure. The picture of the figure was then taken away, and Mr. M. was asked to draw the figure immediately and after a 25-minute delay. Mr. M.'s ability to recall and draw the figure immediately and after a delay was in the superior and high average range, respectively. Taken together, Mr. M.'s visual-spatial memory was very well developed.

Emotional Functioning

Mr. M. provided valid and reliable responses to the MMPI-2. According to the results of the MMPI-2, Mr. M.'s profile suggests that he is currently experiencing anxiety and depression. The profile suggests a tendency to be anxious and insecure. He also may be experiencing some psychosomatic problems, such as trouble sleeping and appetite changes.

This profile also suggests that Mr. M. is introverted and has difficulties meeting other people. He may be shy, uneasy, and somewhat rigid and over-controlled in social situations. He may have high standards and a strong need to achieve, but feels that he falls short of his expectations and blames himself harshly. According to the results, he feels insecure and pessimistic about the future and doubts that he can solve his problems.

The results also suggest that Mr. M. is passive and dependent in interpersonal relationships and does not speak up for himself even when others take advantage of him. He forms deep emotional attachments and tends to be quite vulnerable to being hurt. He also tends to blame himself for interpersonal problems.

On the STAI, a self-report measure of current and general levels of anxiety, Mr. M. also indicated high levels of state and trait anxiety (90th and 96th percentiles, respectively). On the BDI-II, Mr. M. received a score of 28, indicating that he is reporting moderate depressive symptoms. During the clinical interview, Mr. M. was assessed for depression, generalized anxiety disorder, panic disorder, and attention-deficit hyperactivity disorder.

Major Depressive Disorder

Mr. M. indicated that he has been suffering from depressed mood, anhedonia, weight loss, sleep disturbances, guilty feelings, concentration difficulties, and indecisiveness since middle school. He reported that he often felt down because of schoolwork and wondered whether he is "cut out for college." He became somewhat more introverted this past school year and now rarely goes out with friends. He felt cut off from the other students and teachers because guilt surrounding his poor work performance made him want to avoid seeing them. By the end of the school year, he had lost 5–7 lbs., due to a decreased appetite. Mr. M. indicated that he slept fewer hours more than usual. He also indicated that he felt guilty about not making his paper deadlines. He found it difficult to concentrate on completing his papers. He also reported that he usually considers himself an indecisive person, but that decision making was somewhat more difficult than usual. Mr. M. did not indicate any thoughts of death or dying. Based on these responses, Mr. M. meets criteria for a Major Depressive Disorder.

Mr. M. also reported feeling depressed, hopeless, and lonely for 2–3 months starting in October when he broke up with his first serious girlfriend.

Generalized Anxiety Disorder

When assessed for symptoms of generalized anxiety disorder, Mr. M. indicated that he is often consumed with worry, has difficulty controlling his worry, and experiences physical symptoms such as restlessness, fatigue, concentration difficulties, and body tension when he worries. Mr. M. reported that since his sophomore year in high school he has frequently worried about the writing he is required to do at school and work. He finds that after collecting and reading all of the needed research articles, it is difficult for him to write a cohesive essay.

Mr. M. reported that he has always worried about what other people think of him. For example, he often worries about making mistakes in oral presentations. A few times other people have told him that he was too sensitive and should not worry about things so much. He also thinks that he worries too much about what other people think and that the worry may be excessive. Mr. M. reported that he spends 5–6 hours each day worrying. He feels like the worries are on his mind all day, more days than not and are difficult to control.

Mr. M. reported that when he is worrying he has trouble sitting still. He gets tired very easily. It is harder for him to pay attention. He become more introverted and will avoid talking to his roommate. He feels his chest get tight, as if he can feel the burden of stress. He also reported feeling tension in his shoulders and neck. Mr. M. indicated that these physical symptoms occur 1–2 times per week. This worry has had a significant effect on Mr. M.'s life. It bothers him that he feels this way and it has made him question whether he should remain in graduate school. This worry has also affected his social life. He reported that worrying has turned him into a hermit, where he hardly ever leaves the house. Based on these symptoms, Mr. M. meets criteria for Generalized Anxiety Disorder.

Panic Disorder

When assessed for symptoms of panic disorder, Mr. M. reported experiencing several panic attacks at the end of the past school year as he tried to complete his writing assignments. During these attacks, he felt his heart racing. He began to shake. He had trouble catching his breath. He had pains in his chest and feared he was having a heart attack. He also worried whether he would lose control. He reported that all of these physical symptoms came on quickly, within 10 minutes after the attack began. Mr. M. reported having panic attacks three times per week during one month in the fall and as much as three times per day during one recent month. Mr. M. indicated that he does not fear having another attack, but he does believe he will have one again. Based on these symptoms, Mr. M. meets criteria for Panic Disorder Without Agoraphobia.

Attention-Deficit Hyperactivity Disorder

When assessed for symptoms of attention-deficit hyperactivity disorder, Mr. M. reported that has difficulties with listening, finishing assignments, and organizing. He also reported that he avoids activities that require him to sustain attention for long periods and is often forgetful. Mr. M. reported that he has trouble listening and understanding others. He first noticed this behavior when he began his junior year of high school. He feels like it takes him longer to understand things than others, especially when unfamiliar topics are being discussed. This mainly happens with teachers, and he does not have this problem with his parents or peers. Mr. M. also reported that he has more trouble than others finishing long and tedious tasks. He first noticed that he had trouble finishing assignments in elementary school, but this difficulty only causes significant problems for him when he is writing papers. He also reported difficulties with continuing to work on one school assignment for an extended period of time. He indicated that he will start doing one task, get bored, and then switch to another. This problem, however, is specific to schoolwork and he does not have trouble completing chores around the house.

Mr. M. also reported having more difficulties organizing things than others. He often has trouble keeping papers and computer files organized. He is also disorganized with his bills, which are often not paid on time because of this. It is also difficult for him to organize his schedule, and he will often forget deadlines and appointments. He reported that he keeps a calendar, but then will not look at it for a week. When asked how he was able to arrive on time to each of our assessment sessions, he indicated that he set a reminder on his phone. Mr. M. reported that he avoids, dislikes, and is reluctant to engage in activities requiring sustained attention, especially writing and editing papers. He does not find himself avoiding reading assignments, however. Mr. M. also reported that he is somewhat more forgetful than others. He sometimes forgets to complete school and work tasks. He reported that this does not occur frequently, however. On average, he forgets things 1–2 times per month. He does not forget daily chores. Mr. M. did not indorse any hyperactivity or impulsivity symptoms. Results from the T.O.V.A. and the clinical interview indicate that Mr. M. meets criteria for Attention-Deficit Hyperactivity Disorder Inattentive Type. These findings may indicate the presence of ADHD, but the presence of a mood disorder makes this determination problematic and should be more fully explored psychiatrically. In addition, the difficulties were not identified until Mr. M was a sophomore in high school. At this time he does not qualify for a diagnosis of ADHD.

DSM-IV-TR Diagnosis

Axis I: Moderate Major Depressive Disorder, Recurrent (296.32)
            Generalized Anxiety Disorder (300.02)
            Panic Disorder Without Agoraphobia (300.01)
            Possible history of Major Depressive Disorder (311.00; as reported by the client)
Axis II: None
Axis III: None
Axis IV: Academic difficulties
Axis V: Global Assessment of Functioning 54 (current)

Summary and Recommendations

Mr. M. is a 17-year-old, right-handed male who was referred for an evaluation of learning characteristics and attention problems. Mr. M.'s stated goals for the assessment were to determine if he had a writing disability and to receive recommendations on how to improve his writing. During the clinical interview, he reported that he has problems with academic writing in the social sciences especially, due to his difficulties sustaining attention while writing and developing a cohesive argument.

An extensive battery of tests was administered to assess Mr. M.'s current level of intellectual and psychological functioning. During testing, he was somewhat down and stressed due to school concerns, but appeared to work to the best of his abilities on all tasks. Test results are, therefore, believed to be an accurate reflection of his current level of functioning.

Overall, Mr. M. exhibited superior intellectual abilities. His perceptual organization and working memory skills were strengths, while his verbal comprehension was a relative weakness. Mr. M.'s scholastic achievement skills were in the high average range. Specifically, his overall mathematics and written language skills were in the high average range and his reading skills were in the average range. While Mr. M.'s working memory abilities were in the average to superior range, his ability to sustain attention is impaired. Mr. M. demonstrated average to high average executive functioning and his memory abilities were in the high average range to superior range.

Mr. M.'s personality profile suggested that he is introverted, uneasy, and somewhat overcontrolled in social situations. He also may be feeling insecure and pessimistic about whether he can solve his problems. Mr. M. is experiencing significant anxiety and depressive symptoms, and meets criteria for Major Depressive Disorder, Generalized Anxiety Disorder, and Panic Disorder. Although results from the tests of attention and the clinical interview indicate that he meets criteria for Attention-Deficit Hyperactivity Disorder Inattentive Type, these symptoms were not reported until his sophomore year in high school and increased as the writing workload and expectations for academic performance increased. His attention problems are likely exacerbated by his significant anxiety symptoms, especially with regard to writing.

The following recommendations may be useful in dealing with weaknesses, enhancing strengths, and improving Mr. M.'s academic performance:

Recommendations

1. Mr. M. shows significant emotional distress that is likely causing him problems in learning and exacerbating his attentional problems. Given that the attention problems were not identified until he was in high school, it is unlikely that he has ADHD.
2. Mr. M.'s anxiety symptoms are likely exacerbating his attention difficulties and may be preventing him from reaching his full academic potential. Therefore, it is recommended that he seek therapeutic counseling and a psychiatric consult. When an appointment is made, this psychological report can be sent to the assigned therapist to aid in the psychological evaluation.
3. Mr. M.'s academic performance may benefit from extra help with his writing skills. He is encouraged to seek assistance from his community college and to ask for additional support prior to beginning the fall semester.
4. It is recommended that Mr. M. take only one writing-heavy course each term in order to give him ample time to develop the skills required for the specific class. Spreading these types of courses out will likely give Mr. M. extra time to complete his writing assignments.
5. Due to his attention problems, Mr. M. may benefit from taking frequent breaks during class. Because his efficiency wanes over time, a short walk outside of the classroom may give him time to regroup.
6. Additionally, Mr. M. may benefit from having larger projects (e.g., paper deadlines) broken into more manageable tasks with individual deadlines. Mr. M. should speak with his advisor about setting discrete deadlines for separate portions of papers.

References

Achenbach, T. M., & Rescorla, L. (2001). *Manual for the ASEBA school-age forms and profiles* . Burlington: University of Vermont, Research Center for Children, Youth and Families.

Adam, E., Klimes-Dougan, B., & Gunnar, M. R. (2007). Social regulation of the adrenocortical response to stress in infants, children and adolescents: Implications for psychopathology and education. In D. Coch, K. Fischer, & G. Dawson (Eds.), *Human behavior, learning, and the developing brain* (pp. 264–304). New York, NY: Guilford Press.

Albano, A. M., Chorpita, B. F., & Barlow, D. H. (2006). Childhood anxiety disorders. In E. J. Mash & R. A. Barkley (Eds.), *Child psychopathology* (2nd ed., pp 279–329). New York: Guilford Press.

Alessi, N. E., & Magen, J. (1988). Comorbidity of other psychiatric disturbances in depressed psychiatrically hospitalized children. *American Journal of Psychiatry, 145,* 1582–1584.

Allen, J. C., & Hollifield, J. (2003). Using the Rorschach with children and adolescents: The Exner Comprehensive System. In C. R. Reynolds & R. W. Kamphaus (Eds.), *Handbook of psychological and educational assessment of children: Personality, behavior, and context* (2nd ed., pp.182–197). New York: Guilford Press.

Allsop, M., & Verduyn, C. (1990). Adolescents with obsessive compulsive disorder: A case note review of consecutive patients referred to a provincial regional adolescent psychiatry unit. *Journal of Adolescence, 13,* 157–169.

American Psychiatric Association. (2000). *Diagnostic and statistical manual of mental disorders* (4th ed. text revision). Washington, DC: Author.

Anderson, J. C., Williams, S., McGee, R., & Silva, P. A. (1987). DSM-111 disorders in preadolescent children. Prevalence in a large sample from the general population. *Archives of General Psychiatry, 44,* 6–76.

Angold, A., Costello, E. J., & Erkanli, A. (1999). Comorbidity. *Journal of Child Psychology and Psychiatry, 40,* 57–87.

Ashman, S. B., Dawson, G., Panagiotides, H., Yamada, E., & Wilkinson, C. W. (2002). Stress hormone levels of children of depressed mothers. *Development and Psychopathology, 14,* 333–349.

Avenenoli, S., Knight, E., Kessler, R. C., & Merikangas, K. R. (2007). Epidemiology of depression in children and adolescents. In J. R. Z. Abela & B. L. Hankin (Eds.), *Handbook of depression in children and adolescents* (pp. 6–34). NY: Guilford Press.

Barkley, R. A., (2006). *Attention-deficit hyperactivity disorder: A handbook for diagnosis and treatment (3rd ed.).* New York: Guildford Press.

Barlow, D. H. (2002). Anxiety and its disorders (2nd ed.). New York: Guilford Press.

Baxter, L. R., Thompson, J. M., Schwartz, J. M., Guze, B. H., Phelps, M. E., Mazziotta, J. C., et al. (1987). Trazodone treatment response in obsessive-compulsive disorder. *Psychopathology, 20,* 114–422.

Biederman, J., Baldessarini, R. J., Wright, V., Knee, D., & Harmatz, J. E. (1989). A double-blind placebo controlled study of desipramine in the treatment of ADD: I. Efficacy. *Journal of the American Academy of Child and Adolescent Psychiatry, 28,* 777–784.

Biederman, J., Faraone, S., Marrs, A., Moore, P., Garcia, J., Ablon, J. S., Mick, E. Gershon, J., & Kearns, M. E. (1997). Panic disorder and agoraphobia in consecutively referred children and adolescents. *Journal of the American Academy of Child and Adolescent Psychiatry, 36,* 214–223.

Biederman, J., Munir, K., Keenan, K., & Tsuang, M. T. (1991). Evidence of familial association between attention deficit and major affective disorders. *Archives of General Psychiatry, 48*, 633–642.

Birleson, P. (1981). The validity of depressive disorder in childhood and the development of self-rating scale: A research report. *Journal of Child Psychology and Psychiatry, 22*, 73–88.

Birmaher, B., Ryna, N. D., Williamson, D. E., Brent, D. A., Kaufman, J., Dahl, R. E., et al. (1996). Childhood and adolescent depression: A review of the past 10 years. Part I. *Journal of the American Academy of Child and Adolescent Psychiatry, 35*, 1427–1439.

Blanchard, L. T., Gurka, M. J., & Blackman, J. A. (2006). Emotional, developmental, and behavioral health of American children and their families: A report from the 2003 National Survey of Children's Health. *Pediatrics, 117*(6), e1202–e1212.

Caine, E. D. (1986). The neuropsychology of depression: The pseudodementia syndrome. In I. Grant & K. Adams (Eds.), *Neuropsychological assessment of neuro-psychiatric disorders* (pp. 221–243). New York: Oxford University Press.

Checkley, S. (1996). The neuroendocriniology of depression. *International Review of Psychiatry, 8*, 373–378.

Chorpita, B. F., & Southam-Gerow, M. A. (2006). Fears and anxieties. In E. J. Mash & R. A. Barkley (Eds.), *Treatment of childhood disorders*, 3rd ed., (pp. 271–335). New York: Guilford Press.

Chow, T. W., & Cummings, J. L. (2007). Frontal-subcortical circuits. In B. L. Miller & J. L. Cummings (Eds.), *The human frontal lobes: Functions and disorders* (2nd ed., pp. 25–43). New York: Guilfrod Press.

Clarizio, H. F. (1991). Obsessive-compulsive disorder: The secretive syndrome. *Psychology in the Schools, 28*, 106–115.

Clark, D. A., & Bolton, D. (1985). Obsessive-compulsive adolescents and their parents. *Journal of Child Psychology and Psychiatry and Allied Disciplines, 26*, 267–276.

Cohen, R. M., Weingarten, H., Smallberg, S. A., &Murphy, D. L. (1982). Effort and cognition in depression. *Archives of General Psychiatry, 39*, 593–597.

Costello, E. J., Mustillo, S., Erkanli, A., Keeler, G., & Angold, A. (2003). Prevalence and development of psychiatric disorders in childhood and adolescence. *Archives of General Psychiatry, 60*, 837–844.

Cummings, E. M., & Cicchetti, D. (1990). Toward a transactional model of relations between attachment and depression. In M. T. Greenberg, D. Cicchetti, & E. M. Cicchetti (Eds.), *Attachment in preschool years: Theory, research, and intervention* (pp. 339–372). Chicago: University Press.

Davidson, R. J., Abercrombie, H., Nitschke, J. B., & Putman, K. M. (1999). Regional brain function, emotion, and disorders of emotions. *Current Opinion in Neurobiology, 9* (2), 228–234.

Dawson, G., Frey, K., Panagiotides, H., Osterling, J., & Hessl, D. (1997). Infants of depressed mothers exhibit atypical frontal brain activity: A replication and extension of previous findings. *Journal of Child Psychology and Psychiatry, 38*, 179–186.

Dawson, G., Grofer Klinger, L., Pangiotides, H., Hill, D., Spieker, S., & Frey, K. (1992). Infants of mothers with depressive symptoms: Electrophysiological and behavioral findings related to attachment status. *Development and Psychopathology, 4* ,6740.

De Bellis, M. D., Chrousos, G. P., Dorn, L. D., Burke, L., Helmers, K., Kling, M. A., et al. (1994). Hypothalamic-pituitary-adrenal axis dysregulation in sexually abused girls. *Journal of Clinical Endocrinology and Metabolism, 78*, 249–255.

Dencina, P., Kestenbaum, E. J., Farber, S., Kron, L., et al. (1983). Clinical and psychological assessment of children of bipolar probands. *American Journal ofPsychiatry, 140*, 54–558.

Dickstein, D. P., Trelanda, J. E., Snowa, J., McClurea, E. B., Mehtaa, M. S., Towbina, K. E., et al. (2004). Neuropsychological performance in pediatric bipolar disorder. *Biological Psychiatry, 55* (1), 32–39.

Downey, G., & Coyne, J. (1990). Children of depressed parents: An integrative view. *Psychological Bulletin, 108*, 50–76.

Drevets, W. (2001a). Neuroimaging studies of mood disorders. *Biological Psychiatry, 48* (8), 813–829.

Drevets, W. C. (2001b). Neuroimaging and neuropathological studies of depression: Implications for the cognitive-emotional features of mood disorders. *Current Opinion in Neurobiology, 119* (2), 240–249.

DuPree, J. L., & Prevatt, F. (2003). Projective story telling techniques. In C. R. Reynolds & R. W. Kamphaus (Eds.), *Handbook of psychological and educational assessment of children: Personality, behavior, and context* (2nd ed., pp. 66–90). New York: Guilford Press.

Edelbrock, C., Costello, A. J., Dulcas, M. K., Kalas, R., & Conover, N. C. (1986). Parent-child agreement on child psychiatric symptoms assessed via structured interview. *Journal of Child Psychology and Psychiatry, 27*, 181–190.

Firth, C. D., Stevens, M., Johnstone, E. C., Deakin, J. F., Lawler, P., Crow, T. J. (1983). Effects of ECT and depression on various aspects of memory. *Journal of British Psychiatry, 142*, 610–617.

Flament, M. F., Koby, E., Rapoport, J. L., Berg, C. J., Zahn, T., Cox, C., et al. (1990). Childhood obsessive-compulsive disorder: A prospective follow-up study. *Journal of Child Psychology and Psychiatry, 31*, 363–380.

Flament, M. F., Whitaker, A., Rapoport, J. L., Davies, M., Berg, C. Z., Kalikow, et al. (1988). Obsessive compulsive disorder in adolescence: An epidemiological study. *Journal of the American Academy of Child and Adolescent Psychiatry, 27*, 764 – 771.

Francis, G., Last, C. G., & Strauss, C. C. (1992). Avoidant disorder and social phobia in childhood and adolescence. *Journal of the American Academy of Child and Adolescent Psychiatry, 31*, 1086–1089.

Friedman, A. S., Utada, A. T., Glickman, N. W., & Morrissey, M. R. (1987). Psychopathology as an antecedent to, and as a "consequence" of, substance abuse, in adolescence. *Journal of Drug Education, 17*, 233–244.

Geller, B., & Tillman, R. (2005). Prepubertal and early adolescent bipolar I disorder: Review of diagnostic validation by Robins and Guze criteria. *Journal of Clinical Psychiatry, 66* (suppl 7), 21–28.

Gorwood, P. (2004). Confusing clinical presentations and differential diagnosis of bipolar disorder. *Encephale, 30* (2), 182–193.

Gratacos, M., Nadal, M., Martin-Santos, R., Pujana, M. A., Gago, J., & Peral, B. (2001). A polymorphic genome duplication on human chromosome 15 is a susceptibility factor for panic and phobic disorders. *Cell, 106,* 367–379.

Gurley, D., Cohen, P., Pine, D. S., & Brook, J. (1996). Discriminating anxiety and depression in youth: A role for diagnostic criteria. *Journal of Affective Disorders, 39,* 191–190.

Haldane, M., & Frangou, S. (2004). New insights help define the pathophysiology of bipolar affective disorder: Neuroimaging and neuropathology findings. Progress in *Neuropsychopharmacology and Biological Psychiatry, 28* (6), 943–960.

Hamilton, M. (1967). Development of a rating scale for primary depressive illness. *British Journal of Social and Clinical Psychology, 6,* 278–296.

Hammen, C. (1990). Cognitive approaches to depression in children: Current findings and new directions. In B. B. Lahey & A. E. Kazdin (Eds.), *Advances in clinical child psychology* (Vol. 13, pp. 173–202). New York: Plenum Press.

Hammen, C. D., & Brennan, P. A. (2001). Depressed adolescents of depressed and non-depressed mothers: Tests of an interpersonal impairment hypothesis. *Journal of Consulting and Clinical Psychology, 69,* 284–294.

Hammen, C. D., & Rudolph, K. D. (2003). Childhood mood disorders. In E. J. Mash & R. A. Barkley, (Eds.), *Child psychopathology* (2nd ed., pp. 233–278). New York: Guilford Press.

Hankin, J. R., & Abela, J. R. (2005). *Development of psychopathology: A vulnerability stress perspective.* NY: Sage Publications

Hankin, B. L., Abramson, L. Y., Moffitt, T. E., Silva, P. A., McGee, R., & Angell, K. E. (1998). Development of depression from preadolescence to young adulthood: Emerging gender differences in a 10-year longitudinal study. *Journal of Abnormal Psychology, 107,* 128–140.

Hasler, G., Fromm, S., Carlson, P. J., Luckenbaugh, D. A., Waldeck, T., Geraci, M., et al. (2008). Neural response to catecholamine depletion in unmedicated subjects with major depressive disorder in remission and healthy subjects. *Archives of General Psychiatry, 65* (5), 521–31.

Heim, C., & Nemeroff, C. B. (2001). The role of childhood trauma in the neurobiology of mood and anxiety disorders: Preclinical and clinical studies. *Biological Psychiatry, 49,* 1023–1039.

Henriques, J., & Davidson, R. (1990). Regional brain electrical asymmetries discriminate between previously depressed subjects and healthy controls. *Journal of Abnormal Psychology, 99,* 22–31.

Jensen, J. P., Martin, D., & Cantwell, D. P. (1997). Comorbidity in ADHD: Implications for research, practice, and DSM-V. *Journal of the American Academy of Child and Adolescent Psychiatry, 36,* 1065–1079.

Jensen, P. S., Hinshaw, S., Swanson, J., Greenhill, L., Conners, K., Arnold, E., et al. (2001). Findings from the NIMH multimodal treatment study of ADHD (MTA): Implications and applications for primary care providers. *Developmental and Behavioral Pediatrics, 22,* 60–73.

Kagan, J., Arcus, D., Snidman, N., & Feng-Wang-Yu (1994). Reactivity in infants. *Developmental Psychology, 30,* 342–345.

Kaufman, J., Martin, A., King, R. A., & Charney, D. (2001). Are child-, adolescent-, and adult-onset depression one and the same? *Biological Psychiatry, 49,* 980–1001.

Kaufman, J., Yang, B. Z., Douglas-Palumberi, H., Grasso, D., Lipschitz, D., Houshyar, S., et al. (2006). Brain-derived neurotrophic factor-5-HTTLPR gene interactions and environmental modifiers of depression in children. *Biological Psychiatry, 59,* 673–680.

Kazdin, A. E. (1987). *Conduct disorders in childhood and adolescence.* Beverly Hills, CA: Sage Publications.

Kazdin, A. E., French, N. H., Unis, A. S., Esveldt-Dawson, & Sherick, R. B. (1983). The Hopelessness Scale for Children: Psychometric characteristics and concurrent validity. *Journal of Consulting and Clinical Psychology, 51,* 504–510.

Kendler, K. S., Neale, M. C., Heath, A. C., & Eaves, L. J. (1992). Major depression and generalized anxiety disorder: Same genes, (partly) different environments? *Archives of General Psychiatry, 49,* 716–722.

Kendler, K. S., Neale, M. C., Heath, A. C., & Eaves, L. J. (1993). A twin study of recent life events and difficulties. *Archives of General Psychiatry, 50,* 789–796.

Kessler, R. C., & Waters, E. E. (1998). Epidemiology of DSM-III-R major depression and minor depression among adolescents and young adults in the National Comorbidity Survey. *Depression and Anxiety, 7,* 3–14.

Kovacs, M. (1989). Affective disorders in children and adolescents. *American Psychologist, 44,* 201–215.

Kovacs, M. (1992). *Children's Depression Inventory (CDI).* New York: Multi-Health Systems, Inc.

Kusche, C. A., Cook, E. T., & Greenberg, M. T. (1993). Neuropsychological and cognitive functioning in children with anxiety, externalizing, and comorbid psychopathology. *Journal of Clinical Child Psychology, 22,* 172–195.

Last, C. G., Hersen, M., Kazdin, A. E., Finkelstein, R., & Strauss, C. C. (1987). Comparison of DSM-III separation anxiety and overanxious disorders: Demographic characteristics and patterns of comorbidity. *Journal of the American Academy of Child Psychiatry, 26,* 527–531.

Leech, S. L., Larkby, C. A., Day, R., & Day, N. L. (2006). Predictors and correlates of high levels of depression and anxiety symptoms among children at age 10. *Journal of the American Academy of Child and Adolescent Psychiatry, 45,* 223–230.

Lenti, C., Giacobbe, A., & Pegna, C. (2000). Recognition of emotional facial expressions in depressed children and adolescents. *Perceptual and Motor Skills, 91,* 227–236.

Lewinson, P. M., Hops, H., Roberts, R. E., Seeley, J. R., & Andrews, J. A. (1993). Adolescent psychopathology: I: Prevalence, and incidence of depression and other DSM-III-R disorders in high school students. *Journal of Abnormal Psychology, 102,* 133–144.

Loney, B. R., & Frick, P. J. (2003). Structured diagnostic interviewing. In C. R. Reynolds & R. W. Kamphaus (Eds.), *Handbook of psychological & educational assessment of children: Personality, behavior, and context* (2nd ed., pp. 235–247). New York: Guilford Press.

Luxenberg, J. S., Swedo, S. E., Flament, M. F., Friedland, R. P., Rapoport, J., & Rapoport, S. I. (1988). Neuroanatomical abnormalities in obsessive-compulsive disorders detected with quantitative X-ray computed tomography. *American Journal of Psychiatry, 145,* 1089–1093.

Lyoo, I. K., Lee, H. K., Jung, J. H., Noam, G. G., & Renshaw, P. F. (2002). White matter hyperintensities on magnetic resonance imaging of the brain in children with psychiatric disorders. *Comprehensive Psychiatry, 43*, 361–368.

Mash, E. J., & Barkley, R. A. (2006). *Treatment of childhood disorders* (3rd ed.). New York: Guilford Press.

Matthews, K. A., Manuck, S. B., & Saab, P. G. (1986). Cardiovascular responses of adolescents during a naturally occurring stressor and their behavioral and psychophysiological predictors. *Psychophysiology, 23*, 198–209.

Mayberg, H. S. (1997). Limbic-cortical dysregulation: A proposed model of depression. In S. Salloway, P. Malloy, & J. L. Cummings (Eds.), *The neuropsychiatry of limbic and subcortical disorders* (pp. 167–178). Washington, DC: American Psychiatric Press.

McClellan, J., Kowatch, R., & Findling, R. L. (2007). Work group on quality issues. Practice parameter for the assessment and treatment of children and adolescents with bipolar disorder. *Journal of the American Academy of Child & Adolescent Psychiatry, 46* (1), 107–25.

McEwen, B. S. (1998). Protective and damaging effects of stress mediators. *New England Journal of Medicine, 322*, 171–179.

Michael, K. D., & Crowley, S. L. (2002). How effective are treatments for child and adolescent depression?: A meta-analytic review. *Clinical Psychology Review, 22*, 247–269.

Mirescu, C., Peters, J. D., & Gould, E. (2004). Early life experience alters response of adult neurogenesis to stress. *Nature Neuroscience, 7* (8), 841–846.

Moffitt, T. E., Harrington, H. L., Caspi, A., Kim-Cohen, J., Goldberg, D., Gregory, A. M., et al. (2007). Depression and generalized anxiety disorder: Cumulative and sequential comorbidity in a birth cohort followed prospectively to age 32 years. *Archives of General Psychiatry, 64* (6), 651–660.

Munir, K., Biederman, J., & Knee, D. (1987). Psychiatric comorbidity in patients with attention deficit disorder: A controlled study. *Journal of the American Academy of Child and Adolescent Psychiatry, 26*, 844–848.

NIMH Bipolar Facts. (2008). www.nimh.nih.gov/health/topics/bipolar-disorder/index.shtml.

Pennington, B. F. (2002). *The development of psychopathology: Nature and nurture* . New York: Guilford Press.

Perlis, R. H., Miyahara, S., Marangell, L. B., Wisniewski, S. R., Ostacher, M., DelBello, M. P., et al. (2004). Long-term implications of early onset in bipolar disorder: Data from the first 1000 participants in the systematic treatment enhancement program for bipolar disorder (STEP-BD). *Biological Psychiatry, 55*, 875–881.

Phan, K. L., Wager, T., Taylor, S. F., & Liberzon, I. (2002). Functional neuroanatomy of emotion: A meta-analysis of emotion activation studies in PET and fMR. *Neuroimage, 16* (2), 333–348.

Pine, D. S. (2002). Brain development and the onset of mood disorders. *Seminars in Clinical Neuropsychiatry, 7* , 223–233, 57–67.

Pliszka, S. R. (2003). *Neuroscience of mental health clinicians*. New York, NY: Guilford Press.

Pliszka, S. R., Carlson, C. L., & Swanson, J. M. (1999). *ADHD with comorbid disorders* . New York, NY: Guilford Press.

Pomanski, E., Grossman, J. A., Buchsbaum, Y., Banegas, M., Freeman, L., & Gibbons, R. (1984). Preliminary studies of the reliability and validity of the children's depression rating scale. *Journal of the American Academy of Child Psychiatry, 23*, 191–197.

Quay, H. C., Peterson, D. R., Radke-Yarrow, M., Cummings, E., Kuczynski, L., & Chapman, M. (1985). Patterns of attachment in two- and three-year-olds in normal families and families with parental depression. *Child Development, 56*, 884–893.

Rachman, S. J., & Hodgson. (1991). Consequences of panic. *Journal of Cognitive Psychotherapy, 5*, 187–197.

Rapoport, J. L. (1986). Childhood obsessive compulsive disorder. *Journal of Child and Psychology and Psychiatry and Allied Disciplines, 27*, 289–295.

Recklitis, C. J., Lockwood, R. A., Rothwell,M. A., & Diller, L. R. (2006). Suicidal ideation and attempts in adult survivors of childhood cancer. *Journal of Clinical Oncology, 24*, 3852–3857.

Reinherz, Gianconia, Hauf, Wasserman, & Paradis, 2000

Reynolds, C. R., & Kamphaus, R. W. (2004). *Behavior assessment system for children second edition*. Circle Pines, MN: American Guidance Service.

Reynolds, C. R., & Richmond, B. O. (1978). What I think and feel: A revised measure of children's manifest anxiety. *Journal of Abnormal Child Psychology, 6*, 27 1–280.

Reynolds, W. M. (1989). *Reynolds child depression scale*. Odessa, FL: Psychological Assessment Resources.

Ronsaville, D. S., Municchi, G., Laney, C., Cizza, G., Meyer, S. E., Haim, A., et al. (2006). Maternal and environmental factors influence the hypothalamic-pituitary-adrenal axis response to corticotropin-releasing hormone infusion in offspring of mothers with or without mood disorders.*Development and Psychopathology, 18*, 173–194.

Rosenbaum, J. F. (1988). Course and treatment of manic depressive illness. *Journal of Clinical Psychiatr, 49*, Supplement.

Rosso, I. M., Cintron, C. M., Steingard, R. J., Renshaw, P. F., Young, A. D., & Yurgelun-Todd, D. A. (2005). Amygdala and hippocampus volumes in pediatric major depression. *Biological Psychiatry, 57*, 21–26.

Rush, A. J., Trivedi, M. H., Wisniewski, S. R., Nierenberg, A., Stewart, J. W., Warden, D., et al. (2006). Acute and longer-term outcomes in depressed outpatients who required one or several treatment steps: A STAR.D Report. *American Journal of Psychiatry, 163* (11), 1905–17.

Satcher, D. (1999). Mental health: A report of the surgeon general. http://www.mentalhealth.org/special/surgeongeneralreport.

Semrud-Clikeman, M., Bennett, L., & Guli, L. (2003). Assessment of childhood depression. In C. R. Reynolds & R. W. Kamphaus (Eds.), *Handbook of psychological and educational assessment of children: Personality, behavior, and context* (2nd ed., 259–290). New York: Guilford Press.

Semrud-Clikeman, M., & Hynd, G. W. (1991). Review of issues and measures in childhood depression. *School Psychology International, 12*, 275–298.

Shaffer, D., Gould, M. S., Fisher, P., Trautment, P., Moreau, D., Kleinman, M., et al. (1996). Psychiatric diagnosis in child and adolescent suicide. *Archives of General Psychiatry, 53*, 339–348.

Shea, A., Walsh, C., MacMillan, H., & Steiner, M. (2004). Child maltreatment and HPA axis dysregulation: Relationship to major depressive disorder and post traumatic stress disorder in females. *Psychoneuroendocrinology, 30*, 162–178.

Shear, K., Jin, R., Ruscio, A. M., Walters, E. E., & Kessler, R. C. (2006). Prevalence and correlates of estimated DSM-IV child and adult separation anxiety disorder in the National Comorbidity Survey Replication. *American Journal of Psychiatry, 163*, 1074–1083.

Silberg, J. L., Rutter, M., & Eaves, L. (2001). Genetic and environmental influences on the temporal association between earlier anxiety and later depression in girls. *Biological Psychiatry, 49* (12), 1040–1049.

Silberg, J., Pickles, A., Rutter, M., Hewitt, J., Simonoff, E., Maes, H., et al. (1999).The influence of genetic factors and life stress on depression among adolescent girls. *Archives of General Psychiatry, 56*, 225–232.

Silver, L. B. (1988). The scope of the problem in children and adolescents. In J. G. Looney (Ed.), *Chronic mental illness in children and adolescents* (pp. 39–51). Washington, DC: American Psychiatric Press.

Simon, G. E., Savarino, J. Operskalski, B., & Wang, P. (2006). Suicide risk during antidepressant treatment. *American Journal of Psychiatry, 163* (1), 41–47.

Spence, S. H., Rapee, R., McDonald, C., & Ingram, M. (2001). The structure of anxiety symptoms among preschoolers. *Behaviour Research and Therapy, 39*, 1293–1316.

Spencer, T., Wilens, T., Biederman, J., Wozniak, J., & Harding-Crawford, M. (2000). Attention-deficit/hyperactivity disorder with mood disorders. In T. E. Brown (Ed.), *Attention deficit hyperactivity disorders and comorbidities in children, adolescents, and adults* (pp. 79–124). Washington, DC: American Psychiatric Press.

Stark, K. D., Snader, J., Hauser, M., Simpson, J., Schnoebelen, S., Glenn, R., et al. (2006). Depressive disorders during childhood and adolescence. In E. J. Mash & R. A. Barkley (Eds.), *Treatment of childhood disorders* (3rd ed., pp. 336–410). New York: Guilford Press.

Steingard, R. J. (2000). The neuroscience of depression in adolescence. *Journal of Affective Disorders, 61*, 15–21.

Steingard, R., Biederman, J., Doyle, A., & Sprich Buckminster, I. (1992). Psychiatric comorbidity in attention deficit disorder: Impact on the interpretation of child behavior checklist results. *Journal of American Academy of Child and Adolescent Psychiatry, 31*, 449–454.

Steingard, R., Renshaw, P., Yurgelun-Todd, D., Appelmans, K., Lyoo, I. K., Shorrock, K., et al. (1996). Structural abnormalities in brain magnetic resonance images of depressed children. *Journal of the American Academy of Child & Adolescent Psychiatry, 35* (3), 307–311.

Strauss, C. C. (1990). Anxiety disorders of childhood and adolescence. *School Psychology Review, 19*, 142–157.

Strauss, C. S. (1991). Anxiety disorders of childhood and adolescence. *School Psychology Review, 19*, 142–157.

Strauss, C. C., Frame, C. L., & Forehand, R. L. (1987). Psychosocial impairment associated with anxiety in children. *Journal of Clinical Child Psychology, 1*, 235–439.

Strauss, C. C., Last, C. G., Hersen, M., & Kazdin, A. (1988). Association between anxiety and depression in children and adolescents with anxiety disorders. *Journal of Abnormal Child Psychology, 15*, 57–68.

Sullivan, P. F., Neale, M. C., & Kendler, K. S. (2000). Genetic epidemiology of major depression: review and meta-analysis. *American Journal of Psychiatry, 157*, 1552–1562.

Teeter Ellison, P. A., Eckert, L., Nelson, A., Platten, P., Semrud-Clikeman, M., & Kamphaus, R. W. (2009). Assessment of behavior and personality in the neuropsychological diagnosis of children. In C. R. Reynolds & Fletcher-Jensen, E. (Eds.), *Handbook of clinical child neuropsychology* (2nd ed.). New York: Plenum Press.

Teeter Ellison, P. A., & Nelson, A. (2008). Brain development: Evidence of gender differences. In E. Fletcher-Janzen (Ed.), *Introduction to the neuropsychology of women* . New York: Springer

Templer, D. I. (1972). The obsessive-compulsive neurosis: Review of research findings. *Comprehensive Psychiatry, 13*, 375–383.

Torgesen, J. K. (1986). Genetic factors in moderately severe and mild affective disorders. *Archives of General Psychiatry, 43*, 222–226.

Tramontana, M., & Hooper, S. (1989). Neuropsychology of child psychopathology. In C. R. Reynolds & E. Fletcher-Janzen (Eds.), *Handbook of clinical child neuropsychology* (pp. 87–106). New York: Plenum Press.

Treatment for Adolescents with Depression Study Team. (2004). Fluoxetine, cognitive-behavioral therapy, and their combination for adolescents with depression: Treatment for Adolescents with Depression Study (TADS) randomized trial. *JAMA, 292*, 807–820.

Valla, J., Bergerson, L., & Smolla, N. (2000). The dominic-R: A pictorial interview for 6- to 11- year old children. *Journal of the American Academy of Child and Adolescent Psychiatry, 39*, 85–93.

Venken, T., Claes, S., Sluijs, S., Paterson, A. D., van Duijn, C., Adolfsson, R., et al. (2005). Genomewide scan for affective disorder susceptibility loci in families of a northern Swedish isolated population. *American Journal of Human Genetics, 76*, 237–248.

Weaver, I. C., Cervoni, N., Champagne, F. A., D'Alessio, A. C., Sharma, S., Seckl, J. R., et al. (2004). Epigenetic programming of maternal behavior. *Nature Neuroscience, 7* (8), 847–854.

Weingartner, H., Gold, P., Ballenger, J. D., Smallberg, S. A., Summers, R., Rubinow, D. R. (1981). Effects of vasopressin on human memory functions. *Science, 211*, 601–603.

Weissman, M. M., Pilowsky, D. J., Wickramaratne, P. J., Talati, A., Wisniewski, S. R., Fava, M., et al. (2006). Remission in maternal depression and child psychopathology: A STAR*D-Child report. *JAMA, 295*, 1389–1398.

Weissman, M. M., Wolk, S., Goldstein, R. B., Moreau, D., Adams, P., Greenwald, S., et al. (1999). Depressed adolescents grown up. *Journal of the American Medical Association, 281*, 1707–1713.

Zisook, S., Lesser, I., Stewart, J. W., Wisniewski, S. R., Balasubramani, G. K., Fava, M., et al. (2007). Effect of age at onset on the course of major depressive disorder. *American Journal of Psychiatry 164*, 1539–1546.

Chapter 11
Autistic Spectrum Disorders

Research in Autistic Spectrum Disorders (ASD) has greatly increased within the past decade. DSM IV TR (APA, 2000) has grouped autism, Rett's disorder, Asperger's Disorder (AS), and childhood disintegrative disorder under the umbrella term, Pervasive Developmental Disorder (PDD). PDD-NOS (not otherwise specified) is a term and diagnosis with no specific criteria which is often used when a child does not meet full criteria for either diagnosis and is generally used when the child shows some, but not all of the symptoms of either AS or autism.

The main hallmark of these disorders is a severe impairment across situations in social interaction skills as well as significant problems with communication or stereotyped behaviors, interests, and activities. PDD may also be seen with medical and chromosomal abnormalities and has been particularly associated with tuberous sclerosis. Common comorbid diagnoses with ASD are seizures (Volkmar, Klin, & Pauls, 1998), Tourette's syndrome (Baron-Cohen, Scahill, Izaguirre, Hornsey, & Robertson, 1999), ADHD (Ghaziuddin, 2002), anxiety, and mood disorders (Kim, Szatmari, Bryson, Streiner, & Wilson, 2000). Case histories suggest that some children with autism spectrum disorders (ASD) were socially unresponsive from early infancy (Dahlgren, Ehlers, Hagberg, & Gillberg, 2000) while others report the onset of symptoms sometime after the second year of life (Volkmar, Lord, Bailey, Schultz, & Klin, 2004).

Social interaction difficulties such as poor eye contact and difficulty understanding nonverbal communication and social reciprocity are the hallmarks for the diagnosis of autistic spectrum disorder (Semrud-Clikeman, 2007). Delays are often found in spoken and receptive language, pragmatic language, the presence of stereotyped and echolalic speech. A narrow pattern of interests and behavior is frequently present, coupled with repetitive behaviors and preoccupation with objects and items.

Incidence and Prevalence

The overall prevalence of the Autistic Spectrum Disorders (ASD) is approximately 26.1 per 10,000 (Fombonne, 2001) with estimates of prevalence for ASD of 12.7 cases per 10,000 (Fombonne, 2003b). The incidence of ASD appears to be increasing due, in part, to improved diagnostic measures and the tendency for children with autism to be eligible for more services through the public schools than those with mental retardation. It is not uncommon for neuropsychologists, school psychologists and clinical psychologists to be pressured into making a diagnosis of autism to receive these additional services. Children with autism are generally identified earlier compared to diagnoses of PDD or AS, approximately by the age of 30.0 months of age, compared to 37.2 for PDD-NOS and AS.

Epidemiological data reports indicate that the incidence of AS is approximately 8.4 per 10,000 children (Chakrabarti & Fombonne, 2001), while Rett's disorder and Childhood Disintegrative Disorder have lower rates (<1 per 10,000 and 1 per 50,000, respectively). The prevalence of PDD-NOS is more problematic to estimate due to the difficulty

M. Semrud-Clikeman, P.A. Teeter Ellison, *Child Neuropsychology*, DOI 10.1007/978-0-387-88963-4_11,
© Springer Science+Business Media, LLC 2009

with the diagnostic criteria. It has been estimated from an epidemiological stay at 36.1 cases per 10,000 (Chakrabarti & Fombonne, 2001).

Racial and ethnic differences have not been substantiated for the diagnosis of ASD or between social class and ASD (Dyches, Wilder, & Obiakor, 2001; Fombonne, 2003a). More males are identified with autism than girls with the ratios approaching 2:1 (Fombonne, 2003b). There appears to be a difference based on cognitive ability with average or higher ability being related to a higher incidence of ASD in males. When the ability level is in the mentally handicapped range, the ratios approach each other (Volkmar et al., 2004). It has been suggested that boys may be at higher risk for autism while girls require more neurological compromise for autism to be confirmed.

Neuropsychological Aspects of ASD

Asperger Disorder and High Functioning Autism

A more recent conceptualization of autism is that impairments in social reciprocity, communication, and stereotyped behaviors lie on a severity continuum ranging from severely autistic to those individuals classified as high functioning (HFA) (Barrett, Prior, & Manjiviona, 2004; Prior & Ozonoff, 1998). Children with ASD have difficulties with planning, cognitive flexibility, working memory, and verbal fluency, with few differences between HFA and AS found on these measures (Klin, Saulnier, Tsatsanis, & Volkmar, 2005; Klin, Sparrow, Cicchetti, & Rourke, 1995; Miller & Ozonoff, 2000; Ozonoff & Griffith, 2000; Verte et al., 2006).

Presently, the differentiation between AS and children who are classified with HFA is not clear given the overlap in the areas of social reciprocity, communication, and perspective taking found in both disorders (Gillberg, 1999; Macintosh & Dissanayake, 2004). Some neuropsychological differences have been identified between HFA and AS. Strengths on visual-spatial tasks and perceptual reasoning have been found in HFA with weaknesses in obtaining knowledge that requires inferential

thinking (Ehlers et al., 1997). In contrast, the children with AS exhibit the opposite pattern. Further analysis found that these differences were due to higher overall cognitive ability and language skills in the children with AS compared to those with HFA.

Others have found that children with HFA show a higher performance IQ than verbal IQ, with the opposite present for children with AS (Klin et al., 1995). This finding continues to be of interest, but has not been replicated with larger groups of children. Similarly, executive function and social-cognitive abilities were not found to discriminate between HFA and AS (Manjiviona & Prior, 1999; Miller & Ozonoff, 2000). Some behavioral differences do appear to be present. Children with AS have fewer stereotyped behaviors, but more abnormal preoccupations than children with HFA (Kugler, 1998; McLaughlin-Cheng, 1998). Others have suggested that HFA and AS are part of the same disorder, but may differ in severity.

Social Understanding

Children with ASD generally have difficulty with social reciprocity, likely related to challenges in social information processing. The encoding of these social-emotional cues includes processing of nonverbal cues such as facial expressions, gestures, and voice intonation. Nonverbal, novel stimuli are generally processed in the right hemisphere in typically developing children and in adults, while the lexical aspects of language are processed in the left hemisphere. Children with ASD frequently utilize language to process social information and, thus, may use left hemispheric pathways more than children without ASD. Such processing generally requires longer latencies and is not as efficient.

Ashwin, Wheelwright, and Baron-Cohen (2006) studied latency to Stroop-like pictures of emotional faces in adults with AS and controls. Findings indicated that response latencies to angry faces were the longest, followed by response to neutral faces, and fastest for looking at an object (a chair). The control group showed the longest latency for the angry faces while the AS group showed no difference between angry and neutral faces. As predicted, the controls showed more attention to faces that could be considered threatening while the ASD group showed longer latencies to all faces versus the object. These differences may be related to difficulties in encoding any face in participants with ASD, and suggest a threat vulnerability to facial expressions of any type (Schultz, Gauthier et al., 2000).

Ashwin, Wheelwright et al. (2006) suggest that any face may produce anxiety for participants with ASD and that these participants are actually biased toward attempting to decode facial expressions. Thus, it may be that these latency differences are due to perceptual decoding difficulties as well as an innate problem for understanding facial expressions. Williams, Goldstein, and Minshew (2005) studied adults with HFA on measures of auditory and visual memory. Compared to the control sample, deficits were found for memory of faces and the social scenes compared to the controls. These findings implicate difficulty in the area of recalling faces and social scenes that may interfere with social performance in more naturalistic settings.

Children with ASD may have difficulty understanding emotions from standardized facial expressions such as anger, fear, happiness, and sadness when matched to same-aged peers (Castelli, 2005b). Some have hypothesized that these differences are due partially to difficulties with social interaction in children with ASD while others suggest that a visual perceptual deficit contributes to this problem (Behrman, Thomas, & Humphreys, 2006). For some children simple identification may be related to low ability. When children with ASD are matched to peers at the same developmental language level, these differences disappear (Ozonoff, Pennington, & Rogers, 1990), except for young children (Klin et al., 1999).

Castelli (2005) studied children with HFA and found they were as able as control children to identify static pictures of complex and simple emotions. This study differs from other studies because it included only HFA and AS children rather than the full range of abilities that was utilized in earlier studies. It is possible that children with HFA and AS have developed compensatory techniques to identify emotions based on intensive intervention generally provided in early and middle childhood.

Support for this hypothesis comes from an event-related potential study evaluating face processing in children aged 3–4 years prior to having experienced significant amounts of intervention pointed toward emotional identification. In that study slower brain responses to faces and higher activation to objects were found for children with ASD, compared to children who were typically developing and those who were developmentally delayed but not autistic (Webb, Dawson, Bernier, & Panagiotides, 2006). There was a preference for objects over faces implicating both perceptual differences and, possibly, motivation to process social interactions. For this reason it is important to control for ability level as well as age level when studying the ability of a child with ASD to recognize facial expression from pictures.

It has also been hypothesized that children with ASD may prefer fragmented and detail-oriented processing of visual material which interferes with processing of the whole picture; this is also referred to as weak central coherence (Happe & Frith, 2006). Thus, the difficulty present in emotion identification in faces may be due to problems with paying attention to the whole rather than the parts (Mann & Walker, 2003). In support of this hypothesis Baron-Cohen, Wheelwright, and Jolliffe (1997) found that adults with ASD have a problem recognizing feelings when shown the eye region, as compared to the whole face, as well as in understanding more complex emotions such as interest or surprise. These complex emotions require more processing as well as perspective taking as they are related to a metacognitive understanding of why the person may feel what he/she is feeling compared to simple identification ("she's happy"). It may be that the child with ASD is centered on details rather than the whole.

Similarly, Grossman, Klin, Carter, and Volkmar (2000) found that when the label conflicted with the pictured emotion, children with ASD used the verbal label rather than the nonverbal information to define the emotion depicted. Again, the emphasis was on details rather than generalizing or understanding the whole of the nonverbal information presented. Castelli (2005) suggests that these difficulties may be related to executive functioning deficits as well as in perspective taking.

Thus, these studies are of interest to understand facial recognition, but do not provide information about how the child performs in a more naturalistic setting which is, by definition, more fluid and dynamic. While there may not be consistent difficulties for children with ASD in facial identification in a controlled clinical environment, these difficulties are likely to present when the child is faced with a threatening experience or when the facial expressions change quickly as happens in everyday social interactions.

Rett's Disorder/Childhood Disintegrative Disorder

Rett's disorder and childhood disintegrative disorder are included under the PDD umbrella. Rett's disorder is a neurodegenerative disorder and seems out of place in the ASD category. Some have suggested that it is grouped within ASD as a place marker (Volkmar et al., 2004). Rett's disorder is found only in girls and is usually not identified until the child is at least five-months-old (frequently later), but generally before the age of three (Swaiman & Dyken, 1999). Initially the child appears to have difficult with hand control and becomes less interested in observing or interacting with others. Neurological examinations, with MRI confirmation, generally find that the head stops growing due to a lack of brain growth. The child appears to lose language and show significant cognitive decline (Ozonoff & Rogers, 2003). With age the child begins to wring his/her hands, and to clap or rub his/her hands together. In addition, the cognitive decline continues. It is believed that Rett's syndrome is a mutation of the X chromosome (Kerr, 2002).

Childhood Disintegrative Disorder

Childhood disintegrative disorder (CDD) is a rare condition. The child shows a pattern of regression after normal development. It is present in both genders, but more commonly seen in males. In this disorder the regression occurs without warning, is quite severe, and can occur anywhere between the ages of two and 10. Prior to this time the child's development appears normal. The child's ability and adaptive behaviors decrease significantly and communication and social interaction become nonexistent. This process lasts approximately 1–2

months with the child becoming very agitated and difficult to control. After this period the child appears to have severe autism and mental retardation. Unfortunately, there is little improvement with treatment and the condition is irreversible. The cause of this disorder is not presently clear, but it is believed to be genetic (Ozonoff & Rogers, 2003).

Pervasive Developmental Disorders-Not Otherwise Specified (PDD-NOS)

PDD-NOS is very difficult to reliably diagnose and is frequently a fallback diagnosis when the criteria for AS or autism is not met. For the most part, a diagnosis of PDD-NOS indicates that two of the three symptom clusters that identify children with ASD or AS have been met (Ozonoff & Rogers, 2003). These clusters are the social responsiveness cluster, communication skill difficulty, and stereotyped or repetitive behaviors. The diagnosis of PDD-NOS requires that the child have difficulty with social reciprocity and either social communication problems or stereotyped/repetitive behaviors. The incidence of mental retardation is much lower than in autism and is generally around 7.3 percent of the PDD-NOS population (Chakrabarti & Fombonne, 2001). Most children with a diagnosis of PDD-NOS show some autistic-like symptoms, but do not qualify for a diagnosis of autism, or have a language delay and so do not qualify for a diagnosis of AS.

The DSM IV field trials found that the diagnosis of PDD-NOS is one of the more unreliable diagnostic categories (Volkmar et al., 1994). In the field trials one-third of the children diagnosed with PDD-NOS met criteria for autism, while another one-third did not qualify for any diagnosis in the autistic spectrum. The children who did not qualify were generally found to have language and learning problems or had significant symptoms of ADHD.

Developmental Course of Autistic Spectrum Disorders

For most children with ASD onset occurs prior to age three, particularly for those children with a more severe presentation of the disorder. As discussed earlier a sizable majority does not show the disorder until after the age of two, particularly when diagnosed with AS or PDD-NOS. Retrospectively the children who are diagnosed later are reported to show irregularities and delays in development from infancy until diagnosis. Generally these problems are related to difficulty with nonverbal communication, inappropriate responses to facial expressions, and a lack of social responsiveness to caretakers. Approximately one-third of children with autism show regression of skills between the ages of 1–2 years, and some have hypothesized that this regression is due to infections and immunological factors (Hornig & Lipkin, 2001) or to genetic influences (Lainhart et al., 2002).

Qualitative differences are present in the expression of some symptoms at different ages. Stereotyped and repetitive behaviors are most commonly seen in preschool and either improve or significantly decline in elementary school (Semrud-Clikeman, 2007). For children receiving early intervention, it is estimated that 50 percent approach normal functioning by adolescence (McEachin, Smith, & Lovass, 1993). Although improvement is noted, most of these adolescents continue to have difficulty with social interaction and few are able to establish an independent lifestyle in adulthood (Howlin, 2000). The most predictive variable for a positive outcome is the level of intelligence present by the age of five (Howlin, 2000).

Prenatal and Postnatal Factors

An increase in the incidence of prenatal and perinatal complications in autistic individuals compared to normal children has been found (Meyer et al., 2008). Some of the more frequent complications are meconium in the amniotic fluid, bleeding during pregnancy, and use of doctor-prescribed hormones (National Institute of Mental Health, 2006). In a study of mice and their offspring, Meyer et al. (2008) found that prenatal events predispose the child to autism or schizophrenia more so than postnatal events.

Seven studies that met stringent criteria for selection were reviewed to evaluate prenatal and perinatal risk factors for autism (Kolevzon, Gross, &

Reichenberg, 2008). Selected studies needed to have a well-defined sample standardized and data collected during and after pregnancy, a group of comparison subjects who also experienced obstetric complications without resulting autism, and a standardized report of the findings to allow comparisons across studies. Characteristics that were selected were those associated with a 50 percent increase or larger in risk. Factors that emerged for parental characteristics included advanced maternal age, advanced paternal age, and maternal birthplace. Of the seven studies, three showed maternal age to be a significant predictor for autism when confounding variables were covaried. Paternal age has also been identified as a risk factor with a twofold risk found for each 10-year increase in paternal age (Reichenberg et al., 2006).

Other factor that emerged included birth weight and prematurity as well as hypoxia at birth. Low birth weight (defined as less than 2,500 g) was not associated with an increased risk of autism. Four studies reported prematurity with a birth at less than 35 weeks to be at higher risk for autism in two studies. Apgar scores below seven were also associated with autism in all four studies that examined this variable. The authors concluded that hypoxia-related complications appeared to increase the risk of autism. They also concluded that low birth weight and prematurity were not strongly tied to a heightened risk for autism and that further study is needed to more carefully examine these issues (Kolevzon et al., 2008).

Autism and Vaccines

An additional issue that has arisen in the past decade is the relationship between autism and vaccines that contain thimerosal. The media has reported a possible link between autism and these vaccines. The empirical support for such a link is tenuous at best. Thimerosol was removed from vaccines, except for trace amounts, by 2001. The Immunization Safety Review Committee of the Institute of Medicine from the National Academies reviewed the data about thimerosal and autism and did not find a causal relationship (Immunization Safety Review Committee: Board on Health Promotion and Disease Prevention, 2004). Studies that have evaluated the incidence of autism since thimerosal's removal from the vaccines have not found a drop in the incidence of the disorder (Fombonne, 2008; Schechter & Grether, 2008).

Studies that evaluated early thimerosal exposure and neuropsychological functioning in mid-childhood have been conducted in children without autism (Thompson, Price, Goodson, & Shay, 2007). One-thousand-forty-seven children were enrolled in the study and administered several neuropsychological measures. The study did not find a causal association between early exposure to thimerosal and neuropsychological deficits. Thus, the findings, taken as a whole, do not support a link between thimerosal and autism.

Genetics

The heritability of autism is supported by two important findings: (1) the rate of autism in siblings of autistic individuals is approximately 50 times that of the general population (Bailey, Pelferman, & Heavey, 1998), and (2) there is a high concordance rate of autism in monozygotic twins compared to dyzygotic twins (Ozonoff & Rogers, 2003). Recent advances in genetic analysis have found that autism recurs in families at an approximate rate of 3–6 percent, which is higher than the rate found in the general population (Bailey, Le Couteur, & Gottesman, 1995). Twin studies have found that monozygotic twins have a concordance rate for a diagnosis of autism of 60 percent, while the rate was 5 percent for dyzygotic pairs (Bailey et al., 1995). When all types of PDD were included the concordance rate increased to 90 percent for monozygotic pairs, yielding a heritability estimate greater than 0.90 (LeCouteur et al., 1996). In studies that have evaluated familial risk factors in autism, these families have a higher rate of psychiatric and developmental illnesses compared to the general population. In addition, these families also show a higher incidence of medical disorders leading one to suggest that the genetic structures in these families leaves the members vulnerable to many types of disorders (Brimacombe, Ming, & Parikh, 2007)

Ozonoff and Rogers (2003) further point out that autism frequently co-occurs with other chromosomal abnormalities including tuberous sclerosis,

fragile X syndrome and in deletion syndromes including chromosomes 7, 15, and 18 (Semrud-Clikeman & Schaefer, 2000). Fragile X syndrome is a commonly inherited cause of mental retardation that is transmitted by the mother's contribution to the sex chromosomes. Approximately 2–8 percent of boys with autism and Fragile X syndrome are also mentally retarded (Reiss & Hall, 2007; Wassnik, Piven, & Vieland, 2001).

Tuberous Sclerosis (TS) is a genetic disorder where tubers or lesions are present throughout the body, particularly in the brain. Approximately 2–4 percent of children with autism have TS (Hansen & Hagerman, 2003). Although the majority of children with TS are not diagnosed with autism, approximately 43–61 percent show autistic symptoms with a higher than expected percentage showing brain lesions in the temporal lobe, an area of the brain particularly involved in language and emotion recognition (Gillberg & Billstedt, 2000). A possible link between ASD and TS was evaluated in a PET study. Patients with TS, both with and without autism, showed a higher metabolic rate in areas of the brain associated with impaired social interactions, language problems, and stereotyped behaviors (Asano, Chugani, & Muzik, 2001). These are the areas that are specifically problematic for children with ASD.

Neurological Features

Neurodevelopmental anomalies have been identified in children with autism, particularly in the frontal lobes with neural circuits differing as well as frontal lobe enlargement and atypical patterns of brain connectivity (Courchesne, Carper, & Akshoomoff, 2003; Courchesne & Pierce, 2005; Hill, 2004; Murphy et al., 2002). Although the exact etiology of autism is still unknown, results from electrophysiological and dichotic listening techniques suggest that autistic children may not show the expected pattern of hemispheric specialization. Research has documented that normally the two hemispheres are functionally and structurally asymmetric at birth (Gazzaniga, Ivry, & Mangun, 2002). Autistic children do not show such hemispheric specialization and may show less functional asymmetry as evidenced by dichotic listening techniques as well as through electroencephalograms (Coben, Clarke, Hudspeth, & Barry, 2008).

Data from electrophysiological studies indicate that children with autism tended to either have dominant right-hemisphere response to linguistic stimuli with impairment in the left hemisphere or did not show a dominant language hemisphere (Tanguay, 2000). When EEG recordings are made during completion of cognitive tasks, a reversed pattern of brain activity during language tasks and use of the right hand (normally left-hemispheric-mediated tasks) has been found (Dawson, Finley, Phillips, & Galpert, 1986). Moreover, children with autism have been found to show differences when told not to attend to stimuli compared to typically developing children. These differences indicate that children with autism may process auditory signals (i.e., words and sounds) differently than those without autism and that this difference leads to difficulty in processing of information (Dunn, Gomes, & Gravel, 2008).

As you will recall from Chapter 3, the P300 component has been associated with the detection of novel and unpredictable stimuli. In individuals with autism this component has an extended latency; that is, it occurs later than expected and the amplitude (degree of response) is smaller (Dawson et al., 1986). Additional work in this area has led researchers to hypothesize that the foregoing results may be due to the possibility that autistic children react to novel stimuli as aversive and/or as overstimulating (Dawson et al., 2005). Moreover, there is emerging evidence that autistic individuals may be chronically over-aroused (Wolf, Fein, & Akshoomoff, 2007).

It may well be that the connectivity of the brain in children with autism interferes with the crucial aspects of language processing that are so important for social interactions. Differences in the ability to process emotional and non-emotional words as well as possible perceptual difficulty likely interfere with the autistic child's ability to understand the social and general world. Atypical patterns of brain connectivity have indicated an underconnectivity for both inter- and intrahemispheric neuronal signals (Rippon, Brock, Brown, & Boucher, 2007). This underconnectivity has been associated with problems with social cognition (Barnea-Gorly

et al., 2004), frontal lobe connectivity (Belmonte et al., 2004), and facial processing (Dawson & Webb, 2005).

Neuroimaging

Neuroimaging techniques have made it possible to view the developing brain while the child completes various tasks. Thus, the ability to compare brain activity among groups as well as for different tasks allows us to understand some of the differences that are present that may account for problems in reasoning, social interaction, and with executive functioning. One of the more common techniques used to study children and adolescents with autistic spectrum disorders is functional magnetic resonance imaging (fMRI).

Because the behaviors associated with autism vary from social reciprocity/understanding to language, to stereotyped and repetitive behaviors, it is likely that many brain systems are involved and will vary depending on the severity of the autistic symptoms as well as the level of cognitive involvement. Children with autism tend to have larger heads than the general population (Aylward, Minshew, Field, Sparks, & Singh, 2002). Brains of autistic toddlers have measured 10 percent larger than same-aged peers; the largeness of the head decreases with age, but continues to be larger than matched aged peers throughout life (Courchesne et al., 2003). Interestingly, there is no difference in head size at birth (Lainhart, 1997) and the brain growth that later occurs may be due to early overgrowth of neurons, glial cells, and a lack of synaptic pruning (Courchesne & Pierce, 2005). Findings have suggested that this increased brain size indicates that the extra tissue is not well utilized or organized, thus resulting in poorer skill development (Aylward et al., 2002). Specific findings indicate an increase in gray matter volume, particularly in the temporal lobes (Herbert et al., 2002; Rojas et al., 2004). Autopsy studies have found that the cellular columns that make up the frontal and temporal gray matter areas were disrupted, possibly resulting in an inability to inhibit neuronal activity in these areas and, thus, produce cognitive dysfunction and possibly behavioral overflow (Casanova, Buxhoeven, & Brown, 2002; Casanova, Buxhoeven, Switala, & Roy, 2002).

Using structural MRI analyses, Courchesne et al. (2001) found smaller measures of white matter compared to gray matter in toddlers and adolescents. Other studies of adults with autism have found reduced measures of the corpus callosum (Hardan, Minshew, & Keshavan, 2000), a structure that connects the two hemispheres, as well as difficulties with interregional integration. Some have suggested that the larger brain, higher white matter volume, and disrupted gray matter cellular columns may contribute to an autistic person's difficulty in integrating information and generalizing this information to new situations (Schultz, Romanski, & Tsatsanis, 2000). These difficulties may interfere with the person's ability to put information together into an understandable whole—or interfere with establishing central coherence—a theory discussed in an earlier chapter.

Schultz et al. (2003) suggested that the social brain incorporates frontal, limbic, and temporal connectivity and that these regions are integral to socialization. In children with ASD, findings have included hypoactivation in the areas of the superior temporal gyrus (STG), the fusiform face gyrus of the temporal lobe (FG), and regions of the temporal and occipital lobes. These areas are the hypothesized regions for social understanding and comprehension. Schultz et al. (2003) suggest that this hypoactivation is not causative of autism, but rather may be an outcome of autism–less practice may mean less growth in this region.

The amygdala has also been implicated in autism (Adolphs, 2001; Baron-Cohen et al., 2000; Sparks et al., 2002). Patients with damage to the amygdala experience difficulties with some aspects of social impairment including lack of emotional response and problems in recognizing fearful stimuli (Zirlinger & Anderson, 2003). Postmortem analysis of autistic brains have found increased neuronal density in the amygdala in people with autism (Kemper & Bauman, 1993). When the amygdala has been ablated in rhesus monkeys and neonatal rats, social behaviors are poorly developed, particularly if the damage occurred before birth (Baron-Cohen et al., 2000; Wolterink et al., 2001). The amygdala has extensive connections to the cortex, the striatum,

and the hippocampus (Amaral, Price, Pitkanan, & Carmichael, 1992). This connectivity may influence perception as well as perspective taking abilities. If there is a reduction in the functional connectivity for social processing, then there should be differences in these regions on fMRI as well as on Diffusion Tensor Imaging (DTI), a procedure that examines white matter tracts.

MRI Findings in ASD

Structural imaging in ASD has found a variety of cerebral anomalies. Some findings indicate differences in the corpus callosum, particularly in thinning and in the midsagittal area and in white matter density in persons with ASD (Chung, Dalton, Alexander, & Davidson, 2004; Hardan et al., 2000; Vidal et al., 2006). These differences have been linked to difficulties with language processing and in working memory (Just, Cherkassky, Keller, & Minshew, 2004). Structural imaging findings have found increased brain size in children with ASD, specifically enlargement in the regions of the parietal, temporal, and occipital lobes (Courchesne et al., 2003; Piven, Arndt, Bailey, & Andreasen, 1996). The enlargement is due to greater volumes of white matter, but not gray (Filipek, 1999). For adolescents and adults with autism, increased brain size was not found, but increased head circumference was identified (Aylward et al., 2002).

Findings have also implicated the caudate in children with ASD. Sears et al. (1999) found increased volume bilaterally in the caudate of adolescents and young adults with HFA. Caudate enlargement was proportional to the increased total brain volumes also identified. To determine whether these findings were specific to the sample studied, the results were replicated with a different sample of participants with ASD. Previous studies have found that the caudate volume in typically developing children decreases at puberty (Giedd, 2004). For the Sears et al. (1999) study this decrease did not occur.

In typically developing adults, right-sided activation has been found for the FG, the STG, and the amygdala when viewing social faces (Schultz et al., 2003) and social interaction (Semrud-Clikeman,

Fine, & Zhu, submitted). These findings seem to corroborate the hypothesis that the right hemisphere is more heavily involved in social processing than the left (Winner, Brownell, Happe, Blum, & Pincus, 1998). Studies of adults with HFA or AS have found differences in these regions using structural and functional imaging that found less activation or smaller volumes (Abell et al., 1999; Baron-Cohen, Ring et al., 1999).

Some studies have found underactivation in the prefrontal areas in participants with ASD (Schultz et al., 2000) with higher activation in controls particularly in the left prefrontal regions. Significant metabolic reduction has been found in the anterior cingulate gyrus, an area important for error monitoring, and in the frontostriatal networks involved in visuospatial processing (Ohnishi et al., 2000; Silk et al., 2006). The amygdala and striatal regions have been implicated in processing of emotional facial expressions (Canli, Sivers, Whitfield, Gotlib, & Gabrieli, 2002; Killgore & Yurgelun-Todd, 2005; Yang et al., 2002).

Studies involving the amygdala have found that patients with bilateral lesions show difficulty in judging emotional facial expressions (Bechara, Damasio, & Damasio, 2003). Faces that were negative in nature were found to produce slower activation than those which were neutral in controls (Monk et al., 2003; Simpson, Öngür, Akbudak, Conturo, & Ollinger, 2000). Positive stimuli increased activity in the amygdala with happy expressions, resulting in faster response times (Canli et al., 2002; Pessoa, Kastner, & Ungerleider, 2002; Somerville, Kim, Johnstone, Alexander, & Whalen, 2004). Hare, Tottenham, Davidson, Glover, and Casey (2005) found longer latencies for negative facial expressions in activation of the amygdala in normal adult controls, while activation of the caudate was present when the participant was avoiding positive information.

These findings are important because they point to the neural networks that underlie the processing of positive and negative emotions. It is crucial to determine how emotional cues may influence behavior that interferes with this processing which is frequently seen in children and adults with ASD. Similarly, Ashwin, Baron-Cohen, Wheelwright, O'Riordan, and Bullmore (2006) studied the amygdala in adults with HFA and AS using fMRI when

viewing fearful (high and low fear) and neutral faces. Findings indicated that the control sample showed more activation in the left amygdala and left orbitofrontal regions compared to the HFA/AS group when viewing the fearful faces. In contrast, the HFA/AS group showed more activation in the anterior cingulate and the superior temporal cortex when viewing all of the faces.

Specific areas implicated in ASD using fMRI include the superior temporal gyrus (STG) (Allison, Puce, & McCarthy, 2000; Baron-Cohen, Ring et al., 1999) and the amygdala (Amaral et al., 1992; Carmichael & Price, 1995). When a child with ASD is asked to view faces, functional imaging has found less activation in the right fusiform face gyrus (FG) (Critchley et al., 2000; Dierks, Bolte, Hubl, Lanfermann, & Poustka, 2004; Pierce, Muller, Ambrose, Allen, & Courchesne, 2001). The fusiform face gyrus appears to be selectively engaged when the person views faces. Children with ASD appear to pay less attention to the face and may not activate this region in the same manner as typically developing children (Schultz et al., 2003).

Differences in activation have not been found solely for viewing of faces. Just et al. (2004) found more cortical activation in children with HFA when processing verbal material compared to a control group. This finding may indicate that more brain resources are needed to process verbal information in children with ASD. This inefficiency may slow down their processing and take resources away from understanding the intent of the speaker's prosody or interpreting facial expressions. Kana, Keller, Cherkassky, Minshew, and Just (2006) found that children with HFA show poorly synchronized neural connectivity when asked to process material using their imagination. Moreover, children with ASD were also found to use parietal and occipital regions associated with imagery for tasks that had low imagery as well as high imagery requirements. Controls only utilized these regions for the high imagery tasks.

The difference in activation that ASD participants have when viewing faces is important for our understanding of ASD. Animal studies have found that the temporal cortex responds to the perceptual aspects of social stimuli (Hasselmo, Rolls, & Baylis, 1989; Perrett & Mistlin, 1990). Human studies have also found a relationship between the perception of eyes and mouths in the superior temporal cortex

(Adolphs, 2001; Haxby, Hoffman, & Gobbini, 2000). The superior temporal lobe is thought to be involved in perceiving social stimuli with the connections to the amygdala and frontal lobes to interpret these stimuli. Findings from participants with ASD have repeatedly shown that these areas are important for the processing of facial expressions. An area of the temporal lobe that is important for recognizing faces has been studied in children with autism. This area is underactive in people with autism, and the degree of underactivation is highly correlated with the degree of social impairment (Schultz et al., 2001). Additionally, this area of the temporal lobe has also been implicated in successfully solving Theory of Mind tasks, skills that are also impaired in people with autism (Castelli, 2005a; Martin & Weisberg, 2003).

Few studies have used DTI in children with ASD. Alexander et al. (2007) used DTI with children with ASD and found reduced volumes in the corpus callosum and reduced fractional anisotropy (FA) of the genu, splenium, and total corpus callosum in children with ASD. Medication status and the presence of comorbid diagnoses were not found to have an effect on the DTI measures. In a similar vein to these findings, Boger-Megiddo et al. (2006) scanned young children with ASD and found that the corpus callosum area was disproportionately small compared to total brain volume for these children, compared to typically developing children. Children with a more severe form of ASD showed the smallest corpus callosal area. Future research needs to utilize quantitative imaging to more fully capture the relation between the corpus callosum connectivity and ASD. Taken together these findings suggest that children with ASD may be inefficient in their use of neural networks and that their networks show poor connectivity compared to same-aged peers.

The amygdala, anterior cingulate, and hippocampus have also been studied in children with ASD. These two structures are part of the limbic system of the brain—or the emotional part of the brain. The amygdala is important in emotional arousal as well as processing social information. The hippocampus allows for the short-term and eventual long-term storage of information while the anterior cingulate works as a type of central executive directing attention where it is most

required. Abnormalities have been found in these parts of the brain during autopsy with reduced size and fewer connections present (Kemper & Bauman, 1993). These abnormalities may contribute to the behavioral difficulties seen in people with autism in social reciprocity and social awareness. Further study is needed in these areas. Some have suggested that the amygdala may be important for mediating physiological arousal and, if it is not as active, the person may not be as motivated to participate in social activities (Dawson, Meltzoff, Osterling, & Rinaldi, 1998; Klin & Volkmar, 2003).

Areas of the frontal lobes have also been studied in patients with autism. Both the frontal lobes and the superior area of the temporal lobes are important for understanding and perceiving social interactions as well as interpreting facial expressions. The frontal lobes have been particularly implicated in the ability to take another's perspective, or in social cognition. These areas are intimately connected to the limbic system as well as the temporal lobe areas discussed earlier in this section. Studies of brain metabolism have found reduced activity in these regions of the brain in autistic patients, particularly when individuals are asked to perform tasks that tap social cognition and perception (Castelli et al., 2002; Ehlers et al., 1997; Haznedar et al., 2000).

The neuroimaging findings are intriguing and suggest that there are significant differences structurally as well as in neural connectivity of cognitive systems. These differences likely result in neuropsychological challenges for these children as well as for the neuropsychologist. The following section discusses the neuropsychological factors involved in autism.

Neuropsychological Aspects in Diagnosis

The cognitive ability of children within the ASD umbrella varies widely, ranging from significant mental retardation to giftedness. There is no pattern of strengths and abilities within the cognitive measures, although some have found a pattern of performance IQ being stronger than verbal IQ (Akshoomoff, 2005). Some have suggested that children with autism show a VIQ < PIQ profile, and children with AS show the opposite pattern (Klin et al., 1995), while others have not replicated this finding. Instead, children with AS have higher verbal scores compared to those with HFA, but not performance ability (Ghaziuddin & Mountain-Kimchi, 2004). Ability is generally found to be higher in HFA children with some suggesting the neuropsychological differences between AS and HFA are due to ability and not true neuropsychological variation (Miller & Ozonoff, 2000).

A comprehensive neuropsychological evaluation of a child suspected of having an ASD needs to include a measure of communication ability including both receptive and expressive language skills (Kjelgaard & Tager-Flusberg, 2001). Consistent with the discussion presented in earlier sections, children with autism also have difficulty with executive functioning, particularly in cognitive flexibility and working memory (Lord et al., 2006). The difficulties in executive functioning have been equivocal with some studies which have identified problems in these areas (Kleinhans, Akshoomoff, & Delis, 2005; Ozonoff & Jensen, 1999), while others have not (Griffith, Pennington, Wehner, & Rogers, 1999; Liss et al., 2001). Further evaluation of the differences among these studies is that some were with young children who may not evidence executive functioning deficits on standardized measures until a later age (Semrud-Clikeman & Schaefer, 2000), while others did not match the groups on ability (Wolf et al., 2007). These areas require additional study with groups matched by ability as well as evaluating the effect of age on the performance of the child on standardized measures of executive functioning. It is certainly appropriate for an evaluation to include measures of executive functioning as well as problem solving skills. These skills have been tied to the ability to adapt to changing environments; an area of difficulty for many children with ASD.

As discussed earlier in this chapter, many children with ASD have difficulty discerning the whole from the parts. Tests such as block design or copying of figures (VMI, Rey-Osterreith Complex figure) may be particularly difficult for them. It is important to evaluate these skills for the individual. Memory skills is another area that requires evaluation in children with ASD. Verbal memory and spatial memory skills have been reported as an

area of difficulty (Lord et al., 2006; Luna et al., 2002; Toichi & Kamio, 1998) while visual memory skills for designs have been relatively intact. Working memory skills may also be an area of weakness for children with ASD and appear to be very dependent on the context and nature of the skills required (Ozonoff & Strayer, 2001).

Attention is a variable area in the population of children with ASD. Few studies have evaluated the co-occurrence of ADHD and ASD partly due to the exclusion of ADHD in the diagnostic criteria for AS. However, Ghaziuddin, Weidmer-Mikhail, & Ghaziuddin (1998) found a high co-occurrence of ADHD in a sample of children with AS followed by a higher than expected incidence of depression. A significant number of attentional symptoms were found in approximately 33 percent–50 percent of the ASD population in this study. In contrast, the co-occurrence of ASD and hyperactivity/impulsivity symptoms is less (approximately 7–10%). Other studies have found that children diagnosed with HFA and AS appear to share similar attentional difficulties with ADHD children (Ehlers et al., 1997; Nyden, Gillberg, Hjelmquist, & Heiman, 1999).

Leyfer et al. (2006) examined 109 children with autism for comorbid diagnoses. Phobias were the most common co-occurring disorder, followed by obsessive- compulsive disorder and ADHD. Of the 109 children in the sample, 20 percent qualified for a diagnosis of ADHD: predominately inattentive (ADHD:PI). When cases that were one symptom short of diagnosis were included, the rate increased to 55 percent. It is not clear from this study how many of the children with co-occurring ASD and ADHD also had other diagnoses. Studies have found that 40 percent of children aged 3–5, and 50 percent of those aged 6–12 referred to a clinic with ASD showed some form of ADHD (Gadow, DeVincent, & Pomeroy, 2006; Gadow, DeVincent, Pomeroy, & Azizian, 2005). Findings also indicated that these rates of ADHD in children with ASD were similar to children without ASD who were also referred for a clinical evaluation.

One of the concerns about the comorbidity of ADHD and ASD is whether the attentional and hyperactive/impulsive symptoms are part of the ASD diagnosis or are reflective of the ASD diagnosis. Gadow et al. (2006) sought to study DSM IV psychiatric symptoms in children with ASD who referred to a clinic using parent and teacher rating scales. Findings indicated that 20 percent of the younger children qualified for a diagnosis of ADHD:PI, and 12 percent for ADHD:C along with a diagnosis of ASD. For the older group 36 percent qualified for a diagnosis of ADHD:PI and 20 percent for ADHD:C, as well as a diagnosis of ASD. Importantly, there were no differences in severity between the groups of children with ASD and those with a sole diagnosis of ADHD, suggesting that the expression of significant attentional difficulties is similar in the two populations. Gadow et al. (2006) conclude that DSM IV should be considered a blueprint for diagnosing ADHD in this population and not as a firm standard given the dearth of studies with this population. In addition, these findings also lend support to the hypothesis that ADHD co-occurs with ASD and is not just part of the ASD diagnosis. The existing studies used parent and teacher rating scales to determine the existence of ADHD.

Given the hypothesis that children with ASD may have attentional differences, it is important to rule out significant attentional problems for these children. ADHD may interact with ASD and stretch the already depleted attentional resources to the limit. These children's ability to understand social interactions may be further compounded by difficulties with response inhibition as well as with impulse control. These concerns about the comorbidity of ASD and ADHD raise the question about previously equivocal findings of executive functioning in children with ASD. It may be that attentional issues were not controlled in these studies, thus confounding the findings.

As discussed in Chapter 6, many of the neuropsychological measures for memory, attention, and language are presented and are appropriate for use with children with ASD depending on the child's ability level and age. The following section discusses particular instruments that have been developed for children with autism. Most of these measures are parent interview and behavior rating scales. The findings discussed above indicate that there is no current "pattern" of functioning for a child with ASD and, thus, a comprehensive evaluation needs to include measures from the various domains as well as the interviews discussed below.

Diagnostic Instruments

Diagnosing ASD has been somewhat problematic, but the advent of fairly well-standardized measures has improved our ability to reliably diagnose children with ASD. Three diagnostic instruments are considered to be reliable for diagnosis (Wolf et al., 2007): the Childhood Autism Rating Scale (CARS) (Schopler & Reichler, 2004), Autism Diagnostic Observation System (ADOS) (Lord, Rutter, DiLavore, & Risi, 1999), and Autism Diagnostic Interview-Revised (ADI-R) (Rutter, Le Couteur, & Lord, 2003).

Although many children with autism have been diagnosed with mental retardation, there are more children now diagnosed in the average to above average range with autism partly due to improved diagnostic skills as well as in our understanding of the disorder's scope (Volkmar et al., 2004). Previously these children were not diagnosed because they were able to adapt somewhat to the situation at hand or their parents had arranged for early and intense interventions. During the past several years, studies have found that less than half of children with autism now qualify for an additional diagnosis of mental retardation when adequately evaluated (Chakrabarti & Fombonne, 2001, 2005; Howlin, 2000; Tsatsania, 2003).

Psychopharmacological Treatment

Psychopharmacological treatment for ASD has increased by approximately 50 percent in the past 15 years (Aman, Lam, & Van Bourgondein, 2005). Antidepressant medication is the most commonly prescribed medication in children with ASD, followed by psychostimulants and antihypertensive drugs (Aman et al., 2005). Medication to reduce anxiety and compulsive behaviors includes anticonvulsants, stimulants, neuroleptics, fluoxetine and clomipramine, fenfluramine, and most recently opiate antagonists (Wilens, 2004). These medications may assist with obsessions and compulsions as well as anxiety and irritability. Fenfluramine, a serotonin reducer, has had a good effects on early autistic symptoms, but this response diminishes with time and an increasing the dosage has been only moderately helpful (Erickson, Stigler, Posey, & McDougle, 2007). Another type of psychopharmacological intervention is the use of opiate receptor antagonists such as naloxone or naltreione. Opiate receptor antagonists do not allow the postsynaptic receptors to absorb the brain endorphins. Beginning evidence shows that low doses of this agent have reduced many maladaptive behaviors including self-injurious behavior (Benjamin, Seek, Tresise, Price, & Gagnon, 1995), while high doses improve the child's ability to relate to others (Feldman, Kolman, & Gonzaga, 1999).

Atypical antipsychotics have also been studied in children with ASD. These medications, such as haloperidol, have been found to improve symptoms in ASD as well as attentional difficulties, but have also increased dyskinesias and so are used sparingly due to this serious side effect (Barnard, Young, Pearson, Geddes, & O'Brien, 2002; Remington, Sloman, Konstantareas, Parker, & Gow, 2001). Risperidone has also been utilized for children with ASD to control difficult behavior. While the medication has been very helpful in reducing behavioral difficulties in children with ASD (Hanft & Hendren, 2004), side effects such as decreased appetite, weight gain, fatigue, and drooling may counterindicate the use of this medication (Findling et al., 2004; Stigler, Posey, & McDougle, 2004).

Attentional problems are also seen frequently with autistic spectrum disorders. While not diagnosed in the presence of such a disorder, the difficulty they cause for the child is often treated through medication. Approximately 60 percent of children with ASD exhibit attentional problems, and 40 percent of these also have hyperactivity (Hazell, 2007). Improvement in activity level and attention has been found for a majority of children with ASD with attention/hyperactivity symptoms following administration of methylphenidate (Handen, Johnson, & Lubetsky, 2000; Research Units on Pediatric Psychopharmacology Autistic Disorder Network, 2005), but not for dexamphetamine (Handen et al., 2000).

Behavioral Treatments

The treatment options available for autistic children has grown, but no one solution has been found to be appropriate for all children with autism. Areas that require intervention include the domains of language, attention, social cognitive, cognition, learning, and adaptive behavior. These areas require multifaceted treatment that includes working with families, schools, and individuals in order to improve functioning as well as develop skills (Iovannone, Dunlap, Huber, & Kincaid, 2003). There has been an explosion in literature in the area of autism and many of the clinicians and researchers suggest that, based on the literature, no single approach is appropriate for all children with autism. Therefore, programs needs to be tailored to the individual child's needs (National Research Council, 2001). It has been strongly suggested that a combination of approaches be used to support the child's acquisition of basic skills and allow the child to develop more complex social skills and social reciprocity (Volkmar et al., 2004).

Behavioral treatment has by far the most support for interventions for children with autism, although improvement has not been as good as previously was predicted from initial studies (Mudford, Martin, Eikeseth, & Bibby, 2001; Smith, Buch, & Gamby, 2000; Smith, Groen, & Wynn, 2000). Although behavioral treatment improved targeted behaviors, the children required continual support to maintain these gains and cognitive skills did not improve (Bibby, Eikeseth, Martin, Mudford, & Reeves, 2001). Parent satisfaction has been generally good with applied behavior analysis techniques as well as other behavioral treatments, and the maintenance and increase in gains have not been significant when the children are followed 2–3 years later (Volkmar et al., 2004).

One important finding is that to be successful, the child needs to be motivated to participate in the program and that the program needs to be tailored to the specific family's needs (Lord & McGee, 2001; Moes, 1998). Teaching individual skills such as joint attention and social communication skills has led to improved social skills (Drew et al., 2002; Whalen & Schreibman, 2002). However, these skills are often not generalized to the natural setting without directly teaching those skills in that setting (Hwang & Hughes, 2000; Strain & Hoyson, 2000).

A review of 10 studies on the efficacy of communication intervention found that teaching social communication was most successful when it was

262 Autistic Spectrum Disorders

directly related to everyday situations and possible communications to which the child would be exposed (Delprato, 2001). When the communication skills are tied to an interest of the child's (i.e., weather, dinosaurs), language skills improvement is dramatic and appears to be present in long-lasting follow-up evaluations (Siller & Sigman, 2002).

Similar to the findings for language, Gutstein & Whitney (2002) suggest that interventions need to include specific occasions for the child to learn social skills that are apart from the traditionally scripted approaches most commonly seen with social skills programs. Tasks that directly teach appropriate social interaction as well as perspective taking, and are guided by adults, have been most appropriate. These authors suggest that the initial interventions need to be ritualistic and predictable with inconsistency and novelty kept to a minimum. As the child learns these skills, more complexity and novelty is introduced, assisting the child with generalization. The intervention needs to be in a quiet and distraction-free environment where the child feels safe. It is important to restrict the sensory input so that the child does not become overwhelmed. Actions, emotions, intonations, and gestures need to be overdone and amplified so that the child learns what is important. Emotions and environmental input that are subtle may be too difficult for the child to process and will most likely be ignored. Finally the adult coaches need to move the child to a peer coach as readiness is perceived. Using these techniques can assist the child in developing the abilities that are needed, but more importantly to generalize the skills to the more dynamic nature seen in most social exchanges.

Due to the difficult nature of intervention studies, most empirical evidence comes from case studies or small groups. Further study is needed to determine the parameters for the success of many of these interventions, and to move much of the work into public schools. Corbett (2003) has developed a video modeling intervention based on Bandura's social learning theory. Video modeling emphasizes the ability to learn new behaviors by observing a model engaging in a behavior the child would like to emulate. Video modeling involves the child watching a videotape of a desirable model producing a behavior. The behavior is then imitated and practiced with a therapist. The behaviors are repeated and reinforced over time.

Corbett (2003) studied the efficacy of video modeling on social skill acquisition using a single case study design. The child was eight-years, three-months-old and was diagnosed with autism. His IQ was measured at 60 with adaptive behavior being significantly lower at 37. The child watched the videotape showing expressions denoting happy, sad, angry, or afraid. The videotape was shown for 10–15 minutes daily for two weeks. The child quickly mastered identification of the happy face with improvement seen in the other categories over the treatment duration. Certainly this study shows promise and replication, and follow-up of the length of these gains is needed.

Social stories have also been used fairly successfully with ASD children. This method describes a social situation to the child and explains what the child should do and what the appropriate feelings should be. The child is asked for his or her interpretation. Gray & Garand (1993) use four types of sentences for the social stories. The descriptive sentence describes where the situation is occurring and who the main character is. The perspective sentences describe the reactions of others and the feelings that the characters have. The directive sentences provide information about what the child is expected to do or say. Finally, the control sentence is generally written by the child to solve the situation. Most stories have 0–1 control and/or directive sentences for every 2–5 descriptive and perspective sentences. For those children who cannot read the stories can be read to them and discussed as the therapist reads the story.

An example of a social story would be the following:

> John rides the school bus to school every day (descriptive). He sits in the front seat next to the bus driver (descriptive). The ride takes about 20 minutes to get to John's school (descriptive). He knows that he can ask the bus driver for help if he needs it (perspective). John also knows that he can't always have the same seat on the bus if someone gets on before him (perspective). He can ask the other child if he can sit on the seat (descriptive). He is afraid to ask the child to move over (perspective). John asks the child and sits next to her (perspective). Buses have large seats (control). His mother will be proud that he solved his problem (perspective).

Social stories can help the child solve a current problem or resolve an issue that is troublesome to him/her. They can also be tailored to fit the child's particular interests to keep the story relevant to him/her. As with other interventions, this appears promising, but empirical support has not been developed at this time.

Conclusion

The etiology, effective psychopharmacological treatments, and productive educational interventions for autism are currently being developed and researched. Much is unknown about this disorder, but gains are being made in our understanding. It is likely that a transactional approach, utilizing neurological and neuropsychological knowledge of this disorder in conjunction with work in the child's two major environments, namely home and school, will be most effective. Evidence of an exquisite sensitivity to environmental stimulation has led to a new understanding of the autistic child's behavior and language skills. Effective pharmacological treatment continues to elude practitioners, and additional work is needed in that regard. Researchers are beginning to develop programs across the life span for individuals with autism, and promising vocationally based programs have been started for adolescents and adults.

The following case study is an example of a complex scenario that is often referred to a neuropsychologist. The school has repeatedly attempted an evaluation, but the school personnel do not have the requisite knowledge to structure an evaluation. This case was selected to illustrate the difficulties that may be present when evaluating a significantly compromised child, and the need to pursue serial evaluations in order to obtain the most comprehensive and useful assessment of the child's abilities.

A Child with Severe Expressive Aphasia and Motor Apraxia with Pervasive Developmental Delay

This case illustrates the complexity of diagnosing children with severe expressive aphasia with motor apraxia and pervasive developmental delays at an early age. It demonstrates the need for collaboration between neuropsychologists and public school staff

so that neuropsychological findings can be integrated into the classroom. Initial contact with the child came at the family's request to verify previous evaluations and diagnoses conducted at a different clinic. A comprehensive neuropsychological evaluation was conducted to determine the child's neuropsychological, academic, cognitive and social-emotional functioning, and to develop an appropriate intervention program. Serial evaluation results were presented at the school's multidisciplinary team meetings.

Teddy

First and Second Evaluations

Information gathered from the first (age 5 1/2 years) and second (age 7 1/2 years) evaluations was based on observational methods because Teddy was unable to respond adequately to verbal or nonverbal test items. A number of methods were attempted during the first and second evaluations, including items from the Stanford-Binet, the NEPSY II, the Wechsler Scales, the Reitan-Indiana Battery, the French Pictorial Test of Intelligence, and the Leiter International Scales. Severe motor apraxia affected his ability to complete nonverbal measures, and his severe expressive language deficits interfered with verbal measures. On several subtests of the Leiter Scales, however, Teddy showed near average abilities at the age of five and one-half years.

Teddy was enrolled in a preschool program for children with significant developmental delays. He was transferred to a regular elementary school in first grade and received special education services. Speech-language, occupational, and physical therapy were the major interventions in the special education program at the public school. Although he was taught sign language, which he readily picked up, articulating vowels and consonant-vowel combinations was the major focus of speech therapy over a four-year period.

At the time of the last evaluation, the therapy goal was to attain expressive language to the five-year-level. After four years of speech therapy, Teddy had not reached his milestone. Teddy was mainstreamed for part of the day for socialization, but received services for learning disabilities

55 percent to 60 percent of the day, 12 percent to 15 percent of which were for speech. Although he learned to read, Teddy appeared hyperlexic as his rate and speed of reading outpaced his reading comprehension skills.

Despite two years of extensive physical therapy and a full-time aide who helped Teddy trace, cut paper, and draw lines and letters, he was unable to print his name, cut with scissors, or draw simple figures. While he did not approach age-appropriate levels for fine motor skills, Teddy did learn to use a computer and was able to type (one–two finger technique) on the keyboard. Gross motor skills were also delayed, but were not as significantly affected.

Attempts to increase his socialization skills showed some progress in that Teddy became more responsive to others. Although he was encouraged to use a combination of speech and sign language for communication, Teddy remained isolated despite attempts to increase socialization with normal and handicapped peers.

Recommendations at the end of the second evaluation urged the school to make a transition into computer technology so that Teddy could make better progress with communication and academic skills.

Third Evaluation

The third evaluation was conducted when Teddy was 9 years –3 months of age, and in the third grade. This was the first evaluation where Teddy was able to complete subtests on standardized assessment measures. During individual testing sessions, Teddy was able to work for periods up to about 45 minutes long. Teddy's attention span was best when activities required reading or when pictures were used to elicit a response. Teddy was able to indicate when he did not know an answer, and occasionally it appeared that he simply said he didn't know when the answer required a complex verbal response. His expressive language was difficult to understand, and Teddy became frustrated when the examiner could not understand what he was saying. He always repeated his answer, but as the session progressed this was obviously frustrating for him. When speaking, Teddy tried hard to enunciate individual letter sounds, especially the T and C sounds. On numerous occasions, he used the proper speech inflection and rhythm, but it was difficult to

determine if his verbal responses were correct. Because of severe limitations in responding, formal evaluations may underestimate Teddy's actual level of academic and cognitive development. Portions of the Tests of Cognitive Ability from the Woodcock-Johnson Psychoeducational Test Battery (WJIII) were administered in an attempt to determine Teddy's cognitive potential. The following scores were taken from age-based norms and must be analyzed with caution because of Teddy's severe expressive language delays secondary to motor apraxia.

Measure	Standard score	Percentile
Memory for Names	109	73
Memory for Names (delayed)	105	63
Memory for Words	89	17
Picture vocabulary	86	16
Visual Closure	79	8

Teddy's most outstanding strengths were revealed on tests of associational learning and long-term retrieval. Specifically, Teddy was able to learn associations between unfamiliar auditory and visual stimuli, and scores on the subtest reached the average to high average range of ability. He was able to remember these auditory-visual associations after a four-day delay, and his scores fell within the average range compared to same-age peers. Further, his associational learning was much better when pictures were used instead of more abstract visual stimuli, like rebus figures.

On another measure of short-term memory, Teddy scored within the average range of ability as he was able to recall a series of unrelated words in the proper order. Teddy also showed at least average potential on a task measuring comprehension-knowledge or crystallized intelligence (standard score = 86). When asked to name familiar and unfamiliar pictured objects Teddy identified "waterfall," "grasshopper," "magnet," and "theater." While Teddy scored within the average range on this subtest, several of his verbal responses were unintelligible. Thus, his academic potential may be higher than can be measured at this time.

Teddy had more difficulty on tasks that required visual processing when objects were distorted or superimposed on other patterns. He also had trouble on a test where he had to remember a series of objects when similar or "distractor" pictures were included (standard score = 73). While this test is a measure of visual processing, Teddy often did not study the pictures for the full five-second interval before the distractors were presented, so his lack of interest in or attention to this task reduced his score. Subtest scores on the Stanford Binet Intelligence Scale-Fifth Edition revealed similar patterns as did the WJ III Cognitive subtests. Teddy scored above age level on terms where short-term memory for objects was required, and had difficulty on items requiring complex verbal or motor responses.

Educational Implications

Academically, Teddy appears to show improvement in the areas of reading recognition and comprehension. On standardized measures, Teddy identified words such as *special, straight, powder*, and *couple*. While he was able to read sentences, he made errors when responding to questions. For example, he clapped five times instead of two and identified his "eyebrow" instead of his elbow. At other times it was impossible to understand his verbal responses; as a result, Teddy's reading comprehension may be slightly higher than reported. He also showed slightly higher comprehension scores on the Woodcock Reading Mastery Test than on the K-ABC II test. According to his teacher, Teddy is reading and understanding vocabulary slightly above grade level and is reading from a fourth-grade book at school.

Test	Standard score	Percentile
WJ III		
Letter-Word ID	93	18
Reading Comprehension	79	8
Mathematics Calculation	60	1
Mathematics Reasoning	Unable to complete	

Teddy's math skills are less well developed than his reading abilities. While math skills are emerging, this area is a weakness for Teddy (below the 1.0 grade level). Teddy was able to identify numbers and to determine if there were "just as many" puppets and people in different pictures. However, he could not complete simple addition or subtraction, and he was unable to identify the "third" position in a line. Visual-perceptual deficits appear to be having an impact on his ability to develop math skills.

Spelling skills were not formerly measured because severe apraxia interferes with Teddy's printing skills. However, Teddy can spell some words with his Touch Talker that he is unable to write. For example he was able to type the words *to* and *be*. At this point he spontaneously remarked, "To be or not to be. Shakespeare." He obviously associated this phrase with something he had learned at home, and he was able to further associate it in the testing session. Severe motor apraxia severely limits Teddy's written expressive skills, and he remains virtually a non-writer because of his motor limitations.

Classroom Observations

Because standardized assessment tools may be underestimating Teddy's academic progress, a school-based observation was conducted. Teddy seemed aware of the routine and reacted appropriately to directions for small group activities. In large open classroom settings, Teddy was less adaptable, showing more distractibility and off-task behaviors. He was unable to complete worksheets without the help of a teacher's aide, who helped Teddy print the answers on his paper. When working in pairs, Teddy attempted to answer the questions his partner read aloud to him and was more successful when questions were not too complex. Teddy was able to answer 21 percent (3 out of 14) of the questions read to him and guessed at others. He was unable to print any answers on his worksheet, although his aide traced all the answers with him. In less structured story time, Teddy sat on the floor with the rest of his class and showed appropriate behaviors.

Generally, Teddy's behaviors were not distinguishable from those of his peers during story time. He did, however, move close to his teacher and sit up on his knees to see the pictures of the book better. When his classmates signaled for him to sit down, he complied. On several occasions Teddy rested his elbows on his teacher's lap, and he seemed comfortable to be close to her during story time. He smiled spontaneously, and he seemed very attentive throughout this session, which was 25 minutes long.

In speech therapy Teddy was careful when articulating and appeared highly motivated and spontaneous in his interaction with the speech therapist. His articulation of individual sounds was clear, distinct, and at a more normal pace. He played the message on the Touch Talker, and he seemed genuinely spontaneous and interested in interacting. Teddy was able to introduce the neuropsychologist to his teacher when prompted. He practiced muscle control in front of the mirror, and he used the proper hand and finger cues to remind himself where his tongue belonged when reproducing individual sounds. His speech production of individual sounds was about 80 percent intelligible, while his production of c-v-c combinations and words were about 25 percent to 30 percent intelligible. He produced the K sound at the beginning and end of words, he read out of a "book" he created about Mickey Mouse, and he played a Mickey Mouse game.

Teddy showed some signs of anxiety during the speech therapy session that was not present at any other time during the day. Teddy repeatedly stomped his feet, clapped his hands, and laughed out loud. He would stop for a short time when his teacher told him to, but he would continue to act out when frustrated. Despite these problems, Teddy was more intelligible, happy, interactive, and spontaneous during speech therapy then at any other time during the day.

Teddy showed appropriate lunchtime behaviors. He turned in his lunch ticket by himself, carried his tray with some assistance from his aide, ate quietly, and cleaned up by himself. He used his utensils correctly and opened his milk carton on his own. He sat next to his homeroom "buddy" and smiled, but did not communicate further with him. During recess another child gave Teddy a "high five" and he responded appropriately. Other than this 5- or 10-second interchange, Teddy did not interact with anyone else. When left by himself, he walked up and down a square of asphalt. His aide told him to play on the equipment, and he methodically walked over to each piece and climbed up a ladder and over two arches. Before climbing over the ladder, Teddy

walked around a square area for seven minutes waiting for two children to leave. Once they left, he climbed the ladder once and then left.

Although he went through the motions of play, Teddy did not appear enthusiastic or involved. In the afternoon sessions, Teddy worked on a worksheet counting the number of units of 10 and units of one. He was able to count the units by himself, but his aide had to trace the numbers on the worksheet with him. When he played a game of Addition Bingo, the aide helped him count problems like 7 + 3, 1 + 1, 3 + 0, 4 + 5, 3 + 4, 2 + 3, and 5 + 1. Teddy was not independent on any of these problems, but he was able to count out loud when the aide pointed to the edge of each number. No other concrete objects were used during this lesson.

In language arts, Teddy did one computer reading lesson in which he had to read a short passage and answer questions. He was able to turn the computer on, type his first and last name, and select the correct sequence to start the lesson. His accuracy rate was about 75 percent for the comprehension questions following a story about dinosaurs.

In a small group reading lesson with his LD teacher and one other student, Teddy read and answered questions in a fourth-grade book. His intelligibility continues to be a problem, but his teacher appears to understand his responses. His inflections and rhythm follow the sentence structure, which suggests that he is processing written material. He was able to answer questions showing that he understood the difference between fiction and nonfiction, and he was able to answer questions such as "Which animal is extinct?", "Why was the place terrible?", and "Where did the bugs go?" His teacher also reported that his recognition vocabulary is at the level of the fourth-grade reading book, and his comprehension skills are improving.

Developmental Progress

There have been remarkable gains in several areas since Teddy's initial evaluation. First, the most apparent developmental progress is in the area of behavior and classroom adjustment. Teddy seems to be very much aware of classroom expectations, although he is not always able to respond to everything requested of him, especially writing on worksheets. He is able to walk to his different classes without getting lost, make transitions with relative ease, and sit in his seat and attend to lessons for longer periods of time.

Second, Teddy appears to initiate interactions with teachers and several peers at a rate higher than previously observed. Although Teddy is still isolated because of his communication difficulties, he spontaneously interacts and seeks to communicate more often. Third, Teddy seems more tuned into and aware of his surroundings. He responds more appropriately to the directions of his teachers and he redirects quickly when reminded. Fourth, Teddy spends less time daydreaming and staring off. Although he still has a tendency to watch others, he is more attentive to his lessons and to his teachers. Fifth, Teddy has made remarkable academic gains, especially in reading and in reading comprehension. Math continues to be a weakness.

Sixth, Teddy's expressive skills are improving. His sound repertoire is larger than before and his intelligibility is much better. Teddy is also using speech to communicate. Seventh, Teddy has learned to use the Touch Talker to communicate. This involves sequential associative learning whereby icons and words or sentences are combined to communicate. Finally, Teddy shows more independence for everyday activities, such as going to the bathroom and eating lunch. Gains are apparent in speech production and Teddy is communicating with a higher frequency than previously noted. His articulation has improved, although he still has a tendency to speak quickly, which reduces his intelligibility.

Teddy also appears more mature, and his classroom behaviors are more age- appropriate. Although he still is not fully integrated into his surroundings because of his developmental problems, Teddy responds more appropriately to classroom rules, is more attentive, and is more independent for everyday self-help skills at school. Although Teddy remains isolated from his peers, he is more spontaneous than ever and he initiates interactions more frequently. He spontaneously interacts with his teachers more often, and he smiles and laughs appropriately. Although he remains delayed in overall social interaction skills, his progress over the last year has been substantial.

Specific Recommendations

1. The school staff was encouraged to focus on functional communication skills with an integrated speech-language program rather than primarily a therapy-articulation focus.
2. Augmented speech technology should be incorporated throughout Teddy's academic lessons. At this time, the Touch Talker is used as a secondary rather than primary method for inputting and outputting communication. This should be reversed.
3. The educational environment and expectations should be modified to include computer technology for written and reading lessons. Computer technologies are only intermittently used at present. Again, this should be shifted, with the majority of assignments produced on the computer. Efforts to encourage Teddy in social interactions with peers were recommended. Social skills training may be initiated to teach appropriate communication and joining-in skills. Teddy should be reinforced for social interactions and should be assigned a "buddy" for portions of the day during recess or lunchtime. Other cooperative learning experiences should also be incorporated into daily lessons. Socialization should be closely monitored and reassessed periodically to determine whether goals and recommendations are realistic.

References

Abell, F., Krams, M., Ashburner, J., Passingham, R., Friston, K., Frackowiak, R., et al. (1999). The neuroanatomy of autism: A voxel-based whole brain analysis of structural scans. *Cognitive Neuroscience, 10*(8), 1647–1651.

Adolphs, R. (2001). The neurobiology of social cognition. *Current Opinion in Neurobiology Cognitive Neuroscience, 11*(2), 231–239.

Akshoomoff, N. (2005). The neuropsychology of autistic spectrum disorder. *Developmental Neuropsychology, 27*, 307–310.

Alexander, A. L., Lee, J. E., Lazar, M., Boudos, R., Dubray, M. B., Oakes, T. R., et al. (2007). Diffusion tensor imaging of the corpus callosum in Autism. *Neuroimage, 34*(1), 61–73.

Allison, T., Puce, A., & McCarthy, G. (2000). Social perception from visual cues: Role of the STS region. *Trends in Cognitive Sciences, 4*(7), 1364–1366.

Aman, M. G., Lam, K. S., & Van Bourgondein, M. E. (2005). Medication patterns in patients with autistic disorder: Temporal, regional and demographic influences. *Journal of Child and Adolescent Psychopharmacology, 15*, 116–126.

Amaral, D. G., Price, J. L., Pitkanan, A., & Carmichael, S. T. (1992). Anatomical organization of the primate amygdaloid complex. In J. Aggleton (Ed.), *The amygdala: Neurobiological aspects of emotion, memory and mental dysfunction.* New York: Wiley.

American Psychiatric Association (2000). *Diagnostic and statistical manual of mental disorders* (Fourth Text Rev. ed.). Washington, DC: American Psychiatric Association.

Asano, E., Chugani, D. C., & Muzik, O. (2001). Autism in tuberous sclerosis complex is related to both cortical and subcortical dysfunction. *Neurology, 57*, 1269–1277.

Ashwin, C., Baron-Cohen, S., Wheelwright, S., O'Riordan, M., & Bullmore, E. T. (2006). Differential activation of the amygdala and the 'social brain' during fearful face-processing in Asperger Syndrome. *Neuropsychologia, 45*(1), 2–14.

Ashwin, C., Wheelwright, S., & Baron-Cohen, S. (2006). Attention bias to faces in asperger syndrome: A pictorial emotion Stroop study. *Psychological Medicine*, 835–843.

Aylward, E. H., Minshew, N. J., Field, K., Sparks, B. F., & Singh, N. (2002). Effects of age on brain volume and head circumference in autism. *Neurology*, 175–183.

Bailey, A., Le Couteur, A., & Gottesman, I. (1995). Autism as a strongly genetic disorder. Evidence from a British twin study. *Psychological Medicine, 25*, 63–77.

Bailey, A., Pelferman, S., & Heavey, L. (1998). Autism: The phenotype in relatives. *Journal of Autism and Developmental Disorders, 28*, 369–392.

Barnard, L., Young, A. H., Pearson, J., Geddes, J., & O'Brien, G. (2002). A systematic review of the use of atypical antipsychotics in autistic disorder. *Journal of Psychopharmacology, 14*, 233–241.

Barnea-Gorly, N., Kwon, H., Menon, V., Eliez, S., Lotspeich, L., & Reiss, A. L. (2004). White matter structure in autism: Preliminary evidence from diffusion tensor imaging. *Biological Psychiatry, 55*, 323–326.

Baron-Cohen, S., Ring, H. A., Bullmore, E. T., Wheelwright, S., Ashwin, C., & Williams, S. C. R. (2000). The amygdala theory of autism. *Neuroscience & Biobehavioral Reviews, 24*(3), 355–364.

Baron-Cohen, S., Ring, H. A., Wheelwright, S., Bullmore, E. T., Brammer, M. J., Simmons, A., et al. (1999). Social intelligence in the normal and autistic brain: An fMRI study. *European Journal Neuroscience, 11*(6), 1891–1898.

Baron-Cohen, S., Scahill, V. L., Izaguirre, J., Hornsey, H., & Robertson, M. M. (1999). The prevalence of Gilles de la Tourette syndrome in children and adolescents with autism: A large scale study. *Psychological Medicine, 29*, 1151–1159.

Baron-Cohen, S., Wheelwright, S., & Jolliffe, T. (1997). Is there a "language of the eyes"? Evidence from normal adults, and adults with autism or Asperger syndrome. *Visual Cognition, 4*(3), 311–331.

Barrett, S., Prior, M., & Manjiviona, J. (2004). Children on the borderlands of autism. *Autism, 8*(1), 61–87.

Bechara, A., Damasio, H., & Damasio, A. R. (2003). The role of the amygdala in decision making. *Annals of the New York Academy of Sciences, 985*, 356–369.

Behrman, M., Thomas, C., & Humphreys, K. (2006). Seeing it differently: Visual processing in autism. *Trends in Cognitive Sciences, 10*(6), 258–264.

Belmonte, M. K., Allen, G., Beckel-Mitchener, A., Boulanger, L. M., Carper, R. A., & Webb, S. J. (2004). Autism and abnormal development of brain connectivity. *Journal of Neuroscience, 24*, 9228–9231.

Benjamin, S., Seek, A., Tresise, L., Price, E., & Gagnon M.. (1995). Case study: Paradoxical response to naltrexone treatment of self-injurious behavior. *Journal of the American Academy of Child & Adolescent Psychiatry, 34*, 238–242.

Bibby, P., Eikeseth, S., Martin, N. T., Mudford, O. C., & Reeves, D. (2001). Progress and outcomes for children with autism receiving parent-managed intensive interventions. *Research in Developmental Disabilities, 22*, 425–447.

Boger-Megiddo, I. B., Shaw, D. W., Friedman, S. D., Sparks, B. F., Artru, A. A., Giedd, J. N., et al. (2006). Corpus callosum morphometrics in young children with autism spectrum disorder. *Journal of Autism and Developmental Disorders, 36*(6), 733–739.

Brimacombe, M., Ming, X., & Parikh, A. (2007). Familial risk factors in autism. *Journal of Child Neurology, 22*, 593–597.

Canli, T., Sivers, H., Whitfield, S. L., Gotlib, I. H., & Gabrieli, J. D. (2002). Amygdala response to happy faces as a function of extraversion. *Science, 296*, 2191.

Carmichael, S. T., & Price, J. L. (1995). Limbic connections of the orbital and medial prefrontal cortex in macaque monkeys. *The Journal of Comparative Neurology, 363*(4), 615–641.

Casanova, M. F., Buxhoeven, D. P., & Brown, C. (2002). Clinical and macroscopic correlates of minicolumnar pathology in autism. *Journal of Child Neurology, 17*, 692–695.

Casanova, M. F., Buxhoeven, D. P., Switala, A. E., & Roy, E. (2002). Neuronal density and architecture (Gray Level Index) in the brains of autistic patients. *Journal of Child Neurology, 17*, 515–521.

Castelli, F. (2005). Understanding emotions from standardized facial expressions in autism and normal development. *Autism, 9*, 428–449.

Castelli, F., Frith, C., Happe, F., & Frith, U. (2002). Autism, Asperger syndrome and brain mechanisms for the attribution of mental states to animated states. *Brain, 125*, 1839–1849.

Chakrabarti, S., & Fombonne, E. (2001). Pervasive developmental disorders in preschool children. *Journal of the American Medical Association, 285*, 3093–3099.

Chakrabarti, S., & Fombonne, E. (2005). Pervasive developmental disorders in preschool children: Confirmation of high prevalence. *The American Journal of Psychiatry, 162*, 1133–1141.

Chung, M. K., Dalton, K. M., Alexander, A. L., & Davidson, R. J. (2004). Less white matter concentration in autism: 2D voxel-based morphometry. *NeuroImage, 23*(1), 242–251.

Coben, R., Clarke, A. R., Hudspeth, W., & Barry, R. J. (2008). EEG power and coherence in autistic spectrum disorder. *Clinical Neurophysiology, 119*, 1002–1009.

Corbett, V. A. (2003). Video modeling: A window into the world of autism. *The Behavior Analyst Today, 4*, 1–10.

Courchesne, E., Carper, R., & Akshoomoff, N. (2003). Evidence of brain overgrowth in the first year of life in autism. *The Journal of the American Medical Association, 290*(3), 337–344.

Courchesne, E., Karns, C. M., Davis, H. R., Ziccardi, R., Carper, R. A., Tigue, Z. D., et al. (2001). Unusual brain growth patterns in early life in patients with autistic disorder: An MRI study. *Neurology, 57*, 245–254.

Courchesne, E., & Pierce, K. (2005). Why the frontal cortex in autism might be talking only to itself: Local overconnectivity but long-distance connection. *Current Opinion in Neurobiology, 15*, 225–230.

Critchley, H. D., Daly, E. M., Bullmore, E. T., Williams, S. C. R., Van Amelsvoort, T., Robertson, D. M., et al. (2000). The functional neuroanatomy of social behavior: Changes in cerebral blood flow when people with autistic disorder process facial expressions. *Brain, 123*, 2203–2212.

Dahlgren, A. S., Ehlers, S. U., Hagberg, B., & Gillberg, C. (2000). The Rett syndrome complex: Communicative functions in relation to developmental level and autistic features. *Autism, 4*, 249–267.

Dawson, G., Finley, C., Phillips, S., & Galpert, L. (1986). Hemispheric specialization and the language abilities of autistic children. *Child Development, 57*, 1440–1453.

Dawson, G., Meltzoff, A. N., Osterling, J., & Rinaldi, J. (1998). Neuropsychological correlates of early symptoms of autism. *Child Development, 69*, 1276–1285.

Dawson, G., & Webb, S. J. (2005). Understanding the nature of face processing impairment in autism: Insights from behavioral and electrophysiological studies. *Developmental Neuropsychology, 27*(3), 403–424.

Dawson, G., Webb, S. J., Wijsman, E., Schellenberg, G., Estes, A., Munson, J., et al. (2005). Neurocognitive and electrophysiological evidence of altered face processing in parents of children with autism? Implications for a model of abnormal development of social brain circuitry in autism. *Development and Psychopathology, 17*, 679–697.

Delprato, D. J. (2001). Comparisons of discrete-trial and normalized behavioural language intervention for young children with autism. *Journal of Autism and Developmental Disorders, 31*, 315–325.

Dierks, T., Bolte, S., Hubl, D., Lanfermann, H., & Poustka, F. (2004). Alterations of face processing strategies in autism: A fMRI study. *NeuroImage, 13*(6), 1016–1053.

Drew, A., Baird, G., Baron-Cohen, S., Cox, A., Slonims, V., Wheelwright, S., et al. (2002). A pilot randomized control trial for a parent training intervention for preschool children with autism: Preliminary findings and methodological challenges. *European Child and Adolescent Psychiatry, 11*, 266–272.

Dunn, M. A., Gomes, H., & Gravel, J. (2008). Mismatch negativity in children with autism and typical development. *Journal of Autism and Developmental Disorders, 38*, 52–71.

Dyches, T. T., Wilder, L. K., & Obiakor, F. E. (2001). Autism: Multicultural perspectives. In F. Wahlberg, F. E. Obiakor & S. Burkhardt (Eds.), *Educational and clinical interventions*. Oxford, England: Elevier Science Ltd.

Ehlers, S. U., Nyden, A., Gillberg, C., Sandberg, A. D., Dahlgren, S. O., Hjelmquist, E., et al. (1997). Asperger syndrome, autism and attention disorders: A comparative study of the cognitive profiles of 120 children. *Journal of Child Psychology and Psychiatry, 38*(2), 207–217.

Erickson, C. A., Stigler, K. A., Posey, D. J., & McDougle, C. J. (2007). Psychopharmacology. In F. R. Volkmar (Ed.), *Autism and pervasive developmental disorders* (2nd ed., pp. 221–253). New York: Cambridge University Press.

Feldman, H. M., Kolman, B. K., & Gonzaga, A. (1999). Naltexone and communication skills in young children with autism. *Journal of the American Academy of Child & Adolescent Psychiatry, 38*, 587–593.

Filipek, P. A. (1999). Neuroimaging in the developmental disorders: The state of the science. *The Journal of Child Psychology and Psychiatry and Allied Disciplines, 40*(1), 113–128.

Findling, R. L., McNamara, N. K., Gracious, B. L., O'Riordan, M., Reed, M. D., Demeter, C., et al. (2004). Quetiapine in nine youths with autistic disorder. *Journal of Child and Adolescent Psychopharmacology, 14*, 287–294.

Fombonne, E. (2001). What is the prevalence of Asperger disorder? *Journal of Autism and Developmental Disorders, 31*, 363–364.

Fombonne, E. (2003a). Epidemiological surveys of autism and other pervasive developmental disorders: An update. *Journal of Autism and Developmental Disorders, 33*, 365–382.

Fombonne, E. (2003b). The prevalence of autism. *Journal of the American Medical Association, 289*, 87–89.

Fombonne, E. (2008). Thirmerosal disappears but autism remains. *Archives of General Psychiatry, 65*, 15–16.

Gadow, K. D., DeVincent, C. J., & Pomeroy, J. (2006). ADHD symptom subtypes in children with pervasive developmental disorder. *Journal of Autism and Developmental Disorders, 36*(2), 271–283.

Gadow, K. D., DeVincent, C. J., Pomeroy, J., & Azizian, A. (2005). Comparison of DSM-IV symptoms in elementary school-age children with PDD versus clinic and community samples. *Autism*, 392–415.

Gazzaniga, M. S., Ivry, R. B., & Mangun, G. R. (2002). *Cognitive neuroscience: The biology of the mind* (2nd ed.). New York: W.W. Norton & Company.

Ghaziuddin, M. (2002). Asperger syndrome: Associated psychiatric and medical conditions. *Focus on Autism and Other Developmental Disabilities Asperger Syndrome, 17*(3), 138–144.

Ghaziuddin, M., & Mountain-Kimchi, K. (2004). Defining the intellectual profile of Asperger syndrome: Comparison with high-functioning autism. *Journal of Autism and Developmental Disorders, 34*, 279–284.

Ghaziuddin, M., Weidmer-Mikhail, E., & Ghaziuddin, N. (1998). Comorbidity of Asperger syndrome: A preliminary report. *Journal of Intellectual Disability Research, 42*(4), 279–283.

Giedd, J. N. (2004). Structural magnetic resonance imaging of the adolescent brain. *Annals of the New York Academy of Sciences, 1021*, 1308–1309.

Gillberg, C. (1999). Neurodevelopmental processes and psychological functioning in autism. *Development and Psychopathology, 11*(3), 567–587.

Gillberg, C., & Billstedt, E. (2000). Autism and Asperger syndrome: Coexistence with other clinical disorders. *Acta Psychiatrica Scandinavica, 102*(5), 321–330.

Gray, C. A., & Garand, J. (1993). Social stories: Improving responses of students with autism with accurate social information. *Focus on Autistic Behavior, 8*, 1–10.

Griffith, E. M., Pennington, B. F., Wehner, E. A., & Rogers, S. J. (1999). Executive functions in young children with autism. *Child Development, 70*, 817–832.

Grossman, J. B., Klin, A., Carter, A. S., & Volkmar, F. R. (2000). Verbal bias in recognition of facial emotions in children with Asperger syndrome. *Journal of Child Psychology and Psychiatry, 41*(3), 369–379.

Gutstein, S. E., & Whitney, T. (2002). Asperger syndrome and the development of social competence. *Focus on Autism and other Developmental Disabilities, 17*, 161–171.

Handen, B. L., Johnson, C. R., & Lubetsky, M. (2000). Efficacy of methylphenidate among children with autistic disorder and symptoms of attention-deficit hyperactivity disorder. *Journal of Autism and Developmental Disorders, 30*, 245–255.

Hanft, A., & Hendren, R. L. (2004). Pharmacotherapy of children and adolescents with pervasive developmental disorders. *Essential Psychopharmacology, 6*, 12–24.

Hansen, R. L., & Hagerman, R. J. (2003). Contributions of pediatrics. In S. Ozonoff, S. J. Rogers, & R. L. Hendren (Eds.), *Autism spectrum disorders* (pp. 87–110). Washington, DC: American Psychiatric Publishing, Inc.

Happe, F., & Frith, U. (2006). The weak coherence account: Detail-focused cognitive style in autism spectrum disorders. *Journal of Autism and Developmental Disorders, 36*(1), 5–25.

Hardan, A. Y., Minshew, N. J., & Keshavan, M. S. (2000). Corpus callosum size in autism. *Neurology, 55*, 1033–1036.

Hare, T. A., Tottenham, N., Davidson, M. C., Glover, G. H., & Casey, B. J. (2005). Contributions of amygdala and striatal activity in emotion regulation. *Biological Psychiatry, 57*(6), 624–632.

Hasselmo, M. E., Rolls, E. T., & Baylis, G. C. (1989). The role of expression and identity in the face-selective responses of neurons in the temporal visual cortex of the monkey. *Behavioural Brain Research, 32*(3), 203–218.

Haxby, J. V., Hoffman, E. A., & Gobbini, M. I. (2000). The distributed human neural system for face perception. *Trends in Cognitive Sciences, 4*(6), 223–233.

Hazell, P. (2007). Drug therapy for attention-deficit/hyperactivity disorder-like symptoms in autistic disorder. *Journal of Paediatrics and Child Health, 43*, 19–24.

Haznedar, M. M., Buchsbaum, M. S., Wei, T-C., Hof, P. R., Cartwright, C., Bienstock, C. A., Hollander, E. (2000). Limbic circuitry in patients with autism spectrum disorders studied with positron emission tomography and magnetic resonance imaging. *American Journal of Psychiatry, 157*, 1994–2001.

Herbert, M. R., Harris, G. J., Adrien, K. T., Ziegler, D. A., Makris, N., Kennedy, D. M., et al. (2002). Abnormal asymmetry in language association cortex in autism. *Annals of Neurology, 52*, 588–596.

Hill, E. L. (2004). Executive dysfunction in autism. *Trends in Cognitive Science, 8*, 26–31.

Hornig, M., & Lipkin, W. I. (2001). Infectious and immune factors in the pathogenesis of neurodevelopmental disorders: Epidemiology, hypotheses, and animal models. *Mental Retardation and Developmental Disabilities Research, 7*, 200–210.

Howlin, P. (2000). Outcome in adult life for more able individuals with autism. *Journal of Child Psychology and Psychiatry, 39*, 307–322.

Hwang, B., & Hughes, C. (2000). The effects of social interactive training on early social communicative skills of children with autism. *Journal of Autism and Developmental Disorders, 30*, 331–343.

Immunization Safety Review Committee: Board on Health Promotion and Disease Prevention. (2004). *Immunization safety review: Vaccines and autism*. Washington, DC: Institute of Medicine: National Academies http://www.nap.edu/catalog/10997.html#toc.

Iovannone, R., Dunlap, G., Huber, H., & Kincaid, D. (2003). Effective educational practices for students with autism spectrum disorders. *Focus on Autism and other Developmental Disabilities, 18*, 150–165.

Just, M. A., Cherkassky, V. L., Keller, T. A., & Minshew, N. J. (2004). Cortical activation and synchronization during sentence comprehension in high-functioning autism: Evidence of underconnectivity. *Brain, 127*(8), 1811–1821.

Kana, R. K., Keller, T. A., Cherkassky, V. L., Minshew, N. J. , & Just, M. A. (2006). Sentence comprehension in autism: Thinking in pictures with decreased functional connectivity. *Brain, 129*(9), 2484–2493.

Kemper, T. L., & Bauman, M. L. (1993). The contribution of neuropathologic studies to the understanding of autism. *Neurologic Clinics, 11*(1), 175–187.

Kerr, A. (2002). Rett syndrome: Recent progress and implications for research and clinical practice. *Journal of Child Psychology and Psychiatry, 43*, 277–287.

Killgore, W. D., & Yurgelun-Todd, D. A. (2005). Social anxiety predicts amygdala activation in adolescents viewing fearful faces. *Neuroreport, 16*(15), 1671–1675.

Kim, J. A., Szatmari, P., Bryson, S. E., Streiner, D. L., & Wilson, F. J. (2000). The prevalence of anxiety and mood problems among children with autism and Asperger syndrome. *Autism, 4*, 117–132.

Kjelgaard, M. M., & Tager-Flusberg, H. (2001). An investigation of language impairment in autism: Implications for genetic subgroups. *Language and Cognitive Processes, 16*, 287–308.

Kleinhans, N., Akshoomoff, N., & Delis, D. C. (2005). Executive functions in autism and Asperger's disorder: Flexibility, fluency, and inhibition. *Developmental Neuropsychology, 27*, 379–401.

Klin, A., Saulnier, C., Tsatsanis, K. D., & Volkmar, F. R. (2005). Clinical evaluation in autism spectrum disorders: Psychological assessment within a transdisciplinary framework. In F. R. Volkmar, R. Paul, A. Klin, & D. J. Cohen (Eds.), *Handbook of autism and pervasive developmental disorders: Vol. 2. Assessment, interventions, and policy* (3rd ed.). Hoboken, NJ: John Wiley & Sons, Inc.

Klin, A., Sparrow, S. S., Cicchetti, D. V., & Rourke, B. P. (1995). Validity and neuropsychological characterization of Asperger syndrome: Convergence with nonverbal learning disabilities syndrome. *Journal of Child Psychology and Psychiatry, 36,* 1127–1140.

Klin, A., Sparrow, S. S., de Bildt, A., Cicchetti, D. V., Cohen, D. J., & Volkmar, F. R. (1999). A normed study of face recognition in autism and related disorders. *Journal of Autism and Developmental Disorders, 29*(6), 499–508.

Klin, A., & Volkmar, F. R. (2003). Asperger syndrome: Diagnosis and external validity. *Child and Adolescent Psychiatric Clinics of North America, 12,* 1–13.

Kolevzon, A., Gross, R., & Reichenberg, A. (2008). Prenatal and perinatal risk factors for autism. *Archives of Pediatric Adolescent Medicine, 161,* 326–333.

Kugler, B. (1998). The differentiation between autism and Asperger syndrome. *Autism, 2*(1), 11–32.

Lainhart, J. E. (1997). Macrocephaly in children and adults with autism. *Journal of the American Academy of Child & Adolescent Psychiatry, 36,* 282–290.

Lainhart, J. E., Piven, J., Wzorek, M., Landa, R., Santangelo, S. L., Coon, H., et al. (2002). Autism, regression, and the broader autism phenotype. *American Journal of Medical Genetics, 113,* 231–237.

Le Couteur, A., Bailey, A., Good, S., & Pickles, A. (1996). A broader phenotype of autism: The clinical spectrum in twins. *Journal of Child Psychology and Psychiatry, 37,* 785–801.

Leyfer, O. T., Folstein, S. E., Bacalman, S., Davis, N. O., Dinh, E., Morgan, J., et al. (2006). Comorbid psychiatric disorders in children with Autism: Interview development and rates of disorders. *Journal of Autism and Developmental Disorders, V36*(7), 849–861.

Liss, M., Fein, D., Allen, D., Dunn, M. A., Feinstein, C., Morris, R. D., et al. (2001). Executive functioning in high-functioning children with autism. *Journal of Child Psychology and Psychiatry, 42,* 261–270.

Lord, C., & McGee, J. P. (2001). *Educating children with autism.* Washington, DC: National Academy Press.

Lord, C., Risi, S., DiLavore, P. S., Shulman, C., Thurm, A., & Pickles, A. (2006). Autism from 2 to 9 years of age. *Archives of General Psychiatry, 63,* 694–701.

Lord, C., Rutter, M., DiLavore, P. C., & Risi, S. (1999). *Autism diagnostic observation schedule.* Los Angeles, CA: Western Psychological Services.

Luna, B., Minshew, N. J., Garver, K. E., Laza, N. A., Thulborn, K. R., Eddy, W. F., et al. (2002). Neocortical system abnormalities in autism: An fMRI study of spatial working memory. *Neurology, 59,* 834–840.

Macintosh, K. E., & Dissanayake, C. (2004). Annotation: The similarities and differences between autistic disorder and Asperger's disorder: A review of the empirical evidence. *Journal of Child Psychology and Psychiatry, 45*(3), 421–434.

Manjiviona, J., & Prior, M. (1999). Neuropsychological profiles of children with Asperger syndrome and autism. *Autism, 3*(4), 327–356.

Mann, T. A., & Walker, P. (2003). Autism and a deficit in broadening the spread of visual attention. *Journal of Child Psychology and Psychiatry, 44*(2), 274–284.

Martin, A., & Weisberg, J. (2003). Neural foundations for understanding social and mechanical concepts. *Cognitive Neuropsychology, 20,* 575–587.

McEachin, J. J., Smith, T., & Lovass, O. I. (1993). Long-term outcome for children with autism who received early intensive behavioral treatment. *American Journal of Mental Retardation, 97,* 359–372.

McLaughlin-Cheng, E. (1998). Asperger syndrome and autism: A literature review and meta-analysis. *Focus on Autism and Other Developmental Disabilities, 13*(4), 234–245.

Meyer, U., Nyffeler, M., Schwendener, S., Knuesel, I., Yee, B. K., & Feldon, J. (2008). Relative prenatal and postnatal maternal contributions to schizophrenia-related neurochemical dysfunction after in-utero immune challenge. *Neuropsychopharmacology, 33,* 441–456.

Miller, J. N., & Ozonoff, S. (2000). The external validity of Asperger disorder: Lack of evidence from the domain of neuropsychology. *Journal of Abnormal Psychology, 109*(2), 227–238.

Moes, D. R. (1998). Integrating choice-making opportunities within teacher-assigned academic tasks to facilitate the performance of children with autism. *Journal of the Association for Persons with Severe Handicaps, 23,* 319–328.

Monk, C. S., McClure, E. B., Nelson, E. E., Zarahn, E., Bilder, R. M., & Leivenluft, E. (2003). Adolescent immaturity in attention-related brain engagement to emotional facial expressions. *NeuroImage, 20,* 420–428.

Mudford, O. C., Martin, N. T., Eikeseth, S., & Bibby, P. (2001). Parent-managed behavioral treatment for preschool children with autism: Some characteristics of UK programs. *Research in Developmental Disabilities, 22,* 173–182.

Murphy, D. G. M., Critchley, H. D., Schmitz, N., McAlonan, G. M., Van Amelsvoort, T., Robertson, D. M., et al. (2002). Asperger syndrome: A proton magnetic resonance spectroscopy study of the brain. *Archives of General Psychiatry, 59,* 885–891.

National Institute of Mental Health. (2006). *Research on autism and autism spectrum disorders. Program Announcement No. PA-09-390.* Washington, DC: http://www.nimh.nih.gov/grants/guide/pa-files/PA-06-390.html.

National Research Council. (2001). *Educating young children with autism.* Washington, DC: National Academy Press.

Nyden, A., Gillberg, C., Hjelmquist, E., & Heiman, M. (1999). Executive function/attention deficits in boys with Asperger syndrome, attention disorder and reading/writing disorder. *Autism, 3*(3), 213–228.

Ohnishi, T., Matsuda, H., Hashimoto, T., Kunihiro, T., Nishikawa, M., Uema, T., et al. (2000). Abnormal regional cerebral blood flow in childhood autism. *Brain, 123,* 1838–1844.

Ozonoff, S., & Griffith, E. M. (2000). Neuropsychological function and the external validity of Asperger syndrome. In A. Klin, F. R. Volkmar, & S. S. Sparrow (Eds.), *Asperger syndrome.* New York: Guilford Press.

Ozonoff, S., & Jensen, J. (1999). Brief report: Specific executive function profiles in three neurodevelopmental disorders. *Journal of Autism and Developmental Disorders, 29,* 171–177.

Ozonoff, S., Pennington, B. F., & Rogers, S. J. (1990). Are there emotion perception deficits in young autistic children? *Journal of Child Psychology and Psychiatry, and Allied Disciplines, 31*(3), 343–361.

Ozonoff, S., & Rogers, S. J. (2003). Autism spectrum disorders: A research review for practitioners. In S. Ozonoff, S.

J. Rogers, & R. L. Hendren (Eds.), *Review of psychiatry* (pp. 3–33). Washington, DC: American Psychiatric Publishing.

Ozonoff, S., & Strayer, D. L. (2001). Further evidence of intact working memory in autism. *Journal of Autism and Developmental Disorders, 31*, 257–263.

Perrett, D. I., & Mistlin, A. J. (1990). Perception of facial characteristics by monkeys. In W. C. Stebbins & M. A. Berkley (Eds.), *Comparative perception* (pp. 187–215). Oxford, England: John Wiley & Sons.

Pessoa, L., Kastner, S., & Ungerleider, L. G. (2002). Attentional control of the processing of neutral and emotional stimuli. *Cognitive Brain Research, 15*(1), 31–45.

Pierce, K., Muller, R. A., Ambrose, J., Allen, G., & Courchesne, E. (2001). Face processing occurs outside the fusiform 'face area' in autism: Evidence from functional MRI. *Brain, 124*, 2059–2073.

Piven, J., Arndt, S., Bailey, J., & Andreasen, N. (1996). Regional brain enlargement in autism: A magnetic resonance imaging study. *Journal of the American Academy of Child & Adolescent Psychiatry, 35*(4), 530–536.

Prior, M., & Ozonoff, S. (1998). Psychological factors in autism. In F. R. Volkmar (Ed.), *Autism and pervasive developmental disorders* (pp. 64–108). New York, NY: Cambridge University Press.

Reichenberg, A., Gross, R., Weiser, M., Bresnahan, M., Silverman, J., Harlap, S., et al. (2006). Advancing paternal age and autism. *Archives of General Psychiatry, 63*, 1026–1032.

Reiss, A. L., & Hall, S. S. (2007). Fragile X syndrome: Assessment and treatment implications. *Child and Adolescent Psychiatric Clinics of North America, 16*, 663–675.

Remington, G., Sloman, L., Konstantareas, M., Parker, K., & Gow, R. (2001). Clomipramine versus haloperidol in the treatment of autistic disorder: A double-blind, placebo-controlled, crossover study. *Journal of Clinical Psychopharmacology, 21*, 440–444.

Research Units on Pediatric Psychopharmacology Autistic Disorder Network. (2005). Randomized, controlled, crossover trial of methylphenidate in pervasive developmental disorders with hyperactivity. *Archives of General Psychiatry, 62*, 1266–1274.

Rippon, G., Brock, J., Brown, C., & Boucher, J. (2007). Disordered connectivity in the autistic brain: Challenges for the 'new physiology.' *International Journal of Psychophysiology, 63*, 164–172.

Rojas, D. C., Smith, J. A., Benkers, T. L., Camou, S. L., Reite, M. L., & Rogers, S. J. (2004). Hippocampus and amygdala volumes in parents of children with autistic disorder. *The American Journal of Psychiatry, 161*, 2038–2044.

Rutter, M., Le Couteur, A., & Lord, C. (2003). *Autism Diagnostic Interview - Revised (ADI-R)*. Los Angeles, CA: Western Psychological Services.

Schechter, R., & Grether, J. K. (2008). Continuing increases in autism reported to California's developmental services system. *Archives of General Psychiatry, 65*, 19–24.

Schopler, E., & Reichler, J. (2004). *Childhood Autism Rating Scale, revised (CARS)* (Rev. ed.). Los Angeles, CA: Western Psycholgical Services.

Schultz, R. T., Gauthier, I., Klin, A., Fulbright, R. K., Anderson, A. W., Volkmar, F. R., et al. (2000). Abnormal ventral temporal cortical activity during face discrimination among individuals with autism and Asperger syndrome. *Archives of General Psychiatry, 57*(4), 331–340.

Schultz, R. T., Grelotti, D. J., Klin, A., Kleinman, J., Van der Gaag, C., Marois, R., et al. (2003). The role of the fusiform face area in social cognition: Implications for the pathobiology of autism. *Philosophical Transactions of the Royal Society of London, 358*(1430), 415–427.

Schultz, R. T., Grelotti, D. J., Klin, A., Levitan, E., Cantey, T., Skudlarski, P., et al. (2001). *An fMRI study of face recognition, facial expression detection, and social judgment in autism spectrum conditions*. Paper presented at the International Meeting for Autism Research.

Schultz, R. T., Romanski, L. M., & Tsatsanis, K. D. (2000). Neurofunctional models of autistic disorder and Asperger syndrome: Clues from neuroimaging. In A. Klin, F. R. Volkmar, & S. S. Sparrow (Eds.), *Asperger syndrome*. New York: The Guilford Press.

Sears, L. L., Vest, C., Mohamed, S., Bailey, J., Ranson, B. J., & Piven, J. (1999). An MRI study of the basal ganglia in autism. *Progress in Neuro-Psychopharmacology & Biological Psychiatry*, 613–624.

Semrud-Clikeman, M. (2007). *Social competence in children*. New York: Springer.

Semrud-Clikeman, M., Fine, J. G., & Zhu, D. C. (submitted). Brain activation in normal adults to happy and sad photographs and videos. *NeuroImage*.

Semrud-Clikeman, M., & Schaefer, V. (2000). Social competence in developmental disorders. *Journal of Psychotherapy in Independent Practice, 4*, 3–20.

Silk, T. J., Rinehart, N., Bradshaw, J. L., Tonge, B., Egan, G., O'Boyle, M. W., et al. (2006). Visuospatial processing and the function of prefrontal-parietal networks in autism spectrum disorders: A functional MRI study. *American Journal of Psychiatry, 163*(8), 1440–1443.

Siller, M., & Sigman, M. (2002). The behaviors of parents of children with autism predict the subsequent development of their children's communication. *Journal of Autism and Developmental Disorders, 32*, 77–89.

Simpson, J. R., Öngür, D., Akbudak, E., Conturo, T. E., & Ollinger, J. M. (2000). The emotional modulation of cognitive processing: An fMRI study. *Journal of Cognitive Neuroscience, 12*(Suppl2), 157–170.

Smith, T., Buch, G. A., & Gamby, T. E. (2000). Parent-directed, intensive early intervention for children with pervasive developmental disorder. *Research in Developmental Disabilities, 21*, 297–309.

Smith, T., Groen, A. D., & Wynn, J. W. (2000). Randomized trial of intensive early intervention for children with pervasive developmental disorder. *American Journal of Mental Retardation, 105*, 269–285.

Somerville, L. H., Kim, H., Johnstone, T., Alexander, A. L., & Whalen, P. J. (2004). Human amygdala responses during presentation of happy and neutral faces: Correlations with state anxiety. *Biological Psychiatry, 55*, 897–903.

Sparks, B. F., Friedman, S. D., Shaw, D. W., Aylward, E. H., Echelard, D., Artru, A. A., et al. (2002). Brain structural abnormalities in young children with autism spectrum disorder. *Neurology, 59*(2), 184–192.

Stigler, K. A., Posey, D. J., & McDougle, C. J. (2004). Aripiprazole for maladaptive behavior in pervasive developmental disorders. *Journal of Child and Adolescent Psychopharmacology, 14*, 455–463.

Strain, P. S., & Hoyson, M. (2000). The need for longitudinal, intensive social skill intervention: LEAP follow-up outcomes for children with autism. *Topics in Early Childhood Special Education, 20*, 116–122.

Swaiman, K. F., & Dyken, P. R. (1999). Degenerative diseases primarily of gray matter. In K. F. Swaiman & S. Ashwal (Eds.), *Pediatric neurology* (pp. 833–848). St. Louis, MO: Mosby.

Tanguay, P. E. (2000). Pervasive developmental disorders: A 10-year review. *Journal of the American Academy of Child & Adolescent Psychiatry, 39*, 1079–1094.

Thompson, W. W., Price, C., Goodson, B., & Shay, D. K. (2007). Early thimerosal exposure and neuropsychological outcomes at 7 to 10 years. *The New England Journal of Medicine, 357*, 1281–1290.

Toichi, M., & Kamio, Y. (1998). Verbal memory in autistic adolescents. *Japanese Journal of Child and Adolescent Psychiatry, 39*, 364–373.

Tsatsania, K. D. (2003). Outcome research in Asperger syndrome and autism. *Child and Adolescent Psychiatric Clinics of North America, 12*, 47–63.

Verte, S., Geurts, H. M., Roeyers, H., Rosseel, Y., Oosterlaan, J., & Sergeant, J. A. (2006). Executive functioning in children with an autism spectrum disorder: Can we differentiate within the spectrum? *Journal of Autism and Developmental Disorders, 36*(3), 351–372.

Vidal, C. N., Nicolson, R., DeVito, T. J., Hayashi, K. M., Geaga, J. A., Drost, D. J., et al. (2006). Mapping corpus callosum deficits in autism: An index of aberrant cortical connectivity. *Biological Psychiatry, 60*(3), 218–225.

Volkmar, F. R., Klin, A., & Pauls, D. L. (1998). Nosological and genetic aspects of Asperger syndrome. *Journal of Autism and Developmental Disorders, 28*(5), 457–463.

Volkmar, F. R., Klin, A., Siegal, B., Szatmari, P., Lord, C., Campbell, M., et al. (1994). Field trial for autistic disorder in DSM IV. *American Journal of Psychiatry, 151*, 1361–1367.

Volkmar, F. R., Lord, C., Bailey, A., Schultz, R. T., & Klin, A. (2004). Autism and pervasive developmental disorders. *Journal of Child Psychology and Psychiatry, 45*, 135–170.

Wassnik, T. H., Piven, J., & Vieland, J. (2001). Evidence supporting WNT2 as an autism susceptibility gene. *American Journal of Medical Genetics, 105*, 406–413.

Webb, S. J., Dawson, G., Bernier, R., & Panagiotides, H. (2006). ERP evidence of atypical face processing in young children with autism. *Journal of Autism and Developmental Disorders, 36*(7), 881–890.

Whalen, C. K., & Schreibman, L. (2002). Joint attention training for children with autism using behavior modification procedures. *Journal of Child Psychology and Psychiatry, 44*, 456–468.

Wilens, T. (2004). *Straight talk about psychiatric medications for kids* (2nd ed.). New York: Guilford.

Williams, D. L., Goldstein, G., & Minshew, N. J. (2005). Impaired memory for faces and social scenes in autism: Clinical implications of memory dysfunction. *Archives of clinical neuropsychology the official journal of the National Academy of Neuropsychologists, 20*(1), 1–15.

Winner, E., Brownell, H., Happe, F., Blum, A., & Pincus, D. (1998). Distinguishing lies from jokes: Theory of mind deficits and discourse interpretation in right hemisphere brain-damaged patients *Brain Language, 62*(1), 89–106.

Wolf, J. M., Fein, D., & Akshoomoff, N. (2007). Autism spectrum disorders and social disabilities. In S. J. Hunter & J. Donders (Eds.), *Pediatric neuropsychological intervention* (pp. 151–174). Cambridge: Cambridge University Press.

Wolterink, G., Daenen, L. E. W. P. M., Dubbeldam, S., Gerrits, M. A. F. M., van Rijn, R., Kruse, C. G., et al. (2001). Early amygdala damage in the rat as a model for neurodevelopmental psychopathological disorders. *European Neuropsychopharmacology, 11*(1), 51–59.

Yang, T. T., Menon, V., Eliez, S., Blasey, C., White, C. D., Reid, A. J., et al. (2002). Amygdalar activation associated with positive and negative facial expressions. *Neuroreport: For Rapid Communication of Neuroscience Research, 13*(14), 1737–1741.

Zirlinger, M., & Anderson, D. (2003). Molecular dissection of the amygdala and its relevance to autism. *Genes, Brain, and Behavior, 2*, 282–294.

Chapter 12
Language-Related and Learning Disorders

Neurodevelopmental disorders of childhood, including language-related and learning disabilities, constitute a large percentage of the childhood disorders seen by child clinical neuropsychologists. Language impairments and learning disabilities resulting from phonological core deficits are featured, as are mathematics difficulties resulting from nonverbal, reasoning, and perceptual deficits. Recently these disorders have often been combined with the new term, learning and language impaired. A large body of research has burgeoned over the past decade. There are some children who simply exhibit a language delay as well as a few children with a learning disability without a significant language delay. For that reason we will discuss language disability somewhat separate from learning disabilities although they are related and should be viewed as such.

Each of these neurodevelopmental disorders will be explored within a transactional model, where the genetic and prenatal/postnatal history affecting neuropsychological, cognitive, perceptual, and memory functions will be reviewed. The manner in which family, school, and social factors interact with and ultimately influence the manifestation of these disorders will also be discussed. Research and clinical literature will be incorporated, and implications for assessment and intervention will be addressed.

Articulation Impairment

Articulation Impairment (AI) decreases with age and is approximately 2:1 male to female in incidence (Petherham & Enderby, 2001). In the past,

children with AI were considered to have primary motor system problems, and therapies were devised to address motor learning patterns. Recent conceptualizations suggest that linguistic abilities, particularly phonological processing skills, play an important role in AI. From this perspective, speech sound production is viewed in light of global language functions, including syntax, semantics, and pragmatics (Fox & Dodd, 2001).

Research has suggested that there are four types of articulatory difficulty: articulation disorder, delay, consistent use of atypical error patterns, and inconsistent pronunciation (Dodd, 1995). These subtypes have been found in German speaking populations (Fox & Dodd, 2001) as well as Cantonese children (Holm & Dodd, 2001). Further study has found that, in a large sample of English-speaking children referred for a speech evaluation, 57.5 percent had a phonological delay, 20.6 percent had non-developmental errors, 9.4 percent made inconsistent errors on the same sound, and 12.5 percent had an articulation disorder (Broomfield & Dodd, 2004b). In this sample no child had a significant hearing impairment, diagnosed learning disability, or physical disability. Although attempts have been made to determine whether children with articulation disorders also have general language deficits, it is unclear whether AI should be considered a linguistic (phonological disorder) or a neurogenic (developmental motor apraxia) disorder.

M. Semrud-Clikeman, P.A. Teeter Ellison, *Child Neuropsychology*, DOI 10.1007/978-0-387-88963-4_12,
© Springer Science+Business Media, LLC 2009

Neuropsychological Correlates of AI

Children with AI are more similar to typically developing children than to children with language disorders. There are no specific neuropsychological correlates for children with a sole diagnosis of AI. Children that were language impaired (LI) had more trouble with speech perception capabilities, whereas children with AI performed better than control children on these measures (Snow, 2001). AI children generally show fewer omissions, transpositions, and syllable additions, compared to LI children.

In a multivariate analysis differentiating AI from normal children, the following variables were predictive of group membership: weight, temporal ordering of visual graphemes (e and k), and identifying syllables hae/ compared to /dae/ (Stark & Tallal, 1988). In a smaller group of children with AI, weight, family history of speech disorders, history of motor delays, difficulty identifying syllables (/bad /due/), and problems discriminating light flashes were significant in differentiating AI children from normal controls. In this study, AI and LI children were all heavier and taller than the control group. There are no clear-cut answers as to why weight is associated with LI and AI, but speculations suggest that heavy children may be more socially awkward, particularly if they are also clumsy; that low self-esteem may be manifested in less spontaneous speech, especially if accompanied by poor expressive language skills, or that uneven or rapid growth periods may place challenges on speech musculature (Stark & Tallal, 1988).

While children with AI have difficulty controlling involuntary movements of arms as well as with rapid fine motor coordination tasks, they are able to produce CV syllables in rapid succession when speaking (Leonard, 1998). Compared to LI groups, children with articulation disorders did not show difficulty on measures of verbal auditory processing or speech discrimination. Further, children with AI who have mild expressive language problems appear to function more similarly to typically developing children than to LI groups. In general, very few children with articulation disorders are found to show similar difficulties compared to children with more serious language impairment (Tallal & Fitch, 2005).

Language Impairment

Language impairment and speech disorders are considered to be communication disorders, and are often discussed along with reading impairment (Tallal & Gaab, 2006). Language impairment is often difficult to untangle from learning disabilities (or dyslexia) and studies often include participants with both difficulties. While this section will attempt to focus on language impairment, some of the studies will have samples that have both disorders.

The incidence of pediatric speech and language disorders is estimated to be approximately 33 percent of children aged 5–12 years of age (Law, Boyle, Harris, Harkness, & Nye, 2000). The gender ratio has been found to be approximately 3:1 for a language disorder and 2:1 for an articulation disorder, with males more likely to be diagnosed with either disorder than females (Broomfield & Dodd, 2004a). Of the children evaluated in a large clinic in England 28 percent showed a mild disability, 39 percent a moderate disability, and 12 percent had a severe disability (Broomfield & Dodd, 2004a). It was found that children with a severe language disability showed problems with receptive language disorders, a finding not present for those with articulation disorders. Children who showed global language problems were more impaired and at higher risk of later academic difficulties than those with isolated difficulty (Johnson et al., 1999; Shriberg, Tomblin, & McSweeney, 1999).

The main risk factors that have been identified for a language impairment include pre- and perinatal medical problems, otolarynological problems, problems with early feeding due to sucking difficulty, and family history (Johnson et al., 1999). There also appears to be a genetic predisposition to language impairment (Stromsvold, 2001) with monozygotic twins showing a higher concordance rate than dizygotic twins. Most of the studies reviewed on genetics have been from clinic-referred samples. Studies that have used samples from the community have found a modest genetic influence on low vocabulary skills at two years of age (Price et al., 2000), and a stronger relation at older ages (Eley, Dale, Bishop, Price, & Plomin, 2001; Spinath, Ronald, Harlaar, Price, & Plomin, 2003).

Studies of large community-based twin samples have found a relation between language performance and heritability (Spinath, Price, Dale, & Plomin, 2004; Viding et al., 2004). Heritability was found to be greater for children with more severe impairments than for those with mild impairments. It was also found that genetic and environmental influences appeared to be qualitatively and quantitatively similar for boys and girls. Similar to earlier findings, language impairment was present more often in boys than in girls.

Neuropsychological Correlates of LI

Fitch and Tallal (2003) indicate that impairment of spoken language and the underlying neuropsychological mechanisms may be the common thread between production and comprehension language difficulties, reading problems, mathematics problems, written language, and social difficulties in children with learning disabilities. It has been hypothesized that language disorders are a result of impaired temporal processing of auditory information (Tallal, 2004).

Children with specific language impairment (LI) or developmental dysphasia have been to found to have a number of difficulties:

- significant deficits in expressive and/or receptive language, with normal abilities in nonverbal areas;
- deficits in speech perception and poor vocabulary skills, including naming, memory, syntax (grammar), and semantics (word meaning), and
- impaired temporal sequence of nonverbal auditory stimuli and poor discrimination of sounds, particularly when auditory signals are presented rapidly (Semrud-Clikeman, 2006). Speech articulation, syntactic, and semantic deficits may also be present.

It is difficult to determine a causal link between brain functions and language impairment in children. However, several tentative hypotheses have been offered. One is that atypical patterns of symmetry of the planum temporale are associated with verbal comprehension problems, phonological processing deficits, and expressive language difficulties (Foster, Hynd, Morgan, & Hugdahl, 2002; Morgan & Hynd, 1998). The other assumes that perisylvian temporal cortical activation is present for processing auditory speech stimuli . Both the right and left hemisphere temporal regions appear activated, and each hemisphere may have a different role to play in the analysis of sounds (Binder et al., 2000). A study using fMRI technology in adults with normal language abilities suggests that the superior temporal lobes are involved in the decoding of acoustic signals of speech, whereas the left frontal lobes are involved in semantic operations (Eckert, Leonard, Possing, & Binder, 2006). Binder, Frost, Hammeke, Rao, and Prieto (1997) suggest that language processing is probably hierarchical in nature, involving primary sensory levels and intermodal association regions for higher cognitive activities. As processing demands move from simple (unimodal) to complex (multimodal), more brain regions are likely to be involved. Further research into these mechanisms is underway and will undoubtedly shed more light onto the neurological basis of language, and further clarify the role of selective attention, memory, cognitive associations, and semantic functions on language processes.

Other research indicates that children with LI are less efficient on neuropsychological tasks involving rate of motor performance (rapid alternating finger movements); dihaptic stimulation (simultaneous perception of bilateral tactile stimulation), and left-right discrimination (Talcott et al., 2000). LI children also had less control over involuntary movements than control children, and although signs of involuntary movements are observed in both groups, LI children have movements of longer duration.

Studies have indicated that children with LI experience difficulties with working memory and short-term memory (Adams & Gathercole, 2000; Balthazar, 2003; Gathercole, Tiffany, Briscoe, & Thorn, 2005; Montgomery, 2004). Phonological working memory and impaired language ability are related (Marton & Schwartz, 2003; Norrelgen, Lacerda, & Forssberg, 2002). A link has also been found between visual-spatial working memory and language development (Marton & Schwartz, 2003).

A possible link between visual-spatial working memory and language impairment has been found, but requires additional study to fully understand how these difficulties translate into language performance (Adams & Gathercole, 2000; Hoffman & Gillam, 2004). To investigate these relations more closely, a large study of kindergarteners evaluated the relation between working memory and language skills (van Daal, Verhoeven, van Leeuwe, & van Balkom, 2008). Findings indicated that phonological working memory was predictive of semantic and syntactic abilities, while visual memory was weakly related to speech production skills. It was hypothesized that phonological working memory is related to maintaining lexical semantic information while processing the verbal information. Baddeley's model of working memory (discussed in Chapter 6) was confirmed for language ability and disability for the phonological loop and the central executive, but not strongly for the visual sketch pad. These findings are consistent with previous research showing a strong link between phonological working memory and language ability (Alloway & Gathercole, 2005). In conclusion, working memory deficits particularly in phonological coding as well as in lexical retrieval appear to be important for our understanding of language impairment and likely interfere with cognitive processing as well as learning.

Cognitive Processing Features of LI

Children with language impairments exhibit problems with rate processing deficits; that is, children with LI have auditory processing deficits or difficulty in processing auditory signals that have short segments or are presented rapidly in a series (Fitch & Tallal, 2003). Some suggest that this is the basic deficit that underlies many of the neuropsychological and cognitive features associated with LI (Tallal, 2004). Rate processing weaknesses have been found in rapid speech production; finger identification (two fingers); association of consonants and vowels (ba versus da); processing of cross-modal, nonverbal stimuli, and simultaneous tactile stimulation (face and hand). Auditory masking may explain some of the auditory deficits found in LI children, where the rapid presentation of signals runs on top of or masks other, later occurring signals. Masking also may account for other problems observed in both the tactile and motor areas, where a sequence of stimuli or movements interferes with discrete single stimuli. Tallal (2004) concludes that there may be a common thread through interacting neural substrates for both speech and nonverbal processing that "incorporate rapidly changing temporal cues" that appear to be deficient in children with LI (p. 183) (Tallal, 1988). Normal infants discriminate subtle temporal signals (i.e., speech and nonverbal stimuli), that were problematic for LI children 5–9 years of age. Research suggests that children with LI are characterized by deficits in the ability to perceive and to produce information in rapid time sequences. This deficit is not specific to language, but includes other processes (e.g., motor, tactile, memory). Stark and Tallal (1988) hypothesize that "a basic neural timing mechanism" interferes with the simultaneous processing and production of information. While other higher level linguistic deficits may also be present, the timing mechanism deficit seems to have a significant negative impact on various processing skills. Ways to alter the functioning of this "neural timing mechanism" are explored in the discussion on intervention implications.

Rate processing deficits appear in both children with learning and language problems. Tallal and Gaab (2006) have found that these rate processing deficits and sensorimotor delays are consistently found in children with language impairment. Infants with a family history of learning and language problems take longer to learn how to discriminate between two tones than those without such a history (Benasich & Tallal, 2002). The difficulty in learning how to discriminate between the tones was strongly linked to later difficulties with language development independent of the language being learned. Similarly, Foxton et al. (2003) found that problems in the ability to acquire phonological discrimination and speech intonation knowledge were related to later difficulties in language as well as in reading. Children with LI frequently develop later reading problems, and as many as 50 percent of young children with impaired language also show math difficulties and reading problems in elementary school (Tallal, 2004). There have been links between language impairment and reading and writing difficulties.

Social-Psychological Correlates of LI

The psychosocial functioning of children with language problems is often not investigated separately from that of children with learning disabilities. In general, discussions of social difficulties in children with learning disabilities have focused on the communicative competency of children in social situations, level of moral development, perspective taking and empathy for others, understanding of nonverbal cues, and problem solving abilities (Beitchman et al., 2001). Children with LI tend to have a higher rate of emotional and behavioral disorders than would be expected, with some finding that 80 percent of juvenile delinquents either show a current language delay or have a history of language impairment (Beitchman, Nair, Clegg, Ferguson, & Patel, 1986; Hall & Moats, 1999). Children with LI are at a higher risk to develop emotional difficulties compared to typically developing peers (Conti-Ramsden & Botting, 2008).

The extent to which social-emotional difficulties are related to language impaired children without learning disorders in general needs further exploration. It does seem evident that communication and verbal intelligence are important variables in determining social adjustment, in conjunction with other cognitive and behavioral factors. If a child is unable to express what he/she needs, then it is likely he/she will turn to a more physical manner to express feelings or to turn those feelings inward and not express them.

Implications for Assessment

There is a paucity of decent measures for language impairments in both young and older children. It is especially difficult to find one adequate test that measures phonemic awareness, syntax, and semantic skills, and analyzing subtests from more than one instrument presents psychometric measurement problems (e.g., comparison of grade or age levels from different tests with dissimilar reliability and validity standards). Language pragmatics are also often overlooked, so it is difficult to determine the effects of LI on communication in general. Table 6.1 provides a list of commonly used measures for assessing language. It is important to use parts of tests in order to answer particular questions about the child's functioning. For this reason, the astute clinician will be aware of all these measures and select the most appropriate ones for the child at hand.

Implications for Interventions

Interventions for language disorders may be (1) preventive, by reducing the probability of reading disorders; (2) remedial, by addressing the language or communication deficits, or (3) compensatory in nature (Stark, 1988). Early identification and intervention at preschool age are crucial to increase the likelihood of preventing the associated features of severe communication disorders. However, most intervention research has focused on children with cognitive delays or hearing impairments, a fact that complicates the picture when evaluating the efficacy of such research when these disorders are not also present.

Fast ForWord Language (FFW-L) (Scientific Learning Corporation, 1998) is a popular intervention tool that has been suggested to correct difficulties in temporal processing of information thought to be related to learning and language difficulties. Some have found gains of 1–1 ½ years following six weeks of training (Merzenich et al., 1996; Tallal & Gaab, 2006). This program is based on Tallal's theory that language difficulties are due to problems with fast processing of auditory information and that an intense intervention that basically reprograms the brain to recognize sounds and blends will improve language ability. FFW-L consists of two-stage computer-generated lessons. In stage 1 of the training, speech was temporally modified by lengthening the speech signal by 50 percent; during stage 2, fast (3–30 Hz) transitional features of speech were enhanced by as much as 20 db. The speech tracks were presented on CD-ROMs. The speech sounds have a staccato quality, with consonants (usually fast elements of speech sound) exaggerated compared to vowels (typically slower speech sounds). Intervention outcome may be best for children with expressive language problems who do not have accompanying receptive language disorders (Merzenich et al., 1996; Tallal et al., 1996).

Independent researchers have also evaluated the FFW-L program to determine its effectiveness with children who have LLI (learning and language impairment). One study included a group of 54 children with LLI assigned to one of three intervention groups focusing on auditory training: FFW-L, Earobics, or the Lindamood Phoneme Sequencing Program (LiPS) (Pokorni,

Worthington, & Jamison, 2004). All children showed significant difficulties with language and reading ability. Children were tested 4–6 weeks prior to the intervention and 6–8 weeks after the intervention ended. Gains were not found on retesting for any of the interventions.

Similarly, Cohen et al. (2005) compared Fast ForWord to commercially available home programs and no programs in three groups of children with severe mixed receptive and expressive language disabilities. All groups received speech and language intervention services in addition to these programs during the intervention period. At nine weeks and six months after the intervention period all groups showed significant improvement on standardized testing, but no difference was found among the groups. Cohen et al. (2005) suggested that the groups did not provide any additional support apart from the speech and language services that were provided individually.

Gillam et al. (2008) studied 216 children aged 6–9 years in four intervention programs: Fast ForWord Language, academic enrichment, computer-assisted language intervention, or individualized language intervention. Each child had treatment five days per week for six weeks for one hour and 40 minutes each day. All groups showed improvement on a standardized language test after the intervention with no difference among the groups present. These findings indicate that interventions that provide intensive experiences with a great deal of feedback and support improve language functioning. Gillam et al. (2008) concluded that the temporal processing hypothesis of language impairment may not fully explain the difficulties these children have and in and of itself, is not sufficient for our understanding of language impairment. Thus, auditory processing is likely a very important, albeit complex, aspect to language development, and requires one to include many aspects in understanding LI, not solely temporal processing of stimuli (Johnston, 2006).

From the studies, it appears that auditory processing deficits may result in both expressive and receptive language deficits, while speech motor deficits may result in expressive problems. Further, if auditory processing abilities are intact, these abilities may facilitate the development of expressive language and speech motor problems, while the opposite does not appear to be the case. That is,

intact speech motor abilities have little impact on improving language problems resulting from auditory processing deficits. The best treatment approach is not always evident. As discussed briefly earlier, learning and language disabilities go hand in hand, and many children have both disorders. The following section discusses learning disabilities from a neuropsychological point of view.

Learning Disabilities

Children with learning disabilities (LD) constitute the largest and fastest growing population of special needs children in schools. Estimates place the incidence of learning disabilities (LD) in general to be at 5–8 percent of public school students (Semrud-Clikeman, Guy, Griffin, & Hynd, 2000). While there is a large body of research indicating that learning disabilities are more common in males than females with the incidence generally running at 2:1 (Flannery, Liederman, Daly, & Schultz, 2000; Miles, Haslum, & Wheeler, 1999), others have found the ratio between males and females to be relatively closer (Shaywitz et al., 1995). The study that found equal distribution of males and females, however, did find that when looking at the more severe form of a reading disability, males were more affected compared to females by at least 2:1.

Liederman, Kantrowitz, and Flannery (2005) completed a comprehensive review of the literature in male vulnerability for reading disability. The findings from this review indicate that while the literature does support a preponderance of males with reading disabilities, more research is needed to evaluate the incidence using more than one definition of LD, to compare genders based on their own gender rather than across genders, and for researchers to report effect sizes for their findings. Siegel and Smythe (2005) suggest that the discrepancy definition for LD (see below) may bias selection to males. In addition, it has been found that early reading skills (word identification, phonological processing) often differ between the genders until fourth grade when the differences generally disappear for most children (Share & Silva, 2003; Siegel & Smythe, 2005). More research is needed to examine male and female differences based on the definition of a learning disability, and possibly also evaluate differences in severity over development. The definition of a learning disability continues to be an area of contention and the issues are discussed in the next section

Definitions

Currently, the field is replete with controversies affecting how we think about, diagnose, and design educational interventions for children identified as LD. Learning problems can arise from divergent sources including genetic, neuropsychological, cognitive/perceptual, social-psychological, and environmental (i.e., home and school or classroom) factors. The extent to which we can reliably identify which factors or combination of factors affects a child's learning may be helpful in distinguishing children with LD from other slow learners or "garden-variety" poor readers. For example, we might expect to see differences across variables depending on whether the learning difficulties result from neurobiological, cognitive-perceptual, intellectual, or instructional opportunities and experiences.

Learning disabilities have been defined in many different ways over the years. Some have used the term "dyslexia" to be synonymous with learning disabilities when, in fact, dyslexia refers to problems solely with reading. The general term "learning disabilities" refers to problems in any one of seven areas of learning including listening comprehension, expressive language, basic reading skills (word identification, phonological coding), reading comprehension, written language, mathematics calculation, or mathematics reasoning. Many assume that LD is due to a central nervous system difference that contributes to the problems in deciphering both written and oral language (Shaywitz, 2003).

Learning disabilities is a heterogeneous grouping that generally includes children with difficulty learning despite adequate ability and instruction in one of seven areas related to language, reading, and mathematics. The definition generally assumes a significant discrepancy between ability and achievement that is often not well-defined. Differences in defining this discrepancy has led to various incidences of LD across the country, with some states defining the discrepancy conservatively (children achieving below the second percentile for their age) and others more liberally (a difference of 16 standard score points between ability and achievement).

Many children may experience difficulties in more than one area, and have difficulties with attention, emotional adjustment, and/or behavioral problems as well (Lyon, Shaywitz, & Shaywitz, 2003). The majority of children identified with a learning disability have difficulties in reading with many of these also experiencing difficulties with written language. Poor phonological processing is the most predictive of continuing reading difficulty (Shaywitz, Mody, & Shaywitz, 2006).

When a severe learning disability is present, even despite intensive remediation, achieving average reading ability may be questionable (Lyon et al., 2003). It is likely that these children show significant problems with emotional adjustment and with social competence and, thus, academic interventions are complicated by these concomitant difficulties. Comorbidity with other disorders is present with learning disabilities similar to that with ADHD.

One theory for the mechanism that is faulty in learning disabilities is the double-deficit hypothesis (Wolf & Bowers, 1999). This theory suggests that readers be grouped by their ability on measures of phonological coding and automatized naming skills. There are three, suggested subtypes: phonological deficit, naming speed deficit, and phonological and naming speed deficit. The phonological deficit subtype is those children that have difficulty with phonological processing, but have average ability in naming. The naming speed subtype has difficulty in automatized naming, but not in phonological coding. When phonological coding and rapid naming are both present, it is believed that the disorder is of a more severe nature.

Research has supported the finding of naming speed and phonological difficulties in children with learning problems. A sole problem with naming speed, however, has not been found in children with learning problems (Morris et al., 1998). Other studies have found a strong relation between phonological processing and reading ability, and a weak or modest relationship between reading skills and rapid naming ability (Hammill, Mather,

Allen, & Roberts, 2002; Pennington, Cardoso-Martins, Green, & Lefly, 2001). Rapid naming and phonological processing also correlate with poorer phonological coding skills strongly related to poorer automatized naming skills (Compton, DeFries, & Olson, 2001; Schatschneider, Carlson, Francis, Foorman, & Fletcher, 2002).

Comprehensive reviews of research on the double-deficit hypothesis have found that phonological coding and double-deficit subtypes do exist, but that the naming speed subtype has not been confirmed and that naming speed and phonological processing are strongly correlated skills (McCardle, Scarborough, & Catts, 2001; Vukovic & Siegel, 2006). This review also found that phonological interventions improve rapid naming speed, thus supporting the idea that these skills are not independent. The review concludes that naming speed deficits are not characteristic of a reading problem and are only important when they occur in conjunction with phonological processing difficulty. Further discussion of assessment and definition issues is presented below. One of the areas that has challenged the research in learning disabilities is the frequency of other disorders that co-occur with a learning problem.

Diagnostic Issues

One of the major issues in the field of learning disabilities is the precise definition of a learning disability and who should be served under this category. Tied to this difficulty is the problem of appropriately assessing a child to determine whether a significant learning problem does exist. Previous definitions have generally included an IQ-achievement discrepancy that is called "significant," but is not well-defined. As a result, different states and, in some cases, school districts define eligibility for services differently. Other definitions have included the idea that the learning problem is due to a developmental lag. These definitions will be reviewed in the following section.

A meta-analysis of the relation between ability and reading level was conducted to evaluate the use of the IQ-Achievement discrepancy to define a learning disability (Fuchs, Fuchs, Mathes, & Lipsey, 2000a, 2000b). This meta-analysis found that children with the poorest reading ability, compared to poor readers with lower ability levels, were most appropriately served using the discrepancy model. Hoskyn and Swanson (2000) also conducted a meta-analysis looking at children with reading disability and those with reading delays and lower ability. There was no differences between the groups on reading and phonological processing, but the brighter group performed stronger in vocabulary and syntax skills. The difference between these two meta-analysis studies is likely due to differences in sample selection for the studies as well as the emphasis on an ability measure. The Fuchs et al. (2000a, 2000b) study did not restrict the study to a certain IQ level, while the Hoskyn and Swanson (2000) review included studies that utilized significantly below average IQ samples. These differences in study selection changed the findings and account for the findings' discrepancies.

Steubing et al. (2002) conducted a further evaluation of the LD literature with regard to the IQ-discrepancy issue. Their sample included studies that used two groups to classify poor readers (IQ discrepant and concordant), studies were not included that utilized poor readers with significantly below average ability, and additional domains such as behavioral functioning were included in addition to cognition and achievement variables. In addition, effect sizes were evaluated to determine whether the size estimates were consistent across domains.

This analysis found few differences among the IQ discrepant and IQ concordant groups on measures of phonological awareness, rapid naming, verbal short-term memory, and vocabulary ability. The IQ discrepant groups showed stronger effect sizes for the Verbal IQ, Nonverbal IQ, and Full Scale IQ measures. Some studies have shown that once decoding skills have been attained, comprehension skills may be slightly better for children with specific reading disabilities than for children with generalized cognitive deficits (Stanovich, 2005). In addition, the IQ-discrepant group scored better on measures of fine motor skills, concept formation, spatial ability, planning skills, perceptual motor skills, and nonverbal short-term memory. These measures were not believed to affect reading skills, but are separate areas that would discriminate the groups.

One of the issues that arises when IQ discrepancy is utilized to diagnose a child with a learning disability is the difficulty that children with lower ability have to qualify for services. It is much more difficult for a child with an IQ of 85 to qualify for services than a child with an IQ of 110, particularly at a younger age. Some have questioned the discrepancy model's use and argue that it delays services to those children who need help the most at an early age. This concern is particularly apt as interventions have not been found to be as successful if started after second grade, compared to early intervention (Lyon et al., 2001; Torgesen et al., 2001).

The difference between slow learners (those children who do not read well, but read roughly commensurate with their ability) and children with severe learning problems has been evaluated to determine whether differences in reading skills are present as well as response to intervention. Research on this issue has yielded mixed results. LD and non-identified slow learners do not differ in terms of demographics or psychoeducational test scores, including both cognitive and affective measures (Strong, Silver, & Perini, 2008). Further, slow learners and LD groups show similar skills on cognitive tasks related to reading (Lyon et al., 2001), including phonological awareness, and on measures of reading achievement.

LD and garden-variety poor readers differ on cognitive tasks not directly related to reading, such as nonverbal reasoning skills and verbal-conceptual abilities which, in turn, may ultimately affect intervention efficacy (Hulslander et al., 2004). It has been suggested that garden-variety poor readers have global deficits across a variety of cognitive measures, whereas children with reading disabilities have core deficits in the phonological area and, thus, have more domain-specific deficits (Stanovich, Siegel, & Gottardo, 1997). Further, problems in phonological awareness are shared by the two groups and serve as causal factors for reading problems (Stanovich, 2005).

Developmental lag theories may be more appropriate for children with mild reading problems than for children with severe reading deficits or dyslexia (Chiappe, Stringer, Siegel, & Stanovich, 2002). There is evidence that when children who are delayed in reading are compared to children with the same reading level, but who are younger than the children with reading difficulties, the differences between the groups are smaller than when the child is compared to same-aged peers (Stanovich, Siegel, Gottardo, Chiappe, & Sidhu, 1997). Measures of vocabulary development, pseudo-word decoding, phonological processing, verbal fluency, and picture naming tasks are similar in children with the same reading level. Differences are found in vocabulary level and metacognitive ability with children who have reading difficulties scoring higher (Goswami, 2006; Goswami & Bryant, 1990).

Chiappe et al. (2002) studied adults and children with and without reading disabilities to determine whether phonological problems remained throughout the life span. The adults with LD showed poorer performance compared to the typically performing adults on measures of phonology. These difficulties were present even when compared to same reading level children, particularly on phonological processing and on naming tasks.

These findings lend preliminary support to the developmental lag theory for children with mild reading problems. The developmental lag theory is not as robust for severe reading disabled and dyslexic groups. When matched to reading skills with younger children, studies of children with specific reading disabilities show mixed results. In a critical review of studies, Stanovich, Nathan, and Vala-Rossa (1986) concluded that, "The presently available evidence would appear to suggest the hypothesis that the 'garden-variety' poor reader is characterized by a developmental lag; whereas the much rarer, dyslexic child displays a specific phonological deficit, in conjunction with compensatory use of other skills and knowledge sources" (p. 280). Further, although mildly reading-impaired children should not be overlooked in our schools, they may be expected to progress in reading when given instructional resources and will eventually develop reading abilities similar to their other cognitive skills. The same may not be the case for the more severe and specific reading problems found in children with LD.

Best practice now suggests that the technique, Response to Intervention (RTI), is most appropriate for initial work with children with reading problems before these children are identified as having a learning disability. This technique is generally thought to be most appropriate in the initial stages of treatment when it is not clear how the child will respond to treatment. As discussed above many children will respond to treatment, both those with a mild learning disability and those who are considered slower learners. These children benefit from interventions that are designed prior to identification, and an IQ discrepancy is not required to provide such support (Semrud-Clikeman, 2006).

RTI generally consists of three tiers for intervention. Often the first tier provides additional training for teachers in teaching reading. Tier 2 is small group reading instruction which is provided three times per week, and tier 3 is either individual or two group members who meet daily (O'Connor, Harty, & Fulmer, 2005). The tier system improves reading skills in children in early school grades (Vaughn, Linan-Thompson, & Hickman, 2003). There is limited support for RTI for older students, particularly in high school (Kavale, 2005). While the new IDEA re-authorization suggests using empirically validated interventions when working with children with RD, RTI interventions have small to moderate effects, suggesting only modest validation. In addition, these interventions are generally for phonological processing and phonemic awareness only, thus limiting their applicability to all aspects of reading (Scruggs & Mastropieri, 2002; Strauss, 2001). Further work is needed and, based on concerns that RTI may delay support for children with severe RD, the technique should be evaluated for different levels of disability. It is helpful to attempt interventions before a RD or LD diagnosis is made, and RTI can be very helpful to that end. Concern has been expressed that the technique has not been empirically validated beyond the early grades and that it identifies both too many false positives and false negatives to be used as a sole manner for diagnosing RD/LD (Kavale, 2005).

Comorbid Disorders

When a reading disability is coupled with other learning problems, a more severe form of the disorder is likely present (Semrud-Clikeman, 2007). Most children with a language-based learning disability have difficulty with reading as well as with written language (Lyon, 1996b). Difficulties in written language frequently involve problems with

spelling, organization of ideas, planning of the writing process, and ability to utilize appropriate punctuation and grammar (Harder, Semrud-Clikeman, & Maegden, 2006).

Many children who experience difficulty in reading also have problems in mathematics. Approximately 6 percent of children have a learning disability in mathematics (Semrud-Clikeman, 2006). Most often children with reading disabilities also show difficulty with mathematics calculation while those with reading comprehension problems also struggle with mathematics reasoning. Very few children are diagnosed with a sole disability in mathematics. Problems with visual-spatial and visual-motor skills are linked to problems with nonverbal learning disabilities and are discussed later in this chapter.

Approximately 35 percent to 75 percent of children with learning disabilities also have significant problems with attention (Semrud-Clikeman et al., 1992; Spencer, Biederman, & Mick, 2007). It is likely that attentional and impulse difficulties make it problematic for the child to attend to classroom instruction particularly on tasks that are already very difficult for the child. In addition those children with an ADHD diagnosis have a higher risk of having problems with phonological processing, compared to those in the general population (Lyon, 1996a). Children who have ADHD (particularly with the predominately inattentive subtype) and LD show more difficulty with their peers in social desirability as well as significant signs of social anxiety and low self-esteem (Kellner, Houghton, & Graham, 2003). In contrast, children who were diagnosed with ADHD Combined subtype and LD showed problems with externalizing behaviors and with social functioning due to impulse control and hyperactive behaviors. In addition, children with ADHD: Combined subtype also become more resistant to interventions and require more intensive support due to significant behavioral difficulties (Teeter, 1998).

Children with LD also are more susceptible to emotional difficulties (Martinez & Semrud-Clikeman, 2004), and are more likely to show internalizing disorders such as anxiety and depression as well as withdrawal and low self-esteem. These problems may stem from frustration with the learning process as well as lower expectations for employment and financial success (Lyon, 1996b).

Difficulties in emotional adjustment have been found to extend into adulthood and to require ongoing treatment through psychotherapy for low self-esteem and social difficulties (Brieger & Majovski, 2008; Gregg, Coleman, Lindstrom, & Lee, 2007).

Genetic Factors

The search for the genetic basis of reading disabilities has been helpful in determining the relationship between environmental and genetic factors. The Colorado Reading Project (Decker & Vandenberg, 1985; DeFries, Fulker, & LaBuda, 1987), one of the largest studies of its type, found a strong relationship between reading disabilities in identical or monozygotic twins (MZ) and in same-sex fraternal or dyzgotic twins (DZ). The concordance rate was 71 percent for MZ twins and 49 percent for DZ twins, confirming a strong genetic basis for reading disabilities in children. When the proportion of variance accounted for by both genetic and environmental factors was measured, the genetic factors were found to be more important than environmental factors for explaining differences in reading between MZ and DZ twins (DeFries & Alarcon, 1996; DeFries et al., 1997).

When gender differences and severity issues were evaluated using a sample of MZ and DZ twins, heritability and shared environmental influences were not found to differ between the genders (Hawke, Wadsworth, Olson, & DeFries, 2007; Wadsworth & DeFries, 2005). Other researchers have found that the heritability of LD in more severe populations was greater for males than females (Harlaar, Spinath, Dale, & Plomin, 2005). One of the differences was the definition of severity. When a more severe cutoff was utilized (the most severe 5%, rather than 10%) a male gender bias was found (Harlaar et al., 2005). Differences may also be due to the various methodologies and instruments used to measure reading skill. Harlaar et al. (2005) administered timed tests over the phone while Hawke et al. (2007) administered non-timed measures in-person. In addition, the earlier study used younger children while the other study used older children (Hawke et al., 2007). These finding indicate

that further study that controls for the age and type of measure used is needed to determine whether there is a genetic link to severity and gender in LD.

Continuing study in the Colorado longitudinal twin study has followed 124 twins with a history of reading difficulty, and 154 twins with no history of learning problems over 5–6 years. Initial findings of significant learning problems were present at the follow-up testing 5–6 years later. The most stable measure was the reading measure with a stability correlation of 0.80. In addition the shared genetic influences accounted for 86 percent of the phenotypic relations for the twins with reading problems, and 49 percent for the twins without reading problems (Wadsworth, DeFries, Olson, & Willcutt, 2007).

Some studies have also evaluated the shared environment variable for families with twins. Emerging evidence is present that shared environment effects may be important during the early years of development and schooling, particularly for phonemic awareness and letter identification (Byrne et al., 2002; Harlaar et al., 2005; Petrill, Deater-Deckard, Thompson, & DeThorne, 2006). Variables that have been found to be important in the shared environment and reading outcome include parental education and cognitive ability (Christian, Morrison, & Bryant, 1998), and the family environment for promoting reading and parental involvement in schoolwork (Foy & Mann, 2003; Petrill, Deater-Deckard, Schatschneider, & Davis, 2005; Senechal & LeFevure, 2002). A further study of shared environment with adoptive parents of twins was conducted to determine effects that are separate from genetics. This study found that the adoptive parents' skills in pseudo-word decoding and phonological awareness were related to the child's reading skills, but only for the youngest readers (Petrill, Deater-Deckard, Schatschneider, & Davis, 2007). It was also found that these shared environmental influences decrease with adolescence to the point of almost zero.

In addition to a strong genetic influence for reading ability and the contribution of shared environments for younger children, there have also been studies evaluating the various aspects of reading and heritability of those skills. Word reading and reading comprehension are highly correlated in the early grades, but this correlation decreases with mid-elementary school years when reading comprehension becomes paramount for success in school (Catts, Hogan, & Adlof, 2005; Scarborough, 2005).

Orthographic aspects of reading have also been studied to determine the behavioral genetic contribution to these skills. Orthographic processing is the ability to recall the spelling pattern of a word that is retrieved from memory without decoding the word (Ehri, 2005). Adept readers can use rapid and automatized retrieval of words particularly those with irregular spellings or pronunciations (prevalent is not pre' valent) (Byrne et al., 2008). Previous studies have found a genetic correlation between phonological awareness and print knowledge (Samuelsson et al., 2007), combined word and nonword identification and spelling, rapid naming, and reading comprehension (Byrne et al., 2007) and language ability (Bishop, Adams, & Norbury, 2006).

Byrne et al. (2008) evaluated the contribution of genetics to orthographic processing as well as skills such as nonverbal reasoning. Twin pairs (225 MZ and 214 DZ) in the second grade were compared on measures of orthography as well as the Block Design and vocabulary tests from the WPPSI-R. Heritability for orthography was found to be significant, but not shared environment variables. Further analysis found that there is a shared genetic influence between orthography and phonological coding. In addition it was found that while there was some genetic overlap between overall ability and reading skill, reading variables were substantially separate from IQ.

Reading comprehension difficulty exists separately from word reading accuracy (Oakhill, Cain, & Bryant, 2003). Further studies have found that these children experience problems outside of phonological and orthographic (word form) deficits, thus suggesting that reading comprehension and these skills are dissociable (Perfetti, Landi, & Oakhill, 2005; Scarborough, 2005). In addition, these children also experience listening comprehension difficulties, both with and without coexisting problems with phonological working memory (Catts et al., 2005; Kovas, Oliver, Dale, Bishop, & Plomin, 2005; Nation & Norbury, 2005).

Keenan, Betjemann, Wadsworth, DeFries, and Olson (2006) sought to evaluate the genetic involvement in word recognition, listening comprehension,

and reading comprehension. The second part of the study also evaluated the relation between IQ and these reading skills in view of genetic and shared environment contributions. Seventy monozygotic twin pairs, 61 same-sex fraternal twin pairs, and 60 opposite-sex fraternal twin pairs were compared on measures of reading and listening comprehension. Word recognition was found to have a strong genetic influence and was strongly related to reading comprehension and less strongly to listening comprehension. Reading comprehension and listening comprehension were also found to be related in the genetic analysis apart from the relation with word reading. Environmental aspects were equally related to all the reading aspects and not significantly related to genetic influences. IQ was significantly heritable with the genetic path; IQ to listening comprehension was stronger than listening comprehension to word reading. Word recognition had a significant genetic influence after IQ was controlled, which was also true for reading comprehension. In all cases shared environmental influences were not found to be significant for any variable. The authors suggest that lower power may have influenced these findings.

The finding of a relation between IQ, heritability, and reading disability was also evaluated by Wadsworth, Olson, Pennington, & DeFries (2000). This study found that the genetic influences of IQ were a more important cause of reading disability for higher skills, and the environment had less of an impact for those children with higher ability. Conversely, the children with lower ability showed less genetic influences of IQ and more influence from shared environment. These findings suggest that children with lower abilities may require alternative, earlier intervention. Response to intervention in this group has been very successful (MacMillan, Gresham, & Bocian, 1998).

Prenatal/Postnatal Factors

To date, prenatal factors affecting a child's capacity to develop phonological awareness deficits are virtually unknown; however, there are several environmental factors that have been found to be related to general language deficits and reading disabilities.

Although a biogenetic foundation for language is virtually indisputable, postnatal factors associated with language development typically emphasize the influence of environmental stimulation. Infants 1–4 months of age are quite adept at discriminating speech sounds, and can make discriminations between ba and ga, ma and na, and preschool children seem to utilize phonetic representations when processing language in short-term memory (Molfese, Molfese, & Molfese, 2007; Molfese, Molfese, & Pratt, 2007). Studies with newborn infants have found that children at this age may be aware of and able to discriminate phonemes, even though they may not be aware that phoneme units exist (Cheour et al., 2002). It is likely that experience plays a role in the child's development of speech perception and vocabulary, both of which are related to language acquisition and reading; however, the role of the environment on these factors has not been adequately investigated for poor readers. A predictable growth spurt in phonemic awareness occurs in children at about the age of six years, which appears related to efforts in teaching children to read (Guttorm et al., 2005). The genetic studies suggest that while experience plays a prominent role in the development of phonemic awareness, children with phonological deficits appear to have some biogenetic factor that limits their ability to profit from exposure (Petrill et al., 2006).

Prematurity is another prenatal factor that has been evaluated in children with learning disabilities. Preterm infants who were also of low birth weight have different responses to auditory information and detection (Therien, Worwa, Mattia, & deRegnier, 2004). These differences have been tied to problems with recognition memory and, later, reading disabilities (Curtis, Lindeke, Georgieff, & Nelson, 2002; Rose, Feldman, & Jankowski, 2002). It has also found that these neural circuits can discriminate between term and preterm infants and may be reversed with appropriate interventions (Peterson et al., 2002).

Frequent ear infections may possibly relate to later difficulties with auditory comprehension and phonological coding. Children with frequent middle ear infections do not show long-term language impairment, but do show a more pronounced right ear advantage compared to children without such a history (Asbjornsen et al., 2000; Asbjornsen et al., 2005;

Winskel, 2006). It was suggested by these authors that early hearing difficulties relate to differences in how auditory stimuli are processed and that the increased right ear advantage seen in children with early and frequent ear infections relates to compensation for problems with hearing. Further study is needed to more fully understand these mechanisms.

Neuroanatomical Variations and Neuropsychological Correlates

Brain imaging has increased our knowledge of neuroanatomical and neurofunctional contributions to learning and learning disabilities. Early studies found differences in the area of the planum temporale, a structure implicated in phonological processing (Hynd, Semrud-Clikeman, Lorys, Novey, & Eliopulos, 1990; Morgan & Hynd, 1998). The planum temporale in the left hemisphere is consistently larger in a majority of adults (Galaburda, 2005; Geschwind & Galaburda, 1985; Steinmetz et al., 1992) and in fetuses, newborns, and infants (Chi, Dooling, & Gilles, 1977). The left planum temporale is thought to be the primary site for linguistic processes and reading (Morgan & Hynd, 1998) because of its proximity to the auditory association region and Wernicke's area. The expected leftward asymmetry is rare in dyslexics, whereas symmetry in the temporal regions is more frequent (Hynd & Semrud-Clikeman, 1989; Kibby et al., 2004; Shaywitz et al., 2006). A number of studies report that the symmetrical patterns appear to be the result of larger plana in the right hemisphere (Galaburda, Sherman, Rosen, Aboitiz, & Geschwind, 1985; Larsen, Hoien, Lundberg, & Odegaard, 1990). Although others found smaller left plana, different measurement techniques may be responsible for these divergent findings.

Children with reading disabilities have symmetrical or reversed asymmetry (R > L) in parietooccipital regions, which is found less frequently in normal groups (Helenius, Tarkiainen, Cornelissen, Hansen, & Salmelin, 1999; Tarkiainen, Helenius, Hansen, Cornelissen, & Salmelin, 1999). This region of the brain, called the occipitotemporal system, is involved in rapid recognition of words and has been implicated in the orthographic route to reading and spelling (Pugh, Mencl, Jenner, Lee et al., 2001; Shaywitz, 1998). In addition, in the parietal, occipital, and temporal association areas including the angular gyrus (also called the temporoparietal system) are areas that are activated in reading of pseudo-words and phonological processing (Pugh, Mencl, Jenner, Katz et al., 2001). This region is important to translate unfamiliar words by using phonics and step-by-step decoding.

The final area responsible for reading is in the frontal regions of the brain. In children without reading difficulty, this region is well connected to the posterior region by the superior longitudinal fasciulus (see Chapter 2). This system connects the areas of the brain responsible for oral reading in the frontal area to those responsible for reading understanding in the temporal lobe of the brain. It is believed that this system is important to prepare for oral word reading and is related to phonological processing (Pugh, Mencl, Jenner, Lee et al., 2001).

As the child develops these systems also develop interdependently. When first learning to read the posterior regions of the brain responsible for orthographic and phonological coding are activated and allow the child to decode and analyze the word. Once the word has become automatized (that is overlearned), a neural trace is formed and the pronunciation, spelling, meaning, and the way the word looks are all stored in long-term memory within the written lexicon for that child. When the word is then encountered the reading of the word is automatized and fast and the posterior regions of the brain in the occipitotemporal regions are able to fluently read the word quickly (Shaywitz et al., 2006).

Children without reading disabilities develop these systems simultaneously and are able to store words in memory both phonologically and orthographically (Pugh, Mencl, Jenner, Katz et al., 2001). As the child becomes more adept in reading the occiptotemporal region shows increased activation, allowing for smooth access to the word lexicon (Shaywitz, 2003). Children with learning disabilities experience a disconnection between these systems, making word reading labored and effortful. Functional imaging has found that children with dyslexia show hyperactivation in the frontal system (associated with naming and oral reading) which may be related to trying to compensate for hypoactivity with phonological processing subserved by the posterior systems (Fiez, 1997; Milne, Syngeniotis, Jackson, & Corballis, 2002).

Hoeft et al. (2007) sought to evaluate the hypoactivation in the left posterior systems and the left frontal hyperactivation in a group of adolescents with dyslexia. There were four groups: two groups with a diagnosis of dyslexia, one control group matched on age to one of the dyslexic groups, and one control group matched on reading level to the other dyslexic group. Relative to the age-matched group, the dyslexic group showed hypoactivation in the left parietal regions and hyperactivation in the left inferior regions as well as in the caudate and thalamus. When compared to the reading matched group, the dyslexic group showed hypoactivation in the left parietal regions, but similar activation in the frontal regions. The dyslexic group also had reduced gray matter volume compared to both control groups. These researchers concluded that the hyperactivation was a result of an attempt to compensate for the reading problems. The hypoactivation regions were believed to be a true brain abnormality that is associated with reading disabilities and problems with learning to read (Hoeft et al., 2006). To support this view, findings from intervention studies have indicated that increased activation in these regions occurs after intense intervention, thus suggesting that these regions are a core deficit for dyslexia (Aylward et al., 2003; Shaywitz et al., 2004; Simos et al., 2002).

Structural Differences

Differences have been found that discriminate between children with and without learning disabilities at the molecular as well as the structural level. Autopsied brains show misplaced and misaligned cells particularly in the regions of the perisylvian area, the left frontal region, and the language areas (Galaburda et al., 1985; Grigorenko, 2001; Humphreys, Kaufman, & Galaburda, 1990). Structural differences have been found in the planum temporale (Duara et al., 1991; Hynd et al., 1990; Rumsey et al., 1986), the corpus callosum (Duara et al., 1991; Fine, Semrud-Clikeman, Keith, Stapleton, & Hynd, 2006; Hynd et al., 1991; Larsen, Hoeien, & Oedegaard, 1992), and the frontal lobe area (Semrud-Clikeman, Hynd, Novey, & Eliopulos, 1991).

Semrud-Clikeman et al. (1991) found that atypical patterns of symmetry in the planum temporale were related to word attack skills, passage comprehension skills, and rapid naming abilities. Thus, the left planum was postulated as a central language processing center. Researchers have also explored other neuropsychological postulates and have focused on deficient or abnormal patterns of hemispheric lateralization related to attentional activation processes as plausible explanations for the academic deficiencies exhibited by children with LD.

Dichotic listening has also been utilized to evaluate children with reading disabilities and hemispheric specialization for auditory processing. Findings have indicated that typically developing children show greater ease in focusing attention when provided with a verbal cue while children with LD do better when a tone cue is presented (Obrzut, Boliek, & Asbjornsen, 2006). Other studies have found that the usual right ear advantage for language is not present on a dichotic listening task in children with LD (Helland, Asbjornsen, Hushovd, & Hugdahl, 2007). Since there was no cue to trigger attention to the task, children with LD showed less right ear advantage and in some cases heightened left ear advantage due to activating both hemispheres in order to solve the problem. Thus, the child with LD is dividing attention between both ears and is not as efficient as the child without LD.

Therefore, neither ear is as good as when attention is direct and auditory processing is efficiently managed. These difficulties are related to poorer verbal processing of auditory information, an area of significant difficulty for children with a reading problem (Lamm & Epstein, 1997). These findings are consistent with functional neuroimaging studies that have also found lower activation when processing oral information in children with LD (Heiervang, Stevenson, & Hugdahl, 2002; Helenius et al., 1999; Hugdahl et al., 2003)

These studies raise questions about whether children with learning disabilities have attentional imbalances between the two hemispheres or whether there are problems in interconnected attentional systems. Further research is necessary to determine the relationship between morphology and attention control mechanisms during language tasks in children with LD. Padlonsky (2008) found that children with ADHD and LD who had a history of otitis media showed a more severe form of disability characterized by deficits in phonological processing. The extent to which these neuropsychological aspects are further related to the cognitive, academic, and perceptional deficits associated with LD also needs further exploration.

Implications for Assessment

The difficulties that are present with a definition of a learning disability have not been resolved at this point in time. Ongoing research, however, has evaluated the different problematic areas in learning disabilities to attempt not only to understand the problems posed for the child in learning to read and write, but also to design interventions that are helpful to the child.

Reading Disabilities: Phonological Core Deficits

Phonological awareness deficits are a primary cause of reading deficits (Shaywitz et al., 2006). As described earlier in this chapter, children with phonological reading disabilities (PRD) experience trouble in early reading and also have associated difficulties in speech perception, speech production, and naming tasks. Phonological awareness is the ability to use the phonemic segments of speech, including the awareness and use of the sound structure of language. Related difficulties in phonological processing include difficulty understanding how sounds relate to one another (phonemic awareness deficits), problems with auditory discrimination, naming and vocabulary deficits, and problems with working memory for sounds and sound combinations. Reading requires learning the relationship between graphemes (written letters) and phonemes (sound segments). Thus, children with phonological deficits have difficulty applying the alphabetic principle when reading unfamiliar words (Torgesen et al., 2001). Table 12.1 summarizes selected research findings.

Guidelines for classifying and treating LD may be more clearly articulated and systematically investigated within this transactional framework.

Table 12.1 Summary of specific deficits associated with reading disabilities: Phonological Core Deficits (PRD)

Biogenetic Factors	*Environmental Factors: Prenatal and Postnatal*
– 40% variance in word recognition is genetic – h2g = .62 phonology/reading deficits – h2g = .22 orthographic/ reading deficits	– Orthographic deficits related to exposure to print and learning opportunities – Development of speech and vocabulary related to language acquisition and reading – Growth spurt in phonemic awareness at 6 years related to reading efforts – Despite strong heritability of phonological awareness, deficits can be modified
Temperament	*Birth Complications*
– No known correlates	– No known correlates

CNS Factors
– Gray matter dysfunction
– Left temporal anomalies
– Larger plana in right hemisphere
– Symmetrical R/L[a] temporal lobes
– Symmetrical or reversed parieto-occipital regions
– Abnormal asymmetry (R > L) in prefrontal regions
– Abnormal asymmetry in parietal regions

Neuropsychological Factors
– Rapid naming
– Abnormal hemispheric lateralization
– Attention activation of RH interferes with LH verbal processing
– Attentional control mechanisms between hemispheres
– Phonemic hearing, segmenting, and blending

Intellectual	*Perceptual*	*Memory*	*Attentional*
– Verbal weaknesses – Vocabulary knowledge – Verbal associations – Word similarities – Verbal fluency – Receptive language – Expressive language – Verbal IQ – Comprehension	– Phonemic – Speech	– Digit span – Speech sounds – Word series – Letter strings – Phonetic strategies	– Strong comorbidity of reading problems and ADHD – Attention to phonemes

Academic/Behavioral	*Psychosocial*	*Family*
– Motivational problems – Chronic reading problems – Disengaged in learning – Spends less time reading – Reading and spelling	– Research is sparse – RD in general show internalized disorders (e.g., depression)	– Research is sparse on PRD – Prenatal and postnatal risk factors related to general learning and behavioral problems – "Disorganized" and/or poverty, environment more important with age

Note: PRD refers to phonological reading disabilities, while RD refers to reading disabilities in general. L and LH refer to left hemisphere, R and RH to right hemisphere.

Although not every child is expected to demonstrate all of the associated features presented, Table 12.1 suggests an interaction among the neuropsychological, cognitive, academic, and psychosocial problems that may accompany reading disabilities resulting from phonological core deficits.

Intellectual, Perceptual, Memory, and Attentional Functions

Intellectual Functions

Children with phonological core deficits evidence weaknesses on a variety of verbal measures, including vocabulary knowledge (Berninger, Abbott, Abbott, Graham, & Richards, 2002); auditory memory and verbal associations (Shaywitz et al., 2006); receptive vocabulary, word similarities, and verbal fluency (Fletcher, Morris, & Lyon, 2003), and receptive and expressive language (Wills, 2007). Measures of intelligence relate to the child's exposure and experience with language, a skill that is often compromised in children with a learning disability (Siegel & Smythe, 2005). Stanovich (2005) refers to the Matthew effect to describe the reading-IQ relationship, where reading has "reciprocal causation effects" on other cognitive skills. Children with reading deficits read less, acquire less general and specific knowledge, and may fall further and further behind in achievement and verbal skills (Wong, Strickland, Fletcher-Janzen, Ardila, & Reynolds, 2000).

Perceptual Functions

Difficulty in phonemic processing underlies reading deficits in many children. The child's ability to perceive spoken words appears related to reading difficulties and is less than accurate, particularly under adverse or noisy conditions (Riccio, Cohen, Garrison, & Smith, 2005). Deficient speech perception seems evident, but children with phoneme awareness deficits may also have poor memory for speech sounds as well. (Tunmer, Chapman, & Prochnow, 2003).

Memory Functions

Research does provide evidence that children with reading disabilities do poorly on a variety of memory functions, including deficits on digit span, recall of letter strings, nonsense words, and word order (Jarrold, Baddeley, Hewes, Leeke, & Phillips, 2004). The ability to remember a series of words precedes a reading disability diagnosis and appears to be a risk factor rather than a consequence for reading problems (Adams & Gathercole, 2000). Poor readers are unable to use the phonological structure of language to hold letter strings in short-term memory (Riccio, Garland, & Cohen, 2007). Some have suggested that poor readers rely on word meaning in an effort to remember words, and do not appear to use

visual rather than phonetic memory strategies. To support this hypothesis, error pattern analysis suggests that poor readers make errors that are consistent with phonological processing and in a manner similar to good readers, but that their error scores are quite high (Mann, 2003). These findings indicate that they are not using good orthographic coding to recall the spelling and word form in order to read a problematic word.

Academic and School Adjustment

Early reading failure has been shown to create motivational problems in children. Children with chronic reading problems often dislike going to school, and develop secondary self-esteem problems (Martinez & Semrud-Clikeman, 2004). Wills (2007) further reports that remedial classes often drill in phonics or word recognition, but may deemphasize passage comprehension so that the child spends less time reading. Eventually the child develops more generalized cognitive deficits involving numerous subject areas due to delays in reading skills.

Social-Psychological Adjustment

Research addressing the socioemotional functioning of children with phonological core deficits is sparse. Other research shows that children with LD who demonstrate distinctively lower verbal abilities with intact visual-spatial skills were rated by their parents as having more internalizing disorders, particularly depression (Bender, Rosenkrans, & Crane, 1999). The extent to which this applies specifically to children with phonological core deficits is yet to be established. In addition, it appears that children with basic phonological processing disorders are prone to develop psychosocial disturbances if parents and teachers have unrealistic expectations or if acting out serves as a mechanism for avoiding school and/or schoolwork. Others have found that children with conduct disorders (CD) also have lower verbal intelligence (Grigorenko, 2006). The extent to which CD and language-based difficulties are associated with poor achievement and learning problems needs further study (Sundheim & Voeller, 2004).

Children with neurological signs who also have learning disabilities have been found to be at higher risk for emotional disturbance (Glassberg, Hooper, & Mattison, 1999)

Family and Home Factors

There are few studies addressing family home factors and reading disabilities, specifically for children who display phonological awareness deficits. The research that has been conducted generally shows genetic linkage to be stronger than environmental variables (Petrill et al., 2006). Studies investigating family and home influences on learning disabilities in general have found that prenatal and postnatal conditions are highly related to risk factors, including the development of general behavioral or learning problems during the first 20 months of life (Pennington, 2006). Further, risk conditions were found in families that were characterized as disorganized and/or in poverty, and these environmental factors became more significant as the children became older. Children who continued to demonstrate moderate to severe problems tended to come from families with low economic status and with a high degree of disruption and psychopathology in the family. Socioeconomic status, home conditions, and educational attainment of family members may act as compensatory variables for children initially identified as at risk for reading problems, but who later show normal achievement progress (Capozzi et al., 2008). It is premature to generalize conclusions reported in studies investigating children with general learning problems to students with phonological core deficits. However, stable and consistent home situations, strong emotional family bonds, and child characteristics (e.g., easy temperament) appear to be important factors associated with the "resilient" child who appears less susceptible to the adverse effects of risk factors (Elksnin et al., 2001).

Implications for Intervention

Evidence indicates that phonologically impaired children show normal progress in math, but continue to show severe delays in reading despite remedial attempts in school (Torgesen, 2004). When remedial techniques specifically address phonological core deficits, the outcome is more positive for at-risk students and children with PRD. Studies have also shown increased reading abilities when phonological awareness is combined with metacognitive techniques (Cunningham, 2007), and when phoneme awareness is contextualized within the reading curriculum (Cunningham, 2005).

Early identification and remediation have been offered in order to provide the children with early support who may be at risk for reading difficulties (National Reading Panel, 2000). Early remediation has also been suggested to help prevent the Matthew effect which is related to poorer readers reading less than good readers, thus widening the gap between the two groups (Torgesen, 2004). Specific training in phonemic awareness for young children in kindergarten and early elementary grades has proved successful and seems preferable to control conditions where children are not exposed to these skills (Bishop & Snowling, 2004). Further, children as young as two years of age are at extreme risk for severe reading problems when they have a family history of dyslexia and also possess even mild syntactic fluency problems in language development (Olson, 1999; Petrill et al., 2006). Research has suggested that phonological processing is a key deficit and early intervention needs to stress these skills, as well as develop phoneme-grapheme correspondence (Jackson & Coltheart, 2001). A meta-analysis of studies evaluating phonological intervention found large effects for the immediate aspect of the intervention, but weaker long-term effects (Bus & van Ijzendoorn, 1999). The long-term effects on reading, spelling and reading comprehension after one and one-half years following the intervention were very small or nonsignificant. Another study found long-term effects for children who received phonological training in preschool did show significant improvement, but again the long-term effect was small yet significant (effect sizes ranging from 0.33 to 0.39) (Byrne, Fielding-Barnsley, & Ashley, 2000).

Some main types of programs have purported to do so include the Reading Recovery Program, Phonological Awareness plus Synthetic Phonics (PASP) (Torgesen, 2004), Orton-Gillingham approach, Process Assessment of the Learner (PALS) (Berninger, 2001), and the Lindamood Phoneme

Sequencing Program (Lindamood & Lindamood, 1998). The Lindamood and Fast ForWord programs were discussed in the language section of this chapter and will not be discussed further in this section. These programs will not be reviewed in-depth in this section, but will be described and the interested reader is encouraged to seek out further information as wanted. The research indicates that early intervention is important, but it also suggests that intervention needs to continue, particularly for children who are at higher risk for learning problems. This suggestion is supported by a recent study comparing children who showed significant reading problems with those exhibiting milder difficulties. Early intervention improved reading, but did not show long-term effects when intervention ended (Hurry & Sylva, 2007).

Reading Recovery

The Reading Recovery Program (Clay, 1993) effectively increases reading achievement of children in the early grades (Ohio Department of Education, 1995), but does not show continued progress in later grades when the children again fall behind their peers (Venezky, 1998). The program incorporates aspects of whole language while also emphasizing decoding instruction. Decoding is taught in the context of reading and writing, where the teacher selects strategies depending on the child's unique reading problems. It is helpful for early intervention with less support provided for long-term outcome if the program does not continue (Chapman, Tunmer, & Prochnow, 2001). Some have suggested the Reading Recovery does not fully teach phonics, but relies on a whole language approach, thus children who have significant problems with phonological awareness are at a great disadvantage and are not assisted by this approach (Reynolds & Wheldall, 2007).

The research does not support using this program for children with significant phonological processing deficits. It may be helpful for those children with orthographic difficulties, an area that is discussed in the next section of this chapter. The research also supports the idea that while early intervention is good, it needs to be continued in order to affect good long-term outcomes.

Orton-Gillingham

The Orton-Gillingham (OG) method is a systematic and multisensory approach to reading and writing (Gillingham & Stillman, 1997). It is an intensive type of instruction that needs to be accomplished either on a one-to-one basis or in a small group. A phonetic approach to reading, it that stresses sound-symbol correspondence, morphology, syntax, and meaning. It involves training using visual, auditory, and kinesthetic/tactile learning exercises which have also been called the *Language Triangle* (Gillingham & Stillman, 1997). Children are taught the components for learning and provided many opportunities to practice until mastery occurs; assessment of their progress is built into the program.

A meta-analysis of the research with the OG method evaluated 12 studies that utilized a comparison group (Ritchey & Goeke, 2006). Of the 12 studies reviewed five showed OG instruction was more effective, compared to all other interventions. Four studies found improved word reading, word decoding, spelling, and reading comprehension. Two studies found improvement in vocabulary skills and only one study evaluated fluency ability. The conclusion from this review was that there was only one study that evaluated OG in an experimental fashion and whether this program is experimentally validated as required by the No Child Left Behind Law (No Child Left Behind, 2002).

Whether the OG method is feasible for more than a few children has been challenged in the courts, and the school districts have won in over 75 percent of the cases brought before a mediator or a court (Rose & Zirkel, 2007). One of the issues has been the cost of providing the OG method in a regular school district (Torgesen et al., 2001). In addition, response to the intervention (RTI) model and the reauthorization of IDEA have suggested a shift from the discrepancy model to one that includes pre-referral interventions provided in the regular education classroom. Given the shift to early intervention and some funding for this intervention, the OG method may become more common in regular school districts as part of RTI (Rose & Zirkel, 2007). However, IDEA's proposed regulations require research-based interventions and the research supporting most of the interventions is not clear and empirically validated.

The PASP program (Torgesen, 2004) stresses the use of phonological awareness and decoding ability. Similar to OG and Reading Recovery programs it stresses systematic instruction in phonemic decoding as well as in reading comprehension. Research support has not been reported at this point in time and requires additional empirical validation prior to becoming a widely accepted program.

Reading comprehension is another area that requires remediation for many children. Most children that have difficulties with reading comprehension also have trouble with decoding skills. Generally, problems are present in vocabulary, listening comprehension, and working memory and likely underlie problems with reading comprehension (Leach, Scarborough, & Rescorla, 2003). Interventions often require learning how to think about what is being read, mapping advance organizers on the topic at hand, and utilizing strategies for reading and learning (Vaughn & Klingner, 2004). A program developed by Schumaker, Deshler, and McKnight (2002) is designed to directly teach reading comprehension through the use of metacognitive strategies.

Although phonemic awareness is essential for early reading success, several researchers have found that orthographic and visual-spatial deficits are present in some children with severe reading disabilities. These problems have not been as well studied as phonological coding. This type of learning disability will be briefly reviewed next.

Visual/Orthographic Deficits in Reading

Although PRD seems well established, there also appears to be a smaller group of children who have major difficulties accessing the orthographic or visual features of written words (Berninger & Fuller, 1992). Chase and Tallal (1991) describe the sequential order of reading including the logographic, alphabetic, and orthographic. During the logographic stage, reading occurs through a visual or graphic analysis of letters and words (lexical system). Visual memory plays an important role during this stage, and the child begins to develop a sight-word vocabulary. The alphabetic stage is characterized by the phonological decoding (phonological system) of words using grapheme-phoneme (letter-to-sound) conversions. To develop into a fluent reader, the child must then proceed to the orthographic stage, where larger morpheme units (i.e., syllables) are used. Decoding is quicker during this last stage and this model assumes that later stages are dependent on skills acquired at earlier stages. It has been suggested that orthography is a direct route to understanding meaning of a word while phonology first requires decoding of the word and then the orthography/meaning (Harm & Seidenberg, 2004; Seidenberg & McClelland, 1989). The proposed model of Harm and Seidenberg (2004) suggests that orthography and phonology are cooperative and not separate. Both are tied to semantics with orthography being direct and phonology being indirect.

Berninger (2001) describes numerous measures of orthographic coding skills and methods for assessing the lexical processes of reading. A number of research tasks have been employed to measure orthographic coding skills, including pseudohomophone choice (e.g., raiwane), letter verification, homonym verification, recognition of orthographic patterns, rhyme judgments with orthographically dissimilar words (e.g., great-state), and brief exposure of words. Lexical impairments have been found in a small proportion of children with dyslexia, although impairment in the phonological system seems to be a more consistent finding across studies.

There may be a gender difference in orthographic ability. Some evidence show that males have more difficulty with orthographic skills compared to women with no difference between the genders in motor ability (Berninger, Nielsen, Abbott, Wijsman, & Raskind, 2008a). In addition, males had more difficulty with accuracy and rate of reading passages orally both due to orthographic and phonological problems. Further study is needed in the area of orthography and its relation to phonology. One of the major studies conducted has linked orthography to difficulties with written language (Berninger, Nielsen, Abbott, Wijsman, & Raskind, 2008b). The following section discusses written language disorders.

Written Language Disorders

Written language impairments are often overlooked in discussions of learning disabilities. The prevalence of written language disorders is approximately 1.3–2.7 percent for handwriting deficits, 3.7 percent to 4 percent for spelling deficits, and 1 percent to 3 percent for written expression (Berninger & Hart, 1992). The most recent estimates of difficulties in writing have indicated that 69 percent to 77 percent of typically developing students in fourth, eighth, and 12th grades did not meet writing proficiency goals as measured by the National Assessment of Educational Progress (Graham & Perrin, 2007b). Children with specific problems with learning show significant difficulties in composition, spelling, handwriting, and grammar at higher levels due to the learning disability (Graham & Perrin, 2007a).

Written language disorders (WLD) can have profound effects on the academic attainment of older children and adolescents. In fact, young children with learning disabilities differ from typically developing children on writing conventions, while older LD children show significant deficits from typically developing children on composition skills (Berninger et al., 2006). Further, children with LD have difficulty writing narrative text, generating expository, and finding ideas to write about (Berninger et al., 2006). Men had more significant problems in writing and spelling, compared to women (Berninger et al., 2008a). In addition, males had more difficulty with composition and handwriting although they did not differ in motor ability.

Neuropsychological Correlates of Written Language Disorders

The extent to which written language disorders result from right- or left-hemisphere lesions or dysfunction is still not resolved. The two hemispheres appear to play complementary roles in writing, with the right hemisphere (anterior, central, and posterior regions) involved in the visual-spatial, emotional, and affective components of language skills, while the left hemisphere (temporalparietal and anterior regions) is involved in linguistic, speech, and reading processes. Studies have found that the processing of graphics requires quick recognition of the spatial features (Coltheart, Rastle, Perry, Langdon, & Ziegler, 2001) with teaching of handwriting contributing the visual recognition of letters (Longcamp et al., 2008). Areas found through fMRI to be involved in writing include the left Broca's area and bilateral inferior parietal lobe. In addition the fusiform gyrus in the temporal lobe appears to have an area that is dedicated to word forms which is important for spelling as well as for writing (Xue & Poldrack, 2007). This region has been implicated in processing of letter patterns, a skill important for handwriting and spelling (McCandliss, Cohen, & Dehaene, 2003).

The neuropsychological substrates of WLD have not been researched as thoroughly as reading and speech-language disorders. Written language deficits have been found to be associated with right hemispheric lesions (Aram & Ekelman, 1988). Orthographic mapping, a skill important for spelling and writing, has been found to be present in the right frontal gyrus and right posterior parietal gyrus (Cohen et al., 2002). Direct intervention in spelling and writing with dyslexic children found normalization in this region following intensive treatment using fMRI (Richards et al., 2005). These changes were related to improvement in spelling of real and nonwords.

Cognitive Correlates of Written Language

Writing requires motor skills as well as visual-spatial ability. The child begins learning to write by copying and tracing figures, and moves to independent production of these figures as the motor strokes become more automatized. Teaching generally moves from single letters to connecting letters to making words through practice and repetition. Studies have suggested that children respond very well to visual models paired with practice rather than through practice alone (Berninger & Amtmann, 2003).

Hayes (1996) has revised his previous model developed with Flower (Hayes & Flower, 1986) which includes planning, translating and reviewing as key issues in writing. Problem solving and executive functioning skills have also been implicated in writing. Children with writing difficulties may experience problems with selective attention which impacts the ability to plan and write coherently. In addition, there may be problems with organization and spelling that further impede the writing process. Handwriting or keyboarding difficulties arising from motor or visual-spatial challenges can also impede writing progress and interfere with conveying main ideas. Memory problems affect word retrieval; spelling; memory for rules of grammar, punctuation and capitalization, and dysfluent writing. Language problems may result in impoverished vocabulary, decreased written expression, dysphonetic (phoneme–grapheme irregularities), spelling patterns, and poor narration. Working memory is also important for writing because it allows ideas to be utilized as the child/adolescent is writing. It is also important for recalling vocabulary, spelling, and grammar as the writing process continues (Hooper, Swartz, Wakely, de Kruif, & Montgomery, 2002).

An important area for intact writing ability is planning and self-regulation (Harder et al., 2006). Planning is closely related to working memory and the two skills interact. As one writes the ability to plan what is to be said next and to link it to what has been said requires working memory (Gregg & Mather, 2002). These skills have been found to be problematic for children with writing difficulties and have also been the target for interventions.

Assessment of Written Language Disorders

Written language disorders can be measured using writing samples taken from the child's academic work or structured tests. Portfolio or authentic assessment procedures typically include an analysis of writing samples generated by the child. See Table 6.1 for a list of commonly utilized standardized measures.

Informal measures of writing are very helpful in understanding the difficulties a particular child has in writing. Task analysis, error pattern analysis, application of the academic skill, dynamic assessment

(e.g., learning efficiency), and process assessment using the child's curriculum to determine the learning processes used by the child are several alternative measures that can be used informally to evaluate the child's writing skills (Berninger, 2001).

Interventions for Written Language Disorders

Berninger and colleagues have published extensively on interventions for handwriting and spelling as well as for writing composition. A review of the literature as to interventions for WLD has indicated that a tiered model of instruction provides the best results for both children with and without learning disabilities who experience written language deficits (Graham, Olinghouse, & Harris, in press). Particular areas that are important to target for intervention at Tier 1 include direct teaching of the ability to plan, revise, and edit a writing sample. In addition, the ability to set clear goals and develop an outline, as well as understand how to use the outline to write a preliminary draft of the writing sample is important, as is teaching the students how to develop an idea and link it throughout the writing sample are all crucial to developing appropriate writing skills (Mason & Graham, 2008).

The second tier includes teaching the student self-regulation which includes self-monitoring, self-reward, and instructions as the writing process continues. During this period of time it was also suggested to utilize student-teacher conferencing and peer conferencing to discuss progress and any areas of difficulty that were encountered (Mason & Graham, 2008). Reading and writing need to be taught together as they are complementary, and writing cannot be done without also utilizing reading skills (Graves, Valles, & Rueda, 2000).

Using computers, technology, and web-based instruction can support basic writing skills and direct teaching, but cannot be used in isolation (Feretti, MacArthur, & Dowdy, 2000). The use of this technology in isolation is often recommended for working with children with written language disabilities (Freeman, MacKinnon, & Miller, 2004). It is important, however, to emphasize that using computers and technology have not been empirically validated for WLD (Berninger & Hooper, 2006).

Summary

The emerging evidence in WLD is providing support to improve our diagnostic and interventional capacity to assist children in learning how to write. These skills are becoming more and more crucial for functioning in many positions and for success in college. WLD often goes hand in hand with RD and needs to be treated accordingly. There is evidence that utilizing small groups and providing intensive intervention can assist children with the process of writing. Difficulties remain for adolescents and college students with WLD, particularly as writing demands increase (Harder & Semrud-Clikeman, submitted). More work is needed to understand early writing difficulties as well as appropriate interventions for high school and college students.

Learning Disabilities in Mathematics

A sole learning disability in mathematics is unusual and often found in children with nonverbal learning disabilities (NVLD). NVLD will be discussed in the next section of this chapter. The prevalence of mathematics learning disability (MLD) is approximately 5 percent to 8 percent of school-aged children (Geary, 2004). It is unclear from these percentages what proportion of these children also has a learning disability in reading and/or ADHD. It is also not clear how MLD and RD differ and whether they arise from two separate substrates (Mazzocco & Myers, 2003). MLD is similar to RD in that many processes are involved in mathematics knowledge and a definition that encompasses all of the complexity of mathematics is not established at this time. Consequently, the research findings are varied due to differing definitions, cut-offs, and conceptualization of what a MLD is.

Geary (2004) suggests there are three subtypes of MLD. The first is the procedural subtype. These children's performance skills are similar to a developmental delay and their skills often improve with age and grade. They show frequent careless errors, use their fingers to count, and do not fully understand the basic processes behind the task. The second subtype is the semantic memory which continues throughout school. These children frequently also have a RD, show problems with memory and retrieval of math facts. This subtype is hypothesized to be associated with a left hemispheric dysfunction due to problems with retrieval of information. The final subtype is called the visuospatial subtype. These children experience problems with spatial representation, aligning columns, understanding the relationships between number and quantity, and experiencing problems with misperception. These children do not show a RD. The deficit in this subtype is hypothesized to be a right hemispheric dysfunction. It should be cautioned that there is no empirical evidence to support this; therefore these are basically theoretical at this time. The final subtype is reminiscent of the nonverbal learning disability disorder which is discussed later in this chapter.

Development of Mathematics Ability

For the typically developing child counting is an important ability in learning mathematics. Skills such as one-to-one correspondent counting, correct order of numbers, and understanding how objects can be sorted and categorized are important pre-math skills that underlie development. Findings with MLD children indicate that they do not understand the counting process that underlies mathematical skills (Hoard, Geary, & Hamson, 1999).

Arithmetic skills begin with addition which is based on counting ability. Arithmetic facts become memorized and then automatized with practice and exposure. As the child becomes more adept at the calculations, the problems are solved more efficiently and more quickly with fewer errors (Geary, 2004). Children with MLD experience significant problems in solving arithmetic calculation problems. Younger children generally use their fingers to count to solve the problems; a strategy that becomes less useful as the facts are automatized. Children with MLD do not move from the finger counting strategy to automatic processing until the late elementary years (Geary & Hoard, 2002). In addition, problem solving strategies and memory retrieval deficits for number facts are not well established until the MLD child is much older than his/her peers (Hanich, Jordan, Kaplan, & Dick, 2001; Ostad, 2000). These difficulties may be related to problems with storing facts and then retrieving them in an efficient manner (Geary, 2004).

Neuropsychological Correlates of MLD

A review of the literature found that 231 articles were published between 1985 and 2006 studying MLD, compared to 1,077 for RD in the same time period. Thus, the study of MLD is in its infancy compared to that of RD or possibly WLD. Also complicating the situation is the dearth of standardized measures that are specifically designed to evaluate a mathematics-based learning disability. This consideration is important because standardized tests often measure overall calculation and reasoning skills, but do not evaluate number sense, counting skill and other components important for mathematical reasoning (Murphy, Mazzocco, Hanich, & Early, 2008).

Murphy et al. (2008) evaluated three groups of children using varying definitions of MLD. One group had mathematics ability in kindergarten measured at or below the 10th percentile, one group had scores between the 11th and 25th percentile, and the final group had scores above the 25th percentile on the Test of Early Math Ability (TEMA-2) (Ginsberg & Baroody, 1990). These children were evaluated in kindergarten and again in third grade. Measures included reading cluster from the WJ R, visual-spatial ability, rapid automatized naming tasks, and the Contingency Naming Test as a measure of working memory (Anderson, Anderson, Northam, & Taylor, 2000). It was found that the mathematics skills of the two highest scoring groups increased at a faster rate than for the children in the lowest performing group. The middle group did show a lag that continued into third grade, compared to the typically achieving group. These differences continued at the same rate indicating that, while not as severe as the low performing group, the middle group continued to lag in mathematics

ability. In addition, the low achieving group appeared to reach a plateau that wasn't seen in the two higher achieving groups, suggesting that further improvement was unlikely without intensive intervention. All groups differed on the counting task particularly in identifying errors that were made.

An assessment of related neuropsychological factors found that IQ, visual-spatial ability, and rapid number naming predicted group membership at the entry level. IQ and visual-spatial ability were not predictive of growth rates while rapid naming of numbers was particularly for the lowest achieving group. Reading ability was related most strongly to progress for the lowest achieving group and was also present as a predictor for the middle achieving group, albeit in a weaker manner. Working memory skills were related to mathematics difficulty as well as progress for all groups. Poorer working memory ability was related to efficiency in solving mathematical problems.

Executive functioning appears to be a problematic area for children with MLD. In order to solve a mathematical problem one not only needs the basic facts and operations readily at hand, but must also focus attention to the task at hand and inhibit responding to irrelevant material (Blair, Knipe, & Gamson, 2008; Geary, 2004). These skills, plus working memory, are important for success in mathematics, but children with MLD appear to have problems with these skills. Children with MLD show concurrent difficulties on tasks that measure executive functioning, particularly in the areas of working memory and inhibition (Mazzocco & Kover, 2007).

Children with MLD are less accurate, compared to their peers, in evaluating whether answers to specific arithmetic problems are correct or not. This difficulty is related to the MLD child's ability to monitor what is being asked of him/her and evaluating whether the correct response has been provided. Such self-checking is an important aspect of mastering arithmetic facts and processes (Garrett, Mazzocco, & Baker, 2006).

Neurological Contributions to Mathematics Skills

Mathematicians have increased parietal gray matter bilaterally and increased volume of the bilateral inferior frontal lobes. These regions have been implicated in arithmetic calculation and visuospatial processing. Morphometric differences have been found in the brains of accomplished mathematicians, musicians, and scientists in the parietal lobes. Larger parietal regions and more gyral formations have been linked to stronger mathematical skills in adults (Spitzka, 1907; Witelson, Kigar, & Harvey, 1999). Brain differences may be due to experience and/or genetic disposition. Studies have found that brain differences can be associated with intense learning. Studies of children with early and intense musical training have found morphological differences in these children compared to controls (Gaser & Schlaug, 2003; Hutchinson, Lee, & Gaab, 2003; Munte, Altenmuller, & Jancke, 2002). Brain structural changes have also been linked to intensive training in undergraduate and graduate students in medicine, with increases in the bilateral parietal cortex as well and hippocampus in post-versus pre-testing (Dragnanski et al., 2006). These increases were associated with learning abstract material. Whether increased volume in the parietal and hippocampal regions are present at earlier ages has not been studied. What differences may be present at an earlier age in students who are mathematically and scientifically disposed, and how these differences change with exposure and training, are important questions for further study. Long-term training in a mathematical discipline may lead to brain changes that support mathematical ability.

There are studies that link brain changes to practice and experience with mathematical concepts. These studies have generally utilized structural (anatomical) data. While high ability has been linked to expertise in a field, differences in brain structure may be due to more than solely intelligence, and are specific to mathematics-based talent (Rickard et al., 2000). Very few studies have been conducted that involve brain activation in adults with mathematics-based interests, and no studies have linked developmental brain activation and structural changes in participants with math-based skills and interests. No studies were found that evaluate neuroimaging in children with mathematical disabilities.

Implications for Assessment

As described in Chapter 6, there are several standardized measures that evaluate reading, mathematics and written language. There are very few specially developed tests just for mathematics. To evaluate mathematical skills standardized tests need to be supplemented with curriculum-based materials. These materials need to evaluate the child's counting ability, understanding of quantity, knowledge of concepts, and ability to check one's work. One of the main tests used to evaluate mathematics directly include the Key Math Diagnostic Arithmetic Test-3 (Connolly, 2007). The test is designed for students aged four years, six months to 21 years and meets the criteria established by the National Council of Teachers of Mathematics in 2000. Its measures evaluate numeration, algebra, geometry, measurement, probability, mental computation, basic fact knowledge, problem solving, and estimation.

For younger children, the Test of Early Mathematics Ability-3 (Ginsburg & Baroody, 2002) measures basic number understanding as well as beginning comprehension of quantity and mathematical facts. Evaluating the child's ability to count, to understand quantity through a number line, and having the child rapidly name numbers are other methods for understanding a child who is at risk for learning problems in mathematics. There is emerging evidence that children who experience difficulty with phoneme-grapheme correspondence may also have problems associating numbers and symbols (Wills, 2007).

Implications for Interventions

As stated above, drilling on mathematical facts is helpful only up to a point. Using visual cues as well as experiential materials may be very helpful for a child who has not mastered the concepts of basic math (numerosity, quantity, etc.). Cuisenaire rods are a series of color-segmented rods with different colors representing numbers from 1 to 10. Children are able to mix and match the colors to understand adding (2 red rods each equal to

5 make 10) or subtracting rods as desired. Other visual aids such as number lines can also help children understand how numbers relate to each other.

Word problems can be problematic for children who have difficulty understanding the words as well as the processes that are required. Fuchs et al. (2004) evaluated third-grade students to evaluate how word problems are solved. The children were provided with intervention to assist with understanding word problems and developing strategies to solve future problems. This intervention improved functioning in typically developing children apart from knowledge that they would have gained from practice (aligning columns, understanding particular words and symbols, etc.). When these interventions were applied to children who were below grade level in mathematics, they also made improvement following intervention (Fuchs et al., 2003a). When these strategies and self-monitoring strategies were further evaluated in low achieving samples of children in mathematics, these children had more difficulty, particularly in setting realistic goals based on their performance (Fuchs et al., 2003b). Thus, teaching basic executive functions may assist in helping children with MLD to improve.

Summary

Based on this brief review of the literature on MLD, there are many areas of inquiry that are incomplete in our understanding of mathematically based learning disability. Neuroimaging of children with MLD has not been published at this point in time and it is not clear what the neurological contributions to mathematical difficulty are. While there is evidence that excellence in mathematical ability may be related to enhanced parietal lobe functioning, neuroanatomical and neurofunctional differences in children with MLD and those without have not been demonstrated. As the research continues to produce results, findings as to best practices for assessment and intervention will assist in our understanding of this disorder both with and without co-occurring reading disability.

Nonverbal Learning Disabilities

In a series of studies (Rourke, 1989, 1995; Rourke & Tsatsanis, 1996), Rourke and colleagues introduced the concept of a syndrome, nonverbal learning disability (NVLD), based on the presence of an intact left hemisphere with dysfunctional right-hemisphere systems. The interplay between basic neuropsychological deficits and assets result in complex social-emotional and academic difficulties.

The definition of a nonverbal learning disability is problematic and varies among researchers and clinicians. Children with NVLD generally show a different pattern of strengths and weaknesses compared to children with LD. In contrast to children with LD who show difficulties in phonological processing, children with NVLD frequently do fairly well in single word reading and in spelling. Children with NVLD have significant problems with mathematics calculation, frequently misalign the columns in the computations, and have problems learning basic mathematics facts. They have particular difficulty in recalling information that is complex or novel, but do very well with rote memory or information that can be recalled by verbal means (Rourke, 1995). Many children with NVLD have difficulty with fine and gross motor development and experience problems in learning to skip, tie shoes, and to write legibly.

Children with NVLD also have difficulties understanding nonverbal input in social situations and, subsequently, are socially isolated. They are infrequently chosen in games and often socially isolated. Significant problems are described in the child's ability to correctly perceive social relationships and with social judgment. In several instances the child experiences difficulty with relating to peers. Many children with NVLD relate better to adults and may cling to teachers and parents as a way of adapting to a confusing social situation. Many children with NVLD also have a tendency to show attentional difficulties and may qualify for an additional diagnosis of ADHD: predominately inattentive. An increased incidence of mood disorders has been found in older children with NVLD.

Children with NVLD have particular difficulties understanding situations that are novel and complex (Rourke & Fuerst, 1991). Particular difficulty is present in understanding situations that involve cause-effect reasoning and with generating solutions to problems (Semrud-Clikeman, 2001). Language skills are generally well developed for basic skills, but problems are also present with more complex language, understanding figurative language and idioms, and with incongruities frequently seen with the understanding of humor (Semrud-Clikeman & Glass, 2008). Difficulties with social conversation as well as reciprocity in relating to others can significantly affect the NVLD child's ability to enter into peer relations, a skill that becomes more important with adolescence.

Rourke and colleagues (2002) characterize the NVLD disorder as having several principal features, including:

- bilateral tactile-perceptual deficits more pronounced on the left side of the body than the right,
- bilateral coordination problems—again more on the left than right,
- problems with visual, spatial, and organizational abilities,
- problems adapting to novel and complex situations—use of rote or literal interpretation of behaviors that frequently result in inappropriate behavior,
- difficulty with problem solving—more evident with nonverbal than verbal materials and situations,
- problems with benefiting from positive and negative feedback,
- a distorted sense of time,
- well developed rote verbal memory,
- highly verbose with much repetition of previously stated ideas,
- poor speech intonation (prosody),
- problems with mathematics calculation with relative strengths in reading and spelling, and
- problems with social judgment, social perception, and social interaction skills.

Some studies have not supported this conceptualization, particularly in regard to the difficulty in motor and perception skills (Wilkinson & Semrud-Clikeman, 2008). Areas that have received support in research include prosody, attention, mathematics problems, social judgment difficulty, and challenges with problem solving (Semrud-Clikeman & Fine, 2008). Many clinicians and researchers utilize diagnoses that include 3–5 of the symptoms listed above.

There is little empirical evaluation of this process and further study is needed. It is not clear which of the symptoms are required for a diagnosis and which are correlated. For example, some children may show visual-spatial and mathematics problems, but do not have difficulty with social understanding. Others do not show verbal performance differences and yet have social difficulty, visual-spatial problems, and mathematics difficulty. A discriminant analysis of a large database of children with NVLD, ADHD, LD, and ASD found that the single most salient predictor of group membership for NVLD was social functioning (Fine, Semrud-Clikeman, Reynolds, & Smith, submitted). Similar studies need to evaluate which of the symptoms in this disorder are primary and which are correlated in order for a better understanding of what NVLD is and how to diagnose the disorder. See Table 12.2 for a summary of research investigating the neuropsychological, cognitive, academic, and psychosocial features of the NVLD syndrome.

The NVLD model is a culmination of 20 years of research investigating the neurocognitive basis of learning and social-emotional functioning in children (Rourke & Tsatsanis, 2000), and is an extension of the Goldberg and Costa model (Goldberg & Costa, 1981). Rourke (1989) summarizes two major functional-anatomical differences between the hemispheres:

1. The left hemisphere has greater cortical representation in specific sensory modalities (in temporal, occipital, and parietal areas) and in the motor cortex, whereas the right hemisphere has more association cortex (temporoparietal and prefrontal areas) than the left.
2. The left hemisphere has more intraregional connections, while the right has more interregional connections.

These basic differences led Goldberg and Costa (1981) to conclude that the right hemisphere has a greater capacity for dealing with "informational complexity." Rourke (1989) further incorporates neurodevelopmental theory and discusses the role of the right hemisphere cognitive and emotional adjustment in children. Rourke proposes that the right hemisphere is more important than the left for activating the entire cortex, processing novel information, developing new descriptive systems,

Table 12.2 A summary of specific deficits associated with Nonverbal Learning Disabilities (NLD)

Biogenetic Factors		*Environmental Factors/Prenatal/Postnatal*	
– No known correlates		– NLD appear at or soon after birth	
		– Neurodevelopmental disorder or may be caused by traumatic injury	
		– Few details on environmental impact	
Temperament		*Birth Complications*	
– No known correlates		– No known correlates	
		CNS Factors	
		– White matter dysfunction	
		– Intermodal integration (callosal fibers)	
		– Right-hemisphere involvement	
	Neuropsychological Factors		
	– Bilateral tactile deficits (pronounced on left side)		
	– Visual-spatial-organizational deficits		
	– Complex psychomotor deficits		
	– Oral-motor apraxia		
	– Concept formation and problem-solving deficits		
Intellectual	*Perceptual Memory*	*Memory*	*Attentional*
– Concept formation	– Visual discrimination	– Tactile	– Tactile
– Strategy generation	– Visual detail	– Nonverbal	– Visual attention
– Hypothesis testing	– Visual relation	– Complex information	– Attends to simple, repetitive verbal material
– Cause-effect relations			
– Little speech prosody			
– Formal operational thought			
Academic/Behavioral	*Psychosocial*		*Family*
– Graphomotor	– Adapting		– Research is sparse
– Reading comprehension	– Overreliance on rote behaviors		– Social interaction skills
– Mechanical arithmetic	– Externalized disorders (conduct, acting out)		
– Mathematical reasoning	– Social perception and judgment		
– Science	– Social withdrawal or isolation		
	– May develop internalized disorders (e.g., depression, anxiety)		

and processing complex information. The left hemisphere is more adept than the right at applying already learned descriptive systems that use discrete units of information (like language), and for storing compact codes (Rourke, 1989).

Genetic Factors

To date there are no studies addressing the genetic basis for the NVLD syndrome. The extent to which genetic factors play a role in this neuropsychologically based learning disorder certainly warrants investigation. There are indications that some genetic syndromes may have profiles that are similar to those described for nonverbal learning disabilities, including Turner syndrome and Velocardiofacial syndrome.

Turner Syndrome

Turner Syndrome (TS) is the loss of some or all of the X chromosome. It is rarely seen in males and has an incidence of 1 in 3,000–5,000 live births in females (Rovet, 2004). Females with TS lack estrogen and often have ovarian dysgeneration and infertility. The neuropsychological profile present in TS includes significant problems processing social information, visuospatial information, and severe mathematics disabilities. Performance IQ is generally 15 points lower than verbal IQ, which is generally in the average range (Rovet, 2004). Other areas that are frequently affected include working memory, face processing (Lawrence et al., 2003), mental rotation, spatial reasoning, and difficulty processing emotions (Elgar, Campbell, & Skuse, 2002; Lawrence, Kuntsi, Coleman, Campbell, & Skuse, 2003). The mathematics, working memory, and visuo-spatial difficulties have been found to be present developmentally and continue throughout a child's life (Murphy & Mazzocco, 2008; Murphy, Mazzocco, Gerner, & Hendry, 2006).

Structural imaging has found differences in children and adults with TS in smaller volumes in the areas of the occipital and parietal lobe and reduced volume in the caudate, thalamus, and hippocampus (Reiss, Eliez, Schmitt, Patwardhan, & Haberecht, 2000). Larger volumes compared to controls have been found in patients with TS in the temporal lobes, amygdala, and orbitofrontal gray matter (Brown et al., 2002; Good et al., 2003).

The finding of anamolous development in the amygdala is similar to research in autism (see Chapter 10 for further information. Patients with TS have abnormal responses to fear recognition and other types of negative facial expressions which may be related to the anomalous amygdaloid and orbitofrontal regions. These structural differences, coupled with the neuropsychological correlates of NVLD, have lead some to speculate that there may be similar underlying neurological differences between these disorders. Further study is needed to determine whether there is a commonality in connectivity, functionality, and neuropsychological findings that underlie both TS and NVLD.

Velocardiofacial Syndrome

Velocardiofacial syndrome can also exhibit deficits in visual-spatial skills, social processing, and mathematics reasoning (Swillen et al., 1999). Velocardiofacial syndrome occurs with a deletion on chromosome 22 and many of these patients show neurological, cognitive, and behavioral deficits (Murphy, Jones, & Owen, 1999). Imaging has found differences in the white matter, particularly in the parietal regions of the brain (Amelsvoort et al., 2001; Eliez, Schmitt, White, Hu, & Reiss, 2002). Diffusion Tensor Imaging (DTI) has found alterations in the white matter tracts in the parietal lobes as well as in the frontotemporal regions bilaterally (Barnea-Gorly et al., 2003).

Agenesis of the Corpus Callosum

While not a genetic disorder per se, agenesis of the corpus callosum (AC) occurs at some point during gestation when the corpus callosum (a large bundle of fibers that connect the two hemispheres) either forms incompletely or not at all. Children with AC range in ability from mentally retarded to having average ability. For those children with average ability difficulty appears to be present for novel problem solving, as well as social understanding (Brown & Paul, 2000; Paul, Schieffer, & Brown, 2004). In addition, children with AC also have trouble understanding figurative language as well as affect as expressed by speech intonation (Brown, Symingtion, Van Lancker-Sidtis, Dietrich, & Paul, 2005; Paul, Van Lancker-Sidtis, Schieffer, Dietrich, & Brown, 2003).

These findings certainly suggest a similarity to NVLD. Studies that compare children with AC, children with NVLD, and children with other genetic syndromes that have similar features would be informative as to what these disorders have in common and whether there are discriminating aspects of these issues. If there are similar behaviors that arise from similar neurological underpinnings but different causes, it may well be that the disruption of connectivity in particular regions of the brain relates to social, visual-spatial, and mathematical difficulties. Some studies of children with TS have contrasted their functioning in mathematics to that of children with Fragile X and found similarities (Murphy & Mazzocco, 2008). Unfortunately, social functioning measures were not also obtained in these studies. This area of research is ripe for further investigation.

Prenatal/Postnatal Factors

The NVLD syndrome is described as a neurodevelopmental disorder; that is, one that is present at or soon after birth (Rourke, 1989). While Rourke (1989) does assume that the neuropsychological patterns of assets and deficits are developmental in nature, appearing at birth, he does acknowledge that traumatic injury or trauma may result in a similar pattern. Few other details are available describing prenatal and postnatal factors associated with the NLD syndrome.

One of the theories about NVLD is that it involves right hemispheric dysfunction. It has been suggested that development of the right hemisphere can be affected by many issues including hormones during gestation, prematurity, pregnancy and delivery complications, among others (Forrest, 2007). During development the right hemisphere is believed to grow first, followed by the left hemisphere and finally connectivity between the two hemispheres and hemispheric specialization (Thatcher, 1996). Similarly, Luria suggests that within the lobes hierarchical development occurs, moving from primary centers (hardwired centers) to more associative and highly complex areas that are important for problem solving and insight into behavior (Luria, 1980).

Neuropsychological Correlates

Rourke (1989) lists the neuropsychological assets of the child with NVLD as auditory perception, simple motor skills, rote memory, verbal and auditory memory, attention to verbal and auditory information, and verbal reception, storage, and associations. Neuropsychological deficits associated with the right hemisphere NLD syndrome include tactile and visual imperception, impaired complex psychomotor skills, inattention to tactile and visual information, poor memory for tactile and visual information, and some verbal skill deficits (i.e., prosody, semantics, content). Scores are also below average on subtests of the Performance Scale of the WISC-R (Block Design, Picture Arrangement, and Object Assembly): the Tactual Performance Test, left hand; the Pegboard Test, both right and left hands, and the Category test (Rourke, 2000).

Academic and School Factors

The interaction between right hemisphere weaknesses and left hemisphere assets is manifested in good graphomotor skills for right-handed children (usually later in life), word decoding skills, spelling skills, and "verbatim memory" (Rourke, 1989). Because children with NVLD rely heavily on intact left hemisphere functions, they often develop excellent reading, decoding, and spelling skills (Semrud-Clikeman, 2007). Children with NVLD tend to perform well on academic tasks that rely on rote verbal memory.

Academic deficits include poor academic achievement in mathematical reasoning and computation. Initially the child with NVLD shows good reading recognition, but in later grades as reading for meaning becomes more important, the child experiences significant problems with reading comprehension. These academic areas are particularly compromised by difficulties with abstract reasoning and deduction. Children with NVLD fail to develop complex concept formation and problem solving abilities needed for advanced subject matter such as physics (Semrud-Clikeman, 2003).

Although children with NVLD start out with slow development of early graphomotor skills, these abilities improve with age. Academically, children with NVLD appear to be compromised by their extreme difficulties with understanding cause-and-effect relationships, and problems generating age-appropriate problem solving skills. These deficits are particularly evident during novel tasks, and subsequent learning is negatively affected (Semrud-Clikeman, 2007).

Visual-Spatial Ability

Visuospatial skills, visual working memory, and imagery in children with NVLD are areas of significant difficulty (Cornoldi, 1999). Visual imagery and working memory have been linked to the ability to process social information, an area that is difficult for children with NVLD (Logie, 1995). Children with NVLD have trouble recalling visual and spatial information as well as imagery for both verbal and visual information. Thus, difficulty is present on tasks that require the child to learn new information by associating it with previously learned material. It is suggested that visual working memory is an area of particular difficulty and support is required to assist with these abilities.

The ability to integrate information presented visually may be a primary difficulty for children with NVLD who have more difficulty on measures of visual-motor integration and visual-spatial skills, compared to children with ADHD or typically developing children (Wilkinson, & Semrud-Clikeman, 2008). When the performance of children with verbal LD, NVLD and typically developing children were compared on measures of visual motor integration (Foss, 1991; Meyers & Meyers, 1995), the children with learning disabilities performed more poorly than typically developing children. The children with NVLD, however, performed the most poorly. Qualitative analysis of the findings indicated that children with verbal LD were generally able to copy the picture adequately, but missed many details. The children with NVLD copied the picture in a piecemeal fashion with disconnected details. This disjointed understanding of the whole from the parts likely interacts with difficulties with social perception.

An evaluation of the perception of children with NVLD using projective measures found that they had significant difficulties in perceiving the inkblots in a typical manner compared to controls and children with ADHD: PI (Corlett, 2002). The difficulty that was present was characterized by problems with integration. No differences were found between the ADHD: PI and control groups, thus attentional deficits were not at the core of the problems with visual integration. Thus, it is likely that children with NVLD will have difficulties integrating visual input accurately and may react inappropriately. Although children with NVLD scored on indices indicating interest in others, their responses indicated they are likely to react inflexibly to a social situation.

These studies indicate that children with NVLD have difficulty with visual-spatial integration that may relate to the frequently encountered problems with social processing. These difficulties in understanding novel events, processing materials quickly, and putting together parts of a scenario to understand the underlying meaning likely interfere with social processing. In addition, if the infant has difficulty deciphering faces and understanding facial expressions, it is likely that the early building blocks of social understanding are not well established and carry over into later childhood (Semrud-Clikeman & Hynd, 1990).

Attention

Attentional skills are problematic for children with NVLD and many are diagnosed with ADHD: predominately inattentive type (Semrud-Clikeman, Walkowiak, Wilkinson, & Christopher, submitted). Attention to complex, novel information is particularly difficult, and children with NVLD are more attentive to simple, repetitive tasks than to tasks that are verbal or auditory in nature. This attentional bias makes new learning particularly difficult, and becomes more prominent with age. Children with NVLD often appear overactive initially, but this apparent hyperactivity does not persist.

Executive Functioning

The skills of working memory, processing of complex and novel material, and understanding of other's motives and feelings is related to difficulty with executive functioning for these children. Executive functions are those that allow a person to view their behavior, assess its appropriateness, and make changes if required. They differ from cognitive functions somewhat; cognitive functions look at what a person knows while executive functions evaluate the person's ability to carry through with a plan of action (Damasio, Tranel, & Rizzo, 2000). Thus, a child or adolescent can know the appropriate plan of action in a social situation, but be unable to carry through with it in an efficient manner. Often fluid social interaction require the child to process information quickly and efficiently generally using simultaneous evaluation of many aspects of the difficulty.

Children with NVLD perform better skills on measures of sequential processing than those of simultaneous processing. Simultaneous and sequential processing are based on Luria's (1980) model of brain function that conceptualizes the brain function into three networks that function independently and are integrated at higher levels. The three networks are planning, arousal, and processing (simultaneous as well as sequential). Sequential processing is the ability to process information in a step-by-step manner and is primarily based on left hemispheric processing. Simultaneous processing is a right hemispheric function and allows the individual to process information with many facets and form an integrated whole. The individual uses either style depending on the task at hand. Chow and Skuy (1999) evaluated children with NVLD and those with verbal LD on measures of sequential and simultaneous processing. Children with verbal LD were more likely to use the simultaneous processing style while children with NVLD favored the successive processing mode.

This difficulty in understanding the gestalt of a task, or social exchange, likely interferes with the ease of social interactions. If the child with NVLD is attempting to understand a perceptual task using an inefficient method (such as sequential, language-based processing), the behaviors are likely to feel flat and inappropriate to the fellow person in the interaction. Difficulties with fluid reasoning, concept formation, and problem solving have been identified in children with NVLD (Schnoebelen, Semrud-Clikeman, Guli, & Corlett, 2002). These difficulties interact with the problems in processing perceptual information, particularly when it requires the processing of novel and complex social information. The problem that children with NVLD have in social interactions may be a combination of difficulty with attention, executive functioning, and perception (Semrud-Clikeman & Schaefer, 2000).

Social-Psychological Functioning

The difficulty children with NVLD have understanding complex pictures underscores the challenges present in comprehending dynamic social exchanges. These difficulties with integration make it problematic for the child with NVLD to understand facial expressions and pair them with gestures and language. When asked to interpret a scene where the verbal portion of the communication does not match the nonverbal portion, children with NVLD inevitably use the verbal portion to translate meaning. Thus, sarcasm or humor is not understood by children with NVLD and they often

translate this type of communication literally (Semrud-Clikeman & Glass, 2008). Moreover, children with NVLD often make inferences based on language and interpret a situation using details without reference to the context (Worling, Humphries, & Tannock, 1999). Thus, the child's interpretation may not be accurate for the context in which the information is given and, subsequently, his/her behavior is often inappropriate based on misperceptions.

Borod, Andelman, Obler, Tweedy, and Welkowitz (1992) suggest that interpretation of emotion requires the ability to understand the relationship between emotions which in turn requires spatial organization—a right hemispheric integrative function. Working memory deficits present in NVLD also limit the child's ability to apply appropriate emotional inferences to the situation at hand. It is likely that this system becomes overloaded attempting to process the details involved in any social exchange, thus resulting in difficulty with social interacting that is fluid and reciprocal.

To more fully understand the prevalence of psychopathology in children with NVLD compared to those with RD, a study contrasted typically developing children, children with NVLD, RD, a psychiatric control group, and a group of children with velocardiofacial syndrome (VCFS) to determine what differences may be in the prevalence rate of psychiatric disorders (Antshell & Khan, 2008). Each parent was interviewed to determine the presence of psychopathology. The NVLD, RD, and psychiatric control groups were found to show a higher incidence of ADHD and substance abuse/dependence. The psychiatric controls and children with NVLD were also found to have a higher prevalence rate of familial bipolar disorder. This finding was not true for the velocardiofacial group who also had NVLD. It was concluded that the children with VCFS and NVLD were different genetically compared to the NVLD without VCFS. The conclusions from this study are interesting in that the authors related NVLD to bipolar disorder. This conclusion of increased bipolar disorder in the families of children with NVLD has not been replicated (McDonough-Ryan et al., 2002). Further study is needed in these areas to more fully understand the link that may exist between NVLD and other psychiatric disorders.

The areas of attention, executive functioning, social understanding, and academic functioning are domains that need to be evaluated by a neuropsychologist. Each of these regions requires varying types of measures. The following section discusses what measures may be most helpful in this evaluation.

Neuroimaging in NVLD

The only studies completed on neuroimaging in NVLD are case studies. In one case two adolescents with NVLD and two controls were asked to utilize self-talk to complete a task and then to use solely tactile information (Tuller, Jantzen, Olvera, Steinberg, & Kelso, 2007). Each adolescent was asked to touch his thumb to each of his fingertips in the same hand. Results from the fMRI found that the two subjects with NVLD showed a widely distributed network when completing this task, compared to the controls. One of the difficulties with this study is the low number of subjects and the difficulty in knowing whether these results truly represent the functioning of children with NVLD or whether they solely represent normal fluctuation among individuals.

One study evaluated a 14-year-old boy with cerebral palsy who was diagnosed with nonverbal learning disabilities as well as executive function deficits and visual-spatial delays (Gross-Tur, Ben-Bashat, Shalev, Levav, & Sira, 2006). He had a developmental hypoplastic left cerebellum. A reduction in right hemispheric white matter in the cerebrum as well as in the cerebellum was found via DTI. The conclusion from this study was that the disruption of the right hemispheric circuits negatively influenced the child's ability to relate to others, complete visual-spatial tasks, or plan and organize information. There were no other specific studies that evaluated NVLD using neuroimaging in our recent literature review.

Implications for Assessment

Comprehensive neuropsychological assessment is necessary to identify the NVLD syndrome in children. A developmental model of assessment, where evaluations are repeated over time and form the basis for remedial programs, has been recommended (Rourke, 1994). Based on the above descriptions of difficulties children with NVLD experience it would be recommended to include measures of attention, executive functioning, and academic performance. Many of the measures listed in Chapter 6 are appropriate for this evaluation. Particular recommendations would be for the sorting, Stroop, and Tower tests from the Delis-Kaplan Test of Executive Functioning, the Rey-Osterreith, the TOVA, the WJ III Tests of fluid reasoning, and a full evaluation of the child's mathematical and reading abilities.

In addition to these measures, it is also imperative to evaluate the child's social abilities. There are few good direct measures of social functioning. One measure that has been helpful in our work is the Child and Adolescent Social Perception Test (CASP (Magill-Evans, Koning, Cameron-Sadava, & Manyk, 1996). This measure is a series of video-taped vignettes of children, adolescents and adults interacting. The videotape shows the action with the words masked so that what the child hears is the intonation, but not the words. After each of 10 vignettes, the child is asked questions about what happened and what the people were feeling. Two standard scores are provided, one for nonverbal cues and one for emotion recognition. The psychometric properties of the measure are acceptable, but further research is needed to determine whether the scores can discriminate among groups of children with disabilities.

Fine, Semrud-Clikeman, Butcher, and Walkowiak (2008) evaluated the use of the CASP with children with attention problems and those with social competence problems with and without attentional issues. While attention played a part in the performance on this measure, the CASP identified children with social difficulties even with attentional aspects removed. While the CASP is helpful and one of the few things available, the vignettes are a bit dated and its use for younger children may be questionable. It can be ordered by contacting Dr. Magill-Evans at the University of Alberta in Edmonton, Canada.

Other measures that have recently become available include the Social Communication Questionnaire (SCQ) (Rutter, Bailey, Berument, Lord, &

Pickeles, 2003). The SCQ is completed by the parent and provides a total score that indicates the child's likelihood for autism. While it is a screener for autism and shows severity of difficulty, it is a measure that can also be used with children with NVLD to pinpoint problem areas. The authors report that the SCQ is not affected by age, gender, language skills or performance ability. The utility of the SCQ for diagnosis of autism has been established; its use with NVLD would be to assist with understanding the social areas for which the child has difficulty.

The Social Responsiveness Scale (Constantino & Gruber, 2006) is a parent report for children aged 4–18 years. It can be completed by a parent or teacher and evaluates the child's functioning within a natural social setting. The areas of reciprocal social communication, social anxiety/avoidance, preoccupations, social awareness and social impairments are evaluated. It provides information about the level of difficulty in each of the areas of concern. There are five treatment subscales in addition to the total score. These subscales are receptive, cognitive, expression, and motivational aspects of social behavior and autistic preoccupations. It differs from the SCQ in that it doesn't use a cutoff score, but rather utilizes a scale that provides a measure of severity for each of the subscales. This instrument is fairly new and further research is needed to determine how useful it will be for evaluating children with NVLD. It is, however, a measure that can be helpful in evaluating the child's social performance in school and home.

Evaluating the child's functioning in all of these domains should also provide ideas as to appropriate interventions. The interventions often need to be tailored to the individual child and empirical validation of these methods is not as strongly established as for other types of learning disorders. The following section briefly reviews one particular type of intervention that has provided some empirical validation.

Implications for Intervention

According to Rourke, when systems of the right hemisphere are dysfunctional and systems of the left hemisphere are relatively intact, the child tends to engage in perseverative or stereotypic responses because of the over-reliance on information that has already been learned. This often results in difficulties in developing problem solving strategies and generating alternative solutions. Children begin to develop compensatory skills that are primarily verbal in nature, and they begin to avoid novel situations. Because of tactile deficits and slow maturation of early psychomotor skills, children with NVLD have a tendency to avoid active exploration of the environment.

Intervention programs that incorporate early teaching in sensory-motor integration as well as interventions that are implemented across all domains (i.e., academic and psychosocial) include the child as well as the parent. Methods that increase social awareness, teach problem solving strategies, encourage generalization of strategies, and improve verbal skills should be part of the intervention plan. Methods for strengthening areas of weakness in visual-spatial areas, interpreting competing stimuli, teaching nonverbal behaviors, providing structure for exploration, using concrete aids, teaching self-evaluation, and developing life skills are important aims for any intervention.

The social skills curriculum developed for other children has proven to be a successful intervention without tailoring the skills to the child with NVLD (Palombo, 2006; Semrud-Clikeman & Schaefer, 2000). Most social skill programs begin at a level that is likely too advanced for children with NVLD as these programs generally assume that the child is able to accurately interpret facial expressions and body language. For many children with NVLD (and for those with HFA and AS) the interventions need to begin with labeling of emotions and understanding emotional labels to be effective. In addition, interventions need to be based on teaching social perception through the use of practice, modeling, and role-playing. Breaking social perception down into discrete steps and teaching rules to allow the child with NVLD to process the information verbally plays on the strengths that these children bring to the program. Pairing auditory and visual stimuli together may also provide the type of support that is necessary for the child to fully understand the complex nonverbal social communication that is problematic for his/her interpretation (Semrud-Clikeman, 2007).

In order for these interventions to be helpful to children with NVLD it is likely important that the program begin slowly and with a great deal of structure, and then gradually move to the more complex activities that require the building of trust in order to attempt them. Practicing the skills as well as overlearning key social abilities and perceptions is crucial not only for mastering these abilities, but for later generalization. To encourage generalization of the skills, it is important to involve the parents so they can help practice the newly learned skills at home and in school, and teach these children how to apply the social skills appropriately.

Generally the interventions fall into one of three types: parent interventions, social skills curriculum (including coaching and friendship groups), and a group-based intervention based on learning about emotions and social applications. Parents can be very helpful in working with NVLD children as long as additional support is provided. Another method that has been helpful is that of peer or adult coaching. These interventions will be briefly discussed below.

Parent Interventions

Parent Effectiveness Training (PET) (Gordan, 2006) is a program that assists a child to manage his/her relations with others. PET encourages parents to invite children over to play with their child in a structured environment as well as join groups such as 4-H, Cub/Boy Scouts or Brownies/Girl Scouts. The structure of these programs and the emphasis on working together can assist a child with NVLD to enter into more structured, safe settings for social experiences. For parents who also experience social difficulties, family therapy may be the most appropriate mechanism to support the child with similar social difficulties. A frequent clinical observation is that parents with children with NVLD (or ASD) may also experience difficulties with social interactions. Thus, an intervention that expects them to teach the child such skills is problematic.

While parents may not be the best vehicle for teaching social skills, they are very helpful in providing appropriate information about development, new programs, and the child's progress (Semrud-Clikeman & Schaefer, 2000). Parents supplied with suggestions and support can provide additional experiences for their child that is more helpful. Children with NVLD often experience rejection and isolation in school and in unstructured activities. A parent who can provide support through organized activities, a calm demeanor, and a place to decompress is likely giving the best support to the child. Setting up situations where the child is paired with one other child who may be more tolerant of the child's behaviors can also help. Trips to the museum, movies, or a structured activity are proactive for appropriate social exchanges. Situations that don't provide such structure are likely to be more anxiety-producing and possibly less constructive as the child seeks to entertain his/her "friend" (Glass, Guli, & Semrud-Clikeman, 2000; Semrud-Clikeman & Schaefer, 2000).

Coaching

Matching the child with NVLD to a child who is more tolerant for socialization can be helpful. While this type of "friend making" can be somewhat artificial and requires a very special child to support the child with NVLD, it can provide a safe environment in which the child is able to perform skills that have been taught in the clinic or in small groups. The advantages of peer matching are that it occurs in a naturalistic setting and the child learns from a same-aged child. However, it is time consuming and requires a great deal of adult support for success both from the parent and teacher. It may be most successful for children who are in special education programs where there are additional paraprofessionals and support rather than in a larger classroom.

Suggestions in the field have been made for coaching interventions. These interventions occur in the child's environment and the adult observes the child. Following the observation, the child meets with his/her coach and discusses the behaviors seen and the situations. Corrective exercises are provided. It is likely that this method could be quite useful in assisting the child to learn appropriate behaviors in a naturalistic setting. This type of intervention does not have empirical validation and can be costly. However, it may also be helpful for children who are really struggling to relate to other children.

Social Competence Intervention Program

A social competence intervention program (SCIP) designed to work with children with NVLD and Asperger's Disorder has been developed (Guli, Wilkinson, & Semrud-Clikeman, 2008). SCIP is an intervention that is multisensory in nature and targets underlying difficulties in social perception as well as provide exercises to improve the generation of strategies for problem solving. Figure 12.1 illustrates the basic tenet behind this intervention.

Fig. 12.1 Model for Social Perception

PERCEPTION

visual
auditory
tactile
kinesthetic

INTERPRETATION

facial expression
body language
vocal cues

RESPONSE

social interaction
contextual understanding

In SCIP, exercises were adapted from children's creative drama and theater classes to practice the processes fundamental to social competence. These activities were originally designed to help actors develop accurate perception and response to cues, and address various aspects of social perception (Guli et al., 2008). These activities fall into the following categories: sensory games, space/movement games, mirroring activities, communication with sounds, physical control, "part of a whole" and multiple-stimulus games.

The exercises are designed to move from learning how to perceive various emotions to appropriate interpretation of these emotions and then to assisting with choosing the best response to the situation

at hand. In each case the training begins with easily recognized emotions such as happy and sad, and moves to more abstract emotions such as embarrassment, confusion, and frustration. The initial session includes direct teaching of facial expression recognition as well as voice intonation, intent of the speaker, and interpreting body language. As the child moves through the program, role-playing is introduced and the child is exposed to more and more complex situations with significant amounts of adult guidance. The SCIP program provides new experiences that change with time, but are built on situations that are familiar and thus not as anxiety-producing as fully novel experiences would be. The work is constantly reviewed and supported throughout the intervention, thus reviewing and refreshing skills.

One of the difficulties that children with NVLD face is limited exposure to other children to practice skills. They are often isolated and ignored. The intensity of the SCIP program allows the child to experience being with other children as they work toward a common goal; namely, understanding social interactions. The experience of children with SCIP has been a joining together and enjoyment of one another within a safe environment. Activities and role-plays are in a setting which allows the child to experiment, laugh when something goes wrong, and find out that he/she is not the only one struggling with some issues.

Guli et al., (2008) evaluated the efficacy of the SCIP program. A treatment group and a clinical control group with deficits in social perception were compared using several outcome measures before and after participation in the SCIP program. The outcome measures included a test of recognizing facial expressions and voice cues, parent ratings on behavioral checklists of withdrawal and social skills, and direct behavioral observations of peer interactions. Following the intervention, parents and children in the treatment group were interviewed about their experiences.

Quantitative and qualitative support was found. Improvement was found in the child's ability to correctly recognize facial expressions, vocal cues, and social behavior. Approximately three-fourths of the parents reported positive changes in one aspect of their child's social functioning, while 82 percent reported several aspects showed improvement. Moreover, these findings strongly support research that stresses training in perception and integration of nonverbal cues for children with nonverbal learning disabilities (Barnhill, Tapscott, Tebbgenkamp, & Smith, 2002; Bauminger, 2002).

Summary and Comments about NVLD

Emerging research underscores the need to understand the dynamic interaction between psychological and emotional problems in light of neuropsychological assets/deficits in children with learning disabilities. Although further research is necessary to verify these relationships and to determine how learning disabilities change over the ages, an integrated neurodevelopmental model provides the framework for such study. Although Rourke has developed a model based on a series of related studies spanning two decades, sub-typology research has been criticized. Reynolds (2003) asserts that models relying on profile analysis must take into account the reliability (i.e., stability) of profiles. The extent to which profiles change over time and how these changes might affect the original clinical decision need further study. Others have pointed out weaknesses in using correlational methods to imply similarity among subjects (Keith, 2006). Correlational methods are also inappropriate for studies when the linearity of variables is questionable.

Despite criticisms of subtype research, Rourke's NVLD model provides a foundation for further research and contributes to our preliminary understanding of how neuropsychological, cognitive, and social-emotional functioning interacts with and influences the development of children. This model describes a complex interaction among deficient and intact neuropsychological systems, early experiences, and learning that is associated with social-emotional functioning. Rourke does provide a viable model for a "right-hemisphere syndrome" that can be tested empirically with children experiencing academic disabilities (primarily in math) and psychosocial adjustment difficulties using standard neuropsychological and psychological tests.

Recent research indicates that the original belief that motor and tactile issues were primary in NVLD have not been supported and that attention and social-emotional functioning may be important aspects of this disorder. The research does not clarify the main aspects of NVLD or the neural underlays for the difficulty these children have in relating to others in visual-spatial skills and in executive functioning. In addition, when the diagnosis is not clearly defined, it is difficult to compare results across studies. Further validation of the disorder, as well as additional study of the possible causes and interventions, would be increase our understanding of this disorder.

Case Study of a Child with Severe Developmental Dyslexia

The following case describes an assessment of a 10-year-old boy who had received excellent special education services for several years, but who continued to be unable to read beyond a primer level. The case demonstrates the need to evaluate reading difficulties comprehensively, and obtain a family history. Allen is a fourth-grade boy who was referred to the clinic for ongoing reading difficulties despite having had three years of special education services. He had been diagnosed with ADHD and responded favorably to Ritalin. In kindergarten, Allen was first identified as experiencing difficulty with readiness skills. He was very active and had great difficulty staying in a group and participating in activities. He started taking Ritalin in first grade and was kept in first grade an additional year because of significant delays in academics. Allen was evaluated in second grade and placed in a learning disability program. Behaviorally and socially he was reported not to experience any difficulties, and was well accepted by his peers. He was also reported to be hard working and motivated.

Allen was the product of a normal full-term birth, labor, and delivery. Developmental milestones were generally attained within normal limits for age. At an early age Allen was noted to display an extreme level of overactivity and inattention. He was diagnosed with ADHD in first grade. His

Ritalin dosage has gradually increased from 5 milligrams (mg) twice per day to a current dose of 20 mg in the morning, 20 mg at noon, and 15 mg at 3:00 P.M. His paternal history is remarkable for reading difficulties. His father, his stepsister, a paternal uncle, and a grandfather have all experienced significant reading difficulties, which continued throughout school and into adulthood. Although Allen's father's intelligence is above average, he is unable to read and is currently employed as a grocery stocker. Allen's neurological examination and MRI were normal. He has not had any head injuries, seizures, or serious illnesses.

Cognitive Ability

Allen's evaluation indicated an average ability with strengths in vocabulary, social comprehension, perceptual organization and nonverbal reasoning. Significant weakness was present in working memory as well as in memory for previously learned material, abstract language ability, motor speed, and arithmetic reasoning. The following results were obtained on the WISC IV.

Verbal Comprehension	82
Perceptual Reasoning	99
Full Scale IQ	94
Working Memory	78
Processing Speed	75

Information	5	Picture Completion	10
Similarities	6	Coding	4
Arithmetic	5	Matrix Reasoning	10
Vocabulary	9	Block Design	8
Comprehension	10	Object Assembly	9
Digit Span	4	Symbol Search	6

Achievement Testing

Achievement testing indicated severe deficits in all areas of reading, with math skills also depressed, particularly in applied problems. The Woodcock

Johnson Achievement Battery-III was administered and the following scores obtained:

Letter-Word ID	46
Reading Comprehension	64
Reading Fluency	50
Word Attack	51
Applied Problems	75
Arithmetic Calculation	83
Math Fluency	80
Spelling	50
Written Expression	65
Writing Fluency	60

Allen is a choppy and dysfluent reader. He appeared unsure of vowel and consonant sounds and consequently relied on a "best guess" strategy for reading (e.g., using a word's visual characteristics as an aid to decoding). The Lindamood Auditory Concepts test was also administered to further evaluate Allen's word attack skills. Allen performed at the mid-first grade level on this test, with significant difficulties with sound-symbol relationships even at the individual phoneme levels. Blending and the ability to combine sounds were delayed. Allen experienced difficulty at the primary level for distinguishing similar, but different sounds at the beginning and ending of words.

Memory

Allen's memory skills were evaluated using the Children's Version of the California Verbal Learning Test.

Allen's learning of List A fell significantly below average over the five trials. Although the learning curve rose steadily over the five trials, suggesting that Allen benefited from repetition of the words, the number of items recalled after each trial fell below expectations compared to same-aged peers. Allen's recall of List B also fell below average. Both short-term free recall and cued recall fell within average levels for his age. These findings indicate that Allen is able to retain information that he has learned. His memory skills are problematic in that Allen has difficulty encoding new information. In addition, he was unable to utilize memory strategies that would assist him in encoding information; rather he tried to recall the words using rote memory rather than grouping them into categories.

Total Recalled	85
Trial 1 Recall	60
Trial 5 Recall	80
List B	75
Short-term Free Recall	100
Short-term Cued Recall	98
Long-term Free Recall	102
Long-term Cued Recall	103
Learning slope	88

Language Ability

Language assessment indicated that Allen has difficulty in both receptive and expressive language skills. The Clinical Evaluation of Language Fundamentals-3 was administered, and the following results were obtained:

Receptive Language		Expressive Language	
Concepts and Directions	4	Formulated Sentences	5
Word Classes	9	Recalling Sentences	7
Semantic Relationships	3	Sentence Assembly	6

This assessment indicated pervasive language problems in Allen's ability to understand and use language. On receptive language tasks, Allen's ability to follow directions using visual cues that increase in complexity was quite poor, and likely a reflection of his previously identified difficulty with adequately encoding verbally based information. Allen's performance on a task that tapped his understanding of comparative, temporal, quantitative, and spatial concepts in language also fell significantly below average. Allen's ability to see relationships between words was within age expectations.

On the expressive language measures, Allen demonstrated significant weakness on a series of structured tasks that required him to create sentences about pictures using stimulus words. He had difficulty integrating words into a relevant sentence while maintaining appropriate grammatical structure. Consistent with his difficulties with encoding verbally mediated information, Allen evidenced a significant weakness in his ability to repeat progressively longer and syntactically complex sentences.

Attention

The Test of Variables of Attention (TOVA) was used to measure attentional functioning. Testing was done off Ritalin, on 15 mg of Ritalin, and on 20 mg of Ritalin. Measures of vigilance (omissions), impulsivity and inhibition of responding (commission), speed of information processing (reaction times), and variability of reaction time (variability) were obtained with the following results:

Measure	20 mg	15 mg	Off Ritalin
Omissions	98	98	66
Commissions	90	90	98
Response Time	67	54	34
Variability	63	26	< 25

Results indicated that on his current 20 mg dose, Allen demonstrated age-appropriate gross attention to task and impulse control. In contrast, reaction time and sustained attention fell significantly below expected limits for age. On a 15 mg dose of Ritalin, Allen's gross attention and impulse control were identical to that observed on the higher dose. However, his reaction time and sustained attention were much poorer on the lower dose of Ritalin. With the exception of his impulse control, Allen's performance on the TOVA off medication fell significantly below average on all attentional parameters. Overall results indicated that Allen exhibits a beneficial response to his current Ritalin dose of 20 mg. Even with the higher dose, however, his response time and ability to sustain and deploy attention consistently fell significantly below average.

Executive Functioning

Allen completed subtests from the Delis Kaplan Test of Executive Functioning (D-KEFS). The D-KEFS found that Allen's executive functioning ability fell within the average to far below average range. Allen's visual-spatial-motor skills consistently fell in the average range. For example, on a measure that required Allen to connect a series of letters as quickly as possible, his performance fell in the average range. On a similar task, his ability to connect a series of numbers also fell in the average range. He also performed in the average range when asked to sequence between a number and a letter in succession (1-A, 2-B, 3-C, etc). On a measure of verbal fluency, Allen's ability to rapidly name as many words that began with a certain letter, name as many animals, and as many male names as he could in 60 seconds fell within the average range. His ability to repeat a sequence of numbers presented orally fell within the low average range and his ability to repeat a series of numbers and letters was also within the low average range. Allen struggled in a task that required him to rapidly name colors and color word names. His ability to name colors and read color words fell in the average range. However, as the task became more difficult, he struggled when he was asked to name the color of a color word printed in an opposing color (Saying "green" when looking at the word blue printed in green ink). His performance in this response interference task fell in the far below average range. Allen performed in the far below average range on a planning task that required him to plan a set of sequential moves using up to five rings in a predetermined starting point after being shown the correct ending position of the rings.

Taken together these findings indicate that Allen shows relatively better performance on visual-spatial-motor tasks than tasks that require cognitive response interference, set switching, and planning. This finding may mean that since he performed in the average range on visual-motor tasks but not purely cognitive executive measures, Allen may be experiencing specific difficulty with tasks that require him to hold a cognitive task "online" while ignoring distracters. In addition he experiences problems in his ability to successfully plan and execute a set of moves while remembering the directions necessary to complete the task.

Visual-Spatial Skills

Allen's visual-motor integration skills were assessed using the Developmental Test of Visual-Motor Integration. Consistent with teacher reports regarding illegible writing and poor copying skills, Allen's reproductions on this task fell moderately below age expectations (standard scores = 76). On the Judgement of Line Orientation, Allen showed below age level functioning. His finger dexterity as measured by the Purdue Pegboard was within age expectations for either hand and for both hands together. These findings indicate some difficulty with visual-spatial integration, but not with motor skills.

Behavioral/Emotional Functioning

Personality and behavioral assessment indicated no areas of concern. He did not score in the significant range on any portion of the Behavior Assessment Scale for Children II. Teacher reports indicated concerns only in the area of academic progress. These profiles indicated that Allen is perceived as well adjusted, without any behavioral problems.

Summary and Recommendations

Allen is a 10-year-old boy with speech and language problems as well as difficulty with acquiring reading skills. He also has a history of ADHD and is currently being treated with Ritalin. This evaluation was requested by his mother to determine current reading skills and to offer treatment recommendations. Assessment of Allen's academic achievement confirms school and parental reports that he is experiencing persistent and severe difficulties in acquisition of beginning reading skills. Evaluation revealed that his reading skills fell significantly below average, and well below what was to be expected on the basis of his intellectual profile.

Allen's reading skills fall approximately at a mid-first grade level and are limited to inconsistent identification of high frequency sight words. He shows little in the way of word attack skills and is deficient in other phonological coding skills that have been found to be highly related to the normal acquisition of reading. Relative to an assessment completed more than two years ago, Allen shows little progress. Overall, results from the present testing indicate the presence of a verbally based learning disability. Testing of language functions revealed striking weaknesses in both receptive and expressive language skills. Although parental reports indicated that Allen has made a stable pattern of gains since speech therapy was initiated this year; his language problems are of such severity that they are continuing to have an impact on his ability to use and understand language effectively. Testing of memory and learning indicated that Allen experienced difficulties in encoding and memorizing verbal information, such as stories and lists of words. Allen's ability to remember verbal information is constrained by problems with encoding and inputting. He does not have difficulty in retrieving and outputting information from memory; that is, once information is encoded into memory, he can retain it for relatively long periods of time. His encoding problems also affect his ability to process verbal material, such as instructions, adequately. It is important to emphasize that despite his encoding difficulties, Allen has the potential to learn and memorize new information, but he will do so at a rate that is significantly slower than his same-aged peers, and he will require more than the usual amount of repetition. Allen does not appear to have significant difficulty memorizing material that is visual in nature, such as designs and pictures. Recommendations include an intensive learning disabilities program to work on his phonological coding difficulties while simultaneously strengthening his sight word vocabulary. Given Allen's good visual-perceptual and visual-memory abilities, it is recommended that teaching strategies focus on a sight word approach with the high frequency words he encounters. For Allen to become a fully functional reader, it is crucial that he become adept at decoding unknown words. Teaching Allen how to decode words will not be an easy task, given that he lacks a number of the essential phonological processing

skills necessary for effective decoding. To help Allen develop the phonological processing skills that are critical to becoming an effective reader, the Lindamood Auditory Discrimination In Depth Program is recommended. This program, multisensory in nature, recognizes that some children have great difficulty in recognizing and perceiving the association between sequences of sounds in spoken words and sequences of letters in written words. It provides experience at a level prior to that of most beginning phonic programs by teaching sound-symbol correspondences through activities that allow students to hear, see, and feel sound units of language. The program starts with oral motor activities (e.g., noting the position of the mouth and tongue when a certain sound is produced), and gradually builds up to working with words. For the program to be effective for Allen, it should be intensively incorporated into his reading program. For many children with phonological processing difficulties, this program has been helpful in diminishing their decoding difficulties. The Lindamood Program, including the associated manual and step-by-step program instructions, can be obtained through Riverside Press.

It is further recommended that Allen be provided with a computer for rehearsing reading skills. Moreover, a language experience approach should be incorporated into Allen's classroom program. This method, which will encourage Allen to use his own words, includes writing his own book by dictating a story to a teacher or aide who provides him with a written transcript. Allen would then read the story back and accumulate flashcards of unknown words that he encounters. Taped books should also be available for Allen. The benefits of taped books are two-fold. They will assist with the acquisition of information that would ordinarily be available only through written text, and provide a way to enhance Allen's reading skills by allowing him to listen to a tape as he follows along in a book. Language therapy is also required to assist with his skill development. Intervention that focuses on his organization of language output, pragmatics, and repair strategies (e.g., using an alternative word or phrase to accommodate his word finding difficulty), will be especially helpful to him at this point. These recommendations have been put into place. Allen will return to the clinic in approximately six months to assess his progress.

Chapter Summary

The purpose of this chapter was to describe the neuropsychology of language disorders and learning disabilities in children. In all these disorders, the child's genetic inheritance and neurological makeup interact with the environment. A child with language and learning disorders is born with neurological constraints that make up the beginning points of the child's interaction with the world. In these disorders, early interventions that combine phonological awareness training and direct instruction of the child in the context of reading have been most successful. The neurobiological constraints are the backdrop for what develops and, although they are limiting in some manner, they are also malleable through environmental interventions.

A transactional approach allows for a simultaneous understanding of the biology, neuropsychology, and family systems of children with neurodevelopmental disorders. Such an understanding is imperative in order to work effectively with children with neurobiological vulnerabilities. As one parent of a learning disabled child reminded the first author: "You professionals give us [the mother and father] lots of suggestions-do you not recognize that we also have learning disabilities? How do you expect us to follow through when we have the same problem?" The wisdom of this father's statement cannot be lost on us as we work with families of children with neurodevelopmental disorders. Families frequently share, to some degree at least, the problems of their child. Even when they do not, the stress, concern, frustration, and disappointment families routinely feel is often ignored when developing treatment plans for children and adolescents with disorders. These contextual variables also need to be assessed and planned for in effective interventions.

References

Adams, A.-M., & Gathercole, S. E. (2000). Limitations in working memory: Implications for language development. *International Journal of Language and Communication Disorders, 35*, 95–116.

Alloway, T. P., & Gathercole, S. E. (2005). Working memory and short-term sentence recall in young children. *European Journal of Cognitive Psychology, 17*, 207–220.

Amelsvoort, T. V., Daly, E. M., Robertson, D. M., Suckling, J., Ng, V., Critchley, H. D., et al. (2001). Structural brain abnormalities associated with deletion at chromosome 22q11: Quantitative neuroimaging study of adults with velocardiofacial syndrome. *British Journal of Psychiatry, 173*, 412–419.

Anderson, P., Anderson, V., Northam, E., & Taylor, H. G. (2000). Standardization of the contingency naming test (CNT) for school-aged children: A measure of reactive flexibility. *Clinical Neuropsychological Assessment, 1*, 247–273.

Antshell, K. M., & Khan, F. M. (2008). Is there an increased familial prevalence of psychopathology in children with nonverbal learning disorders? *Journal of Learning Disabilities, 42*, 208–217.

Aram, D. M., & Ekelman, B. L. (1988). Scholastic aptitude and achievement among children with unilateral brain lesions. *Neuropsychologia, 26*, 903–916.

Asbjornsen, A., Holmefjord, A., Reisaeter, S., Moller, P., Klausen, O., Prytz, B., et al. (2000). Lasting auditory attention impairment after persistent middle ear infections: A dichotic listening study. *Developmental Medicine & Child Neurology, 42*, 481–486.

Asbjornsen, A., Obzrut, J. E., Boliek, C. A., Myking, E., Holmefjord, A., Reisaeter, S., et al. (2005). Impaired auditory attention skills following middle-ear infections. *Child Neuropsychology, 11*, 121–133.

Aylward, E. H., Richards, T. L., Berninger, V. W., Nagy, W. E., Field, K. M., Grimme, A. C., et al. (2003). Instructional treatment associated with changes in brain activation in children with dyslexia. *Neurology, 61*, 212–219.

Balthazar, C. H. (2003). The word length effect in children with language impairment. *Journal of Communication Disorders, 36*, 487–505.

Barnea-Gorly, N., Menon, V., Krasnow, B., Ko, A., Reiss, A. L., & Eliez, S. (2003). Investigation of white matter structure in velocardiofacial syndrome: A diffusion tensor imaging study. *American Journal of Psychiatry, 160*, 1863–1869.

Barnhill, G. P., Tapscott, K., Tebbgenkamp, K., & Smith, B. (2002). The effectiveness of social skills intervention targeting nonverbal communication for adolescents with Asperger syndrome and related pervasive developmental delays. *Focus on Autism and other Developmental Disabilities, 17*, 112–118.

Bauminger, N. (2002). The facilitation of social-emotional understanding and social interaction in high-functioning children with autism: Intervention outcomes. *Journal of Autism and Developmental Disorders, 32*, 283–298.

Beitchman, J., Adlaf, E. M., Douglas, L., Atkinson, L., Young, A., Johnson, C. J., et al. (2001). Comorbidity of psychiatric and substance use disorders in late adolescence: A cluster analytic approach. *American Journal of Drug and Alcohol Abuse, 27*, 421–440.

Beitchman, J., Nair, R., Clegg, M., Ferguson, B., & Patel, P. G. (1986). Prevalence of psychiatric disorders in children with speech and language disorders. *Journal of the American Academy of Child & Adolescent Psychiatry, 32*, 585–594.

Benasich, A. A., & Tallal, P. (2002). Infant discrimination of rapid auditory cues predicts later language impairment. *Behavioural Brain Research, 136*(1), 31–49.

Bender, W. M., Rosenkrans, C. B., & Crane, M.-K. (1999). Stress, depression, and suicide among students with learning disabilities: Assessing the risk. *Learning Disability Quarterly, 22*, 143–156.

Berninger, V. W. (2001). *Process Assessment of the Learner*. San Antonio, TX: Psychological Corporation.

Berninger, V. W., Abbott, R. D., Abbott, S. P., Graham, S., & Richards, T. (2002). Writing and reading: connections between language by hand and language by eye. *Journal of Learning Disabilities, 35*(1), 39–56.

Berninger, V. W., Abbott, R. D., Thomson, J. B., Wagner, R. K., Swanson, H. L., Wijsman, E., et al. (2006). Modeling developmental phonological core deficits within a working-memory architecture in children and adults with developmental dyslexia. *Scientific Studies of Reading, 10*, 165–198.

Berninger, V. W., & Amtmann, D. (2003). Preventing written expression disabilities through early and continuing assessment and intervention for handwriting and/or spelling problems: Research into practice. In H. L. Swanson, K. R. Harris, & S. Graham (Eds.), *Handbook of Learning Disabilities* (pp. 345–363). New York: Guilford Press.

Berninger, V. W., & Fuller, F. (1992). Gender differences in orthographic, verbal, and compositional fluency: Implications for diagnosis of writing disabilities in primary grade children. *Journal of School Psychology, 30*, 363–382.

Berninger, V. W., & Hart, T. (1992). A developmental neuropsychological perspective for reading and writing acquisition. *Educational Psychologist, 27*, 415–434.

Berninger, V. W., & Hooper, S. R. (2006). Special issue on writing. *Developmental Neuropsychology, 29*, 1–4.

Berninger, V. W., Nielsen, K. H., Abbott, R. D., Wijsman, E., & Raskind, W. (2008a). Gender differences in severity of writing and reading disabilities. *Journal of School Psychology, 46*, 151–172.

Berninger, V. W., Nielsen, K. H., Abbott, R. D., Wijsman, E., & Raskind, W. (2008b). Writing problems in developmental dyslexia: Under-recognized and under-treated. *Journal of School Psychology, 46*, 1–21.

Berninger, V. W., Rutberg, J., Abbott, R. D., Garcia, N., Anderson-Youngstrom, M., Brooks, A., et al. (2006). Tier 1 and Tier 2 early intervention for handwriting and composing. *Journal of School Psychology, 44*, 3–30.

Binder, J. R., Frost, J. A., Hammeke, T. A., Bellgowan, P. S. F., Springer, J. A., Kaufman, J. N., et al. (2000). Human temporal lobe activation by speech and nonspeech sounds. *Cerebral Cortex, 10*, 512–528.

Binder, J. R., Frost, J. A., Hammeke, T. A., Rao, S. M., & Prieto, T. (1997). Human brain areas identified by functional magnetic resonance imaging. *Journal of Neuroscience, 17*, 353–362.

Bishop, D. V. M., Adams, C. V., & Norbury, C. F. (2006). Distinct genetic influences on grammar and phonological short-term memory deficits: Evidence from 6-year-old twins. *Genes, Brain, and Behavior, 5*, 158–169.

Bishop, D. V. M., & Snowling, M. J. (2004). Developmental dyslexia and specific language impairment: Same or different? *Psychological Bulletin, 130*, 858–886.

Blair, C., Knipe, H., & Gamson, D. (2008). Is there a role for executive functions in the development of mathematics ability? *Mind, Brain, and Education, 2*, 79–88.

Borod, J. C., Andelman, F., Obler, L. K., Tweedy, J. R., & Welkowitz, J. (1992). Right hemispheric specialization for the identification of emotional words and sentences: Evidence from stroke patients. *Neuropsychologia, 30*, 827–844.

Brieger, D., & Majovski, L. V. (2008). Neuropsychological assessment and RTI in the assessment of learning disabilities: Are they mutually exclusive? In E. Fletcher-Janzen & C. R. Reynolds (Eds.), *Neuropsychological perspectives on learning disabilities in the era of RTI: Recommendations for diagnosis and intervention*. Hoboken, NJ: John Wiley & Sons, Inc.

Broomfield, J., & Dodd, B. (2004a). Children with speech and language disability: Caseload characteristics. *International Journal of Language and Communication Disorders, 39*, 303–324.

Broomfield, J., & Dodd, B. (2004b). The nature of referred subtypes of primary speech disability. *Child Language Teaching and Therapy, 20*, 135–151.

Brown, W. E., Kesler, S. R., Eliez, S., Warsofsky, I. S., Haberecht, M., Patwardhan, A., et al. (2002). Brain development in Turner syndrome: A magnetic resonance imaging study. *Psychiatry Research: Neuroimaging, 116*, 187–196.

Brown, W. S., & Paul, L. K. (2000). Cognitive and psychosocial deficits in agenesis of the corpus callosum with normal intelligence. *Cognitive Neuropsychiatry, 5*, 135–157.

Brown, W. S., Symingtion, M., Van Lancker-Sidtis, D., Dietrich, R., & Paul, L. K. (2005). Paralinguistic processing in children with callosal agenesis: Emergence of neurolinguistic deficits. *Brain and Language, 93*, 135–139.

Bus, A., & van Ijzendoorn, M. (1999). Phonological awareness and early reading: A meta-analysis of experimental training studies. *Journal of Educational Psychology, 91*, 403–414.

Byrne, B., Coventry, W. L., Olson, R. K., Hulslander, J., Wadsworth, S., DeFries, J. C., et al. (2008). A behavior-genetic analysis of orthographic learning, spelling, and decoding. *Journal of Research in Reading, 31*, 8–21.

Byrne, B., Delaland, C., Fielding-Barnsley, R., Quain, P., Samuelsson, S., Hoien, T., et al. (2002). Longitudinal twin study of early reading development in three countries: Preliminary results. *Annals of Dyslexia, 52*, 49–74.

Byrne, B., Fielding-Barnsley, R., & Ashley, L. (2000). Effects of preschool phoneme identity training after six years: Outcome level distinguished from rate of response. *Journal of Educational Psychology, 92*, 659–667.

Byrne, B., Samuelsson, S., Wadsworth, S., Hulslander, J., Corley, R., DeFries, J. C., et al. (2007). Longitudinal twin study of early literacy development: Preschool through Grade 1. *Reading and Writing, 20*, 77–102.

Capozzi, F., Casini, M. P., Romani, M., De Gennaro, L., Nicolais, G., & Luigi, S. (2008). Psychiatric comorbidity in learning disorder: Analysis of family variables. *Child Psychiatry and Human Development, 39*, 101–110.

Catts, H. W., Hogan, T. P., & Adlof, S. M. (2005). Developmental changes in reading and reading disabilities. In H. W. Catts & A. G. Kamhi (Eds.), *The connections between language and reading disabilities* (pp. 24–51). Mahwah, NJ: Erlbaum.

Chapman, J. W., Tunmer, W. E., & Prochnow, J. E. (2001). Does success in the reading recovery program depend on developing proficiency in phonological processing skills? A longitudinal study in a whole language instructional context. *Scientific Studies of Reading, 5*, 141–176.

Chase, C. H., & Tallal, P. (1991). Cognitive models of developmental reading disorders. In J. E. Obzrut & G. W. Hynd (Eds.), *Neuropsychological foundations of learning disabilities* (pp. 199–240). San Diego, CA: Academic Press.

Cheour, M., Martynova, O., Naatanen, R., Erkkola, R., Sillanpaa, M., Kero, P., et al. (2002). Speech sounds learned by sleeping newborns. *Nature, 415*, 599–600.

Chi, J. G., Dooling, E. C., & Gilles, F. H. (1977). Left-right asymmetries of the temporal speech areas of the human fetus. *Archives of neurology, 34*, 346–348.

Chiappe, P., Stringer, R., Siegel, L. S., & Stanovich, K. E. (2002). Why the timing deficit hypothesis does not explain reading disability in adults. *Reading and Writing, 15*, 73–107.

Chow, D., & Skuy, M. (1999). Simultaneous and successive cognitive processing in children with nonverbal learning disabilities. *School Psychology International, 20*, 219–231.

Christian, K., Morrison, F. J., & Bryant, F. B. (1998). Predicting kindergarten academic skills: Interactions among child care, maternal education, and family literacy environments. *Early Child Research Quarterly, 13*, 501–521.

Clay, M. M. (1993). *Reading recovery: A guidebook for teachers in training*. Auckland, New Zealand: Heinemann Education.

Cohen, L., Lehericy, S., Chhochon, F., Lemer, C., Rivaud, S., & Dehaene, S. (2002). Language-specific tuning of visual cortex? Functional properties of the visual word form area. *Brain, 124*, 1054–1069.

Cohen, W., Hodson, A., O'Hare, A., Boyle, J., Durrani, T., McCartney, E., et al. (2005). Effects of computer-based intervention through acoustically modified speech (Fast ForWord) in severe mixed receptive-expressive language impairment: Outcomes from a randomized controlled trial. *Journal of Speech, Language, and Hearing Research, 48*, 715–729.

Coltheart, M., Rastle, K., Perry, C., Langdon, R., & Ziegler, J. (2001). DRC: A dual route cascaded model of visual word recognition and read aloud. *Psychological Review, 108*, 204–256.

Compton, D. L., DeFries, J. C., & Olson, R. K. (2001). Are RAN and phonological awareness deficits additive in reading disabled individuals? *Dyslexia, 7*, 125–149.

Connolly, A. J. (2007). *Key Math 3*. San Antonio, TX: Pearson Assessments.

Constantino, J. N., & Gruber, C. P. (2006). *Social responsiveness scale*. Los Angeles: Western Psychological Services.

Conti-Ramsden, G., & Botting, N. (2008). Emotional health in adolescents with and without a history of specific language impairment (SLI). *Journal of Child Psychology and Psychiatry, 49*, 516–525.

Corlett, M. (2002). *Visual perceptual processing errors in children with nonverbal learning disabilities*. Unpublished dissertation, University of Texas, Austin.

Cornoldi, C. (1999). Imagery deficits in nonverbal learning disabilities. *Journal of Learning Disabilities, 32*, 48–60.

Cunningham, A. E. (2005). Vocabulary growth through independent reading and reading aloud to children. In E. H. Hiebert & M. H. Kamil (Eds.), *Teaching and learning vocabulary: Bringing research to practice* (pp. 45–68). Mahwah, NJ: Lawrence Erlbaum Associates Publishers.

Cunningham, P. M. (2007). Best practices in teaching phonological awareness and phonics. In L. B. Gambrell, L. M. Morrow, & M. Pressley (Eds.), *Best practices in literacy instruction* (pp. 159–177). New York: Guilford.

Curtis, W. J., Lindeke, L. L., Georgieff, M. K., & Nelson, C. A. (2002). Neurobehavioral functioning in neonatal intensive care unit graduates in late childhood and early adolescence. *Brain, 125*, 1646–1659.

Damasio, A. R., Tranel, D., & Rizzo, M. (2000). Disorders of complex visual processing. In M. M. Mesulam (Ed.), *Principles of behavioral and cognitive neurology* (2nd ed.). Oxford: Oxford University Press.

Decker, S. N., & Vandenberg, S. G. (1985). Colorado twin study of reading disability. In D. B. Gray & J. F. Kavanaugh (Eds.), *Behavioral measures of dyslexia* (pp. 123–135). Parkton, MD: York Press.

DeFries, J. C., & Alarcon, M. (1996). Genetics of special reading disability. *Mental Retardation and Developmental Disabilities Research Reviews, 2*, 39–47.

DeFries, J. C., Filipek, P. A., Fulker, D. W., Olson, R. K., Pennington, B. F., Smith, S. D., et al. (1997). Colorado learning disabilities research center. *Learning Disabilities, 8*, 7–19.

DeFries, J. C., Fulker, D. W., & LaBuda, M. C. (1987). Evidence for a genetic aetiology in reading disability of twins. *Nature, 329*, 537–539.

Dodd, B. (1995). *Differential diagnosis and treatment of children with speech disorder*. London: Whurr Publisher.

Dragnanski, B., Gaser, C., Kempermann, G., Kuhn, H. G., Winkler, J., Buchel, C., et al. (2006). Temporal and spatial dynamics of brain structure changes during extensive learning. *Journal of Neuroscience Methods, 26*, 6314–6317.

Duara, B., Kushch, A., Gross-Glenn, K., Barker, W. W., Jallad, B., Pascal, S., et al. (1991). Neuroanatomic differences between dyslexic and normal readers on magnetic resonance imaging scans. *Archives of Neurology, 48*, 410–416.

Eckert, M. A., Leonard, C. M., Possing, E. T., & Binder, J. R. (2006). Uncoupled leftward asymmetries for planum morphology and functional language processing. *Brain and Language, 98*, 102–111.

Ehri, L. C. (2005). Development of sight word reading: Phases and findings. In M. J. Snowling & C. Hulme (Eds.), *The science of reading: A handbook* (pp. 135–154). Oxford: Blackwell.

Eley, T. C., Dale, P. S., Bishop, D. V. M., Price, T. S., & Plomin, R. (2001). Longitudinal analysis of components of cognitive delay: Examining the aetiology of verbal and performance aspects of cognitive delay. *Journal of Educational Psychology, 93*, 698–707.

Elgar, K., Campbell, R., & Skuse, D. (2002). Are you looking at me? Accuracy in processing line-of-sight in Turner syndrome. *Proceedings of the Royal Society of London, 269*, 2415–2422.

Eliez, S., Schmitt, J. E., White, C. D., Hu, D., & Reiss, A. L. (2002). Velocardiofacial syndrome: Are structural changes in the temporal and mesial temporal regions related to schizophrenia? *American Journal of Psychiatry, 159*, 447–453.

Elksnin, L. K., Bryan, D. P., Gartland, D., King-Sears, M., Rosenberg, M. S., Scanlon, D. M., et al. (2001). LD Summit: Important issues in the field of learning disabilities. *Learning Disability Quarterly, 24*, 297–305.

Feretti, R. P., MacArthur, C. A., & Dowdy, N. S. (2000). The effects of an elaborated goal on the persuasive writing of students with learning disabilities and their normally achieving peers. *Journal of Educational Psychology, 92*, 694–702.

Fiez, J. A. (1997). Phonology, semantics, and the role of the left inferior prefrontal cortex. *Human Brain Mapping, 5*, 79–83.

Fine, J. G., Semrud-Clikeman, M., Butcher, B., & Walkowiak, J. (2008). Brief report: Attention effect on a measure of social perception *Journal of Attention Disorders 38*, 1797–1802.

Fine, J. G., Semrud-Clikeman, M., Keith, T. Z., Stapleton, L., & Hynd, G. W. (2006). Reading and the corpus callosum: An MRI family study of volume and area. *Neuropsychology, 21*(2), 235–241.

Fine, J. G., Semrud-Clikeman, M., Reynolds, M. R., & Smith, S. (submitted). Assessing social competence in ADHD and other disorders: Indirect and direct measures. *Submitted to Journal of Learning Disabilities.*

Fitch, R. H., & Tallal, P. (2003). Neural mechanisms of language-based learning impairments: Insights from human populations and animal models. *Behavioral and Cognitive Neuroscience Reviews, 2*, 155–178.

Flannery, K., Liederman, J., Daly, L., & Schultz, J. (2000). Male prevalence for reading disability is found in a large sample of black and white children free from ascertainment bias. *Journal of the International Neuropsychological Society, 6*, 433–442.

Fletcher, J. M., Morris, M. K., & Lyon, G. R. (2003). Classification and definition of learning disabilities: An integrative perspective. In H. L. Swanson, K. R. Harris, & S. Graham (Eds.), *Handbook of learning disabilities* (pp. 30–56). New York: Guilford Press.

Forrest, B. (2007). Diagnosing and treating right hemisphere disorders. In S. J. Hunter & J. Donders (Eds.), *Pediatric neuropsychological intervention* (pp. 175–192). Cambridge: Cambridge University Press.

Foss, J. M. (1991). Nonverbal learning disabilities and remedial interventions. *Annals of Dyslexia, 41*, 128–140.

Foster, L. M., Hynd, G. W., Morgan, A. E., & Hugdahl, K. (2002). Planum temporale asymmetry and ear advantage in dichotic listening in developmental dyslexia and Attention-Deficit/Hyperactivity Disorder (ADHD). *Journal of the International Neuropsychological Society, 8*, 22–36.

Fox, A. V., & Dodd, B. (2001). Phonologically disordered German-speaking children. *American Journal of Speech-Language Pathology, 10*, 291–303.

Foxton, J. M., Talcott, J. B., Witton, C., Brace, H., McIntyre, F., & Griffiths, T. D. (2003). Reading skills are related to global, but not local, acoustic pattern perception. *Nature Neuroscience, 6*, 343–344.

Foy, J. G., & Mann, V. A. (2003). Home literacy environment and phonological awareness in preschool children: Differential effects for rhyme and phoneme awareness. *Applied Psycholinguistics, 24*, 59–68.

Freeman, A. R., MacKinnon, J. R., & Miller, L. T. (2004). Assistive technology and handwriting problems: What do occupational therapists recommend? *Canadian Journal of Occupational Disabilities: Research and Practice, 18*, 157–171.

Fuchs, D., Fuchs, L. S., Mathes, P. G., & Lipsey, M. W. (2000a). A meta-analysis of reading differences between underachievers with and without the disability label. *Learning Disabilities, 10*, 1–4.

Fuchs, D., Fuchs, L. S., Mathes, P. G., & Lipsey, M. W. (2000b). Reading differences between low-achieving students with and without learning disabilities: A meta-analysis. In R. Gersten, E. P. Schiller, & S. Vaughn (Eds.), *Contemporary special education research: Syntheses of the knowledge base on critical instructional issues* (pp. 81–104). Mahwah, NJ: Erlbaum.

Fuchs, L. S., Fuchs, D., Prentice, K., Burch, M., Hamlett, C. L., Owen, R., et al. (2003a). Explicitly teaching for transfer: Effect on third-grade students' mathematical problem solving. *Journal of Educational Psychology, 95*, 293–305.

Fuchs, L. S., Fuchs, D., Prentice, K., Burch, M., Hamlett, C. L., Owen, R., et al. (2003b). Enhancing third-grade students' mathematical problem solving with self-regulated learning strategies. *Journal of Educational Psychology, 95*, 306–315.

Fuchs, L. S., Fuchs, D., Prentice, K., Hamlett, C. L., Finelli, R., & Courey, S. J. (2004). Enhancing mathematical problem solving among third-grade students with schema-based instruction. *Journal of Educational Psychology, 96*, 635–746.

Galaburda, A. M. (2005). Neurology of learning disabilities: What will the future bring? The answer comes from the successes of the recent past. *Learning Disabilities Quarterly, 28*, 107–109.

Galaburda, A. M., Sherman, G. P., Rosen, G. D., Aboitiz, F., & Geschwind, N. (1985). Developmental dyslexia: Four consecutive patients with cortical anomalies. *Annals of Neurology, 18*, 222–233.

Garrett, A. J., Mazzocco, M. M. M., & Baker, L. (2006). Development of metacognitive skills of prediction and evaluation in children with and without math disability. *Learning Disabilities Research, 21*, 77–88.

Gaser, C., & Schlaug, G. (2003). Brain structures differ between musicians and non-musicians. *Journal of Neuroscience Methods, 23*, 9240–9245.

Gathercole, S. E., Tiffany, C., Briscoe, J., & Thorn, A. (2005). Developmental consequences of poor phonological short-term memory functions in childhood: A longitudinal study. *Journal of Child Psychology and Psychiatry and Allied Disciplines, 46*, 598–611.

Geary, D. C. (2004). Mathematics and learning disabilities. *Journal of Learning Disabilities, 37*, 4–15.

Geary, D. C., & Hoard, M. K. (2002). Learning disabilities in basic mathematics: Deficits in memory and cognition. In J. M. Royer (Ed.), *Mathematical cognition* (pp. 95–115). Greenwich, CT: Information Age.

Geschwind, N., & Galaburda, A. M. (1985). Cerebral lateralization: Biological mechanisms, associations, and pathology: I. A hypothesis and a program for research. *Archives of Neurology, 42*, 521–552.

Gillam, R. B., Loeb, D. F., Hoffman, L. M., Bohman, T., Champlin, C. A., Thibodeau, L., et al. (2008). The efficacy of Fast ForWord language intervention for school-age children with language impairment: A randomized controlled trial. *Journal of Speech, Language, and Hearing Research, 51*, 97–119.

Gillingham, A., & Stillman, B. W. (1997). *The Gillingham manual: Remedial training for children with specific disability in reading, spelling, and writing* (8th ed.). Cambridge, MA: Educators Publishing Service.

Ginsberg, H. P., & Baroody, A. J. (1990). *Test of early mathematics ability* (2nd ed.). Austin, TX: Pro-Ed.

Ginsburg, H. P., & Baroody, A. J. (2002). *Test of Early Mathematics Ability* (3rd ed.). Austin, TX: Pro-Ed.

Glass, K. L., Guli, L. A., & Semrud-Clikeman, M. (2000). Social competence intervention program: A pilot program for the development of social competence. *Journal of Psychotherapy in Independent Practice Social Competence and Developmental Disorders, 1*(4), 21–33.

Glassberg, L. A., Hooper, S. R., & Mattison, R. E. (1999). Prevalence of learning disabilities at enrollment in special education students with behavioral disorders. *Behavioral Disorders, 25*, 9–21.

Goldberg, E., & Costa, L. D. (1981). Hemisphere differences in the acquisition and use of descriptive systems. *Brain and Language, 14*, 144–173.

Good, C. D., Lawrence, K., Thomas, N. S., Price, C. J., Ashburner, J., Friston, K. J., et al. (2003). Dosage-sensitive X-linked locus influences the development of amygdala and orbitofrontal cortex, and fear recognition in humans. *Brain, 126*, 2431–2446.

Gordan, T. (2006). *Parent effectiveness training*. Solana Beach, CA: Gordon Training International.

Goswami, U. (2006). Sensorimotor impairments in dyslexia: Getting the beat. *Developmental Science, 9*(3), 257–259.

Goswami, U., & Bryant, P. E. (1990). *Phonological skills and learning to read*. Hillsdale, NJ: Erlbaum.

Graham, S., Olinghouse, N. G., & Harris, K. R. (in press). Teaching composing to students with learning disabilities: Scientifically-supported recommendations. In G. Troia (Ed.), *Writing instruction and assessment for struggling writers*. New York: Guilford.

Graham, S., & Perrin, D. (2007a). A meta-analysis of writing instruction for adolescent students. *Journal of Educational Psychology, 99*, 445–476.

Graham, S., & Perrin, D. (2007b). *Writing new: Effective strategies to improve writing of adolescents in middle and high school*. Washington, DC: Alliance for Excellence in Education.

Graves, A., Valles, E. C., & Rueda, R. (2000). Variation in interactive writing instruction: A study in four bilingual special education settings. *Learning Disabilities Research and Practice, 15*, 1–9.

Gregg, N., Coleman, C., Lindstrom, J., & Lee, C. (2007). Who are most, average or high-functioning adults? *Learning Disabilities Research and Practice, 22*, 264–274.

Gregg, N., & Mather, N. (2002). School is fun at recess: Informal analyses of written language for students with learning disabilities. *Journal of Learning Disabilities, 35*, 7–22.

Grigorenko, E. L. (2001). Developmental dyslexia: An update on genes, brains, and environments. *Journal of Child Psychology and Psychiatry, 42*(1), 91–125.

Grigorenko, E. L. (2006). Learning disabilities in juvenile offenders. *Child and Adolescent Psychiatric Clinics of North America, 15*, 353–371.

Gross-Tur, V., Ben-Bashat, D., Shalev, R. S., Levav, M., & Sira, L. B. (2006). Evidence of a developmental cerebello-cerebral disorder. *Neuropsychologia, 44*, 2569–2572.

Guli, L. A., Wilkinson, A., & Semrud-Clikeman, M. (2008). *Enhancing social competence on the autism spectrum: A drama-based intervention for youth*. Champaign, IL: Research Press.

Guttorm, T. K., Leppanen, P. H., Poikkeus, A.-M., Eklund, K. M., Lyytinen, P., & Lyytinen, H. (2005). Brain event-related potentials (ERPs) measured at birth predict later language development in children with and without familial risk for dyslexia. *Cortex, 41*, 291–303.

Hall, S. L., & Moats, L. C. (1999). *Straight talk about reading: How parents can make a difference during the early years*. Chicago: Contemporary Books.

Hammill, D. D., Mather, N., Allen, E. A., & Roberts, R. (2002). Using semantics, grammar, phonology, and rapid naming tasks to predict word identification. *Journal of Learning Disabilities, 35*, 121–136.

Hanich, L. B., Jordan, N. C., Kaplan, D., & Dick, J. (2001). Performance across different areas of mathematical cognition in children with learning difficulties. *Journal of Educational Psychology, 93*, 615–626.

Harder, L., & Semrud-Clikeman, M. (submitted). The relation between executive functions and written expression in college students with Attention-Deficit/Hyperactivity Disorder. *Journal of Attention Disorders*.

Harder, L., Semrud-Clikeman, M., & Maegden, J. (2006). *College-age students with ADHD and written language difficulties*. Paper presented at the International Neuropsychological Society.

Harlaar, N., Spinath, F. M., Dale, P. S., & Plomin, R. (2005). Genetic influences on word recognition abilities and disabilities: A study of 7 year old twins. *Journal of Child Psychology and Psychiatry, 46*, 373–384.

Harm, M. W., & Seidenberg, M. S. (2004). Computing the meaning of words in reading: Cooperative division of labor between visual and phonological processes. *Psychological Review, 111*, 662–720.

Hawke, J. L., Wadsworth, S., Olson, R. K., & DeFries, J. C. (2007). Etiology of reading difficulties as a function of gender and severity. *Reading and Writing, 20*, 13–25.

Hayes, J. R. (1996). A new framework for understanding cognition and affect in writing. In C. M. Levy &

S. Ransdell (Eds.), *The science of writing: Theories, methods, individual differences, and applications* (pp. 1–27). Mahwah, NJ: Lawrence Erlbaum and Associates.

Hayes, J. R., & Flower, L. S. (1986). Writing research and the writer. *American Psychologist, 41*, 1106–1113.

Heiervang, E., Stevenson, J., & Hugdahl, K. (2002). Auditory processing in children with dyslexia. *Journal of Child Psychology and Psychiatry, 43*, 931–938.

Helenius, P., Tarkiainen, A., Cornelissen, P. L., Hansen, P. C., & Salmelin, R. (1999). Dissociation of normal feature analysis and deficient processing of letter-strings in dyslexic adults. *Cerebral Cortex, 9*(5), 476–483.

Helland, T., Asbjornsen, A., Hushovd, A. E., & Hugdahl, K. (2007). Dichotic listening and school performance in dyslexia. *Dyslexia, 14*, 42–53.

Hoard, M. K., Geary, D. C., & Hamson, C. O. (1999). Numerical and arithmetical cognition: Performance of low- and average-IQ children. *Mathematical Cognition, 5*, 65–91.

Hoeft, F., Hernandez, A., McMillon, G., Taylor-Hill, H., Martindale, J. L., Meyler, A., et al. (2006). Neural basis of dyslexia: A comparison between dyslexic and nondyslexic children equated for reading ability. *The Journal of Neuroscience, 26*, 10700–10708.

Hoeft, F., Meyler, A., Hernandez, A., Juel, C., Taylor-Hill, H., Martindale, J. L., et al. (2007). Functional and morphometric brain dissociation between dyslexia and reading ability. *Proceedings of the National Academy of Science USA, 104*, 4234–4239.

Hoffman, L. M., & Gillam, R. B. (2004). Verbal and spatial information processing constraints in children with specific language impairment. *Journal of Speech, Language, and Hearing Research, 47*, 114–125.

Holm, A., & Dodd, B. (2001). Comparison of cross-language generalisation following speech therapy. *Folia Phoniatrica et Logopaedica, 53*, 166–172.

Hooper, S. R., Swartz, C., Wakely, M. B., de Kruif, R. E. L., & Montgomery, J. W. (2002). Executive functions in elementary school children with and without problems in written expression. *Journal of Learning Disabilities, 35*, 57–68.

Hoskyn, M., & Swanson, H. L. (2000). What definitions of learning disability say and don't say: A critical analysis. *Journal of Learning Disabilities, 33*, 239–256.

Hugdahl, K., Heiervang, E., Ersland, L., Lundervold, A., Steinmetz, H., & Smievoll, A. I. (2003). Significant relation between MR measures of planum temporale area and dichotic processing of syllables in dyslexic children. *Neuropsychologia, 41*, 666–675.

Hulslander, J., Talcott, J. B., Witton, C., DeFries, J. C., Pennington, B. F., Wadsworth, S., et al. (2004). Sensory processing, reading, IQ, and attention. *Journal of Experimental Child Psychology, 88*, 272–295.

Humphreys, P., Kaufman, W. E., & Galaburda, A. M. (1990). Developmental dyslexia in women: Neuropsychological findings in three cases. *Annals of Neurology, 28*, 727–738.

Hurry, J., & Sylva, K. (2007). Long-term outcomes of early reading intervention. *Journal of Research in Reading, 30*, 227–248.

Hutchinson, S., Lee, L. H., & Gaab, N. (2003). Cerebellar volume of musicians. *Cerebral Cortex, 13*, 943–949.

Hynd, G. W., & Semrud-Clikeman, M. (1989). Dyslexia and brain morphology. *Psychological Bulletin, 106*, 447–482.

Hynd, G. W., Semrud-Clikeman, M., Lorys, A. R., Novey, E. S., & Eliopulos, D. (1990). Brain morphology in developmental dyslexia and attention deficit disorder/hyperactivity. *Archives of neurology, 47*, 919–926.

Hynd, G. W., Semrud-Clikeman, M., Lorys, A. R., Novey, E. S., Eliopulos, D., & Lyytinen, H. (1991). Corpus callosum morphology in attention deficit-hyperactivity disorder: Morphometric analysis of MRI. *Journal of Learning Disabilities, 24*(3), 141–146.

Jackson, N. W., & Coltheart, M. (2001). *Routes to reading success and failure.* New York: Psychology Press.

Jarrold, C., Baddeley, A. D., Hewes, A. K., Leeke, T. C., & Phillips, C. E. (2004). What links verbal short-term memory performance and vocabulary level? Evidence of change relationships among individuals with learning disability. *Journal of Memory and Language, 50*, 134–148.

Johnson, C. R., Beitchman, J., Young, A., Escobar, M. D., Atkinson, L., Wilson, B., et al. (1999). Fourteen year follow-up of children with and without speech/language impairments: Speech/language stability outcomes. *Journal of Speech and Hearing Research, 42*, 744–760.

Johnston, J. R. (2006). *Thinking about child language: Research to practice.* Eau Claire, WI: Thinking Publications.

Kavale, K. A. (2005). Identifying specific learning disability: Is responsiveness to intervention the answer? *Journal of Learning Disabilities, 38*, 553–562.

Keenan, J. M., Betjemann, R. S., Wadsworth, S., DeFries, J. C., & Olson, R. K. (2006). Genetic and environmental influences on reading and listening comprehension. *Journal of Research in Reading, 29*, 75–91.

Keith, T. Z. (2006). *Multiple regression and beyond.* Boston: Pearson/Allyn & Bacon.

Kellner, R., Houghton, S., & Graham, D. (2003). Peer-related personal experiences of children with attention-deficit/hyperactivity disorder with and without comorbid learning disabilities. *International Journal of Disability, Development and Education, 50*, 119–136.

Kibby, M., Kroese, J. M., Morgan, A. E., Heimenz, J. R., Cohen, M. J., & Hynd, G. W. (2004). The relationship between perisylvian morphology and verbal short-term memory functioning in children with neurodevelopmental disorders. *Brain and Language, 89*, 122–135.

Kovas, Y., Oliver, B., Dale, P. S., Bishop, D. V. M., & Plomin, R. (2005). Genetic influences in different aspects of language development: The etiology of language skills in 4.5 year-old twins. *Child Development, 76*, 632–651.

Lamm, O., & Epstein, R. (1997). Dichotic listening in children: The reflection of verbal and attentional changes with age. *Journal of Experimental Child Psychology, 65*, 25–42.

Larsen, J. P., Hoeien, T., & Oedegaard, H. (1992). Magnetic resonance imaging of the corpus callosum in developmental dyslexia. *Cognitive Neuropsychology, 9*(2), 123–134.

Larsen, J. P., Hoien, T., Lundberg, I., & Odegaard, H. (1990). MRI evaluation of the size and symmetry of the planum temporale in adolescents with developmental dyslexia. *Brain and Language, 39*, 289–301.

Law, J., Boyle, J., Harris, F., Harkness, A., & Nye, C. (2000). Prevalence and natural history of speech and language delay: Findings from a systematic review of the literature. *International Journal of Language and Communication Disorders, 35*, 165–188.

Lawrence, K., Campbell, R., Swettenham, J., Terstegge, J., Akers, R., Coleman, M., et al. (2003). Interpreting gaze in Turner syndrome: Impaired sensitivity to intention and emotion, but preservation of social cueing. *Neuropsychologia, 41*, 894–905.

Lawrence, K., Kuntsi, J., Coleman, M., Campbell, R., & Skuse, D. (2003). Face and emotion recognition deficits in Turner syndrome: A possible role for X-linked genes in amygdala development. *Neuropsychology, 17*, 39–49.

Leach, J. M., Scarborough, H. S., & Rescorla, L. A. (2003). Late-emerging reading disabilities. *Journal of Educational Psychology, 95*, 211–214.

Leonard, L. B. (1998). *Children with specific language impairment*. Cambridge, MA: MIT Press.

Liederman, J., Kantrowitz, L., & Flannery, K. (2005). Male vulnerability to reading disability is not likely to be a myth: A call for new data. *Journal of Learning Disabilities, 38*, 109–129.

Lindamood, P. C., & Lindamood, P. D. (1998). *The Lindamood phonemic sequencing (LIPS) for reading, spelling, and speech*. Austin, TX: Pro-Ed.

Logie, R. H. (1995). *Visual-spatial working memory*. Mahwah, NJ: Erlbaum.

Longcamp, M., Boucard, C., Gilhodes, J.-C., Anton, J.-L., Roth, M., Nazarian, B., et al. (2008). Learning through hand-or typewriting influences visual recognition of new graphic shapes: Behavioral and functional imaging evidence. *Journal of Cognitive Neuroscience, 20*, 802–815.

Luria, A. B. (1980). *Higher cortical functions in man* (2nd ed.). New York: Basic Books.

Lyon, G. R. (1996a). Learning disabilities. *Special Education for Students with Disabilities, 6*, 54–76.

Lyon, G. R. (1996b). Learning disabilities. In E. Marsh & R. Barkely (Eds.), *Child Psychopathology* (pp. 390–434). New York: Guilford Press.

Lyon, G. R., Fletcher, J. M., Shaywitz, S. E., Shaywitz, B. A., Torgesen, J. K., Wood, F. B., et al. (2001). Rethinking learning disabilities. In C. E. Finn, A. J. Rotherhan & C. R. Hokanson (Eds.), *Rethinking special education for a new century* (pp. 259–287). Washington, DC: Fordham Foundation.

Lyon, G. R., Shaywitz, S. E., & Shaywitz, B. A. (2003). A definition of dyslexia. *Annals of Dyslexia, 53*, 1–14.

MacMillan, D. L., Gresham, F. M., & Bocian, K. M. (1998). Discrepancy between definitions of learning disabilities and school practices: An empirical investigation. *Journal of Learning Disabilities, 31*, 314–326.

Magill-Evans, J., Koning, C., Cameron-Sadava, A., & Manyk, K. (1996). *Manual for the child and adolescent social perception measure*: Unpublished test.

Mann, V. A. (2003). Language processes: Keys to reading disability. In H. L. Swanson, K. R. Harris, & S. Graham (Eds.), *Handbook of learning disabilities* (pp. 213–228). New York: Guilford.

Martinez, R., & Semrud-Clikeman, M. (2004). Emotional adjustment of young adolescents with different learning disability subtypes. *Journal of Learning Disabilities, 37*, 411–420.

Marton, K., & Schwartz, R. G. (2003). Working memory capacity and language processes in children with specific language impairment. *Journal of Speech, Language, and Hearing Research, 46*, 1138–1153.

Mason, L. H., & Graham, S. (2008). Writing instruction for adolescents with learning disabilities: Programs for intervention research. *Learning Disabilities Research and Practice, 23*, 103–112.

Mazzocco, M. M. M., & Kover, S. T. (2007). A longitudinal assessment of executive function skills and their association with math performance. *Child Neuropsychology, 13*, 18–45.

Mazzocco, M. M. M., & Myers, G. F. (2003). Complexities in identifying and defining mathematics learning disability in the primary school-age years. *Annals of Dyslexia, 53*, 218–253.

McCandliss, B., Cohen, L., & Dehaene, S. (2003). The visual word form area: Expertise for reading in the fusiform gyrus. *Trends in Cognitive Science, 7*, 293–302.

McCardle, P., Scarborough, H. S., & Catts, H. W. (2001). Predicting, explaining, and preventing children's reading difficulties. *Learning Disabilities Research & Practice, 16*(4), 230–239.

McDonough-Ryan, P., Delbello, M., Shear, P. K., Ris, D. M., Soutullo, C., & Strakowski, S. M. (2002). Academic and cognitive abilities in children of parents with bipolar disorder: A test of the nonverbal learning disability model. *Journal of Clinical and Experimental Neuropsychology, 24*, 280–285.

Merzenich, M. M., Jenkins, W. M., Johnson, P., Scheiner, C., Miller, S. L., & Tallal, P. (1996). Temporal processing deficits of language-learning impaired children ameliorated by training. *Science, 271*, 77–81.

Meyers, J. E., & Meyers, K. R. (1995). Rey Complex Figure Test under four different administration procedures. *Clinical Neuropsychologist, 9*, 63–67.

Miles, T. R., Haslum, M. N., & Wheeler, T. J. (1999). Gender ratio in dyslexia. *Annals of Dyslexia, 48*, 27–56.

Milne, R. D., Syngeniotis, A., Jackson, G., & Corballis, M. C. (2002). Mixed lateralization of phonological assembly in developmental dyslexia. *Neurocase, 8*, 205–209.

Molfese, D. L., Molfese, V. J., & Molfese, P. J. (2007). Relation between early measures of brain responses to language stimuli and childhood performance on language and language-related tasks. In D. Coch, G. Dawson & K. W. Fischer (Eds.), *Human behavior, learning, and the developing brain: Atypical development* (pp. 191–211). New York: Guilford Press.

Molfese, D. L., Molfese, V. J., & Pratt, N. L. (2007). The use of event-related evoked potentials to predict developmental outcomes. In M. deHaan (Ed.), *Infant EEG and event-related potentials. Studies in developmental psychology* (pp. 199–225). New York: Psychology Press.

Montgomery, J. W. (2004). Sentence comprehension in children with specific language impairment: Effects of input rate and phonological working memory. *International Journal of Language and Communication Disorders, 39*, 115–133.

Morgan, A. E., & Hynd, G. W. (1998). Dyslexia, neurolinguistic ability, and anatomical variation of the planum temporale. *Neuropsychology Review, 8*, 79–93.

Morris, R. D., Stuebing, K. K., Fletcher, J. M., Shaywitz, S. E. , Lyon, G. R., Shankweiler, D. P., et al. (1998). Subtypes of reading disability: Variability around a phonological core. *Journal of Educational Psychology, 90*, 347–373.

Munte, T. F., Altenmuller, E., & Jancke, L. (2002). The musician's brain as a model of neuroplasticity. *Nature Review of Neuroscience, 3*, 473–478.

Murphy, K. C., Jones, L. A., & Owen, M. J. (1999). High rates of schizophrenia in adults with velocardiofacial syndrome. *Archives of General Psychiatry, 56*, 940–945.

Murphy, M. M., & Mazzocco, M. M. M. (2008). Mathematics learning disabilities in girls with Fragile X or Turner syndrome during late elementary school. *Journal of Learning Disabilities, 41*, 29–46.

Murphy, M. M., Mazzocco, M. M. M., Gerner, G., & Hendry, A. E. (2006). Mathematics learning disability in girls with Turner syndrome or Fragile X syndrome. *Brain and Cognition, 61*, 195–210.

Murphy, M. M., Mazzocco, M. M. M., Hanich, L. B., & Early, M. C. (2008). Cognitive characteristics of children with mathematics learning disability (MLD) vary as a function of the cutoff criterion used to define MLD. *Journal of Learning Disabilities, 40*, 458–478.

Nation, K., & Norbury, C. F. (2005). Why reading comprehension fails: Insights from children with developmental disorders. *Topics in Language Disorders, 25*, 21–32.

National Reading Panel. (2000). *Teaching children to read: An evidence-based assessment of the scientific research literature on reading and its implications for reading instruction.* Washington, DC: National Institute of Child Health and Human Development.

No Child Left Behind. (2002). http://www.ed.gov/policy/elsec/leg/egsea02.html. Washington, DC: U.S. Government

Norrelgen, F., Lacerda, F., & Forssberg, H. (2002). Temporal resolution of auditory perception and verbal working memory in 15 children with language impairment. *Journal of Learning Disabilities, 35*, 540–546.

O'Connor, R. E., Harty, K. R., & Fulmer, D. (2005). Tiers of intervention in kindergarten through third grade. *Journal of Learning Disabilities, 38*, 532–538.

Oakhill, J., Cain, K. E., & Bryant, P. E. (2003). The dissociation of word reading and text comprehension: Evidence from component skills. *Language and Cognitive Processes, 18*, 443–468.

Obrzut, J., Boliek, C. A., & Asbjornsen, A. (2006). Does attentional cueing affect dichotic listening performance in children? *Developmental Neuropsychology, 30*, 791–800.

Ohio Department of Education. (1995). *Longitudinal study of reading recovery 1990–1991 though 1993–1994.* Battelle, OH: Final Report.

Olson, R. K. (1999). Genes, environment, and reading disabilities. In R. Sternberg & L. Spear-Swerling (Eds.), *Perspectives on learning disabilities* (pp. 3–22). Oxford: Westview Press.

Ostad, S. A. (2000). Cognitive subtraction in a developmental perspective: Accuracy, speed-of-processing and strategy-use differences in normal and mathematically disabled children. *Focus on Learning Problems in Mathematics, 22*, 18–31.

Padlonsky, I. (2008). The neuropsychological and neurobehavioral consequences of ADHD comorbid with LD and otitis media. *Journal of Developmental and Physical Disabilities, 20*, 11–20.

Palombo, J. (2006). *Nonverbal learning disabilities: A clinical perspective.* New York: W.W. Norton & Co.

Paul, L. K., Schieffer, B., & Brown, W. S. (2004). Social processing deficits in agenesis of the corpus callosum: Narratives from the thematic apperception test. *Archives of Clinical Neuropsychology, 19*, 215–225.

Paul, L. K., Van Lancker-Sidtis, D., Schieffer, B., Dietrich, R., & Brown, W. S. (2003). Communicative deficits in agenesis of the corpus callosum: Nonliteral language and affective prosody. *Brain and Language, 85*, 313–324.

Pennington, B. F. (2006). From single to multiple deficit models of developmental disorders. *Cognition, 101*(2), 385–413.

Pennington, B. F., Cardoso-Martins, C., Green, P. A., & Lefly, D. (2001). Comparing the phonological and double deficit hypotheses for developmental dyslexia. *Reading and Writing, 14*, 707–755.

Perfetti, C. A., Landi, N., & Oakhill, J. (2005). The acquisition of reading comprehension skill. In M. J. Snowling & C. Hulme (Eds.), *The science of reading: A handbook* (pp. 227–247). Oxford: Blackwell.

Peterson, B., Vohr, B., Kane, M. J., Whalen, D. H., Schneider, K. C., Katz, K. H., et al. (2002). A functional magnetic resonance imaging study of language processing and its cognitive correlates in prematurely born children. *Pediatrics, 110*, 1153–1162.

Petherham, B., & Enderby, P. (2001). Demographic and epidemiological analysis of patients referred to speech and language therapy at eleven centres. *International Journal of Language and Communication Disorders, 36*, 515–525.

Petrill, S. A., Deater-Deckard, K., Schatschneider, C., & Davis, C. (2005). Measured environmental influences on early reading: Evidence from an adoption study. *Scientific Studies of Reading, 9*, 237–260.

Petrill, S. A., Deater-Deckard, K., Schatschneider, C., & Davis, C. (2007). Environmental influences on reading-related outcomes: An adoption study. *Infant and Child Development, 16*, 171–191.

Petrill, S. A., Deater-Deckard, K., Thompson, L. A., & DeThorne, L. S. (2006). Reading skills in early readers: Genetic and shared environmental influences. *Journal of Learning Disabilities, 39*, 48–55.

Pokorni, J. L., Worthington, C. K., & Jamison, P. J. (2004). Phonological awareness intervention: Comparison of Fast ForWord, Earobics, and LiPs. *Journal of Educational Research, 97*, 147–157.

Price, T. S., Eley, T. C., Dale, P. S., Stevenson, J., Saudino, K., & Plomin, R. (2000). Genetic and environmental covariation between verbal and non-verbal cognitive development in infancy. *Child Development, 71*, 941–959.

Pugh, K. R., Mencl, W. E., Jenner, A. R., Katz, L., Frost, S. J., Lee, J. R., et al. (2001). Neurobiological studies of reading and reading disability. *Journal of Communication Disorders, 34*, 479–492.

Pugh, K. R., Mencl, W. E., Jenner, A. R., Lee, J. R., Katz, L., Frost, S. J., et al. (2001). Neuroimaging studies of reading development and reading disability. *Learning Disabilities Research & Practice, 16*(4), 240–249.

Reiss, A. L., Eliez, S., Schmitt, J. E., Patwardhan, A., & Haberecht, M. (2000). Brain imaging in neurogenetic conditions: Realizing the potential of behavioral neurogenetics research. *Mental Retardation and Developmental Disabilities Research, 6*, 186–197.

Reynolds, C. R. (2003). Conceptual and technical problems in learning disability diagnosis. In C. R. Reynolds & R. W. Kamphaus (Eds.), *Handbook for psychological and educational assessment of children: Intelligence, aptitude and achievement* (2nd ed., pp. 474–497). New York: Guilford Press.

Reynolds, M. R., & Wheldall, K. (2007). Reading recovery 20 years down the track: Looking forward, looking back. *International Journal of Disability, Development and Education, 54*, 199–223.

Riccio, C., Cohen, M. J., Garrison, T., & Smith, B. (2005). Auditory processing measures: Correlation with neuropsychological measures of attention, memory, and behavior. *Child Neuropsychology, 11*, 363–372.

Riccio, C., Garland, B. H., & Cohen, M. J. (2007). Relations between the Test of Variables of Attention (TOVA) and the Children's Memory Scale (CMS). *Journal of Attention Disorders, 11*, 167–171.

Richards, T. L., Aylward, E. H., Berninger, V. W., Field, K., Grimme, A. C., Richards, A. L., et al. (2005). Individual fMRI activation in orthographic mapping and morpheme mapping after orthographic or morphological spelling treatment in child dyslexics. *Journal of Neurolinguistics, 19*, 56–86.

Rickard, T. C., Romero, S. G., Basso, G., Wharton, C., Flitman, S., & Grafman, J. (2000). The calculating brain: An fMRI study. *Neuropsychologia, 38*, 325–335.

Ritchey, K. D., & Goeke, J. L. (2006). Orton-Gillingham and Orton-Gillingham-based reading instruction: A review of the literature. *Journal of Special Education, 40*, 171–184.

Rose, S. A., Feldman, J. F., & Jankowski, J. J. (2002). Processing speed in the 1st year of life: A longitudinal study of preterm and full-term infants. *Developmental Psychology, 38*, 895–902.

Rose, T. E., & Zirkel, P. (2007). Orton-Gillingham methodology for students with reading disabilities. *Journal of Special Education, 41*, 171–185.

Rourke, B. P. (1989). *Nonverbal learning disabilities: The syndrome and the model.* New York: Guilford Press.

Rourke, B. P. (1994). Neuropsychological assessment of children with learning disabilities: Measurement issues. In G. R. Lyon (Ed.), *Frames of reference for the assessment of learning disabilities: New views on measurement issues* (pp. 475–514). Baltimore, MD: Paul H. Brookes Publishing Co.

Rourke, B. P. (1995). The NLD syndrome and the white matter model. In B. P. Rourke (Ed.), *Syndrome of nonverbal learning disabilities: Neurodevelopmental manifestations.* New York: Guilford Press.

Rourke, B. P. (2000). Neuropsychological and psychosocial subtyping: A review of investigations within the University of Windsor laboratory. *Canadian Psychology, 41*(1), 34–51.

Rourke, B. P., Ahmad, S. A., Collins, D. W., Hayman-Abello, B. A., & Warriner, E. M. (2002). Child clinical/pediatric neuropsychology: Some recent advances. *Review of Psychology, 53*, 309–339.

Rourke, B. P., & Fuerst, D. R. (1991). *Cognitive processing, academic achievement, and psychosocial functioning: A neurodevelopmental perspective.* New York: Guilford Press.

Rourke, B. P., & Tsatsanis, K. D. (1996). Syndrome of nonverbal learning disabilities: Psycholinguistic assets and deficits. *Topics in Language Disorders, 16*(2), 30–44.

Rourke, B. P., & Tsatsanis, K. D. (2000). Nonverbal learning disabilities. In A. Klin, F. R. Volkmar, & S. S. Sparrow (Eds.), *Asperger syndrome.* New York: The Guilford Press.

Rovet, J. (2004). Turner Syndrome: Genetic and hormonal factors contributing to a specific learning disability profile. *Learning Disabilities Research and Practice, 19*, 133–145.

Rumsey, J. M., Dorwart, R., Vermess, M., Denckla, M. B., Kruesi, M. J. P., & Rappoport, J. L. (1986). Magnetic resonance imaging of brain anatomy in severe developmental dyslexia. *Archives of neurology, 43*, 1045–1046.

Rutter, M., Bailey, A., Berument, S. K., Lord, C., & Pickeles, A. (2003). *Social Communication Questionnaire (SCQ).* Los Angeles: Western Psychological Services.

Samuelsson, S., Byrne, B., Wadsworth, S., Corley, R., DeFries, J. C., Willcutt, E., et al. (2007). Genetic and environmental influences on prereading skills and early reading and spelling development in the United States, Australia, and Scandinavia. *Reading and Writing, 20*, 51–75.

Scarborough, H. S. (2005). Developmental relationships between language and reading: Reconciling a beautiful hypothesis with some ugly facts. In H. W. Catts & A. G. Kamhi (Eds.), *The connections between language and reading disabilities* (pp. 3–24). Mahwah, NJ: Erlbaum.

Schatschneider, C., Carlson, C. D., Francis, D. J., Foorman, B. R., & Fletcher, J. M. (2002). Relationship of rapid automatized naming and phonological awareness in early reading development: Implications for the double-deficit hypothesis. *Journal of Learning Disabilities, 35*, 245–256.

Schnoebelen, S., Semrud-Clikeman, M., Guli, L. A., & Corlett, M. (2002). *Planning and organization in children with learning disabilities.* Paper presented at the American Psychological Association.

Schumaker, J. B., Deshler, D. D., & McKnight, P. (2002). Ensuring success in the secondary general education curriculum through the use of teaching routines. In M. A. Shinn, H. M. Walker, & G. Stoner (Eds.), *Interventions for academic and behavior problems II: Preventive and remedial approaches* (pp. 403–424). Bethseda, MD: NASP Publications.

Scientific Learning Corporation. (1998). *Fast ForWord Language (Computer software).* Berkeley, CA: Author.

Scruggs, T. E., & Mastropieri, M. A. (2002). On babies and bathwater: Addressing the problems of identification of learning disabilities. *Learning Disability Quarterly, 25*, 155–168.

Seidenberg, M. S., & McClelland, J. L. (1989). A distributed, developmental model of word recognition and naming. *Psychological Review, 96*, 523–568.

Semrud-Clikeman, M. (2001). *Traumatic brain injury in children and adolescents.* New York: Guilford Press.

Semrud-Clikeman, M. (2003). Executive functions and social communication disorders. *Perspectives, 29*, 20–22.

Semrud-Clikeman, M. (2006). Neuropsychological aspects for evaluating LD. *Journal of Learning Disabilities, 38*, 563–568.

Semrud-Clikeman, M. (2007). *Social competence in children*. New York: Springer.

Semrud-Clikeman, M., Biederman, J., Sprich-Buckminster, S., Krifcher Lehman, B., Faraone, S. V., & Norman, D. (1992). The incidence of ADHD and concurrent learning disabilities. *Journal of the American Academy of Child and Adolescent Psychiatry, 31,* 439–448.

Semrud-Clikeman, M., & Fine, J. G. (2008). *A meta-analysis of the neuropsychology of NVLD*. Paper presented at the International Neuropsychological Society.

Semrud-Clikeman, M., & Glass, K. L. (2008). Comprehension of humor in children with nonverbal learning disabilities, verbal learning disabilities and without learning disabilities. *Annals of Dyslexia, 58,* 163–180.

Semrud-Clikeman, M., Guy, K., Griffin, J. D., & Hynd, G. W. (2000). Rapid naming deficits in children and adolescents with reading disabilities and attention deficit hyperactivity disorder. *Brain and Language, 74,* 70–83.

Semrud-Clikeman, M., & Hynd, G. W. (1990). Right hemispheric dysfunction in nonverbal learning disabilities: Social, academic, and adaptive functioning in adults and children. *Psychological Bulletin, 107*(2), 196–209.

Semrud-Clikeman, M., Hynd, G. W., Novey, E. S., & Eliopulos, D. (1991). Dyslexia and brain morphology: Relationships between neuroanatomical variation and neurolinguistic tasks. *Learning and Individual Differences, 3*(3), 225–242.

Semrud-Clikeman, M., & Schaefer, V. (2000). Social competence in developmental disorders. *Journal of Psychotherapy in Independent Practice, 4,* 3–20.

Semrud-Clikeman, M., Walkowiak, J., Wilkinson, & Christopher (submitted). Neuropsychological findings in nonverbal learning disabilities. *Developmental Neuropsychology*.

Senechal, M., & LeFevure, J. (2002). Parental involvement in the development of children's reading skills: A five-year longitudinal study. *Child Development, 73,* 445–460.

Share, D. L., & Silva, P. A. (2003). Gender bias in IQ-discrepancy and post-discrepancy definitions of reading disability. *Journal of Learning Disabilities, 36,* 4–14.

Shaywitz, B. A., Shaywitz, S. E., Blachman, B. A., Pugh, K. R., Fulbright, R. K., Skudlarski, P., et al. (2004). Development of left occipitotemporal systems for skilled reading in children after a phonologically-based intervention. *Biological Psychiatry, 55,* 926–933.

Shaywitz, B. A., Shaywitz, S. E., Pugh, K. R., Constable, R. T., Skudlarski, P., Fulbright, R. K., et al. (1995). Sex differences in the functional organization of the brain for language. *Nature, 373,* 607–60.

Shaywitz, S. E. (1998). Dyslexia. *The New England Journal of Medicine, 338*(5), 307–312.

Shaywitz, S. E. (2003). *Overcoming dyslexia: A new and complete science-based program for reading problems at any level*. New York: Alfred A. Knopf.

Shaywitz, S. E., Mody, M., & Shaywitz, B. A. (2006). Neural mechanisms in dyslexia. *Current Directions in Psychological Science, 15*(6), 278–281.

Shriberg, L., Tomblin, J., & McSweeney, J. (1999). Prevalence of speech delay in six-year-old children and comorbidity with language impairment. *Journal of Speech, Language, and Hearing Research, 42,* 1461–1484.

Siegel, L. S., & Smythe, I. S. (2005). Reflections on research on reading disability with special attention to gender issues. *Journal of Learning Disabilities, 38,* 473–477.

Simos, P. G., Fletcher, J. M., Bergman, E., Breier, J. I., Foorman, B. R., Castillo, E. M., et al. (2002). Dyslexia-specific brain activation profile becomes normal following successful remedial training. *Neurology, 58,* 1203–1213.

Snow, D. M. (2001). Imitation of intonation contours by children with normal and disordered language development. *Clinical Linguistics and Phonetics 15,* 567–584.

Spencer, T. J., Biederman, J., & Mick, E. (2007). Attention-deficit hyperactivity disorder: Diagnosis, lifespan, comorbidities, and neurobiology. *Journal of Pediatric Psychology, 32,* 631–642.

Spinath, F. M., Price, T. S., Dale, P. S., & Plomin, R. (2004). The genetic and environmental origins of language disability and ability. *Child Development, 75,* 445–454.

Spinath, F. M., Ronald, A., Harlaar, N., Price, T. S., & Plomin, R. (2003). Phenotypic 'g' early in life: On the etiology of general cognitive ability in a large population sample of twin children aged 2 to 4 years. *Intelligence, 31,* 195–210.

Spitzka, E. A. (1907). A study of the brains of six eminent scientists belonging to the American Anthropometric Society: Together with a discussion of the skull of Professor E.D. *Cope Transaction on American Philosophical Society, 21,* 175–208.

Stanovich, K. E. (2005). The future of a mistake: Will discrepancy measurement continue to make the learning disabilities field a pseudoscience? *Learning Disability Quarterly, 28,* 103–106.

Stanovich, K. E., Nathan, R., & Vala-Rossa, M. (1986). Developmental changes in the cognitive correlates of reading ability and the developmental lag hypothesis. *Reading Research Quarterly, 21,* 267–283.

Stanovich, K. E., Siegel, L. S., & Gottardo, A. (1997). Converging evidence for phonological and surface subtypes of reading disability. *Journal of Educational Psychology, 89,* 114–128.

Stanovich, K. E., Siegel, L. S., Gottardo, A., Chiappe, P., & Sidhu, R. (1997). Subtypes of developmental dyslexia: Differences in phonological and orthographic coding. In B. A. Blachman (Ed.), *Cognitive and linguistic foundations of reading acquisition* (pp. 115–141). Hillsdale, NJ: Erlbaum.

Stark, R. E. (1988). Implications for clinical management: A perspective. In R. E. Stark & P. Tallal (Eds.), *Language, speech, and reading disorders in children: Neuropsychological studies* (pp. 169–180). Boston: College-Hill.

Stark, R. E., & Tallal, P. (1988). *Language, speech, and reading disorders in children: Neuropsychological studies*. Boston: College-Hill.

Steinmetz, H., Jäncke, L., Kleinschmidt, A., Schlaug, G., Volkmann, J., & Huang, Y. (1992). Sex but no hand difference in the isthmus of the corpus callosum. *Neurology, 42*, 749–752.

Steubing, K. K., Fletcher, J. M., LeDoux, J. M., Lyon, G. R., Shaywitz, S. E., & Shaywitz, B. A. (2002). Validity of IQ-discrepancy classifications of reading disabilities: A meta-analysis. *American Education Research Journal, 39*, 469–518.

Strauss, S. L. (2001). An open letter to Reid Lyon. *Educational Researcher, 30*, 26–33.

Stromsvold, K. (2001). The heritability of language: A review and meta-analysis of twin, adoption and linkage studies. *Language, 77*, 647–723.

Strong, R. W., Silver, H. F., & Perini, M. J. (2008). *Reading for academic success, grades 2–6: Differentiated strategies for struggling, average, and advanced readers*. Thousand Oaks, CA: Corwin Press.

Sundheim, S. T. P. V., & Voeller, K. K. S. (2004). Psychiatric implications of language disorders and learning disabilities: Risks and management. *Journal of Child Neurology, 19*, 814–826.

Swillen, A., Vandeputte, L., Cracco, J., Maes, B., Ghesquiere, P., Devriendt, K., et al. (1999). Neuropsychological, learning, and psychosocial profile of primary school-aged children with the velocardiofacial syndrome (22q11 deletion): Evidence for a nonverbal learning disability. *Neuropsychology, 5*, 230–241.

Talcott, J. B., Witton, C., McClean, M., Hansen, P. C., Rees, A., Green, G. G. R., et al. (2000). Dynamic sensory sensitivity and children's word decoding skills. *Proceedings of the National Academy of Science USA, 97*, 2952–2957.

Tallal, P. (1988). Developmental language disorders. In J. F. Kavanagh & T. J. Truss (Eds.), *Learning disabilities: Proceedings of the National Conference* (pp. 181–272). Parkton, MD: York Press.

Tallal, P. (2004). Improving language and literacy is a matter of time. *Nature Reviews: Neuroscience, 5*, 721–728.

Tallal, P., & Fitch, R. H. (2005). Central auditory processing and language learning impairments: Implications for neuroplasticity research. In J. Syka & M. M. Merzenich (Eds.), *Plasticity and signal representation in the auditory system* (pp. 355–385). New York: Springer Publishing Company.

Tallal, P., & Gaab, N. (2006). Dynamic auditory processing, musical experience, and language development. *Trends in Neurosciences, 29*, 382–390.

Tallal, P., Miller, S. L., Bedi, G., Byma, G., Wang, X., Nagarajan, S. S., et al. (1996). Language comprehension in language learning impaired children improved with acoustically modified speech. *Science, 271*, 81–84.

Tarkiainen, A., Helenius, P., Hansen, P. C., Cornelissen, P. L., & Salmelin, R. (1999). Dynamics of letter string perception in the human occipitotemporal cortex. *Brain, 122*, 2119–2131.

Teeter, P. A. (1998). *Interventions for ADHD*. New York: Guilford.

Thatcher, R. W. (1996). Neuroimaging of cyclic cortical reorganization during human development. In R. W. Thatcher, G. R. Lyon, J. Rumsey & N. A. Krasnegor (Eds.), *Developmental neuroimaging: Mapping the development of brain and behavior* (pp. 91–106). San Diego: Academic Press.

Therien, J. M., Worwa, C. T., Mattia, F. R., & deRegnier, R. A. (2004). Altered pathways for auditory discrimination and recognition memory in preterm infants. *Developmental Medicine & Child Neurology, 46*, 816–824.

Torgesen, J. K. (2004). Lessons learned from research on interventions for students who have difficulty learning to read. In P. McCardle & V. Chhabra (Eds.), *The voice of evidence in reading research* (pp. 355–382). Baltimore, MD: Paul H. Brookes.

Torgesen, J. K., Alexander, A. L., Wagner, R. K., Rashotte, C. A., Voeller, K. K. S., & Conway, T. (2001). Intensive remedial instruction for children with severe reading disabilities: Immediate and long-term outcomes from two instructional approaches. *Journal of Learning Disabilities, 34*, 33–58.

Tuller, B., Jantzen, K. J., Olvera, D., Steinberg, F., & Kelso, J. A. S. (2007). The influence of instruction modality on brain activation in teenagers with nonverbal learning disabilities: Two case histories. *Journal of Learning Disabilities, 40*, 348–359.

Tunmer, W. E., Chapman, J. W., & Prochnow, J. E. (2003). Preventing negative Matthews effects in at-risk readers: A retrospective study. In B. R. Foorman (Ed.), *Preventing and remediating reading difficulties* (pp. 121–164). New York: York Press.

van Daal, J., Verhoeven, L., van Leeuwe, J., & van Balkom, H. (2008). Working memory limitations in children with severe language impairment. *Journal of Communication Disorders, 41*, 85–107.

Vaughn, S., & Klingner, J. K. (2004). Teaching reading comprehension to students with learning disabilities. In C. Stone, E. Silliman, B. Ehren & K. Apel (Eds.), *Handbook of language and literacy development and disorders*. New York: Guilford.

Vaughn, S., Linan-Thompson, S., & Hickman, P. (2003). Response to treatment as a means of identifying students with reading/learning disabilities. *Exceptional Children, 69*, 391–409.

Venezky, R. (1998). An alternative perspective on success for all. In K. Wong (Ed.), *Advances in educational policy* (pp. 145–165). New York: JAI Press.

Viding, E., Spinath, F. M., Price, T. S., Bishop, D. V. M., Dale, P. S., & Plomin, R. (2004). Genetic and environmental influence on language impairment in 4-year-old same-sex and opposite-sex twins. *Journal of Child Psychology and Psychiatry, 45*, 31–325.

Vukovic, R. K., & Siegel, L. S. (2006). The double-deficit hypothesis. *Journal of Learning Disabilities, 39*, 25–47.

Wadsworth, S., & DeFries, J. C. (2005). Genetic etiology of reading difficulties in boys and girls. *Twin Research and Human Genetics, 8*, 594–601.

Wadsworth, S., DeFries, J. C., Olson, R. K., & Willcutt, E. (2007). Colorado longitudinal twin study of reading disability. *Annals of Dyslexia, 57*, 139–160.

Wadsworth, S., Olson, R. K., Pennington, B. F., & DeFries, J. C. (2000). Differential genetic etiology of reading disability as a function of IQ. *Journal of Learning Disabilities, 33*, 192–199.

Wilkinson, A., & Semrud-Clikeman, M. (2008). *Motor speed in children and adolescents with nonverbal learning disabilities.* Paper presented at the International Neuropsychological Society,.

Wills, K. (2007). Remediating specific learning disabilities. In S. J. Hunter & J. Donders (Eds.), *Pediatric neuropsychological intervention* (pp. 224–252). Cambridge, UK: Cambridge University Press.

Winskel, H. (2006). The effects of an early history of otitis media on children's language and literacy skill development. *British Journal of Educational Psychology, 76,* 727–744.

Witelson, S. F., Kigar, D. L., & Harvey, T. (1999). The exceptional brain of Albert Einstein. *Lancet, 353,* 2149–2153.

Wolf, M., & Bowers, P. G. (1999). The double-deficit hypothesis for the developmental dyslexics. *Journal of Educational Psychology, 91,* 415–438.

Wong, T. M., Strickland, T. L., Fletcher-Janzen, E., Ardila, A., & Reynolds, C. R. (2000). Theoretical and practical issues in the neuropsychological assessment and treatment of culturally dissimilar patients. In E. Fletcher-Janzen, T. L. Strickland, & C. R. Reynolds (Eds.), *Handbook of cross-cultural neuropsychology* (pp. 3–18). New York: Kluwer Academic/Plenum publishers.

Worling, D. E., Humphries, T., & Tannock, R. (1999). Spatial and emotional aspects of language inferencing in nonverbal learning disabilities. *Brain and Language, 70,* 220–239.

Xue, G., & Poldrack, R. A. (2007). The neural substrates of visual perceptual learning of words: Implications for the visual word form area hypothesis. *Journal of Cognitive Neuroscience, 19,* 1643–1655.

Chapter 13
Metabolic, Biogenetic, Seizure, and Neuromotor Disorders of Childhood

Various metabolic, biogenetic/chromosomal, seizure and neuromotor disorders (e.g., cerebral palsy) are the focus of this chapter. These neurological disorders frequently result in accompanying neuropsychological, social/emotional, and behavioral difficulties that place stress on the child, family, and school. As with other neurological and neurodevelopmental disorders, the pediatric neuropsychologist needs to be particularly sensitive to these stressors when assessing and planning intervention programs. Study of these variables is just beginning, but clinical practice indicates that children with these various disorders require support in all environments: home, school, and social. A transactional approach to the deficits experienced by children with these disorders would be most ecologically valid while also providing information for the most appropriate interventions. A number of select metabolic, biogenetic, seizure, and neuromotor disorders will be discussed in this chapter, with attention not only to the neuropsychological assessment of deficits, but also to the contributions of the family and school for remediating these difficulties. Research on intervention outcome is sparse and is sorely needed. For each of these disorders, a review of the literature indicates that more knowledge is needed, not only concerning the neuropsychology of the disorder, but also in planning for these children throughout the life span. The demarcation of biogenetic, neurocutaneous, and metabolic disorders is one of convenience and does not imply that a biogenetic basis underlies all of these conditions. The demarcations are used only for ease of discussion.

Metabolic Disorders

Metabolic disorders have been linked to various neurological disorders including cognitive retardation; over 200 genes have been identified that produce hereditary diseases (Phelps, 1998a). Phenylketonuria (PKU) and Lesch-Nyhan syndrome (LNS) are only two metabolic disorders that will be discussed here. These disorders could easily be listed under chromosomal abnormalities, as each has a genetic basis (Cook & Leventhal, 1992). See Hynd and Willis (1988), Goldstein and Reynolds (1999), and Phelps (1998a) for an in-depth treatment of other disorders affecting metabolic processes that ultimately result in neuropsychiatric disorders in children and adolescents.

PKU

Phenylketonuria (PKU) is a rare (affecting 1:15,000 to 1:18,000) autosomal recessive disorder that affects males and females equally (Carey & Lesen, 1998; Cook & Leventhal, 1992; Hynd & Willis, 1988). PKU is a chronic disorder that affects the metabolism of phenylalanine to tyrosine (Fehrenbach & Peterson, 1989). Tyrosine is a precursor to dopamine (DA), and when phenylalanine is too low, the production of DA may be altered and may result in changes in bones, anemia, antibodies, and cognitive development. Phenylalanine is a protein and, when it is not metabolized, it begins to be stored in the body. Characteristics of the disorder, and assessment and intervention practices are briefly discussed.

M. Semrud-Clikeman, P.A. Teeter Ellison, *Child Neuropsychology*, DOI 10.1007/978-0-387-88963-4_13,
© Springer Science+Business Media, LLC 2009

Characteristics and Associated Features of PKU

When phenylalanine levels are too high they can produce serious negative consequences, including cognitive retardation (Carey & Lesen, 1998; Hynd & Willis, 1988; Michaels, Lopus, & Matalon, 1988; Waisbren, 1999). PKU can produce neuropsychiatric disorders in children, including behavioral disruption and antisocial problems (Fehrenbach & Peterson, 1989). Cognitive retardation is usually avoided when PKU is appropriately treated (Waisbren, 1999). Lifetime ADHD was also associated with PKU even after successful dietary control (Realmuto et al., 1986). In rare instances, PKU can result in death (Hanley, Linsoa, Davidson, & Moes, 1970) or in seizure activity, abnormal EEGs, spasticity, and reflex and tremor disorders (Hynd & Willis, 1988). The development of neural tissues appears to be affected, with cellular abnormalities and incomplete myelination resulting.

Waisbren (1999) suggests that executive control functions are affected by PKU, including planning skills, integrative processing, and sustained attention. These deficits are particularly acute when information is presented rapidly or when the cognitive load is high—as tasks become more complex and processing time is fast. Deficits of this nature may also be present in early-treated children.

Implications for Assessment

Early medical screening for PKU is widespread and can be extremely effective in reducing the progressive, deleterious developmental and medical difficulties associated with the disorder (Hynd & Willis, 1988). Since universal screening in newborns was implemented in the 1960 s, the severe symptoms of PKU are rarely seen (NIH, 2008).

Neuropsychological assessment may also be important to identify cognitive, reasoning, and visuospatial deficits that have been reported in some children with PKU. Psychoeducational evaluation is effective to determine academic (e.g., learning disabilities, deficits in mathematics), and behavioral adjustment difficulties (e.g., disruptiveness, antisocial behavior, low self-esteem). Waisbren (1999) also suggests that ADHD may result in elevated blood levels of phenylalanine.

Effective interventions focus on dietary control and compliance with these restrictions. Family issues appear to affect dietary compliance, so strategies that address these related factors are discussed.

Implications for Interventions

The negative effects of PKU can be controlled through dietary changes whereby foods containing high levels of phenylalanine (e.g., meats, milk, and milk products) are reduced or eliminated (Carey & Lesen, 1998; Fehrenbach & Peterson, 1989). Thus, PKU is clearly a genetic disorder that is influenced by environmental factors (intake of foods), which directly affect the manifestation and control of the disorder. It is important to initiate dietary treatment early in life (within the first three months) to reduce the possibility of cognitive retardation (Waisbren, 1999). Although early treatment appears to reduce significant cognitive impairment, children with PKU may still have minor cognitive deficits, and the long-term consequences of early treatment are still relatively unknown. Some evidence suggests that the child's cognitive outcome is dependent on a number of factors, including maternal IQ level, the age at which treatment is initiated, and dietary compliance (Waisbren, 1999; Williamson, Koch, Azen, & Chang, 1981).

Waisbren (1999) suggests that compliance to food regimens may become problematic as children struggle with the development of their own identity. Waisbren provides an outline for developing treatment plans for PKU from infancy to adolescence. Many of the strategies shown help the children become more knowledgeable and involved with their own treatment. With age, children become more self-sufficient when taught self-management strategies for monitoring blood levels, selecting appropriate foods, and coping with peer pressure.

Family Factors Related to Dietary Compliance

Fehrenbach and Peterson (1989) investigated the affects of other family factors, including organization, cohesion, stress, and conflict, on the child's compliance with dietary restrictions. The families of 30 children were followed, and the level of parental problem solving was related to disease control. Specifically, Fehrenbach and Peterson (1989) found that verbal problem solving abilities were related to children's compliance. Further, parents with highly compliant children were able to provide a number of solutions and parenting options available in problem situations. Family cohesion, level of conflict, and support were not related to compliance. Although family SES, age, and education of parents were unrelated to problem solving measures, these variables were related to stress levels and family functioning (Fehrenbach & Peterson, 1989). Induced stress conditions affected both groups of families (high- and low-compliant groups), and were not considered predictive of compliance. While stress did reduce the number of alternative strategies that were generated by both groups, the high-compliant parent group demonstrated higher quality solutions and reported stressful situations as less stressful. These findings are important because they point out the need to consider family members in the treatment plans for children with PKU.

Preventive Measures

Recent research suggests that maternal hyperphenylalanemia should be monitored during pregnancy (Waisbren, 1999). Dietary control (i.e., phenylalanine-restrictions) during pregnancy does have preventive effects, thereby reducing fetal complications including microcephaly. Ongoing treatment monitoring appears prudent and may increase children's compliance with dietary restrictions and other intervention strategies. Medical, psychological, and educational interventions should be coordinated, with the child and the family as the focus of treatment.

Lesch-Nyhan Syndrome

Lesch-Nyhan syndrome (LNS) is a progressive metabolic disorder that results in cognitive retardation and is often accompanied by choreoathetoid movements (Little & Rodemaker, 1998; Matthews, Solan, & Barabas, 1995). The way that LNS affects development of the nervous system remains unknown, but evidence suggests that abnormal adhesion processes occur during neuronal migration and differentiation (Stacey, Ma, & Daley, 2000). LNS causes a build up of uric acid, which produces gout, poor muscle control and cognitive retardation in the 1st or 2nd decade of life. In addition to neurological symptoms, patients with LNS often have swelling of joints and severe kidney problems. Renal failure is the major cause of early death (Little & Rodemaker, 1998). Seizure disorders are common in LNS patients (maybe as high as 50%). Other neuropsychiatric problems may include self-injury and aggression.

LNS is a sex-linked disorder that is usually inherited, although it can occur through a spontaneous genetic mutation (Davidson et al., 1991). Females rarely have LNS, but can be carriers of the disorder. LNS is associated with an abnormality or near absence of an enzyme [hypoxanthine-guanine phosphoribosynltransferase (HGPRT)] that appears prominent on the X chromosome (Cook & Leventhal, 1992). This abnormality has an effect on the individual's ability to metabolize purines, which in turn has profound neurological and behavioral consequences (Matthews et al., 1995).

Dopamine activity appears altered in various brain regions (i.e., putamen, caudate, and nucleus accumbens), with other neurochemical imbalances that may explain the movement and psychiatric problems associated with LNS (Jankovic et al., 1988). Positron emission tomography showed decreased levels of dopamine in all dopaminergic pathways of the brain (i.e., the putamen, caudate nucleus, frontal cortex, substantia nigra and ventral tegmentum) (Ernest et al., 1996). Researchers are investigating the role of dopamine in self-injurious behaviors, and the degree to which medications alter dopamine and serotonin may be useful for the treatment of LNS (Morales, 1999).

Characteristics and Associated Features of LNS

At birth, there are no abnormal characteristics, but motor delays and choreoathetoid movements appear within the first year and progressively worsen for infants with LNS (Cook & Leventhal, 1992; Morales, 1999). Children with LNS often develop normally until about eight–24 months of age, when choreoathetosis appears and earlier motor milestones are lost (Matthews et al., 1995). Hypotonia may be present in infants, but hypertonia and hyperreflexia develop. Communication is also hampered because of poor articulation from the palsy in speech musculature (Matthews et al., 1995).

Self-mutilation is characteristic of children between the ages of three and five years, when injuries to facial areas (i.e., eyes, nose, and lips) and appendages (fingers and legs) result from chewing and biting oneself (Hynd & Willis, 1988). Almost all children with LNS show self-injurious behaviors by age eight–10 years, with spasticity, choreoathetosis, opisthotonos, and facial hypotonia also evident (Matthews et al., 1995). Malnutrition may result from severe self-injury to the mouth or from vomiting (Nyhan, 1976).

Although cognitive retardation has been reported, individuals with LNS may be brighter than measured abilities suggest (Nyhan, 1976). Using the Stanford Binet Intelligence Scale, fourth edition (SB-IV), Matthews et al. (1995) investigated intellectual levels for seven subjects. Subjects showed ability levels ranging from moderate cognitive retardation to low average ability. As a group, the sample performed equally well on verbal and nonverbal tasks, although individually they did show a strong preference for either the visual or the verbal modality. Further, attention and higher level intellectual abilities appeared most compromised in this group. Memory, word definitions, and comprehension of complex speech were impaired. Memory deficits affected mental computation, recall of digits backward, visual reasoning, and verbal reasoning. The youngest children performed the best, suggesting that there may be a ceiling for cognitive development for individuals with LNS.

Matthews et al. (1995) caution that standardized tests may not be appropriate for determining functional capacity, educational goals and occupational plans for children with LNS because significant motor difficulties interfere with their performance. Baseline information can be gathered from standardized tests to determine effects of medical, behavioral and educational interventions.

Implications for Assessment

Neuropsychologists play a role in the treatment of children with LNS by providing baseline data to substantiate initial cognitive and psychiatric features of the disorder. To date there is no prescribed assessment protocol for this group, but comprehensive, multifactorial assessment is needed to evaluate the full range and extent of deficits across motor, cognitive, academic, and psychosocial areas. Significant motor impairments may restrict the type of intellectual and neuropsychological measures that can reliably be used with this population. Therefore, the clinician needs to incorporate functional, ecologically based assessment procedures to ascertain skill levels. Efforts should be made to assess functional skills through interview and observation of the individual in a natural setting (e.g., in a classroom or home environment). Careful evaluation of family stress and coping patterns will also be helpful to aid in the planning of interventions.

Implications for Interventions

LNS can be detected during the fetal stage, and research into various medical interventions is underway. Psychopharmacotherapy may be helpful in treating individuals with LNS, but haloperidol, L-dopa, pimozide, diazepam, and clomipramine have been limited in there effectiveness (Watts et al., 1982). Serotonin reuptake inhibitors (e.g., fluoxetine) may help reduce the compulsively self-injurious behaviors (Cook, Rowlett, Jaselskis, & Leventhal, 1992), and other medications have been suggested for use (i.e., 5-hydroxytryptophan, fluphenazine, and naltreone; Cook & Leventhal, 1992). Controlled research into psychopharmacological trials is needed before these avenues can be fairly assessed.

Treatment most often occurs in acute settings where medical professionals work with families to improve the quality of life for individuals with LNS (Bernal, 2006). To date, behavioral interventions have been effective for reducing self-mutilation, although in rare cases self-restraints may be required (Little & Rodemaker, 1998). Residential care or homebound education programs may also be appropriate for some children with LNS. Family members may also require emotional support and additional therapy to deal with the stress that is placed on parents and siblings.

Chromosomal Syndromes

Selected biogenetic disorders of childhood, including Down, Fragile X, and Klinefelter syndromes, are reviewed next. See Dill, Hayden, and McGillivray (1992), Goldstein and Reynolds (1999), Whittle, Satori, Dierssen, Lubec, and Singewald (2007) and Engidawork and Lubec (2003) for a more extensive review of chromosomal abnormalities.

Down Syndrome

Down syndrome, the most common chromosomal disorder, occurs when there is a triplication of a chromosome which may result from trisomy 21 or a fragment of 21q22 during meiosis (Cook & Leventhal, 1992; Lubec, 2003). Down syndrome is the most common genetic cause of cognitive retardation, and occurs in one out of 800 births (NIH Down Syndrome, 2008). NIH has launched a major initiative to map the genome of Down syndrome, and labs across the country are investigating animal models to better understand and ultimately treat individuals with this disorder.

Although Down syndrome can be inherited, the majority of cases result from a random event in the chromosomal distribution in the development of the ovum, sperm, or zygote (NIH Down Syndrome, 2008). Risk factors increase dramatically depending on the age of the mother, from one in 800 births in mothers in their 20 s, to one in 400 for mothers at age 35 years, and one in 20 by age 46 (NIH Down Syndrome, 2008). Although the mother is typically implicated, the syndrome also increases (20%–30% greater chance of occurrence) when fathers are between the age of 50 and 55 (Erickson & Bjerkedal, 1981). Less frequently, occurrences of Down syndrome are associated with translocation of chromosomes other than 21 (Cody & Kamphaus, 1999).

Characteristics and Associated Features of Down Syndrome

Down syndrome is a disorder associated with mild to severe cognitive retardation (NIH Down Syndrome, 2008). Physical anomalies include small head, flat nose, folds at the corners of the eyes, protruding tongue, and heart, eye, and ear defects. Although infants with Down syndrome may show slower development, they follow the same sequence of development as control children.

Children with Down syndrome are also prone to spinal cord injuries due to lax ligaments between the first and second cervical vertebrate (Heller, Alberto, Forney, & Schwartzman, 1996). Dislocation of this area may weaken the child's arms and legs or, in rare instances, may result in paralysis; thus, some activities that put strain on the neck (e.g., diving and tumbling) should be avoided (Shapiro, 1992). Children with Down syndrome also have higher than normal rates of hip dislocation and dysplasia (Shaw & Beals, 1992). Alzheimer's disease may be linked to the same chromosome associated with Down syndrome. Alzheimer's is a progressive loss of memory and brain function associated with tangling/plaguing of nerve tissue. Older individuals with Down syndrome have shown physiological abnormalities similar to those seen in Alzheimer's patients, and apparently the underlying pathology in both disorders occurs from a defective gene on chromosome 21 (Goldgarber, Lerman, McBride, Saffiotti, & Gajdusek, 1987).

Other medical problems include heart disease, pulmonary hypertension, seizure disorders, hypothyroidism, gastrointestinal, orthopedic, vision disorders, and dermatological conditions (NIH Down Syndrome, 2008). Individuals with Down syndrome are at risk for shorter life spans due to medical complications particularly from congenital heart problems, respiratory illness, and gastrointestinal complications (Cody & Kamphaus, 1999). Even those without heart complications have a higher mortality rate than individuals with cognitive retardation, especially after the age of 35 (Strauss & Eyman, 1996). Data compiled by NIH Down Syndrome (2008) indicate that individuals with Down syndrome also have a 12-fold higher mortality rate from various infectious diseases. Abnormalities in the immune system may account for chronic respiratory and ear infections. Children also have recurring tonsillitis and high rates of pneumonia.

Implications for Assessment

During pregnancy there are a number of diagnostic tests for Down syndrome including amniocentesis and chorionic villus sampling (CVS; NIH Down Syndrome, 2008). In amniocentesis, amniotic fluid is drawn and fetal cells are examined for the presence of chromosomal abnormalities. CVS also involves testing of fetal cells, but these are drawn from samples of chorion which precedes the placenta (Liu, 1991). CVS can be performed early (within seven weeks after conception) and tests can be conducted on the same day. Amniocentesis requires two- to three-weeks of laboratory time to grow cultures, so results are not available until well into the second trimester of the pregnancy (NIH Down Syndrome, 2008). However, CVS may carry a higher risk for complications, resulting in a loss of the fetus in 1 percent–4 percent of cases (Gilmore & Aitken, 1989; NIH Down Syndrome, 2008). Percutaneous umbilical blood sampling (PUBS) is the most accurate diagnostic method, but this technique cannot be performed until later in the pregnancy (18th–22nd week) and has increased risk for miscarriage (NIH Down Syndrome, 2008). Newer diagnostic tests are being developed that detect a number of genetic syndromes (e.g., cystic fibrosis, Lesch-Nyhan syndrome) for mothers undergoing in vitro fertilization.

Assessment of Children with Down Syndrome

Early developmental milestones may be delayed for young children with Down syndrome, particularly with motor, language and speech delays. Ongoing developmental assessment in early childhood and later into adolescence is generally recommended to measure cognitive, emotional, behavioral and other academic growth.

Implications for Interventions

While long-term outcomes for early intervention programs are difficult to measure (NIH Down Syndrome, 2008), supportive, enriched environments are recommended for young children with Down syndrome (Cody & Kamphaus, 1999). Children with Down syndrome may experience multiple disabilities that influence their physical, communication, cognitive, and psychosocial performance (Heller et al., 1996). The design of an intervention program depends upon the unique combination of disabilities and the severity of symptoms the child displays. Cognitive retardation affects learning in general and may result in longer learning curves, necessitating repetition and increased drill and practice for academic and/or self-help, daily living skills. Antecedent or response cues appear to be effective for children with cognitive disabilities (Heller et al., 1996), although increased rates of reinforcement may also be required. Basic instruction in daily self-care skills may be necessary and reinforcement and modeling techniques have proven effective. Social interaction skills may also be enhanced through direct instruction in specific skills and reinforcement of appropriate behaviors in naturally occurring situations.

Heller et al. (1996) suggest that children with congenital heart disorders need to be monitored carefully in the classroom depending on the nature and severity of the heart defects. 504 Plans would be appropriate to outline both medical and educational goals. Physical restrictions may be necessary for those with severe forms of heart defects, while milder forms may not necessitate such restrictions. Adaptive physical education, shortened days or special rest times, and homebound education may be needed in some cases. Further, Heller et al. (1996) suggest that children with congenital heart problems should be taught about heart defects, how to identify their own symptoms, what their own limitations are, and how to be their own advocates when decisions about the level of their activities are discussed.

Although Carr (1985) found that individuals with Down syndrome are living longer lives and are in better health than in past years, the long-term outcome is still unsettling. Cody and Kamphaus (1999) suggest that career and vocational planning help older teens and young adults with Down syndrome have more opportunities than they did in the past. Transition into adulthood can be facilitated with post-secondary vocational schooling, on-the-job training, sheltered workshop or other programs that promote independent or semi-independent living.

Fragile X Syndrome

Fragile X occurs from a permutation or full mutation of the X chromosome, and is the most common form of inherited cognitive retardation (Crawford, Acuña, & Sherman, 2001). Although Fragile X occurs in females, it is more common in males and may be one reason why cognitive retardation is more frequent in males than in females (Crawford et al., 2001). Females with Fragile X syndrome appear to have higher rates of normal intelligence (70%) than males (20%) affected by the disorder (Dill, Hayden, & McGillivray, 1992). As a sex-linked genetic disorder, where the X chromosome is abnormal, the defective gene appears to have more of a profound effect on males, who have only one X chromosome, whereas females may inherit one good X chromosome to counterbalance the other defective gene (LeFrancois, 1995). The full mutation of Fragile X is found more frequently in Caucasian males and is found in other races (Crawford et al., 2001). Females appear to have a higher prevalence rate as carriers than males (1/246 to 1/468 in females versus 1/1,000 in males) (Crawford et al., 2001). Fragile X syndrome also increases in frequency for mothers over the age of 40 (Hsu, 1986).

Characteristics and Associated Features of Fragile X

Fragile X syndrome is associated with mild to severe retardation and is considered to be the most common cause of inherited cognitive retardation (Crawford et al., 2001). Although Down syndrome may account for more cases of cognitive retardation, it is not considered to be inherited from parent to child, but occurs from abnormal chromosomal divisions (LeFrancois, 1995). Unlike Down syndrome, cognitive retardation in Fragile X may not be obvious until later stages of development, where marked intellectual deterioration may occur between the ages of 10 and 15 years of age (Silverstein & Johnston, 1990). Dykens et al. (1989) suggest that the drop in IQ, which may drop from a high of 54 points (between ages five and 10) to 38 points (at older ages), may be due to a "plateau" effect rather than a loss of previously acquired intellectual skills. Nevertheless, impairments in visual and sequential processing skills appear prominent (Cook & Leventhal, 1992).

Hypersensitivity to auditory stimuli, self-injury, and interest in unusual sensory stimuli (smell) may be present. Fragile X is also one of the primary causes of autism (Hessl et al., 2007), with as many as 12 percent of children with autism displaying Fragile X (Wolf-Schein, 1992). Males appear to have more severe symptoms, including language delays, slow motor development, speech impairments, and hyperactivity. Rapid speech, echolalia, and impaired communication skills have been reported (Cook & Leventhal, 1992). Social interactions also appear compromised.

Neuropsychological Functions

Widespread structural anomalies have been found in males with Fragile X syndrome, including in the cerebellum, hippocampus, and the superior temporal gyrus (Klaiman & Phelps, 1998). These variations may account for the deficits in attention, memory, visual-spatial reasoning, language skills and mathematics that often accompany the disorder.

In an fMRI study investigating affected males, Hessl et al. (2007) found diminished activation patterns in the amygdala and other brain regions known to regulate social cognition. There was less activation of these brain regions when males were observing fearful stimuli, less startle effect, and reduced skin conduction compared to controls.

Male and female carriers are known to acquire Fragile X-associated tremor/ataxia syndrome (FXTAS) later in life (Adams et al., 2007). This is a neurodegenerative disorder with evidence of brain differences in males and females. Volumetric MRI studies show: less reduction in cerebellar volume in affected females compared to affected males, and reduced brain volume and more white matter diseases in affected females compared to controls. Further, the severity of FXTAS symptoms were associated with reductions in cerebellar volume and the form of permutation in male carriers, but not in females (Adams et al., 2007). While females appear to have milder brain changes than males, the pattern of findings is similar.

Implications for Assessment

Specific genetic tests are available to diagnose Fragile X syndrome (NIH Fragile X, 2008). There are few outward signs of Fragile X syndrome in newborns, but some physical characteristics may be observed, including large head circumference; long face; prominent ears, jaw, and forehead, and hypermobility and hypertonia (NIH Fragile X, 2008).

Implications for Interventions

While there are no effective cures for Fragile X syndrome and syndrome-specific treatments have not been found, children are eligible for early intervention services including special education (Crawford et al., 2001). The extent to which social interaction, intellectual, and communication abilities are involved may determine the long-term outcome.

Research suggests that individuals with Fragile X syndrome may need treatment for autism and/or pervasive developmental disorders (NIH Fragile X, 2008). While there is evidence that hyperactivity and attentional problems improve with stimulant medications (Hagerman, Murphy, & Wittenberger, 1988), other medications are being investigated to improve behaviors and/or cognitive functioning (NIH Fragile X, 2008). Therapeutic interventions are not well investigated to date, and Cook and Leventhal (1992) suggest that "molecular understanding of pathogenesis may contribute directly to the development of therapeutic strategies" (p. 657).

Klinefelter Syndrome

Klinefelter syndrome (KS), also known as the XXY condition, is a chromosomal variation whereby an extra X chromosome is present on most cells (NIH Klinefelter Syndrome, 2008). KS is considered the most common of the chromosomal abnormalities, and estimates suggest that it occurs in approximately one in every 500 male births (NIH Klinefelter Syndrome, 2008). KS, like other autosomal abnormalities, including Down syndrome (trisomy 2 1), Edward syndrome (trisomy 18), Patua syndrome (trisomy 13), Cri du Chat syndrome (deletion on

Chromosome 5), and Turner syndrome (XO), affect CNS development and are characterized by physical variations (Hynd & Willis, 1988). During puberty, boys are more likely to exhibit above average height, breast enlargement, less body and facial hair, wider hips, and heavier and less muscular bodies (Ginther & Fullwood, 1998; NIH Klinefelter Syndrome, 2008). By adulthood XXY males look similar to non-affected males, but tend to have higher rates of autoimmune disorders, breast cancer, vein diseases, bone weakness, and dental problems (NIH Klinefelter Syndrome, 2008).

Although scientists believe that one in 500 males have an extra X chromosome, not all will have symptoms of KS (NIH Klinefelter Syndrome, 2008). Symptom presentation appears related to the number of XXY cells, the level of testosterone, and the age of diagnosis. The risks for KS increase with the age of the mother (see Ginther & Fullwood, 1998).

Characteristics and Associated Features of KS

Characteristics of KS include infertility, male breast development, underdeveloped masculine build, and social-cognitive-academic difficulties (Grumbach & Conte, 1985). Physical characteristics (e.g., long legs, tall stature, small testes and penis for body) may be distinguishing features for diagnosing KS (Ratcliffe, Butler, & Jones, 1990).

Psychosocial and Psychoeducational Correlates of KS

Males with KS often have associated behavioral difficulties (i.e., anxiety, immaturity, passivity, and low activity levels), and may present with various problems in peer relations as well as academic, and behavioral problems including impulsivity, aggressiveness, and withdrawal (NIH Klinefelter Syndrome, 2008). Because some children with KS appear shy and withdrawn, teachers may describe these boys as lazy or day dreamy. Many males with KS have difficulties with psychosocial adjustment because of passivity and withdrawal (Robinson, Bender, & Linden, 1990). Further, schizophrenia appears higher among children with KS (Friedman & McGillivray, 1992).

Language and speech delays may be present in anywhere from 25 percent to 85 percent of XXY males (NIH Klinefelter Syndrome, 2008). Children typically have average IQ (Pennington, Bender, Puck, Salbenblatt, & Robinson, 1982). Fine and gross motor delays have been found in some individuals, where dexterity, speed, coordination, and strength may be affected (Mandoki & Sumner, 1991). Children with KS often have a number of academic weaknesses, including difficulty in reading (Netley, 1987; Ratcliffe et al., 1990), spelling (Netley, 1987), and reading comprehension (Graham, Bashir, Stark, Silbert, & Walzer, 1988).

Implications for Assessment

Sandberg and Barrick (1995) indicate that most males with KS are not identified in adolescence or in adulthood, so present research may be skewed toward those individuals with more medical and/or psychological difficulties. Chromosomal analysis is necessary to identify KS, but is not routinely conducted. Careful history taking, in light of psychosocial, behavioral, and academic problems, may suggest the need for a medical consultation and genetic screening. Thorough psychological and educational assessment may shed light on other language and academic delays.

Implications for Interventions

Medical interventions may include testosterone replacement (NIH Klinefelter Syndrome, 2008), and, in cases where gynecomastia (breast development) is present, surgery may be warranted (Sandberg & Barrick, 1995). Although some individuals have been successfully treated with testosterone replacement, not all males have favorable outcomes (Nielsen, 1991). It is important to begin replacement therapy early in life for the most favorable outcomes.

Individual and family therapy may be needed to address the psychosocial needs of the individual with KS. Sandberg and Barrick (1995) suggest implementing opportunities for structured social interactions. Finally, special education interventions may address cognitive, language, and speech-related difficulties.

Neurofibromatosis, tuberous sclerosis, and Sturge Weber syndrome are among the more common neurocutaneous syndromes. These disorders are discussed separately.

Neurocutaneous Syndromes/Disorders

Tuberous sclerosis and neurofibromatosis both involve the failure of cells to differentiate and/or proliferate during early neurodevelopmental stages (Cook & Leventhal, 1992). Morphological changes in the brain occur following these early developmental abnormalities, and these morphological differences result primarily from a failure of control of cell differentiation and proliferation. Hynd and Willis (1988) suggest that these abnormalities may occur during the eighth and 24th week of gestation, when migration of embryonic cells is at its height. Most of these neurocutaneous disorders are genetically transmitted through autosomal dominant means. Thus, neurocutaneous disorders could just as easily be discussed under biogenetic diseases.

Neurofibromatosis

Neurofibromatosis (NF) is a rare disorder and has been referred to as Von Recklinghausen's disease in honor of the physician who first identified the disorder (Hynd & Willis, 1988). The disorder is "considered to be a peripheral neuropathy, brain tumors and other lesions within the brain" (Nilsson & Bradford, 1999, p. 350). There are two major forms of NF—NF1 and NF2—involving either chromosome 17 (NF1) or chromosome 22 (NF2; Phelps, 1998b). NF1 is a dominant, autosomal (nonsex) inherited disorder and occurs in approximately one in 3,000–4,000 individuals in the world, while NF2 is more rare [one in 25,000 (NIH Neurofibromatosis, 2008)]. NF1 and NF2 have different features, although NF2 occurs rarely in pediatric populations.

While NF1 increases the risk for benign and malignant tumors, most NF1- type neurofibromas are non-cancerous (NIH Neurofibromatosis, 2008). Cancerous tumors do occur in some individuals with NF1 along spinal cord nerves or other brain regions, and in the blood system (leukemia). NF2 signs and symptoms typically appear in adolescence or early adulthood, but onset can occur at any age (NIH Neurofibromatosis, 2008). Early symptoms of vestibular schwannomas are difficulty with balance, hearing loss and ringing in the ears.

The manner in which NF is expressed varies dramatically; parents may show few abnormalities, while one child may show severe symptoms and a sibling may show no signs (Hynd & Willis, 1988). When the child's father is affected by NF, the child tends to have less severe symptoms than when the mother is affected (Miller & Hall, 1978). Furthermore, children with affected mothers have higher morbidity, and show symptoms at an earlier age (38% show signs in infancy and 76% by age three years). For a more detailed discussion of neurofibromatosis, see NIH Neurofibromatosis (2008).

Characteristics and Associated Features of NF Features of NFI

NF1 is characterized by the following: spots of skin pigmentation that appear like birthmarks (cafe au lait maculas); benign tumors on or under the skin (neurofibromas); tumors in the iris that are also benign (Lisch nodules); focal lesions in various brain regions (e.g., basal ganglia, subcortical white matter, brain stem, and cerebellum), and freckles in unexposed body areas (e.g., armpit or groin area) (NIH Neurofibromatosis, 2008; Nilsson & Bradford, 1999). NF1 is also associated with learning problems, anxiety related to physical appearance, cluster tumors (plexiform neurofibromas), optic tumors, and seizure disorders. Other signs include high blood pressure, short stature, macrocephaly (large head), and curvature of the spine (NIH Neurofibromatosis, 2008).

North, Joy, Yuille, Cocks, and Hutchins (1995) found that children with NF1 displayed high rates of learning disabilities, poor adaptive social functioning, and high rates of behavioral problems. A bimodal distribution in intelligence scores was found suggesting that the group may have subtypes, specifically those with and without cognitive deficits. Individuals with lower IQs do show abnormal MRI scans (increased T, signal intensity) (North

et al., 1995). These lesions are thought to arise from glial proliferation and aberrant myelination. Speech-language, attentional, organizational, and social difficulties were present, although hyperactivity and oppositional and conduct disorders were not apparent.

The physical features of NF1 vary from mild, with cafe au lait spots, to extensive pigmentation and neurofibromas all over the body (Phelps, 1998b). Neurofibromas and brain lesions may not appear until later childhood and adolescence, and with the onset of puberty they have a tendency to increase. While the cafe au lait spots may be present immediately, they too increase with age, along with increased Lisch nodules (Listernick & Charrow, 1990). Symptoms may become so severe in a large number of adolescents that by the age of 15 as many as 50 percent of individuals with NF1 may have health-related problems (Riccardi, 1992).

Cognitive and Psychosocial Correlates of NF1

Academic problems, including a variety of learning disabilities, occur in about 50 percent of children with NF1 (Nilsson & Bradford, 1999; Riccardi, 1992). Visual-spatial disorders, with accompanying reading problems, are common (Hofman et al., 1994; Riccardi, 1992). Compared to noninvolved siblings, NF1 patients have lower cognitive skills (Hofman et al., 1994), but the IQ range varies from cognitive retardation to giftedness (Nilsson & Bradford, 1999). Global and verbal intelligence appear somewhat compromised, although these skills are within the average range (Phelps, 1998b). Nilsson and Bradford (1999) suggest that both language-based and visual perceptual deficits are present, which is consistent with nonverbal learning disabilities (NVLD).

Psychosocial adjustment appears problematic in that NF1 children are often teased because of their appearance, which worsens with age. Children with NF1 often do poorly in school and have trouble establishing friendships. NF is a disfiguring disorder that produces stress and anxiety in afflicted individuals (Benjamin et al., 1993). Attempts to hide the condition often lead to isolation, and high levels of anxiety are not uncommon in adolescents (Benjamin et al., 1993).

Features of NF2

NF2 involves the eighth cranial nerve, resulting in hearing loss, imbalances, pain, headaches, and ringing in the ears (NIH Neurofibromatosis, 2008; Phelps, 1998b). These are late appearing tumors (in the 20 s or 30 s), although it is possible to diagnose NF2 in children, particularly when there are multiple skin (absent cafe au lait or Lisch nodules) or CNS tumors. Complications of tumor growth may also affect numbness and/or weakness in arms and legs, and a buildup of fluid in the brain (NIH Neurofibromatosis, 2008).

Implications for Assessment

The presence of cafe au lait spots is often used as a clinical marker for the presence of NF1. However, the number of spots needed to make a diagnosis is controversial, ranging from five to six distinct spots at least 1.5 cm in diameter (Hynd & Willis, 1988). Diagnosis of NF2 is often made following MRI scans, genetic testing, and a review of family history of the disorder, particularly when the physical appearances described above are present (Mautner, Tatagiba, Guthoff, Samii, & Pulst, 1993). MRI, CT scans, X-rays and blood tests may also be used to identify defects in the NF1 gene (NIH Neurofibromatosis, 2008). Doctors also look for hearing loss, conduct audiometry and brainstem evoked potential response tests to determine damage to the 8th cranial nerve, and investigate family history when making a diagnosis of NF2. Prenatal genetic testing may be used for both NF1 and NF2 when there is a history of NF in the family.

Neuropsychologists may assess the child to establish a base rate of cognitive and academic deficits, and to ascertain subsequent neurodevelopmental deterioration that may occur. Thus, the use of a broad-based assessment protocol is advised, including measures of intellectual, language, motor, academic, and psychosocial functioning (Nilsson & Bradford, 1999; North et al., 1995). Executive functions and reasoning skills should also be assessed.

Implications for Interventions

Although specific treatment plans have not been investigated, techniques for addressing learning, behavioral, and academic difficulties may prove helpful. Access to special education services may be appropriate under the category of "Other Health Impaired" (Nilsson & Bradford, 1999; Phelps, 1998b). Children with NF require academic as well as psychological support. Educational staff may need to be informed about the nature, course and features of NF in order to design appropriate interventions. Nilsson and Bradford suggest that interventions for NVLD may be helpful for some children. Compensatory, adaptive strategies may be helpful to increase skills and avoid frustrations.

Surgical removal of tumors may be necessary (Hynd & Willis, 1988). Long-term follow-up is needed because children with NF may show deficits at a later age as demands increase (Montgomery, 1992). Parents may also benefit from counseling and realistic planning for the child's future. Family education and support is also recommended, as families often are not well informed about the disorder (Benjamin et al., 1993; Nilsson & Bradford, 1999). Further research is needed to more clearly establish how these factors affect interventions with this population of children and adolescents.

Tuberous Sclerosis

Tuberous sclerosis (TS) is a genetic condition characterized by numerous nonmalignant tumors on various body parts (i.e., skin, brain, kidneys, lungs, retina, and other organs), and affects about one in 6,000 infants (NIH Tuberous Sclerous, 2008). CNS symptoms are common (i.e., seizures, cognitive retardation), and a majority of individuals develop significant medical problems involving the heart, lungs, bones, and kidneys. Symptom presentation varies depending on the tumor location. Distinct facial lesions—adenoma sebaceum—that appear like acne are present in approximately 53 percent of five-year-olds and 100 percent of 35-year-olds with the disorder (Bundey & Evans, 1969). Other white spots—amelanotic naevus—may be present on the face, trunk, or limbs in half of patients with TS (Chalhub, 1976). A rough discolored patch also may be observed in the lumbar region in a smaller number of individuals (20–50%).

CNS lesions result from an abnormal proliferation of brain cells and glia during embryonic development (Chalhub, 1976). Cortical tubers often
occur in the convulsions of brain tissue and ultimately interfere with the lamination of the cortex.
Tumor-like protrusions also may enter the ventricular regions from an outgrowth of astrocytes.
These calcium-enriched tubers are visible on CT
scans. White matter heterotopias also may be one
of the CNS lesions found in patients with TS. When
tumors are present near the lateral ventricular
region, hydrocephalus may appear.

Characteristics and Associated Features of TS

Children with TS often have cognitive retardation,
epilepsy, and hemiplegia (Hynd & Willis, 1988).
Seizure activity is common in individuals with TS,
and may be as high as 85 percent to 95 percent of
those affected. Infantile spasms are common and
may worsen with age (NIH Tuberous Sclerous,
2008). However, there appears to be little connection between physical signs (lesions), seizure activity, and intracranial lesions. Psychological and
behavioral characteristics have been noted in children with TS, including hyperactivity, aggression,
destructive tantrums, and other behavioral control
problems (NIH Tuberous Sclerous, 2008; Riccio &
Harrison, 1998). Autism has been associated with
TS and schizophrenia also appears in some individuals (Cook & Leventhal, 1992; NIH Tuberous
Sclerous, 2008).

Implications for Assessment

Surgical removal of CNS tumors (near the ventricular region) may be necessary, but does not always
produce good results and may have a high morbidity rate (Hynd & Willis, 1988). Children may require
medical evaluations including ultrasound to identify tumors in visceral regions, and EEGs for seizure
activity or spasms. Children with TS and severe
seizure disorders are also likely to have significant
cognitive retardation (Riccio & Harrison, 1998).

Neuropsychological assessment, including academic and psychological evaluation to identify
associated features such as hyperactivity,
aggression, autism, and other behavioral/psychia-
tric disorders, is recommended. It is important to
identify the full range of associated difficulties prior
to designing effective interventions.

Implications for Interventions

Similar to other neurocutaneous disorders, little is
known about a specific course of action to take for
interventions, other than medical treatment and
seizure control. Although psychoeducational interventions for school-related difficulties seem reasonable, efficacy and outcome research has not been
conducted. Thus, careful follow-up and monitoring
of specific interventions should be conducted on an
individual basis to determine which strategies and
approaches are most effective for addressing educational and psychological problems. Medical follow-
up is essential, and may help determine the long-
term outcome of children with TS.

Sturge-Weber Syndrome

Sturge-Weber syndrome (SWS) is characterized by
a number of significant neurodevelopmental
anomalies, including seizure disorders, cognitive
retardation, behavioral difficulties, and infantile
hemiplegia. These anomalies appear to result from
various neuropathologies involving (1) intracranial
calcification in the occipital and parietal regions,
and sometimes in the temporal region, and (2)
abnormal production of endothelial cells, which
leads to leptomeningeal angioma and, in some
cases, to subarachnoid or subdural hemorrhage
(Cody & Hynd, 1998; NINDS Sturge-Weber,
2008). Calcification usually is not observable during
infancy, but can be seen with neuroimaging at a
later age. Vascular lesions and abnormal blood
flow have also been found using carotid angiography. Facial naevus (port wine staining) is characteristic of SWS (Cody & Hynd, 1998).

Seizures usually occur in the hemisphere opposite the birthmark (NINDS Sturge-Weber, 2008).
Children with SWS are also at risk for glaucoma—
this increased pressure causes the eye to enlarge,
often resulting in a bulging outside the eye socket.

Characteristics and Associated Features of SWS

SWS is associated with seizure activity usually occurring within the first two years of life, and progressively worsening with age (NINDS Sturge-Weber, 2008). The extent to which seizures can be controlled often predicts later outcome of the disorder. Cognitive and behavioral problems are common, and the risk for cognitive impairment especially when seizures occur before the age of two years (NINDS Sturge-Weber, 2008).

Implications for Assessment and Intervention

Medical follow-up is required to identify the nature of neuropathology and to treat seizure activity. In rare cases, hemispherectomy may be necessary to control intractable seizures. While the outcome of neurosurgery has been variable, seizure control has been effective, although severe cognitive retardation was an outcome when the left hemisphere was removed early in life (Falconer & Rushworth, 1960). Severe behavioral disturbances were also reduced following surgery. Neurosurgical intervention is used with caution because of the serious complications associated with hemidecortication, including hemorrhaging into the open cavity, hydrocephalus, and brainstem shifts (Falconer & Wilson, 1969). Furthermore, improved medications for seizure control have reduced the need for invasive surgical techniques (Hynd & Willis, 1988).

Educational services are appropriate to address cognitive and behavioral problems. Disruptive, acting out problems may be reduced with behavior management strategies (Cody & Hynd, 1998). Physical therapy may be needed for some children with muscle weakness (NINDS Sturge-Weber, 2008). Research is currently underway with NINDS support to better understand, diagnose, treat, and prevent this disorder.

Seizure disorders are reviewed next, with attention paid to the transactional nature of the associated features and the need for a transactional, multifaceted intervention plan including medical, academic, and psychosocial approaches.

Seizure Disorders

Seizure disorders can occur in children with developmental disorders and may be caused by metabolic disorders, hypoxia, or other congenital problems (Teeter & Semrud-Clikeman, 1998). *Epilepsy* refers to chronic disturbances in brain functions affecting perceptions, movements, consciousness, and other behaviors, while *seizures* refer to individual episodes (NIH Seizures, 2008). Neppe (1985) describes seizures as paroxysmal firing of neurons, which may cause perceptual, motor disturbances or loss of consciousness. Although epilepsy occurs in only 1 percent–2 percent of the population (Hynd & Willis, 1988), it is considered to be the most prevalent of childhood neurological disorders (Black & Hynd, 1995). National data suggest that approximately 2 million individuals have epilepsy and one-half of those are children (NICHY, 2004).

Seizures, or single episodes, caused by high fevers (above 102°F) are the common cause of convulsions. Febrile seizures are most common in children between three months and five years of age (Hynd & Willis, 1988). Most children (70%) experience only one seizure episode; when a second seizure does occur, it is usually within a year of the first episode (Hynd & Willis, 1988).

There are several classification systems based on changes in EEG activity during (ictal) and between (interictal) seizures (Neppe & Tucker, 1992). Most recent systems ignore neuroanatomical sites of seizure activity, age, gender, and pathological explanations of epileptic seizures, and emphasize major descriptions, including partial (i.e., simple, complex, generalized tonic-clonic), generalized (i.e., absence, myoclonic, clonic, tonic, etc.), or unclassified generalized seizures (Neppe & Tucker, 1992). McDonald and Saykin (2007) indicate that temporal lobe seizures are the most common form of complex partial seizures. Older classification systems for seizure disorders (grand mal, petit mal, psychomotor), have been replaced (Hartlage & Hartlage, 1989). Seizures that appear for unknown reasons (idiopathic) typically are differentiated from those occurring for known reasons such as brain trauma or tumor activity (Hynd & Willis, 1988).

Stages of Seizure Activity

The seizure itself may be divided into stages: the prodome, aura, automatism, and postictal changes (Besag, 1995). According to Besag (1995), the *prodome* is the time before a seizure or cluster of seizures occurs. The child may show irritability, lethargy, or apathy during this period, with these symptoms ending when the seizure begins. The *aura* occurs just prior to the seizure and has been described as a seizure itself. The aura is a simple partial seizure type that can lead to a complex partial seizure. The aura, which occurs while the child is fully conscious, has been described as more distressing to the child than the actual tonic-clonic seizure (Besag, 1995). The aura is actually a seizure with a focal charge, lasts a few seconds, and can occur many times a day. Besag (1995) reports that auras can result in mood (mainly anxiety) and behavioral change; thus, the aura may herald not only the beginning of a seizure, but also significant behavioral change in the child.

Automatisms have been defined as a "clouding of consciousness, which occurs during or immediately after a seizure and during which the individual retains control of posture and muscle tone but performs simple or complex movements and actions without being aware of what is happening" (Fenton, 1972, p. 59). Automatisms may include lip smacking, hand flapping, eye blinking, twirling, and other similar behaviors.

Postictal changes are behaviors that occur after the seizure and vary depending on the parts of the brain involved, the duration of the seizure, and whether the seizures come in clusters. Behaviors during the postictal stage can range from drowsiness to significant behavioral and cognitive changes such as paranoid ideation. Usual symptoms include irritability and confusion. Besag (1995) strongly recommends that parents and teachers realize that these postictal changes *are* related to the seizure and require understanding and empathy for the child.

Partial Seizures

Partial seizures are associated with diagnosable structural lesions. These seizures do not involve a loss of consciousness, but can evolve into generalized clonic-tonic seizures (Dreifuss, 1994).

Simple Partial Seizures

This type of seizure results from a specific focus in the gray matter of the brain, which causes an abnormal electrical discharge. The most commonly seen seizure of this type involves the jerking of one part of the body without loss of consciousness. The simple partial seizure foci is in the motor strip area. Other types of simple partial seizures include sensory (simple hallucinations), autonomic (sweating, pallor, hair standing on end on limbs), and psychic (affective problems, speaking, distortion of time sense) seizures with no impairment of consciousness (Hartlage & Telzrow, 1984).

Complex Partial Seizures

Complex partial seizures generally involve a loss or impairment of consciousness. This alteration of consciousness occurs before the attack or shortly after its beginning. These seizures involve behavioral automatisms such as lip smacking, hair twirling, and hand patting. Problems in orientation in time and space also occur. The focus of this type of seizure is in the temporal lobe as well as the frontal lobes. Some believe the complex partial seizures arising from the frontal lobes are associated with automatisms, while those with a temporal focus relate to a cessation of activity (Delgado-Escueta, Bascal, & Treiman, 1982).

Generalized Seizures

There are three main types of generalized seizures. Of the three, febrile seizures are not considered a seizure disorder. This type of seizure is associated with a fever experienced by a previously neurologically intact child. Although these seizures may reoccur, medication is not used due to the benign nature of the seizure (Hartlage & Telzrow, 1984). The other two types of generalized seizures are absence and tonic-clonic.

Absence Seizures

This type of seizure was previously labeled petit mal. Seizures of this kind involve an abrupt loss of consciousness. The child's eyes may flicker, roll back, or blink rapidly. When the seizure ceases, the child resumes his or her activity as if nothing unusual has occurred. These seizures may occur very frequently; some children have been known to have over 100 in a day (Hartlage & Telzrow, 1984). Age of onset is 4–8 years. School performance is often seen to fall off, and the child may be described as dreamy or unmotivated. The diagnosis of absence seizures is confirmed by EEG. The EEG will show spikes that are synchronized bilaterally and frontally (normal brain activity is *not* synchronized), with alternating spike and slow wave patterns (Lockman, 1993). To induce a seizure during an EEG, hyperventilation is used whereby the child is asked to take 60 deep breaths for three or four minutes (Lockman, 1993). Although the etiology of absence seizures is suspected to be genetic in origin, the genetic mechanism has not yet been identified. The risk of siblings also showing absence seizures is approximately three times greater than for the general population (Ottman et al., 1989). Absence seizures are generally treated with one medication. Zarontin is the medication with the fewest side effects (Dooley et al., 1990), followed by valproate (Sato et al., 1982) and clonazepam (Hartlage & Telzrow, 1984). Absence seizures have been known to worsen with the use of carbamazepine (Horn, Ater, & Hurst, 1986). The prognosis for absence seizures is favorable, with approximately half of affected children becoming seizure-free. The other 50 percent may develop tonic-clonic seizures or may continue to experience absence seizures (Lockman, 1993). Sato et al. (1983) found that 90 percent of children of normal intelligence and neurological function with no history of tonic-clonic seizures were seizure-free in adolescence. Conversely, those children with automatisms and motor responses during the absence seizures had a poorer prognosis. Lockman (1994) concluded that typical absence seizures are not necessarily benign and that medical management of these seizures does not necessarily influence the eventual outcome.

Tonic-Clonic Seizures

Further, increased seizure activity correlated with this type of seizure was formerly called grand mal seizure. Epidemiological studies have shown this type of seizure to be the most commonly found in children (Ellenberg, Hirtz, & Nelson, 1984). Tonic-clonic seizures begin with a loss of consciousness and a fall accompanied by a cry. The limbs extend, the back arches, and breathing may cease for short periods of time. This phase can last from several seconds to minutes. The limb extension is then followed by jerking of the head, arms, and legs. This is the clonic phase, which can last for minutes or may stop with intervention (Dreifuss, 1994). Most commonly, the jerking decreases and the child regains consciousness. Headaches and confusion usually ensue. Generally, the child falls into a deep sleep lasting from 30 minutes to several hours. Tonic-clonic seizures can occur after focal discharges and then are labeled as secondary generalization (Dreifuss, 1994). Tonic-clonic seizures are related to metabolic imbalances, liver failure, and head injury. On rare occasions, tonic-clonic seizures may persist for extremely long periods of time or may be repeated so close together that no recovery occurs between attacks. This type of seizure is called *status epilepticus* (Lockman, 1994). Underlying conditions such as subarachnoid hemorrhage, metabolic disturbances, and fevers (e.g., bacterial meningitis) can trigger status epilepticus in children (Phillips & Shanahan, 1989). Treatment for status epilepticus includes very high dosages of medication and, in some cases, inducing a coma (Young, Segalowitz, Misek, Alp, & Boulet, 1983).

Associated Features

While seizures can occur in children with normal cognitive abilities (Hartlage & Hartlage, 1989), seizure disorders occur more frequently in individuals with depressed intelligence (Cook & Leventhal, 1992). Low IQ (less than 80) with intractable epilepsy usually has a poor outcome for remission (Huttenlocher & Hapke, 1990). Further, increased seizure activity is correlated with more severe cognitive deficits (Farwell, Dodrill, & Batzel, 1985). It is also important to note that children with early seizure onset are likely to have lower IQ (Aldenkamp, Gutter, & Beun, 1992).

Curatolo, Arpino, Stazi, and Medda (1995) investigated risk factors associated with the comorbidity of partial seizures, cerebral palsy (CP), and cognitive retardation in a group of children from Italy. Cerebral malformations (e.g., agenesis of the corpus callosum, NF, cortical dysplasia, lissencephaly) were found in half of the group. Children with an early onset of seizures were likely also to have CP and cognitive retardation. Children with a family history of epilepsy may have a "genetic predisposition to neurological disorders in general which range from epilepsy to CP" to cognitive retardation (Curatolo et al., 1995, p. 779). Cardiopulmonary resuscitation was also found to be a risk factor only in the group of children who did not have cerebral malformations. These authors suggest that resuscitation may be the first neurological abnormality that appears in this group, rather than a cause of the cerebral palsy.

Academic problems may also occur in children with seizure disorders (Pazzaglia & Frank-Pazzaglia, 1976), and LD may occur in approximately 15 percent–30 percent of children with epilepsy (Matthews, Barabas, & Ferrai, 1983). Epidemiologic studies of children with epilepsy have found that approximately 50 percent have school difficulty ranging from mild to severe (Pazzaglia & Frank Pazzaglia, 1976; Sillanpaa, 1992). In a study of Finnish children with epilepsy compared to non-epileptic controls, Sillanpaa (1992) found that the most frequent associated problems were mental (cognitive) retardation (31.4%), speech disorders (27.5%), and specific learning disorders (23.1%).

Children with seizure disorders have shown impaired performance on tests of reading, written language, and spelling (Seidenberg et al., 1986), as well as on teacher reports of attention, concentration, and information processing (Bennett-Levy & Stores, 1984). Reading comprehension appears to be more compromised than word recognition skills. However, social and cultural factors may also influence academic outcome and IQ for children with epilepsy-related disorders, as family factors (e.g., family setting and parental attitudes) were significantly correlated with underachievement. Finally, psychomotor and visual-motor coordination

problems have also been found to be poorer in children with seizure disorders than in typically developing children (Cull, 1988).

Psychosocial Correlates

Although children with epilepsy differ from normal peers on a number of social-emotional variables, they do not appear to have higher rates of psychopathology than children with other chronic medical or neurological conditions (Hartlage & Hartlage, 1989). Psychosocial features often include external locus of control, poor self-esteem (Matthews, Barabas, & Ferrai, 1982), and increased dependency (Hartlage & Hartlage, 1989). Neppe (1985) indicates that individuals with epilepsy do experience psychosocial stress due to the effects of having a chronic illness, anxieties over social interactions, and restrictions in everyday activities (e.g., driving). Seizure disorders in childhood are related to other psychiatric conditions. The majority of children (85%) with temporal lobe epilepsy have cognitive retardation (25%) and disruptive behavior disorders, including hyperactivity and "catastrophic rage" (Cook & Leventhal, 1992). Psychopathology, including psychoses, has been described in individuals with epilepsy (Neppe & Tucker, 1992), and psychiatric disorders (i.e., cognitive retardation, hyperkinesis, and rage disorders) have been reported in 85 percent of children with temporal lobe epilepsy (Lindsay, Ounstead, & Richards, 1979). Cook and Leventhal (1992) suggest that the loss of control children may experience as a result of epilepsy may be a special challenge during development, and children may react either passively or aggressively. However, these reactions may be related to how seizure activity affects cognition and impulse control.

Implications for Assessment

Children with seizure disorders require medical diagnosis and follow-up by a child neurologist. Ongoing assessment of neuropsychological, cognitive, and psychosocial functioning is useful for measuring the long-term effects of chronic seizure disorders. Because many children with epilepsy are not easily categorized, each child would benefit from a team that includes a physician, psychologist, teacher, and counselor (Black & Hynd, 1995).

Moderator Variables

There are a number of moderator variables which need to be recognized when evaluating the performance of a child with a seizure disorder. These variables are etiology of the seizure disorder, age of onset, seizure type, seizure frequency, medication, and family environment. Each of these moderator variables will be discussed in the following sections.

Etiology

The main classes of etiology for seizure disorders are idiopathic, where the cause is unknown, and symptomatic, where the cause is associated with organic and/or identified neurological problems (Cull, 1988). Children with symptomatic epilepsy generally have lower IQ scores, with many showing cognitive retardation (Sillanpaa, 1992), whereas those with idiopathic epilepsy show normal distribution of intellectual ability. Symptomatic epilepsy is also associated with poorer academic and intellectual outcome. Recently, neural developmental abnormalities have been implicated in the development of seizure-related disorders. Specifically, abnormal cell migration has been associated with both mental retardation and epilepsy (Falconer et al., 1990). As cells migrate and move into their final destinations during embryonic development, genetic and/or environmental factors may disrupt this process and ultimately result in epilepsy.

Age of Onset

The majority of studies evaluating the significance of age of onset in relation to cognitive development have found a direct relationship between the two, with children with early onset generally showing poorer cognitive attainment (Seidenberg, 1988). Ellenberg and Nelson (1984) reported that children

with normal neurological development prior to the first seizure have a better prognosis for intellectual development at age seven than those who had earlier seizures *and* poorer neurological attainment. O'Leary, Seidenberg, Berent, and Boll (1981) compared the performance of children with tonic-clonic seizures on the Halstead-Reitan Test Battery for Children. Those children with seizure onset before the age of five years were more impaired on measures of motor speed, attention and concentration, memory, and complex problem solving than those with a later onset. These researchers then evaluated the relationship between age of onset and partial seizure type. O'Leary et al. (1981) found that children with partial seizures and early onset performed more poorly than those with later onset, regardless of whether their seizures were partial or generalized. Similarly, Hermann, Whitman, and Dell (1988) found that children with early onset performed more poorly on eight of 11 scales of the LNNB-C. Evaluating age of onset with seizure type found that children with complex-partial seizures *and* early onset performed more poorly on Memory, Expressive Speech, and Reading, whereas generalized seizures *and* early onset were associated with poorer performance on Receptive Speech, Writing, Mathematics, and Intelligence Scales.

Duration of seizure has been found to co-occur with age of onset as a crucial variable and is frequently difficult to evaluate apart from age of onset. Generally it has been found that the earlier the onset of seizures, the longer the duration (Black & Hynd, 1995). Early onset and long duration appear to be associated with a poorer prognosis for learning. The number of seizures over the life span is a contributing factor to poor outcome as well. Seidenberg (1988) makes the point that further study is needed in this area to determine whether the neuropsychological impairment is broad-based and general, or whether there are specific areas of functioning that are more vulnerable during specific periods of development. This may be a likely case given what we know about neurodevelopment and increased cognitive, language, memory, and reasoning abilities in children. Thus, age of onset and seizure duration are important variables to consider when evaluating children with seizure disorders, particularly when planning for their educational and vocational needs.

Seizure Type

The relationship between seizure type and intellectual and educational attainment is currently unclear. Some investigators have found memory deficits to be associated with partial-complex seizures with a temporal lobe focus, whereas others have found that children with mixed seizures perform more poorly on measures of ability and achievement (Seidenberg et al., 1986). However, O'Leary et al. (1981) found few differences between seizure types, and those significant differences that did appear occurred more frequently in children with generalized seizures. Seidenberg (1988) concluded from his review of this literature that further study is needed using subtypes of seizure disorders. Most research has not identified subtypes of the seizure disorders when evaluating neuropsychological functioning.

Seizure Frequency

The relationship between seizure frequency and cognitive development is presently unclear. Methodological considerations may account for this difficulty, as many studies have not investigated subtypes of seizures, thereby possibly obscuring important findings.

Studies that have looked at seizure subtypes have generally found an inverse relationship between seizure duration and cognitive performance (longer duration = poorer test performance). Seidenberg (1988) found that with increasing frequency of seizure activity, performance on the full, verbal, and performance intelligence scales (FSIQ, VIQ, and PIQ) of the Wechsler, and the Trailmaking and Tactual Performance of the Reitan Battery declined significantly. When seizure type was also factored into the analysis, significant correlations for seizure duration, seizure frequency, and seizure type were found only for the tonic-clonic subtype.

Seizure control is also related to seizure frequency. Hermann et al. (1988) found that poor seizure control was related to poorer neuropsychological performance *only* for generalized epilepsies. Such a finding was not present for those children with partial seizures.

Seidenberg (1988) suggests that not only is subtyping of seizures important, but that researchers need to pay attention to seizure frequency, age of onset and duration, seizure type, and seizure control when evaluating neuropsychological functioning. He also suggests that seizure severity may be an overlooked variable in all investigations. Thus, etiology, age of onset of a seizure disorder, duration and frequency, type of seizure disorder, and possibly severity of the seizure all appear to contribute to the neuropsychological impairments that children may experience. In addition to these intraindividual variables, two major extra individual variables interact with the seizure disorder—namely, medication effects and family environmental influences. Each of these will be developed in the following sections.

Medication

Antiepileptic drugs such as Phenobarbital and clonazepam have been associated with cognitive difficulties (Besag, 1995). Others, including ethosuximide, sodium valporate, and carbamazepine generally have been found to be beneficial (Cull, 1988). Carbamazepine has been found to impair memory (Forsythe, Butler, Berg, & McGuire, 1991). Some researchers have found that decreases in dosage are associated with better performance, while increases show no such effects (Cull, 1988). Moreover, children with more than one antiepileptic medication show more cognitive impairment. Whether polydrug treatment is related to a more severe seizure disorder and, therefore, to more cognitive impairment, this is currently unclear.

Family Influences

Family and environmental influences on children with seizure disorders are just beginning to be explored. Given our transactional model, it is important to gather information concerning family and school environment influences.

Preliminary data indicate that negative reactions to the child's behaviors from peers and teachers can have a significant deleterious effect on the child's school attainment (Dreifuss, 1994). As discussed earlier, behavioral changes during aura and postictal stages are frequently seen. When peers and teachers interpret these behaviors as willful and deviant, significant adjustment problems can arise. Research evaluating interventions such as educating the child's peers about seizure disorders and any resulting changes in attitudes has not been conducted. Such investigations are sorely needed. These influences on the child with a seizure disorder are probably more easily solved than variables such as age of onset, frequency of seizures, and severity of seizures.

Socioeconomic status (SES) is significantly related to intelligence. In a study with Indian children, Singhi, Bansal, Singhi, and Pershad (1992), found that SES was the second most powerful indicator of cognitive impairment, second only to status epilepticus. This finding is similar to that of Caucasian and African-American children (Dodson, 1993).

Family variables such as stress, divorce, parental control and dependency, financial difficulty, and fewer family social supports have been shown to have a negative impact on cognitive development in children with seizure disorders (Teeter & Semrud-Clikeman, 1998). Austin, Risinger, and Beckett (1992) sought to evaluate the relative importance of demographics, seizure, and family variables on the behaviors of children with seizure disorders. In this study, no differences were found between boys and girls, children with mono- versus polydrug therapy, one-parent versus two-parent homes, or seizure type in behavioral problems. Significant findings were present for age, seizure frequency, family stress, and extended family social support. When stepwise multiple regression techniques were employed, intrafamily strain and marital strain emerged as the most significant predictors of behavioral problems. This finding is similar to those linking family discord to psychopathology in children without seizures (Breslau, 1985; Austin, 1988).

Hoare and Russell (1995) describe an assessment measure for identifying quality-of-life issues for children with chronic epilepsy and their families. This scale measures the impact of the illness on the child, the parents, and the family, and the cumulative impact. Further research is needed to determine the efficacy of this scale for intervention planning, but initial reports suggest that parents do have significant concerns, and these appear related to age of onset and seizure frequency.

Summary

Seizure variables interact with family variables to influence the child's intellectual and educational attainment as well as his or her emotional adjustment. Investigators are just beginning to evaluate these transactional relationships and their contributions to appropriate interventions. It is not clear, at present, whether interventions that target environmental (school and family) influences can improve the child's eventual cognitive attainment. However, it is important to consider these variables when designing treatment plans for these children, as they have been found to be potent predictors. The following section discusses intervention strategies for children with seizure disorders.

Implications for Intervention

Interventions addressing pharmacological, environmental, and educational strategies are briefly reviewed. In many cases, a dynamic plan may include one or more of the following strategies.

Pharmacological and Surgical Treatments

While anticonvulsant medications are commonly prescribed for children with nonfebrile seizure disorders, these medications (e.g., Phenobarbital) produce adverse side effects (e.g., sedation) that interfere with academic performance (Cook & Leventhal, 1992), and may increase hyperactivity (Vining et al., 1987) or depression (Brent, Crumrine, Varma, Allan, & Allman, 1987). Newer medications (lamotrigine and felbamate) may be used when side effects are not well tolerated or when traditional medications (i.e., valporate and carbamazepine) do not control seizure activity (Williams & Sharp, 2000).

In a review of pediatric pharmacology, DuPaul, McGoey, and Mautone (2003) list common anticonvulsant mediations for treating various seizure types: (1) Phenobarbitol, phenytoin, carbamazepine, and valporate for clonic-tonic seizures; (2) ethosuximide or valporate for absence seizures; (3)

carbamazepine, phenytoin, and valporate for partial seizures, with (4) gabapentine or felbamate as
second line medications.

In rare cases of intractable seizures, surgical
transactions may be an option when the seizures
are localized to one region in the brain. In a
meta-analysis of studies, it was concluded that
surgery produces long-term seizure-free outcomes,
especially for temporal lobe resective surgery
(Tellez-Zenteno, Dhar, & Wiebe, 2005); however,
it is clear that not all children who undergo brain
surgery are seizure-free. Studies appear to document resiliency in the developing brain, where
intact brain regions compensate for regions that
have been removed. For example, Meyer, Marsh,
Laws, and Sharbrough (1986) found that children
who had undergone surgical removal of the dominant temporal lobes, including the hippocampus
and amygdala, showed no significant decline in
verbal, performance, or full-scale IQ scores.
Smith, Walker, and Myers (1988) also found
that a six-year-old made remarkable postopera-
tive recovery following surgical removal of the
right hemisphere. The child had perinatal epilep-
togenic seizures that worsened and spread from
the right to the left hemisphere. Post-surgical test
scores showed average verbal intelligence (96),
low average performance abilities (87), and average full-scale (90) potential. The extent to which
cognitive abilities improve or develop following
surgical interventions depends on a number of
factors, including the age of the child and the
location of the lesion, once intact brain regions
are freed from the abnormal influences of the
lesioned regions.

Alternative Interventions

Recent studies have investigated the kerogenic diet
(KD) to determine safety and efficacy for treating
intractable epilepsy (Kang & Kim, 2006). The diet
has a ratio of 1:4 fat to nonfat foods, is high in
protein and restricts carbohydrate intake, and
has both anticonvulsant properties and also reduces
the development of recurring seizures and epilepsy
(Freeman, Kossoff, & Hartman, 2007). In a review
of patients treated with the kerogenic diet at
St. John's Hospital, Groesbeck, Bluml, and Kossoff

(2006) found that after six years, seizure activity
was significantly reduced in children on the diet.
Side effects included kidney stones, slowed growth,
and bone fractures. Other studies document early
onset (i.e., gastrointestinal disturbances, dehydra-
tion, biochemical disturbances) as well as late
onset (i.e., heptic failure, mineral and vitamin deficiencies) symptoms which require scheduled medical assessments to evaluate adverse effects of the
diet (Freeman et al., 2000). Henderson et al. (2006)
found children with generalized seizures and
those who showed more than a 50 percent reduction in seizure activity were more likely to remain
on the diet.

Despite their efficacy, neurologists are not likely
to prescribe kerogenic diets for patients, even
though they adhere to other evidence-based practices (i.e., antiepileptic medications) when treating
children with epilepsy (Mastriani, Williams, Hulsey,
Wheless, & Maria, 2008). See Freeman et al. (2007)
for a more extensive review of the KD treatment for
seizure disorders.

Environmental Interventions

Given previous research, it appears imperative to
assess variables such as family strain, behavioral
concerns, and discipline, and to plan interventions
taking these factors into consideration. Parenting,
stress management, and epilepsy education are
likely avenues for intervention. It is important in
the course of epilepsy education to discuss the
potential for parents to overcompensate for their
child's illness and the possible guilt that may
accompany a diagnosis. Parents who expect to
provide lifetime care for their child do not facilitate the development of independent behaviors.
Moreover, parents may lower expectations for
their child's academic performance. Therefore, it
is crucial to discuss these possibilities with parents
and to help them set realistic goals for their child
and encourage coping skills for the child with
epilepsy and seizure disorders (Freeman, Vining,
& Pillas, 2003). When a transactional approach is
not taken, the child's program will be incomplete
and most likely will be at least partially
unsuccessful.

Educational Interventions

Students with seizure disorders or epilepsy may access educational services under "other-health impaired" as defined by the Individuals with Disabilities Act (IDEA; NICHY, 2004). The school should not only be aware of the diagnosis of epilepsy, but educational staff should develop and institute a plan for working effectively with the child who has a seizure disorder. 504 plans may also be helpful to address medication issues (i.e., efficacy and side effects), and to establish home-school-physician communication.

The pediatric neuropsychologist can be helpful in the initial planning and implementation phase of the educational program. At the very least, medication monitoring is important. Sachs and Barrett (1995) list behavioral side effects of medication, such as drowsiness, lethargy, overactivity, confusion, and motor signs (e.g., clumsiness), and suggest that teachers should be on the look-out for these signs. Moreover, information on what action should be taken in the event of a seizure in school is very important for teachers and staff. Generally, little action is needed except when the child needs to be protected from injury. It is not appropriate to place items in the child's mouth, to restrain the child, or to perform cardiopulmonary resuscitation (NICHY, 2004).

Communication between the school and the physician is important for monitoring the child's seizure frequency and medication response (Lechtenberg, 2002; NICHY, 2004). The pediatric neuropsychologist may serve a much needed service in interpreting medical information for school personnel and parents. Linking these services is desirable to understand the child's needs and to develop a comprehensive intervention program for the child. Formulating the program can assist in planning for psychosocial stressors that may occur at home or in school, monitoring medication compliance and effectiveness, and enhancing the child's school performance in either special or regular education (Teeter & Semrud-Clikeman, 1998). Helping peers to understand the child's needs and his or her occasional unusual behaviors (during seizure activity) may smooth the way for children with seizure disorders to develop healthy peer relationships.

In summary, a transactional approach is an important vehicle for understanding and planning for the needs of children with seizures disorders. Similarly, children with head injuries would benefit from this type of integrated approach. See Chapter 14 for a discussion of interventions for children sustaining traumatic brain injury. Cerebral palsy is reviewed next.

Cerebral Palsy

Cerebral palsy (CP) is a neurological disorder that first appears in infancy or early childhood (NINDS Cerebral Palsy, 2008). Body movements and muscle coordination are permanently damaged and typically do not worsen with age. CP is caused by an insult to the developing brain usually between prenatal development and age three. Birth complications are a major cause of CP in newborns, although encephalitis, meningitis, and traumatic brain injury (from car accidents, falls, or abuse) may also cause CP in early childhood. Maternal and infant infections are also associated with increased risk for CP.

Muscle coordination is particularly compromised during voluntary movements (ataxia). Other motor signs include tight muscles and exaggerated reflexes (spasticity); walking on toes, on one foot or leg dragging; crouched or "scissor" gait, and floppy or stiff muscle tone (NINDS Cerebral Palsy, 2008). Other health problems have been found in children with CP including the need for feeding tubes, respiratory problems, and lower global health scores (Liptak et al., 2007). Liptak et al. found that children with the most severe disability who also have feeding tubes are particularly fragile children with other health problems.

Etiology of Cerebral Palsy

Prevalence rates for CP range from 2.12 to 4.45 per 1,000 births, in six countries (Odding, Roebroeck, & Stam, 2006). Incidence rates appear higher in less affluent communities where pre-pregnancy and pregnancy risk factors may be higher, including poor maternal health and access to quality health care. A minority of identified cases can be traced to documented brain injury from infection or trauma after four months of life.

A two-fold increase in the rate of CP across the spectrum has also been reported in England (Colver et al., 2000). Colver et al. found that low weight newborns (< 2,500 g) now represent one-half of the cases, where past data showed they accounted for one-third of cases. They suggest that modern neonatal care for babies < 2,500 g are now surviving at higher rates than previously reported, and these infants are surviving with CP. Males also appear to have an increased risk for CP compared to females, most likely because of other biological vulnerabilities including preterm births and mortality due to stillbirth and neonatal strokes (Johnston & Hagberg, 2007; Odding et al., 2006).

Low Birth Weight Factors

Low birth weight babies are at high risk for developing CP. As a result of increased rates of survival, CP in low birth weight babies is increasing (Colver et al., 2000). Survival rates for CP appear to depend on the severity of the disorder and the level of intelligence. Children with severe motor involvement and extremely low IQ have a shorter life expectancy.

Premature infants who are significantly smaller than expected appear to be at high risk for CP (Colver et al., 2000). Frequent medical difficulties found in these infants may contribute to the development of CP. These complications include intraventricular hemorrhage, white matter necrosis, and variation in cerebral blood flow (Leviton & Paneth, 1990). Evidence for the involvement of these complications in CP has been found by ultrasonography in infants and neuroimaging for older children and adults (Krageloh-Mann et al., 1992).

Twins who are low birth weight appear to be at special risk for CP as well (Nelson Swaiman, & Russman, 1994). If one of the twins dies at or before birth, the remaining twin appears to be at high risk for CP (Szymonowicz, Preston, & Yu, 1986). In fact, the incidence of twins in the general population is 2 percent, with a 10 percent incidence rate of CP within this sample (Grether et al., 1992).

Pregnancy and Birth Complications

Babies who sustain brain damage during delivery are at high risk for CP. Occlusion of a cerebral artery or prenatal strokes that restrict blood flow to the brain are the most common causes of hemiparetic CP (Lee et al., 2005). Strokes were most common in first born children and other birth complications (i.e., emergency C-section, ruptured membranes, prolonged second stage labor, and vacuum extraction). Infants sustaining strokes appear to have heart anomalies, inflammation of the placenta, and umbilical cord abnormalities. More than half of infants with one of these risk factors did not suffer a perinatal stroke.

Infants born with brain damage frequently show low tone, breathing problems, low APGAR scores, delayed reflexes, and seizures (Nelson & Leviton, 1991). When all these symptoms are present, the child is at greater risk for CP, with the risk decreasing as the number of presenting symptoms decreases (Ellenberg & Nelson, 1984; Seidman et al., 1991).

While subtypes of CP appear related to different causes, most children and adults with CP did not experience oxygen deprivation during birth. Asphyxia has been most closely related to quadriplegia (Nelson & Leviton, 1991). In most cases, however, it is not possible to determine the cause of CP.

Pre- and Postnatal Medical Complications

There are a number of pre- and postnatal complications that increase the risk for CP. In a review of research investigating pregnancy and pre-pregnancy infections, Dammann and Leviton (2006) reported that maternal infections place fetal brains at risk for neonatal white matter damage, including CP. New research investigating how to prevent infections to the mother prior to and during pregnancy is needed as well as an investigation of effective methods to protect the developing fetus. Wu and Colford (2000) also found that inflammation of the fetal membrane (chorioamnionitis) is associated with an increased risk for cystic periventricular leukomalacia and CP in pre-term and full-term babies. Other studies have shown that intra-amniotic inflammation following amniocentesis and subsequent inflammatory responses in the fetus (funisitis) place newborns at higher risk for CP by the age of three years (Hun et al., 2000).

Pre-term infants (before 12 hours of age) who received a three-day course of dexamethsone to prevent chronic lung diseases were at a risk for a range of medical problems including hypertension, gastrointestinal hemorrhage, and hyperglycemia (Shinwell et al., 2000). Stoll et al. (2004) also found that pre-term infants are at risk for infections (e.g., sepsis, meningitis), which increases the risk for CP. It has been hypothesized that cytokines, chemicals that fight the infections, may cause damage to the brain. These young infants were also at greater risk for CP, with the most common form being spastic diplegia, and developmental delays were also higher (Shinwell et al., 2000). Maternal infections (i.e., bladder or kidney) appear to be risk factors of infants with normal birth weight (Grether & Nelson, 1997).

Brain Malformations

Children with CP appear to have structural brain disorders which may be related to abnormal neuronal migration (Volpe, 1992). In these cases cells have migrated to the wrong place and, thus, brain layers are disordered, cells are out of place, and/or there are too many or not enough cells in certain critical brain regions. Volpe (1992) estimates that approximately 33 percent of CP in full-term infants involves some disordered cells and layers due to cortical malformation deficits.

Cerebral palsy is not a unitary disorder; rather, it consists of many subtypes, which share the common symptoms of movement disorder, early onset, and no progression of the disorder (Nelson et al., 1994). Cerebral palsy is generally subtyped by the area of the body involved, level of difficulty experienced, and concomitant disorders.

Subtypes of Cerebral Palsy

Six subtypes of CP are currently identified, although some controversy exists in the field as to their delineation. The subtypes presented in this book have been adopted by many pediatric neurologists (Nelson et al., 1994; Thorogood & Alexander, 2007). They are spastic hemiplegia, spastic quadriplegia, spastic diplegia, extrapyramidal, atonic, ataxic, and mixed. These subtypes are based on the motor systems, the body regions, and the amount of impairment involved.

Spastic Hemiplegia

Children with this subtype show difficulties on one side of their body, with more arm than leg involvement. The right side of the body (left hemisphere) appears to be at the highest risk for involvement and is found in two-thirds of patients (Crothers & Paine, 1959). The child's walk is characterized by toe walking and swinging the affected leg in a semicircular movement when taking steps. Moreover, the affected arm does not follow the reciprocal movement usually seen in walking. The foot faces in toward the middle of the body, with hypotonia present throughout the limbs. The affected side often appears smaller and during development becomes noticeably smaller than the unaffected side. This condition frequently causes lower spinal and walking difficulties as the child develops (Nelson et al., 1994). Children with this type of CP may show cognitive retardation (28%) and seizure disorders (33%) (Aicardi, 1990). In addition, brain studies using MRI and CT scans have frequently found atrophy of the affected hemisphere with areas of cortical thinning, loss of white matter, and expansion of the same-side lateral ventricle (Uvebrandt, 1988).

Spastic Quadriplegia In contrast to spastic hemiplegia, spastic quadriplegia is characterized by increased muscle tone, with the legs the most involved (Nelson et al., 1994). Some difficulty with articulation and swallowing may be present when the corticospinal tract is involved. Almost half of children with this subtype are cognitively retarded or learning disabled (Robinson, 1973), and a large percentage have tonic-clonic seizure disorders (Ingram, 1964). These children also frequently have visual impairments. Children with this type of CP often have morphological abnormalities, generally in the white matter, including death of white matter, edema, and cysts (Chutorian, Michener,

Defendini, Hilal, & Gamboa, 1979). In addition to missing white matter in specific areas, the cortex underlying the white matter exhibits a thickening of the meninges and gliosis in the white matter (Nelson et al., 1994). Nelson et al. (1994) further report that these lesions can vary from one full hemisphere to one lobe, to a specified portion of a lobe. Some structural deviations are also found in the brainstem (Wilson, Mirra, & Schwartz, 1982).

Spastic Diplegia

Spastic diplegia generally involves both legs, with some arm involvement. This type of CP is commonly found in premature infants, with approximately 80 percent of infants with motor abnormalities showing this type of CP (Hagberg, Hagberg, & Zetterstrom, 1989). These children may later develop ataxia and frequently toe walk (Nelson et al., 1994). The clinical picture of children with spastic diplegia includes hypertonia with rigidity. Many children show generalized tonic-clonic seizures (27%) (Ingram, 1955), strabismus (43%) (Ingram, 1955), and cognitive retardation (30%, with increasingly higher rates as more extremely low birth weight babies survive) (Hagberg et al., 1989).

The brains of these children often evidence porencephalic cysts and microgyria (many small gyri) with abnormalities in tracts which serve the legs as they transverse the internal capsule (Christensen & Melchior, 1967). Atrophy, abnormal cortical formation, and periventricular lesions have been found to strongly correlate with severe impairment (Hagberg et al., 1989).

Extrapyramidal Cerebral Palsy

This type of CP involves problems with posture, involuntary movements, hypertonia, and rigidity (Nelson et al., 1994). Extrapyramidal CP can be further divided into choreoathetotic and dystonic CP.

Choreoathetotic Cerebral Palsy

This type of CP is characterized by involuntary movements that are very large and marked by slow, irregular, twisting movements seen mostly in the upper extremities. This type of CP has been most clearly associated with birth asphyxia and oxygen deprivation (Nelson et al., 1994). Use of ventilation and brain lesions due to asphyxia are frequently seen immediately after birth. Changes in the caudate nucleus are generally found, with cysts present where arteries and veins have swelled and neighboring cells are negatively affected (Volpe, 1987). Demyelinization is often present, with deviations in critical columns and neuronal loss in corticospinal tracts. An MRI study by Yokochi, Aiba, Kodama, and Fujimoto (1991) reported that a majority of children have basal ganglia, thalamic, and white matter lesions. In this subtype of CP, muscle tone will fluctuate between hypertonic, normal, and hypertonic. Choreiform movements are present in the face and limbs, and are asymmetric, involuntary, and uncoordinated (Nelson et al., 1994). Children with choreoathetotic CP frequently have speech production problems, with unexpected changes in rate and volume. The upper motor neuron unit appears to be affected, and this is frequently accompanied by seizures and cognitive retardation (Nelson et al., 1994).

Dystonic Cerebral Palsy

This form of CP is believed to be uncommon, with the trunk muscles being mostly affected. The trunk may be twisted and contorted, which affects the head's movement (Nelson et al., 1994).

Atonic Cerebral Palsy

Children with atonic CP have hypertonic and muscle weakness in the limbs. This type of CP is less common than the other subtypes and is associated with delayed developmental motor milestones. Its cause is unknown, and it is not known which brain region is affected in this subtype of CP (Nelson et al., 1994).

Ataxic Cerebral Palsy

Ataxic CP is associated with dysfunction of the cerebellum leading to difficulty with skilled movements (Hagberg, Hagberg, Olow, 1975). Hypotonia, poor fine motor skills, and clumsiness are seen and identified late in the first year of life. Walking develops very late (three or four years of age), and frequent falling is observed in children with ataxic CP (Nelson et al., 1994). Findings of brain pathology in ataxic CP are inconsistent. Some researchers have found abnormality in the cerebellar vermis (Bordarier & Aicardi, 1990), while others have found differences in the cerebral hemispheres (Miller & Cala, 1989).

Neuropsychological Aspects of Cerebral Palsy

Neurocognitive deficits seem to progress as high risk children mature (Majnemer, Rosenblatt, & Riley, 1994). In a study by Majnemer et al. (1994), 23 healthy and 51 high risk neonates were tested at birth, one year, and three years. Findings included 13 (7%) delayed at age one year, increasing to 39 percent at age three. Those subjects who were high risk *and* normal at the neonatal stage had the most favorable outcome. Additional studies have found a decline in abilities in life (ages 18–25 years) that is attributed to ongoing psychological stress rather than to medical reasons (Pirnm, 1992).

The finding that many children with CP have concomitant learning disabilities, cognitive retardation, and attention-deficit disorders has implications for educational planning (Blondis, Roizen, Snow, & Accardo, 1993). This result, coupled with the finding by Majnemer et al. (1994), indicates not only that the needs of these children are multiple, but that they become more evident as the child matures.

In addition, localization of brain damage also has an impact on the type of learning difficulties experienced by children with CP. Children with motor difficulties appear to be at higher risk for deficits in arithmetic and visual-spatial skills than those who do not have such difficulties (Roussounis, Hubley, & Dear, 1993). In a further study of motor effects on visuospatial abilities, Howard and Henderson (1989) found that compared to athetoid CP and normal children, children with spastic CP showed more difficulty in visual-spatial judgment.

These researchers also found that experience and training can improve skills dramatically.

Right-sided hemiplegia (left-hemisphere involvement) has been found to result in language impairment in girls, but not in boys (Carlsson et al., 1994). Similarly, in a study by Feldman, Janosky, Scher, and Wareham (1994) preschool boys with CP did not show language impairment. In children with right and left hemiplegia, both boys and girls showed significant impairment on nonverbal tasks. It was not clear why boys showed less language impairment. The extent to which these findings are related to other research showing gender differences between normal males and females for language lateralization is unknown. For example, Witelson (1990) indicates that women have more focused representation of language and speech functions in the anterior left frontal regions than men. Further research may add to our understanding of these gender differences in language deficits in children with CP.

Working memory, a skill associated with attention, has not been found to be an area of impairment for children with CP (White, Craft, Hale, & Park, 1994). White et al. (1994) taught children with spastic CP to utilize memory strategies such as covert and overt rehearsal in order to improve articulation skills. Impairment was found in phonemic discrimination in children with CP and speech impairment. Bishop, Brown, and Robson (1990) also reported that children with impaired speech and CP have difficulty discriminating same-different nonwords. There were no difficulties found in receptive language skills or in their ability to discriminate altered sounds in real words. Therefore, it appears that CP children with speech impairment do *not* show concomitant language problems, but do show phonological processing difficulty. Speech production ability has been found to correlate significantly with sound blending skills. Reading difficulties have not been found in this population to the same degree as arithmetic-based learning disabilities and visual-perceptual deficits (Rowan & Monaghan, 1989). This is somewhat surprising given the relationship between phonemic awareness deficits and reading disabilities in learning disabled samples. Reading deficits have also been shown in children who have both phonological and visuospatial deficits; so the absence of high rates of reading problems in CP groups is interesting.

Attentional skills in children with CP have been found to be deficient (Blondis et al., 1993). White et al. (1994) found that children with bilateral anterior lesions showed significant problems in focusing attention, while those with bilateral posterior lesions showed slower reaction times. These researchers interpreted their findings to indicate problems in visual attention when anterior lesions, particularly in the left hemisphere, occur. Using a dichotic listening paradigm, Hugdahl and Carlsson (1994) found significant auditory attentional difficulties in children with both left and right hemiplegia.

The most striking finding in the neuropsychology of CP children is the heterogeneity of problems experienced by this varied population. Early identification of CP, development of appropriate intervention program, and the use of a multidisciplinary team approach have been found to relate strongly to later success in school and life (Rowan & Monaghan, 1989). Kohn (1990) found a strong link between psychoeducational, family, and vocational support and positive outcome. She strongly recommends that pediatricians acquaint themselves with community resources and utilize early referrals to appropriate early childhood programs for young children with CP.

Psychosocial Correlates of Cerebral Palsy

Although parents of children with motor disabilities have been found to report more sadness, these symptoms have not been found to be strongly related to the child's rate of development or to parent-child interactions (Smith, Innocenti, Boyce, & Smith, 1993). Further studies of mothers with CP children have found that professionals who interact with these families disregard information provided by mothers (Case-Smith & Nastro, 1993). These difficulties are compounded by the frequent change in professionals who work with families. Perrin, Ayoub, and Willett (1993) found that mothers' feelings of control over their child's program were a potent predictor of the child's adjustment. This finding is important to consider when designing intervention programs for children with CP, and provides further evidence of the need for an integrated, transactional model.

Family interactions have been linked to the psychological adjustment of children, regardless of age and socioeconomic status (Perrin et al., 1993). Dallas, Stevenson, and McGurk (1993a) found that children with CP often are more passive and less assertive than their siblings and generally were treated as if they were younger than their chronological age. Maternal intervention between children with CP and siblings was found to be more common than with non-disabled siblings. Similarly, Dallas, Stevenson, and McGurk (1993b) found that the tendency toward sibling and maternal control of interactions resulted in lower self-efficacy and poorer development of social skills in children with CP.

The findings of Dallas et al. (1993a, 1993b) were supported by results of a study by King et al. (1993), who found lower self-efficacy and self-control on self-report measures in a group of male and female children with CP. Level of social self-efficacy was found to be a good predictor of the adolescent's later independence and persistence. A follow-up study of adults with motor disabilities found that they were more frequently unemployed, left the parental home at a later age than normal peers, and completed less schooling (Kokkonen et al., 1991). Recommendations were for earlier vocational training and support and additional family assistance for individuals with CP. Moreover, for adults who received such support in adolescence, self-esteem and self-efficacy measures have not found them to differ from typical adults (Magill-Evans & Restall, 1991). A cognitive-behavioral approach to social skills and assertiveness training appears to meet the needs of adolescents with CP.

Implications for Treatment

Many children with CP receive comprehensive services in educational settings, including physical and occupational therapy, language and communication therapy, and academic instruction (Thorogood & Alexander, 2007). Assistive technologies, including augmented communication devices, have revolutionized treatment options and the functional abilities of children with CP. Synthesized and augmented speech devices, specially designed computers and other electronic devices are commonly used.

Physical and occupational therapy often centers on movement therapy as well as adaptive equipment to improve motor development and mobility. Stretching, range of motion, progressive resistance and strengthening, postural and motor control are typical physical therapy activities (Thorogood & Alexander, 2007). Orthotic devices may also be helpful. Occupational therapy generally focuses on increasing daily living skills and may also incorporate adaptive equipment.

In a study to determine the effects of constraint-induced movement therapy, Sutcliffe, Gaetz, Logan, Cheyne, and Fehlings (2007) found increased motor function in a child with hemiplegia CP. Three weeks of therapy also produced changes in brain activity and cortical reorganization six months following therapy. This is the first study to document cortical reorganization and shows great promise for other children with hemiplegia CP.

Other researchers have established motor development curves for children with CP. Five distinct patterns of motor development were created after careful assessment of a full spectrum of CP in children from one to 13 years of age (Rosenbaum et al., 2002). These curves can be helpful for parents, therapists, and educators for planning short- and long-term treatment plans for children with CP, and to measure therapeutic progress.

Finally there are several medical treatments that may be necessary for some children with CP, including surgery to reduce spasticity, skeletal muscle relaxants and neuromuscular blocker agents (e.g., baclofen, dantrolene, diazepam, botulinum).

Conclusions

Children with CP are more different from one another than the same on neuropsychological measures. What they seem to have in common is the need for early intervention that is tailored to their specific needs and provides vocational and family support. A transactional approach is particularly relevant for this population given the findings that when psychoeducational objectives, vocational training, and parental support are interwoven, the child's later outcome is most optimal. For these children, the neuropsychologist needs to move beyond the diagnostic role into the role of advocate and counselor. The Americans with Disabilities Act of 1990 empowers disabled adults, children, and adolescents to gain the vocational and educational training needed for life success. The extent to which we can foster this kind of ecologically valid intervention may mean the difference between developing individuals who are self-reliant, self-sufficient, and independent or semi-independent.

References

Adams, J. S., Adams, P. E., Nguyen, D., Brunberg, J. A., Tassone, F., Zhang, W., et al. (2007). Volumetric brain changes in females with fragile X-associated tremor/ataxia syndrome (FXTAS). *Neurology, 69*, 851–859.

Aicardi, J. (1990). Epilepsy in brain-injured children with cerebral palsy. *Developmental Medicine in Clinical Neurology, 32*, 191–202.

Aldenkamp, A. P., Gutter, T., & Beun, A. M. (1992). The effect of seizure activity and paroxysmal electroencephalographic discharges on cognition. *Acta Neurologia, 86*(Supp. 140), 111–121.

Austin, J. K. (1988). Childhood epilepsy: Child adaptation and family resources. *Child and Adolescent Psychiatric Mental Health in Nursing, 1*, 18–24.

Austin, J. K., Risinger, M. W., & Beckett, L. A. (1992). Correlates of behavior problems in children with epilepsy. *Epilepsia, 33*, 115–122.

Benjamin, C. M., Colley, A., Donnai, D., Kingston, H., Harris, R., & Kerzin-Storrar, L. (1993). Neuro-fibromatosis type 1: Knowledge, experience, and reproductive decisions of affected patients and families. *Journal of Medical Genetics, 30*, 567–574.

Bennett-Levy, J., & Stores, G. (1984). The nature of cognitive dysfunction in school children with epilepsy. *Acta Neurologica Scandinavica, Supplement, 99*, 79–82.

Bernal, C. (2006). Managing difficult behavior in the acute setting. In H. K. Warner (Ed.), *Meeting the needs of children with disabilities: Families and professionals facing the challenges together* (pp. 119–128). New York: Routledge.

Besag, F. M. C. (1995). Epilepsy, learning, and behavior in childhood. *Epilepsia, 36* (Suppl. I), S5–63.

Bishop, D. V. M., Brown, B. D., & Robson, J. (1990). The relationship between phoneme discrimination, speech production, and language comprehension in cerebral-palsied individuals. *Journal of Speech and Hearing Research, 33*, 210–219.

Black, K., & Hynd, G. W. (1995). Epilepsy in the school aged child: Cognitive-behavioral characteristics and effects on academic performance. *School Psychology Quarterly, 10*, 345–358.

Blondis, T. A., Roizen, N. J., Snow, J. H., & Accardo, P. J. (1993). Developmental disabilities: A continuum. *Clinical Pediatrics, 32*, 492–498.

Bordarier, C., & Aicardi, J. (1990). Dandy-Walker syndrome and agenesis of the cerebellar vermis: Diagnostic problems and genetic counseling. A review. *Developmental Medicine Child Neurology, 32*, 285–294.

Brent, D. A., Crumrine, P. K., Varma, R. R., Allan, M. A., & Allman, C. (1987). Phenobaribitol treatment and major depressive disorder in children with epilepsy. *Pediatrics, 80*, 900–917.

Breslau, N. (1985). Psychiatric disorder in children with physical disabilities. *Journal of the American Academy of Child and Adolescent Psychiatry, 24*, 87–94.

Bundey, S., & Evans, K. (1969). Tuberous sclerosis: A genetic study of chronic proximal spinal muscular atrophy. *Brain, 98*, 45–72.

Carey, K. T., & Lesen, B. M. (1998). Phenylketonuria. In L. Phelps (Ed.), *A guide for understanding and educating health-related disorders in children and adolescents* (pp. 519–523). Washington, DC: American Psychological Association.

Carlsson, G., Uvebrant, P. Hugdahl, K., Arvidsson, J., Wiklund, L. M. & Von Wendt, L. (1994). Verbal and non-verbal function of children with right- versus left-hemiplegic cerebral palsy of pre-and perinatal origin. *Developmental Medicine and Child Neurology, 36*, 503–512.

Carr, E. G. (1985). Behavioral approaches to language and communication. In E. Shopler & G. Mesibov (Eds.), *Communication problems in autism* (pp. 37–57). New York: Plemun Press.

Case-Smith, J., & Nastro, M. A. (1993). The effect of occupational therapy intervention on mothers of children with cerebral palsy. *American Journal of Occupational Therapy, 47*, 811–4317.

Chalhub, E. G. (1976). Neurocutaneous syndromes in children. *Pediatric Clinics of North America, 23*, 499–516.

Christensen, E., & Melchior, J. (1967). Cerebral palsy–a clinical and neuropathological study. *Clinical Developmental Medicine, 25*, 1–10.

Chutorian, A. M., Michener, R. C., Defendini, R., Hilal, S. K., & Gamboa, E. T. (1979). Neonatal polycystic encephalomalacia: Four new cases and review of the literature. *Journal of Neurology, Neurosurgery, and Psychiatry, 42*, 154–160.

Cody, H., & Hynd, G. W. (1998). Sturge-Weber syndrome. In L. Phelps (Ed.), *A guide for understanding and educating health-related disorders in children and adolescents* (pp. 624–628). American Psychological Association: Washington, DC.

Cody, H., & Kamphaus, R. W. (1999). Down syndrome. In S. Goldstein & C. R. Reynolds (Eds.), *Handbook of neurodevelopmental and genetic disorders in children* (pp. 385–405). New York: Guilford Press.

Colver, A. F., Gibson, M., Hey, E. N., Jarvis, S. N., Mackie, P. C., & Richmond, S. (2000). Increasing rates of cerebral palsy across the severity spectrum in northeast England 1964–1993. *Archives of Disease in Childhood Fetal & Neonatal Edition, 83*(1), F7–F12.

Cook, E. H., & Leventhal, B. L. (1992). Neuropsychiatric disorders of childhood and adolescence. In S. C. Yudofsky & R. E. Hales (Eds.), *The American psychiatric press textbook of neuropsychiatry* (pp. 63–662). Washington, DC: American Psychiatric Press.

Cook, E. H., Rowlett, R., Jaselskis, C., & Leventhal, B. L. (1992). Fluoxetine treatment of patients with autism and mental retardation. *Journal of American Academy of Child and Adolescent Psychiatry, 31*, 73S745.

Crawford, D. C., Acuña, J. M., & Sherman, S. L. (2001). FMR1 and the fragile X syndrome: human genome epidemiology review. FMR1 and the fragile X syndrome: human genome epidemiology review. *Genetic Medicine 3*(5), 359–71.

Crothers, B., & Paine, R. S. (1959). *The natural history of cerebral palsy*. Cambridge, MA: Harvard University Press.

Cull, C. A. (1988). Cognitive function and behavior in children. In M. R. Trimble & E. H. Reynolds (Eds.), *Epilepsy: Behavior and cognitive function* (pp. 97–111). New York: Wiley.

Curatolo, P., Arpino, C., Stazi, M. A., & Medda, E. (1995). Risk factors for the co-occurrence of partial epilepsy, cerebral palsy, and mental retardation. *Developmental Medicine and Child Neurology, 3*(7), 776–782.

Dallas, E., Stevenson, J., & McGurk, H. (1993a). Cerebral-palsied children's interactions with siblings: I. Influence of severity of disability, age, and birth order. *Journal of Child Psychology and Psychiatry and Allied Disciplines, 34*, 621–47.

Dallas, E., Stevenson, J., & McGurk, H. (1993b). Cerebral-palsied children's interactions with siblings: 11. Interactional structure. *Journal of Child Psychology and Psychiatry and Allied Disciplines, 34*, 64–71.

Dammann, O., & Leviton, A. (2006). Infection remote from the brain, neonatal white matter damage, and cerebral palsy in the preterm infant. *Seminars in Pediatric Neurology, 5*(3), 190–201.

Davidson, B. L., Tarle, S. A., Van Antwerp, M., Gibbs, D. A., Watts, R. W., Kelly, W. N., et al. (1991). Identification of 17 independent mutations responsible for human hypoxanthineguanine phosphoriribosyl-transferase (HGPRT) deficiency. *American Journal of Human Genetics, 48*, 951–958.

Delgado-Escueta, A. V., Bascal, F. E., & Treiman, D. M. (1982). Complex partial seizures in closed-circuit television and EEG: A study of 691 attacks in 79 patients. *Annals of Neurology, 11*, 292–296.

Dill, F. J., Hayden, M. R., & McGillivray, B. (1992). *Genetics*. Baltimore, MD: Williams & Wilkins.

Dodson, W. E. (1993). Epilepsy and IQ. In W. E. Dodson & J. M. Pellock (Eds.), *Pediatric epilepsy: Diagnosis and therapy* (pp. 373–385). New York: Demos Publications.

Dooley, J. M., Camfield, P. R, Camfield, C. S., et al. (1990). Once-daily ethosuximide in the treatment of absence epilepsy. *Pediatric Neurology, 6*, 38–45.

Dreifuss, F. E. (1994). Partial seizures (focal and multifocal). In K. Swaiman (Ed.), *Pediatric neurology* (pp. 509–530). St. Louis, MO: Mosby.

DuPaul, G. W., McGoey, K. & Mautone, J. A. (2003). Pediatric pharmacology and psychopharmacology. In M. C. Roberts (Ed.), *Handbook of paediatric psychology* (pp. 234–252). NY: Guilford Press.

Dykens, E. M., Hodapp, R. M., Ort, S., Finacane, B., Shapiro, L. R., & Leckman, J. F. (1989). The trajectory of cognitive development in males with fragile X syndrome. *Journal of American Academy of Child and Adolescent Psychiatry, 28*, 422–426

Ellenberg, J. H., Hirtz, D. G., & Nelson, K. B. (1984). Age at onset of seizures in young children. *Annals of Neurology, 15,* 27–134.

Ellenberg, J. H., & Nelson, K. B. (1984). Cluster of perinatal events identifying infants at high risk for death or disability. *Journal of Pediatrics, 113,* 546–552.

Engidawork, E., & Lubec, G. (2003). Molecular changes in fetal Down syndrome brain. *Journal of Neurochemistry, 84(5),* 895–905.

Erickson, J. D., & Bjerkedal, T. (1981). Down's syndrome associated with father's age in Norway. *Journal of Medical Genetics, 18,* 22–28.

Ernest, M., Zametkin, A. J., Matochik, J. A., Pascualvaca, D., Jons, P. H., Hardy, K., et al. (1996). Presynaptic dopamine deficits in Lesch-Nyhan disease. *New England Journal of Medicine, 334*(24), 1568–1572.

Falconer, M. A., & Rushworth, R. G. (1960). Treatment of encephalotrigeminal angiomatosis (Sturge-Weber disease) by hemispherectomy. *Archives of Disease in Children, 35,* 43–47.

Falconer, J., Wada, J. A., Martin, W., et al. (1990). PET, CT, and MR imaging of neuronal migration abnormalities in epileptic patients. *Canadian Journal of Neurological Science, 17,* 35–39.

Falconer, M. A., & Wilson, P. J. E. (1969). Complications related to delayed haemorrhage after hemispherectomy. *Journal of Neurosurgery, 30,* 41–26.

Farwell, J. R., Dodrill, C. B., & Batzel, L. W. (1985). Neuropsychological abilities of children with epilepsy. *Epilepsia, 26,* 3–9

Fedio, P., & Mirsky, A. F. (1969). Selective intellectual deficits in children with temporal lobe or centrencephalic epilepsy. *Neuropsychologia, 7,* 395–400.

Fehrenbach, A. M. B., & Peterson, L. (1989). Parental problem solving skills, stress, and dietary compliance in phenyketonuria. *Journal of Consulting and Clinical Psychology, 57,* 237–241.

Feldman, H. M., Janosky, J. E., Scher, M. S., & Wareham, N. L. (1994). Language abilities following prematurity, perventribular brain injury, and cerebral palsy. *Journal of Communication Disorders, 27,* 71–4.

Fenton, G. W. (1972). Epilepsy and automatism. *British Journal of Hospital Medicine, 7,* 57–64.

Forsythe, I., Butler, R., Berg, I., & McGuire, R. (1991). Cognitive impairment in new cases of epilepsy randomly assigned to carbamazepine, phenytoin and sodium valporate. *Developmental Medicine and Child Neurology, 33,* 526–534.

Friedman, J. M., & McGillivray, B. (1992). Genetic paradigms in human disease. In J. M. Friedman, F. J. Dill, M. R. Hayden, & B. McGillivray (Eds.), *Genetics*. Baltimore, MD: Williams & Wilkins.

Freeman, J. M., Kossoff, E. H., & Hartman, A. L. (2007). The kerotogenic diet: One decade later. *Pediatric, 119,* 535–543.

Freeman, J. M., Vining, E. P. G., & Pillas, D. J. (2003). *Seizures and epilepsy in childhood: A guide for parents* (3rd ed.). Baltimore, MD: Johns Hopkins University Press.

Gilmore, D. H., & Aitken, D. A. (1989). Specific diagnostic techniques. In M. J. Whittle & J. M. Connor (Eds.), *Prenatal diagnosis in obstetric practice*. Boston: Blackwell Scientific Publications.

Ginther, D. W., & Fullwood, H. (1998). Klinefelter syndrome. In L. Phelps (Ed.), *A guide for understanding and educating health-related disorders in children and adolescents* (pp. 359–363). Washington, DC: American Psychological Association.

Goldgarber, D., Lerman, M. I., McBride, O. W., Saffiotti, U., & Gajdusek, D. C. (1987). Characterization and chromosomal location of a DNA encoding brain amyloid of Alzhemer's disease. *Science, 235,* 877–880.

Goldstein, S., & Reynolds, C. (1999). *Handbook of neurodevelopmental and genetic disorders in children.* NY: Guilford press.

Graham, J. M., Bashir, A. S., Stark, R. E., Silbert, A., & Walzer, S. (1988). Oral and written language abilities of **XXY**boys: Implications for anticipatory guidance. *Pediatrics, 81,* 795–806.

Grether, J. K., Cumrnins, S. K., & Nelson, K. B. (1992). The California cerebral palsy project. *Paediatric Perinatal Epidemiology, 6,* 335–351.

Grether, J. K., & Nelson, K. B. (1997). Maternal infection and cerebral palsy in infants of normal birth weight. *JAMA, 278*(3), 207–211.

Groesbeck, D. K., Bluml, R. M., & Kossoff, E. H. (2006). Long term use of the kerotogenic diet in the treatment of epilepsy. *Developmental Medicine and Child Neurology, 48*(12), 978–981.

Grumbach, M. M., & Conte, F. A. (1985). Disorders of sexual differentiation. In J. D. Wilson & D. W. Foster (Eds.), *Williams textbook of endocrinology* (7th ed., pp. 312–401). Philadelphia: W. B. Saunders.

Hagberg, B., Hagberg, G., & Olow, I. (1975). The changing panorama of cerebral palsy in Sweden 1954–1970: II Analysis of the various syndromes. *Acta Paediatrica Scandinavia, 73,* 433–438.

Hagberg, B., Hagberg, G., & Zetterstrom, R. (1989). Decreasing perinatal mortality-increase in cerebral palsy morbidity? *Acta Paediatrica Scandinavia, 78,* 664–670.

Hagerman, R. J., Murphy, M. A., & Wittenberger, M. D. (1988). A controlled trial of stimulant medication in children with the fragile X syndrome. *American Journal of Medical Genetics, 30,* 377–392.

Hanley, W. B., Linsoa, L., Davidson, W., & Moes, C. A. (1970). Malnutrition with early treatment of phenylketonuria. *Pediatric Research, 4,* 18–27.

Hartlage, P. L., & Hartlage, L. C. (1989). Neuropsychological aspects of epilepsy: Introduction and overview. In C. R. Reynolds & E. Fletcher-Janzen (Eds.), *Handbook of clinical child neuropsychology* (pp. 409–418). New York: Plenum Press.

Hartlage, L. C., & Telzrow, C. F. (1984). Neuropsychological aspects of childhood epilepsy. In R. Tarter & G. Goldstein (Eds.), *Advances in clinical neuropsychology* (pp. 159–179). New York: Plenum Press.

Heller, K. W., Alberto, P. A., Forney, P. E., & Schwartzman, M. N. (1996). *Understanding physical, sensory, and health impairments: Characteristics and educational implications.* Pacific Grove, CA: Brooks/Cole.

Henderson, C. B., Filloux, F. M., Alder, S. C., Lyon, J. L., & Caplin, D. A. (2006). Efficacy of the ketogenic diet as a treatment option for epilepsy: Meta-analysis. *Journal of Child Neurology, 21*(3), 193–198.

Hermann, B. P., Whitman, S., & Dell, J. (1988). Correlates of behaviour problems and social competence in children with epilepsy, aged 6–11. In B. P. Hermann & M. Seidenberg (Eds.), *Childhood epilepsies: Neuropsychological, psychosocial and intervention aspects* (pp. 143–158). New York: Wiley.

Hessl, D., Rivera, S., Koldewyn, K., Cordeiro, L., Adams, J., Tassone, F., Hagerman, P. J., & Hagerman, R. J. (2007). Amygdala dysfunction in men with the fragile X permutation. *Brain, 130*(2), 404–416.

Hoare, P., & Russell, M. (1995). The quality of life of children with chronic epilepsy and their families: Preliminary findings with a new assessment measure. *Developmental Medicine and Child Neurology, 37*, 689–696.

Hofman, K., Harris, E. L., Bryan, R. N., & Denckla, M. B. (1994). Neurofibromatosis type 1: The cognitive phenotype. *Journal of Pediatrics, 124*, Sl–48.

Horn, C. S., Ater, S. B., & Hurst, D. L. (1986). Carbamazepine-exacerbated epilepsy in children and adolescents. *Pediatric Neurology, 2*, 340–347.

Howard, E. M., & Henderson, S. E. (1989). Perceptual problems in cerebral-palsied children: A real-world example. *Human Movement Science, 8*, 141–160.

Hsu, L. Y. F. (1986). Prenatal diagnosis of chromosomal abnormalities. In A. Milunsky (Ed.), *Genetic disorders and the fetus* (2nd ed.). New York: Plenum Press.

Hugdahl, K., & Carlsson, G. (1994). Dichotic listening and focused attention in children with hemiplegic cerebral palsy. *Journal of Clinical and Experimental Neuropsychology, 16*, 84–92.

Huttenlocher, P. R., & Hapke, R. J. (1990). A follow-up study of intractable seizures in childhood. *Annals of Neurology, 28*, 699–705.

Hynd, G. W., & Willis, W. G. (1988). *Pediatric neuropsychology*. Orlando, FL: Grune & Stratton.

Ingram, T. T. S. (1955). A study of cerebral palsy in the childhood population of Edinburgh. *Archives of Disabled Children, 117*, 395.

Ingram, T. T. S. (1964). *Paediatric aspects of cerebral palsy*. Edinburgh: Churchill-Livingston.

Jankovic, J., Caskey, T. C., Stout, J. T., et al. (1988). Lesch Nyhan syndrome: A study of motor behavior and cerebrospinal fluid neurotransmitters. *Annals of Neurology, 23*, 466–469.

Johnston, M. V., & Hagberg, H. (2007). Sex and the pathogenesis of cerebral palsy. *Developmental Medicine & Child Neurology, 49*, 74–78.

Kang, H. C., Chung, D. E., Kim, D. W., et al. (2004) Early- and late-onset complications of the ketogenic diet for intractable epilepsy. *Epilepsia, 45*, 1116–24.

Kang, H. C., & Kim, H. D. (2006). Diet therapy in refractory pediatric epilepsy: Increased efficacy and tolerability. *Epileptic Disorders, 8*(4), 309–16.

King, G. A., Schultz, I. Z., Steel, K., Gilpin, M., & Cathers, T. (1993). Self-evaluation and self-concept of adolescents with physical disabilities. *American Journal of Occupational Therapy, 47*, 132–140.

Klaiman, R. S., & Phelps, L. (1998). Fraigle X syndrome. In L. Phelps (Ed.), *A guide for understanding and educating health-related disorders in children and adolescents* (pp. 299–308). Washington, DC: American Psychological Association.

Kohn, J. G. (1990). Issues in the management of children with spastic cerebral palsy. *Pediatrician, 17*, 230–236.

Kokkonen, J., Saukkonen, A. L., Timonen, E., Serlo, W., Kinnunen, P. (1991). Social outcome of handicapped children as adults. *Developmental Medicine and Child Neurology, 33*, 1095–1100.

Krageloh-Mann, I., Hagberg, B., Petersen, D., Riethmuller, J., Gut, E., Michaelis, R., (1992). Bilateral spastic cerebral palsy-pathogenetic aspects from MRI. *Neuropediatrics, 20*, 46–48.

Lechtenberg, R. (2002). *Epilepsy and the family: A new guide* (2nd ed.). Cambridge, MA: Harvard University Press.

Lee J., Croen L. A., Backstrand, K. H., Yoshida C. K., Henning, L. H., Lindan, C., et al. (2005). Maternal and infant characteristics associated with perinatal arterial stroke in the infant. *JAMA, 293*(6), 723–729.

LeFrancois, G. R. (1995).*An introduction to child development* (8th ed.). Belmont, CA: Wadsworth.

Leviton, A., & Paneth, W. (1990). White matter damage in preterm newborns-An epidemiologic perspective. *Early Human Development, 24*, 1–22

Lindsay, J., Ounstead, C., & Richards, P. (1979). Long-term outcome in children with temporal lobe seizures: *III.* Psychiatric aspects in childhood and adult life. *Developmental Medicine and Child Neurology, 21*, 63M36.

Liptak, G. S., O & Donnell, M., Conaway, M., Chumlea, W. C., Worley, G., Henderson, R. C., Fung, E., Stallings, V. A., Samson-Fang, L., Calvert, R., Rosenbaum, P., & Stevenson, R. D. (2007). Health status of children with moderate to severe cerebral palsy. *Developmental Medicine & Child Neurology, 43*(6), 364–370.

Listernick, R., & Charrow, J. (1990). Neurofibromatosis type 1 in childhood. *Journal of Pediatrics, 116*, 845–853.

Little, S. G., & Rodemaker, J. E. (1998). Lesch-Nyhan disease. In L. Phelps (Ed.), *A guide for understanding and educating health-related disorders in children and adolescents* (pp. 386–391). Washington, DC: American Psychological Association.

Liu, D. T. (1991). Introduction and historical perspectives. In D. T. Liu (Ed.), *A practical guide to chorion villus sampling*. New York: Oxford University Press.

Lockman, L. A. (1993, November). *Pediatric brain tumors: The role of the Pediatric Brain Tumor Task Force*. Paper presented at the Cancer Center Symposium on Cancer and the Nervous System, Minneapolis, MN.

Lockman, L. A. (1994). Absence seizures. In K. Swaiman (Ed.), *Pediatric neurology* (pp. 531–536). St. Louis, MO: Mosby.

Magill-Evans, J. E., & Restall, G. (1991). Self-esteem or persons with cerebral palsy: From adolescence to adulthood. *American Journal of Occupational Therapy, 45*, 819–825.

Majnemer, A., Rosenblatt, B., & Riley, P. (1994). Predicting outcome in high-risk newborns with a neonatal neurobehavioral assessment. *American Journal of Occupational Therapy, 48*, 723–732.

Mandoki, M. W., & Sumner, G. S., (1991). Klinefelter Syndrome: The need for early identification and treatment. *Clinical Pediatrics, 3*, 161–164.

Mastriani, K. S., Williams, V. C., Hulsey, T. C., Wheless, J. L., & Maria, B. L. (2008). Evidence-based versus reported epilepsy management practices. *Journal of Child Neurology, 23*(5), 507–514.

Matthews, W. S., Barabas, G., & Ferrai, M. (1982). Emotional concomitants of childhood epilepsy. *Epilepsia, 23*, 671–681.

Matthews, W. S., Barabas, G., & Ferrai, M. (1983). Achievement and school behavior in children with epilepsy. *Psychology in the Schools, 26*, 10–13.

Matthews, W. S., Solan, A., & Barabas, G. (1995). Cognitive functioning in Lesch-Nyhan syndrome. *Developmental Medicine and Child Neurology, 37*, 715–22.

Mautner, V. F., Tatagiba, M., Guthoff, R., Samii, M., & Pulst, S. M. (1993). Neurofibromatosis 2 in the pediatric age group. *Neurosurgery, 33*, 92–96.

Meyer, F. B., Marsh, W. R., Laws, E. R., & Sharbrough, F. W. (1986). Temporal lobectomy in children with epilepsy. *Journal of Neurosurgery, 64(33)*, 371–376.

McDonald, B. C., & Saykin, A. J. (2007). Functional magnetic neuroimaging in neurosurgical planning for temporal lobe epilepsy. In F. G. Hillary, & J. DeLuca (Eds.), *Functional neuroimaging in clinical populations* (pp. 185–218). NY: Guilford Press.

Michaels, K., Lopus, M., & Matalon, R. (1988). Phenylalanine metabolites as indicators of dietary compliance in children phenylketonuria. *Biochemical Medicine and Metabolic Biology, 39*, 18–23.

Miller, G., & Cala, L. A. (1989). Ataxic cerebral palsy Clinico-radiological correlations. *Neuropediatrics, 20*, 84–49.

Miller, M., & Hall, J. G. (1978). Possible maternal effect on severity of neurofibromatosis. *Lancet, 2*, 84–89.

Montgomery, J. W. (1992). Easily overlooked language disabilities during childhood and adolescence: A cognitive linguistic perspective. *Pediatric Clinics of North America, 39*, 513–524.

Morales, P. C. (1999). Lesch-nyhan syndrome. In S. Goldstein & C. Reynolds (Eds.), *Handbook of neurodevelopmental and genetic disorders in children* (pp. 478–498). New York: Guilford Press.

Nelson, K. B., & Leviton, A. (1991). How much of neonatal encephalopathy is due to birth asphyxia? *American Journal of Disabled Children, 145*, 132–1331.

Nelson, K. B., Swaiman, K. F., & Russman, B. S. (1994). Cerebral palsy. In K. F. Swaiman (Ed.), *Pediatric neurology* (pp. 471–488). St. Louis, MO: Mosby.

Neppe, V. M. (1985). Epilepsy and psychiatry: Essential links. *Psychiatric Insight, 2*, 18–22.

Neppe, V. M., & Tucker, G. J. (1992). Neuropsychiatric aspects of seizure disorders. In S. C. Yudofsky & R. E. Hales (Eds.), *The American psychiatric press textbook of neuropsychiatry* (2nd ed., pp. 397–425). Washington, DC: American Psychiatric Press.

Netley, C. (1987). Predicting intellectual functioning in 47, XXY boys from characteristics of siblings. *Clinical Genetics, 32*, 24–47.

NICHY. (2004). Epilepsy fact sheet. www.nichy.org/pubs/factshe/fs6.pdf.

Nielsen, J. (1991). *Klinefelter's syndrome: An orientation* (2nd ed.). Denmark: Novo Nordisk AIS.

NIH Down Syndrome. (2008). Facts about Down Syndrome. www.nichd.nih.gov/publications/pubs/downsyndrome.cfm.

NIH Fragile X Syndrome (2008). Facts about Fragile X Syndrome. www.nih.gov/publications/pubs/fragileX/sub1/cfm.

NIH Klinefelter Syndrome. (2008). Facts about Klinefelter Syndrome. www.nichd.nih.gov/publications/pubs/Klinefelter_syndrome.cfm.

NIH Neurofibromatosis. (2008). www.ninds.nih.gov/disorders/neurofibromatosis.htm.

NIH PKU (2008). Facts about PKU. www.nichd.nih.gov/health/topics/phenylketonuria.cfm.

NIH Seizures. (2008). Seizures and epilepsy: Hope through research. www.NINDS.NIH.gov/disorders/epilepsy/detail_epilepsy.htm.

NIH Tuberous Sclerosis. (2008). http://ghr.nlm.nih.gov/condition = tuberoussclerosis.

Nilsson, D. E., & Bradford, L. W. (1999). Neurofibromatosis. In S. Goldstein & C. Reynolds (Eds.), *Handbook of neurodevelopmental and genetic disorders in children* (pp. 350–367). New York: Guilford Press.

NINDS Cerebral Palsy, 2008). www.ninds.nih.gov/disorders/cerebral_palsy.htm.

NINDS Authors. (2008). Sturge Weber fact sheet. www.ninds.nih.gov/disorders/sturge_weber/sturge_weber.htm.

North, K., Joy, P., Yuille, D., Cocks, N., & Hutchins, P. (1995). Cognitive function and academic performance in children with neurofibromatosis type 1. *Developmental Medicine and Child Neurology, 37*, 427–436.

Nyhan, W. L. (1976). Behavior in the Lesch-Nyhan syndrome. *Journal of Autism and Childhood Schizophrenia, 6*, 235–252.

Odding, E., Roebroeck, M. E., & Stam, H. J. (2006). The Epidemiology of cerebral palsy: incidence, impairments and risk factors. *Disability Rehabilitation, 28*(4), 183–91.

O'Leary, D. S., Seidenberg, M., Berent, S., & Boll, T. J. (1981). The effects of age of onset of partial and generalized seizures on neuropsychological performance in children. *Journal of Nervous and Mental Disease, 141*, 624–629.

Ottman, R., Annegers, J. F., Hauser, W. A., Kurland, L. T., Dansky, L. V., Andermann, E., et al. (1989). Seizure risk in offspring of parents with generalized versus partial epilepsy. *Epilepsia, 30*, 157–165.

Pazzaglia, P., & Frank-Pazzaglia, L. (1976). Record in grade school of pupils with epilepsy: An epidemiological study. *Epilepsia, 17*, 361–366.

Pennington, B., Bender, B., Puck, M., Salbenblatt, J., & Robinson, A. (1982). Learning disabilities in children with sex chromosome anomalies. *Child Development, 53*, 1182–1192.

Perrin, E. C., Ayoub, C. C., & Willett, J. B. (1993). In the eyes of the beholder: Family and maternal influences on perceptions of adjustment of children with chronic illness. *Journal of Developmental and Behavioral Pediatrics, 14*, 94–105.

Phelps, L. (1998a). A guide to genetics. In L. Phelps (Ed.), *A guide for understanding and educating health-related disorders in children and adolescents* (pp. 6–14). Washington, DC: American Psychological Association.

Phelps, L. (1998b). Neurofibromatosis. In L. Phelps (Ed.), A guide to genetics. In L. Phelps (ed.), *A guide for understanding and educating health-related disorders in children and adolescents* (pp. 459–462). Washington, DC: American Psychological Association.

Phillips, S. A., & Shanahan, R. J. (1989). Etiology and mortality of status epilepticus in children: A recent update. *Archives of Neurology, 46*, 74–76.

Pirnm, P. (1992). Cerebral palsy: "A non-progressive disorder?" *Educational and Child Psychology, 9*, 27–33.

Ratcliffe, S. G., Butler, G. E., & Jones, M. (1990). Edinburgh study of growth and development of children with sex chromosome abnormalities. In J. A. Evans, J. L. Hamerton, & A. Robinson (Eds.), *Birth defects: Original article series: Vol. 26. Children and young adults with chromosome aneuploidy* (pp. 1–44). New York: Wiley-Liss.

Realmuto, G. M., Garfinkel, B. D., Tuchman, M., Tsai, M. Y., Chang, P.-N., Fisch, R. O., et al. (1986). Psychiatric diagnosis and behavioral characteristics of phenylketonuric children. *Journal of Nervous and Mental Disorders, 174*, 536–540.

Riccardi, V. M. (1992). *Neurofibromatosis, natural history, and pathogenesis*. Baltimore, MD: John Hopkins University Press.

Riccio, C. A., & Harrison, P. L. (1998). Tuberous sclerosis. . In L. Phelps (Ed.), *A guide for understanding and educating health-related disorders in children and adolescents* (pp. 683–690). Washington, DC: American Psychological Association.

Robinson, R. (1973). The frequency of other handicaps in children with cerebral palsy. *Developmental Medicine in Child Neurology, 15*, 305–312.

Robinson, A., Bender, B., & Linden, M. (1990). Summary of clinical findings in children and young adults with chromosome anomalies. In J. A. Evans, J. L. Hamerton, & A. Robinson (Eds.), *Birth defects: Original article series: Vol. 26 Children and young adults with sex chromosome aneuploidy* (pp. 225–228). New York: Wiley-Liss.

Rosenbaum, P. L., Walter, S. D., Hanna, S. E., Palisano, R. J., Russell, D. J., Raina, P., et al. (2002). Prognosis for gross motor function in cerebral palsy: Creation of motor development curves. *JAMA, 288*, 1357–1363.

Roussounis, S. H., Hubley, P. A., & Dear, P. R. (1993). Five-year-follow-up of very low birthweight infants: Neurological and psychological outcome. *Child Care, Health and Development, 19*, 45–49.

Rowan, N., & Monaghan, H. (1989). Reading achievement in pupils with cerebral palsy (hemiplegia). Special Issue: Dyslexia: Current research issues. *Irish Journal of Psychology, 10*, 615–621.

Sachs, H. T., & Barrett, R. P. (1995). Seizure disorders: A review for school psychologists. *School Psychology Review, 24*, 131–145.

Sandberg, D., & Barrick, C. (1995). Endocrine disorders in childhood: A selective survey of intellectual and educational sequelae. *School Psychology Review, 24*, 146–170.

Sato, S., Dreifuss, F. E., Penry, J. K. et al. (1983). Long-term follow-up of absence seizures. *Neurology, 33*, 1590–1600.

Sato, S., White, B. G., Penry, J. K., et al. (1982). Valporic acid versus ethosuximide in the treatment of absence *seizures. Neurology, 32*, 157–165.

Seidenberg, M. (1988). Neuropsychological functioning of children with epilepsy. In B. P. Hermann & M. Seidenberg

(Eds.), *Childhood epilepsies: Neuropsychological, psychosocial and intervention aspects* (pp. 71–81). New York: Wiley.

Seidenberg, M., Beck, N., Geisser, M., Giordani, B., et al. (1986). Academic achievement of children with epilepsy. *Epilepsia, 27*, 75S759.

Seidman, D. S., Paz, I., Laor, A., Gale, R., Stevenson, D. K., & Danon, Y. L. (1991). Apgar scores and cognitive performance at 17 years of age. *Obstetrics and Gynecology, 77*, 875–78.

Shapiro, B. (1992). Normal and abnormal development. In M. L. Batshaw & Y. M. Perret (Eds.), *Children with disabilities: A medical primer*. Baltimore, MD: Paul H. Brooks.

Shaw, E. D., & Beals, R. K. (1992). The hip joint in Down's syndrome: A study of its structure and associated disease. *Clinical Orthopaedics and Related Research, 278*, 100–107.

Shinwell, E. S., Karplus, M., Reich, D., Weintraub, Z., Blazer, S., Bader, D., et al. (2000). Early postnatal dexamethasone treatment and increased incidence of cerebral palsy. *Archives of Disease in Childhood Fetal & Neonatal Edition, 83*(3), F177–F181.

Sillanpaa, M. (1992). Epilepsy in children: Prevalence, disability and handicap. *Epilepsia, 33*, 444–449.

Silverstein, F. S., & Johnston, M. V. (1990). Neurological assessment of children: The damaged child. In R. D. Eden, F. H. Boehm, & M. Haire (Eds.), *Assessment and care of the fetus: Physiological, clinical, and methodological principles*. Nonvalk, CT: Appleton & Lange.

Singhi, P. D., Bansal, U., Singhi, S., & Pershad, D. (1992). Determinants of IQ profile in children with idiopathic generalized epilepsy. *Epilepsia, 33*, 1106–1114.

Smith, M. N. (1989). Reading without speech: A study of children with cerebral palsy. Special Issues: Dyslexia: Current research issues. *Irish Journal of Psychology, 10*, 601–614.

Smith, T. B., Innocenti, M. S., Boyce, G. C., & Smith, C. S. (1993). Depressive symptomatology and interaction behaviors of mothers having a child with disabilities. *Psychological Reports, 73*, 1184–1186.

Smith, A., Walker, M. L., & Myers, G. (1988). Hemispherectomy and diaschisis: Rapid improvement in cerebral functions after right hemispherectomy in a six year old child. *Archives of Clinical Neuropsychology, 3*, 1–4.

Stacey, N. C., Ma, M. H. Y., & Daley, J. A. (2000). Abnormalities in cellular adhesion of neuroblastoma and fibroblast models of Lesch Nyhan Syndrome. *Neuroscience, 98(2)*, 397–401.

Stoll, B. J., Hansen, N. I., Adams-Chapman, I., Fanaroff, A. A., Hintz, S. R., Vohr, B., et al. (2004). Neurodevelopmental and growth impairment among extremely low-birth-weight infants with neonatal infection. *JAMA, 292*(19), 2357–2401.

Strauss, D., & Eyman, R. (1996). Mortality of people with mental retardation in California with and without Down syndrome, 1986–1991. *American Journal of Mental Retardation, 100*, 643–651.

Sutcliffe, T. L., Gaetz, W. C., Logan, W. J., Cheyne, D. O., & Fehlings, D. L. (2007). Cortical reorganization after modified constraint-induced movement therapy in pediatric hemiplegic cerebral palsy. *Journal of Child Neurology, 22*(11), 1281–1287.

Szymonowicz, W., Preston, H., & Yu, V. Y. (1986). The surviving monozygotic twin. *Archives of Disabled Children, 61*, 454–458.

Teeter, P. A. & Semrud-Clikeman, M. (1998). Seizure disorders. In L. Phelps (ed.), *A guide for understanding and educating health-related disorders in children and adolescents* (pp. 583–595). Washington, DC: American Psychological Association.

Tellez-Zenteno, J. F., & Dhar, R., & Wiebe, S. (2005). Long-term seizure outcome following epilepsy surgery: A systematic review of meta-analysis. *Brain, 128*(5), 1188–1198.

Thorogood, C., & Alexander, M. A. (2007). Cerebral palsy. www.emedicine.com/pmr/topic24.htm.

Uvebrandt, P. (1988). Hemiplegic cerebral palsy aetiology and outcome. *Acta Paediatrica Scandinavia, 345* (Suppl.), 1–100.

Vining, E. P. G., Mellits, D., Dorsen, M. M., Cataldo, M. F., Quaskey, S. A., Spielberg, S. P., et al. (1987). Psychologic and behavioral effects of antiepileptic drugs in children: A double-blind comparison between phenobarbitol and valporic acid. *Pediatrics, 80*, 165–174.

Volpe, J. J. (1987). *Neurology of the newborn* (2nd ed.). Philadelphia: W. B. Saunders.

Volpe, J. J. (1992). Value of MR in definition of the neuropathology of cerebral palsy in vivo. *American Journal of Neuroradiology, 13*, 7 M.

Waisbren, S. E. (1999). Phenylketonuria. In S. Goldstein, & C. R. Reynolds (Eds.), *Handbook of neurodevelopmental and genetic disorders in children* (pp. 433–458). New York; Guilford Press.

Watts, R. W., Spellacy, E., Gibbs, D. A. Allsop, J., McKeran, R. O., & Slavin, G. E. (1982). Clinical, post-mortem, biochemical and therapeutic observations on the Lesch-Nyhan syndrome with particular reference to the neurological manifestations. *Quarterly Journal of Medicine, 51*, 43–78.

White, D. A., Craft, S., Hale, S., & Park, T. S. (1994). Working memory and articulation rate in children with spastic diplegic cerebral palsy. *Neuropsychology, 8*, 180–186.

Whittle, N., Satori, S., Dierssen, M., Lubec, G., & Singewald, N. (2007). Fetal down syndrome brains exhibit aberrant levels of neurotransmitters critical for normal brain development. *Pediatrics, 120(6)*, 1465–1471.

Williams, J., & Sharp, G. B. (2000). Epilepsy. In K. O. Yeates, M. D. Ris, & H. G. Taylor (Eds.), *Pediatric neuropsychology: Research, theory, and practice* (pp. 47–73). New York: Guilford Press.

Williamson, M. L., Koch, R., Azen, C., & Chang, C. (1981). Correlates of intelligence test results in heated phenylketonuric children. *Pediatrics, 68*, 161–167.

Wilson, E. R., Mirra, S., & Schwartz, J. F. (1982). Congenital diencephalic and brain stem damage: Neuropathologic study of three cases. *Acta Neuropathologica, 57*, 70–74.

Witelson, S. (1990). Structural correlates of cognitive function in the human brain. In A. B. Scheibel & A. F. Wechsler (Eds.), *Neurobiology of higher cognitive function* (pp. 167–184). New York: Guilford Press.

Wolf-Schein, E. G. (1992). On the association between Fragile X chromosome, mental handicap, and autistic disorder. *Developmental Disabilities Bulletin, 20*, 13–30.

Wu, Y. W., & Colford, J. M. (2000). Chorioamnionitis as a risk factor for cerebral palsy: A meta-analysis. *JAMA, 284*(11), 1417–1424.

Yokochi, K., Aiba, K., Kodama, M., & Fujimoto, J. M. (1991). Magnetic resonance imaging in athetotic cerebral palsied children. *Acta Paediatrica Scandinavia, 80*, 818–4323.

Yoon, B. H., Romero, R., Park, J. S., Kim, C. J., Kim, S. H., Choi, J. H., Han, T. R. (2000). Fetal exposure to an intra-amniotic inflammation and the development of cerebral palsy at the age of three years. *American Journal of Obstetrics & Gynecology, 182(3)*, 675–681.

Young, G., Segalowitz, J., Misek, P., Alp, I. E., & Boulet, R. (1983). Is early reaching left-handed? Review of manual specialization research. In G. Young, S. J. Segalowitz, C. Corter, & S. E. Trehaub (Eds.), *Manual specialization and the developing brain* (pp. 13–32). New York: Academic Press.

Chapter 14
Acquired Neurological Disorders and Diseases of Childhood

Though relatively rare compared to neurodevelopmental disorders, acquired neurological disorders and diseases represent some of the more common disorders seen by child clinical neuropsychologists. This chapter uses a transactional neuropsychological approach to review traumatic brain injury in children; exposure to teratogenic agents, including alcohol and cocaine; childhood cancer, and infectious diseases of the CNS, including meningitis and encephalitis. Research into these various disorders and diseases suggests the need for a transactional approach to assessing and treating children with these neurological conditions. Such an approach is particularly appropriate given the complexity of these disorders as well as the long-term effects that are present during and following recovery.

injury is from impact and is localized to a specific region of the brain. Diffuse injury is the result of shearing white matter and gray matter due to the acceleration/deceleration of the brain and is often seen as a result of car accidents or severe falls. In diffuse injury the axons are stretched and distorted and the child often falls into a coma from the neuronal damage. The main structures involved are important for information processing and involve the transfer of information from one area of the brain including the corpus callosum, internal capsule, cerebellum, frontal and temporal lobes. Seizures are not uncommon as a result of head trauma and most children are either carefully monitored following the injury or are placed on antiepileptic medications as a precaution.

Traumatic Brain Injury

Traumatic brain injury (TBI) is a relatively common occurrence in childhood. There are two types of head injury: closed and open. An open head injury involves an open type of wound and is caused by a missile or some type of object penetrating the skull and entering the brain. These types of injuries are rarer than closed head injuries and will not be discussed in this text in any great detail. For a closed head injury the child's head has struck another surface or is a result of child abuse such as in shaken baby syndrome. For a head trauma to occur it is generally the result of acceleration/deceleration forces with or without impact of the skull. The head injury may be either diffuse or focal. Focal

Neurobehavioral Sequelae of Head Injury

The neurobehavioral sequelae of head injury may include declines in nonverbal intelligence; visual-motor impairment; attentional and memory deficits; decreases in oral fluency, comprehension, and verbal association; achievement declines in reading, and an increase in psychiatric disorders (Coelho, 2007; Tonks, Williams, Frampton, Yates, & Slater, 2007). Obviously, deficits will vary among children depending on their age at injury and on the nature, type, and severity of injury sustained. The extent to which TBI alters brain development and functional capacity of the CNS depends on a variety of factors, including the age of injury, the etiology and severity of the injury sustained, the neurological

M. Semrud-Clikeman, P.A. Teeter Ellison, *Child Neuropsychology*, DOI 10.1007/978-0-387-88963-4_14,
© Springer Science+Business Media, LLC 2009

complications, and the treatment protocol. These factors are reviewed in the following sections.

Incidence

The incidence of children and adolescents experiencing TBI has increased and head injury has become the leading cause of death in those under age 35, with children under 15 years of age with head injuries accounting for over half of the deaths due to trauma (Fletcher, Ewing-Cobbs, Francis, & Levin, 1995). The incidence of TBI is approximately 180 per 100,000 for children and adolescents aged 1–15 years (Langlois, Rutland-Brown, & Thomas, 2004). Of this number 475,000 are children between the ages of 0–14 years, and 160,000 are between 15 and 19 (Jantz & Coulter, 2007). This incidence is significantly higher than deaths from the second leading cause of death, childhood leukemia. For those children who do not die from their injuries, a significant proportion results in learning and behavioral difficulties.

Of those children with severe TBI, 80 percent have educational needs or require modified educational environments two years post-injury (Rao & Lyketsos, 2000). Behavioral difficulties are also relatively prevalent even among those children with mild head injuries (Stavinhoa, 2005). The majority of children admitted alive to the hospital are discharged with a prognosis for good recovery. However, good recovery does not mean full recovery and many of the children have been later found to develop temporary to permanent difficulties in cognition, memory, or physical disability (Semrud-Clikeman, 2001).

Age

The age of the child is closely related to the type of injury sustained. For the youngest children severe head trauma is generally due to child abuse or car accidents. For those between four and 11 the cause is generally due to pedestrian and bike accidents, while for teenagers it is generally due to automobile accidents that involve teenage drivers. For infants and toddlers the most common cause of head

trauma is a fall with few long-term consequences. Severe head trauma at this age is generally due to child abuse or automobile injury. For young children through elementary school the most common type of head injury is pedestrian and bicycle accidents. For teenagers injury is generally due to automobile accidents particularly when the teenager is the driver.

Age is an important variable in understanding the sequelae that follow TBI. Younger children show different patterns of recovery and future learning is more impacted due to the incomplete development. An injury that occurs at an early age is generally associated with more significant deficits than one that occurs later on (Morgan, Ward, Murdoch, Kennedy, & Murision, 2003). In this case, the developing brain may be more vulnerable to damage due to the rapid growth spurts that occur during early development. In addition, the early ages are most vulnerable because the child is learning so many new things. With neuronal disruption, such learning is not present and key structures such as the hippocampus and others that are responsible for new learning may be damaged. Research has indicated that damage occurring prior to age one results in significant impairment because there is little that has been previously learned including language. From the ages of 1–5 years of age reorganization of functions and recovery of language ability appear to be more likely. Damage after the age of five is also problematic as the brain is not as plastic as it was earlier and, thus, reorganization is not as readily obtained.

Structures that do not generally develop until later in life may be compromised by early damage and this injury may not be obvious until years later (Baron, 2008). Executive functioning tasks that develop with myelination are particularly vulnerable to damage from head injury. These abilities allow the adolescent to self-monitor behavior, have insight into behavior, and integrate information from simultaneous sources.

Child abuse is the most common reason for head injury in infants with 64% of infant head injuries due to abuse (Starling, Sirotnak, Heisler, & Barnes-Eley, 2007). Injury rates decrease for females during the first 15 years, while incidence rates increase for males between five and 15 years. Children and adolescents may be at risk for TBI as a result of sports activities, including football and soccer.

Nature, Type, and Severity of Injury

The nature, type, and severity of brain injury affect the outcome and long-term sequelae associated with such injury in children. Further, injury type (e.g., falling versus being hit on the head) may produce very different cognitive, behavioral, and neuropsychological impairment, which should be carefully assessed and monitored. The mechanisms of closed head injury involve several factors, including compression of neural tissues, which are pushed together; tension as tissues are torn apart; shearing as tissues slide over other tissue, and skull deformations that change the volume of cerebrospinal fluid (Semrud-Clikeman, 2001).

Brain injury may occur in three basic ways. First, acceleration occurs when a moving object (e.g., baseball bat) makes sudden contact with the skull. This type of injury may result in bruising or contusions in the brainstem, under the corpus callosum, in the cerebellum, or in the occipital lobes. Contre coup is common in these conditions and results in more severe damage in regions opposite the point of contact. McCrea (2008) indicates that pressure waves spread out from the injury site and cause tissue tearing. The frontal lobes are particularly sensitive to this kind of injury because of the bony protrusions in the anterior skull. Second, deceleration occurs when the head is moving faster than a stationary object (e.g., the dashboard of an automobile), causing abrupt deceleration of the skull. Contusions occur at the site of injury, and contre coup may also result as the brain is thrust back against the skull. Occipital impact may cause frontal and temporal involvement. Midbrain injury also may involve temporal lobe injury to the opposite lobe, while impact to the frontal regions is less likely to result in occipital damage because the surface of the posterior skull is smooth (McCrea, 2008). Third, rotations of the neck or head may occur when there is both acceleration and deceleration, and this rotation results in shearing. Although the skull is less rigid in children than in adults, shearing may still cause significant distortions and damage.

There are basically three levels of head injury. The Glasgow Coma Scale (GCS) (Jennett & Teasdale, 1981) is frequently utilized to ascertain the level of head injury. The child's level of

Table 14.1 Glasgow coma scale

Behavior	Points
Eye Opening (E)	
Spontaneous	4
In response to speech	3
In response to pinprick (pain)	2
No response	1
Motor (M)	
Follows commands	6
Can localize pain	5
Withdraws from painful stimulus	4
Abnormal flexion to pain	3
Extensor response to pain	2
No response	1
Verbal (V)	
Oriented	5
Confused conversation	4
Inappropriate words	3
Incomprehensible sounds	2
No response	1

Coma Score = E + M + V
Source: Jennett & Teasdale (1981)

consciousness and response is evaluated by this scale and is predictive of recovery and disability level. It assesses nonverbal response to stimuli, motor responses, and verbal responses, and ranges from a score of 3–15. A higher score is desirable. Table 14.1 presents the behaviors assessed by the GCS.

The duration of impaired consciousness is used to gauge severity of head trauma and involves the number of days from the injury until the child is able to follow commands. Severe injuries are generally seen when impaired consciousness exceeds 24 hours. The highest rates of fatality are for those patients with a GCS of eight or less (Donders, 2007). The time required for the child to be able to understand time and spatial orientation as well as memory for prior events [post-traumatic amnesia (PTA)] is another measure of the injury's severity.

Levels of Head Injury

Mild head injury compromises approximately 50–75 percent of all traumatic head injuries (Semrud-Clikeman, 2001). Many of these are not fully evaluated by medical personnel or are dismissed as non-remarkable. Mild head injuries are those that result in a loss of consciousness, or PTA, for less than one hour and a GCS score of 13–15. Many children have minor blows to the head throughout development that are not considered problematic by most personnel and are not often evaluated. Research has generally not supported long-term neuropsychological deficits as present from mild injury (Anderson & Yeates, 2007). Mild head injuries may be accompanied by headache, lethargy, irritability, withdrawal, and/or lability.

For head injuries where the loss of consciousness or PTA lasts from one to 24 hours, with a GCS score of 9–12, the injury is considered moderate in nature. Headache, memory deficits, and behavioral difficulties persist over time as the child recovers from the head injury. In addition, secondary symptoms such as hematomas and edema (brain swelling) that require surgery are more frequently present than for mild head injury. Early signs include difficulty with problem solving, memory, and attention/concentration which often improve with time (Yeates et al., 2007).

Severe head injury is one with a loss of consciousness or PTA for more than 24 hours and a GCS of 3–8. Medical treatment is often immediate and intensive, and roughly half of the children brought to the emergency room with severe head injuries die (Wade et al., 2008). For those who survive, the deficits are more severe both physically and neuropsychologically. Children with severe head injury remain in the hospital and often have additional injuries.

Recovery for children with severe head injuries is often compromised with intellectual impairment and co-occurring psychiatric disabilities. School achievement is problematic and difficulties are found in naming objects and/or pictures, verbal fluency and writing skills (Yeates et al., 2004). Additional deficits in memory, mathematics, attention, and organization have repeatedly been found with children suffering from severe head injuries (Ayr, Yeates, & Enrile, 2005). The length of the coma is associated with enduring cognitive impairment, and the ability to return to school after a longer coma is associated with poorer outcome (Yeates et al., 2005).

Adults generally regain the skills that will be obtained within 180 days of injury; the likely extent of recovery will be present within 6–9 months of the injury (Lezak, Howieson, & Loring, 2004). For children, recovery from severe TBI can span 5–6 years post-injury with most improvement seen within 2–3 years after injury (Draper, Ponsford, & Schonberger, 2007).

Unilateral Damage

The effects of lateralized damage has been investigated extensively and it has been found that functional loss following injury may be recovered by the intact hemisphere when injury occurs early (Donders, 2007). While the right hemisphere can assume language functions following damage to the left hemisphere, it does so at the expense of reduced right hemisphere (i.e., visual-spatial) functions. Thus, transfer of language occurs primarily when the speech regions of the left hemisphere are involved. In instances where the Broca's area remains intact, the left hemisphere may reorganize rather than transfer language functions to the right hemisphere.

Although the two hemispheres are functionally specialized at birth, both are relatively flexible in their capacity to pick up functions for the hemisphere that has been surgically removed (Lettori et al., 2008). The price of transfer, however, seems to be a loss of higher level abilities and generalized lower intelligence. For example, simple language functions appear intact following left hemispherectomy, but complex language skills (e.g., complex syntax) are compromised. Conversely, right hemispherectomy results in normal language functions and decreased complex visual-spatial skills (e.g., visual organization, perception of mazes) (Fournier, Calverley, Wagner, Poock, & Crossley, 2008). Thus, while both hemispheres can assume functions of the opposite hemisphere if it has been removed early, neither can mediate all of these functions. While these findings support the notion of brain plasticity, Fournier et al. (2008) cite studies indicating that surgical removal of one hemisphere following injury may actually produce fewer problems than when surgical removal is not feasible. It may be that the damaged hemisphere exerts abnormal influence as the intact hemisphere attempts to assume the functions of the damaged hemisphere, an influence that is not possible when the damaged hemisphere is removed.

Transactional Features of TBI

The neuropsychological, academic, and psychosocial sequelae of TBI depend on numerous factors (e.g., age, severity and site of injury). Further, environmental and premorbid status, including IQ level and presence of psychiatric or behavioral problems, is an important factor affecting outcome. Table 14.2 presents a summary of select research findings for children sustaining TBI. This summary suggests that a variety of domains are affected by traumatic injury. Individual children will vary in terms of the specific features and dysfunctions manifested following injury. The various domains are reviewed next.

Genetic Factors

Although traumatic brain injury is not a result of genetic factors, there is some evidence that certain children may be at higher risk for sustaining brain injury. In a discussion of risk factors associated with TBI, Goldstein and Levin (1990) indicate that children who sustain injuries may not be a random group. Preexisting conditions often include hyperactivity and antisocial behavioral problems; developmental learning problems, particularly in young males; reading difficulties, impulsivity, and overactivity (Farmer et al., 2002; Max et al., 2004; Yeates et al., 2005). Preexisting behavioral patterns may increase risk taking behaviors leading to traumatic injuries and exacerbating previous psychiatric diagnoses (Hayman-Abello, Rourke, & Fuerst, 2003; Max, Robertson, & Lansing, 2001).

Prenatal Postnatal Factors

There are no known prenatal factors that predispose a child to TBI, although brain damage can occur during the birth process. Postnatal factors generally are most important, including both child and family characteristics associated with increased rates of TBI in children. The level of violence and child-related homicides appears to be on the rise, and one can only wonder how many children and adolescents sustain TBI as a result of gunshot wounds and physical attacks.

Parental behaviors, avoidable situations such as drinking and driving or not restraining children while driving, may also place children at risk for TBI. However, family socioeconomic status and parental employment history do not appear related to increased rates of TBI, but these variables may increase problems during recovery and exacerbate neuropsychological deficits (Donders, 2007). Child abuse victims do sustain high levels of brain injury, especially among young children (Anderst, 2008).

Neuropsychological Correlates

Neuropsychological correlates usually relate to the major areas that have been damaged. Patterns of neuropsychological performance of children with head injury begin to mimic those of adults when injury is sustained in late childhood or early adolescence (Armstrong, Allen, Donohue, & Mayfield, 2008). Particular issues that arise in severe head injury for children are in the domains of attention, memory, and executive functioning. The following sections discuss neuropsychological domains involved in TBI in more detail.

Intellectual, Perceptual, Memory, and Attentional Functions

Intellectual Functions

Persistent intellectual deficits have been found in children sustaining brain injury with coma status for more than 24 hours (Wood & Rutherford, 2006). Performance IQ is lower than Verbal IQ in children suffering posttraumatic amnesia, particularly with lower Glasgow Coma scores (7 or less) and with severe head injury (Campbell, Kuehn, Richards, Venuevra, & Hutchison, 2004). Specifically, on the WISC lower scores on the processing speed (PS) and the perceptual organization (PO) factors relate to the severity of TBI (Donders, 1997; Donders & Warschausky, 1996). Further study comparing moderate and severe head injury

Table 14.2 Transactional features of traumatic brain injury in children

Genetic	*Environmental*
– No genetic linkage	– No known prenatal factors
– TBI children may not be random group	– Birth process may produce brain damage
• Hyperactivity	– Level of violence in environment
• Antisocial behavioral problems	– Parental behaviors place child at risk
• Reading problems, impulsivity, and hyperactivity	• Child abuse
	• Drinking while driving
	• Not restraining child in car

Neuropsychological Correlates
- Patterns depend on site and type of injury.
- Begin to mimic adult patterns in later childhood.
- Mild injury show few NP deficits

Intelligence	*Perceptual*	*Memory*
– Persistent deficits coma (24 hrs +)	– Severity of injury	– Common in TBI
– PIQ >VIQ with amnesia	– Timed conditions	– Verbal learning and memory
– Low PIQ with low Glascow (7 or less)	– Visual-spatial	– Visual-spatial
– Less specific cognitive deficits		– Selective reminding
– Laterlized damage not always clear-cut		– Memory improves first year
– Left hemisphere—language deficits		– Verbal learning of new information deficits persist with severe injury
– Right hemisphere—design deficits		– Even mild injury can affect
– Laterlization of higher level skills not always predictable		
– Laterlization of sensory-perceptual and motor deficits more clear-cut		

Attentional and Executive Functions
- Disinhibition
- Impulsivity
- Attentional deficits
- Excessive verbalization
- Socially inappropriate
- Insensitivity

Academic	*Psychosocial*	*Family*
– Not well researched	– Changes in personality	– Discruptive to relationships
– Recognized as handicapping condition (IDEA, 1990)	– Increased psychiatric disorders in severe injury (not mild)	– Home environment impacts
– Problems persist after EEGs and neurological exams appear normal		
– Language difficulties		
– Writing to dictation and copying		
– Verbal associations		
– Left hemisphere damage—deficits across all areas (injury before 5 years of age)		

found statistically lower scores on the perceptual organization and processing speed factors of the WISC III for the severe group, but not for the mild and moderate groups (Donders & Warschausky, 1996). Moreover, selective impairment on the PO and PS indices was found to be specific to the TBI group, but not to the WISC III standardization sample (Donders, 1996; Hoffman, Donders, & Thompson, 2000).

While personality factors following injury in children are somewhat similar to patterns found in adults, the cognitive deficits appear less specific and not as clearly lateralized (Max et al., 2001). For example, there is only a mild tendency for injury to the left hemisphere to produce language-related deficits, and for right hemisphere injury to produce deficits in memory for designs. Donders and Warschausky (1996) found a distinct pattern on intelligence testing where children scoring poorly on the PO and PS indices showed a disproportionate incidence in the severe head injury group. This group, as a whole, showed diffuse lesions on CT/

MRI with lesions mostly present in the right hemisphere. Because these children experienced more difficulty on tasks that required visual-spatial reasoning (perceptual organization index) and processing speed, it was suggested from these findings that damage to the right hemisphere was related to these difficulties.

IQ abilities also change over time with decreasing IQ seen in children with focal lesions and with those experiencing damage prior to the age of three (Donders, 2007; Semrud-Clikeman, 2001). These differences are present to a lesser degree for older children and adolescents. Gains in ability have been found after recovery and are maintained into adulthood (Campbell et al., 2004). A quantitative MRI study of moderate and severe closed head injury found structural differences in patients with IQs less than 90 with enlarged ventricles and atrophy in the temporal regions (Bigler, Johnson, & Blatter, 1999). Those with higher IQs did not show compromised structures.

Academic and School Adjustment

Children with TBI have difficulties with language and reading, arithmetic calculation, writing, and spelling (Levin, Ewing-Cobbs, & Eisenberg, 1995). Studies have found significant difficulties in reading recognition, spelling and arithmetic scores in children with severe head injury compared to those with mild to moderate TBI (Arroyos-Jurado, Paulsen, Merrell, Lindgren, & Max, 2000; Ewing-Cobbs et al., 2004). Significant long-term effects were found for reading, arithmetic and spelling with the most significant weaknesses present in children with the more severe injury. Impairment was also seen for children with mild/moderate injury—although not to the degree shown in the severe TBI group. Children injured at a younger age showed a deceleration in academic growth for all groups compared to older children. Phonological processing and verbal memory were variably affected in these children. These findings suggest that all children with TBI need intensive and ongoing support for continued academic growth to occur. This support appears particularly crucial for children injured at a younger age as their skills do not show the same rate of growth as those children injured at older ages.

A longitudinal study also found these weaknesses (Ewing-Cobbs, Fletcher, Levin, Iovino, & Miner, 1998). Older children were also found to score more poorly on measures of numerical operations and reading comprehension compared to the younger children. Achievement improved during the initial six-month recovery period with improvement showing less recovery after the first six-month period. After two years, 79 percent of the severely injured children had either been retained in a grade or had received special education services.

Although language deficits are reported to be present in many adults and children with TBI, it appears that receptive language skills are frequently spared following injury while expressive language skills are significantly impacted. For younger children, particularly those injured during the 6–8-year-old period, problems are present in the development of abstract language abilities, written language, and the ability to express complex ideas (Levin et al., 1995). These difficulties with expressive and written language likely disrupt the child's academic progress, particularly in reading and in writing. It is also important to note that when injury occurs prior to the expectation for performance on measures of inferential reading comprehension and higher level writing skills, the child may perform adequately on a usual achievement test, but show a decline in later grades that is indicative of the aforementioned problems. For a child with TBI it is particularly important to conduct serial evaluations in order to assess these skills which are not expected at younger ages, but are crucial for performance at older ages.

Perceptual Functions

Perceptual problems appear related to the severity of injury, particularly under timed conditions, and visual and visual-spatial impairment have been identified in children following injury (Lehnung et al., 2003). Difficulties are found in motor speed and in the ability to process information quickly following severe TBI (Anderson & Catroppa, 2007). Perceptual difficulties are generally studied in relation to memory and cognition rather than separately. Visual-motor deficits are dependent on whether motor areas of the brain and parietal regions are impacted. These regions are less likely to be injured in TBI, compared to frontal and temporal regions that are related to difficulties with memory, executive functioning, and attention.

Memory Functions

Memory deficits appear to be fairly common in children following TBI (Catroppa, Anderson, Ditchfield, & Coleman, 2008). Verbal learning and verbal memory, and working memory deficits have been reported in children following TBI while visual-spatial memory and immediate memory are not as affected (Anderson & Catroppa, 2007; Lehnung et al., 2003). Visual spatial memory is when a child is asked to recall where something is on a page while immediate memory is similar to that tapped by Digit span. Working memory is generally memory that requires the child to hold something in mind while solving a problem. Working memory and complex auditory-verbal memory (learning of word lists) have consistently been found to be problematic for children with severe TBI (Anderson & Catroppa, 2007; Vakil, Blachstein, Rochberg, & Vardi, 2004). Further study has indicated that memory difficulties continue after 24 months for those children with severe TBI. In addition, pre-injury academic skills and verbal memory ability was highly predictive of academic success after injury (Catroppa & Anderson, 2007).

Attentional and Executive Control Functions

Children who experience TBI have difficulty with attention and executive functioning. In the area of executive functioning particular difficulty is found on measures of problem solving and planning, and processing speed (Brookshire, Levin, Song, & Zhang, 2004). Children with severe head injuries frequently exhibit problems with disinhibition, impulsivity, and problems with working memory compared to mild injury TBI and control children, and these difficulties continue into adulthood (Mangeot, Armstrong, Colvin, Yeates, & Taylor, 2002; Nybo & Koskiniemi, 1999). Children who experienced TBI in preschool and who were studied as adults showed continuing problems with executive functioning. Those who had made improvements in

cognitive flexibility were found to show the best outcome vocationally (Nybo, Sainio, & Muller, 2004)

Attentional difficulties, as measured by continuous performance tasks, have also been documented in children sustaining brain damage, and require special education support (Schachar, Levin, Max, Purvis, & Chen, 2004; Vriezen & Pigott, 2000). Disinhibition has been frequently found in children with TBI, particularly with those children with severe head injuries (Wassenberg, Max, Lindgren, & Schatz, 2004). The prevalence of acquired ADHD is seen in 20% and 50% of children with TBI, with higher rates found in those children with severe TBI (Bloom, Levin, & Ewing-Cobbs, 2001; Max et al., 2004). Studies have also found that when a child has premorbid symptoms of ADHD, he/she is more likely to showed acquired ADHD following injury (Bloom et al., 2001; Max et al., 2004). Thus, children with ADHD or several symptoms of ADHD are at higher risk for experiencing TBI and once they have TBI are more likely to have significant problems with attention.

Yeates et al. (2005) studied long-term attentional functioning in children with TBI longitudinally over four years and compared their functioning with children with orthopedic injuries. Findings indicated that 20 percent of the severe TBI group showed ADHD: combined subtype, where 4 percent of the orthopedically injured children did. In addition, premorbid attentional difficulties predicted the level of attentional problems after injury. It was suggested by these authors that the underlying difficulties with executive functioning (working memory, disinhibition) significantly impacted the child's attentional difficulties apart from cognitive factors.

Taken together these findings indicate that attentional issues are an important consideration when evaluating children with TBI. In addition, they indicate that children with premorbid problems with attention are more likely to show significant attentional difficulties after injury. These problems are more pronounced for children with severe TBI. In addition, attentional problems do not appear to improve dramatically with recovery for these children and continue to be an area that is significantly impacted. It is also highly likely that these problems interact with learning difficulties to further complicate recovery and success in school.

Social-Psychological Adjustment

New psychiatric disorders post-injury appear significantly more often in children with severe head injury (in 50% of cases), whereas children with mild head injury have not been found to differ from a control group (Janusz, Kirkwood, Yeates, & Taylor, 2002). Disorders most frequently seen in children with TBI are in externalizing behaviors including ADHD, oppositionality, irritability, and aggression (Bloom et al., 2001; Janusz et al., 2002; Max et al., 2001). While depression and anxiety are seen in adults with TBI, these disorders are much less common in children (Robin, Temkin, & Machamer, 1999).

One of the issues that is most troubling for children with TBI is difficulty in relating to others and social competence issues (Semrud-Clikeman, 2007). The difficulties that are seen with lability and aggression certainly impair the child's ability to form and maintain friendships. In addition, these problems are exacerbated by difficulties these children have in being critical of their own abilities and having insight into their contribution to the social difficulties. This area makes treatment very difficult for the children, particularly as many of them exhibit an aggressive style toward their peers (Poggi et al., 2005). Most studies investigating head injury in children stress the importance of considering premorbid status in order to assess the full impact of injury on the child (Goldstein & Levin, 1990).

Family and Home Factors

TBI can disrupt family interactions and the home environment can have an impact on the recovery process following TBI. Families that have children with moderate and severe TBI frequently experience not only the stress from the injury and anxiety about the child's future, they also experience significant problems with financial and time obligations during the child's recovery. Continuing difficulties with the child's behavior and adjustment following TBI have been linked to familial functioning, family cohesion, and increased divorce rates (Wade, Taylor, Drotar, Stancin, & Yeates, 1996; Wade et al., 2008). Moreover, severe injury coupled with premorbid family

dysfunction and social disadvantage have been linked to a poorer prognosis (Taylor et al., 2002). Children who have experienced severe TBI, had poorer performance premorbidly, and whose family was coping poorly have had the poorest recovery both for the immediate and long-term time periods (Anderson et al., 2006).

Studies that have evaluated the child's functioning within the family have found that an open communication style, flexibility, and positive coping strategies are associated with improved adjustment for the child (Benn & McColl, 2004; Hawley, 2003). Mothers and fathers cope with a disability differently. Mothers focus on the needs of the child and the family while fathers focus on the long-term financial aspects of the child's injury and recovery (Minnes, 1998). Parents often are important for determining how the child eventually adapts to his/her injury and the recovery period. Training for this role is often rudimentary and parents often seek additional information in order to cope with the child's difficulty (Semrud-Clikeman, 2001). Findings that help the parent learn helpful coping strategies and manage their own anxiety and concern about the child indicate that supporting the family in the development of coping strategies is a crucial aspect for the child's rehabilitation (Benn & McColl, 2004; Minnes, Graffi, Nolte, Carlson, & Harrick, 2000).

Implications for Assessment

Due to the various neuropsychological, cognitive, academic, memory, and psychosocial disorders accompanying TBI, a broad-based evaluation is imperative. Areas that should be included are attention, executive functioning, language, cognition, memory, visual-perception, adaptive behavior, and psychosocial functioning. Tests that are discussed in Chapter 6 need to be included in the evaluation of a child with TBI. In addition to the initial evaluation, serial evaluations need to be conducted to monitor the child's progress. Research has indicated that the largest amount of recovery occurs in the first six months following the accident, with additional recovery found 2–5 years post-injury. Not only should the neuropsychologist investigate the standard and scaled scores that are obtained, but comparison of the raw scores is also desirable. In some cases, children with TBI may appear to decline in ability due to a lowering of standardized scores. However, if the raw scores are compared the neuropsychologist may find that the raw scores have plateaued, indicating that the child has neither progressed nor made progress. This difference is important particularly when developing treatment options.

Neuroimaging is generally part of the assessment process for the neurologist and medical team. Obtaining the reports of these results is crucial for understanding the damage that may have occurred. Scans obtained right after the injury will generally differ from those taken 6–12 months later when damage may be more readily seen (Donders & Nesbit-Greene, 2004; Wilde et al., 2005). As the child grows and develops it is helpful to obtain the follow-up neurological and neuroradiological studies to further inform the neuropsychological testing results.

Implications for Intervention

Cognitive and personality characteristics of the child, as well as family resources, marital stability, and socioeconomic status, have an impact on outcome variables measuring the child's recovery. With this in mind, developmental history and circumstances in the child's environment must be carefully considered. Further, teacher reports and a review of history help to determine the presence of preexisting disorders like hyperactivity, attentional problems, social interaction, and academic difficulties. Many teachers have had little training in TBI, and information that can be provided to the parent and the teacher can be invaluable in assisting the development of an appropriate individual educational plan. Emerging research using web-based applications that provide information as well as video conferencing for family interventions is promising and may provide the support that families need (Braga, Da Paz Junior, & Ylvisaker, 2005; Wade, Carey, & Wolfe, 2006; Wade, Wolfe, & Pestian, 2004).

Medications may be helpful for some of the symptoms seen in children with TBI, including attention and aggression. Some studies have found modest improvement with stimulant medication (Jin & Schachar, 2004). Other medications for internalizing and externalizing disorders have found small to modest improvement (Beers, Skold, Dixon, & Adelson, 2005) with few studies solely targeting TBI using selective serotonin reuptake inhibitors (SSRIs) (Donders, 2007). In summary, studies indicate the need to integrate data from various sources in order to measure the full impact of head injury on children, and support the need for an integrated paradigm for developing educational and psychosocial treatment programs for brain-injured children.

Fetal Alcohol Syndrome

Prenatal exposure to teratogenic agents, including alcohol and cocaine, has been known to produce various neuropsychological, neurocognitive, and neurobehavioral disorders in children. Fetal alcohol syndrome disorders (FASD) describe children who exhibit a growth deficiency, facial anomalies, and CNS dysfunction (Premj, Benzies, & Hayden, 2007). FASD is an umbrella term and describes the continuum of difficulties found when a fetus is exposed to alcohol. It includes Fetal Alcohol Syndrome (FAS), Fetal Alcohol Effects (FAE), Partial Fetal Alcohol Syndrome (PFAS) and miscellaneous conditions included in the spectrum (Alcohol-related Neurodevelopmental disorder, Alcohol-related birth defects, and static encephalopathy) (Streissguth & O'Malley, 2000).

Children with FASD frequently show delayed development, overactivity, motor clumsiness, attention deficits, learning problems, cognitive retardation, and seizure disorders. The prevalence of FAS is estimated to be between 0.5 per 1,000 live births (May & Gossage, 2001) to 25 per 1,000 for children from alcoholic mothers (Canadian Pediatric Society, 2002). Differences in incidence rates of FAS depend on community, ethnic, and cultural mores, and on geographical area.

Etiology of Fetal Alcohol Syndrome

The type and severity of FAS depends upon when the mother drank during gestation, how much alcohol was consumed, how frequently it was used, and the age of the mother. During the first few weeks of prenatal development, alcohol (ethanol) is thought to cause either cell death or modify chromosomes in such a way as to precipitate a miscarriage (Nichols, 2007). Heavy alcohol consumption from weeks four to 10 of gestation has been found to cause disorganization of cells due to disruption of cell migration and severe cell loss leading to microcephaly (small brain). From eight to 10 weeks and upward during pregnancy, ethanol disorganizes cell migration and development and neural synapses are not formed, thus preventing appropriate neuronal transmission (Nichols, 2007). Finally, alcohol consumption in the third trimester interferes with the development of the cerebellum, hippocampus, and prefrontal cortex, thus setting the stage for later problems with balance, attention, and new learning (Livy, Miller, Maier, & West, 2003).

Exposure to alcohol in utero has a wide range of consequences to the child, from no problems to fetal death, and the probability of a child experiencing FASD from a mother who drank ranges from 1 to 7 percent (Clarren, Randels, Sanderson, & Fineman, 2001; May et al., 2006). The threshold for alcohol use during pregnancy appears to be between seven and 28 drinks per week in early and mid-pregnancy. This level of alcohol intake is highly related to neurobehavioral sequalae (May et al., 2008). Although the mechanism behind FAS is not fully understood, nutritional and metabolic effects of alcoholism, age of the mother, whether the mother binged or drank steadily, and maternal and fetal metabolism, along with the teratogenic effects of the alcohol itself, are believed to play a role (Jacobson, Jacobson, Sokol, Chiodo, & Corobana, 2004).

Animal models are being used in order to understand the etiology of FAS. Rats prenatally exposed to alcohol were found to be highly irritable and to have difficulty with regulating their sleep and eating adequate amounts of food (Kelly, Day, & Streissguth, 2000). Studies with animals have also found that damage to the hippocampus occurs with alcohol ingestion during pregnancy (Berman &

Hannigan, 2000), as well as the frontal cortex (Mihalick, Crandall, Langois, Krienke, & Dube, 2001).

Studies of the brains of children diagnosed with FAS show decreases in total brain size, particularly in the cerebrum and the cerebellum (Riley & McGee, 2005; Spandoni, McGee, Fryer, & Riley, 2007). Moreover, smaller volume of the basal ganglia has also been found, particularly in the caudate nucleus (Archibald et al., 2001), as well as reduced metabolic activity in the caudate in children with FASD (Clark et al., 2000). The corpus callosum has been affected in individuals with FASD. Agenesis of the corpus callosum has been found as well as thinning of the regions near the genu and splenium (Sowell et al., 2001). Asymmetry of the hippocampus has also been found to differ in FASD children, showing a smaller left hippocampus than right compared to typically developing children (Riikonen, Salonen, Partanen, & Verho, 1999). This increase in asymmetry is related to poorer memory skills. Reduced volume of the frontal lobes, particularly in the left, has also been found, particularly in the ventral portions of the frontal lobes (Archibald et al., 2001; Malisza et al., 2005). These regions were found to show less activation in children with FASD when performing a working memory task compared to typically developing children (Connor & Mahurin, 2001). These regions that are compromised in FASD children are important for the development and maintenance of attention, executive function, and memory skills – all areas found to be compromised in children with FASD.

Implications for Assessment and Diagnosis

Facial features usually assist in the diagnosis and are more prominent on the left side of the face. The discriminating facial features of FAS include a shorter than expected eye opening, flattening of the midface, a short nose, indistinct ridges between nose and mouth, and a tiny upper lip. Associated features include small folded skin at the inner corner of the eye, low nasal bridge, ear anomalies, and an abnormally small jaw (Sokol, Delaney-Black, & Nordstrom, 2003). In addition, the child's growth is generally delayed. The facial features generally become less evident after puberty, and diagnosis at that point becomes problematic (Astley & Clarren, 2001). A small head continues to be a distinguishing feature, with only 28 percent of samples showing normal head size (Hoyme et al., 2005). FAS is diagnosed when the facial characteristics are present, a growth deficiency is present, and CNS malfunctioning occurs in conjunction with a maternal history of alcohol abuse. If the child shows some of the facial characteristics of FAS and/or CNS signs along with maternal drinking, the diagnosis of fetal alcohol effect (FAE) is given (Autti-Ramo et al., 2006).

Hoyme et al. (2005) have suggested that the criteria established by the Institute of Medicine be revised to be more specific. The original criteria basically are an umbrella term that includes most of the symptoms. Hoyme et al. (2005) suggests that FAS includes the minor facial anomalies, growth retardation, and deficient brain growth while partial fetal alcohol syndrome (PFAS) includes the minor facial anomalies and either growth retardation or structure brain abnormalities/smaller brain with or without confirmed maternal alcohol use. For a diagnosis of alcohol-related birth defects (ARBD) there must be characteristic facial features, a confirmed history of prenatal alcohol exposure, and at least one organ system showing significant structural defects. Alcohol-related neurodevelopmental disorder (ARND) requires documented maternal alcohol use, deficient brain growth, and evidence for behavioral and cognitive difficulties that are not within age expectations.

Ervalahti et al. (2007) compared dysmorphic features and cognitive functioning in children with FASD. It was found that dysmorphic features and growth deficiency were significantly related to cognitive ability. The more dysmorphic the child appeared, the lower the ability level. The relation was found to be modest indicating that facial features and growth retardation alone were not highly predictive of cognitive ability. The risk, however, for significant learning disabilities, ADHD, social skills deficits, and mental retardation increased by 37–82 percent for children with FAS/PFAS (Burd, Klug, Martsolf, & Kerbeshian, 2003). In order to more fully understand why types of neuropsychological problems may be present in FASD, it is important to briefly review the basic neuropsychological domains.

Neuropsychological Aspects of FASD

Longitudinal studies of children with FAS indicate that this disorder persists throughout the life span. Difficulties are present with cognitive retardation, attention, and adaptive behaviors. Information processing skills also appear to be significantly affected and sensitive to the effects of maternal binge drinking (Nichols, 2007). Newborns of alcoholic mothers have been found to be delayed in their response to the environment and to be born with low birth weights (Jacobson et al., 2004). These difficulties continue into adulthood. It is accepted by researchers and clinicians that interventions need to begin early to assist with adaptation to problems most frequently seen cognitively and behaviorally for these children (Green, Diaz-Gonzalez de Ferris, Vasquez, Lau, & Yusim, 2001; Zevenbergen & Ferraro, 2001).

There is a high incidence of cognitive retardation and ADHD in children with FAS and ability is generally lower for children with FAS than those with PFAS, ARBD, or ARND. Streissguth and O'Malley (2000) reviewed the literature on FAS and found that IQs ranged from 29 to 120 with a mean of 70 for children with FAS, and from 42 to 142 with a mean of 90 for those with PFAS. When children with FAS, PFAS, and ARND were compared using a Finnish sample, there was no difference in Full Scale IQ (FSIQ) or Verbal IQ (VIQ) on the WISC III. However, there was a significant difference on Performance IQ (PIQ), with the FAS group scoring significantly more poorly compared to the PFAS group. For all groups, the scores were significantly poorer than the standardization sample, with the FAS group scoring more poorly on all indices (Ervalahti et al., 2007). Ability scores were fairly stable throughout the life span (Niccols, 2007).

Thus, these findings indicate that for the severely affected children with FAS, cognitive retardation is common. For those with PFAS and ARND retardation is not as clear-cut and some children function within the average to above average range in cognitive ability. In addition, the degree of dys-morphic features appears to be related to the level of cognitive functioning, with more dysmorphic features associated with poorer performance. It is likely that the children who are exposed throughout pregnancy and whose mothers may binge drink or are older, are at highest risk for the most severe form of FAS.

Attentional and Executive Functioning

Attentional problems are frequently found in chil-dren with FASD (Riley & McGee, 2005). Compar-ing children with FASDs to those who do not have a history of alcohol exposure, but have ADHD using a computerized attention test, found that children with FASDs showed more inattention problems while those with a sole diagnosis of ADHD showed more impulsivity (Mattson, Calarco, & Robertson, 2006). When FAS children were compared to those without FAS on attentional measures the FAS chil-dren had significant visual attention problems. Their auditory attention was average unless they were asked to listen to long and complex material (Mattson, Lang, & Calarco, 2002).

It has been suggested that executive functioning is a core deficit in children with FASD (Kodituwakku, Kalberg, & May, 2001; Schonfeld, Mattson, Lang, Delis, & Riley, 2001). Cognitive flexibility, response inhibition, planning, and concept formation were evaluated in children with FASDs compared to typi-cally developing children (Mattson, Goodman, Caine, Delis, & Riley, 1999). The children with FASDs had marked deficits in cognitive flexibility, response inhibition, and planning skills. Additional problems were found on measures of abstract pro-blem solving. When children with FASD, ADHD, and typically developing controls were compared on measures of executive functioning, both clinical groups had difficulty on measures of cognitive flex-ibility. The FASD children had additional problems on measures of working memory, compared to those with a sole diagnosis of ADHD. In addition, both the ADHD and FASD groups had difficulty with verbal fluency, with the FASD group scoring the poorest, although actually functioning above ability level (Vaurio, Riley, & Mattson, 2008). These results were also found when children with heavy prenatal exposure to alcohol were compared to those without on measures of verbal and nonverbal fluency (Schon-feld et al., 2001). In this case the children with and without FAS, but with prenatal alcohol exposure, showed problems on measures of fluency compared to controls. The alcohol-exposed groups did not dif-fer from each other. IQ was not a significant predic-tor for difficulties on these measures, while it was for the diagnostic group.

The above findings indicate that executive func-tion deficits and attentional problems are key diffi-culties in FASDs. These disorders are relatively independent of IQ and are present even when the full diagnosis of FAS is not. The finding of pro-blems with cognitive flexibility and response inhibi-tion are important for the development of appro-priate interventions; a topic discussed later in this section.

Adaptive Behavior

Adaptive behavior skills appear to be most proble-matic for FAS children and appear related to the problems cited above with executive functioning. The finding that adaptive behavior difficulties are present is true for those children who were and those who were not cognitively retarded (Riley & McGee, 2005). Areas that were particularly difficult for chil-dren with FASDs were acting without considering the consequences, problems with initiative, inap-propriateness of behaviors due to an inability to read social cues, and inability to establish social relationships (Whaley, O'Connor, & Gunderson, 2001). These findings were present for those chil-dren with mental retardation and FASDs as well as those without these disorders. In addition, these difficulties tend to increase in severity with age so that the FASD child's adaptive behavior does not progress at the same rate as those without FASDs.

Academic Achievement

Academic achievement also poses difficulty for chil-dren with FASDs. A large study of children with FASDs found that approximately 50 percent of the sample were retained at least once, 40 percent were receiving special education services at some point in school, and 65 percent were receiving additional support in reading and mathematics (Streissguth, Barr, Kogan, & Bookstein, 1996; Streissguth & O'Malley, 2000). Children with FASDs have difficulties particularly in new learning and in arithmetic (Kodituwakku et al., 2006). A relation between how much alcohol has been imbibed during gestation in the second trimester of pregnancy and mathematics ability with IQ controlled has been found (Goldschmidt, Richardson, Stoffer, Geva, & Day, 1996). Mathematics appears to be the most vulnerable as reading and spelling skills were not as directly affected. In addition, children with pronounced dysmorphic features also had more difficulties in mathematics calculation and reasoning compared to those with fewer dysmorphic features (Howell, Lynch, Platzman, Smith, & Coles, 2006).

Language Skills

Language skills in FAS children have not been found to be generally deficient. Language development seems more closely related to the quality of caretaking, independent of SES and/or alcohol exposure. As discussed in the executive function section, verbal fluency appears to be the most affected in the language area (Schonfeld et al., 2001). Language comprehension difficulties are problematic for children with FAS (May et al., 2006). In addition both verbal and nonverbal IQ scores were significantly below average for children with FASDs who also showed significant dysmorphic facial features. These findings indicate that verbal skills are compromised in the more significantly affected children. These challenges likely interact with learning difficulties to further complicate the establishment of intervention strategies. It is important to evaluate children with suspected or confirmed FASD for possible language difficulties, particularly those involved in language comprehension.

Motor

Difficulties in motor functioning have been found in children with FASD particularly in the areas of balance, visual-motor integration, fine motor dexterity and gross motor skills (Adnams et al., 2001;

Connor, Sampson, Streissguth, Bookstein, & Barr, 2006; Roebuck, Mattson, Marion, Brown, & Riley, 2004). These difficulties continue into adulthood with FASD adults exhibiting significant problems with balance and fine motor control (Connor et al., 2006). The difficulties that continue to be present in motor skills are likely to compromise the individual's ability to readily complete activities of daily living such as buttoning, writing, and walking smoothly. Continued evaluation and support for motor skills would appear to be appropriate for the more severely affected individuals with FASD.

Psychosocial Considerations

Many FAS children come from chaotic home environments where alcohol and other drugs are used. In addition, there is a relation between poor executive functioning and social skills attainment for children with FAS (Schonfeld, Paley, Frankel, & O'Connor, 2006). Attachment difficulties have been confirmed in many children with FASDs, as well as in animals exposed to prenatal alcohol (Kelly et al., 2000). Children with FASDs have been found to be very outgoing, affectionate, socially engaging, and relate to both familiar and unfamiliar people similarly. It has been suggested that children with FASDs do not understand the perspective of another person and, thus, act on their own impulses without a clear understanding of boundaries between themselves and others (Coggins, Olswang, Olson, & Timler, 2003).

Individuals with FASDs appear at higher risk for psychiatric disorders throughout adolescence and adulthood (Niccols, 2007). In addition, many experience problems with substance abuse, criminal behavior, and disruptive behavior (Streissguth et al., 2004). These difficulties relate to problems with learning from previous mistakes, disinhibition, and likely poor school achievement, yielding fewer vocational options.

Many of these deficits appear to be related to a form of disinhibition and executive control problems, particularly where higher level functions are required (e.g., in social relations). It is also difficult to ascertain the degree to which psychopathology is a function of abnormal neuropsychological and cognitive development, and where it reflects the troubled family environment. At any rate, the interaction of these factors should be considered when designing intervention programs.

Implications for Interventions

Studies evaluating interventions with FAS children are just beginning to establish treatment paradigms. For preschool children, early identification is crucial. Many children are cognitively retarded, show language delays, have problems with attention and memory, and have delayed social skills (Streissguth et al., 2004). Interventions such as early referral by physicians to the school or educational multidisciplinary team is improving, but continues to be below the incidence levels (Clarren et al., 2001; Eriksson, 2007). Medical education in this regard is sorely needed.

Early childhood special education services are invaluable for these children and their families. It is particularly important to involve families in any intervention program. Federal regulations provide for Individual Family Service Plans (IFSPs) as part of special education for young children (see P.L. 94–357). For elementary-aged children, continued special education services are needed for academic and social support. Medication for distractibility and overactivity may be considered for ADHD symptoms. Social skills training can be helpful to assist with development. Skills training needs to focus on foundational skills of learning social cues and gestures, and should be conducted in a school setting or in another setting where natural, ecologically valid social situations serve as the training ground. Minimizing sensory overload, recognizing sleep and eating disorders, and establishing a specialized curriculum are helpful (Riley et al., 2003). Emphasis should be placed on appropriate vocational training for adolescents. In addition, structured behavioral and vocational training is crucial for these students because social judgment, consequential thinking, and risk taking behaviors are problematic for FAS adolescents (Zevenbergen & Ferraro, 2001).

There is no research currently published that evaluates intervention programs with families. Interventions would differ depending on whether the child remains in a chaotic home or is placed in

a more stable environment. Some success has been found in utilizing cognitive-behavioral techniques to prevent alcohol use in women who are drinking during pregnancy. Additional research is sorely needed in both intervention efficacy and family interventions. Prevention seems to be a more effective way to reduce the very serious deleterious effects to unborn infants, and should be a priority. A critical review of FASD interventions found limited scientific evidence for efficacy (Premj et al., 2007) and recommended a comprehensive research agenda developed by the main researchers in the area of FASD.

Conclusions

FASD is a preventable cause of cognitive retardation in children. Research has pinpointed difficulties for FAS children, specifically in terms of attention, self-regulation, problem solving, and social awareness. These difficulties continue into adulthood and create significant adjustment problems. Intervention programs have been developed for academic skills, but progress in adaptive behavior skills and basic living skills have been sorely lacking. Research investigating appropriate vocational training is needed, and the need for earlier training in this area is probably necessary. Moreover, using a transactional approach to the neuropsychology of FAS necessitates that interventions be developed for both the child and the family. Community-based interventions that recognize the particular values and culture of the community are also needed. Efforts to alert the medical profession to the need for early educational interventions is also advised.

Cocaine-Exposed Infants

The incidence of infants born exposed to cocaine, either during gestation or passively after birth, has risen in the past decade particularly, in the inner city where this is estimated to occur in one out of 3–6 infants (Lustbader, Mayes, McGee, Jatlow, & Roberts, 1998). Estimates indicate that more than 100,000 babies are born with exposure to cocaine and/or other drugs annually. Research investigating the effects of cocaine exposure to the developing fetus has produced mixed results. Early studies indicated that there were statistically significant abnormalities across many measures of behavior, temperament, and cognition in early development (Singer, Farkas, & Kliegman, 1991). These abnormalities were well publicized, and many believed that the school systems would be flooded with "crack cocaine children" with severe developmental and behavioral disabilities.

Children with prenatal exposure to cocaine were initially characterized as listless, without affect, difficult to soothe, unmotivated, unable to establish attachments to caregivers, and hyperactive or aggressive (Coles, Platzman, Smith, James, & Falek, 1992). More recent findings have indicated that the effects of prenatal exposure to cocaine include intrauterine growth retardation, low birth weight, and problems with attention, arousal, and reactivity to stimuli (Kliegman, Madura, Kiwi, Eisenberg, & Yamashita, 1994; Mayes & Bornstein, 1995). Exposure to cocaine also increases the risk for sudden infant death syndrome either through active or passive exposure as an infant (Mirchandani, Mirchandani, & Hellman, 1991).

Effects of Cocaine

Cocaine is a powerful stimulant that can be ingested by snorting, "freebasing," or smoking. Crack is a form of cocaine that is increasingly popular because of its lower cost. Cocaine or crack produces an intense feeling of euphoria, with increased energy and self-esteem, and decreased anxiety. The rebound effects, which include increases in anxiety, exhaustion, and depression, are so emotionally painful that the addicted person will continually smoke cocaine or crack to avoid them. Chronic use is associated with paranoid and affective disorder, weight loss, and poor judgment and insight (Ahmadi, Kampman, Dackis, Sparkman, & Pettinati, 2008). Thus, cocaine's effect on the CNS is evident in adults and is related to the chemical properties of the drug.

Cocaine is water and lipid soluble and passes easily across the placenta (Behnke, Eyler, Garvan, Wobie, & Hou, 2002). Moreover, the fetus is exposed for a longer period of time than adults because of a deficiency in the mother's ability to chemically deactivate the drug action (Buck &

Gurwitch, 2003). The cocaine also causes uterine vessel vasoconstriction, which results in reduced blood and oxygen flow to the fetus.

Variables that are just beginning to be studied include individual differences in one's ability to metabolize cocaine, the difference in frequency of cocaine use, and variations in placental perfusion. Koren (1993) suggests that these variables may account for the variation in severity of symptoms in children prenatally exposed to cocaine. Use of cocaine at high levels and at frequent intervals appears to have more adverse effects on the fetus than low level use. Some pregnant women using cocaine appear to have a lower activity level of a primary enzyme (cholinesterase) that metabolizes cocaine. For these women's babies, there is an increased risk of high exposure. Additionally, the human placenta varies in its ability to metabolize cocaine (Hoffman et al., 1992). Some fetuses have had higher exposures to cocaine compared to others when mothers from both groups consumed equivalent doses. Moreover, some fetal placental vessels appear to restrict blood and oxygen flow more than others when cocaine is ingested by the mother (Simone, Derewlany, Knie, & Koren, 1992). This variable may have significant effects on the level of exposure to cocaine, regardless of the amount of cocaine taken. To understand the effect of cocaine on the developing nervous system, it is important to evaluate a number of related variables before describing existing research on behavioral and cognitive outcome for these children. The following sections will discuss environmental variables, pre- and postnatal complications, animal models examining cocaine exposure on a fetus, previous studies on the result of cocaine exposure on the fetus, and current knowledge of the behavioral and cognitive status of these children.

Environmental Variables

Socioeconomic status has been frequently cited as an important variable in the evaluation of newborns for cocaine exposure. Many studies used nonrandom subject selection from large urban hospitals that primarily have indigent and minority women as patients. Results from these studies indicated that minority and poor women were more likely to have drug-exposed children

(Minnes, Singer, Humphrey-Wall, & Satayathum, 2008). The use of cocaine in pregnant minority women has been found to interact with such variables as polydrug use, less prenatal care, lower weight at time of delivery, and less weight gain during pregnancy (Arendt et al., 2004a). These women are more likely to provide a poorer caregiving environment for the infant, possibly due to poor maternal mental status (Beeghly et al., 2006).

Mothers who used cocaine during and after pregnancy were studied to evaluate environmental aspects present in these homes (Minnes et al., 2008). Mothers who lost custody of their child were compared to those who maintained custody. The mothers who had their child removed from the home showed more childhood neglect and physical abuse in their history. In addition, these mothers were more likely to not have had prenatal care, used more cocaine during pregnancy, and showed greater psychological distress compared to the mothers that maintained custody. The use of crack cocaine was detrimental to the mother's functioning, a problem that increases in severity over time. Thus, understanding the dynamics of cocaine use during pregnancy depends on a systems model that interrelates polydrug use with environmental and/or lifestyle issues. It is not clear what difficulties may be found between the children removed from these homes and those who remained with the mother. This type of study would be interesting, particularly given the higher rate of cocaine use in the mothers who lost custody.

One issue that is important to note is the preponderance of studies of non-white women who use cocaine. Population demographics indicate that addiction is color-blind. However, babies born to non-white women addicted to cocaine are more likely to be removed from the home than those of white women also addicted to cocaine (Neuspiel, 1996). One issue that needs to be further evaluated are the environmental and societal reasons for such addiction as well as the paucity of services for poor, ethnic women with addictions.

Animal Models

Animal models help us understand the mechanisms underlying the effects of various neurotoxic agents. Applying the results of animal studies to human behavior has been found to be helpful with these agents. A study of offspring from Sprague-Dawley CD rats given multiple daily doses of cocaine found that exposure to cocaine produced poorer performance on more complicated cognitive tasks when the rats were fully mature (Smith & Morrell, 2008). Problem solving and socialization behaviors were particularly susceptible to cocaine exposure in utero (Seymour & Wagner, 2008).

Alterations in neural function have also been found, lending support to the hypothesis that cocaine, used frequently and in large doses, acts as a neurobehavioral teratogen (Thomas, Kalivas, & Shaham, 2008). Controlled studies utilizing animal models have been conducted only in the past six to eight years, and data are continuing to emerge. These findings can inform clinicians about the possible affects cocaine has on the developing nervous system.

Pre- and Postnatal Medical Effects

Prenatal exposure to cocaine is believed to disrupt blood flow in the fetus, which in turns interferes with organ development (Rizk, Atterbury, & Groome, 1996). Cocaine also causes vasoconstriction in the placenta, thus reducing blood flow to the fetus and likely contributing to increased birth defects in cocaine-exposed fetuses (Minnes et al., 2006). Cocaine use in the early stage of pregnancy places the fetus at high risk for changes in brain growth, synaptic formation, and cell migration (Bandstra, Morrow, Anthony, Churchill et al., 2001).

Increased risk of spontaneous abortions, abrupted placentas, and meconium stained amniotic fluid is associated with maternal cocaine use (Volpe, 1992). Increased rates of prematurity have been confirmed, and may be related to the early neurodevelopmental effects found in these children (Bada et al., 2005). Premature birth has been associated with a history of heavier drug abuse and/or significant socioeconomic disadvantage. Intrauterine growth retardation has been present in cocaine-exposed infants, when compared to non-cocaine-exposed infants, as well as small head size and slower brain growth (Singer et al., 2002). When very low birth weight babies were studied on follow-up who had been diagnosed with chronic lung disease, 25 percent of these babies had been cocaine-exposed; double the rate of cocaine exposure generally seen (Singer et al., 1991).

Neurological abnormalities found in neonates prenatally exposed to cocaine include cerebral infarcts and EEG abnormalities (Chiriboga, 1998; Jones, Field, Davalos, & Hart, 2004). Cocaine-exposed children show greater right frontal EEG asymmetry when confronted with stimuli requiring an empathic response. In addition quantitative EEG (QEEG) studies have found that children with utero cocaine exposure show differences in response to stimuli that is similar to that of adults who are addicted to cocaine (Prichep, Kowalik, Alper, & de Jesus, 1995). These findings indicate that neuronal transmission differs in children with exposure to cocaine. No longitudinal study was found that evaluated whether these differences continue in childhood or whether there is a relation between EEG abnormalities and neuropsychological deficits.

Neuroimaging Findings

Rivkin et al. (2008) studied children with in utero exposure to cocaine, alcohol, tobacco, and marijuana using volumetric MRI. In the sample of 14 children, nine had exposure to cocaine and alcohol, 12 to cocaine and tobacco, and eight to cocaine and marijuana. For the control group 13 had no exposure to substances while two had exposure to alcohol, six to tobacco, and three to marijuana. The mean age of the children is 12.3 years, with a range from 10 to 14. As a whole, children with intrauterine exposure to cocaine showed smaller gray matter volumes, smaller head circumferences and smaller deep gray matter volumes compared to those without cocaine exposure. In addition, for children with more types of substance exposure cortical gray matter volume and deep gray matter volume, as well as head circumference, declined significantly with the smallest volume present for children who were exposed to all four substances. While this study has very small numbers, the findings suggest that polydrug abuse during pregnancy is related to significant declines in gray matter, particularly that in the subcortical regions that are responsible for response inhibition, gating of stimuli, and reactivity. These findings, while suggestive, need to be replicated with larger samples and possibly by age.

A large scale study of children exposed to cocaine in utero utilized diffusion tensor imaging (DTI) when the children were between the ages of 10 and 12 (Warner et al., 2006). Findings indicated that DTI of children exposed to cocaine found more diffusion in the left frontal callosal and right frontal projection fibers. When the sample was analyzed including additional substances of marijuana, alcohol, and tobacco use, it was found that prenatal exposure to cocaine, alcohol and marijuana affected the left frontal callosal fibers. In addition, for children exposed to both cocaine and marijuana, the connectivity was much poorer than for those children solely exposed to cocaine. In addition, the children completed executive functioning measures and these measures were correlated with the DTI measures. It was found that, for the sample as a whole, children who performed better on the executive functioning tasks had greater diffusion in the left frontal callosal fibers. In addition, faster performance on the Trail Making test was associated with better diffusion in the right frontal regions. These findings were taken to suggest that hemispheric connectivity is not as well developed in children with cocaine exposure, and that their brains may be neurologically immature for their age.

In sum the neuroimaging studies have just begun to evaluate the neurological integrity of the brains in children with cocaine exposure. These findings are intriguing and suggest that the trajectory for developing white matter tracts through DTI analysis may be different and is particularly compromised for children with exposure to both marijuana and cocaine. Moreover, there appears to be a compromise in the gray matter both cortically and subcortically for these children indicating, again, that those exposed to several substances exhibit the most effect. Given that many individuals who use substances during pregnancy are often polysubstance abusers, these findings are important for our understanding of the child's development and difficulties (Minnes, Singer, Arendt, & Satayathum, 2005). These aspects of neurological development are likely related to neuropsychological functioning in children with cocaine exposure. The following section provides a brief overview of the literature describing what has been found in the major domains in children exposed to cocaine.

Neuropsychological Functioning

Cognitive Development

The early development in utero of cocaine-exposed babies has been studied more extensively than later development. Infant development has been evaluated to determine whether cognitive delays are present early on and whether they continue over time. These studies have been difficult to fully conduct in order to determine cognitive challenges due to confound factors such as low socioeconomic status, poor prenatal care, low maternal education and IQ, and negative environmental factors that have all been linked to lower ability without the additional substance abuse issue (Singer, 1999). Studies that seek to isolate these additional environmental causes of cognitive difficulty apart from the cocaine exposure are difficult to conduct. Singer et al. (2008) sought to control these additional variables and studied children with cocaine exposure during the first two years of life. Results found that children with cocaine exposure showed significant delays on the Bayley Mental Scales of Development, with scores generally below 80 that continued through the first two years of life. There was a 13.7 percent rate of mental retardation in the group, which is significantly higher than the 2 percent that would be expected in the population. In addition, 38 percent of the children had mild to moderate delays significant enough to warrant special education. These findings were true even when the variables of the home environment were controlled. These results were related to the amount of cocaine the mother used during pregnancy and the frequency of the use suggested that the fetal brain was directly affected by the cocaine, possibly due to hypoxemia (lack of oxygen in the blood). No motor difficulties were found.

Children at five years of age have had difficulties on measures of language, school readiness, impulse control and visual attention (Pulsifer, Butz, O'Reilly, & Belcher, 2008; Richardson, Goldschmidt, & Willford, 2008). Global ability, visual-motor skills, fine motor skills and sustained attention were found to be within normal limits. Early elementary school-aged children exposed to cocaine have not exhibited significant intellectual difficulties, but did have an increased risk for learning disabilities, particularly in the area of reading (Morrow et al., 2006).

When the cognitive ability of prenatally cocaine-exposed preschool children was evaluated, their ability measures did not differ from non-exposed children within the same socioeconomic status. However, children exposed prenatally to cocaine were found to be less likely to have average ability and more likely to show ability measures in the below average range. Differences were found on measures of visual-spatial ability, general knowledge, and arithmetic skills. Those children exposed to cocaine prenatally who were removed from their home were found to show better vocabulary scores and higher ability levels compared to those who remained with the biological parent. These findings are consistent with a study that found the biological mother's vocabulary ability and home environment to be stronger predictors of developmental outcome than prenatal drug exposure (Arendt et al., 2004b).

Language. When the confounding effects of environmental contributions to language skill development was controlled, the more heavily exposed infants had poorer auditory comprehension skills compared to control children (Singer et al., 2001). In addition, more heavily exposed infants showed poorer total language skills compared to lighter exposed infants and control children. Auditory comprehension is an important aspect for development of receptive language; a skill that generally develops prior to expressive language. Other studies have not found an effect on language, but these studies generally did not control for parental cocaine use and caregiving factors, nor did they evaluate severity of cocaine use and the effect on language abilities (Bland-Steward, Seymour, Beeghly, & Frank, 1998; Hawley, Halle, Drasin, & Thomas, 1993; Nulman et al., 1994).

For older children aged 6–9 years studies of prenatal cocaine exposure have found lower receptive language abilities for six-year-olds, but not for nine-year-olds (Beeghly et al., 2006). In addition, children with prenatal exposure had poorer scores on measures of expressive language if they also had a low birth weight. Females also showed poorer expressive and total language scores compared to males with prenatal exposure to cocaine. Those children who had been exposed to violence in the home scored more poorly across the groups, while children who had preschool experiences scored better across the groups.

Similarly, when preschoolers were studied it was found those exposed to cocaine prenatally scored more poorly on all aspects of language skills over development. However, environmental influences were also found to be important, particularly as the children grew. Both groups of children were mainly from an urban setting, low income, and African-American. These aspects were found to negatively influence language development for all children beyond the influence of cocaine exposure.

These findings indicate that while there are language difficulties, particularly for complex language at later years, these deficits may be more due to caregiving, economic status, and exposure to learning than to cocaine exposure, particularly for those children with light to moderate exposure. In this case, widespread intervention for children in lower socioeconomic situations would likely benefit all of these children with regard to language development.

The additional finding that girls may show more detrimental effects on language than boys is also interesting. It may well be that language is less lateralized in girls and, thus, the diffuseness of language skills is more affected by hypoxia seen in children with cocaine exposure than for boys whose language skills are more lateralized. Boys had more externalizing behaviors than girls, thus possibly affected differentially by cocaine exposure.

Attention/Executive Functioning

Children with prenatal exposure to cocaine have exhibited difficulty in the domains of inhibitory control and attention. It is thought that prenatal cocaine exposure changes the level of specific neurotransmitters important for these abilities during gestation, thereby altering brain organization (Lewis et al., 2004; Stanwood & Levitt, 2004). Studies have found difficulty with disinhibition in children with cocaine exposure at five years of age

(Bendersky, Gambini, Lastella, Bennett, & Lewis, 2003), and with sustained attention in children aged 6–10 years (Bandstra, Morrow, Anthony, Accornero, & Fried, 2001; Richardson, Conroy, & Day, 1996).

Selective attentional difficulties have been found in preschoolers with polydrug prenatal exposure to marijuana and cocaine. Children whose mothers had utilized these substances had more difficulty with selective attention while those who had utilized marijuana showed significant problems with sustained attention (Accornero et al., 2007; Noland et al., 2005). These findings were independent of confounding variables such as maternal psychological distress, maternal IQ, and caregiver level of functioning.

Executive functioning has also been found to be problematic for children with prenatal cocaine exposure. Children with such exposure process information much more slowly and show more difficulties with working memory, particularly with problem solving skills (Mayes, Snyder, Langlois, & Hunter, 2007), and with reaction time and motor/response speed (Mayes, Molfese, Key, & Hunter, 2005; Noland et al., 2003). These skills are particularly important as the child develops and is required to respond quickly both socially and academically. Further study is needed to more fully understand what aspects of executive functioning are particularly compromised for these children.

Social/Emotional/Behavioral Development

Studies of the neonatal behavior of cocaine-exposed infants have found that these children may show no to mild withdrawal behaviors (Singer et al., 2008). Sensory and behavioral deficits consistently have been found with irritability and difficulty with self-soothing was found more often for these children by parent report. In particular, these children had difficulty screening out upsetting stimuli and decreased habituation to environmental stimuli. (Mayes, Cicchetti, Acharyya, & Zhang, 2003). Children at six months of age who were exposed to cocaine in utero had temperamental differences, primarily in their difficulties with cooperation, manageability, and responsiveness to routine. These children were also less responsive and showed less interest in communication and participation in activity, while their cognitive development did not differ from that of non-exposed six-month-olds (Edmondson & Smith, 1994). Reactivity differences have been found using physiological response measures that persist into middle childhood (Kable, Coles, Lynch, & Platzman, 2008). The children with behavioral disturbance showed more extreme behavior problems compared to those with cocaine exposure. These differences were in contrast to children with behavioral disturbance in that children with prenatal cocaine exposure did not show a general level of hyperarousal, but did have increased skin conductance levels to stressors. As a result of these findings, children with cocaine exposure may well respond differently to stress and may overreact to these types of experiences. In comparison to the control group, the cocaine-exposed group had more difficulty controlling their arousal, but not nearly as much difficulty as the behavioral disturbance group had. These findings suggest that children with cocaine exposure may well show more fearfulness and/or anxiety to stressful situations and may need additional assistance in calming themselves down.

In controlled testing sessions others have not found these behaviors when trained observers rated the child's behavior (Frank et al., 2002; Messinger et al., 2004). It may well be that the parent ratings are reflecting the stress the mother is under, coupled with environmental variables, thus lowering the scores. It may also be that the child's behaviors are more difficult in an unstructured setting than when in a structured setting with trained professionals.

When infants have been studied and environmental factors carefully controlled, cocaine use during the second and third trimesters was associated with fussier babies that had a difficult temperament. In addition, these behaviors were most evident at a very young age, and seemed to improve as the infants got older. Parental aspects such as lower educational levels in the home, more hospitalizations, maternal depression, and third trimester marijuana exposure with current substance use placed the child at higher risk for behavioral difficulties (Richardson et al., 2008).

It is likely that methodological differences in these studies may account for these equivocal findings. It may be that controlling for home environment as well as caregiver current use of substances may help explain these differences. In addition, it may be important to evaluate when the mother used cocaine (throughout the pregnancy, variably, etc.) and what effect this had on the subsequent behaviors of the child. Further study is needed, particularly in identifying those children most at risk, but also to assist with appropriate interventions.

Summary

Contrary to the concerns of the 1980s and early 1990s, these children are not showing the long-term global cognitive deficits that were predicted. It is too early to say that these children will have no deficits. Current evidence suggests that cocaine exposure during pregnancy may predispose the child to later difficulties in attention, social development, and emotional regulation and development. Some children appear to have subtle language deficits in the preschool years. Abilities that are unable to be measured in the first three years of life may emerge poorly at later ages. The subtle deficits in organization, regulation of behavior, and problem solving may later translate into difficulty with abstract thinking skills. Moreover, one of the best predictors of later social and emotional adjustment is attachment to the caregiver (Stroufe, Fox, & Pancake, 1983). As we have seen from the foregoing review, cocaine-exposed children not only have difficulty with attachment, but their caretakers are frequently unavailable to them because of the addiction.

A transactional approach to understanding these children is paramount. It appears from the emerging research that the environment the child is in may be just as important as whether he or she was exposed to cocaine in utero. Children from impoverished, chaotic, abusive homes will do poorly, regardless of pregnancy history. To understand the functioning of these children, the clinician must take these variables into consideration in interpreting the data. Moreover, these children should be monitored for progress, as early subtle deficits may translate into later difficulties with more complex learning. Although further study is needed on the long-term effects of cocaine exposure, control of these moderator variables (maternal addiction, poverty, nutrition, etc.) is necessary in order to isolate the effects of cocaine on the fetus.

CNS Infectious Diseases: Meningitis and Encephalitis

Infections of the brain at an early age may result in a variety of outcomes ranging from mental retardation to normal development, and from schizophrenia to affective disorders depending on the type of infection (Dalman et al., 2008). Central nervous system infections can be the result of bacterial, viral, and/or fungal invasions of the brain and spinal cord through the sinuses, ears, nose, and mouth.

In addition to the medical conditions, social and environmental factors have been found to be predictive of later sequelae from early infections (Kopp & Kralow, 1983). Thus, the infections interface with environmental factors in the resulting deficits, if any, for these children. The social factors cannot, of course, fully account for the deficits, as children with early insults to the brain have constraints placed on their development, and such constraints are tempered by how the environment handles them (Sameroff & Chandler, 1975). Thus, a transactional model for understanding these infectious processes is important. Both meningitis and encephalitis will be discussed briefly.

Meningitis

The meninges, as mentioned in Chapter 2, protect the brain from infections, cushion it from injury, and serve as a barrier to foreign objects. However, they are not impervious to damage or disease, and meningitis results when the meninges become inflamed, particularly in the arachnoid and pia mater layers. Meningitis refers to an inflammation of the meninges or protective layers of the brain and spinal cord, whereas encephalitis is a generalized inflammation of the brain. Viral or bacterial infections are the main cause of meningitis. Children

older than two years of age generally show initial symptoms of a headache, stiff neck, vomiting, high fever, and joint pain as well as a sensitivity to light. For infants and neonates symptoms may include lethargy, failure to eat and vomiting (Hilliker & Whitt, 2003).

The incidence of bacterial meningitis is 2.5–3.5 per 100,000. Prior to the introduction of the haemophilus influenzae type b (Hib) immunization, Hib was the most common cause of bacterial meningitis. For neonates Group B streptococcus (GBS) is the most common cause of meningitis and is passed from the mother to the infant at delivery. Most cases of meningitis are currently caused by Streptococcus pneumoniae or Neisseria meningitides. Viral meningitis is more common, but is generally less severe than bacterial meningitis. This type of meningitis is generally spread through direct contact with saliva and mucus and results in fever, headache, and fatigue for about 7–14 days.

Bacterial meningitis disrupts the cerebrovascular and CSF relation. The most frequent site for meningitis is in the pia mater and the arachnoid layer and space. The diagnosis is confirmed by a sample of cerebrospinal fluid (CSF) taken through a lumbar puncture; bacterium is assayed in the sample. In meningitis the CSF is generally cloudy, and pressure is elevated. Neurological indicators are present through CT scans, including hydrocephalus, edema, or cortical atrophy with abnormal EEG results (Anderson & Taylor, 2000).

Treatment generally consists of high doses of antibiotics, frequently ampicillin, for 10 days. Chloramphenicol is also often prescribed in the event that the bacteria are resistant to ampicillin. Fluids are carefully monitored, and CT, MRI, and EEG studies are ordered as needed. The sequelae from meningitis depend on the age of onset, how long before the disorder is diagnosed, the infectious agent and severity of infection, and the treatment used.

Among children with meningitis, 40 percent will experience seizures, hearing loss, and/or hemiparesis with neurological complications seen in approximately half of these children. The mortality rate for bacterial meningitis is 5–10 percent (Anderson & Taylor, 2000).

Neonates are at highest risk for mortality from meningitis. Children who experienced coma and subdural infections have had the most severe neurological and neuropsychological sequelae (V. Anderson et al., 1997). Moreover, those children who had seizures prior to the onset of meningitis, had a longer duration of illness and higher fevers, and those who were younger at onset had the poorest cognitive result following treatment (P. Anderson et al., 1997). Studies looking at long-term effects of meningitis found that 50 percent of the children showed significant cognitive and physical difficulty, with language difficulty, hearing problems, cognitive delays, motor delays, and visual impairments being the most frequent complications (P. Anderson et al., 1997).

Children who have recovered from the disease process need a comprehensive neuropsychological battery to monitor their progress. Such an assessment should be accomplished serially in order to detect any difficulties. The child should be screened repeatedly, and parent and school personnel need to be well versed in attending to possible difficulties in these areas. Moreover, given the importance of parental support and social development, these areas need to be attended to not only in any evaluation, but also in any proposed treatment paradigm.

Encephalitis

Encephalitis refers to a generalized inflammatory state of the brain. This disorder is frequently associated with an inflammation of the meninges as well. The incidence of encephalitis is reported to be approximately 1,400–4,300 cases in the United States annually (Anderson, Northam, Hendy, & Wrennall, 2001). Viruses are frequently the culprit in this disease, which can occur perinatally or postnatally. Encephalitis can be caused by viral diseases such as Herpes simplex or through insect bites. For the majority of cases, however, no cause can be pinpointed (Hooper, Williams, Sarah, & Chua, 2007).

There are two forms of the disease: acute and chronic. Acute forms are evidenced within days or weeks of infection, whereas chronic forms can take months to become symptomatic. Fever, headache, vomiting, loss of energy, lassitude, irritability, and depressive-like symptoms are frequently seen, with increasing confusion and disorientation as the disease progresses. At times speech processes are affected, paralysis or muscle weakness is seen, and gait problems occur (Hooper et al., 2007). Encephalitis is related to later problems with respiratory ailments, particularly when it co-occurred with influenza (Armin et al., 2008). In addition, the children affected prior to age two had brain development abnormalities, while these abnormalities were not as present in children above the age of two.

Diagnosis is through examination of the CSF for viral agents, CT scans and EEG analysis. Treatment includes antiviral agents if a viral cause has been discovered, or through the monitoring of the disease process, antibiotics, and fluids if no virus has been identified. Sequelae are generally related to the type of infection and the duration of the infectious process (Arvin & Whitley, 2001; Kimberlin, 2007). Generally, mental retardation, irritability and lability, seizure disorder, hypertonia, and cranial nerve involvement can be seen with the more severe disease process, while in mild to moderate cases there are few, if any, sequelae (Engman et al., 2008). A review of the literature found very few studies of encephalitis in children and the neuropsychological effects of this disorder. Further investigation is needed to more fully understand the results of these disorders as well as appropriate interventions. Encephalitis associated with herpes virus results in mortality 4–14 percent of the time, and further results in neuropsychological difficulty in 56–69 percent of cases, suggesting that these children require further study.

Chapter Summary

Children with various acquired neurological disorders and diseases have become a focus of study, and researchers have investigated the links between psychological, behavioral, and neuropsychological functioning in traumatic injury, infectious diseases, and prenatal exposure to teratogenic agents, including alcohol and cocaine. Children who experience congenital brain dysfunction tend to have problems with neuropsychological development. These difficulties are frequently subtle and appear related to difficulty in learning new material. Attentional and organizational skills are also sensitive to these disorders and may emerge at older ages when these skills normally develop. These deficits have a negative impact on the adolescent and eventually the adult, and interfere with adjustment and overall adaptation.

In children and adolescents exposed to toxins, traumatic brain injury, and other CNS infectious diseases, it is recommended that frequent neuropsychological evaluations be conducted to monitor progress and to evaluate possible regression. The use of ability and achievement tests needs to be suspended because the performance of children with neurological problems can *not* be predicted as it can be for typically developing children. Parents and teachers play crucial roles in the adjustment and recovery of children with various neurological disorders and diseases. Too often support for the home and school environments are not present, although research indicates the need for this type of service in the treatment plan. If the educational needs of the child are not sufficiently impaired to qualify for special education services, modifications of the regular education program are mandated under Section 504 of the Americans with Disabilities Act of 1973. Children with TBI may qualify for services under P.L. 94–142 or Section 504, while children with other neurological diseases/disorders may be considered as "Other Health Impaired" under the same legislation. In any case, regular education teachers need in-service training to help them recognize the needs of neurologically-impaired children and also during the development of effective intervention strategies for the classroom.

Parents need support not only for the stress the disorder places on the family, but also to plan for the child's long-term development. A transactional approach to neuropsychological assessment can provide the needed support for the parent, school, and child by assisting not only during the diagnostic phase, but also during the planning and implementation phase. Serial assessments can be helpful in this process and can assist in planning appropriate interventions. These evaluations can also be sensitive to the not-always-anticipated changes in the child's development. The following case presentation illustrates the need for comprehensive evaluations as well as parental support.

Case Illustration

Stan's car was hit head-on by a drunken driver. He was 17-years-old at the time of the accident, and he had been a straight A student in his junior year of high school. He was comatose at the accident site, but was moving and breathing spontaneously on the trip to the ER. Intracranial pressure was initially a problem, but improved during his hospitalization. An intracerebral hematoma in the left basal ganglia and internal capsule was diagnosed. Stan had right-sided hemiparesis with a mild right facial droop. Oral motor skills were observed to be below average and speech production was difficult. Stan's hearing and vision were normal.

Stan was hospitalized for five weeks after the accident. He underwent neuropsychological assessment during his stay at the hospital. Findings at that time included difficulties with attention, memory and verbal learning problems, and difficulty with verbal concept formation, with abstract reasoning and visual-spatial skills intact. Stan was reevaluated three months later by a private neuropsychologist using the WMS III and the Woodcock-Johnson Achievement Battery III-Reading Subtests. Scores showed average skills in all areas of memory, with relative strengths in visual memory. Achievement testing showed average performance in reading with slight difficulties in writing. Attentional difficulties continued to be present.

Stan was referred for reevaluation 11 months after his discharge from the hospital. He was succeeding in a limited educational program and was slated to graduate from high school that spring. Continued weakness was present in his right arm and leg, and writing was extremely painstaking and difficult for him. Stan's purpose in obtaining this evaluation was for additional information to aid in his selection of a college as well as assistance in obtaining help for his college program.

Stan presented as a well-groomed young man with a ready wit and smile. He was cooperative throughout the assessment and was well motivated. Stan's attention was good, and he was not easily distracted by extraneous noises. Stan achieved a Full Scale IQ of 106 on the WAIS-III, which placed him in the average range of ability for his age. His verbal IQ of 99 was also in the average range, with more well developed skills found on the performance subtests, resulting in an IQ of 116. His working memory skills and processing speed were in the average range. The following subtest scores were obtained:

Information	9	Picture Completion	15
Digit Span	9	Matrix Reasoning	11
Vocabulary	13	Block Design	14
Arithmetic	14	Letter-No. Sequencing	11
Comprehension	7	Digit Symbol	11
Similarities	11	Symbol Search	10

Language assessment found Stan's receptive language to be in the above average range on the PPVT-III (standard score = 115). His ability to name objects was also well within the average range on the Boston Naming Test (raw score = 55). Performance on the Boston Aphasia Screening Test was well within normal levels and showed good ability to compose paragraphs and stories.

Verbal fluency scores as measured by the Controlled Word Association test were in the low average range and below what would be expected given his previous history. Stan experienced difficulty naming words beginning with the letters F, A, and S. This finding was consistent with a below average performance on the Rey Auditory Verbal Learning Test. Stan was able to remember 11 of 15 words over five trials. His performance did not improve with a second trial. When asked to recall these words after a 20-minute delay, Stan was able to recall 10 correctly which placed him in the average range of functioning.

Motor testing indicated significant right-sided weakness. On the Grooved Pegboard, Stan's right hand performance was over two standard deviations below expectations for his age. He had been right-handed prior to the accident. His performance with his left hand was within normal limits. He used his left hand to complete the VMI as he was continuing to experience right-sided hemiparesis. His performance on the VMI with his left hand was well within the normal range (standard score = 115).

Executive function assessment indicated above average performance on the Wisconsin Card Sorting Test. This finding was consistent with the results of testing during his hospitalization. He showed average performance on measures of problem solving as well as in response inhibition. Moreover, Stan's attentional skills were also within average limits and no difficulties were found in this area.

Social-emotional assessment found that Stan shows some expected emotional distress over his difficulties, but that he has coped well with these challenges. He is currently working with a therapist to assist him in adjusting to changes both in his social and academic life. He did not qualify for any psychiatric diagnoses based on interview, behavior rating scales, or the MMPI.

Impressions were of a young man with at least average ability who has shown improvement in all areas. Continued difficulty was present in word retrieval and motor skills. These motor difficulties were hampering Stan's progress in school, and it was recommended that a peer note taker be secured for him and that alternative methods be provided for him to demonstrate his knowledge. Writing could be accomplished on a specially designed computer for ease of writing. It was further recommended that Stan attend a college with support present for students with disabilities. It was also suggested that he take no more than two reading courses per quarter. Follow-up of Stan's progress indicated that he has made the transition to college, that he has a peer note taker, and that his professors have adapted their requirements to fit. He continues to be well motivated and has decided to major in special education.

References

Accornero, V. H., Amado, A. J., Morrow, C. E., Xue, L., Anthony, J. C., & Bandstra, E. S. (2007). Impact of prenatal cocaine exposure on attention and response inhibition as assessed by continuous performance tests. *Journal of Developmental and Behavioral Pediatrics, 28*, 195–205.

Adnams, C. M., Kodituwakku, P. W., Hay, A., Molteno, C. D., Viljoen, D. L., & May, P. A. (2001). Patterns of cognitive-motor development in children with fetal alcohol syndrome from a community in South Africa. *Alcoholism, Clinical and Experimental Research, 25*, 557–562.

Ahmadi, J., Kampman, K., Dackis, C., Sparkman, T., & Pettinati, H. (2008). Cocaine withdrawal symptoms identify "Type B" cocaine-dependent patients. *The American Journal on Addictions, 17*, 60–64.

Anderson, P., Anderson, V., Grimwood, K., Nolan, T., Catroppa, C., & Keir, E. (1997). Neuropsychological consequences of bacterial meningitis: A prospective study.

Journal of the International Neuropsychological Society, 3, 47–48.

Anderson, V., Bond, L., Catroppa, C., Grimwood, K., Keir, E., & Nolan, T. (1997). Childhood bacterial meningitis: Impact of age at illness and medical complications on long-term outcome. *Journal of the International Neuropsychological Society, 3,* 147–158.

Anderson, V., & Catroppa, C. (2007). Memory outcome at 5 years post-childhood traumatic brain injury. *Brain Injury, 21,* 1399–1409.

Anderson, V., Catroppa, C., Dudgeon, P., Morse, S. A., Haritou, F., & Rosenfeld, R. V. (2006). Understanding predictors of functional recovery and outcome 30 months following early head injury. *Neuropsychology, 20,* 42–57.

Anderson, V., Northam, E., Hendy, J., & Wrennall, J. (2001). Cerebral infections. In V. Anderson, E. Northam, J. Hendy, & J. Wrennall (Eds.), *Developmental neuropsychology: A clinical approach* (pp. 221–248). East Sussex, England: Psychology Press, Ltd.

Anderson, V., & Yeates, K. O. (2007). New frontiers in pediatric traumatic brain injury. *Developmental Neurorehabilitation, 10,* 269–270.

Anderson, V. A., & Taylor, H. G. (2000). Meningitis. In K. O. Yeates, M. D. Ris & H. G. Taylor (Eds.), *Pediatric neuropsychology: Research, theory, and practice.* New York: Guilford.

Anderst, J. D. (2008). Assessment of factors resulting in abuse evaluations in young children with minor head trauma. *Child Abuse and Neglect, 32,* 405–413.

Archibald, S. L., Fennema-Notestine, C., Famst, A., Riley, E. P., Mattson, S. N., & Jernigan, T. L. (2001). Brain dysmorphology in individuals with severe prenatal alcohol exposure. *Developmental Medicine and Child Neurology, 43,* 148–154.

Arendt, R. E., Short, E. J., Singer, L. T., Minnes, S., Hewitt, J., Flynn, S., et al. (2004a). Children prenatally exposed to cocaine: Developmental outcomes and environmental risks at seven years of age. *Developmental and Behavioral Pediatrics, 25,* 83–90.

Arendt, R. E., Short, E. J., Singer, L. T., Minnes, S., Hewitt, J., Flynn, S., et al. (2004b). Children prenatally exposed to cocaine: Developmental outcomes and environmental risks at seven years of age. *Journal of Developmental and Behavioral Pediatrics, 25,* 83–90.

Armin, R., Ford-Jones, E., Richardson, S. E., Macgregor, D., Tellier, R., Heurter, H., et al. (2008). Acute childhood encephalitis and encephalopathy associated with influenza: A prospective 11-year review. *The Pediatric Infectious Disease Journal, 27,* 390–395.

Armstrong, C. M., Allen, D. N., Donohue, B. C., & Mayfield, J. (2008). Sensitivity of the comprehensive Trail Making test to traumatic brain injury in adolescents. *Archives of Clinical Neuropsychology, 23,* 351–358.

Arroyos-Jurado, E., Paulsen, J. S., Merrell, K. W., Lindgren, S. D., & Max, J. E. (2000). Traumatic brain injury in school-age children academic and social outcome. *Journal of School Psychology, 38,* 571–587.

Arvin, A., & Whitley, R. (2001). Herpes, simplex virus infections. In J. Remington & J. Klein (Eds.), *Infectious diseases of the fetus and newborn infant* (5th ed., pp. 425–446). Philadelphia: W.B. Saunders.

Astley, S., & Clarren, S. K. (2001). Measuring the facial phenotype of individuals with prenatal alcohol exposure: Correlations with brain dysfunction. *Alcohol and Alcoholism, 36,* 147–159.

Autti-Ramo, I., Fagerlune, A., Ervalahti, N., Loimu, L., Korkman, M., & Hoyme, H. E. (2006). Fetal alcohol spectrum disorders in Finland: Clinical delineation of 77 older children and adolescents. *American Journal of Medical Genetics, 140A,* 137–143.

Ayr, L. K., Yeates, K. O., & Enrile, B. G. (2005). Arithmetic skills and their cognitive correlates in children with acquired and congenital brain disorder. *Journal of the International Neuropsychological Society, 11,* 249–262.

Bada, H. S., Das, A., Bauer, C. R., Shankaran, S., Lester, B. M., Gard, C. C., et al. (2005). Low birth weight and preterm births: Etiologic fraction attributable to prenatal drug exposure. *Journal of Perinatology, 25,* 631–637.

Bandstra, E. S., Morrow, C. E., Anthony, J. C., Churchill, S. S., Chitwood, D. C., Steele, B. W., et al. (2001). Intrauterine growth of full-term infants: Impact of prenatal cocaine exposure. *Pediatrics, 108,* 1309–1319.

Bandstra, E. S., Morrow, E. C., Anthony, J. C., Accornero, V. H., & Fried, P. A. (2001). Longitudinal investigation of task persistence and sustained attention in children with prenatal cocaine exposure. *Neurotoxicology and Teratology, 23,* 545–559.

Baron, I. S. (2008). Maturation into impairment: The merit of delayed settlement of pediatric forensic neuropsychology cases. In R. L. Heilbronner (Ed.), *Neuropsychology in the courtroom: Expert analysis of reports and testimony* (pp. 66–78). New York: Guilford Press.

Beeghly, M., Martin, B., Rose-Jacobs, R., Cabral, H., Heeren, T., Augustyn, M., et al. (2006). Prenatal cocaine exposure and children's language functioning at 6 and 9.5 years: Moderating effects of child age, birthweight, and gender. *Journal of Pediatric Psychology, 31,* 98–115.

Beers, S. R., Skold, A., Dixon, C. E., & Adelson, P. D. (2005). Neurobehavioral effects of Amantadine after pediatric traumatic brain injury: A preliminary report. *Journal of Head Trauma Rehabilitation, 20,* 450–463.

Behnke, M., Eyler, F., Garvan, K., Wobie, W., & Hou, C. (2002). Cocaine exposure and developmental outcome from birth to 6 months. *Neurotoxicology and Teratology, 24,* 282–295.

Bendersky, M., Gambini, G., Lastella, A., Bennett, D. S., & Lewis, M. (2003). Inhibitory motor control at five years as a function of prenatal cocaine exposure. *Journal of Developmental and Behavioral Pediatrics, 24,* 345–351.

Benn, K. M., & McColl, M. A. (2004). Parental coping following childhood acquired head injury. *Brain Injury, 18,* 239–255.

Berman, R. F., & Hannigan, J. H. (2000). Hippocampal damage following prenatal alcohol exposure in rats. *Hippocampus, 10,* 94–110.

Bigler, E. D., Johnson, S. C., & Blatter, D. D. (1999). Head trauma and intellectual status: Relation to quantitative magnetic resonance imaging findings. *Applied Neuropsychology, 6,* 217–225.

Bland-Steward, L. M., Seymour, H. N., Beeghly, M., & Frank, D. A. (1998). Semantic development of

African-American children prenatally exposed to cocaine. *Seminars in Speech and Language, 19,* 167–186.

Bloom, D. R., Levin, H. S., & Ewing-Cobbs, L. (2001). Lifetime and novel psychiatric disorders after pediatric brain injury. *Journal of the American Academy of Child & Adolescent Psychiatry, 40,* 572–579.

Braga, L. W., Da Paz Junior, A. C., & Ylvisaker, M. (2005). Direct clinician-delivered versus indirect family-supported rehabilitation of children with traumatic brain injury: A randomized controlled trial. *Brain Injury, 19,* 819–831.

Brookshire, B., Levin, H. S., Song, J., & Zhang, L. (2004). Components of executive function in typically developing and head-injured children. *Developmental Neuropsychology, 25,* 61–83.

Buck, L., & Gurwitch, R. H. (2003). Cocaine, Prenatal exposure. In T. H. Ollendick & C. S. Schroeder (Eds.), *Encyclopedia of clinical child and pediatric psychology* (pp. 119–120). New York: Kluwer.

Burd, L., Klug, M. G., Martsolf, J. T., & Kerbeshian, J. (2003). Fetal alcohol syndrome: Neuropsychiatric phenomics. *Neurotoxicology and Teratology, 25,* 697–705.

Campbell, C. G. N., Kuehn, S. M., Richards, P. M. P., Venuevra, E., & Hutchison, J. S. (2004). Medical and cognitive outcome in children with traumatic brain injury. *Canadian Journal of Neurological Sciences, 31,* 213–219.

Canadian Pediatric Society. (2002). Fetal alcohol syndrome. *Paediatrics and Child Health, 7,* 161–174.

Catroppa, C., & Anderson, V. (2007). Recovery in memory function, and its relationship to academic success, at 24 months following pediatric TBI. *Child Neuropsychology, 13,* 240–261.

Catroppa, C., Anderson, V., Ditchfield, M., & Coleman, L. (2008). Using magnetic resonance imaging to predict new learning outcome at 5 years after childhood traumatic brain injury. *Journal of Child Neurology, 23,* 486–496.

Chiriboga, C. A. (1998). Neurological correlates of fetal cocaine exposure. *Annals of the New York Academy of Sciences, 846,* 109–125.

Clark, R. S., Kochanek, P. M., Watkins, S. C., Chen, M., Dixon, C. E., Seidberg, N. A., et al. (2000). Caspase-3 mediated neuronal death after traumatic brain injury in rats. *Journal of Neurochemistry, 74,* 740–753.

Clarren, S. K., Randels, S. P., Sanderson, M., & Fineman, R. M. (2001). Screening for fetal alcohol syndrome in primary schools: A feasibility study. *Teratology, 63,* 3–10.

Coelho, C. A. (2007). Management of discourse deficits following traumatic brain injury: Progress, caveats, and needs. *Seminars in Speech and Language, 28,* 122–135.

Coggins, T., Olswang, L., Olson, H. C., & Timler, G. (2003). On becoming socially competent communicators: the challenge for children with fetal alcohol exposure. In L. Abbeduto (Ed.), *International review of research in mental retardation. Language and communication in mental retardation* (pp. 121–150). San Diego, CA: Academic Press.

Coles, C. D., Platzman, K. A., Smith, I., James, M. E., & Falek, A. (1992). Effects of cocaine and alcohol use in pregnancy on neonatal growth and neurobehavioral status. *Neurotoxicology and Teratology, 14,* 23–33.

Connor, P. D., & Mahurin, R. (2001). A preliminary study of working memory in fetal alcohol damage using fMRI.

Journal of the International Neuropsychological Society, 7, 206–210.

Connor, P. D., Sampson, P. D., Streissguth, A., Bookstein, F. L., & Barr, H. M. (2006). Effects of prenatal alcohol exposure on fine motor coordination and balance: A study of two adult samples. *Neuropsychologia, 44,* 744–751.

Dalman, C., Allebeck, P., Gunnell, D., Harrison, G., Kristensson, K., Lewis, G., et al. (2008). Infections in the CNS during childhood and the risk of subsequent psychotic illness: A cohort of more than one million Swedish subjects. *American Journal of Psychiatry, 156,* 59–65.

Donders, J. (1996). Cluster subtypes in the WISC III standardization sample: analysis of factor index scores. *Psychological Assessment, 8,* 312–318.

Donders, J. (1997). Sensitivity of the WISC III to injury severity in children with traumatic head injury. *Assessment, 4,* 107–109.

Donders, J. (2007). Traumatic brain injury. In S. J. Hunter & J. Donders (Eds.), *Pediatric neuropsychological intervention* (pp. 91–111). Cambridge: Cambridge University Press.

Donders, J., & Nesbit-Greene, K. (2004). Predictors of neuropsychological test performance after pediatric traumatic brain injury. *Assessment, 11,* 275–284.

Donders, J., & Warschausky, S. (1996). A structural equation analysis of the WISC III in children with traumatic brain injury. *Child Neuropsychology, 2,* 185–192.

Draper, K., Ponsford, J., & Schonberger, M. (2007). Psychosocial and emotional outcomes 10 years following traumatic brain injury. *Journal of Head Trauma Rehabilitation, 22,* 278–287.

Edmondson, R., & Smith, T. (1994). Temperament and behavior of infants prenatally exposed to drugs: Clinical implications for the mother-infant dyad. *Infant and Child Development, 15,* 368–374.

Engman, M.-L., Adolfsson, I., Lewensohn-Fuchs, I., Forsgren, M., Mosskin, M., & Malm, G. (2008). Neuropsychologic outcomes in children with neonatal herpes encephalitis. *Pediatric Neurology, 38,* 398–405.

Eriksson, U. J. (2007). Fetal ethanol exposure during pregnancy-how big is the problem and how do we fix it? *Acta Paediatrica, 96,* 1557–1559.

Ervalahti, N., Korkman, M., Fagerlund, A., Autti-Ramo, I., Loimu, L., & Hoyme, H. E. (2007). Relationship between dysmorphic features and general cognitive function in children with fetal alcohol spectrum disorders. *American Journal of Medical Genetics, 143A,* 2916–2923.

Ewing-Cobbs, L., Barnes, M., Fletcher, J. M., Levin, H. S., Swank, P. R., & Song, J. (2004). Modeling of longitudinal academic achievement scores after pediatric traumatic brain injury. *Developmental Neuropsychology, 25,* 107–133.

Ewing-Cobbs, L., Fletcher, J. M., Levin, H. S., Iovino, I., & Miner, M. E. (1998). Academic achievement and academic placement following traumatic brain injury in children and adolescents: A two-year longitudinal study. *Journal of Clinical and Experimental Neuropsychology, 20,* 769–781.

Farmer, J. E., Kanne, S. M., Haut, J. S., Williams, J., Johnstone, B., & Kirk, K. (2002). Memory functioning following traumatic brain injury in children with premorbid learning disabilities. *Developmental Neuropsychology, 22*, 455–469.

Fletcher, J. M., Ewing-Cobbs, L., Francis, D. J., & Levin, H. S. (1995). Variability in outcomes after traumatic brain injury in children: A developmental perspective. In S. H. Broman & M. E. Michel (Eds.), *Traumatic head injury in children* (pp. 3–21). New York: Oxford University Press.

Fournier, N. M., Calverley, K. L., Wagner, J. P., Poock, J. L., & Crossley, M. (2008). Impaired social cognition 30 years after hemispherectomy for intractable epilepsy: The importance of the right hemisphere in complex social functioning. *Epilepsy and Behavior, 12*, 460–471.

Frank, D. A., Jacob, S., Beeghly, M., Augustyn, M., Bellinger, D., Cabral, H., et al. (2002). Level of prenatal cocaine exposure and scores on the Bayley Scales of Infant Development: Modifying effects of caregiver, early intervention, and birth weight. *Pediatrics, 110*, 1143–1152.

Goldschmidt, L., Richardson, G. A., Stoffer, D. S., Geva, D., & Day, N. L. (1996). Prenatal alcohol exposure and academic achievement at age 6: A nonlinear fit. *Alcoholism, Clinical and Experimental Research, 20*, 763–770.

Goldstein, F. C., & Levin, H. S. (1990). Epidemiology of traumatic brain injury: Incidence, clinical characteristics, and risk factors. In E. D. Bigler (Ed.), *Traumatic brain injury: Mechanisms of damage, assessment, intervention, and outcome* (pp. 51–68). Austin, TX: Pro-Ed.

Green, H. L., Diaz-Gonzalez de Ferris, M. E., Vasquez, E., Lau, E., & Yusim, J. (2001). Long-lasting care for the child exposed to alcohol in utero. *Contemporary Paediatrics, 18*, 72–80.

Hawley, C. A. (2003). Reported problems and their resolution following mild, moderate, and severe traumatic brain injury amongst children and adolescents in the UK. *Brain Injury, 17*, 1–23.

Hawley, T. L., Halle, T. G., Drasin, R. E., & Thomas, N. G. (1993). Children of addicted mothers: Effects of the 'crack epidemic' on the caregiving environment and the development of preschoolers. *Journal of Orthopsychiatric Association, 65*, 364–379.

Hayman-Abello, S. E., Rourke, B. P., & Fuerst, D. R. (2003). Psychosocial status after pediatric traumatic brain injury: A subtype analysis using the Child Behavior Checklist. *Journal of the International Neuropsychological Society, 9*, 887–898.

Hilliker, D. R., & Whitt, J. K. (2003). Meningitis. In T. H. Ollendick & C. S. Schroeder (Eds.), *Encyclopedia of clinical child and pediatric psychology*. New York: Kluwer.

Hoffman, N., Donders, J., & Thompson, E. H. (2000). Novel learning abilities after traumatic head injury in children. *Archives of Clinical Neuropsychology, 15*, 47–58.

Hoffman, R. S., Henry, G. C., Howland, M. A., Weisman, R. S., Weil, L., & Goldfrank, L. R. (1992). Association between life-threatening cocaine toxicity and plasma cholinesterase activity. *Annals of Emergency Medicine, 21*, 247–253.

Hooper, L., Williams, W. H., Sarah, E. W., & Chua, K. C. (2007). Caregiver distress, coping, and parenting styles in cases of childhood encephalitis. *Neuropsychological Rehabilitation, 17*, 621–637.

Howell, K. K., Lynch, M. E., Platzman, K. A., Smith, G. H., & Coles, C. D. (2006). Prenatal alcohol exposure and ability, academic achievement, and school functioning in adolescence: A longitudinal follow-up. *Journal of Pediatric Psychology, 31*, 116–126.

Hoyme, H. E., May, P. A., Kalberg, W. O., Kodituwakku, P. W., Gossage, J. P., Trujillo, P. M., et al. (2005). A practical clinical approach to diagnosis of fetal alcohol spectrum disorders: Clarification of the 1996 Institute of Medicine criteria. *Pediatrics, 115*, 39–47.

Jacobson, S. W., Jacobson, J. L., Sokol, R. J., Chiodo, L. M., & Corobana, R. (2004). Maternal age, alcohol abuse history, and quality of parenting as moderators of the effects of prenatal alcohol exposure on 7.5-year intellectual function. *Alcoholism, Clinical and Experimental Research, 28*, 1732–1745.

Jantz, P. B., & Coulter, G. A. (2007). Child and adolescent traumatic brain injury: Academic, behavioural, and social consequences in the classroom. *Support for Learning, 22*, 84–89.

Janusz, J., Kirkwood, M. W., Yeates, K. O., & Taylor, H. G. (2002). Social problem-solving skills in children with traumatic brain injury: Long-term outcomes and prediction of social competence. *Child Neuropsychology, 8*, 179–194.

Jennett, B., & Teasdale, G. (1981). *Management of head injuries*. Philadelphia, PA: Davis.

Jin, C., & Schachar, R. J. (2004). Methylphenidate treatment of attention-deficit/hyperactivity disorder secondary to head injury in childhood: A long-term follow-up of 318 children. *Disability and Rehabilitation, 23*, 665–669.

Jones, N. A., Field, T., Davalos, M., & Hart, S. (2004). Greater right frontal EEG asymmetry and nonempathic behavior are observed in children prenatally exposed to cocaine. *The International Journal of Neuroscience, 114*, 459–480.

Kable, J. A., Coles, C. D., Lynch, M. E., & Platzman, K. A. (2008). Physiological responses to social and cognitive challenges in 8-year olds with a history of prenatal cocaine exposure. *Developmental Psychobiology, 50*, 251–265.

Kelly, S. J., Day, N., & Streissguth, A. (2000). Effects of prenatal alcohol exposure on social behavior in humans and animals. *Neurotoxicology and Teratology, 22*, 143–149.

Kimberlin, D. (2007). Herpes simplex infections of the newborn. *Seminars in Perinatology, 31*, 19–25.

Kliegman, R., Madura, D., Kiwi, R., Eisenberg, I., & Yamashita, T. (1994). Relation of maternal cocaine use to the risks of prematurity and low birth weight. *Journal of Pediatrics, 124*, 751–756.

Kodituwakku, P. W., Coriale, G., Fiorentino, D., Aragon, A. S., Kalberg, W. O., Buckley, D., et al. (2006). Neurobehavioral characteristics of children with fetal alcohol spectrum disorders in communities from Italy: Preliminary results. *Alcoholism, Clinical and Experimental Research, 30*, 1551–1561.

Kodituwakku, P. W., Kalberg, W. O., & May, P. A. (2001). The effects of prenatal alcohol exposure on executive functioning. *Alcohol Research and Health, 25*, 192–198.

Kopp, C., & Kralow, J. (1983). The developmentalist and the study of biological residual in children after recovery from bacterial meningitis. *Archives of Pediatrics, 79*, 63–71.

Koren, G. (1993). Cocaine and the human fetus: The concept of teratophilia. *Neurotoxicology and Teratology, 15,* 301–304.

Langlois, J. A., Rutland-Brown, W., & Thomas, K. E. (2004). *Traumatic brain injury in the United States: Emergency department visits, hospitalizations, and deaths.* Atlanta, GA: Centers for Disease Control and Prevention, National Center for Injury Prevention and Control.

Lehnung, M., Leplow, B., Ekroll, V., Benz, B., Ritz, A., Mehdorm, M., et al. (2003). Recovery of spatial memory and persistence of spatial orientation deficits after traumatic brain injury during childhood. *Brain Injury, 17,* 855–869.

Lettori, D., Battaglia, D., Sacco, A., Veredice, C., Chieffo, D., Massimi, L., et al. (2008). Early hemispherectomy in catastrophic epilepsy: A neuro-cognitive and epileptic long-term follow-up. *Seizure, 17,* 49–63.

Levin, H. S., Ewing-Cobbs, L., & Eisenberg, H. M. (1995). Neurobehavioral outcome of pediatric closed head injury. In S. H. Broman & M. E. Michel (Eds.), *Traumatic head injury in children* (pp. 70–94). New York: Oxford University Press.

Lewis, B. A., Singer, L. T., Minnes, S., Arendt, R. E., Weishampel, P., Short, E. J., et al. (2004). Four-year language outcomes of children exposed to cocaine in utero. *Neurotoxicology and Teratology, 26,* 617–627.

Lezak, M. D., Howieson, D. B., & Loring, D. W. (2004). *Neuropsychological assessment* (4th ed.). New York: Oxford University Press.

Livy, D. J., Miller, E. K., Maier, S. E., & West, J. R. (2003). Fetal alcohol exposure and temporal vulnerability: Effects of binge-like alcohol exposure on the developing rat hippocampus. *Neurotoxicology and Teratology, 25,* 447–458.

Lustbader, A. S., Mayes, L. C., McGee, B. A., Jatlow, P., & Roberts, W. L. (1998). Incidence of passive exposure to crack/cocaine and clinical findings in infants seen in an outpatient service. *Pediatrics, 102,* 1–7.

Malisza, K. L., Allman, A., Shiloff, D., Jakobson, L., Longstaff, S., & Chudley, A. E. (2005). Evaluation of spatial working memory function in children and adults with fetal alcohol spectrum disorders: A functional magnetic resonance imaging study. *Pediatric Research, 58,* 1150–1157.

Mangeot, S., Armstrong, K., Colvin, A. N., Yeates, K. O., & Taylor, H. G. (2002). Long-term executive function deficits in children with traumatic brain injuries: Assessment using the Behavior Rating Inventory of Executive Function (BRIEF). *Child Neuropsychology, 8,* 271–284.

Mattson, S. N., Calarco, K. E., & Robertson, B. A. M. (2006). Focused and shifting attention in children with heavy prenatal alcohol exposure. *Neuropsychology, 20,* 361–369.

Mattson, S. N., Goodman, A. M., Caine, C., Delis, D. C., & Riley, E. P. (1999). Executive functioning in children with heavy prenatal alcohol exposure. *Alcohol Clinical, Experimental Research, 23,* 1808–1815.

Mattson, S. N., Lang, A. R., & Calarco, K. E. (2002). Attentional focus and attentional shift in children with heavy prenatal alcohol exposure. *Journal of the International Neuropsychological Society, 8,* 295–303.

Max, J. E., Lansing, A. E., Koele, S. L., Castillo, C. S., Bokura, H., Schachar, R., et al. (2004). Attention deficit hyperactivity disorder in children and adolescents following traumatic brain injury. *Developmental Neuropsychology, 25,* 159–177.

Max, J. E., Robertson, B. A. M., & Lansing, A. E. (2001). The phenomenology of personality change due to traumatic brain injury in children and adolescents. *Journal of Neuropsychiatry and Clinical Neurosciences, 13,* 161–170.

May, P. A., Fiorentino, D., Gossage, J. P., Kalberg, W. O., Hoyme, H. E., Robinson, L. K., et al. (2006). Epidemiology of FASD in a province in Italy: Prevalence and characteristics of children in a random sample of schools. *Alcoholism, Clinical and Experimental Research, 30,* 1562–1575.

May, P. A., & Gossage, J. P. (2001). Estimating the prevalence of fetal alcohol syndrome: A summary. *Alcohol Research and Health, 25,* 159–167.

May, P. A., Gossage, J. P., Marais, A. S., Hendricks, L. S., Snell, C. L., Tabachnick, B. G., et al. (2008). Maternal risk factors for fetal alcohol syndrome and partial fetal alcohol syndrome in South Africa: A third study. *Alcoholism, Clinical and Experimental Research, 32,* 738–753.

Mayes, L. C., & Bornstein, M. H. (1995). Developmental dilemmas for cocaine-abusing parents and their children. In M. Lewis & L. M. Bendersky (Eds.), *Mothers, babies, and cocaine: The role of toxins in development.* Hillsdale, NJ: Lawrence Erlbaum Associates.

Mayes, L. C., Cicchetti, D. V., Acharyya, S., & Zhang, H. (2003). Developmental trajectories of cocaine-and-other-drug-exposed and non-cocaine-exposed children. *Journal of Developmental and Behavioral Pediatrics, 24,* 323–335.

Mayes, L. C., Molfese, D. L., Key, A. P. F., & Hunter, N. C. (2005). Event-related potentials in cocaine-exposed children during a Stroop task. *Neurotoxicology and Teratology, 27,* 797–813.

Mayes, L. C., Snyder, P. J., Langlois, E., & Hunter, N. (2007). Visuospatial working memory in school-aged children exposed in utero to cocaine. *Child Neuropsychology, 13,* 205–218.

McCrea, M. A. (2008). *Mild traumatic brain injury and post-concussion syndrome.* New York: Guilford Press.

Messinger, D., Bauer, C. R., Das, A., Seifer, R., Lester, B. M., Lagasse, L., et al. (2004). The Maternal Lifestyle Study: Cognitive, motor, and behavioral outcomes of cocaine-exposed and opiate-exposed infants through three years of age. *Pediatrics, 113,* 1677–1685.

Mihalick, S. M., Crandall, J. E., Langois, J. C., Krienke, J. D., & Dube, W. V. (2001). Prenatal alcohol exposure, generalized learning impairment, and medial prefrontal cortical deficits in rats. *Neurotoxicology and Teratology, 23,* 453–462.

Minnes, P. (1998). Family resources and stress associated with having a mentally retarded child. *American Journal on Mental Retardation, 93,* 184–192.

Minnes, P., Graffi, S., Nolte, M. L., Carlson, P., & Harrick, L. (2000). Coping and stress in Canadian family caregivers of persons with traumatic brain injuries. *Brain Injury, 14,* 737–748.

Minnes, S., Robin, N. H., Alt, A. A., Kirchner, H. L., Satayathum, S., Salbert, B. A., et al. (2006). Dysmorphic and anothropmetric outcomes in 6-year-old prenatally cocaine-exposed children. *Neurotoxicology and Teratology, 28*, 28–38.

Minnes, S., Singer, L. T., Arendt, R. E., & Satayathum, S. (2005). Effects of prenatal cocaine/polydrug use on maternal-infant feeding interactions during the first year of life. *Journal of Developmental and Behavioral Pediatrics, 26*, 194–200.

Minnes, S., Singer, L. T., Humphrey-Wall, R., & Satayathum, S. (2008). Psychosocial and behavioral factors related to the post-partum placements of infants born to cocaine-using women. *Child Abuse and Neglect, 32*, 353–366.

Mirchandani, H., Mirchandani, I., & Hellman, F. (1991). Passive inhalation of free-base cocaine ("crack") smoke by infants. *Archives of Pathological Laboratory Medicine, 115*, 494–498.

Morgan, A. T., Ward, E., Murdoch, B., Kennedy, B., & Murision, R. (2003). Incidence, characteristics and predictive factors for dysphagia following paediatric traumatic brain injury. *Journal of Head Trauma Rehabilitation, 18*, 239–251.

Morrow, C. E., Culbertson, J. L., Accornero, V. H., Xue, L., Anthony, J. C., & Bandstra, E. S. (2006). Learning disabilities and intellectual functioning in school-aged children with prenatal cocaine exposure. *Developmental Neuropsychology, 30*, 905–931.

Neuspiel, R. R. (1996). Racism and perinatal addiction. *Ethnicity and Disease, 6*, 47–55.

Niccols, A. (2007). Fetal alcohol syndrome and the developing socio-emotional brain. *Brain and Cognition, 65*, 135–142.

Nichols, A. (2007). Fetal alcohol syndrome and the developing socio-emotional brain. *Brain and Cognition, 65*, 135–142.

Noland, J. S., Singer, L. T., Arendt, R. E., Minnes, S., Short, E. J., & Bearer, C. (2003). Executive functioning in preschool-age children prenatally exposed to alcohol, cocaine, and marijuana. *Alcoholism, Clinical and Experimental Research, 27*, 647–656.

Noland, J. S., Singer, L. T., Short, E. J., Minnes, S., Arendt, R. E., Kirchner, H. L., et al. (2005). Prenatal drug exposure and selective attention in preschoolers. *Neurotoxicology and Teratology, 27*, 429–438.

Nulman, I., Rovet, J., Altmann, D., Bradley, C., Einarson, T., & Koren, G. (1994). Neurodevelopment of adopted children exposed in utero to cocaine. *Canadian Medical Association Journal, 151*, 1591–1597.

Nybo, T., & Koskiniemi, M. (1999). Cognitive indicators of vocational outcome after severe traumatic brain injury (TBI) in childhood. *Brain Injury, 13*, 759–766.

Nybo, T., Sainio, M., & Muller, K. (2004). Stability of vocational outcome in adulthood after moderate to severe preschool brain injury. *Journal of the International Neuropsychological Society, 10*, 719–723.

Poggi, G., Liscio, M., Adduci, A., Galbiati, S., Massimino, M., Sommovigo, M., et al. (2005). Psychological and adjustment problems due to acquired brain lesions in childhood: A comparison between post-traumatic patients and brain tumour survivors. *Brain Injury, 19*, 777–785.

Premj, S., Benzies, K. S., K., & Hayden, K. A. (2007). Research-based interventions for children and youth with Fetal Alcohol Spectrum Disorder: Revealing the gap. *Child care, health, and development, 33*, 389–397.

Prichep, L. S., Kowalik, S. C., Alper, K., & de Jesus, C. (1995). Quantitative EEG characteristics of children exposed in utero to cocaine. *Clinical Electroencephalogy, 26*, 166–172.

Pulsifer, M. B., Butz, A. M., O'Reilly, F. M., & Belcher, H. M. (2008). Prenatal drug exposure: Effects on cognitive functioning at 5 years of age. *Clinical Pediatrics, 47*, 58–65.

Rao, S., & Lyketsos, C. (2000). Neuropsychiatric sequelae of traumatic brain injury. *Psychosomatics, 41*, 95–103.

Richardson, G. A., Conroy, M. L., & Day, N. L. (1996). Prenatal cocaine exposure: Effects on the development of school-age children. *Neurotoxicology and Teratology, 18*, 627–634.

Richardson, G. A., Goldschmidt, L., & Willford, J. (2008). The effects of prenatal cocaine use on infant development. *Neurotoxicology and Teratology, 30*, 96–106.

Riikonen, R., Salonen, I., Partanen, K., & Verho, S. (1999). Brain perfusion SPECT and MRI in fetal alcohol syndrome. *Developmental Medicine & Child Neurology, 41*, 652–659.

Riley, E. P., Guerri, C., Calhoun, F., Charness, M. E., Foroud, T. M., Li, T. K., et al. (2003). Prenatal alcohol exposure: Advancing knowledge through international collaborations. *Alcoholism, Clinical and Experimental Research, 27*, 118–135.

Riley, E. P., & McGee, C. L. (2005). Fetal alcohol spectrum disorders: An overview with emphasis on changes of alcohol related neurodevelopmental disorder. *Teratology, 56*, 317–326.

Rivkin, M. J., Davis, P. E., Lemaster, J. L., Cabral, H. J., Warfield, S. K., Mulkern, R. B., et al. (2008). Volumetric MRI study of brain in children with intrauterine exposure to cocaine, alcohol, tobacco, and marijuana. *Pediatrics, 121*, 741–750.

Rizk, B., Atterbury, J. L., & Groome, L. J. (1996). Reproductive risks of cocaine. *Human Reproduction, 2*, 43–55.

Robin, A. H., Temkin, N. R., & Machamer, J. (1999). Emotional and behavioral adjustment after traumatic brain injury. *Archives of Physical Medicine and Rehabilitation, 80*, 991–999.

Roebuck, T., Mattson, S. N., Marion, S., Brown, W. S., & Riley, E. P. (2004). Bimanual coordination in alcohol exposed children: role of the corpus callosum. *Journal of the International Neuropsychological Society, 10*, 536–548.

Sameroff, A. J., & Chandler, M. J. (1975). Reproductive risk and the continuum of caretaking casualty. In F. D. Horowitz (Ed.), *Review of child development research* (Vol. 4, pp. 187–244). Chicago: University of Chicago Press.

Schachar, R., Levin, H. S., Max, J. E., Purvis, K. L., & Chen, S. H. (2004). Attention deficit hyperactivity disorder symptoms and response inhibition after closed head injury in children: do pre-injury behavior and injury severity predict outcome? *Developmental Neuropsychology, 25*, 179–198.

Schonfeld, A. M., Mattson, S. N., Lang, A. R., Delis, D., & Riley, E. P. (2001). Verbal and nonverbal fluency in children with heavy prenatal alcohol exposure. *Journal of Studies on Alcohol, 62*, 239–246.

Schonfeld, A. M., Paley, B., Frankel, F., & O'Connor, M. J. (2006). Executive functioning predicts social skills following prenatal alcohol exposure. *Child Neuropsychology, 12,* 438–452.

Semrud-Clikeman, M. (2001). *Traumatic brain injury in children and adolescents.* New York: Guilford Press.

Semrud-Clikeman, M. (2007). *Social competence in children.* New York: Springer.

Seymour, C. M., & Wagner, J. J. (2008). Simultaneous expression of cocaine-induced behavioral sensitization and conditioned place preference in individual rats. *Brain Research, 1213,* 57–68.

Simone, C., Derewlany, L., Knie, B., & Koren, G. (1992). Can the human placenta biotransform cocaine? *Clinical Investigations in Medicine, 21,* 247–253.

Singer, L. T. (1999). Advances and redirections in understanding effects of fetal drug exposure. *Journal of Drug Issues, 29,* 253–262.

Singer, L. T., Arendt, R. E., Minnes, S., Farkas, K., Salvator, A., Kirchner, H. L., et al. (2008). Cognitive and motor outcomes of cocaine-exposed infants. *Journal of the American Medical Association, 287,* 1952–1960.

Singer, L. T., Arendt, R. E., Minnes, S., Salvator, A., Siegel, C., & Lewis, B. A. (2001). Developing language skills of cocaine-exposed infants. *Pediatrics, 107,* 1057–1064.

Singer, L. T., Farkas, K., & Kliegman, R. (1991). Childhood medical and behavioral consequences of maternal cocaine use. *Journal of Pediatric Psychology, 17,* 389–406.

Singer, L. T., Salvator, A., Arendt, R. E., Minnes, S., Farkas, K., & Kliegman, R. (2002). Effects of cocaine/polydrug exposure and maternal psychological distress on infant birth outcomes. *Neurotoxicology and Teratology, 24,* 127–136.

Smith, K. S., & Morrell, J. I. (2008). Behavioral responses during the initial exposures to a low dose of cocaine in late preweaning and adult rats. *Neurotoxicology and Teratology, 30,* 202–212.

Sokol, R. J., Delaney-Black, V., & Nordstrom, B. (2003). Fetal alcohol spectrum disorder. *Journal of the American Medical Association, 290,* 2996–2999.

Sowell, E. R., Mattson, S. N., Thompson, P. M., Jernigan, T. L., Riley, E. P., & Toga, A. W. (2001). Mapping callosal morphology and cognitive correlates: Effects of heavy prenatal alcohol exposure. *Neurology, 57,* 235–244.

Spandoni, A. D., McGee, C. L., Fryer, S. L., & Riley, E. P. (2007). Neuroimaging and fetal alcohol spectrum disorders. *Neuroscience & Biobehavioral Reviews, 31,* 238–245.

Stanwood, G. D., & Levitt, P. (2004). Drug exposure early in life: Functional repercussions of changing neuropharmacology during sensitive periods of brain development. *Current Opinions in Pharmacology, 4,* 65–71.

Starling, S. P., Sirotnak, A. P., Heisler, K. W., & Barnes-Eley, M. L. (2007). Inflicted skeletal trauma: The relationship of perpetrators to their victims. *Child Abuse and Neglect, 31,* 993–999.

Stavinhoa, P. L. (2005). Integration of neuropsychology in educational planning following traumatic brain injury. *Preventing School Failure, 49,* 11–16.

Streissguth, A., Barr, H. M., Kogan, J., & Bookstein, F. L. (1996). *Understanding the occurrence of secondary disabilities in clients with fetal alcohol syndrome (FAS) and fetal alcohol effects (FAE).* Seattle, WA: University of Washington Publication Services.

Streissguth, A., Bookstein, F. L., Barr, H. M., Sampson, P. D., O'Malley, K., & Young, J. K. (2004). Risk factors for adverse life outcomes in fetal alcohol syndrome and fetal alcohol effects. *Journal of Developmental and Behavioral Pediatrics, 25,* 228–238.

Streissguth, A., & O'Malley, K. (2000). Neuropsychiatric implications and long-term consequences of fetal alcohol spectrum disorders. *Seminars in Clinical Neuropsychiatry, 5,* 177–190.

Stroufe, L. A., Fox, N. E., & Pancake, V. R. (1983). Attachment and dependency in developmental perspectives. *Child Development, 54,* 1615–1627.

Taylor, H. G., Yeates, K. O., Wade, S. L., Drotar, D., Stancin, T., & Minich, N. (2002). A prospective study of short- and long-term outcomes after traumatic brain injury in children: Behavior and academic achievement. *Neuropsychology, 16,* 15–27.

Thomas, M. J., Kalivas, P. W., & Shaham, Y. (2008). Neuroplasticity in the mesolimbic dopamine system and cocaine addiction. *British Journal of Pharmacology, 154,* 327–342.

Tonks, J., Williams, W. H., Frampton, I., Yates, P., & Slater, A. (2007). Reading emotions after child brain injury: A comparison between children with brain injury and non-injured controls. *Brain Injury, 21,* 731–739.

Vakil, E., Blachstein, H., Rochberg, J., & Vardi, M. (2004). Characterization of memory impairment following closed-head injury in children using the Rey Auditory Verbal Learning Test (AVLT). *Child Neuropsychology, 10,* 57–66.

Vaurio, L., Riley, E. P., & Mattson, S. N. (2008). Differences in executive functioning in children with heavy prenatal alcohol exposure or attention-deficit/hyperactivity disorder. *Journal of the International Neuropsychological Society, 14,* 119–129.

Volpe, J. (1992). Effect of cocaine use on the fetus. *New England Journal of Medicine, 327,* 399–407.

Vriezen, E. R., & Pigott, S. (2000). Sensitivity of measures of attention to pediatric brain injury. *Brain and Cognition, 44,* 67–82.

Wade, S. L., Carey, J., & Wolfe, C. R. (2006). The efficacy of an online cognitive-behavioral, family intervention in improving child behavior and social competence following pediatric brain injury. *Rehabilitation Psychology, 5,* 179–189.

Wade, S. L., Taylor, H. G., Drotar, D., Stancin, T., & Yeates, K. O. (1996). Childhood traumatic brain injury: Initial impact on the family. *Journal of Learning Disabilities, 29,* 652–666.

Wade, S. L., Taylor, H. G., Walz, N. C., Salisbury, S., Stancin, T., Bernard, L. A., et al. (2008). Parent-child interactions during the initial weeks following brain injury in young children. *Rehabilitation Psychology, 53,* 180–190.

Wade, S. L., Wolfe, C. R., & Pestian, J. P. (2004). Web-based family problem-solving intervention for families of children with traumatic brain injury. *Behavior Research, Methods, Instruments & Computers, 36,* 261–169.

Warner, T. D., Behnke, M., Eyler, F. D., Padgett, K., Leonard, C. M., Hou, W., et al. (2006). Diffusion tensor imaging of frontal white matter and executive functioning in cocaine-exposed children. *Pediatrics, 118*, 2014–2024.

Wassenberg, R., Max, J. E., Lindgren, S. D., & Schatz, A. (2004). Sustained attention in children and adolescents after traumatic brain injury: relation to severity of injury, adaptive functioning, ADHD, and social background. *Brain Injury, 18*, 51–64.

Whaley, S. E., O'Connor, M. J., & Gunderson, G. (2001). Comparison of the adaptive functioning of children prenatally exposed to alcohol to an unexposed clinical sample. *Alcoholism: Clinical and Experimental Research, 25*, 118–124.

Wilde, E. A., Hunter, J. V., Newsome, M. R., Scheibel, R. S., Bigler, E. D., Johnson, J. L., et al. (2005). Frontal and temporal morphometric findings on MRI in children after moderate to severe traumatic brain injury. *Journal of Neurotrauma, 22*, 333–344.

Wood, R. L., & Rutherford, N. A. (2006). Long-term effect of head trauma on intellectual abilities: A 16-year outcome study. *Journal of Neurology, Neurosurgery, and Psychiatry, 77*, 1180–1184.

Yeates, K. O., Armstrong, K., Janusz, J., Taylor, G. H., Wade, S. L., Stancin, T., et al. (2005). Long-term attention problems in children with traumatic brain injury. *Journal of the American Academy of Child & Adolescent Psychiatry, 44*, 574–584.

Yeates, K. O., Bigler, E. D., Dennis, M., Gerhardt, C. A., Rubin, K. H., Stancin, T., et al. (2007). Social outcomes in childhood brain disorder: A heuristic integration of social neuroscience and developmental psychology. *Psychological Bulletin, 133*, 535–556.

Yeates, K. O., Swift, E., Taylor, H. G., Wade, S. L., Drotar, D., Stancin, T., et al. (2004). Short- and long-term social outcomes following pediatric traumatic brain injury. *Journal of the International Neuropsychological Society, 10*, 412–426.

Zevenbergen, A., & Ferraro, F. (2001). Assessment and treatment of fetal alcohol syndrome in children and adolescents. *Journal of Developmental and Physical Disabilities, 13*, 123–136.

Chapter 15
Childhood Cancer

Childhood cancers, though relatively rare, are found in children at all ages. The two most common forms of childhood cancer are childhood leukemia and brain tumors. Although the etiologies for these disorders differ, treatment frequently involves chemotherapy and cranial irradiation. The chemotherapy regimen has not been found to have the same effects on later outcome that irradiation produces. It is these "late effects" that most concern the child neuropsychologist. Many more children are surviving given the improvement in treatment over the past few decades. Survival for brain tumors is approximately 70 percent (Brenner, 2003) and above 70 percent for acute lymphoblastic leukemia (ALL) (Gatta, Capocaccia, Coleman, Ries, & Berrino, 2002).

Childhood cancer includes leukemia, brain tumors, and tumors outside the CNS (i.e., kidney). These diseases are, by definition, life threatening and pose challenges in all areas of the child's life as well as in family functioning. Initially the emphasis is on securing appropriate treatment and undergoing procedures which are unpleasant and frequently painful. These treatments can extend for years in the child's life and are fraught with anxiety and stress. For example, treatment for acute lymphoblastic leukemia (ALL) can last for 3–4 years prior to remission. During this time there are numerous doctor visits, hospitalizations, and procedures.

Treatment of childhood cancer in the central nervous system (CNS) varies depending on the type of tumor, the level of malignancy, the location of the tumor, the age of the child, and how much tissue is involved. Treatments include surgery and irradiation as well as chemotherapy. Damage from surgery depends on the extent of the tumor and the involvement in the CNS. Surgery has proven to be less damaging, generally, than radiation and/or chemotherapy (Beebe et al., 2005; Moore, 2005). Surgery is utilized for brain tumors while ALL is treated via radiation and/or chemotherapy. Each of these types of childhood cancers will be discussed in the following sections. Emphasis will be on the neuropsychological aspects of brain tumors and ALL, as well as the family and psychosocial variables in the treatment and recovery for these children.

Neuroimaging in Childhood Cancer

Studies of brain imaging with children with ALL and brain tumors have found that the treatment has significant effects on the brain. Demyelination and lesions in the white matter are found following chemotherapy and irradiation (Burger & Boyko, 1991). Difficulties have also been found in the white matter with intrathecal chemotherapy (ITC), and particularly with the chemotherapy agent, methotrexate (Hudson, 1999).

In the past 10 years, methotrexate treatment was associated with a stroke-like syndrome that included hemiparesis and aphasia and occurs in 3–10 percent of the ALL population (Creutzig et al., 2005; Pui & Evans, 2006). It has been suggested that these difficulties are due to problems with blood perfusion (Laningham et al., 2007). These difficulties are generally monitored and treatment is stopped temporarily for approximately a week until the symptoms subside.

M. Semrud-Clikeman, P.A. Teeter Ellison, *Child Neuropsychology*, DOI 10.1007/978-0-387-88963-4_15,
© Springer Science+Business Media, LLC 2009

Another issue is the significantly increased risk of CNS neoplasms in children who have undergone cranial irradiation for brain tumors or leukemia (Neglia et al., 2006; Paako, Talvensaari, Pyhtinen, & Lanning, 1999). Leukemia survivors had more gliomas than meningiomas (tumors in the meninges) while children with previous brain tumors developed more meningiomas. These tumors occurred within the first nine years following diagnosis for gliomas, and 17 years for meningiomas (Laningham et al., 2007). Approximately 20 percent of survivors were found to develop neoplasms (Pui et al., 2003).

White matter involvement appears to be present in children with ALL or brain tumors following treatment, particularly with methotrexate. Findings of a smaller volume in the cerebral white matter suggest white matter injury following the major treatments (Reddick et al., 2005). A relation between this white matter injury and cognitive ability has been found, particularly for patients with medulloblastomas (Mulhern, Reddick, & Palmer, 1999). When the white matter is compromised in the cerebral hemispheres, particularly in the frontal lobes and the anterior cingulate gyrus, attention and executive functioning abilities are affected (Mulhern, White, & Glass, 2004; Reddick et al., 2005).

This change in white matter may well interfere with normal development once treatment has ended. The disruption to the brain in its ability to transfer neuronal impulses likely interferes with learning as well as with speed of information processing. As is evident from the following sections on brain tumors and ALL, difficulties are frequently present in attention and problem solving skills that are associated with frontal white matter development (Semrud-Clikeman, Pliszka, Lancaster, & Liotti, 2006).

Brain Tumors

Brain tumors are estimated to constitute 20 percent of malignancies of childhood, and are most frequently diagnosed in children between the ages of three and nine years (Sklar, 2002). Treatment protocols often include whole-brain radiation, chemotherapy, and/or surgical interventions, and 50 percent to 60 percent of children are cancer-free after five years (Butler & Haser, 2006).

Survival from brain tumors varies depending on the type of tumor present. Medulloblastoma is the most common type of malignant tumor in children and the survival rate is approximately 65 percent. In contrast, children with brain stem gliomas show a less than 10 percent survival rate. For the majority of children with brain tumors of all types, the survival rate is approximately 65 percent.

Associated Features

Risk factors associated with the development of brain tumors include: (1) genetic syndromes, including neurofibromatosis and tuberous sclerosis; (2) presence of epilepsy and stroke in families of children with brain tumors; (3) immunosuppression prior to organ transplant, and (4) infections (Connelly & Malkin, 2007; Shaw & Infante-Rivard, 2006). Some environmental toxins (e.g., aromatic hydrocarbons) have been implicated, as have maternal use of barbiturates, heat, and prenatal exposure to X-rays (Bunin, Robison, Biegel, Pollack, & Rorke-Adams, 2006; Umansky, Shoshan, Rosenthal, Fraifield, & Spektor, 2008).

Types of Tumors

The most frequently diagnosed type of tumor is the astrocytoma. In an epidemiological study of malignant brain tumors in children under the age of 15, astrocytomas accounted for 57 percent of the tumors, while 23 percent were medulloblastomas and 8 percent were ependymomas (Briere, Scott, McNall-Knapp, & Adams, 2008; Burzynski, 2006; Lum, Halliday, Watson, Smith, & Law, 2006). Although brain tumors can occur at any age, the five- to nine-year-old interval shows the largest occurrence, followed closely by ages 0–4 years and 10–14 years of age (Scott, Elkin, & Thompson, 2001). Poorer outcome, particularly in cognitive development, has been found for children diagnosed at an early age (Mulhern et al., 1998).

In children under age two, the most common types of tumors are medulloblastomas (in the medulla portion of the brainstem), low-grade astrocytomas, and ependynomas (arising from the lining of the ventricles and spinal cord or ependyma). At ages 5–9, the most commonly diagnosed tumors are low-grade astrocytomas, medulloblastomas, high-grade astrocytomas, and cerebellar astrocytomas (Zhou et al., 2008). Children with astrocytomas in the cerebellum have had the highest survival rates, while those with brainstem gliomas have the poorest survival rate. Astrocytomas are graded from 1 to 4, depending on the degree of malignancy. The lower grade of a tumor indicates less malignancy.

Implications for Assessment

Accurate and timely diagnosis of brain tumors is especially important. Clinical manifestations may include changes in personality and cognition, and neuropsychological changes, depending on the type, size, and location of the tumor, and on the presence of cerebral edema (e.g., hydrocephalus and/or increased intracranial pressure). Tumors may be preceded by nausea, headaches, visual deficits (e.g., blurred or double vision, visual field blindness), lateralized sensory or motor impairments, vomiting, or seizures. Presence of these symptoms warrants immediate referral to a child neurologist and may necessitate CT scans or other neuroradiological scans (e.g., MRI). Low-grade tumors often have a gradual rather than acute onset, with neural tissues becoming compressed or displaced at a slow rate (Nortz, Hemme-Phillips, & Ris, 2007). Consequently, neurological signs may not always appear early. Brain tumors have been shown to produce behavioral, personality, academic, intellectual, and neuropsychological deficits in children (Butler & Haser, 2006).

Implications for Assessment

Cognition

Intellectual and academic declines have consistently been found for children who had cranial radiation therapy (CRT) (Reimers et al., 2003). The age at which treatment commences appears to have a significant effect on resulting intelligence test scores. Some have found that the late effects that occur after radiation begin approximately one year after treatment and can steadily worsen with development (Ris, Packer, Goldwein, Jones-Wallace, & Boyett, 2001).

A review of 12 studies of children treated for medulloblastoma or ependymoma found that those treated with CRT showed IQ declines over time, with the youngest patients showing the greatest decline in ability (Mulhern, Merchant, Gajjar, Reddick, & Kun, 2004). Those who had surgery or irradiation confined to the back of the brain (posterior fossa) showed less decline in IQ. The declines that have been found after treatment appear to be in the first few years after treatment (Spiegler, Bouffet, Greenberg, Rutka, & Mabbott, 2004). These declines are not due to regression, but rather to an inability to learn new skills and information (Palmer et al., 2003). In addition, children with higher ability levels have been found to show the most decrement in ability (Ris et al., 2001).

Academically children with brain tumors have significant deficits in learning, particularly in mathematics (Buono, Morris, & Morris, 1998). Those who have an accompanying diagnosis of hydrocephalus show the most difficulty in academics and often require special education (Mabbott et al., 2005). For all of the children with cancer, younger children were found to be at highest risk for later reading difficulties, spelling, and mathematics, while behavioral functioning was found to be within normal limits by parent and teacher report.

Attention

Additional difficulties have been found in memory, attention, and processing speed. Children treated at the youngest ages had the most severe deficits in these areas (Maddrey et al., 2005). Focused and sustained attention appear to be most directly affected in these children (Reddick et al., 2005). In addition, problems have been found in selective attention, cognitive flexibility, and processing speed (Briere et al., 2008; Reeves et al., 2005).

Visual-Spatial Perception

Difficulties have also been found in visual-motor integration, visuo-spatial organization, and poorer performance IQ abilities (Beebe et al., 2005; Carpentieri et al., 2003), particularly when these problems were present comorbidly. This profile is similar to that of children diagnosed with nonverbal learning disabilities and is found most frequently in children treated with radiation therapy and chemotherapy (Anderson, Godber, Smibert, Weiskop, & Ekert, 2000). Girls may be at higher neuropsychological risk following treatment for brain tumors compared to boys (Ris et al., 2001).

Memory

Memory skills have been problematic for children following brain tumor treatment. Children treated with radiotherapy have exhibited poorer memory skills on all aspects. Radiotherapy treatment, location of the tumor, and shunt for hydrocephalus were strong risk factors for memory difficulties (Reimers, Mortensen, & Schmiegelow, 2007). When FSIQ was used as a covariate, the presence of a shunt or tumor location within the hemispheres became more predictive of memory difficulties than did radiotherapy.

Pathways involved in memory are located in the temporal lobe extending into the third ventricle region. Children who had a tumor in this region showed poorer verbal memory skills than those with cerebellar tumors (King et al., 2004; Mickelwright, King, Morris, & Morris, 2007). In addition, those children with tumors in the cerebellum were found to experience significant problems with repetition and attention span (Steinlin et al., 2003).

Social-Emotional

Findings have indicated that there are social, emotional, and behavioral difficulties following treatment for brain tumors. Among children who had surgical treatment, 56 percent of the participants showed sufficient psychological distress that qualified for diagnoses of depression or externalizing behavioral difficulties (i.e., oppositional defiant disorder)(Meyer & Kieran, 2002). Another study found that children with a brain tumor history were evaluated for social skills difficulties. Findings indicated significant problems with socialization as well as a decrement in nonverbal reasoning abilities (Carey, Barakat, Foley, Gyato, & Phillips, 2001).

Most have not found lasting social-emotional dysfunction in children following cancer (Nortz et al., 2007). Some difficulties have been found in social withdrawal and in social skills for some children with brain tumors (Poggi et al., 2005). Family dysfunction following a child's brain tumor treatment has been found, with post-traumatic stress disorder being reported in families of cancer survivors (Kazak, Alderfer, Rourke et al., 2004; Streisand, Kazak, & Tercyzak, 2003). Poorer adjustment was found for children with lower IQs and poorer adaptive functioning, single-parent families, a chaotic family environment, and low socioeconomic status (Carlson-Green, Morris, & Krawiecki, 1995).

Summary

Thus, late effects of brain tumor treatment generally have an impact on academic, intellectual and neuropsychological functioning. Mediating factors such as the amount of radiation, pre- and post-operative status, complications (e.g., shunts, infections), and the extent of the tumor, as well as the age of onset, all affect the child's outcome. Additional study is needed on the quality of life children with brain tumors enjoy and on the level of their psychosocial functioning.

Childhood Leukemia

Leukemia means white blood. There are two types of blood forming cells, myeloid and lymphoid. Myeloid cells mature into red blood cells while lymphoid cells mature into white blood cells, including

B cells and T cells. This maturation is altered in leukemia and the ability of these cells to mature is impaired. There are two types of leukemia based on the cells that are affected: acute lymphocytic leukemia (ALL) which is 75–80 percent of all childhood leukemias, and acute myelogenous leukemia (AML) which is 20–25 percent of all cases (Colby-Graham & Chordas, 2003). Chronic forms of leukemia are uncommon in childhood and will not be discussed in this chapter. AML is less common and less is known about the neuropsychology of this disorder. The emphasis in this chapter will be on ALL.

Children with acute lymphocytic leukemia (ALL) experience significant learning difficulties similar to those of children with brain tumors. ALL accounts for approximately 75 percent of leukemia in children and is the most common type of cancer in childhood (Butler & Haser, 2006). ALL generally presents with initial symptoms of bleeding, fever, irritability, fatigue, and bone pain. Ninety-five percent of children with ALL survive, and 55 percent of those continue in remission five years after treatment (Spix, Eletr, Blettner, & Kaatsch, 2008; Yamamoto & Goodman, 2008). The peak age of onset is between the ages of three and five. ALL is more common in Hispanics and whites than in African–Americans, and in boys more than in girls. Genetics, environmental factors, and viruses have been implicated in the etiology of ALL. There is a one in five chance that an identical twin of a child with ALL will also have the disease (Zipf et al., 2000).

Belson, Kingsley, and Holmes (2007) report that many heritable syndromes as well as immunodeficiency disorders may be related to an increased risk of developing leukemia. Exposure to X-rays either pre- or postnatally is also associated with a higher risk for leukemia. Finally, several viral infections seem to co-occur with childhood leukemia (e.g., Epstein-Barr, human T lymphonea-leukemia virus). Environmental risk factors include radiation, hydrocarbons, and pesticides. Additional risk factors that have been identified are present for mothers who are 35 years or older at conception, large birth weight, neonatal jaundice and women who had two previous pregnancies which ended in early fetal death (Podvin, Kuehn, Mueller, & Williams, 2006).

Important Variables

Important prognostic indicators are initial white blood cell count, sex, age at diagnosis, CNS therapy, degree of lymph node enlargement, hemoglobin level, and platelet count at diagnosis. Initial white blood cell count (WBC) and age at diagnosis are strong predictors for length of remission and survival (Brenner et al., 2001). Patients who are younger than two or older than 10 and who have high WBC have the poorest prognosis.

Symptoms usually occur 1–6 weeks prior to diagnosis and can vary from child to child. During this time the bone marrow has been replaced by the leukemic cells which decrease red blood cells, white blood cells and platelets. Anemia is frequently present, which decreases the oxygen carrying ability of the red blood cells. Symptoms accompanying anemia include fatigue, lethargy, and headache as well as pale skin, nail beds, and the inner lining of the mouth. Cranial nerves can also be involved, particularly in the third (eye movement), sixth (tongue and pharynx), and seventh (face) nerves (Margolin, Steuber, & Poplack, 2002).

Treatment

Treatment differs depending on the risk factors, and patients with more risk factors are generally more aggressively treated. In contrast, those children who are at lower risk are treated by less toxic and less intensive means. There are three stages of treatment: remission induction, consolidation, and maintenance. The first stage, based on National Cancer Institute guidelines, uses age and white blood cell count as indicators to determine the degree of treatment. Children aged 1–9 years of age and with a white blood cell count less than 50,000 mm^3 show the best prognosis and are treated with less chemotherapy during induction than those outside of these guidelines (National Cancer Institute, 2002). Generally, post induction begins 29 days after induction has started. It is determined by how the child responds to treatment, the child's age, and the white blood cell count at diagnosis (Colby-Graham & Chordas, 2003).

The goal of treatment is to induce a remission, and approximately 95 percent of children with ALL are in remission 3–4 weeks after treatment begins (Chessells, 2000). During consolidation treatment the remission is strengthened through intensification of treatment. Methotrexate is the most common medication used during this time and has been found to be highly effective (Pui, 2000). During maintenance therapy a long-term, low dose treatment regimen is used often with daily doses of a cancer medication (often 6-mercaptopurine) and weekly doses of methotrexate with additional steroids as needed. Treatment occurs over a period of 2–3 years and has resulted in fewer relapse rates than those with shorter treatment periods (Chessells, 2000). Children who have had chemotherapy for ALL are at a higher risk for the development of brain tumors.

Intrathecal chemotherapy is used to reduce the possible spread of leukemia to the CNS (Westlake & Bertolone, 2002). For those children at highest risk additional cranial spinal radiation is used. Such treatment is used cautiously since it can cause lowered cognitive functioning, poorer psychomotor skills, and disruptions in neuroendocrine functioning (Margolin et al., 2002).

Neuropsychological Effects of Treatment

Neuropsychological impairment has been found in children treated with low doses of cranial radiation (1,800 rads). Declines in intelligence have been found in children who have undergone cranial radiation, with the most profound effects in younger and brighter patients. Studies in the 1980 s and 1990 s found that cranial radiation therapy was very detrimental to the child's cognitive and neuropsychological deficits (Butler & Haser, 2006). CRT is not used as often, except for children who do not respond well to the traditional methods. Chemotherapy has been evaluated with regard to late effects and, generally, has not been found to be as detrimental to the child's cognitive and neuropsychological development as CRT, although some difficulties are present even with chemotherapy (Espy et al., 2001).

Attentional deficits that affect the encoding of new materials have been found to be the most significantly affected in children following treatment for ALL (Lockwood, Bell, & Colegrove, 1999). Particular problems were found for those children who received CRT prior to five years of age. Difficulties were found in focusing and shifting of attention, cognitive flexibility and problem solving skills. Those children who had CRT at age five years or older had milder problems with attention, sustained attention and cognitive flexibility (Schatz, Kramer, & Albin, 2004).

When children are treated with intrathecal chemotherapy (ITC) alone, findings are of average academic attainment and normal cognitive development. Declines are found in visual-motor integration, verbal fluency, and arithmetic skills (Buizer, de Sonneville, van den Heuvel-Eibrink, & Veeman, 2005; Espy et al., 2001). Girls are more significantly affected on nonverbal skills while boys with ALL have not shown such difficulties (Brown, Madan-Swain, & Walco, 1998).

A meta-analysis of the studies evaluating neurocognitive outcome following treatment of ALL evaluated 28 empirical studies (Campbell et al., 2007). The effects were uniformly negative with significant deficits present for survivors of ALL in cognitive ability and academic achievement in the areas of reading, arithmetic, and spelling. In addition, significant deficits were found in attention, speed of information processing, visuo-spatial ability, verbal memory, visual memory, and fine motor skills. Therefore, these results suggest that these domains that should be particularly evaluated during a neuropsychological assessment. Difficulties with mathematics for children with ALL were found to be related to attentional problems (Buizer, de Sonneville, Van den Heuvel-Eibrink, & Veerman, 2006). Difficulties have also been found in speed of information processing (Reeves et al., 2007). Sluggish cognitive tempo was found in survivors of ALL which, in turn, creates problems following lectures and completing homework; all difficulties that impact the child's functioning in the classroom. Some difficulties have also been found in visuomotor control, particularly when it requires the child to quickly trace a figure that is moving around a screen (Buizer, de Sonneville, Van den Heuvel-Eibrink, Njiokiktjien, & Veerman, 2005).

Analysis of the behavioral functioning of children with childhood cancer has found symptoms that are consistent with a diagnosis of ADHD (Mulhern et al., 2004a). Further study has found that childhood cancer survivors frequently have problems with attention, oppositional behavior, and in cognition (Helton, Corwyn, Bonner, Brown, & Mulhern, 2006). Children with childhood cancer are also more likely to be compared to their siblings to reveal problems with mood, antisocial behaviors, and attention-deficit (Schultz et al., 2008). In this study survivors from brain tumors and ALL were not differentiated.

Based on the current state of the research, many unknowns remain. While it is fairly clear that there are some neuropsychological problems associated with treatment, the range of the difficulty, relation to dose and type of treatment has not been established. Further study is needed to more completely understand the areas of difficulty that continue to be present for the child and his/her family.

Family Issues

The ability of parents to cope with the child's disease appears strongly related to the child's coping level (Kazak et al., 2001). Some of the difficulties found in these families include increased marital discord, financial difficulty brought on by medical costs, anxiety, sibling adjustment problems, and discordant family life. Mothers appear to be at highest risk for developing depression following treatment, possibly due to being most responsible for the daily care of the child and the demands required by the medical care for the cancer (Sahler et al., 2005). Financial issues are also present, as well as the fear of the child's death. These issues affect the entire family including the siblings. Despite all of these stressors, nearly 70 percent of these parents report stable and close marriages (Manne et al., 2001). For families with limited English fluency, lower socioeconomic status, lower educational levels, and lack of insurance, the difficulties are compounded when a child is very ill, particularly with cancer (Kodish et al., 2004; Kouyoumdjian, Zamboanga, & Hansen, 2003). Certainly further study is needed in these areas in order to provide support for the child as well as his/her family.

Interventions for Childhood Cancer

One of the main psychological treatments for childhood cancer survivors is the use of cognitive remediation. Reviews of the literature have found that brain injury rehabilitation shows mild to moderate improvement of functioning (Ciccerone et al., 2000; Cicerone et al., 2005). A major program that has been developed is the Cognitive Remediation Program (CRP)(Butler, 2007) which has adapted practices from brain injury rehabilitation, special education, and clinical psychology sources. This program consists of 25 two-hour sessions and significant improvement has been found on attention and response inhibition following the program (Butler & Copeland, 2002; Butler & Mulhern, 2005). It includes practicing specific skills, teaching of problem solving strategies, and cognitive-behavioral interventions. In addition, it includes the Attention Process Training cognitive remediation program developed by Sohlberg and colleagues (Sohlberg & Mateer, 1999). A multicenter clinical trial of this program found improved attention and academic achievement skills in children with childhood cancer (Butler et al., 2008). The findings were of modest effects and the authors caution researchers and clinicians against the belief that the child's functioning will return to pre-disease states.

Another approach to cognitive rehabilitation involves teaching problem solving skills directly to mothers of children newly diagnosed with cancer (Sahler et al., 2002). The eight-week group experience utilizes a cognitive behavioral approach and includes homework assignments that are tailored to the individual mother's difficulty. Empirical validation of the program has found moderate effect sizes for improvement. In addition, the improvement continued on reevaluation three months later, particularly in the areas of problem orientation as well as in ability to take responsibility and control of areas of difficulty (Sahler et al., 2005).

Another program that has been used to reduce the distress felt by families and survivors after treatment ends is the Surviving Cancer Competently Intervention Program (SCCIP) (Kazak et al., 1999). This intervention involves four sessions conducted over one day. Sessions 1 and 2 teach the use of cognitive-behavioral principles to help relieve sadness and emotional distress and generally involve separate groups of survivors, parents, and siblings. Sessions 3 and 4 utilize family therapy with the entire family unit. For session 1 the discussion is conducted for each group on "how cancer has affected me and my family." In session 2, in the separate groups, specific cognitive-behavioral techniques are taught, including self-talk issues, adversity-beliefs-consequences model, and reframing of issues. For session 3 the families are reconstituted and meet all together. Information about cancer and recovery is provided, andfamilies have an opportunity to role-play different situations. For example, some would be selected to play the 'mother' role, and as they talk about how cancer has affected them (as mothers), the rest of the group listens. This exercise is repeated for survivors, fathers, and siblings. In session 4 the individual families work together on a task that involves the family members' different perceptions about what has happened and how others are coping with the problem. These questions are formulated by the family and put into writing; at the end of this session all families come back together and share their answers. Empirical validation of this approach has found that emotional adjustment and post-traumatic stress improved directly after the intervention, and again when retested 3–5 months later (Kazak, Alderfer, Streisand et al., 2004).

Social skills training has also been emphasized as a supportive intervention during school reintegration. The training program that has been designed includes social-cognitive problem solving, assertiveness training, and how to manage teasing and bullying (Barakat et al., 2003). This program was found to improve functioning for children with brain tumors in social competence and in emotional distress.

Educational Interventions

In addition to the emotional and adjustment issues, educational interventions have also been utilized. One of the major difficulties is reintegration into school following treatment. Many cancer centers have a protocol for such re-entry. These programs raise awareness for parents and teachers about the child's needs, both educational and medical,

provide information for the child's peers, and develop an appropriate IEP (Mitby et al., 2003). A comprehensive program involves school personnel for further information and offers consultation for issues that can arise. Studies have found that children who receive appropriate interventions upon school re-entry exhibit improved reading and written language skills during the first two years of re-entry (Anderson et al., 2000). Others have found that close monitoring of the child's progress and direct teaching of skills does not increase the child's ability to progress in mathematics and reading (Goldman, Briery, Ward, Delgado, & Armstrong, in press; Nortz et al., 2007).

Pharmacological Interventions

Methylphenidate (Ritalin) has been utilized to treat the attentional problems frequently seen in children recovering from childhood cancer and has been fairly successful in alleviating these difficulties. In one study of 32 children with a history of brain tumors or ALL who were administered methylphenidate, improvement was found for every child on sustained attention tasks, compared to placebo (Thompson et al., 2001). These findings were further replicated in a study utilized a three-week, randomized and placebo double-blind procedure (Mulhern et al., 2004b).

Case Illustration

Brian was 14-years- and eight-months-old when seen for a neuropsychological evaluation. He was diagnosed with a cancerous brain tumor at age eight which was removed from the posterior right area of his brain. Chemotherapy was utilized for treatment and the cancer was not evident in the past three MRI scans. His initial neuropsychological examination conducted at age 10 indicated some difficulty with language, processing speed, and with sadness. He was being reevaluated at his mother's request due to concerns about increased feelings of anxiety, withdrawal, and possible depression. Brian had completed eighth grade the past year and was entering high school in the fall. His mother reported that he was in speech and language services as well as in occupational therapy in middle school. Brian's current IEP called for support in all academic classes in high school through a study hall, as well as continued language therapy. He was dismissed from occupational therapy classes. He was not prescribed any medications and has not entered into therapy.

Behavioral Observations

Brian came to the testing session willingly and was cooperative and forthcoming on all measures. He was attentive to the work at hand and was diligent in completing the tasks presented to him. Brian's mood was somber and quiet. While he answered all questions, he did not readily volunteer any additional information. Brian's language was to the point and he did not elaborate on any ideas or thoughts. He became somewhat frustrated on the language portion of the WISC IV and at times would answer "I don't know" very quickly. However, when pressed to answer, Brian would provide a reasonable answer.

Tests Administered

WISC IV, WJ III, Children's Memory Scale, Sensory Perceptual Examination, CELF-3, Purdue Pegboard, DKEFS Trails, Sorting, and Color-Word Interference test, BASC—parent, adolescent, teacher forms.

Test Interpretations

Brian achieved a Full Scale IQ of 81 on the WISC III which places him at the 10th percentile and in the below average range of intellectual functioning. His verbal comprehension score of 77 is in the below average range while his perceptual reasoning score of 92 is in the average range. There is a difference of 15 points between these abilities which is significant,

but not unusual. His working memory scores are in the average range at a standard score of 97 while his processing speed abilities are in the below average range at 78. There is a significant difference between his perceptual reasoning skills and all of the indices indicating that Brian's nonverbal abilities are relatively better developed than his language skills.

Brian's achievement skills indicate that his overall achievement is in the low average range with a standard score of 87 and a percentile of 20. His skills in reading are in the low average range overall and commensurate with his ability. This finding is true in his broad mathematics skills as well as in his writing ability. His poorest score is in the area of reading fluency and in story recall. In order to further evaluate Brian's language and memory skills, the Children's Memory Scale and the CELF-3 were administered.

On the Children's Memory Scale Brian scored in the average range on all tasks. His verbal memory was in the average range for both immediate and delayed conditions. His visual memory was also in the average range for all conditions. Brian showed some difficulty with attention and concentration on the CMS, particularly when asked to complete work in a distracting environment.

On the CELF 3 Brian achieved scores in the below average range for expressive language and in the low average range on measures of receptive language. He showed particular difficulty on tasks that required him to understand relationships between words, and categorize words into appropriate semantic relationships. He had great difficulty in constructing sentences using selected words as well as in using correct nouns and verbs. These scores are consistent with the difficulty Brian experienced on the WISC III in the areas of vocabulary and comprehension.

The TOVA was also administered to determine whether Brian was experiencing significant problems with attention. His scores were in the at risk range, but not significantly indicative of an attentional difficulty. An interview with his mother indicated that Brian met five of the nine inattention criteria, and two of the impulsivity/hyperactivity criteria. Although he does not meet criteria for a diagnosis of ADHD, his attention difficulty is present and particularly evident in situations that require complex processing or processing of material quickly.

Parts of the Delis-Kaplan Test of Executive Functioning (DKEFS) were also administered to evaluate Brian's cognitive flexibility, working memory, and ability to inhibit. On the Trails portion of the DKEFS Brian showed good ability in all areas. On the measure of verbal fluency Brian found it difficult to generate as many words as possible to a selected letter. Brian's response inhibition on the Color-Word Interference subtest was well within the average range. These findings are consistent with the results of the WISC IV working memory subtests which were within the average range for Brian's age.

The Purdue Pegboard was administered in order to determine whether Brian showed any difficulty in the area of fine motor dexterity. Brian showed significant problems with his dominant (right) hand on this measure, but not with his nondominant hand. These findings are consistent with right-sided difficulty on the measure of fingertip writing. Brian experienced 13 errors with his right hand, but none with his left. On the tactile, auditory, and visual tests Brian scored well within the average range.

Psychosocial evaluation indicated concerns by his mother as to Brian's feelings of anxiety and depression. He scored in the significant range on these scales on the BASC-Parent form. The teacher forms indicated significant concerns about anxiety, depression, and withdrawal. Brian achieved no scores in the clinically significant or at risk range on the self-report.

An interview with his mother indicated the likely presence of a mood disorder for Brian as well as significant problems with language. Although Brian scored within the average to low average range on achievement tests, his mother and teacher reported significant problems in the classroom with processing instruction, following directions, and completing homework appropriately. These findings are consistent with the difficulties identified by the neuropsychological evaluation of left-hemispheric dysfunction. Brian's problems with language, right-handed fine motor tasks, and processing of information quickly are all consistent with this area of concern. Given that the tumor was located in the left temporal region, it is likely that these difficulties are related to the treatment of the tumor as well as to residual difficulties. It was recommended that Brian have a follow-up MRI to evaluate the integrity of his brain at the current time. At follow-up it was found that Brian's tumor had recurred and surgery was again needed to resect it. Radiation was utilized at that time to further treat the tumor and Brian was scheduled for a reevaluation of his abilities in three months following the end of treatment. It was also strongly recommended that Brian begin treatment for his mood disorder. In addition, consultation with his school and teacher was strongly recommended. Following treatment for his brain tumor and the subsequent radiation treatment, Brian re-entered his ninth grade year and was provided additional support on his IEP. Although he continued to struggle with his language skills and his right-sided coordination, he responded very well to therapy and was placed on an antidepressant which lightened his mood. He also reported that he was experiencing improvement in his ability to complete his work and participate in class. He went on his first date to the homecoming dance and had re-established friendships with his peers.

Psychometric Summary

WISC IV

Scale/Subtest	Standard/Scaled score	Percentile
Full Scale IQ	81	10
Verbal Comprehension	77	6
• Similarities	7	16
• Vocabulary	6	9
• Comprehension	5	5
• Information	7	16
• Word Reasoning	9	37
Perceptual Reasoning	92	30
• Block Design	7	16
• Picture Completion	13	84
Working Memory	97	42
• Digit Span	11	63
• Letter-Number Sequencing	8	25
• Arithmetic	6	9
Processing Speed	78	7
• Coding	4	2
• Symbol Search	8	25
• Cancellation	9	37

WJ III Achievement

Cluster/Test	Standard score	Percentile
Total Achievement	87	20
Broad Reading	91	14
• Letter-Word ID	88	21
• Passage Comp	93	31
• Reading Fluency	80	9
Oral Language	86	18
• Story Recall	82	11
• Understanding Directions	91	27
Broad Math	93	33
• Calculation	99	47
• Math Fluency	90	25
• Applied Problems	92	30
Broad Written Language	101	53
• Spelling	98	45
• Writing Samples	112	79
• Writing Fluency	100	50
Supplemental Test		
• Word Attack	94	35

Children's Memory Scale

	Standard score	Percentile
General Memory	93	32
Verbal Memory Immediate	103	58
Verbal Memory Delayed	88	21
Visual Memory Immediate	94	34
Visual Memory Delayed	94	34
Learning	88	16
Attention/Concentration	82	12
Delayed Recall	94	34

CELF-3

Scale	Standard score	Percentile
Total Language Score	81	10
Receptive Language Score	86	18
• Concepts and Directions	10	50
• Word Classes	7	16
• Semantic Relationships	6	9
Expressive Language Score	78	7
• Formulated Sentences	6	9
• Recalling Sentences	8	25
• Sentence Assembly	5	5

Delis-Kaplan Test of Executive Functioning

Scale	Scaled score
Trailmaking	
• Visual Scanning	12
• Number Sequencing	14
• Letter Sequencing	14
• Number-Letter Sequencing	12
• Motor Speed	12
Verbal Fluency	
• Letter Fluency	7
• Category Fluency	12
• Category Switching	9
• Category Switching Accuracy	10
Color-Word Interference	
• Color Naming	11
• Word Reading	11
• Inhibition	12
• Inhibition/Switching	12

Purdue Pegboard

Dominan	Z score	−1.7
Nondominant	Z score	.2
Both Hands	Z score	−1.22

Behavior Assessment System for Children (BASC)-Parent

Scale	T Score	Percentile
Internalizing Problems	76	98
Anxiety	76	99
Depression	71	96
Somatization	66	92
Atypicality	65	90
Attention Problems	60	83
Teacher Scales		
Internalizing Problems	75	98
Behavioral Symptoms Index	62	89
Anxiety	80	99
Depression	70	94
Somatization	63	91
Atypicality	68	93
Withdrawal	63	90

Chapter Summary

Childhood cancer and its treatment pose a myriad of challenges for the child and the family. Initial concern about the child's survival, financial pressures, and medical challenges contribute to difficulty with adjustment for the entire family. In addition, there are indications of neuropsychological difficulty following treatment, particularly in the areas of attention, memory, mathematics, social skills, and speed of information processing. These domains contribute to difficulties with adjustment and school re-entry for many children who are survivors. White matter changes following treatment have been linked to difficulties in attention and speed of information processing. The neurological differences do not change over time and likely impact the child's development at older ages. In addition, females appear to be more affected than males in development of necessary skills. Research has indicated that the problems that arise following treatment continue throughout the life span and many childhood survivors of cancer have difficulty with vocational and educational attainment.

For the neuropsychologist, the challenge is providing appropriate evaluation and remediation support as well as assisting the child and his/her family in adjusting to the aftermath of treatment. A transactional approach would be most appropriate for working with survivors of childhood cancer. Such an approach would assist in understanding the 'whole' child. Evaluating a child without input from the school or understanding the social relations with peers prevents a full understanding of the challenges faced by the child. Similarly, evaluating a child without understanding the family dynamics will not assist in developing appropriate interventions.

Emerging research indicates that working with parents, siblings, and survivors of childhood cancer can help the family utilize the available remediation supports in the school and community more effectively. Such time-limited interventions have been shown to be very helpful. Major cancer centers are adept at providing support for the child upon re-entry to school. However, many families do not live near major cancer centers and need information and support that may not be accessible in more rural areas. Such support can be provided by the neuropsychologist who has an understanding of the various systems that are needed to assist the child.

Particular interventions that are helpful for re-entry include educating school professionals and developing an appropriate IEP. The IEP needs to be tailored to the individual child's needs and the neuropsychologist can be instrumental in its development. In many cases school personnel are not trained to work with children with a history of cancer. Thus, it is important to not only provide this information, but to approach key school personnel and suggest a teacher in-service on these issues. Many of these children would not have survived in the past. Training of regular education teachers (and most special education teachers) does not routinely include information about medically involved children.

Finally, it is important to provide serial evaluations of the child's progress in order to monitor any possible problems that may occur as the child ages. Difficulties in executive functioning, inferential reasoning, and higher order cognitive skills may not appear until several years after treatment ends. These difficulties are associated with the decrease in white matter volume that has been found in cancer survivors. Flexible programming and support to develop compensatory strategies in adolescence to support these difficulties is important, and the serial evaluation can assist in the development of these programs.

Research is needed to continue understanding the challenges these children and their families face, as well as to validate appropriate treatments. Neuroimaging can also provide support for our understanding. Current research is generally restricted to volumetric imaging and DTI. Functional imaging may assist in understanding how the brain is processing information and, eventually, what interventions are most appropriate.

References

Anderson, V., Godber, T., Smibert, E., Weiskop, S., & Ekert, H. (2000). Cognitive and academic outcome following cranial irradiation and chemotherapy in children: A longitudinal study. *British Journal of Cancer, 82,* 255–262.

Barakat, L. P., Hetzke, J. D., Foley, B., Carey, M. E., Gyato, K., & Phillips, P. C. (2003). Evaluation of a social-skills training group intervention with children treated for brain tumors: A pilot study. *Journal of Pediatric Psychology, 28,* 299–307.

Beebe, D. W., Ris, M. D., Armstrong, F. D., Fontanesi, J., Mulhern, R., Holmes, E., et al. (2005). Cognitive and adaptive outcome in low-grade pediatric cerebellar astrocytomas: Evidence of diminished cognitive and adaptive functioning in National Collaborate Research Studies (CCG 9891/POG9130). *Journal of Clinical Oncology, 23,* 5198–5204.

Belson, M., Kingsley, B., & Holmes, A. (2007). Risk factors for acute leukemia in children: A review. *Environmental Health Perspectives, 115,* 138–145.

Brenner, H. (2003). Up-to-date survival curves of children with cancer by period analysis. *British Journal of Cancer, 8,* 1693–1697.

Brenner, H., Kaatsch, P., Burkhardt-Hammer, T., Harms, D. O., Schrappe, M., & Michaelis, J. (2001). Long-term survival of children with leukemia achieved by the end of the second millennium. *Cancer, 92,* 1977–1983.

Briere, M.-E., Scott, J. G., McNall-Knapp, R. Y., & Adams, R. L. (2008). Cognitive outcome in pediatric brain tumor survivors: Delayed attention deficit in long-term follow-up. *Pediatric Blood Cancer, 50,* 337–340.

Brown, R. T., Madan-Swain, A., & Walco, G. A. (1998). Cognitive and academic late effects among children previously treated for acute lymphocytic leukemia receiving chemotherapy as CNS prophylaxis. *Journal of Pediatric Psychology, 23,* 333–340.

Buizer, A. I., de Sonneville, L., Van den Heuvel-Eibrink, M. M., Njiokiktjien, C., & Veerman, A. J. P. (2005). Visuomotor control in survivors of childhood acute lymphoblastic leukemia treated with chemotherapy only. *Journal of the International Neuropsychological Society, 11,* 554–565.

Buizer, A. I., de Sonneville, L., Van den Heuvel-Eibrink, M. M., & Veerman, A. J. P. (2006). Behavioral and educational limitations after chemotherapy for childhood acute lymphoblastic leukemia or Wilms tumor. *Cancer, 106,* 2067–2075.

Buizer, A. I., de Sonneville, L. M. J., van den Heuvel-Eibrink, M. M., & Veeman, A. J. (2005). Chemotherapy and attentional dysfunction in survivors of childhood acute lymphoblastic leukemia: Effect of treatment intensity. *Pediatric Blood Cancer, 45,* 281–290.

Bunin, G. R., Robison, L. L., Biegel, J. A., Pollack, I. F., & Rorke-Adams, L. B. (2006). Parental heat exposure and risk of childhood brain tumor: A Children's Oncology Group Study. *American Journal of Epidemiology, 164,* 222–231.

Buono, L. A., Morris, M. K., & Morris, R. D. (1998). Evidence for the syndrome of nonverbal learning disabilities in children with brain tumors. *Child Neuropsychology, 4,* 144–157.

Burger, P. C., & Boyko, O. B. (1991). The pathology of CNS radiation injury. In P. H. Gutin, S. A. Leibel, & G. E. Sheline (Eds.), *Radiation injury to the nervous system* (pp. 3–15). New York: Raven Press.

Burzynski, S. R. (2006). Treatments for astrocytic tumors in children: Current and emerging strategies. *Paediatric Drugs, 8,* 167–178.

Butler, R. W. (2007). Cognitive rehabilitation. In S. J. Hunter & J. Donders (Eds.), *Pediatric neuropsychological intervention* (pp. 444–464). Cambridge: Cambridge University Press.

Butler, R. W., & Copeland, D. R. (2002). Attentional processes and their remediation in children treated for cancer: A literature review and the development of a therapeutic approach. *Journal of the International Neuropsychological Society, 8,* 115–124.

Butler, R. W., Copeland, D. R., Fairclough, D. L., Mulhern, R. K., Katz, E. R., Kazak, A. E., et al. (2008). A multicenter, randomized clinical trial of a cognitive remediation program for childhood survivors of a pediatric malignancy. *Journal of Consulting and Clinical Psychology, 76,* 367–378.

Butler, R. W., & Haser, J. K. (2006). Neurocognitive effects of treatment for childhood cancer. *Mental Retardation and Developmental Disabilities Research, 12,* 184–191.

Butler, R. W., & Mulhern, R. K. (2005). Neurocognitive interventions for children and adolescents surviving cancer. *Journal of Pediatric Psychology, 30,* 65–78.

Campbell, L. K., Scaduto, M., Sharp, W., Dufton, L., Van Slyke, D., Whitlock, J. A., et al. (2007). A meta-analysis of the neurocognitive sequelae of treatment for childhood acute lymphocytic leukemia. *Pediatric Blood Cancer, 49,* 65–73.

Carey, M. E., Barakat, L. P., Foley, B., Gyato, K., & Phillips, P. C. (2001). Neuropsychological functioning and social functioning of survivors of pediatric brain tumors: Evidence of nonverbal learning disability. *Child Neuropsychology, 7,* 265–272.

Carlson-Green, B., Morris, R. D., & Krawiecki, N. S. (1995). Family and illness predictors of outcome in pediatric brain tumors. *Journal of Pediatric Psychology, 20,* 769–784.

Carpentieri, S. C., Waber, D. P., Pomeroy, S. L., Scott, R. M., Goumnerova, L. C., Kieran, M. W., et al. (2003). Neuropsychological functioning after surgery in children treated for brain tumor. *Neurosurgery, 52,* 1348–1356.

Chessells, J. M. (2000). Recent advances in management of acute leukemia. *Archives of Disease in Childhood, 82,* 438–442.

Ciccerone, K. D., Dahlberg, C., Kalmar, K., Langenbahn, D. M., Malec, J. F., Bergquist, T. F., et al. (2000). Evidence-based cognitive rehabilitation: Recommendations for clinical practice. *Archives of Physical Medicine and Rehabilitation, 81,* 1596–1615.

Cicerone, K. D., Dahlberg, C., Malec, J. F., Langenbahn, D. M., Felicetti, T., Kneipp, S., et al. (2005). Evidence-based cognitive rehabilitation: Updated review of the literature from 1998 through 2002. *Archives of Physical Medicine and Rehabilitation, 86,* 1681–1692.

Colby-Graham, M. F., & Chordas, C. (2003). The childhood leukemias. *Journal of Pediatric Nursing, 18,* 87–95.

Connelly, J. M., & Malkin, M. G. (2007). Environmental risk factors for brain tumors. *Current Neurology and Neuroscience Reports, 7,* 208–214.

Creutzig, U., Zimmermann, M., Ritter, J., Reinhardt, D., Hermann, J., Henze, G., et al. (2005). Treatment strategies and long-term results in paediatric patients treated in four consecutive AML-BFM trials. *Leukemia, 19,* 2030–2042.

Espy, K. A., Moore, I. M., Kaufman, P. M., Kramer, J. H., Matthay, K., & Hutter, J. J. (2001). Chemotherapuetic CNS prophylaxis and neuropsychologic change in children with acute lymphoblastic leukemia: A prospective study. *Journal of Pediatric Psychology, 26,* 1–9.

Gatta, G., Capocaccia, R., Coleman, M. P., Ries, L. A. G., & Berrino, F. (2002). Childhood cancer survival in Europe and the United States. *Cancer, 95,* 1767–1772.

Goldman, M. L., Briery, B., Ward, M. W., Delgado, I., & Armstrong, F. D. (in press). Neurocognitive and educational outcomes of childhood cancer: A longitudinal study. *Journal of the International Neuropsychological Society*

Helton, S. C., Corwyn, R. F., Bonner, M. J., Brown, R. T., & Mulhern, R. (2006). Factor analysis and validity of the Conners Parent and Teacher rating scales in childhood cancer survivors.*Journal of Pediatric Psychology, 31,* 200–208.

Hudson, M. (1999). Late complications after leukemia therapy. In C. H. Pui (Ed.), *Childhood leukemias. Cambridge, MA: Cambridge University Press.*

Kazak, A. E., Alderfer, M. A., Rourke, M. T., Simms, S., Streisand, R., & Grossman, J. R. (2004). Posttraumatic stress disorder (PTSD) and posttraumatic stress symptoms (PRSS) in families of adolescent childhood cancer survivors. *Journal of Pediatric Psychology, 29,* 211–219.

Kazak, A. E., Alderfer, M. A., Streisand, R., Simms, S., Rourke, M. T., Barakat, L. P., et al. (2004). Treatment of posttraumatic stress symptoms in adolescent survivors of childhood cancer and their families: A randomized clinical trial. *Journal of Family Psychology, 18,* 493–504.

Kazak, A. E., Barakt, L., Alderfer, M. A., Rourke, M. T., Meeske, K., Gallagher, P., et al. (2001). Posttraumatic stress in survivors of childhood cancer and mothers: Development and validation of the Impact of Traumatic Stressor Interview Schedule (ITSIS). *Journal of Clinical Psychology in Medical Settings, 8,* 307–323.

Kazak, A. E., Simms, S., Barakat, L. P., Hobbie, W., Foley, B., Golomb, V., et al. (1999). Surviving cancer competently intervention program (SCCIP): A cognitive-behavioral family therapy intervention for adolescent survivors of childhood cancer and their families. *Family Process, 38,* 175–191.

King, T. Z., Fennell, E. B., Williams, L., Algina, J., Boggs, S., Crosson, B., et al. (2004). Verbal memory abilities in children with brain tumors. *Child Neuropsychology, 10,* 76–88.

Kodish, E., Eder, M. A., Noll, R. B., Ruccione, K., Lange, B., Angiolillo, A., et al. (2004). Communication of randomization in childhood leukemia trials. *Journal of the American Medical Association, 291,* 470–475.

Kouyoumdjian, H., Zamboanga, B. L., & Hansen, D. J. (2003). Barriers to community mental health services for Latinos: Treatment considerations. *Clinical Psychology, Science, & Practice, 10,* 394–422.

Laningham, F. H., Kun, L. E., Reddick, W. E., Ogg, R. J., Morris, E. B., & Pui, C. H. (2007). Childhood central nervous system leukemia: Historical perspectives, current therapy, and acute neurological sequelae. *Neuroradiology, 49,* 873–888.

Lockwood, K. A., Bell, T. S., & Colegrove, R. W. (1999). Long-term effects of cranial radiation therapy on attention functioning in survivors of childhood leukemia. *Journal of Pediatric Psychology, 24,* 55–66.

Lum, D. J., Halliday, W., Watson, M., Smith, A. B., & Law, A. (2006). Cortical ependymoma or monomorphous angiocentric glioma. *Neuropathology, 28,* 81–86.

Mabbott, D. J., Spiegler, B. J., Greenberg, M. L., Rutka, J. T., Hyder, T. J., & Bouffet, E. (2005). Serial evaluation of academic and behavioral outcome after treatment with cranial radiation in childhood. *Journal of Clinical Oncology, 23,* 2256–2263.

Maddrey, A. M., Bergeron, J. A., Lombardo, E. R., McDonald, N. K., Mulne, A. F., Barenberg, P. D., et al. (2005). Neuropsychological performance and quality of life of 10 year survivors of childhood medulloblastoma. *Journal of Neuro-oncology, 72,* 245–253.

Manne, S., Nereo, N., DuHamel, K., Ostroff, J., Parsons, S., Martini, R., et al. (2001). Anxiety and depression of mothers of children undergoing bone marrow transplant: Symptom prevalence and use of the beck depression and beck anxiety inventories as screening instruments. *Journal of Consulting and Clinical Psychology, 69,* 1037–1047.

Margolin, J. F., Steuber, C. P., & Poplack, D. G. (2002). Acute lymphoblastic leukemia. In P. A. Pizzo & D. G. Poplack (Eds.), *Principles and practice of paediatric oncology. Philadelphia, PA: Lippincott Williams & Wilkins.*

Meyer, E. A., & Kieran, M. W. (2002). Psychological adjustment of 'surgery-only' pediatric neuro-oncology patients: A retrospective analysis. *Psycho-Oncology, 11,* 74–79.

Mickelwright, J. L., King, T. Z., Morris, R. D., & Morris, M. K. (2007). Attention and memory in children with brain tumors. *Child Neuropsychology, 13,* 522–527.

Mitby, P. A., Robison, L. L., Whitton, J. A., Zevon, M. A., Gibbs, I. C., Tersak, J. M., et al. (2003). Utilization of special education services and educational attainment among long-term survivors of childhood cancer: A report from the Childhood Cancer Survivor Study. *Cancer, 97,* 1115–1126.

Moore, B. D. (2005). Neurocognitive outcomes in survivors of childhood cancer. *Journal of Pediatric Psychology, 30,* 51–63.

Mulhern, R. K., Kepner, J. L., Thomas, P. R., Armstong, F. D., Friedman, H. S., & Kun, L. E. (1998). Neuropsychologic functioning of survivors of childhood medulloblastoma randomized to receive conventional or reduced-dose craniospinal irradiation: A Pediatric Oncology Group Study. *Journal of Clinical Oncology, 16,* 1723–1728.

Mulhern, R. K., Khan, R. B., Kaplan, S., Helton, S., Christensen, R., Bonner, M., et al. (2004a). Short-term efficacy of methylphenidate: A randomized, double-blind, placebo-controlled trial among survivors of childhood cancer. *Journal of Clinical Oncology, 22,* 4795–4803.

Mulhern, R. K., Khan, R. B., Kaplan, S., Helton, S., Christensen, R., Bonner, M., et al. (2004b). Short-term efficacy of methylphenidate: A randomized, double-bind, placebo-controlled trial among survivors of childhood cancer. *Journal of Clinical Oncology, 22,* 4743–4751.

Mulhern, R. K., Merchant, T. E., Gajjar, A., Reddick, W. E., & Kun, L. E. (2004). Late neurocognitive sequelae in survivors of brain tumours in childhood. *The Lancet Oncology, 5,* 399–408.

Mulhern, R. K., Reddick, W. E., & Palmer, S. L. (1999). Neurocognitive deficits in medulloblastoma survivors and white matter loss. *Annals of Neurology, 46,* 834–841.

Mulhern, R. K., White, H. A., & Glass, J. O. (2004). Attentional functioning and white matter integrity among survivors of malignant brain tumors of childhood. *Journal of the International Neuropsychological Society, 10,* 180–189.

National Cancer Institute. (2002). Childhood acute lympho-cytic leukemia (PDQ), treatment and health professionals http://cancernet.nci.nih.gov.

Neglia, J. P., Robison, L. L., Stovall, M., Liu, Y., Packer, R. J., Hammond, S., et al. (2006). New primary neoplasms of the central nervous system in survivors of childhood cancer: A report from the Childhood Cancer Survivor Study. *Journal of the National Cancer Institute, 98,* 1528–1537.

Nortz, M. J., Hemme-Phillips, J. M., & Ris, D. M. (2007). Neuropsychological sequelae in children treated for cancer. In S. J. Hunter & J. Donders (Eds.), *Pediatric neuropsychological intervention* (pp. 112–132). Cambridge: Cambridge University Press.

Paako, E., Talvensaari, K., Pyhtinen, J., & Lanning, M. (1999). Late cranial magnetic resonance imaging after cranial irradiation in survivors of childhood cancer. *Neuroradiology, 36,* 652–655.

Palmer, S. L., Gajjar, A., Reddick, W. E., Glass, J. O., Kun, L. E., Wu, S., et al. (2003). Predicting intellectual outcome among children treated with 35–40 Gy craniospinal irradiation for medulloblastoma. *Neuropsychology, 17,* 548–555.

Podvin, D., Kuehn, C. M., Mueller, B. A., & Williams, M. (2006). Maternal and birth characteristics in relation to childhood leukemia. *Paediatric and Perinatal Epidemiology, 20,* 312–322.

Poggi, G., Liscio, M., Adduci, A., Galbiati, S., Massimino, M., Sommovigo, M., et al. (2005). Psychological and adjustment problems due to acquired brain lesions in childhood: A comparison between post-traumatic patients and brain tumour survivors. *Brain Injury, 19,* 777–785.

Pui, C. H. (2000). Acute lymphoblastic leukemia in children. *Current Opinion in Oncology, 12,* 3–12.

Pui, C. H., Cheng, C., Leung, W., Rai, S. N., Rivera, G. K., Sandlund, J. T., et al. (2003). Extended follow-up of long-term survivors of childhood acute lymphoblastic leukemia. *New England Journal of Medicine, 349,* 640–649.

Pui, C. H., & Evans, W. E. (2006). Treatment of acute lymphoblastic leukemia. *New England Journal of Medicine, 354,* 166–178.

Reddick, W. E., Glass, J. O., Palmer, S. L., Wu, S., Gajjar, A., Langston, J. W., et al. (2005). Atypical white matter development in children following craniospinal irradiation. *Neuro-Oncology, 7,* 12–19.

Reeves, C. B., Palmer, S. L., Gross, A. M., Simonian, S. J., Taylor, L., Willingham, E., et al. (2007). Brief report: Sluggish cognitive tempo among pediatric survivors of acute lymphoblastic leukemia. *Journal of Pediatric Psychology, 32,* 1050–1054.

Reeves, D., Palmer, S. L., Reddick, W. E., Merchant, T. E., Buchanan, G. M., Gajjar, A., et al. (2005). Attention and memory functioning among pediatric patients with medulloblastoma. *Journal of Pediatric Psychology, 31,* 272–280.

Reimers, T. S., Ehrenfels, S., Mortensen, E. L., Schmieglow, M., Sonderkaer, S., Carstensen, H., et al. (2003). Cognitive deficits in long-term survivors of childhood brain tumors: Identification of predictive factors. *Medical and Pediatric Oncology, 40,* 26–34.

Reimers, T. S., Mortensen, E. L., & Schmiegelow, K. (2007). Memory deficits in long-term survivors of childhood brain tumors may primarily reflect general cognitive dysfunction. *Pediatric Blood Cancer, 48,* 205–212.

Ris, D. M., Packer, R., Goldwein, J., Jones-Wallace, D., & Boyett, M. (2001). Intellectual outcome after reduced-dose radiation therapy plus adjuvant chemotherapy for medulloblastome: A Children's Cancer Group study. *Journal of Clinical Oncology, 19,* 3470–3476.

Sahler, O. J. Z., Fairclough, D. L., Phipps, S., Mulhern, R. K., Dolgin, M. J., Noll, R. B., et al. (2005). Using problem-solving skills training to reduce negative affectivity in mothers of children with newly diagnosed cancer: Report of a multisite randomized trial. *Journal of Consulting and Clinical Psychology, 73,* 272–283.

Sahler, O. J. Z., Varni, J. W., Fairclough, D. L., Butler, R. W., Noll, R. B., Dolgin, M. J., et al. (2002). Problem-solving skills training for mothers of children with newly diagnosed cancer: A randomized trial. *Journal of Developmental and Behavioral Pediatrics, 23,* 77–86.

Schatz, J., Kramer, J. H., & Albin, A. R. (2004). Visual attention in long-term survivors of leukemia receiving cranial radiation therapy. *Journal of the International Neuropsychological Society, 10,* 211–220.

Schultz, K. A. P., Ness, K. K., Whitton, J. A., Reckilitis, C., Zebrack, B., Robison, L. L., et al. (2008). Behavioral and social outcomes in adolescent survivors of childhood cancer: A report from the childhood cancer survivor study. *Journal of Clinical Oncology, 25,* 3649–3656.

Scott, J. G., Elkin, T. D., & Thompson, M. (2001). Treatment factors predicting neuropsychological outcomes in pediatric cancer survivors. *Journal of the International Neuropsychological Society, 7,* 140–148.

Semrud-Clikeman, M., Pliszka, S. R., Lancaster, J., & Liotti, M. (2006). Volumetric MRI differences in treatment-naïve vs chronically treated children with ADHD. *Neurology, 67,* 1023–1027.

Shaw, A. K., & Infante-Rivard, C. (2006). Early infection and risk of childhood brain tumors. *Cancer Causes and Control, 17,* 1267–1274.

Sklar, C. A. (2002). Childhood brain tumors. *Journal of Pediatric Endocrinology and Metabolism, 15,* 669–673.

Sohlberg, M. M., & Mateer, C. A. (1999). *Attention Process Training I (APT-I).* Wake Forest, NC: Lash & Associates.

Spiegler, B. J., Bouffet, E., Greenberg, M. L., Rutka, J. T., & Mabbott, D. J. (2004). Change in neurocognitive functioning after treatment with cranial radiation in childhood. *Journal of Clinical Oncology, 22,* 706–712.

Spix, C., Eletr, D., Blettner, M., & Kaatsch, P. (2008). Temporal trends in the incidence rate of childhood cancer in Germany, 1987–2004. *International Journal of Cancer, 122,* 1859–1867.

Steinlin, M., Imfield, S., Zulauf, P., Boltshauser, E., Lovlad, K. O., Ridolfi, L. A., et al. (2003). Neuropsychological long-term sequelae after posterior fossa tumour resection during childhood. *Brain, 126,* 1998–2008.

Streisand, R., Kazak, A. E., & Tercyzak, K. P. (2003). Pediatric-specific parenting stress and family functioning in children treated for cancer. *Children's Health Care, 32,* 245–256.

Thompson, S. J., Leigh, L., Christensen, R., Xiong, X., Kun, L. E., Heideman, R. L., et al. (2001). Immediate neurocognitive effects of methylphenidate on learning-impaired survivors of childhood cancer. *Journal of Clinical Oncology, 19,* 1802–1808.

Umansky, F., Shoshan, Y., Rosenthal, G., Fraifield, S., & Spektor, S. (2008). Radiation-induced meningioma. *Neurosurgical Focus, 24,* E7.

Westlake, S., & Bertolone, K. (2002). Acute Lymphoblastic Leukemia. In C. R. Baggott, K. P. Kelly, D. Gochtman & G. V. Foley (Eds.), *Nursing care of children and adolescents with cancer.* Philadelphia: W.B. Saunders Company.

Yamamoto, J. F., & Goodman, M. T. (2008). Patterns of leukemia incidence in the United States by subtype and demographic characteristics, 1997–2002. *Cancer Causes and Control, 19,* 379–390.

Zhou, D., Zhang, Y., Liu, H., Luo, S., Luo, L., & Dai, K. (2008). Epidemiology of nervous system tumors in children: A survey of 1,485 cases in Beijing Tiantan Hospital from 2001 to 2005. *Pediatric Neurosurgery, 44,* 97–103.

Zipf, T. F., Berg, S., Roberts, W. M., Poplack, D. G., Steuber, C. P., & Bleyer, W. A. (2000). Childhood leukemias. In M. D. Abeloff, J. O. Armitage, A. S. Lichter, & J. E. Niederhuber (Eds.), *Clinical oncology.* Philadelphia: Churchill Livingston.

Part IV
An Integration Intervention Paradigm

Chapter 16
Neuropsychological Intervention and Treatment Approaches for Childhood and Adolescent Disorders

Information about the child's neuropsychological, cognitive, academic, and psychosocial status forms the basis for designing integrated intervention and treatment plans for children and adolescents with brain-related disorders. Efforts to develop models of neuropsychological intervention have been expanding in recent years. In an effort to provide a framework for linking assessment to interventions, the Multistage Neuropsychological Assessment-Intervention Model is presented. Specific techniques for designing intervention programs addressing academic, psychosocial, and executive function (EF) deficits associated with various childhood and adolescent disorders are summarized.

Multistage Neuropsychological Model: Linking Assessment to Intervention

While the need for neuropsychological and neuroradiological evaluations may be obvious for conditions where traumatic brain injury or CNS disease is suspected, there also may be reasons to use these techniques for neurodevelopmental disorders, such as learning disabilities and attentional disorders. It is sometimes difficult to determine when to proceed with a comprehensive neuropsychological evaluation, particularly for school-related problems, and how to integrate neuropsychological evaluations into ongoing intervention plans. Teeter (1992) first described a multistage neuropsychological model as a guideline for linking neuropsychological assessment and intervention, and it serves as a foundation for the expanded model to be described (See Table 16.1).

The multistage neuropsychological model begins with structured behavioral-observational assessment techniques, and proceeds to more extensive cognitive and psychosocial, neuropsychological and/or neuroradiological evaluations if problems are not effectively remediated at any given stage. This model recommends that systematic interventions be developed and implemented at each stage based on evaluation results.

The following multistage neuropsychological assessment-intervention model (MNM) should be considered when treating children and adolescents with neurodevelopmental and/or neuropsychiatric disorders. This paradigm assumes a linkage between assessment and intervention, where competent evaluation of a problem or disorder leads to effective intervention strategies or plans. It is possible that at early stages of this model effective interventions may eliminate the necessity for further, more in-depth evaluation of the child. However, ongoing treatment evaluation is needed to verify the efficacy of the problem identification-intervention link at all stages. For some childhood problems (e.g., traumatic brain injury, CNS diseases, seizure activity), the clinician is advised to immediately proceed to more advanced stages of the MNM model (i.e., neuropsychological evaluation and neurodiagnostic examination). The MNM paradigm comprises eight assessment-intervention stages. Stages 1 through 4 can reasonably be conducted by school-based professionals, including school psychologists and educational diagnosticians. Stages 5 and 6 should be conducted by trained clinical child neuropsychologists in private practice, university, or medical clinics.

M. Semrud-Clikeman, P.A. Teeter Ellison, *Child Neuropsychology*, DOI 10.1007/978-0-387-88963-4_16,
© Springer Science+Business Media, LLC 2009

Table 16.1 Viodels for neuropsychological remediation and rehabilitation: Linking assessment to interventions

Models	Stages	Description
MNM[a]		
	Stage 1: Problem identification	Behavioral assessment
	Stage 2: Behavioral-based intervention	Self-management
		Contingency-management
		Learning strategies
		Peer tutoring
	Stage 3: Cognitive child study	Comprehensive congnitive, academic, psychosocial assessment
	Stage 4: Cognitive-based intervention	Pattern analysis
		Phonological awareness
		Activating schemata
		Organizational strategies
	Stage 5: Neuropsychological assessment	Comprehensive neurocognitive assessment
	Stage 6: Integrated neuropsychological intervention	Compensatory skills
		Psychopharmacology
	Stage 7: Neurological and neuroradiological assessment	Neurological, CT, MRI
	Stage 8: Medical-neurological rehabilitation	Rehabilitation and medical management
DNNR (Rourke, 1994)[b]	Step 1: Neuropsychological assets, deficits; academic and psychosiclal assessment	Neuropsychological profile
		Ecologically based evaluation
	Step 2: Demands of environment	Behavioral, academic, and psychosocial challenges within contextual framework
	Step 3: Short and long-term	Formulate short- and long-range predictions
		Which deficits will decrease?
		Specific treatment straegies
	Step 4: "Ideal" remedial plans	"Ideal" plans
		Monitoring and modification
	Step 5: Availability of resources	Therapeutic goals
		Prognosis
		Reduce redundant services
	Step 6: Realistic remedial plan	Compare differences between steps 4 and 5
	Step 7: Ongoing assessment and intervention	
REHABIT (Reitan & Wolfson, 1992)[c]	Tract A: Verbal-language	Materials to increase expressive-receptive skills
	Tract B: Abstraction and reasoning	Materials to increase analysis, organization
	Tract C: General reasoning	Materials for general reasoning
	Tract D: Visual-spatial	Visual-spatial manipulation
		Sequential skills
	Tract E: Visual-spatial and manipulation	

[a] Multistage Neuropsychological Model (developed by Teeter & Semrud-Clikeman).
[b] Developmental Neuropsychological Remediation/Rehabilitation Model (Rourke, 1994).
[c] Reitan Evaluation of Hemispheric Abilities and Brain Improvement Training (Reitan & Wolfson, 1992).

Stage 7 is reserved for physicians in hospitals or medical centers and Stage 8 most likely requires at least short-term hospitalization in a medical or rehabilitation center. At each stage of the MNM, accurate diagnosis or problem identification forms the basis for developing specific intervention strategies and for conducting ongoing monitoring and modification of intervention plans. One of the most common errors in implementing intervention programs occurs when treatment strategies are continued long after they are effective. This may occur when evaluations are scheduled years apart without systematic documentation of how the child is actually progressing (e.g., triennial evaluations conducted by schools when children are placed in special education classrooms). Therefore, ongoing assessment and modification of the intervention plan is essential.

Stage 1: Problem Identification

During Stage 1, children with mild neurodevelopmental disorders (i.e., mild academic delays or deficits) may undergo an initial evaluation using well established behavioral and curriculum-based assessment (CBA) approaches. There are excellent resources describing these procedures, including work by Shapiro (2004) and Shinn (1989). Shapiro (2004) provides a flowchart indicating the steps involved in CBA, including (1) a teacher interview; (2) classroom observation and examination of the child's class work; (3) CBA procedures (e.g., problem identification, problem analysis, problem verification, and remediation); (4) analysis of classroom resources, and (5) remedial decisions. Data gathered from these steps would then be used to develop Stage 2 intervention plans.

Stage 2: Behavioral-Based Intervention Plan

In Stage 2, educational professionals develop and implement an intervention plan based on data derived from the initial behavioral-observational assessment. CBA and ecobehavioral procedures can be helpful to determine a child's instructional, frustrational, and mastery levels for academic materials (Shapiro, 2004). Once specific strategies are selected (e.g., self-management or contingency management techniques), a task analysis of the skill to be taught is conducted. Specific learning strategies may also be the focus of instruction (e.g., summarizing and memory strategies), and other curricular procedures may be implemented (e.g., peer tutoring). Intervention monitoring, use of CBA and behavioral measures, and modification of the instructional plan would be ongoing during this phase. Curriculum-based procedures contribute a number of important factors to the assessment-intervention process, including a means for (1) identifying current levels of academic skills; (2) monitoring intervention strategies or plans; (3) assessing the instructional context, particularly related to ecobehavioral factors (e.g., rate of presentation, reinforcements, contingencies, prompting, cueing, and feedback mechanisms) that affect learning; (4) assessing

mild to moderate reading/learning problems; (5) evaluating skills, particularly at the elementary level; (6) reducing time consuming and expensive evaluation, and (7) conducting data-based consultation for remediating academic difficulties in children (Shapiro, 2004). These contributions are important and may alleviate the need for more in-depth evaluations. In some cases, Stage 1 evaluation and Stage 2 intervention may not be sufficient, and learning problems may persist that require further clinical evaluation and intensive remediation.

Stage 3: Cognitive Child Study

Some conditions (e.g., reading disabilities resulting from phonological core deficits) may not respond to interventions developed from behavioral assessments and, thus, may require more in-depth evaluations. In these instances a comprehensive psychoeducational evaluation is warranted. Measures of intellectual, academic, and psychosocial functioning usually make up this phase of assessment. Evaluation at this stage would seek to identify underlying cognitive, perceptual, memory, and reasoning deficits associated with particular academic deficiencies. Word fluency, phonological awareness, prior knowledge (e.g., vocabulary knowledge), and listening comprehension skills are also of interest in this phase. The child's metacognitive strategies and approaches to learning tasks may be helpful for understanding the nature and extent of their learning difficulties. Intervention plans would incorporate information gleaned during this stage, and may include multiple targets (i.e., academic, cognitive, and psychosocial) for intervention.

Stage 4: Cognitive-Based Intervention Plan

Interventions developed at this stage would address patterns of the child's specific cognitive strengths and weaknesses as the basis for designing effective academic programming. Depending on the patterns of strengths/weaknesses, efforts at this level may include training in phonological awareness for explicit decoding skills, strategic instruction in comprehension (e.g., use of context for gleaning meaning from text), and methods for developing and activating schemata for learning new information. Study skills and organizational strategies may also be targeted. Specific techniques for various academic deficits (e.g., reading) are discussed in subsequent sections of the chapter. Attention would also be paid to the child's psychosocial functioning, and attempts to increase the child's self-esteem, social interaction, and psychological well-being may be a focus. Although Stage 4 interventions would systematically address psychosocial factors, these could also be the focus of intervention in Stage 2. In cases where interventions are not initially effective, however, there is an increased probability that the child will develop secondary psychological problems, as a cycle of academic failure, social rejection, and low self-esteem often ensues with repeated or prolonged academic deficiencies. Intervention plans would be systematically monitored and modified based on the child's progress. There are instances in which traditional psychoeducational evaluations and interventions are not sufficient, and some children require more in-depth neuropsychological evaluations.

Stage 5: Neuropsychological Evaluation

Children with traumatic brain injury or CNS diseases typically require more in-depth neuropsychological evaluations, and would benefit from baseline information about how the brain is functioning and about changes in this baseline over time and after effective interventions. Neuropsychological testing may also be necessary for children sustaining birth complications (e.g., prematurity, hypoxia) or exposure to teratogenic agents. Children with severe speech-language, learning, and/or motor difficulties may also require neuropsychological evaluations in an effort to effectively assess the nature of their delays or deficits. In these instances clinical child neuropsychological assessment is warranted. The need for neuropsychological assessment is particularly crucial for children who do not respond to the

interventions described in earlier stages in the MNM model, or for children who have neurological symptoms associated with their learning and/or psychosocial problems.

Stage 6: Integrated Neuropsychological Intervention Plan

Bergquist and Malec (2002) suggest that neuropsychological assessment serves as the foundation for treatment planning. Interventions developed from neuropsychological data typically address compensatory skills and long-term management. Psychopharmacology may also be needed by some children at this level. See discussions in later sections of the chapter for more details about neuropsychological interventions.

Stage 7: Neurological and/or Neuroradiological Evaluation

Finally, some children may need intensive medical and/or neuroradiological evaluations and interventions. Although only a small portion of children require this stage of evaluation, this stage is crucial for some childhood disorders. Oftentimes children with life threatening conditions (e.g., tumors, injury, and/ or intractable seizures) need ongoing Stage 7 evaluations and medical treatment (e.g., neurosurgery, chemotherapy, and/or CNS irradiation). However, evaluations and interventions described at other levels may also be incorporated into treatment plans for children with these conditions.

Stage 8: Medical-Neurological Rehabilitation

Medical-neurological rehabilitation efforts may be required for a small number of children with severe brain injuries or CNS diseases. These services may require placement in a rehabilitation center for short-term or long-term medical management. In these cases, a medical team including physicians (e.g., pediatric neurologists, neurosurgeons, radiologists, and pediatricians), neuropsychologists, psychologists, speech-language and physical therapists, and social workers design interventions to help remediate or rehabilitate the child's problems. Programs are generally comprehensive in nature and include the child and his or her parent. In summary, the MNM describes a process for linking multiple stages of evaluation into intervention plans.

Neuropsychological Framework for Remediation

Interest in neuropsychological rehabilitation has grown significantly over the past 20 years, and there has been an increase in research in cognitive neuroscience and clinical rehabilitation (Ponsford, 2004). Eslinger and Oliveri (2002) suggest that clinicians should apply rigorous evidence-based analysis to design and evaluate neuropsychological interventions using multiple baseline assessment to determine treatment efficacy. Neuropsychological interventions generally focus on the restoration of functions to improve skill deficits, and/or compensatory training to adapt to behavioral and cognitive deficits (Eslinger & Oliveri, 2002). It is important to set both short-term and long-term goals for clinical interventions and to address the full spectrum of neurocognitive deficits. See Hirschberg, Chui and Frazier (2005) for an overview of emerging brain-based interventions for children and adolescents.

Specific Strategies for Improving Cognitive, Academic, Social-Emotional, and Executive Control Deficits

Various techniques should be carefully selected following a comprehensive, multimethod evaluation, a clear understanding of the child's neuropsychological assets and deficits, and an assessment of his or her developmental, cognitive, academic, and social-emotional needs.

Neurocognitive Deficits

Although neurocognitive deficits are commonly found in a number of pediatric disorders (e.g., TBI), not all deficits are associated with traumatic insult (e.g., learning disabilities, ADHD) (Butler, 2006). Common neurocognitive deficits include problems with attention, learning and memory, language, and self regulation. Specific interventions with proven efficacy are briefly reviewed.

Interventions to Improve Attention Difficulties

Interventions to improve attention difficulties adopt a componential approach that recognizes different forms of attention. Attention may well contain multiple aspects, which are arranged in hierarchical order and may interact with motor, cognitive, and social development (Sohlberg & Mateer, 1989, 2001). Thus, disruption of any component may compromise the efficiency of the total attention system. Moreover, disruption of a component will have a negative impact on aspects lower in the hierarchical chain of attention (e.g., ability to shift set may be disturbed and consequently affect responses to temporally presented information or vigilance). It is likely that a breakdown in processing of temporal information would have an impact on classroom learning which requires processing of sequential instructional language.

A system that combines training on the aspects of attention involving selective and sustained attention was developed by Sohlberg and Mateer (1989, 1996), and later revised by Sohlberg, Johnson, Paule, Raskin, and Mateer (2001)—The Attention Process Training–II (APT-II). The APT-II was designed to rehabilitate mild brain dysfunction (i.e., attention and concentration difficulties) resulting from hear injuries. The program contains five components of attention, including: focused attention, sustained attention, selective attention, alternating attention and divided attention.

- **Focused Attention**: is the ability to focus on specific sensory information including visual, auditory or tactile stimuli

- **Sustained Attention:** is the ability to maintain attention during continuous and repetitive activity; incorporates the concepts of vigilance, persistence and task consistency; includes the ability of *mental control* or *working memory* incorporating the notion of holding and manipulating information in one's head, such as doing mental math
- **Selective Attention:** is the ability to selectively process target information and inhibits responding to nontarget information; incorporates the notion of "freedom from distractibility"
- **Alternating Attention: is** the ability to shift one's focus of attention; includes the capacity for mental flexibility
- **Divided Attention:** is the ability to simultaneously respond to two or more events or stimuli; capacity that allows an individual to divide his or her attention between two or more ongoing events. Deficits in this ability are evident when an individual can only process one (adapted from Sohlberg et al., 2001)

Research on Attention Training

Although sparse, research on the efficacy of attention training has produced promising results for children with TBI, cancer survivors, developmental dyslexia, and ADHD. To date, most research has been case studies with few large scale efforts in progress.

The Amsterdam attention and memory training program is based on a modified version of the Sohlberg and Mateer (1996, 2001) model. The program contains elements that address: process training for attention and memory; metacognitive strategy training; social contact and support, and weekly therapeutic interventions at the hospital clinic. Sessions are 30 minutes per day, over a 20-week period. In a series of case studies, Hooft et al. (2003) found that, following treatment, children with TBI showed: marked improvement on neuropsychological measures of sustained and selective attention; modest improvement on memory tests, and improvement on teacher and parent reports of behaviors, learning and social-emotional factors. Although children commented that the training was hard to integrate into daily school activities

(the sessions were too long and sometimes seemed too easy) they did indicate that it was easier to study for exams after the training. The authors recommended that the 20-week program be shortened, individualized and adapted to the child, and reinforcers should be incorporated into training.

In a review of research on attention training, Penkman (2004) indicated that there have been a few published accounts of rehabilitation for pediatric cancer survivors. Attention training did produce positive effects on arithmetic skills, scores on the Conners' Continuous Performance Test (CPT), and memory for sentences and digits for a young cancer survivor (Butler, 1998). In a larger study, following attention training, pediatric cancer survivors showed positive outcomes on measures of attention and concentration and CPT scores (Butler & Copeland, 2002). In an innovative study where teachers administered rehabilitation training on alertness, attention, concentration, perception and memory, and executive processes, teens with pediatric TBI also showed modest but significant improvements. Penkman conducted a small clinical study of a child who received cranial radiation treatment for acute lymphoblastic leukemia (ALL) with similar results. Modest gains were noted on a number of attention tasks, but attention problems did persist.

In a study investigating attention training for children with dyslexia, Chenault, Thomson, Abbott, and Berninger (2006) found that attention training facilitated composition skills and verbal fluency once composition training was introduced. The authors suggest that attention training can be helpful, but the sequencing of interventions is also important.

Several studies have explored the utility of attention training for children with ADHD. Kerns, Eso, and Thompson (1999) also reported that the Pay Attention! program was effective for 14 children (7–11 years of age) with ADHD. Children who received training improved on measures of attention and academic efficiency. While there were some signs of improvement in inattention-impulsivity, rating scales did not evidence positive changes post-treatment. However, Kerns et al. (1999) found that cognitive efficiency can be improved with direct training. Semrud et al. (1999) adapted tasks that were originally designed for adults with head injuries.

Children with teacher- and parent-identified attention difficulties received during 24 sessions, over a 12-week period. Each child worked in a group of five to six children, and charts were kept of the child's progress. The charts were reviewed at each session, and problem solving techniques were discussed to help the child consider the most efficient alternative, as well as to learn to self-monitor his or her progress. At the end of the 12-week period, teachers reported on the child's ability to complete assignments. In 20 of the 22 cases, improvement was seen in the number of completed assignments. Of the 22 children enrolled in the study, approximately 50 percent were on medication for ADHD. At the end of the study, there was no difference between the medicated and the non-medicated children in their performance on measures of selective and sustained attention. Moreover, there was a significant improvement in the auditory attention of children who participated in the groups. Such improvement on the auditory attention task was not found for children without attention problems or for the ADHD control children. Therefore, it would appear that children with attention and work completion problems can benefit from direct teaching in problem solving skills and practicing selective attention. Semrud et al. (1999), concluded that attention can improve when specific training is provided. Second, the extent to which improvement in attention persists over time needs to be carefully studied. Third, although stimulant medications reduce core ADHD symptoms, medication alone does not improve academic performance. Though preliminary, this research appears promising, and attention training (with problem solving techniques) may prove useful as an intervention strategy for children with attention deficits.

Tamm et al. (in press) are currently developing and examining the effect of a unique attention training program for preschool children with ADHD. This team has modified laboratory activities from a nonhuman primate study, and developed computer-based games that are highly motivating. The program targets attention, planning, and maintaining information over a delay time. Initial pilot study results suggest that AT training in preschool children can produce improvements after five sessions.

Despite these promising findings, Riccio and French (2004) caution that further research is needed to determine the efficacy of attention training programs. In a review of 83 studies, Riccio and French indicated that current research has not adequately measured outcomes at baseline and post-treatment. Further, attention training groups have not been contrasted to control groups or groups who receive alternative treatments. "The ultimate goal is to carry out large scale controlled clinical trails examining the effectiveness of specific interventions. However, these types of studies demand considerable resources from both a financial and time perspective. Single case studies can fill in the gaps in the knowledge base and help guide work that is taking place on a daily basis until there is more solid research" (Penkman, 2004, p. 120).

Interventions to Improve Working Memory and Learning Deficits

Interventions to improve working memory and learning have focused primarily on children with language and attentional difficulties. Children with specific language impairment (SLI) have a number of cognitive deficits, including lexical/morphological learning and sentence comprehension difficulties that may be related to working memory (WM) deficits (Montgomery, 2003). Montgomery reviews current theories of SLI that focus on problems in WM, including the Baddeley (1986) phonological loop model. Baddeley suggests that there is a "central executive" that regulates information within WM, retrieves information from other memory systems (i.e., short-term memory), and processes and stores phonological information. Phonological short-term memory (PWM) and verbal rehearsal is part of the phonological loop, where verbal information is stored for a limited time period and allows the listener to create long-term memory of information by rehearsing. The model suggests that PWM has a limited capacity. Children with SLI have been shown to have weak PWM, which interferes with vocabulary learning.

Daneman and Carpenter (1980) suggest a computational WM model where storage and processing functions share a limited amount of attentional energy during comprehension. This model has been referred to as functional working memory (FWM), where verbal information is both processed (for lexical, morphological, and grammatical representations) and temporally stored/retained and processed [see (Montgomery, 2003) for a more detailed discussion]. Daneman and Carpenter assume there is a trade-off between storing and processing information; as the complexity of the task increases, previously stored information is forgotten. Poor FWM has been associated with difficulties in word recall.

In terms of intervention, Montgomery (2003) argues that "it is important to point out that intervention that does not address the bidirectional influences of memory and language will likely fall short in promoting language learning and processing" (p. 228). Activities to help develop and enhance WM in young children include naming letters and objects, and listening to rhymes and stories; while teaching verbal rehearsal, paraphrasing, and creating manageable chunks of information are helpful for older children and teens.

Klingberg et al. (2005) developed a computerized program to improve the working memory (WM) of children with ADHD. The computer program developed for this study (RoboMemo(R), Cogmed Cognitive Medical Systems AB, Stockholm, Sweden) includes visuospatial (remembering the position of objects) and verbal tasks (remembering phonemes, letters, or digits). The program is described in more detail in Olesen, Westerberg, and Klingberg (2004). The training was spread over 25 days, with 90 WM trials on each day of training (approximately 40 minutes in length). Post-intervention data were collected 5–6 weeks after the baseline data, and the follow-up assessment was completed three months after post-intervention data were gathered. Students were randomly assigned to treatment or a control group who received the same treatment, but had tasks of less difficulty that were not matched to the child's working memory span.

Students who received intensive WM training did show significant improvement on WM tasks compared to the control group. Treated students also showed improvement on measures of response inhibition (scores on the Stroop task), verbal WM (digit-span scores from the WISC-III), complex reasoning (scores on the Raven's Colored Progressive Matrices), and decreased parent ratings of ADHD symptoms. Although the study was conducted on a relatively small group of children (50 completed all phases of the study), it does seem promising. Future studies will investigate the combination of WM training with medication. The next series of studies also need to determine whether improvements in WM generalize to real-life situations that require executive functions and strong WM (e.g., academic tasks).

Interventions to Improve Speech and Language Deficits

Various models of language rehabilitation have been advanced and have received research and clinical attention (Hinckley, 2002). Select therapeutic models include neuropsychological, cognition and learning, linguistic, compensatory, social, and neurological approaches. Each approach emphasizes different goals and treatment procedures. For example, the cognitive neuropsychological model seeks to identify the processes underlying language problems, remediate the impaired component or develop compensatory strategies. Assessing the component deficits allows the clinician to arrange a hierarchy of specific tasks that will be taught during therapy. Treatment could include strategies such as naming, semantic cueing, phonological cueing, and constructing sentences, etc. Conversely the cognition and learning model seeks to understand the underlying cognitive and learning deficits, utilizes theories of learning and skills acquisition, and focuses treatment on developing specific language abilities. Treatment using this model would also address specific cognitive skills including attention, memory, and executive functions. The compensatory model incorporates strategies to enhance functional communication rather than specific component deficits, and may bypass speech-language modalities directly (e.g., gesturing, drawing, or a visual representation of language). Models of learning have dominated the special education and rehabilitation centers where skill acquisition during rehabilitation parallels normal language development. Hinckley argues that "cognitive/learning theories, in conjunction with neurological evidence, offer the best current step toward a theory of therapy" (p. 213). See Hinckley for a more detailed description of various models.

Nadeau and Gonzalez (2004) offer another approach to explain language processing – the parallel distributed process model (PDP). PDP models are "neural-like in that they incorporate large arrays of simple units that are heavily interconnected with each other" (2004, p. 131). Further, Nadeau and Gonzalez explain that "in PDP models of language, memories of language units (e.g., stored knowledge of phonemes, joint phonemes, syllables, words, and sentence constituents) are represented in the same neural networks that support linguistic processing" (2004, p. 131). Nadeau and Gonzalez outline strategies for addressing impairments in phonological and lexical semantic (anomia and word finding difficulties), grammatical (organization of words and words within sentences), working memory, concept manipulation, and word-sequence knowledge.

Studies investigating interventions for speech and language impairments have focused primarily on children with development delays and those with deficits from traumatic events. Several studies are summarized.

In a study to address morphological and phonological processing deficits in preschool children with co-occurring speech and language impairment, Tyler, Lewis, Haskill, and Tolbert (2003) found that an approach that alternated strategies produced the best results. The study compared four conditions: phonological training for 12 weeks followed by 12 weeks of morphosyntax training; morphosyntax training first then phonological training; the alternating condition, one week of phonological training followed by one week of morphosyntax strategies, and, a simultaneous condition. All treatment groups received 24 weeks of training and were compared to a no-treatment control group. At the end of the study children who received the alternating condition (one week of phonological intervention, then one week of morphosyntax) showed the greatest improvement in morphosyntactic and phonological skills, and both the morphological fist condition and the alternating conditions were better than the no-treatment condition. The phonological strategy training did produce changes in phonological skills, but this did not produce a cross-domain effect on morphosyntax.

A large sample of children with language impairments (216, ages 6 and 9 years) were randomly assigned to the Fast ForWord Language (FFW-L) program, general academic enrichment, computer assisted language instruction, or individualized language therapy by a speech-language pathologist (Gillam et al., 2008). Components of the FFW-L training include five language targets: narratives, semantics, syntax (grammatical morphology), syntax (clause structure) and phonological awareness. The FFW-L program provides specific computer games to improve underlying auditory processing deficits, and target discrimination of tones, detection of phonemic changes, phonemic matching, word discrimination, recalling commands, and comprehension of complex sentences. The computer-assisted condition also provided various strategies targeting discrimination and memory, phoneme awareness, recall, and comprehension. The individualized language therapy condition targeted semantics, syntax, narration, and phonological awareness. The academic enrichment condition served as a comparison group, and tasks were similar to those in the FFW-L and computer-assisted conditions (computer games), but none of the computer games were designed to improve language or auditory processing skills. Children received six weeks of therapy, five days per week, for one hour and 40 minutes per week. See Gillam et al. (2008) for more details on the strategies used in each condition.

All treatment groups showed improvement on measures of global expressive and receptive language skills (Gillam, et al, 2008). Children assigned to the FFW-L and the computer assisted learning conditions had significantly better improvements on phonological awareness. In general, children in the FFW-L group did not have significantly better language outcomes than academic enrichment, or methods addressing specific language deficits (computer-assisted and individualized therapy). Gillam et al. concluded that "results of this study suggest that intensive language intervention experiences that require close attending and immediate responding to auditory and visual stimuli in combination with opportunities for socialization with same-ability peers and a great deal of positive attention from caring and interested adults should result in clinically relevant improvements in language and auditory processing skills with language impairments" (2008, p. 114).

Interventions to Improve Self Regulation and Self-control Deficits

Self-management techniques have grown in popularity in an effort to help children develop control over their own behavior. Self-control techniques generally include self-assessment (observing one's own behavior), self-evaluation (comparing one's behavior to a "standard"), self-recording, and self-reinforcement (DuPaul & Stoner, 2003). Although these techniques have been used for a variety of behaviors, attending to task has been a major thrust in the literature. Lloyd and Landrum (1990) surveyed 37 studies using self-recording techniques for children with learning, cognitive, and behavioral disorders from four years of age to adolescence. Self-recording was effective for the following variables: increasing attention to task, decreasing disruption, work productivity, work accuracy, task completion, and sustained schoolwork. Depending on the child's individual needs, self-recording can focus on academic accuracy, productivity, or attention to task, and all areas seem to improve regardless of which is targeted (Lloyd & Landrum, 1990; DuPaul & Stoner, 2003).

Typically, self-recording is most effective when cueing occurs (Heins, Lloyd, & Hallahan, 1986), and may take many forms (e.g., tape recorded beeps at one-, two-, or three-minute intervals, or kitchen timers that ring every five minutes). Fading of taped cues is often built into self-recording procedures, and maintenance appears quite good after the treatment has been discontinued (Lloyd & Landrum, 1990). See DuPaul and Stoner (2003) for a more in-depth treatment of self-management techniques for the classroom.

Treating Academic Deficits

There are number of intervention strategies with documented efficacy for reducing academic deficits in children and adolescents. Techniques for addressing reading, written language, and arithmetic disorders are reviewed, including strategies for improving executive control deficits, study, and organizational skills. Interventions for improving social skills are also discussed briefly. These techniques are offered as possible strategies based on the child's particular neuropsychological, cognitive, and psychosocial profile, and should not be automatically adopted for every child. An in-depth interview with the child's teacher and a record review is critical to determine remedial techniques that have been attempted in the past and have proved effective or ineffective.

Reading Disorders

McCandliss and Nobel (2003) outline a neurocognitive, developmental model for understanding and treating dyslexia. Further, they argue that methodologies and approaches from the neurosciences can be applied to better understand how early phonological processes influence visual processes for rapid recognition of written words.

Phonemic Awareness

Research suggests that "the phonological coding deficit is clearly established as the strongest predictor and correlate of reading disabilities" (Wise & Olson, 1991, p. 638). Remedial techniques that have proved most effective incorporate strategies for teaching children phonemic awareness skills and typically include segmenting, blending, and analyzing sounds (Fletcher, Lyon, Fuchs, & Barnes, 2007).

Lovett and colleagues have been studying the effects of intensive reading remediation for children with severe reading disabilities using a modification of the Reading Mastery, a Direct Instruction program (Fletcher et al. 2007). Two programs were developed, Phonological Analysis and Blending/ Direct Instruction (PHAB/DI) and the Word Identification Strategy Training (WIST), which focus on metacognitive strategies (Lovett, Barron & Benson, 2003). Although both programs feature transfer of learning sessions, neither normalized reading after 35 hours of instruction for children in upper to middle elementary grades. Lovett et al. (2000) combined both programs and extended the training for younger children with better results. The combination of 35 hours of training with PHAB/DI and 35 hours of instruction with WIST was more effective than 70 hours of training with either program alone.

PHAST (phonological and strategy training) is a new reading program that combines the PHAB/DI and WIST programs (Fletcher et al. 2007). Initial findings of school-based training with PHAST have proven to be effective for reading recognition and comprehension skills. The study also examined the effects of a training program emphasizing reading fluency. The RAVE-O (Retrieval, Automaticity, Vocabulary elaboration, and Enrichment with language Orthography) program was developed to increase reading fluency in decoding and comprehension, and to improve reading interest and engagement [see (Fletcher et al., 2007) for more details]. Multidimensional approaches have produced effective outcomes including children from lower socioeconomic backgrounds.

Preventive efforts have also effective, increasing phonemic awareness skills in preschool children (Byrne & Fielding-Barnsley, 1993; Lundberg, Frost, & Petersen, 1988; Torgesen, 2004). Phonological recoding skills are stressed, where the child is taught to translate letters and letter patterns into phonemes. Knowledge of the grapheme-phoneme correspondences are usually integrated within reading instruction, and are not taught in isolation. Phonograms, common sound elements in word families (e.g., "ight" in light and fight), may also be stressed in beginning stages to increase vowel generalizations (Iversen & Tunmer, 1993). While children are instructed to categorize words on the basis of their phonemic similarity (Bradley & Bryant, 1983), phonemic awareness is most effective when contextualized using words taken from regular reading lessons (Cunningham, 1989).

Peer-assisted Learning Strategies (PALS) has been systematically studied for the past 20 years, and shown to be effective for students with weak academic skills (Fuchs & Fuchs, 2005). McMaster, Fuchs, Fuchs, and Compton (2005) extended treatment for children who did not respond favorably to the PALS program. Children who received adult tutoring focusing on word recognition, storytelling practice, and self monitoring improved reading at higher rates than those who received no further adaptations (continued PALS program), or a classroom modification of the PALS.

Training programs in phonological awareness and phonological recoding often incorporate metacognitve strategies. Children are made aware of the visual and phonological similarities in words, and are taught how and when to use this knowledge (Iversen & Tunmer, 1993). Cunningham (1990) incorporated similar metacognitive techniques and found this instruction extremely beneficial.

Reading Comprehension

Strategies to improve reading comprehension have been effective, particularly when metacognitive techniques are used (Fletcher et al., 2007; Wise & Olson, 1991). Palincsar, Brown, and Martin (1987) used a "reciprocal teaching" method whereby teachers used predicting, questioning, and clarifying strategies to improve comprehension skills in slow readers. Comprehension skills were maintained two months after instruction and were generalized to other content areas [see (Wise & Olson, 1991) for a review]. Bos and Van Reusen (1991) describe several techniques that have effectively increased comprehension and vocabulary knowledge, including "interactive learning strategies." This model emphasizes cooperation between the student and the teacher, where the student helps to identify their prior knowledge about a topic and then proceeds to link that prior knowledge with new information. Students are then taught how to scan reading material, to develop "clue lists," "relationship maps," or charts, and to predict relationships across concepts (Bos & Van Reusen, 1991). The teacher's role begins as an instructor working together with the student through these stages, then moves to facilitator when students begin to work with each other. These techniques have been effective in bilingual LD classes for social studies and reading (Bos & Van Reusen, 1991), and for middle school children for science (Bos & Anders, 1990).

Melzer, Pollica, and Barzilla (2007) describe excellent strategies for increasing executive control of reading comprehension for elementary aged students. Planning, prioritizing, organizing, flexibility in shifting mental sets, and self-checking strategies are all important EF skills (see Meltzer, 2007). Many of the EF strategies teach students how to use efficient and effective self-assessment techniques to monitor comprehension during the reading process. "Seven principles for understanding the relationship between reading comprehension and executive control are: 1. Reading must make sense. 2. Understanding is the result of planning to understand. 3. Accessing background information helps organize new information. 5. Self-checking enhances goal achievement. 6. Having a flexible mindset provides opportunities for increased understanding. 7. Understanding is improved by self –assessing" (Gaskin, Satlow, & Pressley, 2007. p. 213). See Gaskin et al. for other metacognitive strategy methods.

Computer and Speech Feedback

Olson and Wise (2006) have conducted a number of studies investigating computer-based programs to increase word recognition and decoding skills. Olson, Foltz, and Wise (1986) developed a reading program for the microcomputer utilizing a speech synthesizer (i.e., DECtalk). Wise et al. (1989) found that below average readers (lowest 10% of readers from selected classrooms) improved in phonological coding and word recognition skills using a computer reading program. When children were unable to read a word, segmented feedback was available whereby the computer highlighted and simultaneously "spoke" the word with the child. Comprehension questions were also incorporated into the program, and corrective feedback was provided. These results are promising and efforts are underway to improve these computer-based technologies (Olson et al., 1994; Wise & Olson, 1991).

Lewandowski and his colleagues at the Syracuse Neuropsychology Laboratory have found that students with reading disabilities also recall more words when stimuli are presented in two modalities–computer screen and computer voice synthesizer–simultaneously. Montali and Lewandowski (1996) showed a memory advantage for students with reading disabilities who experience short-term memory weaknesses, when words were presented bimodally. The performance of the reading-disabled group approached that of normal readers. Further, this performance advantage was also shown for reading conditions. When text was highlighted on the computer screen and the computer also read (spoke) the words at the same time, spontaneous word recall and reading comprehension improved. Students with reading disabilities expressed a preference for this computer-based reading format. Steele, Lewandowski, and Rusling (1996) replicated these findings with a mixed (LD, ADHD, and emotionally disturbed) group of children with reading problems. Bimodal facilitation was found in almost every student when data were analyzed using single-subject methodology. In summary, Lewandowski and colleagues suggest that bimodal computer reading methods can be helpful for a variety of poor readers in grades three through 12. Future research needs to address the issue of long-term benefits for such

methods and to identify which children specifically benefit the most from these procedures. At present, there are a number of commercial computer programs available that combine highlighted and/or bigger text with speak-aloud capacities for spelling, writing, and literacy activities for Macintosh or IBM computers. These commercial programs may prove useful when incorporated into remedial programs for poor readers, and certainly warrant further research.

More recently Wise, Ring, & Olson (2000) developed an intensive computer-based instructional program focusing on phonological awareness and decoding (50–60 ½-hour sessions). Students in grades 2–3 who received this intervention did show phonological improvement 1–2 years after completing the program, but gains for children in grades 4–5 were not as impressive. Older children benefited from computer sessions emphasizing accurate story reading. Even though phonological skills increased for the younger children, these did not transfer to other reading and spelling skills. Long-term transfer is apparently best when word recognition training is combined with reading comprehension strategies (i.e., reflective reading).

Whole Language Programs

Advocates of whole language programs stress the importance of teaching reading as a language activity, linking reading to writing, and incorporating children's literature as a source for reading activities. Wise and Olson (1991) describe whole language techniques as a "strength" approach and further suggest that word recognition and metacognitive techniques can be incorporated into this framework.

Written Language Disorders

Many techniques to improve written language skills use cognitive and metacognitive strategies (Graham, Harris, & Olinghouse, 2007). Strategy instruction usually involves teaching students how to plan, organize, write, edit, and revise their writing samples. Several structured curricular programs are available, including Cognitive Strategy Instruction

Writing (Englert, 1990) and self-regulated strategy development (SRSD) (Graham & Harris, 2003, 2005). The SRSD teaches students to apply writing strategies such as goal setting, self-monitoring, and self-regulation to improve writing (Graham & Harris, 2003, 2005). The SRSD has evolved over the years and includes two major strategies: the POW and the TREE. Strategies that plan (e.g., who are the characters, what is the setting, etc.), organize, and write more ideas (POW) have been combined with other strategies (TREE, Tell what you believe in a topic sentence; give reasons to support your beliefs; end or wrap up your story, and examine the story or edit). The SRSD program has improved performance in students with learning disabilities (Graham & Harris, 2003, 2005).

Mathematic Disorders

Mathematic problem solving difficulties have not been as well researched as reading deficits (Bos & Van Reusen, 1991). Reasoning, metacognitive processing, and reading delays have been associated with deficits in solving word problems (Bos & Van Reusen, 1991). Remedial techniques designed to address mathematical problem solving disorders often reflect cognitive and metacognitive approaches, where students are taught to understand the nature of the problem, plan a solution, carry out the solution, and assess the accuracy of the solution. Similar problem solving strategy instruction has been proven effective in a number of studies (Montague & Bos, 1986). Fleischner (1994) cautions that few studies with math learning disabilities have adequately addressed the neuropsychological characteristics of the subjects, or, when these data are available, the cognitive strategies employed by the subjects are not described. Fletcher et al. (2007) suggest that a number of cognitive difficulties interfere with the development of mathematics, including working memory, language, nonverbal problem solving, phonological decoding, attention, and reading sight words. In this regard, Fleischner (1994) suggests using the Test of Early Mathematics Ability (TEMA-2) or the Diagnostic Test of Arithmetic Strategies to gain information about which strategies are being employed.

In a review of studies on mathematics disabilities, Baker, Gersten and Lee (2002) report that several approaches can be helpful including: providing student progress to the teacher and the student; using peer tutoring; giving performance feedback to parents, and explicit teaching of math concepts and processes. Fuchs et al. (2003a, 2003b) successfully applied a cognitive framework for a classroom-based approach to improve the math problems, particularly when combined approaches were used (e.g., teacher instruction of math concepts, teaching students to solve word problems, word problem solving with specific strategies for transfer). See Fletcher et al. (2007) for a more detailed review of strategy instruction for mathematics disabilities.

Rourke (1989) provides an extensive description of the neuropsychological characteristics of children with specific deficits in the math area, with relative strengths in reading and spelling, and describes a comprehensive intervention program for this problem.

NLD Syndrome

Rourke (1989) and his colleagues (Rourke et al., 1983; Rourke, Del Dotto, Rourke, & Casey, 1990; Rourke & Fuerst, 1991) have described numerous remedial techniques that address the academic and psychosocial problems experienced by children with nonverbal learning disabilities (NLD). NLD children have the most difficulty in the academic areas of mathematics reasoning, calculation, and problem solving, with basic social-emotional problems (Rourke, 1989). These problems appear related to a pattern of right-hemisphere weaknesses (e.g., tactile and visual perception, concept formation, novelty, and complex psychomotor skills), with relative strengths in left-hemisphere activities (e.g., phonological skills, verbal abilities, reading, spelling, verbatim memory) (Rourke, 1994). Rourke (1989) suggests a remedial approach that acknowledges these assets and deficits and encompasses techniques for improving academic skills as well as social relationships. Strang and Rourke (1985) describe a series of teaching strategies to enhance mathematics calculation and reasoning, which involve verbal elaboration of the steps, written cue cards with the rules for solving the problem, and concrete aids (e.g., graph paper and color-coded columns). Students are encouraged to use calculators to check for errors, and teachers use error pattern analysis to modify the remedial plan (Teeter, 1989). Lessons utilize relevant and practical problem solving situations (e.g., shopping). Further, Rourke (1989) describes techniques for increasing problem solving skills, generalization of strategies and concepts, appropriate nonverbal skills, accurate self-evaluation, and life skills that prepare for adulthood. Rourke (1989) stresses the need for social problem solving skills, social awareness, structured peer interactions, and parent involvement in the treatment plan because of the serious psychosocial limitations inherent in the NLD syndrome. Techniques are also developed to increase the child's exploratory behaviors and interactions with the environment. Rourke's (1989) methods emphasize the need for a step-by-step problem solving approach, in which feedback is provided in a supportive manner. Children are encouraged to "lead with their strong suit" and are also taught more appropriate ways to utilize their relative strengths (i.e., verbal language skills). Rourke (1994) has used single-subject investigations to validate his remedial techniques, finding support for treatment plans that are based on a model of identifying the interactions of neuropsychological assets and deficits on academic and psychosocial functioning. Rourke (1994) acknowledges the need for more systematic empirical study of remedial strategies based on neuropsychological findings, particularly to investigate whether interventions should be deficit-driven or compensatory in nature. Developmental considerations appear important in this decision, as Rourke (1994) suggests that when deficits result from early white matter disease or dysfunction, remediation might focus on attacking the deficit. If the diagnosis is made later or if the syndrome persists, compensatory strategies are most likely the best approach.

Interventions for Executive Control Deficits

Dawson and Guare (2004) have written a useful handbook that describes a number of promising interventions for increasing executive skills that focus on the environment and the individual. First, changes in the environment are made to adjust to the limitations of the child. These include: (1) changing the physical environment in the classroom which may include changing the child's seating, matching the child with a highly structured teacher, and/or reducing the number of children in the classroom and increasing the amount of supervision; (2) changing the nature of the task by making it shorter, making steps more explicit, making the task closed ended (e.g., fill-in-the-blank or true-false), building in choice, and providing scoring rubrics with each assignment; (3) changing the way in which cues are given by using verbal prompts and reminders, using visual cues, creating schedules, making lists, using audio taped cues for self-monitoring, and using pager systems for older youth, and (4) changing the way adults interact with the child by anticipating problems and modifying the environment, by intervening early before the problem gets too big, by reminding and prompting the child, and by designing interventions that address the child's individual weaknesses.

Interventions that promote executive control skills that focus on the child teach planning, organization, and follow specified directions (see Dawson & Guare, 2004). Initially these steps are followed under the direction of parents (or teachers); then supervision is faded. For example, specific steps include: describing the problem behavior; setting a goal; establishing steps to meet the goal; supervising the child to meet goals; evaluating the strategies and making changes if needed, and fading the supervision. These steps move the child to self-directed or self-monitored problem solving. An incentive system (i.e., behavioral contracts) is built into the steps to increase saliency of the strategies that are being taught. Other strategies include targeting skills for response inhibition, working memory, self-regulation of emotions, sustained attention, initiating tasks, planning goals, organization, time management, and goal-directed persistence. The techniques that are described utilize a number of behavioral and cognitive-behavioral strategies that may prove to be helpful in assisting children with ADHD. Other coaching techniques are suggested, including ways to integrate these into educational plans.

Study and Organizational Skills

Systematic strategy instruction for high school students has been the focus of a program—the Strategies Intervention Model—developed by the University of Kansas Institute for Research on Learning Disabilities (Ellis & Lenz, 1991). This program was developed to teach learning strategies that enable students to acquire and store knowledge, and demonstrate this knowledge (Ellis & Friend, 1991). For strategies to be effective, they must be useful, efficient, and memorable. Ellis and Friend (1991) describe several effective strategies, including setting priorities; reflecting upon how a task can be attacked and accomplished, and analyzing the task, setting goals, monitoring, and checking to see if goals were accomplished. Archer and Gleason (1989) also developed Skills for Success (Grades 3–6), a structured curriculum to teach students study and organization skills. This program features lessons on reading, organizing and summarizing information, test-taking, anticipating test content, how to study, and responding to various test formats (DuPaul & Stoner, 2003). DuPaul and Stoner (2003) also describe a program for organizing school materials, making an assignment calendar, and organizing and completing a paper for children with ADHD. Although these study and organizational skills have not been thoroughly researched, initial evidence suggests that they are promising procedures that can be employed for learning disabled youth (Ellis & Friend, 1991), and warrant further investigation for children with ADHD (DuPaul & Stoner, 2003).

Social Skills Training

Interest in the remediation of social skills deficits has increased over the years, due to the growing awareness that social skill development is linked to learning disabilities (Semrud-Clikeman & Hynd, 1991); school dropout rates, delinquency, and emotional disturbance (Barclay, 1966), and attention-deficit disorders (Carlson, Lahey, Frame, Walker, & Hynd, 1987). Specifically, it has been shown that peer rejection as a result of aggression is predictive of criminal behavior later in adulthood (Parker &

Asher, 1987). Recently, proposed definitions suggest including social problems as characteristics of learning disabilities (Lerner, 1993). Advocates of this proposal assert that to focus solely on academic gains in reading and math, while ignoring social interaction skills, will limit the usefulness of our remediation efforts for children with learning disabilities (Rourke, 1994). Social skills problems appear related to a number of factors including self-efficacy, self-esteem, locus of control, social cognition, comprehension of nonverbal cues, moral development, comprehension of social rules, problem solving skills, communication disorders, and classroom behaviors (Bryan, 1991). Semrud-Clikeman and Hynd (1991) further describe several neuropsychological syndromes resulting from involvement of either the right or the left hemisphere. Right-hemisphere dysfunction was postulated in learning-disabled children with a variety of deficits, including math, visual-spatial, and social perception, and left-sided motor weaknesses, with verbal reasoning, social gesturing, and social linguistic problems (Denckla, 1978, 1983). Voeller (1986) also described a group of children with abnormal right-hemisphere signs based on CT scans, EEGs, and neuropsychological measures. These children were unable to interpret others' emotions and had trouble displaying appropriate emotions. Further, there was an increased rate of attentional and hypermotoric behaviors as well in children with right-hemisphere involvement.

There are a number of social skills training programs, including the ACCEPTS program for elementary children (Walker, McConnell, Todis, Walker, & Golden, 1988), and the ACCESS program for adolescents (Walker, Holmes, Todis, & Horton, 1988), to name a few. These programs are highly structured, and have proven efficacy for children with mild to moderate handicaps.

Interventions designed to address social skills deficits in children with various learning and social interaction problems have met with mixed if not disappointing results (Vaughn, McIntosh, & Hogan, 1990). When positive behavioral changes have been noted in children with social skills problems, peers and teachers do not readily acknowledge or perceive these gains (Northcutt, 1987). Another concern that is often raised by researchers is that children "trained" in social skills often display appropriate social skills in controlled, therapeutic settings, but fail to interact appropriately in natural settings.

A couple of therapy caveats illustrate this point. One of the authors conducted a 15-week social skills training program with four monthly booster sessions for children with ADHD. At the end of the 15-week sessions, one 12-year-old girl threw her "graduation" gift on the floor. When confronted about her inappropriate behavior, she commented, "Well, you told me I should be honest. Did you want me to lie when I didn't like my present?" Despite weeks of modeling, role-playing, corrective feedback, videotaping, and behavioral reinforcement on expressing feelings appropriately, when disappointed in a "real-life" situation, she was unable to apply the skills she had demonstrated on numerous occasions during group sessions. When processing the incident, she could generate alternative behaviors, but in the heat of her emotions she was unable to exercise control over her disappointment. On another occasion, a 13-year-old ADHD male pushed one of his peers and kicked his books across the parking lot on his way out of the hospital. This situation followed an evening when alternatives to anger were the focus of the group session. This adolescent wasn't even an aggressive child, but when he was teased about something that was particularly painful for him, he reacted inappropriately. Not to be overlooked was the other 12-year-old who was baiting his peer. He, too, was part of the group and obviously was acting inappropriately. Even though both boys were progressing nicely in therapy, in a more natural, less structured situation both were unable to generalize skills that had been the focus of numerous sessions.

In a critical review of 20 studies conducted between 1982 and 1989, Vaughn et al. (1990) did indicate that programs for students with LD were most effective when the following conditions were in place:

1. Students with LD received part-time versus full-time LD services.
2. Students with LD were in either elementary or high school; middle school students showed fewer gains.
3. Regular class students were included in the intervention program.

4. Programs were individualized to the student's needs.
5. Children were selected for social skills training based on deficits rather than LD placement alone.
6. Training programs were long-term (average nine weeks, 23.3 hours) and included follow-up sessions.
7. Instruction is conducted in small groups or one-to-one.
8. Programs included coaching, modeling, corrective feedback, rehearsal, and strategy instruction.

La Greca (1993) indicates the need for training programs that address the broader social milieu of the child. Rather than focusing solely on the social skills deficits of the "problem child," programs should also include high status or non-problem peers. La Greca (1993) recommends the following: (1) changing peer acceptance through multisystemic intervention models; (2) employing prevention models at the school level; (3) utilizing peer pairing or cooperative activities with children of mixed social status; (4) changing the way teachers select groups in the classroom to avoid cliques and child-picked teams; (5) on-going teacher monitoring of social skills interventions in the classroom, and (6) involving parents in intervention efforts. La Greca (1993) also suggests that one or two close friends might buffer a child who does not enjoy peer acceptance with the larger group. Helping the child develop supportive friendships might be worthwhile to reduce anxiety, stress, depression, and low self-esteem.

Stein and Krishnan (2007) provided an overview of strategies to improve the social success of students with NLD. Improvement depends upon interventions that focus on classroom, individual, and small group instruction. It is critical to design classrooms and schools that promote, teach, and reinforce positive social interactions. School environments should provide structure in the classroom and the playground, organize cooperative play, teach social problem solving skills, and implement anti-bullying programs.

In summary, social skills training can be effective when it involves broader goals than increasing skill deficits in the targeted child. By expanding treatment goals to include peers, teachers, parents, and the school environment, social skills intervention can be helpful for many children with learning problems.

Classroom and Behavior Management

Behavior management has long been used as an effective remediation strategy for a variety of learning and behavioral problems in the classroom. The literature base demonstrating the positive effects of behavior management are too extensive to review here. The reader is referred to DuPaul and Stoner (2003) for a detailed review of research on token economies, contingency contracting, cost response, and time-out from positive reinforcement. This section reviews selected strategies that have proved helpful for classroom management and instructional techniques, including self-management, attention training, home-based contingencies, and peer tutoring.

Home-Based Contingencies

Home-based contingencies are frequently used as a supplement to school-based token systems (DuPaul & Stoner, 2003). Generally, these procedures employ daily or weekly rating forms that are filled out by the teacher. Several classroom or academic behaviors can be targeted, including attention to task, work completion, homework completion, compliance, and social interactions. The teacher rates the child by class periods or subject areas, using a point scale (e.g., 5 = excellent, 1 = terrible), and provides written comments. The child is responsible for taking the rating form to the parent, and the parent then discusses the child's performance with the child and provides reinforcement based on the points earned at school. DuPaul and Stoner (2003) indicate that delay of reinforcement can be a problem for children with ADHD, particularly with younger children. However, home-based contingencies have proved effective for increasing school performance, particularly when used with classroom behavior management techniques.

Peer Tutoring

Peer tutoring techniques have been developed for reading, spelling, and math activities, and participants have demonstrated significant gains (Greenwood, Maheady, & Carta, 1991). DuPaul and Stoner (2003) indicate that peer tutoring is an attractive technique because it is time- and cost-efficient. In peer tutoring the class is divided into dyads, and tutor-pairs work together during learning activities (Shapiro, 2004). The Class Wide Peer Tutoring (CWPT) program provides systematic and detailed training guidelines for implementing this intervention technique (Greenwood, Delquardi, & Carta, 1988).

Shapiro (2004) indicates that these procedures have produced positive academic and behavioral gains for children with a variety of disorders, including slow learners, learning disabled children, and behaviorally disordered children. DuPaul and Henningson (1993) also reported positive gains for a young child with ADHD when a class-wide peer tutoring program was initiated. The second-grade child with ADHD showed less hyperactivity and improved on-task behavior and academic performance in math.

These techniques offer a number of viable strategies to improve the academic, behavioral, and social functioning of children and adolescents with various disorders. Individual educational planning is necessary to decide which of these techniques are most appropriate. These interventions are usually used in combination, and careful monitoring is essential to determine their effectiveness. See DuPaul and Stoner (2003) and Shapiro (1989) for detailed information on intervention monitoring.

Other studies have shown that the following behavioral treatments are highly effective for youth with ADHD.

(1) Contingency Management includes the application of positive (token or point systems) and negative consequences (time-out and response cost) in highly structured environments. Pelham and associates developed a summer treatment program that incorporates these principles with other psychosocial and academic interventions (Pelham, Wheeler, & Chronis, 1998). To be effective, behavioral strategies must be used consistently.

(2) Behavioral therapy has been shown to be effective in both the home and school environments

(DuPaul & Stoner, 2003; Teeter, 1998). Parent training programs and teacher consultation to reduce disruptive behaviors generally include the use of token systems with rewards for targeted behaviors. When necessary punishment can be effective when it is nonphysical and consistently applied to a reward-rich environment. Homeschool contingency plans also utilize these behavioral techniques with success.

(3) Social skills training has produced mixed results, but when applied more systematically, positive results have been more robust [see (Pfiffner & McBurnett, 1997; Pfiffner, Barkley, & DuPaul, 2006)].

(4) Peer tutoring of children with ADHD is an effective intervention in the classroom (DuPaul, Ervin, Hook, & McGoey, 1998).

(5) Self-management, self-instruction and self-reinforcement techniques are also promising (DuPaul & Stoner, 2003).

While we do not have an extensive research base to determine efficacy to date, there are some promising interventions that appear effective for promoting self-control and other executive skills in children. Strayhorn (2002) reviewed the empirical evidence of a number of systematic strategies for children with self-control difficulties. In general, the methods incorporate goal setting, determining and arranging task difficulty, changing attributional style, modeling desired behaviors, practicing skills (rehearsal), reinforcement and punishment to foster delay gratification, and self-instruction.

Summary

This chapter provided a brief overview of interventions for various cognitive, academic, social-emotional and executive control difficulties that occur in childhood. Although the strategies cross various paradigms, we suggest that a comprehensive neuropsychological model would advance the science of understanding and treating childhood disorders. It will be important for future research to better determine the extent to which interventions impact brain functions. "While it is possible that some intervention approaches may reverse the

core deficits in abnormal patterns of functional activity, others may achieve their effects by recruiting compensatory mechanisms or have no measurable effect on the underlying brain mechanism" (McCandliss & Noble, 2003, p. 202).

In their elegant review of dyslexia, McCandliss & Noble (2003) concluded, "We believe, however, that a more complete theoretical treatment of the neurobiological basis of reading ability and disorder will require an account of the mechanisms by which the functional properties of these brain areas change with learning, development and intervention" (p. 203). We believe that this statement could easily apply to other cognitive and academic problems.

References

Archer, A., & Gleason, M. (1989). *Skills for school success (grades 3–6)*. North Billerica, MA: Curriculum.

Baddeley, A. D. (1986). *Working memory*. Oxford: Clarendon Press.

Baker, S., Gersten, R., & Lee, S. (2002). A synthesis of empirical research on teaching mathematics to low achieving students. *The Elementary School Journal, 103*(1), 51–73.

Barclay, J. R. (1966). Sociometric choices and teacher ratings as predictors of school dropout. *Journal of Social Psychology, 4*, 40–45.

Bergquist, T. E., & Malec, J. F. (2002). Neuropsychological assessment for treatment planning and research. In P. J. Eslinger (Ed.), *Neuropsychological interventions: Clinical research and practice* (pp. 38–58). New York, NY: Guilford Press.

Bos, C. S., & Anders, P. L. (1990). Interactive teaching and learning: Instructional practices for teaching content and strategic knowledge. In T. E. Scruggs & B. Y. L. Wong (Eds.), *Intervention research in learning disabilities* (pp. 166–185). New York: Springer-Verlag.

Bos, C. S., & Van Reusen, A. K. (1991). Academic interventions with learning-disabled students: A cognitive/metacognitive approach. In J. E. Obrzut & G. W. Hynd (Eds.), *Neuropsychological foundations of learning disabilities* (pp. 659–683). San Diego, CA: Academic Press.

Bradley, L., & Bryant, P. E. (1983). Categorizing sounds and learning to read – A causal connection. *Nature, 301*, 41–21.

Bryan, T. (1991). Social problems and learning disabilities. In B. Y. L. Wong (Ed.), *Learning about learning disabilities* (pp. 195–229). San Diego, CA: Academic Press.

Butler, R. W. (1998). Attentional processes and their remediation in childhood cancer. *Medical and Pediatric Oncology Supplement, 1*, 75–78

Butler, R. W. (2006). Cognitive and behavioral rehabilitation. In J. E. Farmer, J. Donders, & S. Warschausky (Eds.), *Treating neurodevelopmental disabilities: Clinical research and practice* (pp. 186–207). New York, NY: Guilford Press.

Butler, R. W., & Copeland, D. R. (2002). Attentional processes and their remediation in childhood cancer: A literature review and the development of a therapeutic approach. *Journal of the International Neuropsychological Society, 8*, 115–124.

Byrne, B., & Fielding-Barnsley, R. (1993). Evaluation of a program to teach phonemic awareness to young children: A one-year follow-up. *Journal of Educational Psychology, 85*, 104–111.

Carlson, C. C., Lahey, B. B., Frame, C. L., Walker, J., & Hynd, G. W. (1987). Sociometric status of clinic – referred children with attention deficit disorders with and without hyperactivity. *Journal of Abnormal Psychology, 15*, 537–547.

Chenault, B., Thomson, J., Abbott, R. D., & Berninger, V. W. (2006). Effects of prior attention training on child dyslexics' response to composition instruction. *Developmental Neuropsychology, 29*(1), 243–260.

Cunningham, A. (1989). Phonemic awareness: The development of early reading competency. *Reading Research Quarterly, 24*, 471–472.

Cunningham, A. E. (1990). Explicit versus implicit instruction in phonemic awareness. *Journal of Experimental Child Psychology, 50*, 429–4.

Daneman, M., & Carpenter, P. (1980). Individual differences in working memory and reading. *Journal of Verbal Learning and Verbal Behavior, 19*, 450–466.

Dawson, P. & Guare, R. (2004). *Executive skills in children and adolescents.* New York, NY: Guilford Press.

Denckla, M. B. (1978). Minimal brain dysfunction. In J. S. Chall & A. F. Mirsky (Eds.), *Education and the brain* (pp. 223–268). Chicago: University of Chicago Press.

Denckla, M. B. (1983). The neuropsychology of social-emotional learning disabilities. *Archives of Neurology, 40*, 461–462.

DuPaul, G., Ervin, R. A., Hook, C. L., & McGoey, K. (1998). Peer tutoring for children with attention-deficit hyperactivity disorder: Effects on classroom behavior and academic performance. *Journal of Applied Behavioral Analysis, 31*, 579–592.

DuPaul, G, & Henningson, P. N. (1993). Peer tutoring effects on the classroom performance of children with attention deficit hyperactivity disorder. *School Psychology Review, 22*, 134–143.

DuPaul, G. J., & Stoner, G. (2003). *ADHD in the schools: Assessment and intervention strategies* (2nd ed.). New York: Guilford Press

Ellis, E. S., & Friend, P. (1991). Adolescents with learning disabilities. In B. Y. L. Wong (Ed.), *Learning about learning disabilities* (pp. 506–563). San Diego, CA: Academic Press.

Ellis, E. S., & Lenz, B. K. (1991). *The development of learning strategy interventions.* Lawrence, KS: Edge Enterprise.

Englert, C. S. (1990). Unraveling the mysteries of writing through strategy instruction. In T. E. Scruggs & B. Y. L. Wong (Eds.), *Intervention research in learning disabilities* (pp. 186–223). New York: Springer-Verlag.

Eslinger, P. J., & Oliveri, M. V. (2002). Approaching interventions clinically and scientifically. In P. J. Eslinger (Ed.), *Neuropsychological interventions: Clinical research and practice* (pp. 3–15). New York, NY: Guilford Press.

Fleischner, J. E. (1994). Diagnosis and assessment of mathematics learning disabilities. In G. R. Lyon (Ed.), *Frames of reference for the assessment of learning disabilities: New views on measurement issues* (pp. 441–458). Baltimore, MD: Paul H. Brooks.

Fletcher, J. M., Lyon, G. R., Fuchs, L. S., & Barnes, M. A. (2007). *Learning disabilities: From identification to intervention.* New York, NY: Guilford Press.

Fuchs, D., & Fuchs, L. (2005). Peer-Assisted learning Strategies: Promoting word recognition, fluency, and reading comprehension in young children. *Journal of Special Education, 39*, 34–44.

Fuchs, L., Fuchs, D., Prentice, K., Burch, M., Hamlett, C. L., Owen, R., et al. (2003a). Explicitly teaching for transfer: Effects on third grade students' mathematical problem solving. *Journal of Educational Psychology, 95*, 292–305.

Fuchs, L., Fuchs, D., Prentice, K., Burch, M., Hamlett, C. L., Owen, R., et al. (2003b). Enhancing third grade students' mathematical problem solving with self regulation learning strategies. *Journal of Educational Psychology, 95*, 306–326.

Gaskin, I. W., Satlow, E., & Pressley, M. (2007). Executive control of reading comprehension in the elementary school. In L. Meltzer (Ed.), *Executive function in education* (pp. 194–215). New York, NY: Guilford Press.

Gillam, R. B., Loeb, D. F., Hoffman, L. V., Bohman, T., Champlin, C. A., Thibodeau, L., et al. (2008). The efficacy of fast forward language intervention in school-age children with language impairment: A randomized controlled trial. *Journal of Speech, Language, and Hearing Research, 51*(1), 97–119.

Graham, S., & Harris, K. R. (2003). Students with learning disabilities and the process of writing: A meta-analysis of SRSD studies. In L. Swanson, K. R. Harris, & S. Graham (Eds.), *Handbook of research on learning disabilities* (pp. 383–402). New York, NY: Guilford Press.

Graham, S., & Harris, K. R. (2005). *Writing better: Teaching writing processes and self-regulation to students with learning problems.* Baltimore: Brookes.

Graham, S., Harris, K. R., & Olinghouse, N. (2007). Addressing executive function problems in writing. In L. Meltzer (Ed.). *Executive function in education* (pp. 216–236). New York, NY: Guilford Press.

Greenwood, C. R., Delquardi, J., & Carta, J. J. (1988). *Classwide peer tutoring.* Seattle: Educational Achievement Systems.

Greenwood, C. R., Maheady, L., & Carta, J. J. (1991). Peer tutoring programs in the regular education classroom. In G. Stoner, M. R. Shinn, & H. M. Walker (Eds.), *Interventions for achievement and behavior problems* (pp. 179–200). Silver Spring, MD: National Association of School Psychologists.

Heins, E. D., Lloyd, J. W., & Hallahan, D. P. (1986). Cued and noncued self-recording to task. *Behavior Modification, 10*, 235–254.

Hinckley, J. J. (2002). Models of language rehabilitation. In P. J. Eslinger (Ed.), *Neuropsychological interventions: Clinical research and practice* (pp. 182–221). New York, NY: Guilford Press.

Hirshberg, L. M., Chui, S., & Frazier, J. A. (2005). Emerging brain-based interventions for children and adolescents: Overview and clinical perspective. *Child and Adolescent Psychiatric Clinics of America, 14*, 1–19.

Hooft, I. A., Andersson, T., Sejersen, T., Bartfai, A., & von Wendt, L. (2003). Attention and memory training in children with acquired brain injuries. *Acta Paediatrica, 92*, 935–940.

Iversen, S., & Tunmer, W. E., (1993). Phonological processing skills and the reading recovery program. *Journal of Educational Psychology, 85*, 112–126.

Kerns, K. A., Eso, K., & Thompson, J. (1999). Investigation of a direct intervention for improving attention in young children with ADHD. *Developmental Neuropsychology, 16*(2), 273–295.

Klingberg, T., Fernell, E., Olesen, P.J., Johnson, M., Gustafsson, P., Dahlstrom, K., et al. (2005). Computerized training of working memory in children with ADHD–A randomized, controlled trial. *Journal of the American Academy of Child and Adolescent Psychiatry, 44*(2), 177–86F.

La Greca, A. M. (1993). Social skills training with children: Where do we go from here? Presidential Address. *Journal of Clinical Child Psychology, 22*, 288–298.

Lerner, J. (1993). *Learning disabilities: Theories, diagnosis, & teaching strategies* (6th ed.). Boston: Houghton Mifflin.

Lovett, M. W., Barron, R. W., & Benson, N. J. (2003). Effective remediation of word identification and decoding difficulties in school-age children with reading disabilities. In H. L. Swanson, K. Harri, & S. Graham (Eds.), *Handbook of learning disabilities* (pp. 273–292). New York: Gilford Press.

Lovett, M. W., Lacerenza, L., Borden, S. L., Frijters, J. C., Steinbach, K. A., DePalma, M. (2000). Components of effective remediation for developmental reading disabilities: Combining phonological and strategy-based instruction to improve outcomes. *Journal of Educational Psychology, 92*, 262–283.

Lloyd, J. E., & Landrum, T. J. (1990). Self-recording of attending to task: Treatment components and generalization of effects. In T. E. Scruggs & B. Y. L. Wong (Eds.), *Intervention research in learning disabilities* (pp. 235–262). New York: Springer-Verlag.

Lundberg, I., Frost, J., & Petersen, O. P. (1988). Effects of an extensive program for stimulating phonological awareness in preschool children. *Reading Research Quarterly, 23*, 267–284.

McCandliss, B. D., & Noble, K. G. (2003). The development of reading impairment: A cognitive neuroscience model. *Mental Retardation and Developmental Disabilities Research Reviews, 9*(3), 196–204.

McMaster, K. L., Fuchs, D., Fuchs, L. S., & Compton, D. L. (2005). Responding to nonresponders: An experimental field trial of identification and intervention methods. *Exceptional Children, 71*, 445–463.

Meltzer, L. (2007). *Executive function in education.* New York, NY: Guilford Press.

Melzer, L. Pollica, L. S., & Barzilla, M. (2007). Executive function in the classroom: Embedding strategy instruction into daily teaching practices. In L. Meltzer (Ed.), *Executive function in education* (pp. 165–193). New York, NY: Guilford Press.

Montague, M., & Bos, C. (1986). The effect of cognitive strategy training on verbal math problem solving performance of learning disabled adolescents. *Journal of Learning Disabilities, 19*, 26–33.

Montali, J., & Lewandowski, L. (1996). Bimodal reading: Benefits of a talking computer for average and less skilled readers. *Journal of Learning Disabilities, 29*, 271–279.

Montgomery, J. W. (2003). Working memory and comprehension in children with specific language impairment: What we know so far. *Journal of Communications Disorders, 36*, 221–231.

Nadeau, S. E., & Gonzalez Rothi, L. J. (2004). Rehabilitation of language disorders. In J. Ponsford (Ed.). *Cognitive and behavioral rehabilitation: From neurobiology to clinical practice* (pp. 129–174). New York, NY: Guilford Press.

Northcutt, T. E. (1987). The impact of a social skills training program on the teacher-student relationship. *Dissertation Abstracts International, 46*, 1231A.

Olesen, P., Westerberg, H., & Klingberg, T. (2004). Increased prefrontal and parietal brain activity after training of working memory. *Nature Neuroscience, 7*, 75–79.

Olson, R., Foltz, G., & Wise, B. (1986). Reading instruction and remediation with the aid of computer speech. *Behavior Research Methods, Instruments, & Computers, 18*, 9 M

Olson, R., Fosberg, H., Wise, B., & Rack, J. (1994). Measurement of word recognition, orthographic, and phonological skills. In G. R. Lyon (Ed.), *Frames of reference for the assessment of learning disabilities: New views on measurement issues* (pp. 243–278). Baltimore, MD: Paul H. Brooks.

Olson, R. K., & Wise, B. (2006). Computer-based remediation for reading and related phonological disabilities. In M. McKenna, L. Labbo, R. Kieffer, & D. Reinking (Eds.), *Handbook of literacy and technology* (Vol. 2, pp. 57–74). Mahwah, NJ: Erlbaum.

Palincsar, A., Brown, A., & Martin, S. (1987). Peer interaction in reading comprehension instruction. *Educational Psychologist, 22*, 231–253.

Parker, J. G., & Asher, S. R. (1987). Peer relations and later personal adjustment: Are low-accepted children at risk? *Psychological Bulletin, 102*, 357–389.

Pelham, W. E., Wheeler, T., & Chronis, A. (1998). Empirically supported treatments for attention deficit hyperactivity disorder. *Journal of Clinical Child Psychology, 27*(2), 190–205.

Penkman, L. (2004). Remediation of attention deficits in children: A focus on childhood cancer, traumatic brain injury and attention deficit disorder. *Pediatric Rehabilitation, 7*(2), 111–123.

Pfiffner, L., Barkley, R. A., & DuPaul, G. J. (2006). Treatment of ADHD in school settings. In R. A. Barkley, *Attention-deficit hyperactivity disorder: A handbook for diagnosis and treatment* (3rd ed., pp. 547–589). New York: Guildford Press.

Pfiffner, L., & McBurnett, K. (1997). Social skills training with parent generalization: Treatment effects for children with attention deficit disorder. *Journal of Consulting and Clinical Psychology, 65*, 749–57.

Ponsford, J. (2004). *Cognitive and behavioral rehabilitation: From neurobiology to clinical practice.* NY: Guilford Press.

Riccio, C. A., French, C. L. (2004). The status of empirical support for treatments of attention deficits. *The Clinical Neuropsychologist, 18*(4), 528–558.

Rourke, B. (1994). Neuropsychological assessment of children with learning disabilities: Measurement issues. In C. R. Lyon (Ed.), *Frames of reference for the assessment of learning disabilities: New views on measurement issues* (pp. 475–514). Baltimore, MD: Paul H. Brooks.

Rourke, B. (1989). *Nonverbal learning disabilities: The syndrome and the model.* New York: Guilford Press.

Rourke, B., Bakker, D., Fisk, J., & Strang, J. (1983). *Child neuropsychology: An introduction to theory, research, and clinical practice.* New York: Guilford Press.

Rourke, B., Del Dotto, J. E., Rourke, S. B., & Casey, J. E. (1990). Nonverbal learning disabilities: The syndrome and a case study. *Journal of School Psychology, 28*, 361–385.

Rourke, B., & Fuerst, D. R. (1991). *Learning disabilities and psychosocial functioning: A neuropsychological perspective.* New York: Guilford Press.

Semrud-Clikeman. M., & Hynd, G. W. (1991). Specific nonverbal and social skills deficits in children with learning disabilities. In J. E. Obrzut & G. W. Hynd (Eds.), *Neuropsychological foundations of learning disabilities: A handbook of issues, methods, and practice* (pp. 603–430). San Diego, CA: Academic Press.

Semrud-Clikeman, M., Nielsen, K. H., Clinton, A., Sylvester, L., Parle, N., & Connor, R. T. (1999). An intervention approach for children with teacher- and parent identified attentional difficulties. *Journal of Learning Disabilities, 32*, 581–590.

Shapiro, E. S. (2004). *Academic skills problems: Direct assessment and intervention* (3rd ed.). New York: Guilford Press.

Shinn, M. R. (1989). *Curriculum-based measurement: Assessing special children.* New York: Guilford Press.

Sohlberg, M. M., & Mateer, C. A. (1989). *Introduction to cognitive rehabilitation.* New York: Guilford Press.

Sohlberg, M. M., & Mateer, C. A. (1996). *Attention Process Training II (APT-II).* Puyallup, WA: Association for Neuropsychological Research and development.

Sohlberg, M. M., & Mateer, C. A. (2001). *Introduction to cognitive rehabilitation.* New York: Guilford Press.

Sohlberg, M., Johnson, L., Paule, L., Raskin, S. A., & Mateer, C. A. (2001). *Attention Process Training APT-II for persons with mild cognitive dysfunction (2nd Edition).* Wake Forest, NC: Lash & Associates Publishing/ Training Inc.

Steele, E., Lewandowski, L., & Rusling, E. (1996, March). *The effectiveness of bimodal text presentation for poor readers.* Paper presented at the meeting of the National Association of School Psychologists. Atlanta, GA.

Stein, J., & Krishnan, K. (2007). Nonverbal learning disabilities and executive function: The challenges of effective assessment and teaching. In L. Meltzer (Ed.), *Executive function in education* (pp. 106–132). New York, NY: Guilford Press.

Strang, J. D., & Rourke, B. (1985). Adaptive behavior of children with specific arithmetic disabilities and associated neuropsychological abilities and deficits. In B. P. Rourke (Ed.), *Neuropsychology of learning disabilities: Essentials of subtype analysis* (pp. 302–328). New York: Guilford Press.

Strayhorn, J. M. (2002). Self-control: Toward systematic training programs. *Journal of the American Academy of Child and Adolescent Psychiatry, 41*, 17–27.

Tamm, L., McCandliss,B., Liang, A., Wigal, T., Posner, M. & Swanson, M. (in press). Can attention be trained? Attention training for children at-risk for ADHD. In K. McBurnett (Ed.), Attention *deficit/hyperactivity disorder: A 21st century perspective.* New York: Marcel Dekker.

Teeter, P. A. (1992, March). *Medical and behavioral paradigms: A false dichotomy.* Symposia conducted at the meeting of the National Association of School Psychologists, Washington, DC.

Teeter, P. A. (1998). *Interventions for ADHD: Treatment in developmental context.* New York: Guilford Press.

Torgesen, J. K. (2004). Lessons learned from research on intervention for students who have difficulty learning to read. In P. McCardle & V. Chharab (Eds.), *The voice of evidence in reading research* (pp. 355–382). Baltimore, MD: Brookes.

Tyler, A. A., Lewis, K. E., Haskill, A., & Tolbert, L. C. (2003). Outcomes of different speech and language goal attack strategies. *Journal of Speech, Language, and Hearing Research, 46*(5), 1077–1094.

Vaughn, S., McIntosh, R., & Hogan, A. (1990). Why social skills training doesn't work: An alternative model. In T. E. Scruggs & B. Y. L. Wong (Eds.), *Intervention research in learning disabilities* (pp. 263–278). New York: Springer-Verlag.

Voeller, K. K. S. (1986). Right hemisphere deficit syndrome in children. *American Journal of Psychiatry, 143*, 1004–1011.

Walker, H. M., McConnell, S. R., Todis, B., Walker, J., & Golden, H. (1988). *The Walker social skills curriculum: The ACCEPTS program.* Austin, TX: Pro-Ed.

Walker, H. M., Holmes, D., Todis, B., & Horton, G. (1988). *The Walker social skills curriculum. The ACCESS Program: Adolescent curriculum for communication and effective social skills.* Austin, TX: PRO-ED.

Wise, B. W., & Olson, R. K. (1991). Remediating reading disabilities. In J. E. Obrzut & G. W. Hynd (Eds.), *Neuropsychological foundations of learning disabilities: A handbook of issues, methods, and practice* (pp. 631–658). San Diego, CA: Academic Press.

Wise, B. W., Olson, R. K., Anstett, M., Andrews, L., Terjak, M., Schneider, V., et al. (1989). Implementing a long-term remedial reading study in the public schools: Hardware, software, and real world issues. *Behavior Research Methods, & Instrumentation, 21*, 173–180.

Wise, B., Ring, J., & Olson, R. K. (2000). Individual differences in gains from computer-assisted remedial reading with more emphasis on phonological analysis or accurate reading in content. *Journal of Experimental Child Psychology, 77*, 197–235.

Chapter 17
Pediatric Psychopharmacological and Combined Interventions

Some pediatric disorders with biogenetic or neuropsychological causes may require medical treatments (Wilens, 2001). Most of these disorders, however, require multimodal treatments, where medication is used in combination with other psychosocial and behavioral interventions or therapies. A select list of common medications will be reviewed, including those designed to control ADHD, major depressive disorders, bipolar disorders, psychotic disorders, Tourette syndrome, and seizure disorders. The National Institute of Mental Health (NIMH) has funded a number of studies to investigate the safety and efficacy of medications and psychosocial interventions for common childhood and adolescent disorders. These will be briefly reviewed.

Specific Classes of Medication

Medications are typically classified as stimulants, antipsychotics, antidepressants (i.e., tricylics, serotonin reuptake inhibitors, atypical antidepressants, and monoamine oxidase inhibitors); antioxiolytics, and antiepileptic medications, depending on their behavioral effects on the CNS (Wilens, 2001). Table 17.1 lists medications currently used to treat children and adolescent disorders. Potential benefits and possible adverse effects are also summarized. Psychopharmacological agents may affect more than one neurotransmitter, and specific neurotransmitters may be implicated in more than one neuropsychiatric disorder (Pliszka, 2003). CNS affects will be discussed in the following sections.

Stimulant Medications

Stimulant medications are the most common psychotropic drugs to treat ADHD in preschool children (Greenhill et al., 2006), school-aged (Barkley, 2006), adolescents (Connor, 2006), and more recently adults (Barkley, Murphy, & Fischer, 2006). Although a majority of children with ADHD respond positively to stimulant medications, approximately 25–30 percent do not (Connor, 2006). Schaughency and Hynd (1989) suggest that "perhaps there are correlated, parallel, or even orthogonal neurotransmitter systems implicated in ADD that account for these differences in response rates" (p. 436). Further, Hunt, Mandl, Lau, and Hughes (1991) propose that "multiple neurotransmitter systems may be involved in integrated cognitive/behavioral functioning," and "the relative balance of these transmitters and these neurofunctional systems determines the modulation of behavior" (p. 272). Thus, individual response rates may be a function of the child's primary dysfunction in cognitive/perceptual systems, arousal systems, or inhibitory systems. This perspective still needs further study in controlled studies. Others suggest that the presence of comorbid disorders may affect the variability in individual response rates (Pliszka, Carlson, & Swanson, 1999). Specifically, Ghurman et al. (2007) did find that preschool children with AD/HD with three or more disorders did not respond to stimulant medications. While demographics were not predictive of medication responses, children with high comorbidity had higher rates of family/environmental risk factors (i.e., lower socioeconomic status, lower

M. Semrud-Clikeman, P.A. Teeter Ellison, *Child Neuropsychology*, DOI 10.1007/978-0-387-88963-4_17,
© Springer Science+Business Media, LLC 2009

Table 17.1 Common uses, benefits, and side effects of medications for neuropsychiatric disorders of childhood

Drugs	Common use	Manifestations	Side effects
Stimulants			
Methylphenidate (Ritalin)	ADHD	75% children responders	Insomnia, appetite loss, nausea, vomiting, abdominal pains, thirst, headaches
		Decreased motor activity, impulsivity, and disruptive behaviors	
		Increased attention	Tachycardia, change in blood pressure
		Improved socialization	Irritability, moodiness
		Improved ratings (teacher, physician, parent)	Rebound effects
		Increased work completion and accuracy	Growth suppression (can be monitored)
		Improved test scores (mazes, PIQ, and visual memory)	Lower seizure threshold
			Exacerbate preexisting tics
Dextroamphetamine (D-amphetamine)	ADHD	Similar to methylphenidate	Similar to methylphenidate
		Subdued emotional response	Hallucinations, seizures, and drug-induced psychosis (rare occurrences)
		Increased reflectivity and ability to monitor self	
		Increased interest level	
		Improved school performance	
		Improved parent ratings (conduct, impulsivity, immaturity, antisocial, and hyperactivity)	
Magnesium pemoline (Cylert)	ADHD	Similar to methylphenidate	Similar to methylphenidate
		Improved teacher ratings (defiance, inattention, and hyperactivity)	
		Improved parent ratings (conduct, impulsivity, and antisocial behaviors)	
		Improved test scores (mazes, PIQ, visual memory)	
Antipsychotics			
Haloperidol (Haldol)	Psychosis	Reduces aggression, hostility, negativity, and hyperactivity	Behavioral toxicity with pre-existing disorders
	Tourette		Dystonia, loss of tone in tongue and trunk)
	Autism	Reduces psychotic symptoms	
	PDD	Reduces Tourette symptoms	Parkinsonian symptoms (tremors, mask face, and drooling)
	ADD with CD	Reduces fixations, withdrawal stereotypes, anger, and fidgetiness in autism	Dyskinesis (mouth, tongue, and jaw)
		Increases social responsivity and reality testing in PDD	Dose reduction decreases motor side effects
			Intellectual dulling and disorganized thoughts
Chlorpromazine (Thorazine)	Psychosis	Reduces hyperactivity	Similar to haloperidol
	Severe aggression, explosiveness, and hyperexcitability in MR children	Reduces tantrums, aggression, self-injury	Dermatological problems
		Not effective for young autistic	Cardiovascular problems
			Lowers seizure threshold
			Endocrinological problems
			Ophthalmological problems
			Hematological problems
Thioridazine (Mellaril)	Psychosis	Reduces hyperactivity	Similar to haldol
	Severe behavior disorders (extreme)	Improves schizophrenic symptoms	Sedation, cognitive dulling, and impaired arousal
		Similar to Thorazine	
Thiothixene (Navane)	Psychosis	Similar to Mellaril	Less sedating than Mellaril

Table 17.1 (continued)

Drugs	Common use	Manifestations	Side effects
Loxapine Succinate (Loxitane)	Psychosis	Similar to haldol	Similar to haldol
Fluphenazine Hydrochloride (Prolixin, Permitil)	Psychosis		
Pimozide (Orap)	Psychosis Tourette (resistant type)	Clinical improvement	High doses-death and seizures
Clozapine (Clozaril)	Severe psychosis (resistant type)	Clinical improvement	Life-threatening Hypertension, tachycardia, and EEG change Seizures
Tricyclic antidepressants			
Imipramine hydrochloride (Tofranil)	Depression Enuresis ADHD School phobia	Improves depression (not severe) Reduces hyperactivity Reduces separation anxiety Improves sleep disorders)	Potentially life-threatening cardiovascular problems Inhibits bladder muscles CNS symptoms (EEG changes, confusion, lowers seizure threshold, incoordination, drowsiness, delusions, and psychosis) Blurred vision, dry mouth, and constipation
Nortriptyline hydrochloride (Pamelor)	Depression	Low rate of clinical improvement in children and adolescents	Withdrawal symptoms
Desipramine hydrochloride (Norpramine)	ADHD ADHD with Tics	Improved ratings (parents and teachers Conners) Clinical improvement	Dry mouth, decreased appetite, tiredness, dizziness, insomnia EEG changes at high doses
Clomipramine hydrochloride (Anafranil)	Obsessive-compulsive disorders Severe ADHD Enuresis School phobia	Reduces obsessions Reduces school phobia/anxiety Reduces aggression, impulsivity, and depressive/affective symptoms	Withdrawal symptoms Seizures Somnolence, tremors, dizziness, headaches, sweating, sleep disorder, gastrointestinal problems, cardiovascular effects, anorexia, and fatigue
Monoamine osidase inhibitors			
Fluoxetine hydrochloride (Prozac)	Depression Obsessive-compulsive	Effective for adults Clinical improvement for OCD	Nausea, weight loss, anxiety, nervousness, sweating, sleep disorders
Bupropion hydrochloride (Wellbutrin)	Depression ADHD	Adolescents 18 + improve Improved global ratings Not Conners	Seizures, agitation, dry mouth, insomnia, nausea, constipation, tremors
Anxiolytics			
Chlordiazepoxide (Librium)	Anxiety with hyperactivity and irritability School phobia	Clinical improvement Reduced hyperactivity, fears, enuresis, truancy, bizarreness Decreases emotional overload	Drowsiness, fatigue, muscle weakness, ataxia, anxiety, and depression with high doses
Diazepam (Valium)	Mixed psychiatric DX Anxiety and sleep	Improved global ratings Better results for adolescents	Relatively low toxicity
Alprazolam (Xanax)	Anxiety Panic attacks Separation anxiety	Clinical improvements Responders (premorbid, personality were shy, inhibited, nervous)	Mild drowsiness

Table 17.1 (continued)

Drugs	Common use	Manifestations	Side effects
Anticonvulsants			
Phenobarbital	Seizure disorders	Reduces seizures	Lethal at high doses
			Cognitive impairment, rigidity, and depression
Diphenylhydantoin sodium (Phenytoin)	Seizure disorders	Reduces tonic-clonic seizures	Cognitive impairment
			Drug toxicity
Carbamazepine	Seizure disorders	Reduces generalized and tonic-clonic seizures	Fewer adverse side effects than other drugs
	Manic-depression		
		Psychotropic effects	Less cognitive dulling, motoric and affective
Sodium valporate	Seizure disorders	Reduces seizures	Low cognitive symptoms
		Petit mal + tonic-clonic	Relatively nontoxic in adults
			Rare but potentially fatal hepatoxicity in children

Note: Data taken from Green (1991), Neppe and Tucker (1992), and Dubovsky (1992).

parental education and unemployment, and lived in single-parent families).

Disturbances in dopamine (DA) and norepinephrine (NE) levels have been carefully studied in ADHD children, including how stimulants affect these catecholamines for the ultimate control of attention and movement (Barkley, 2006; Pliszka, 2003). DA systems are involved in a variety of cognitive and perceptual functions, including attentional gaiting, sustaining focus, short-term memory, and allocation of memory, while NE systems are involved in cortical arousal, filtering of incoming stimuli, excessive arousal, restlessness, and hyperactivity (Pliszka, 2003).

Serotonin has also been implicated in ADHD, particularly as it relates to cortical inhibition, direction of motor activity, control of impulses and aggression, and complex judgment (Pliszka, 2003). Increased levels of serotonin produce obsessional thoughts, while decreased levels result in increased impulsivity, violent antisocial behavior, criminality, and suicide attempts. Comings (1990) suggests that serotonin may be less important in understanding ADHD, but may be more useful for children with conduct disorders and aggression.

Although biochemical research is difficult to conduct because of developmental changes in neurotransmitters systems, the use of peripheral measures, and the complexity of neurotransmitter action (Zametkin & Rapoport, 1986; Zametkin & Liotta, 1998), several hypotheses have been generated to explain how stimulant medications affect various neurotransmitters.

1. Stimulants bind to the presynapse, thereby increasing the concentrations of catecholamines at the postsynapse (Pliszka, 2003; Volkow et al., 2002).
2. Stimulants increase the release of DA presence at the presynapse and block the reuptake of DA at the postsynapse (see Barkley, 2006).

These various actions facilitate neural transmission by either increasing the amount of neurotransmitters or prolonging the amount of time transmitters are active at the synapse (Pliszka, 2003). Pliszka (2003) suggests that "it is necessary to affect both NE and DA to fully attenuate the symptoms of ADHD" (p.154).

Stimulant Preparations/ Delivery Systems

Stimulant medications can be delivered in a variety of ways, including immediate release, intermediate, extended release, and transdermal patches (Connor, 2006; Wilens, 2001). The main differences in the preparation of stimulants have to do with how quickly the medication is absorbed by the central nervous system, the rate of absorption, or peak plasma or brain concentration of the stimulant (Connor, 2006). Immediate release preparations include: methylphenidate (brand name, Ritalin, Methylin, Metadate), dextromethylphenidate (brand name Focalin), dextroamphetamine (brand name Dextrostat, Dexedrine), and mixed amphetamine salts (brand name Adderall). Intermediate release preparations include: methylphenidate (brand name, Ritalin SR, Methylin ER, Metadate ER), and dextromethylphenidate (brand name Dexedrine spansule). Methylphenidate can also be delivered in quicker acting, longer lasting intermediate formulas (brand name Metadate CD, Ritalin LA). Extended release formulas include methylphenidate (brand name Concerta) and mixed amphetamine salts (brand name Adderall XR). See Connor (2006) for additional information about onset of action, peak clinical effect, serum half-life, duration of behavioral effects and required number of daily doses. Transdermal patches have also been developed that deliver methylphenidate for up to 12-hour periods.

Standard dosing practices have changed over the years, from BID (morning and noon administration) to TID which includes a three-times-per-day dosing with a late afternoon dose (Corkum, Panton, Ironside, MacPherson, & Williams, 2008). Long acting or sustained release formulas also treat symptoms after school. Research to date shows that the long acting delivery systems appear to be effective (Biederman, Faraone, Monuteaux, & Grossbard, 2004).

The transdermal methylphenidate system also seems effective for improving core symptoms of ADHD, academic performance, and deportment based on teacher and parent ratings (McGough et al., 2006). The patch was well tolerated and, when present, adverse effects were mild to moderate in intensity. The adverse effects were similar to those reported in oral delivery systems, and abated after several weeks.

Benefits, Potential Side-Effects and Medication Management

The potential benefits of stimulant medications are well documented and include enhanced performance on the major symptoms of ADHD, including impulse control, motor coordination, and vigilance (Connor, 2006; Pliszka, 2003); improved cognitive functioning (Barkley, DuPaul, & McMurray, 1991); increased academic productivity and accuracy (Balthazor, Wagner, & Pelham, 1991); decreased off-task behaviors (Barkley & Cunningham, 1979); decreased aggression (Hinshaw, Henker, Whalen, Erhardt, & Dunnington, 1989); improved peer relations (Hinshaw, 1991); fewer negative commands from teachers (Barkley, 2006), and improved interactions with parents (Barkley, 2006).

In general stimulant medications produce improvement in compliance, impulsive aggression, social interactions and academic performance (Wilens & Spencer, 2000). Many of the improvements in interpersonal domains occur not only because the child's behaviors improve, the behaviors of the adults supervising the child are indirectly affected (e.g., fewer negative interactions, less hostility) (Connor, 2006). Social skills, per se, do not necessarily improve without specific skill development and contingencies to support these new skills.

Despite positive results, individual response remains highly variable (DuPaul, Barkley, & McMurphy, 1991), and children should be carefully monitored for adverse side effects (Connor, 2006; Wilens, 2001). Also, a number of environmental factors may affect a child's positive response to stimulant medication. For example, Barkley and Cunningham (1980) found that the better the mother-child relationship, the greater the positive response rate in the child.

Potential Adverse Side effects

Stimulant medications are considered to be well tolerated by most individuals (Connor, 2006). In large clinical trials, common side effects include: abdominal pain, headache, anorexia, vomiting, insomnia, and nervousness. Reduced prosocial behaviors have been reported in children, particularly when given high doses (Jacobvitz, Sroufe, Stewart, & Leffert, 1990), while a reduction in total sleep time and sleep onset (Corkum et al., 2008) have been found in some children. Young children taking stimulant medications for ADHD also appear to have higher rates of adverse effects, particularly in preschool children. Crying, irritability and temper outbursts have been documented in young children (Connor, 2006).

NIMH sponsored a large scale study of stimulant medication efficacy in preschool children with ADHD (PATS). Children were considered for medication trials only after 10 weeks of behavioral treatment. Greenhill et al. (2006) reported that 89 percent of the study children 3–5 years of age responded positively to immediate release methylphenidate, while 11 percent discontinued medication because of intolerable side effects. These adverse effects included insomnia, loss of appetite, moodiness, nervousness, worry, and skin picking. Swanson et al. (2006) also found that 95 percent of preschool children who remained on medication for 12 months grew 20.3 percent less than expected in height and had a 55.2 percent reduction in weight. The study authors concluded that preschoolers can benefit from stimulant treatment if carefully monitored and if medication benefits are balanced against negative side effects. Other studies have reported chronic height and weight effects in older children. See the discussion of the MTA study in the next section.

Other rare, acute side effects include: motor and vocal tics; sudden death in children with "silent cardiac abnormalities," and psychosis in children with underlying psychotic disorders [see (Connor, 2006) for a review]. While more serious cardiovascular events have been reported in rare cases, cardiovascular effects are minimal in healthy children (Wilens & Spencer, 2000). Recently, the American Heart Association (AHA) recommended that all children on stimulant medications receive an electrocardiogram (ECG) (Vetter et al., 2008). In contrast, the American Academy of Pediatrics (AAP) argues that ECGs be administered only to children with known heart risks. The AHA and AAP later released a clarification of the recommendation stating that physicians may consider an ECG when prescribing stimulant medications, but these are not mandatory. Medical history of the child and family (including sudden deaths) and physician judgment should guide the need for an ECG. The clarification statement indicated that treatment for ADHD should not be withheld if an ECG is not done.

Combined Pharmacological and Psychosocial Interventions

Pharmacotherapy is rarely advised in isolation. Earlier reviews have shown that most childhood and adolescent disorders are complex and affect multiple facets of the child's cognitive, academic, and psychosocial adjustment. Medications also have their limitations and may not uniformly improve all areas of the child's functioning; thus, most physicians combine pharmacological interventions with psychosocial interventions. Psychosocial interventions may include behavioral treatments (e.g., contingency management, home-school notes), individual or group therapy for the child or adolescent, parent training, and family therapy. Combined therapeutic interventions have been more thoroughly researched with ADHD than with other childhood disorders. Early studies showed that medication combined with parent training and behavior management was more effective than either medication or behavior management alone for "normalizing" children with ADHD (Pelham et al., 1988). Low doses of medication (methylphenidate) were considerably enhanced with combined behavioral interventions. Pelham (1993) suggests that "an important result of combined treatments may be that maximal improvement in behavior may be reached without resorting to high dosages of stimulant medication," which may lower adverse medication effects (p. 220). Further, combined behavioral-medication interventions for children with ADHD appear to complement the shortcomings of either treatment alone (Carlson, Pelham, Milich, & Dixon, 1992), and add incremental effects that do not occur with either intervention alone (Pelham, 1993).

The extent to which similar effects will be shown for combined pharmacological-psychosocial-behavioral interventions with other childhood disorders needs further investigation. Research investigating combined interventions is needed to determine the short-term and long-term effects of psychopharmacotherapy and individual responsivity to various aspects of the other behavioral, academic, and psychosocial interventions.

Multimodal Treatment with Stimulant Medications for ADHD

Multimodal treatment generally includes parent and child education about ADHD, stimulant medication, behavioral therapy, and educational interventions for psychosocial and academic difficulties. The Multimodal Treatment Study of Children with ADHD (MTA Cooperative Group, 2004a, b) investigated the efficacy of medication alone (MedMgt), behavioral and psychosocial treatments alone (Beh), combined medication with behavioral interventions (Comb), and a control group who received treatment in a community setting (CC) or treatment as usual. The study is complex in design and is ongoing, following study participants from childhood into early adulthood.

Initial findings after 14 months of treatment showed that all four groups improved (MTA Cooperative Group, 2008a). However, there were some significant findings that are summarized: (1) MedMgt produced larger benefits than behavior therapy; (2) Comb treatment did not significantly increase the overall benefits of MedMgt alone; (3) participants in the Comb treatment group had 20 a percent lower dose of medication with similar results as those children in the MedMgt group who had higher doses; (4) Comb treatment was superior to other treatments for children in families on public assistance; (5) Comb treatment was superior to other treatments for children with ADHD and comorbid anxiety, and (6) families with higher rates of attendance at monthly clinic visits had better treatment outcomes. Medication as prescribed in the MTA study produced clinical improvement in the core symptoms of ADHD – hyperactivity, inattention and impulsivity. Comb treatment (medication and behavioral therapy) was relatively superior to Beh therapy alone and to CC. Even though some children in CC care received medication (38%), they fared less well compared to those in the MedMgt group. These differences may be the result of lower medication doses prescribed in CC compared to those receiving the MTA MedMgt algorithm. The Beh therapy was also found to be more effective than CC – treatment as usual.

Youth receiving medication in CC group had better outcomes than the non-medicated CC youth, and outcomes were similar to those in the Beh group. However, children in the MedMgt had better outcomes than those receiving treatment as usual in the CC group. It is likely that the manner in which medications are administered and monitored in the community affects long-term outcomes.

The MTA did a 24-month follow-up to measure the long-term outcome of treatment (MTA Cooperative Group, 2008a). The major outcomes include the following. (1) There was a persistent relative superiority of MedMgt and Comb groups over the Beh and CC treatment groups, although effect size was lower than 14-month analyses. (2) While participants taking medication at 24 months had better outcomes than those who were not medicated, there was a partial loss of the relative benefits of medication compared to the data from the 14-month interval. (3) Youths who were continually medicated had slower growth gains compared to non-medicated

youths (1 cm/year reduction; 1.2 kg/year in weight gain), and stimulant growth suppression may continue when medication treatment is maintained. (4) The compliance with assigned medication doses dropped at the 24-month follow-up, while the percentage of children in the Beh group increased their use of medication. This may have affected the results between the treatment groups (see #1 above). (5) Children who stopped medication at the 24-month follow-up had greater overall deterioration in outcomes, while those children starting medication after the initial study phase improved during the 10-month interval.

The 36-month follow-up of the MTA study revealed interesting and sometimes confusing results at the 2nd follow-up (MTA Cooperative Group, 2008a, 2008b). The relative superiority of Comb and MedMgt over the Beh and CC was completely lost at 36 months. The relative superiority of the MTA medication algorithm was lost, and continued medication was a marker of deterioration in some children. There were three different outcome trajectories that are important. Two groups (66% of sample) showed large initial improvement on medication. Class 1 (52%) had a large initial improvement that was maintained over time, while another Class 3 (14%) had large initial improvement that was not maintained at 36 months. In fact, Class 2 showed deterioration at the 36-month follow-up. Family demographics showed that this group had higher rates of adversity than the other groups. Further, Class 2 (34% of sample), had initial modest improvement on medication that gradually increased over time, and was significantly better than those who were not medicated. The first two groups (66%) of the sample had a large and significant improvement with medication over time, and for Class 1 the magnitude of improvement was even greater at 36 months.

The MTA Cooperative Group (2008b) also investigated moderator variables to determine how comorbidity factors impact outcomes. Children with comorbid anxiety had improved outcomes when given Beh therapy, and with outcomes similar to both the MedMgt and the Comb therapies. The Beh, Comb, and MedMgt were superior to treatment as usual (CC therapy) for children with anxiety. Children with disruptive disorder, ADHD and anxiety also fared better with Comb treatment compared to the other therapies. Further, Comb, but not MedMgt, therapies reduced the persistence of oppositional defiant disorder (ODD) and mood disorders.

Family demographics appeared to impact the effectiveness of various treatment modalities. Children from families with income challenges (receiving public assistance versus those who were not) had better outcomes in the Comb therapy compared to other treatments (MTA Cooperative Group, 2008b). Significant reductions in negative/ineffective discipline practices only occurred in the Comb treatment group. In general, families with socioeconomic disadvantage responded most favorably to Beh treatment. In addition, children receiving Comb and Beh therapies had some protection against substance experimentation and delinquency compared to MedMgt and CC groups that were not protected.

While the MTA study has been the most comprehensive of its kind, there are complexities to the data and analyses that have created controversies and confusion. The study is ongoing, and eight-year follow-up data were presented at the MTA Research Symposium (2007), 10-year data analyses have been completed, and 12-year follow-up is in progress (MTA Cooperative Group, 2008b). To date the study has shown long-term benefits of stimulants over a one-year period. These findings are consistent with those reported by Abikoff et al. (2004) which documented benefits of stimulant medications over a two-year period when medications are properly monitored and adjusted. At the 24-month follow-up, the MTA data found that the relative benefits of stimulants were gradually reduced when children return to community care. In the three-year follow-up, treatment benefits dissipated completely for some children, while others continued to improve. In the future, the MTA study will address important questions about quality care for ADHD, the ultimate effects on height and weight for children who show stimulant-related growth suppression, and long-term functional outcomes of treatment (MTA Cooperative Group, 2008b).

Non-Stimulant Medications for ADHD

A non-stimulant medication, atomoxetine hydrochloride (brand name Strattera) was recently approved and has shown to be effective for reducing the core symptoms of ADHD (Kelsey et al., 2004). Comparison studies are somewhat inconsistent, with some reports showing greater improvements on Adderall (extended release mixed amphetamine salts) compared to Strattera (Faraone, Wigal, & Hodgins, 2007), while others show that Strattera is comparable to that of methylphenidate (Kratochvil et al., 2002). Barkley, Anderson, and Kruesi (2007) also found that Strattera improved self-ratings of ADHD symptoms in adults with ADHD and self-evaluations in a driving simulator, although these improvements were not noted for examiner-rated driving performance. Bohnstedt et al. (2005) also found that parent and teacher ratings of ADHD showed significant improvement for children on atomoxetine compared to placebo. Parent ratings appeared to detect "a larger effect and accounted for more unique variance in the prediction of treatment type, independent of teacher-based ratings" (p. 158).

Other medications used for children who are considered non-responders to stimulant medications include imipramine (Connor, 2006), and MAOI (Zametkin, Rapoport, Murphy, Linnoila, & Ismond, 1985). Desipramine selectively blocks the uptake of NE, and imipramine may block the uptake of serotonin. While antidepressants may increase NE availability at the synapse (Hunt et al., 1991), these are not the frontline medications of choice for most children with ADHD.

Wood, Crager, Delap, and Heiskell (2007) reviewed non-stimulant medications that have been used to treat ADHD. Tricyclic antidepressants have been used to treat individuals with ADHD, particularly those with comorbid disorders including mood, anxiety, oppositional and tic disorders. Selective serotonin reuptake inhibitors (SSRIs) have a more cautioned tale. In 2004, the FDA issued a "black box" warning about the risk for suicide in youths taking SSRIs. "The implementation of an SSRI in treating ADHD should only be considered when there is a dual diagnosis of ADHD with depression or anxiety" (Wood et al., 2007, p. 344). Other side effects for SSRIs (increased mania, agitation, insomnia, akathisia, and sleep difficulties) should be carefully monitored. Other antidepressants (i.e., bupropion, venlafaxine) block the reuptake of serotonin and norepinephrine, but children on these medications require regular electroencephalogram (EEG) monitoring to assess the risk for seizure activity in a very small percentage of individuals.

Studies of antihypertensive medications show that clonidine (CLN) reduces ADHD symptoms (Wilens & Spencer, 1999). Clonidine appears to successfully reduce aggression, sleep disturbances, and tics [see (Wood et al., 2007) for a review]. While improvement in conduct-related problems has been shown when CLN is used in combination with stimulants, serious side effects have been reported. In rare instances, sudden death in children has been reported when stimulants and CLN are combined, but evidence for the linkage is not well established (Taylor et al., 2004). Although promising, less research has been conducted testing the efficacy of guanfacine (GFN).

A number of atypical antipsychotic drugs have been used for children experiencing high levels of behavioral problems, including aggression and disruptiveness. Risperidone (RPD) and aripiprazole (ARP) seem to improve severe behaviors, but are less helpful for core ADHD symptoms (hyperactivity and cognition) (Wood et al., 2007). Serious side effects reduce the widespread use of these medications, except for children with extreme behavioral problems. Carbamazepine (CBZ), a seizure medication, appears to be safe and effective for children, but serious side effects (i.e., dizziness, headaches, drowsiness, ataxia, blurred vision, nausea, vomiting, rash, heptic abnormalities) limit their widespread use as an alternative medication for ADHD (Silva, Munoz, Alpert, 1996; Pellock, 1987). Wood et al. (2007) conclude "Despite their variability as alternatives, each type of medication has certain limitations, side effects, and varying amounts of research available to substantiate its use for the treatment of ADHD. These medications offer several potentially successful options to those who fail to respond to stimulants or those who find the side effects of stimulants bothersome" (p. 341).

Antidepressant Medications

There are three main classes of antidepressants, including: Tricyclic antidepressants (TCAs), selective serotonin reuptake inhibitors (SSRIs), atypical antidepressants, and monoamine oxidase inhibitors (MAOIs) (Wilens, 2001). Tricyclic antidepressants (e.g., imipramine, desipramine, nortriptyline, and clomipramine) act on DA and selectively block the reuptake of NE and serotonin (Pliszka, 2003). TCAs have been used to treat a variety of childhood and adolescent disorders, including (1) imipramine for depression, enuresis, school phobia, and sleep disorders; (2) desipramine for ADHD and ADHD with tics; (3) nortriptyline for major depressive disorder, and (4) clomipramine for obsessive-compulsive disorders (Phelps et al., 2002; Wilens, 2001). Plasma levels should be monitored to identify toxic effects, including affective (mood, concentration, lethargy, social withdrawal), motor (i.e., tremor, ataxia, seizures), psychotic (thought disorders, hallucinations, delusions), and organic (disorientation, memory loss, agitation, confusion) symptoms, or to identify subtherapeutic levels of medication (Phelps et al., 2002). Bostic, Prince, Frazier, DeJong, and Wilens (2003) found that TCAs were less effective for young children with depression, while studies with teens show more promise (Brent et al., 2008).

SSRIs, newer agents that inhibit the reuptake of serotonin, include fluoxtine (Prozac), sertraline (Zoloft), fluvoxamine (Luvox), citalopram (Celexa), sertraline (Zoloft), and paroxetine (Paxil) (Pliszka et al., 1999; Wilens, 2001). Fluoxetine (Prozac) is effective for the treatment of depression and obsessive-compulsive disorders (Phelps et al., 2002). Side effects include nausea, decreased appetite, and insomnia, and are usually mild and transient in nature (Phelps et al., 2002). While SSRIs are considered to be frontline treatments for children and adolescents with depression (Birmaher & Brent, 2003), Safer (2006) reports that SSRIs are not more effective than placebo for treating preadolescent youths and they produce increased adverse effects in children.

Atypical antidepressants have been used to treat children with depression including Wellbutrin, Effexor, Remeron, and trazodone (Wilens, 2001). Wellbutrin (bupropion), similar to amphetamines, works on dopamine and has also been found to be useful for smoking cessation (Wilens, 2001). Wellbutrin is frequently used for children with comorbid depression and ADHD, and/or depression and serious mood swings. The major side effects are irritability, appetite suppression, insomnia, tics and, when given in high doses, Wellbutrin can produce drug-related seizures (Wilens, 2001). In rare cases, self-injury and manic episodes have been reported in children on SSRIs (Pliszka et al., 1999).

MAOIs have recently been investigated for treating childhood disorders including depression, anxiety, panic attacks, and ADHD (Wilens, 2001). The most common MAOIs are phenelzine (Nardil) and tranylcypromine (Parnate). Because of their potential for hepatotoxicity, the need for food restrictions, and questionable effectiveness MAOIs were not commonly administered to children, although this trend has recently been reversed (Wilens, 2001). MAOI-Type A deactivates NE and serotonin, while MAOI-Type B deactivates DA and phenylethylamine (Zametkin & Rapoport, 1987). Food restrictions include aged foods particularly cheeses, certain drugs (cocaine), and cold medicines due to the possibility of increased blood pressure. Other side effects that have been reported include, blood pressure changes, weight gain, drowsiness, and dizziness [see (Wilens, 2001) for more details]. Green (1991) suggests that MAOIs should be tried before starting a trial of Wellbutrin. Like other antidepressants, MAOIs also require careful plasma level monitoring.

In 2004, the U.S. Food and Drug Administration (FDA) announced a "black box warning" on the administration of antidepressants due to an increased risk for suicidal thoughts and behaviors (Bhatia et al., 2008). Studies investigating the risk for suicide in medicated children and adolescents report mixed findings, with some indicating an increased risk (Olfson, Marcus, & Shaffer, 2005; Simon, Savarino, Operskalski, & Wang, 2006), while others suggest the benefits of antidepressants outweigh the risks in pediatric populations (Bridge et al., 2007; Gibbons, Hur, Bhaumik, & Mann, 2006). In a meta-analysis of studies investigated the safety and efficacy of SSRIs, nefazodone, venlafaxine, mirtazapine in children younger than 19. Bridge et al. (2007) indicate that antidepressants are efficacious for pediatric patients with major mood disorders, obsessive-compulsive disorders (OCD), and non-OCD anxiety, while Olfson, Marcus, and Shaffer (2006) support careful clinical monitoring in depressed children (6–18 years of age) due to increased suicide attempts and deaths.

NIMH has funded a number of large-scale investigations to study the effects on antidepressants alone and in combination with cognitive behavioral therapy for reducing depression in young children. These studies provide evidence for the efficacy of antidepressants in teens, while others call for caution when using SSRIs with children and adolescents.

Treatment for Adolescents with Depression Study (TADS)

NIMH funded a large scale, multi-site study of the treatment of depression in teens (TADS, 2004). Treatment conditions were medication (fluoxetine) alone; cognitive behavioral therapy (CBT) alone; combined treatment (fluoxetine plus CBT) and placebo. The study found that antidepressant medication was effective for treating youths with depression, but the combined treatment produced the greatest improvement. CBT alone was less effective than medication alone, although both treatments were better than the placebo condition.

The combined treatment significantly reduced depressive symptoms, and was superior to medication and CBT alone (TADS, 2004). Teens in the study were carefully monitored for adverse side effects including gastrointestinal track events, sedation, and insomnia. Medication doses were adjusted to reduce these effects.

While 30 percent of teens had suicidal ideation at the start of the study, suicidal ideation was reduced in all groups. Decreases in suicidal ideation were greatest for teens in the combined treatment condition, while medication alone was not as protective. Based on this study, CBT appears to be an effective treatment for depression and protects teens with SI with carefully monitored medication (prozac).

STAR*D Sequenced Treatment Alternatives to Relieve Depression

The National Institute of Mental Health (NIMH) funded the nation's largest study investigating 18–75-year-olds with treatment-resistant depression (Rush et al., 2004; Weissman et al., 2006). STAR*D data show that about half of all individuals with difficult to treat depression reached remission with additional treatment, but the odds were reduced with each new trial of medication (Rush et al., 2006). Approximately one-third of participants reached remission at Level 1 treatment when given Celexa (citalopram), an antidepressant. CBT was used either as a switch or add-on treatment during Level 2 of the study, while at Levels 3 and 4 new medications were either switched or added on. Drop-out of the study also increased when additional treatments were not effective. It is important to note that patients who have not responded positively to two prior antidepressants and then switch to a different class of antidepressants have only a minimal chance at remission by taking the new medication (Rush et al., 2004, 2006). Additional research is being conducted on the STAR*D sample to determine the efficacy of either adding on or switching to CBT, and to determine who responds to what treatment sequence.

In another phase of the STAR*D study, Zisook et al. (2007) investigated the impact of early versus late onset of depression to determine medication response across five age groups: childhood onset (ages <12), adolescent onset (ages 12–17), early adult onset (ages 18–44), middle adult onset (ages 45–59), and late adult onset (ages ≥ 60). "No group clearly stood out as distinct from the others. Rather, the authors observed an apparent gradient, with earlier ages at onset associated with never being married, more impaired social and occupational function, poorer quality of life, greater medical and psychiatric comorbidity, a more negative view of life and the self, more lifetime depressive episodes and suicide attempts, and greater symptom severity and suicidal ideation in the index episode compared to those with later ages at onset of major depressive disorder" (Zisook et al., 2007, p. 1539). Thus, age of onset was not associated with a difference in treatment response to the initial trial of citalopram.

Treatment of Resistant Depression in Adolescents, TORDIA

In a study of 12–18 year olds who were non-responders to one SSRI, Brent et al. (2008) investigated other antidepressants, with and without CBT. Teens in the TORDIA study were exposed to the following treatments: (1) switch to a 2nd SSRI (i.e., paroxetine, citalopram, or fluoxetine); (2) switch to different antidepressant medication plus CBT; (3) switch to venlafaxine, and (4) switch to venlafaxine plus CBT. Those teens who had switch to 2nd SSRI

and also received CBT showed the most improvement. Treatment with venlafaxine (compared to another SSRI) was just as efficacious with fewer adverse effects than the other SSRIs.

In summary, continued research on the safety and efficacy of all antidepressants in children and adolescents is needed. While research has shown that some antidepressants can effectively treat depression in teens, especially when combined with cognitive behavioral therapy, the findings for young children are more equivocal. Regardless of the study, clinicians are advised to carefully monitor the adverse events that accompany antidepressants, particularly suicidal ideation and/or behaviors.

Antipsychotic Medications

Antipsychotic medications have been classified as typical (1st generation) and atypical (2nd generation), and are used to treat a variety of neuropsychiatric disorders in children and adolescents, including schizophrenia (Wilens, 2001); pervasive developmental delays (Joshi, Cappozzoli, & Coyle, 1988); chronic motor tics and Tourette syndrome (Comings, 1990); severe aggression and conduct disorders (Green, 1991); cognitive retardation with psychotic symptoms (Gadow & Poling, 1988), and excessive or severe hyperactivity, low frustration tolerance, and poor attention (Wood et al., 2007). While the first generation antipsychotics were effective, the adverse side effects were often intolerable, thus the need to find other safe alternatives.

The typical antipsychotics include butyrophenones (e.g., haldol), phenthiazines (e.g., Thorazine), and thioxanthenes (i.e., navane), while the atypical antipsychotics include clozaril, resperidal, ziprasidone, seroquel, and geodone (NIMH, 2007). The major differences between the classes of medications are the side effects, doses, and potency. While both classes of antipsychotics have receptor blocking properties in the dopamine (DA) and serotonin (5-HT) systems, the medications have different actions in the frontal -hippocampal systems [see (Pliszka, 2003) for a more detailed discussion]. Pliszka (2003) indicates that a new class of drugs are being developed (aripiprazole) that have minimal effects on the 5-HT, but stabilizes the DA system (e.g., increases DA in the cortex while reducing activity in the mesolimbic system).

Weizman et al. (1984) indicate that neuroleptics, in combination with stimulants, might be effective for a small number of ADHD children who do not respond to either medication alone. Apparently, when these drugs are used in combination, the stimulants increase the release of DA while the neuroleptics block DA, thereby suggesting synergetic effects between the two agents (Green, 1991). Zametkin and Rapoport (1987) indicate that antipsychotics are not as effective as stimulants, but these medications do seem to decrease motoric activity and inattention.

Because of the serious side effects associated with antipsychotics, these medications require careful monitoring. Green (1991) suggests that cognitive dulling, sedation, and irreversible tardive dyskinesia (abnormal involuntary movements) are of particular concern when treating children and adolescents. Children and adolescents are prone to exhibit acute dystonic reactions (e.g., neck spasms, mouth and tongue contractions, eyes rolling upward) within the first five hours of ingestion, and are more at risk when taking high potency, low dose antipsychotics, versus low potency, high dose regimens.

Antioxiolytic Medications

Antioxiolytics, specifically benzodiazepines (BZDs), are typically administered to control of severe anxiety, sleep disorders (e.g., insomnia, sleep terrors, and/or sleep walking), and over-inhibition disorders (Wilens, 2001). Relatively little research has been conducted on these medications with children and adolescents, although the American Psychiatric Association Task Force on Benzodiazepines reported that these drugs have low toxicity and abuse potential (Salzman, 1990).

The most common medication of benzodiazepines include Valium (diazepam), Librium (chlordiazepoxide), and Klonopin (clonazepam; Wilens, 2001). Other antioxiolytics medications are antihistamines (i.e., Benadryl, Vistaril, and Chlor-Trimeton), and atypical antioxiolytics (Buspar).

Benzodiazepines appear to affect GABA receptors, which in turn enhance chloride channels to produce hyperpolarization of neurons (Pliszka, 2003). This neurochemical (BZD-GABA) process has inhibitory affects in arousal and affective brain

centers, thus reducing anxiety. In addition, benzodiazepines are also effective antiepileptic medications. For example, Valium enhances GABA's inhibitory action to terminate seizures. Potential side effects (e.g., sedation, muscle relaxation, and elevated seizure threshold) appear related to the effects BZD receptors have on cortical, pyramidal, and spinal neurons throughout the brain (Wilens, 2001).

Withdrawal symptoms (e.g., dysphoria, anxiety, heightened sensitivity to light and sound, headaches, sweating, tremors, insomnia, nightmares, delirium, and paranoia) have been reported with BZDs and are similar to the effects of withdrawal from other CNS depressants. Further, long-term use of the BZDs may result in tolerance to the medications, thereby reducing the benefits (Wilens, 2001). Care must be taken when discontinuing BZDs, particularly at high doses. Withdrawal symptoms are common if the medication is stopped too quickly, including mental confusion, increased blood pressure, and, in some cases, seizure activity.

Buspar, a newer antioxiolytic medication, has been used to treat children with severe aggression (Wilens, 2001). Buspar works differently than the BZDs and does not produce anticonvulsant, sedative or muscle relaxing effects. Buspar apparently works on serotonin, but may not be as effective as the typical BZDs. However, side effects for Buspar are not as adverse as the BZDs. Buspar has lower abuse potential, and does not require blood monitoring (Wilens, 2001).

Antiepileptic Medications

Antiepileptic medication is the major form of therapeutic intervention for children and adolescents with nonfebrile seizure disorders. Phenobarbital and phenytoin both have adverse affects on academic work, due to their sedative affects. Phenobarbital has been known to decrease memory in some children and contribute to disturbed behaviors in other children (Wilens, 2001). However, when the children are given other antiepileptic medications, these behavioral and cognitive side effects improve. Carbamazepine also has adverse side effects, but these seem to be less severe than those of the other two agents. All three medications are commonly used, either in combination or as single agents, and require careful blood level monitoring. Antiepileptic medications act as enzyme-inducing agents in the liver, which in turn appears to reduce the "bioavailability of almost all psychotropic agents" (Neppe & Tucker, 1992, p. 4 17). Antiepileptic medications appear to modulate DA, serotonin, and GABA receptor sites.

There has been a trend to use the antiepileptic medications to treat other childhood psychiatric disorders, especially valporic acid/divalproex sodium, carbamazepine, and oxcarbazepine (Handen & Gilchrist, 2006). Valproate has been used to treat children with cognitive retardation who also have aggression, but adverse effects should be carefully monitored, including hepatic failure and hemorrhagic pancreatic which can be life threatening.

Mood Stabilizers: Medications for Bipolar Disorders

Early reports from the STEP-BD study indicate that participants with early onset bipolar disorder (BD) have higher rates of comorbid disorders (i.e., anxiety disorders and substance abuse), higher and shorter periods of euthymia, higher rates of suicide attempts, and increased mood episodes upon entering the study. Thus, bipolar disorders are more complex, severe forms of childhood psychopathology. Mood stabilizers are used for bipolar disorders, seizures, aggression, and self-injurious behaviors (Handen & Gilchrist, 2006). Mood stabilizers include: lithium (Lithobid), oxcarbazepine (Trileptal), valporic acid (Depakene), carbamazine (Tegretol), lamotrigine (Lamictal), and topirmate (Topamax). Divalproex and carbamazepine were first developed as anticonvulsants, while other mood stabilizers are also "atypical" antipsychotics. Adverse side effects have been reported and are often difficult to tolerate, including dizziness, drowsiness, cognitive sedation, vomiting, diarrhea, insomnia, loss of appetite, and extrapyramidal effects (Phelps et al., 2002).

While TCAs and SSRIs have been effective treatments for adults with bipolar disorder, these antidepressants are less effective for treating pediatric populations (Birmaher, 1998). Scheffer, Kowatch, Carmody, and Rush (2005) investigated treatments for youths between the ages of 6–17 years with bipolar disorder with comorbid ADHD. Using a placebo-controlled crossover design, Scheffer et al. (2005) found that mixed amphetamine salts were significantly more effective than placebo for ADHD symptoms. In addition, there were no significant adverse effects and manic symptoms did not increase. In this study, manic symptoms were first controlled with divalproex sodium, which did not effectively reduce ADHD.

NIMH has funded three major studies investigating the treatment options for children and adolescents with bipolar disorders, including the Systematic Treatment Enhancement Program for Bipolar Disorder (STEP-BD), Treatment of early Age Mania (6–15-year-olds), and Effectiveness of Family-focused Therapy (13–17-year-olds). These studies are ongoing and will no doubt shed needed light onto the most effective treatment options for pediatric bipolar disorder.

Regardless of the prescribed medication, there is agreement that benefits must be carefully weighed against adverse effects. Clinicians must strategically monitor medication effects and determine the need for medication, appropriate doses and the need for other combined treatments.

Monitoring Medication Efficacy

A key question prior to selecting pharmacological intervention is whether medication is warranted. This decision typically requires a comprehensive assessment of the problem and a careful review of the child's medical, educational, and psychosocial history (DuPaul et al., 2003). It is important to determine the exact nature and severity of the disorder prior to medicating and, in some cases, to determine if other psychosocial or behavioral interventions have been attempted. Information concerning previous non-medical interventions is particularly important for such pediatric disorders as ADHD, depression, anxiety, and conduct disorders.

When non-medical interventions are not successful in ameliorating the child's problems, then a controlled trial of medication may be considered. Physicians usually obtain baseline data prior to medication trials, which may include electrocardiogram (ECG); electroencephalogram (EEG); urinalysis; liver, thyroid, and renal function tests; blood pressure, and serum blood levels when administering antipsy-chotics, antiepileptics, and antidepressants (Green, 1991). Other baseline behavioral data (rating scales, questionnaires, etc.) are also collected in order to measure the effects of medication. Once psychophar-macotherapy is initiated, objective measures of med-ication effects are needed to determine individual response rates and to assess the side effects of various medications (Barkley, 2006; DuPaul & Stoner, 2003; Wilens, 2001). A number of rating scales are avail-able to measure classroom behaviors and side effects for ADHD (see Barkley, 2006; DuPaul & Stoner, 2003), but fewer scales are available for other child-hood disorders.

Pelham (1993) suggests that when monitoring medication it is advisable to measure ecologically valid behaviors in order to assess the effects of med-ication on a child's performance in the classroom and in social situations. Pelham (1993) employs daily report cards that target behaviors such as work com-pletion, compliance, and accuracy in order to deter-mine the effects of stimulant medications. Although Pelham (1993) specifically addresses medication monitoring of stimulants for ADHD children, eco-logically valid measurements would also seem ap-propriate for other childhood disorders, including depression, anxiety, and conduct-related problems. To assess whether a particular medication is helping a child, the behaviors of concern (e.g., sadness, panic attacks, or anger outbursts) may need to be defined more explicitly and monitored on a regular basis. Thus, for medication monitoring to be ecologically valid, it should occur in the child's natural setting (home and school) and not solely in the clinic or the doctor's office.

Given the need for assessing medication affects in the child's natural setting, it is important that schools, physicians, and parents work together to produce the most benefits from pharmacological approaches. The following section discusses these partnerships.

Home-School-Physician Partnerships

Home-school-physician partnerships are necessary for several reasons. First, children often receive psychosocial, behavioral, and medical interventions from a number of different professionals, and coor-dination of these services is required. It is not uncom-mon for a child with a neuropsychiatric disorder to have a psychiatrist or physician prescribe medica-tion, a clinical psychologist conduct therapy, and a school psychologist and/or counselor address school-related academic and psychosocial problems. These various professionals often target the same behaviors and have similar therapy goals, but they may use different techniques. Therapeutic efforts in one setting should not be counterproductive to the efforts in another. These situations occur when professionals have diametrically opposed theoretical orientations or utilize drastically different approa-ches for the same behavioral, psychological, and/ or academic problem. Parents may pursue the course recommended by one professional, only to hear a completely opposite opinion from another. This not only creates stress and confusion for the parent, it may set a course of action that is comple-tely counterproductive for the child.

Second, because of the concern over high costs of comprehensive assessments and interventions, dupli-cation of services should be avoided whenever possi-ble. Professionals in different settings may utilize similar evaluation procedures (e.g., rating scales, intellectual measures). It is not uncommon for a child to be assessed using the same instruments, for parents to fill out the same rating scales, and for teachers to respond to the same questionnaires for different professionals (e.g., psychiatrist, clinical psychologist, and school psychologist) within a rela-tively short period of time. Interventions may also be similar across therapeutic settings. Coordinating ser-vices and communication between professionals and parents helps to reduce needless redundancy.

Third, a number of children receive medication on a daily basis. Medication monitoring is an impor-tant element of pharmacotherapy and is most helpful when conducted in the child's natural environment, the home or the school, where the behaviors of con-cern can be systematically observed. Physicians need careful and systematic information about how the child is responding to medication, and whether there are side effects at various dosage levels. Properly trained school professionals (e.g., school psycholo-gists) can be extremely helpful in this process. School psychologists may observe the child, collect beha-vioral data (e.g., work completion rates), and assess psychosocial adjustment at various dosage levels. These data can be communicated directly to the physician (with parental permission), or to the parent for proper medication monitoring. Information concerning individual responsivity needs to be communicated on a regular basis in order to ascertain the child's progress.

Fourth, when children with various brain-related diseases or disorders (e.g., brain tumors, traumatic brain injury) reenter the school system, the professional staff needs to be knowledgeable about the child's medical, psychosocial, academic and behavioral needs. In order to be knowledgeable about the ramifications of brain-related disorders, educational professionals need to be in regular contact with attending physicians (e.g., neurologists, neurosurgeons) and other medical specialists (e.g., speech and physical therapists). Information in these situations needs to be bidirectional – from the physician to the teacher or school psychologist, and vice versa. Physicians need information from the school about how the child is progressing and if relapses or other secondary problems are emerging. Educational professionals need to understand the nature and course of recovery of the child's injury or disease.

Fifth, parents and family members may need help coping with the demands and stresses of the child's neuropsychiatric disorders, diseases, or trauma. While each professional may play a different role in this process, each may also possess important information that may be useful to the other. Again, communication between the physician and the school is essential.

It is important to remember that when developing home-school-physician partnerships, confidentiality is required. Parental permission is needed before obtaining and sharing information, and sensitive or personal information should be discussed only on a need-to-know basis. That is, teachers and other school personnel may be informed when information directly affects the intervention or treatment plan; otherwise, personal information should be kept confidential. A case illustration may help clarify this point. A child had been severely beaten by his mother's boyfriend and sustained serious brain trauma. When the child reenters school, should the source of the child's injury be shared with school personnel (e.g., child's teacher, school psychologist)? If there is continued concern about the safety of the child or concern about the psychological

trauma suffered by the child, then sharing this information with the educational professionals is appropriate. If psychoeducational services are needed, then the school psychologist and other educational professionals may also need to know. If the child has already stabilized (i.e., medically, neuropsychologically, and emotionally), then the cause of the injury may not be all that pertinent. Most often the school administrator would be informed under both conditions.

Most of the reasons discussed here suggest the need for communication and coordination of services across agencies. Many parents feel that they have been placed in the role of services coordinator for their child–a role that parents do not always want to assume. Thus, it is imperative that school and medical professionals discuss these issues and identify an individual who will be responsible for coordinating assessment and intervention plans across the various settings. Regular communication among all parties is needed, and a plan or systematic schedule may be helpful, particularly during the assessment and early intervention stages. Contact may be less frequent once the child stabilizes and shows steady progress in meeting the therapeutic or intervention goals. Regular follow-up at six-, 12-, 18-, and 24-month intervals may be sufficient in later stages when the child has shown adequate recovery or is progressing on target.

Summary and Conclusions

This chapter presented a model for comprehensive, multimethod assessment and intervention for children. Five basic assumptions underlie this model. First, the model assumes that many childhood disorders have a biogenetic basis, such that neuropsychological as well as cognitive, behavioral, and psychosocial factors must be considered for assessment and treatment. Second, a single theoretical paradigm (e.g., behavioral, cognitive, or neuropsychological) is rarely defensible when applied in isolation. One-dimensional explanations for complex, multidimensional conditions are not scientifically founded. Third, developmental disorders of childhood present early in life and respond favorably to early intervention. Neurocognitive paradigms offer strong theories and methods for addressing childhood disorders within a developmental framework. Fourth, various paradigms make important contributions for different reasons and, when combined, increase the probability of obtaining the best treatment for children with serious disorders. Finally, advancing the science of childhood disorders will not occur in the form of dramatic discoveries from or within a single paradigm, but will occur through patient working and reworking of complex sets of experimental variables, with clinical validation (Doehring, 1968).

References

Abikoff, M., Hechtman, L., Klein, R., Weiss, K., Fleiss, K., Etcovitch, J., et al. (2004). Symptomatic improvement in children with ADHD treated with long-term methylphenidate and multimodal psychosocial treatment. *Journal of the American Academy of Child and Adolescent Psychiatry, 43,* 802–811.

Balthazor, M. J., Wagner, R. K., & Pelham, W. E. (1991). The specificity of the effects of stimulant medications on classroom-learning related measures of cognitive processing for attention deficit disorder children. *Journal of Abnormal Child Psychology, 19,* 35–52.

Barkley, R. A., (2006). *Attention-deficit hyperactivity disorder: A handbook for diagnosis and treatment* (3rd ed.). New York: Guilford Press.

Barkley, R. A., Anderson, D. L., & Kruesi, M. (2007). A pilot study of the effects of Atomexetine on driving in adults with ADHD. *Journal of Attention Disorders, 10,* 306–316.

Barkley, R. A., & Cunningham, C. E. (1979). Stimulant drugs and activity level in hyperactive children. *American Journal of Orthopsychiatry, 49,* 491–499.

Barkley, R. A., & Cunningham, C. E. (1980). The parent-child interactions of hyperactive children and their modification by stimulant drugs. In R. Knights & D. Bakker (Eds.), *Treatment of hyperactive and learning disabled children* (pp. 219–236). Baltimore, MD: University Park Press.

Barkley, R. A., DuPaul, G. J., & McMurray, M. B. (1991). Attention deficit disorder with and without hyperactivity: Clinical response to three doses of methylphenidate. *Pediatrics, 87,* 519–531.

Barkley, R. A., Fischer, M., Smallish, L., & Fletcher, K. (2006). Young adult outcome of hyperactive children: Adaptive functioning in major life activities. *Journal of the American Academy of Child and Adolescent Psychiatry, 45,* 192–202.

Barkley, R. A., Murphy, K. R., & Fischer, M. (2008). *ADHD in adults: What the science says.* New York: Guilford Press.

Bhatia, S. K., Rezac, A. J., Vitiello, B., Sitorius, M. A., Buehler, B. A. & Kratochvil, C. J. (2008). Antidepressant prescribing practices for the treatment of children and

adolescents. *Journal of Child and Adolescent Psychopharmacology, 18(1),* 70–80.

Biederman, J., Faraone, S., Monuteaux, M., & Grossbard, J. (2004). How informative are parent reports of ADHD symptoms for assessing outcome in clinical trials of long-acting treatments? A pooled analysis of parents' and teachers' reports. *Pediatrics, 113*(6), 1667–1671.

Birmaher, B. (1998). Should we use antidepressant medications for children and adolescents with depression? *Psychopharmacology Bulletin, 34,* 245–251.

Birmaher, B., & Brent, D. A. (2003). Antidepressants: II: Tricylic agents. In A. Martin, L. Scahill, D. S. Chaney, & J. F. Leckman (Eds.), *Pediatric psychopharmacology: Principles and practice* (pp. 466–483). New York: Oxford University Press.

Bohnstedt, B. N., Kronenberger, W. G., Dunn, D. W., Giaugue, A. L., Wood, E. A., Rembusch, M. E., et al. (2005). Investigator ratings of ADHD symptoms during a randomized trial of Atomoxetine: A comparison of parents and teachers as informants. *Journal of Attention Disorders, 8*(4), 153–159.

Bostic, J. Q., Prince, J., Frazier, J., DeJong, S., & Wilens, T. E. (2003). Pediatric psychopharmacology update. *Psychiatric Times, 20,* 9.

Brent, D., Emslie, G., Clarke, G., Wagner, K., Asarnow, J., Keller, M., et al. (2008). Switching to another SSRI or to Venlafaxine with and without cognitive behavioral therapy for adolescents with SSRI-resistant depression. *JAMA, 299*(8), 901–913.

Bridge, J. A., Iyengar, S., Salary, C. B., Barbe, R. P., Birmaher, B., Pincus, H. A., et al. (2007). Clinical response and risk for reported suicidal ideation and suicide attempts in pediatric antidepressant treatment: A meta-analysis of randomized controlled trials. *JAMA, 297*(15), 1683–1696.

Carlson, C. L., Pelham, W. E., Milich, R., & Dixon, M. (1992). Single and combined effects of methylphenidate and behavior therapy on the classroom behavior, academic performance, and self-evaluations of children with attention deficit hyperactivity disorder. *Journal of Abnormal Child Psychology, 202,* 213–232.

Comings, D. E. (1990). Tourette syndrome and human behavior. Durante, CA; Hope Press.

Connor, D. F. (2006). Stimulants. In R.A. Barkley, *Attention-deficit hyperactivity disorder: A handbook for diagnosis and treatment* (3rd ed., pp. 608–647). New York: Guilford Press.

Corkum, P., Panton, R., Ironside, S., MacPherson, M., & Williams, T. (2008). Acute impact of immediate release methylphenidate administered three times a day on sleep in children with attention-deficit/hyperactivity disorder. *Journal of Pediatric Psychology, 33*(4), 368–379.

Doehring, D. G. (1968). *Patterns of impairment in specific reading disability: A neuropsychological investigation.* Bloomington: Indiana University Press.

Dubovsky, S. L. (1992). Psychopharmacological treatment in neuropsychiatry. In S. C. Yudofsky & R. E. Hales (Eds.), *The American Psychiatric Press textbook of neuropsychiatry* (2nd ed., pp. 663–702). Washington, DC: American Psychiatric Press.

DuPaul, G., & Stoner, Ga. (2003). ADHD in the schools: Assessment and intervention strategies (2nd ed.). New York: Guilford Press.

DuPaul, G., Barkley, R. A., & McMurphy, M. B. (1991). Therapeutic effects of medication on ADHD: Implications for school psychologists. *School Psychology Review, 20*,203–219.

DuPaul, G. J., McGoey, K. E., & Mautone, J. A. (2003). Pediatric pharmacology and psychopharmacology. In M. C. Roberts (Ed.), *Handbook of pediatric psychology* (3rd ed. pp. 234–252). New York: Guilford Press.

Faraone, S. V., Wigal, S. B., & Hodgins, P. (2007). Forecasting three-month outcomes in a laboratory school comparison of mixed amphetamine salts extended release (Adderall XR) and Atomoxetine (Stratttera) in school-aged children with ADHD. *Journal of Attention Disorders, 11*(1), 74–82.

Gadow, K. D., & Poling, A. G. (1988). *Pharmacotherapy and mental retardation.* Boston: College Hill Press.

Ghuman, J. K., Riddle, M. A., Vitiello, B., Greenhill, L. L., Ghuang, S., Wigal, S. et al. (2007). Comorbidity moderates response to methylphenidate in the preschoolers with attention deficit/hyperactivity disorder. *Journal of Child and Adolescent Psychopharmacology, 17*(5), 563–580.

Gibbons, R. D., Hur, K., Bhaumik, D. K., & Mann, J.J. (2006). The relationship between antidepressant prescription rates and rate of early adolescent suicide. *American Journal of Psychiatry 163*, 1898–1904.

Green, W. H. (1991). *Child and adolescent clinical psychopharmacology.* Baltimore, MD: Williams & Wilkins.

Greenhill, L., Kollins, S., Abikoff, H., McCracken, J., Riddle, M., Swanson, J., et al. (2006). Efficacy and safety of immediate-release methylphenidate treatment for preschoolers with ADHD. *Journal of the American Academy of Child & Adolescent Psychiatry. 45*(11), 1284–1293.

Handen, B. L., & Gilchrist, R. (2006). Practitioner review: Psychopharmacology in children with mental retardation. *Journal of Child Psychology and Psychiatry, 47*(9), 871–882.

Hasler, G., Fromm, S., Carlson, P. J., Luckenbaugh, D. A., Waldeck ,T., Geraci, M.,et al. (2008). Neural response to catecholamine depletion in unmedicated subjects with major depressive disorder in remission and healthy subjects. *Archives of General Psychiatry, 65*(5), 521–531.

Hinshaw, S. P. (1991). Stimulant medication and the treatment of aggression in children with attention deficits. *Journal of Clinical Child Psychology, 20*, 301–312.

Hinshaw, S. P., Henker, B., Whalen, C. K., Erhardt, D., & Dunnington, R. E. (1989). Aggressive, prosocial, and nonsocial behavior in hyperactive boys: Dose effects of methylphenidate in naturalistic settings. *Journal of Consulting and Clinical Psychology, 57*, 636–443.

Hunt, R. D., Mandl, L., Lau, S., & Hughes, M. (1991). Neurobiological theories of ADHD and Ritalin. In L. Greenhill (Ed.), *Ritalin theory and practice* (pp. 267–287). New York: Mary Ann Leibert Press

Jacobvitz, D., Sroufe, L. A., Stewart, M., & Leffert, N. (1990). Treatment of attentional and hyperactivity problems in children with sympathomimetic drugs: A comprehensive review. *Journal of the American Academy of Child & Adolescent Psychiatry. 29*(5), 677–688.

Joshi, P. T., Cappozzoli, J. A., & Coyle, J. T. (1988). Low-dose neuroleptic therapy for children with child-onset pervasive developmental disorder. *American Journal of Psychiatry, 145*,335–338.

Kelsey, D. K., Sumner, C. R., Casat, C. D., Coury, D. L., Quintana, H., Saylor, K. E., et al. (2004). Once-daily Atomoxetine treatment for children with attention-deficit/hyperactivity disorder, including an assessment of evening and morning behavior: A double-blind, placebo controlled trial. *Pediatrics, 114* (1), e1–e8.

Kratochvil, C., Heiligenstein, J., Dittmann, R., Spencer, T. J., Biederman, J., Wernicke, J., et al. (2002). Atomoxetine and methylphenidate treatment in children with ADHD: A prospective, randomized, open-label trial. *Journal of the American Academy of Child & Adolescent Psychiatry. 41*(7), 776–784.

McGough, J. J., Wigal, S., Abikoff, H., Turnbow, J. M., Posner, K., & Moon, E. (2006). A randomized, double-blind, placebo-controlled, laboratory classroom assessment of methylphenidate transdermal system in children with ADHD. *Journal of Attention Disorders, 9*(3), 476–485.

MTA Cooperative Group. (2004a). National Institute of Mental Health Multimodal Treatment Study of Attention-deficit/hyperactivity disorder. *Pediatrics, 113*, 754–761.

MTA Cooperative Group. (2004b). National Institute of Mental Health Multimodal Treatment Study of ADHD follow-up: Changes in effectiveness and growth after the end of treatment. *Pediatrics, 113*, 762–769.

MTA Cooperative Group. (2008a). Evidence, interpretation, and qualification from multiple reports of long-term outcomes in the Multimodal Treatment Study of Children with AD/HD (MTA): Part I: Executive summary. *Journal of Attention Disorders, 12*(1), 3–13.

MTA Cooperative Group. (2008b). Evidence, interpretation, and qualification from multiple reports of long-term outcomes in the Multimodal Treatment Study of Children with AD/HD (MTA): Part II: Supporting details. *Journal of Attention Disorders, 12*(1), 14–41.

MTA Research Symposium (2007, November). *Key impact of the MTA study: What is the take-home message.* Paper presented at the 20th Anniversary Hall of Fame Conference, CHADD. Crystal City, VA.

Neppe, V. M., & Tucker, G. J. (1992). Neuropsychiatric aspects of seizure disorders. In S. C. Yudofsky & R. E. Hales (Eds.), *The American Psychiatric Press textbook of neuropsychiatry* (2nd ed., pp. 397–425). Washington, DC: American Psychiatric Press.

NIMH. (2007). Medications with Adendum January 2007. Department of Health and Human Services. National Institute of Health.

Olfson M., Marcus S. C., & Shaffer D. (2006). Antidepressant drug therapy and suicide in severely depressed children and adults. *Archives of General Psychiatry, 63*, 865–872.

Pelham, W. E. (1993). Pharmacotherapy for children with attention deficit-hyperactivity disorder. *School Psychology Review, 22*, 1–227.

Pelham, W. E., Schnedler, R, W., Bender, M. E., Nilsson, D. E., Miller, J., Budrow, M. S., et al. (1988). The combination of behavior therapy and methylphenidate in the treatment of attention deficit disorders. In L. Bloomingdale (Eds.), *Attention deficit disorder* (Vol. 3, pp. 29–48). New York: Pergamon Press.

Pellock, J. M. (1987). Carbamazepine side effects in children and adults. *Epilepsia, 28*, S64–S70.

Phelps, L., Brown, R. T., & Power, T. J. (2002). *Pediatric psychopharmacology: Combining medical and psychosocial interventions.* NY: Guilford Press.

Pliszka, S. R. (2003). *Neuroscience of mental health clinicians.* New York: Guilford Press.

Pliszka, S. R., Carlson, C. L., & Swanson, J. M. (1999). *ADHD with comorbid disorders.* New York: Guilford Press.

Rush, A. J., Fava, M., Wisniewski, S. R., Lavori, P. W., Trivedi, M. H., Sackeim, H. A., et al. (2004). Sequenced treatment alternatives to relieve depression (STAR*D): Rationale and design. *Controlled Clinical Trials, 25*(1), 119–142.

Rush, A. J., Trivedi, M. H., Wisniewski, S. R., Nierenberg, A., Stewart, J. W., Warden, D., et al. (2006). Acute and longer-term outcomes in depressed outpatients who required one or several treatment steps: A STAR*D report. *American Journal of Psychiatry, 163*(11), 1905–1917.

Salzman, C. (1990). Benzodiazepine dependency: Summary of the APA task force on benzodiapines. *Psychopharmacology Bulletin, 26*, 61–62.

Safer, D. (2006). Should selective serotonin reuptake inhibitors be prescribed for children with major depressive and anxiety disorders? *Pediatrics, 118*(3), 1248–1251.

Schaughency, E. A., & Hynd, G. W. (1989). Attentional control systems and the attentional deficit disorders (ADD). *Learning and Individual Differences, 4*, 42–449.

Scheffer, R. E., Kowatch, R. A., Carmody, T., & Rush, A. J. (2005). Randomized, placebo-controlled trial of mixed amphetamine salts for symptoms of comorbid ADHD in pediatric bipolar disorder after mood stabilization with divalproex sodium. *American Journal of Psychiatry, 162*(1):58–64.

Silva, R. R., Munoz, D. M., & Alpert, M. (1996). Carbamazepine use in children: Adolescents with features of attention-deficit hyperactivity disorders: A meta-analysis. *The American Academy of Child and Adolescent Psychiatry, 35*(3), 352–358.

Simon, G. E., Savarino, J., Operskalski, B., & Wang, P. (2006). Suicide risk during antidepressant treatment. *American Journal of Psychiatry, 163*(1), 41–47.

Swanson, J., Greenhill, L. L., Wigal, T., Kollins, S., Stehli, A. M., Davies, M., et al. (2006). Stimulant-related reductions of growth rates in the PATS. *Journal of Child and Adolescent Psychopharmacology, 45*(11), 1304–1313.

Treatment for Adolescents with Depression Study (TADS) Team. (2004). Fluoxetine, cognitive-behavioral therapy, and their combination for adolescents with depression: Treatment for Adolescents with Depression Study (TADS) randomized controlled trial. *Journal of the American Medical Association, 292*(7):807–820.

Taylor, E. Anderson, P., Banaschewski, T., Buitelaar, J., Coghill, D., Dopfner, M., et al. (2004). Clinical guidelines for hyperkinetic disorder. *European Child and Adolescent Psychiatry, 13*(Suppl. 1), 17–130.

US Food & Drug Administration. (2004). Background on suicidality associated with antidepressant drug treatment. Retrieved from www.fda.gov/ohrms/dockets/ac/04/briefing/2004-4065b1-04-Tab02-Laughren-Jan5.pdf

Vetter, V. L., Elia, J., Erickson, C., Berger, S., Nathan Blum, N., Uzark, K., et al. (2008). Cardiovascular monitoring of children and adolescents with heart disease receiving medications for attention deficit/hyperactivity disorder: A scientific statement from the American Heart Association Council on Cardiovascular Disease in the Young Congenital Cardiac Defects Committee and the Council on Cardiovascular Nursing. *Circulation; 117*, 2407–2423.

Volkow, N. D., Wang, G. J., Fowler, J. S., Logan, J., Franceschi, D., Maynard, L., et al. (2002). Relationship between blockade of dopamine transporters by oral methylphenidate and the increases in extracellular dopamine: Therapeutic implications. *Synapse, 43*, 181–187.

Weissman, M. M., Pilowsky, D. J., Wickramaratne, P. J., Talati, A., Wisniewski, S. R., Fava, M., et al. (2006). Remission in maternal depression and child psychopathology: A STAR*D-Child report. *JAMA, 295*, 1389–1398.

Weizman, A., Weitz, R., Szekely, G. A., Tyana, S., & Belmaker, R. H. (1984). Combination of neuroleptic and stimulant treatment in attention deficit disorder with hyperactivity. *Journal of American Academy of Child Psychiatry, 23*,295–298.

Wilens, T. E. (2001). *Straight talk about psychiatric medications for kids.* New York: Guilford Press.

Wilens, T. E., & Spencer, T. J. (1999). Debate: Combining methylphenidate and clonidine: A clinically sound medication option. *Journal of the Child and Adolescent Psychiatry, 38*, 614–622.

Wilens, T. E., & Spencer, T. J. (2000). The stimulants revisited. *Child and Adolescent Psychiatric Clinics of North America, 9*(3), 573–603.

Wood, J. G., Crager, J. L., Delap, C. M., & Heiskell, K. D. (2007). Beyond methylphenidate: Nonstimulant medications for youths with ADHD. *Journal of Attention Disorders, 11*(3), 341–350.

Zametkin, A. J., & Liotta W. (1998). The neurobiology of attention-deficit/hyperactivity disorder. *Journal of Clinical Psychiatry, 59*(Suppl 7), 17–23.

Zametkin, A. J., & Rapoport, J. L. (1986). The pathophysiology of attention deficit disorder with hyperactivity. In B. B. Lahey & A. E. Kazdin (Eds.), *Advances in clinical child psychology* (Vol. 9, pp. 177–216). New York: Plenum Press.

Zametkin, A., & Rapoport, J. L. (1987). Noradrenergic hypothesis of attention deficit disorder with hyperactivity: A critical review. In H. Y. Meltzer (Ed.), *Psychopharmacology: The third generation of progress* (pp. 837–842). New York: Raven Press.

Zametkin, A., Rapoport, J. L., Murphy, D. L., Linnoila, M., & Ismond, D. (1985). Treatment of hyperactive children with monamine oxidase inhibitors: I. Clinical efficacy. *Archives of General Psychiatry, 42*, 962–966.

Zisook, S., Lesser, I., Stewart, J. W., Wisniewski, S. R., Balasubramani, G. K., Fava, M., et al. (2007). Effect of age at onset on the course of major depressive disorder. *American Journal of Psychiatry 164*, 1539–1546.

Author Index

Subject Index